INTERIOR DESIGN

INTERIOR

PRENTICE-HALL, INC., ENGLEWOOD CLIFFS, N.J.

HARRY N. ABRAMS, INC., NEW YORK

DESIGN

BY JOHN F. PILE

Project Director: Sheila Franklin Lieber
Editor: Lory Frankel
Picture Editor: J. Susan Sherman
Designer: Bob McKee
Assistant Designer: Maria Miller
Original artwork:
  Steve A. Broback
  Stuart H. McFeely
  Bob McKee
  Raymond Skibinski

Library of Congress Cataloging-in-Publication Data

Pile, John F.
  Interior design.

  Bibliography: p. 527
  1. Interior decoration.   I. Title.
NK2110.P55   1987   729   87-1184
ISBN 0-13-469248-9

A Times Mirror Company

Printed and bound in Japan

Page 3: United Ceramic Tile Showroom, New York. Paul
Haigh, architect, 1986. (Photograph: © Elliott Kaufman)

CONTENTS

PREFACE

Interior design touches the lives of all of us in a very direct way. We all live in interiors, and most of us work, study, shop, and travel inside various buildings, vehicles, and other enclosures. At one time or another, almost everyone has been an interior designer on a limited scale, when choosing a paint color or a rug, when buying furniture, or when arranging furniture in a new living place. For these reasons, interior design is—or should be—of interest to everyone.

A complex and constantly changing field, interior design overlaps and interlaces with related professions, architecture in particular and, to a lesser degree, industrial design, exhibition design, stage design, and other more specialized fields. No one book of reasonable size can deal with every aspect of interior design in full detail at a level that will support professional practice.

This book is concerned with the range of interior design from the modest and everyday experiences at home and at work to full professional involvement in large projects. It is not a collection of decorating suggestions, nor is it a complete "how-to-do-it" book, nor is it a substitute for the level of professional training offered in design schools. It is, rather, a survey of the field as it now exists. Readers interested in learning how to organize residential interiors will find that it presents the basic principles they need to know. It will also prove a useful guide to those who will be dealing with professionals in the field from time to time. Others may find it an introduction to professional study leading to a career in design.

As with any creative endeavor, reading a book, however helpful in learning about a subject and in establishing a point of view, is no substitute for direct, practical experience. Readers who have a real project in mind are urged to augment their reading by trying out some design assignments. Measuring an existing space, making some drawings, putting together color schemes—all these exercises can be done on one's own or in a class with the guidance of an instructor and the stimulation of fellow students doing the same work.

Design schools develop the student's experience through what is often called the *clinical method*. Students are given a *problem*, that is, a space to be designed, with a plan of that space and a set of requirements to be filled. The first problem is usually a single room. As the student gains experience, more complex problems are introduced. The space is never built, but the student receives ongoing criticism and advice from an experienced and skilled critic or teacher and classmates. Putting designs into realized form is the most exciting step of all. It carries its own problems and hazards, but it also promises unique satisfaction.

Earlier books that survey interior design tend to reflect a division in the field that appeared almost from its emergence. There are, on the one hand, *decoration* books that usually focus on the reproduction of historical styles in interiors that are most often residential. In contrast, *architecturally* oriented interior design is more closely allied to the movement known as modernism that surfaced early in the twentieth century as a challenge to historicism. This orientation is usually more concerned with the larger and more public projects such as offices, hotels, restaurants, and public buildings, although residential work of this character also abounds.

Within the last few years, this polarization into two conflicting approaches to interior design has begun to break down. Modern architecture has taken a turn away from an exclusive focus on the more mechanistic expression of modern life and developed a new interest in historicism, not in terms of imitation, but with a willingness to learn from the past and incorporate historical references into contemporary design. At the same time, the general public, long uninterested in the concepts of modernism, is moving toward an awareness and acceptance of modern design even in residential spaces, for many a last holdout against anything contemporary. Even as these changes in attitude continue to develop and merge, they have given rise to a new design vocabulary less concerned with formal styles as such and more focused on developing good solutions to the real problems of modern environmental circumstances.

At the same time, design, long isolated in the esoteric reaches of art, where it was regarded with suspicion by a large segment of the general public, is becoming more involved with the insights of various non-art fields such as sociology, economics, and psychology. Buildings and the spaces within them are, after all, intended to serve people in some advantageous way, and designers seem to be increasingly willing to seek help from other specialized fields in an effort to bring creative artistic expression and practical service into a stronger unity. In this book, there is no intention to take sides in a conflict of views that is rapidly becoming obsolete. The intention is rather to introduce the reader to the best of past and present thinking and to provide a starting point for further reading, study, studio work, and practice.

Unlike most professions (medicine, law, and architecture, for example), interior design is not regulated by legal restrictions. No license or degree has been required to use the title and to practice. Some regulation to protect the public against incompetents has been introduced in some states, and perhaps such regulation will someday come into general acceptance. For the present, anyone can work as an interior designer, with no limitations except those imposed by one's own levels of skill and experience. Prospective clients, at least those who are knowledgeable, may inquire about training, experience, and certification. For most people with career objectives in interior design, study in a good school is probably the most reliable route to full involvement in the field. It should be noted, however, that some well-known interior designers—including several who are impressively able—have developed their abilities without formal training.

Formal training may begin with a single course or may involve a complete college program. In order to gain full professional status, it is usual to spend at least four years in an established design school that awards a diploma and prepares the student to begin work in a design office. In addition, many professionals elect to take an accrediting examination that leads to a certificate of competence. Designers who wish to join one or another professional organization must demonstrate their skills, after which they can legitimately use the organization's name as evidence of a proven level of ability.

Those who wish to learn about interior design outside the professional schools would most reasonably begin with the problems set by their own living circumstances. Most self-taught interior designers have started with a room or two, perhaps designing and redesigning the same space until they find workable, satisfying solutions. As experience develops, a sense of what training will be most helpful may also evolve. Formal study is often more helpful and more meaningful when it follows or is simultaneous with practical experience.

The learning process cannot stop at any fixed point, after reading a particular number of books or after graduating from even the finest of design schools. The identification, observation, and study of good work remain the most useful and significant form of education in any design field. Whether it takes place in school or out, it is essential to the development of a truly personal way of working at the highest possible level of quality.

INTRODUCTION

In our modern, technological world, most of us spend a major part of our lives indoors. In the nature of things, *home* means an indoor place—a room, an apartment, a house, a mobile home, even a trailer or a van. We study in schools and colleges, eat in restaurants, work in shops, factories, or offices. We are born in hospitals and may die there, too. While most of us spend time out-of-doors, walking from one place to another, attending or participating in sports events, enjoying a garden, sailing, hiking, or even camping for a more extended period, these all tend to be brief interludes in lives spent largely inside some human-created structure.

Some working careers still entail being outside—on a farm, on construction sites, or delivering the daily mail. Statistical evidence, however, suggests that work of this kind is decreasing proportionately, while office work and indoor activities are on the rise. Even today's farmer may ride the enclosed cab of a tractor, while the mail may be delivered from a car or truck. When we travel, we say that we are going "out," but cars, trains, buses, ships, and airplanes are almost as totally enclosed as buildings. Even wilderness camping is likely to involve a significant amount of time spent inside a comfortable and often beautiful tent.

If we estimate the portion of an average day spent inside some sort of enclosing space, we will probably find we typically spend about 90 percent of our time inside, with only 10 percent outside (except, perhaps, on vacation, when the balance may tip closer to 50-50). However much we may love nature, most of us must face the reality that modern life goes on, most of the time, inside. If we are to be honest, we must also face the reality that many, perhaps even most of the inside spaces where we spend our time are unsatisfactory. The rooms, corridors, and lobbies of typical schools, hospitals, offices, shops, and factories are all too often crowded, disorganized, unattractive, and depressing. We commute in trains or buses that are often agonizingly uncomfortable. At home, where interiors should be the way we want them, limitations often lead us to settle for compromises. It sometimes seems that we are best off in an automobile or traveling on an ocean liner.

It can be an interesting exercise to make a rating chart evaluating the *quality* of the various indoor spaces in which we spend time, with, for example, a scale of 1 to 10 representing the range from worst experience to ideal. It is a fortunate person who reports an average much above 5. How does it come about that we subject ourselves to being shut up inside so many spaces that are so far from ideal—even downright unpleasant? We have, after all, constructed the enclosures that we live and work in and have done so, presumably, to make life better.

Obviously, any enclosure serves several basic purposes. It protects us against the weather; it provides privacy; it gives us places where we can keep the things we need in some more or less convenient relationship. While enclosure is basic to these needs, it is only a first necessity. Within enclosure we need equipment; places to sit and lie down; surfaces where food and drink can be prepared and served; places for work, reading, conversation, and music. Increasingly, all of these activities demand special technology—for storage and communication; for cooking and refrigeration; for reproduction of sound and image.

THE DEVELOPMENT OF INTERIOR DESIGN

Historically, most interiors were put together, and put together very successfully, as a natural part of building structures. Ancient and still-surviving primitive societies developed various forms of huts, tents, igloos, tepees, and yurts to solve the problems of shelter in a particular climate with particular available materials. They then simply took their few possessions inside, much as we might arrange our affairs in a tent while camping. The resulting interior was practical and often, in its own way, handsome.

Developing civilizations found appropriate ways of building more elaborate structures, which created their own kinds of interior space. One cannot think of a Gothic cathedral's interior apart from the structure of the building itself, and the glass, additions of carved wood, and other decorative elements create a consistent whole, inside and out. At least until modern times, cottages and farm buildings have always been designed and built according to traditions that took into account the occupants' way of life. The furnishings evolved from similar traditions, creating interiors thoroughly compatible with both the enclosing structures and the inhabitants' needs and customs.

It is with the development of more elaborate buildings for aristocratic, often royal owner-occupants that the idea of an interior as a designed unit, comparable to a fashionable costume as an expression of wealth and power as well as taste, emerged. The design professions began to take form in the Renaissance as strictly traditional practices yielded to a more personal way of thinking about design of every sort. Modern industrial society has added tremendous technical complications, both in the nature of buildings themselves and in the variety of specialized purposes that buildings are expected to serve.

Whatever the gains and losses of our modern civilization, we are clearly not likely to turn back to simpler ways of life; our modern habits of living indoors are destined to remain the

1. A variety of elements and objects generate an atmosphere that is comfortable and snug. Classical columns suggest the historic origins of the space; the warm colors of wood and fabrics suggest warmth and comfort; incandescent light from the lamps adds an additional glow of warmth; while the curving form of the seating suggests softness and relaxation. The collected objects reflect the personal interests and history of the occupants. It may come as a surprise to learn that this interior is in the home of a modern designer, Adriano Magistretti of Pediment Designs (New York), in Rome. (Photograph: Isidoro Genovese)

2

norm. This gives us a powerful motive for attempting to make the indoor spaces we occupy as satisfactory, useful, pleasant, and generally supportive as possible. Since this seems overwhelmingly obvious, it takes some questioning to discover why we must so often settle for spaces that fall so far short of these goals.

Every situation will suggest its own list of reasons—historic, economic, social, technical, or various combinations of such realistic pressures—but, in truth, many of these explanations will turn out to be, on close examination, excuses. As a society, we have overcome historical, economic, and technological hurdles to attain all sorts of astonishing achievements. We are able to travel in outer space, communicate instantly over vast distances, manipulate staggering masses of data automatically—in fact, we can, almost as a matter of course, do any number of things once considered miraculous.

We are also able to create spaces in which people can live comfortably, work well, and have pleasant experiences, as a large number of examples can demonstrate. These examples remain extraordinary, however, in a world in which our artificial environments are all too often anything but comfortable and

pleasant. We have lost connection with traditions that provide familiar, accessible answers to the problems of living space, and our industrialized civilization has done poorly at providing worthwhile alternatives.

We seem to suffer from some limitations in thinking, from a sort of block that makes us indifferent to our environment or, when we are not indifferent, that makes us inept to a degree that would never be tolerated in factory production, in financial management, or in scientific research. Towns, cities, and (often worst of all) suburbs are allowed to grow in chaos or to fall into decay. Buildings are erected with some care for their technical qualities (structural strength, mechanical systems) but with only the most minimal concern for design in any larger sense. In fact, the primary motivation for building is often quick profit-making rather than any concern for real use over a longer term. The spaces inside such buildings often limit the possibilities for making truly satisfactory settings for living or work.

Even when we build with good motives—schools, hospitals, or other public buildings or houses for our own occupancy—it often seems that the complicated tasks of putting together good interior spaces are botched in any number of ways. Because they are so familiar, the things that make up an interior space—a room, an office, a living room, a bedroom, a kitchen—seem obvious and easy to arrange. All the evidence shows that this is not so. An interior turns out to be a very complex entity made up of many elements that, to be successful in terms of usefulness, comfort, and beauty, must somehow work together.

Probably the great majority of residential interiors are arranged by their occupants. Offices and other working spaces are also designed, at least to some degree, by the people who use them. While this is most likely among the self-employed or among people who work at home, even business offices are frequently designed, or at least modified, by their user-occupants. Quite standard offices often provide for some level of personalization, which allows the user to adjust the interior to his or her own tastes.

It is an unfortunate reality that a very large number of interiors can hardly be said to have been designed at all. Many people live in interiors composed of rooms left as they found them plus some paint from the painter's standard color card, rugs and curtains inherited, borrowed, or casually picked out at a local store, and furniture acquired in one way or another set about in any way it will fit in. With luck, the results may have some level of rough-and-ready comfort; unfortunately, more often the space is disorganized, inconvenient, and uncomfortable, if not depressing and ugly.

If this is true of living spaces whose occupants are in full control, it is not surprising that public spaces fare even

2. A store's design is all-important: it can set off merchandise to its best advantage and make shopping an agreeable experience. In Contemporary Porcelain, a shop in New York's SoHo that features the work of ceramicists Marek and Lanie Cecula, the flexible display elements and lighting make endless variation possible. This is by William Ruggieri, designer, 1985. (Photograph: © Frederick Charles)

3. A restaurant's design can be a major factor in its success, as the dining experience is enhanced by the color, light, and quality of the surroundings. Open, informal, and verdant, the Chaya Brasserie Restaurant in Los Angeles expresses place and character in a positive way. Grinstein/Daniels, Inc., designer, 1985. (Photograph: Tim Street-Porter)

4

worse. Too many small shops and offices, restaurants and luncheonettes, school and college classrooms, hospitals, factories, airport terminals, bus stations turn out to be chaotic jumbles of unrelated elements that seem to have no connection with the advanced civilization that has produced them.

Our modern world is also full of spaces that have been designed with some effort and concern, but effort that has been misdirected. Restaurants and shops, hotels and motels, offices

and public buildings usually reflect some kind of design effort, but it is often aimed at promoting some product or service and at pleasing what is thought of as "public taste"—defined as a lowest common denominator. Many motel interiors and fast-food outlets exemplify this kind of misdirected design effort, which usually relies on busy patterns, harsh color schemes, and fussy details that are thought to be charming in some commercially defined way. Exceptions to this rather gloomy evaluation of our

4. Brian A. Murphy was the designer for this 1986 interior of his own house in Santa Monica Canyon in California. Seating furniture with an Art Deco flavor, two triangular coffee tables (of his own design), the fireplace mantel, and the keyhole arch of the doorway give this space an unusual, somewhat whimsical flavor. (Photograph: © Tim Street-Porter, courtesy House & Garden)

current norms for interior design exist, but they remain the exceptions. We have to seek out fine buildings and strain to remember offices, restaurants, and, particularly, homes that can truly be described as well designed.

When interiors *are* well designed, the success is rarely the result of chance. Most good interiors result from one of two approaches. The first is the use of skilled, talented, and well-trained professionals. Most modern, complex tasks are dealt with by experts with a very high level of specialized skill. We turn to experts for medical treatment, for financial guidance, even for automobile repair. We accept the idea that becoming a good cook, an able tennis player, or a passable musician will take study and practice. The same attitude should govern our approach to interior design, which must deal with furniture and lighting, color and layout, storage and art, among other elements.

The second approach, by untrained private individuals, is to learn something about what it takes to design an interior well and to give careful thought to the decision-making necessary. Becoming a qualified professional takes as much effort as becoming qualified in any other complex field, but learning to deal with the typical interior problems of home and office is within the reach of any reasonably intelligent person who wants to take the trouble.

THE PRACTICE OF INTERIOR DESIGN

The term *interior design* has come to describe a group of related projects that are involved in making any interior space into an effective setting for whatever range of human activities are to take place there. It can be the name of the profession that concerns itself with these matters, but that profession is not as clearly defined as that of lawyer or doctor. Many people may contribute to the interior design of large and complex spaces.

This book is concerned with exploring the issues that all interior designers, whether professional or amateur, must face. No book can pretend to offer a complete professional design education, but the basics are offered here in a way that can serve as a beginning for a professional design education, as a framework for dealing with one's own living and working situations, and as a background for selecting and working with design professionals if and when that turns out to be a wise course of action.

Making decisions about what interior design problems to deal with alone on a "do-it-yourself" basis, about when to call for professional help, and about when to consider turning professional oneself is not always as simple as it might seem.

Many of the bad interiors we have referred to are the results of wrong decisions on these questions. The best way to begin looking at these issues is to consider the way in which the field is currently organized, into a maze of overlapping (and sometimes conflicting) specialized trades, professions, and practices.

The practice of interior design has not been controlled by any legal restrictions, although some recent state laws establish regulations similar to those in effect in many European countries that require the *professional* interior designer to meet some standards of competence. (See Appendix 8, "Licensing and Professional Organizations.") Except where such new regulation has been adopted, anyone is free to design interiors and even to establish a professional business in the field without any qualifications beyond the necessary level of self-confidence. This situation contributes to the rather confusing nature of the field, in which many designers with varied backgrounds and with varied professional titles work on whatever projects they can sign up. The following listing sorts out and identifies the various professional titles in use in the interior field and defines what each title usually describes.

5

5. In an office area in the New York showrooms of Caroline Herrera, striking art dominates the space—while the bolts of fabric in the corner recall the work in hand. Robert Metzger, designer, 1982. (Photograph: Jaime Ardiles-Arce)

6

7

Decorator
(*or* Interior Decorator)

This is the designation most widely used and understood by the general public today. The title gained currency in the late nineteenth and early twentieth centuries, applied to the large group of designers who were specialists in putting together interiors in the various traditional styles (Colonial, Louis XIV, XV, or XVI, Tudor, Georgian, or even "modernistic," for example) that it became popular to imitate. The term implies a focus on the decorative, ornamental, and movable aspects of interior design: color, furniture, rugs, drapery, and the fixed details of moldings, paneling, and similar small elements that can be introduced into an existing space with relative ease.

Many decorators were also dealers in the elements used in interiors, buying and reselling furniture and rugs and contracting for whatever on-site work needed to be done to pull together a finished project. This latter practice called into question the decorator's status as an independent professional, and with a decline in the emphasis on traditional stylistic work,

6. *Active forms and textures, together with luxurious lounge seating, make this main banking room of the First City Bank, New Orleans, memorable. R. Clay Markham, architect; Tom R. Collum, interior designer, 1985. (Photograph: © Alan Karchmer. All rights reserved)*

7. *In the fields of fashion and style, the ambience reinforces the client's sense of the product's or service's quality. In Janice Julian's hair salon, New York, a cluster of five styling stations uses glittering mirrors, tile, and metallic materials to provide a setting suited to the salon's work. Stepped fin partitions assure each customer's privacy, while enclosed storage for materials and equipment keeps the space looking neat. Ari Bahat, designer, 1978. (Photograph: Mark Ross)*

8

9

8. This living space in the New York apartment of the late Billy Baldwin, one of the best-known American decorators of his time, takes a typically eclectic approach, combining such diverse elements as modern painting, a French provincial chair, a carved Chinese teak table, modern upholstery, and wall-to-wall carpeting. (Photograph: Horst)

9. David Salomon designed this richly luxurious traditional space as a Kips Bay Show House model interior in New York, 1987. The fabric on the sofas and the matching drapery fabric use a typical kilim pattern. The paneled walls, chandelier, painting, tapestry, decorative vases, and other accessories contribute to the sense of opulence. (Photograph: © Robert Levin, appeared in the New York Times, April 30, 1987)

10

the term has tended to take on some negative implications. At best, a decorator can produce work of top quality, but self-appointed decorators who may really be only painting contractors or salespeople in drapery outlets have discouraged others from using the term. Most decorators now prefer to call themselves interior designers, although it is more accurate to reserve that term for work approached in a somewhat different way, as described below.

Interior Designer

This term describes a professional approach to interiors that puts more emphasis on basic planning and functional design than *decoration* implies. In Europe, the term *interior architect* refers to designers who deal with the basic arrangement of spaces, lay out room arrangements, and manage technical issues (such as lighting and acoustics), much as architects design entire buildings. In the United States, where the term *architect* is legally limited (as described below), *interior designer* has become the accepted term for this kind of practice. Interior designers may work as individuals, in partnerships, or in firms that can grow quite large (with dozens

of staff members). These last tend to work on larger projects in commercial, institutional, and office areas. The term *contract design* is also used for this type of practice. It refers to the fact that components and construction work are arranged for under contracts, not simply bought at retail.

Specialization is, perhaps unfortunately, an increasing fact of life in interior design. Some modern fields, such as health-care facilities, have become so complex as to demand specialization. Other fields, such as office design, do not require specialization but have nevertheless attracted a specialized practice.

Space Planner *and* Office Planner

Firms specializing in these fields have surfaced in recent years to handle the development of large corporate and institutional offices that fill whole floors, many floors, or entire buildings with offices and their related services. Since office buildings are usually constructed as floors of open, undivided space, layout planning becomes an important first step in their design. Space and office planners also provide full interior design (or decoration) service.

10. Elegance and reserve, hallmarks of the work of Andrée Putman, interior designer, are evident in this living area of a San Francisco apartment. The rug is a design of Eileen Gray. (Photograph: © Grant Mudford, courtesy House & Garden)

11

In addition to these professionals who specialize in interior design, several other design professions overlap the interior field, sometimes providing interior design. These include:

Architect

An architect must have formal training and experience and must pass an examination leading to *registration,* a type of license to practice. Trained in basic building construction, architects are prepared to design buildings from the foundation up. In many cases, the architect's design includes many interior elements: room shapes, door and window locations, details and selection of materials, and such elements as lighting, heat, air conditioning, plumbing, and related fixtures.

Traditionally, architects provided fairly complete interior

11. In a lounge of the Auberge du Soleil in Rutherford, California, the contrasts between the rough walls and chimney breast and the polished floor, the unfinished log column and the furniture's classic lines give this space a unique character. Michael Taylor, designer, 1981. (Photograph: Russell MacMasters, courtesy Auberge du Soleil)

design, sometimes stopping short of furniture and decorative elements and sometimes including these as well. In modern practice, architects design some buildings as shells (office buildings, for example), leaving the interior design to others. In other situations—a museum, church, or school, for example— they provide complete interior design. Some architectural offices are large organizations (a few employ hundreds of designers, draftsmen, and other specialists), some of which include interior design departments that are actually complete interior design firms within the larger organization.

Industrial Designer

Designers or design firms specializing in industrially produced objects typically work on *products* such as appliances,

12

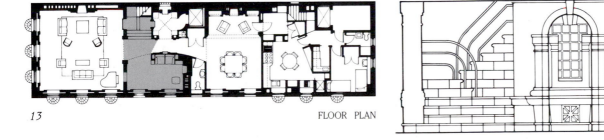

13   FLOOR PLAN

14   ELEVATION

12–14. Robert A. M. Stern Architects designed a large and elaborate duplex apartment in a 1920s New York landmark residential building. Fig. 12 shows a small, parlor-like sitting room at the entrance to the apartment; a stairway across the hall leads to the upper floor. The 1980–82 mix of modern architec- tural elements and more traditional details is in keeping with the building's eclectic style. In the plan of the apart- ment (fig. 13), the room illustrated is shaded. Fig. 14 depicts the hallway in elevation. (Photograph: Jaime Ardiles- Arce)

furniture, machinery, and automobiles. Some products of industrial design, such as furniture, hardware, and light fixtures, become elements used in interior design. Since industrial designers also deal with the interiors of automobiles, ships, and aircraft, many go one step further to design shops, restaurants, and similar projects. Exhibition design, although sometimes considered a specialized type of interior design, often comes within the province of industrial designers.

Other Specialists

In addition to the professional interior design fields described above, a number of specialists may make contributions to interior design projects in specific, limited ways. Although architects can and do undertake complete interior design assignments, they also often participate in the work of interior designers as specialists. This occurs when an interior project involves structural changes (moving a wall or adding a staircase, for example) or when the technical problems extend beyond the scope of the interior designer's training. Legal restrictions in many localities call for *filing plans* with a building department—plans that must be prepared by an architect or engineer to assure that a licensed professional is taking responsibility for the safety of the project and its compliance with all legal requirements. The interior designer may retain an architect to deal with these matters.

Both architects *and* interior designers turn to the still more specialized professional skills of engineers to manage complex and extensive technical issues. Among the many areas of specialization, architectural engineers are concerned with the structural and mechanical engineering of buildings. *Structural engineering* specialization is required for larger buildings with a complex framing of steel or concrete. Designs for simpler structures are often checked by an engineer to assure sound construction. *Mechanical engineering* deals with the plumbing and electrical systems of buildings, heating, ventilating, and air-conditioning systems (known as HVAC), and such special

15

15. Contract design addresses commercial and institutional spaces. These are often large—such as this 1983 multilevel interior, designed by ISD Incorporated for the Continental National Bank of Fort Worth, Texas. (Photograph: Jaime Ardiles-Arce)

16

17

16. A living room in an austere modern house becomes a comfortable environment, rich with plants and a lively mix of attractive objects, including native American pottery, a Turkish kilim rug (above the fireplace), an antique cabinet, and objects from a collection of old tools. Robert Luzzi, a graphic and package designer, acted as his own interior designer for this summer house in East Hampton, New York. (Photograph: Anthony Pettinato, courtesy Metropolitan Home Magazine)

17. Colorful luxury brightens a modern railway car of the French national railroad, the SNCF. The seating design clearly suits its transport function, yet the final effect is appealing rather than institutional. Jacques Catroux, designer, 1985. (Photograph courtesy French National Railroads)

elements as elevators and escalators. Interior designers may turn to engineering consultation for help with such matters or they may work through an architect to obtain engineering advice. Many larger architectural offices employ on-staff engineers. Engineers may file plans for legal approval and often design such buildings as factories and powerhouses.

Other specialized consultants may contribute to interior projects. *Lighting consultants* plan good functional lighting for offices and schools or attractive lighting for stores and restaurants. They are often helpful in aspects of residential design work. *Acoustical consultants* deal with problems of noise (in a restaurant or cafeteria, for example), of good sound in a theater or concert hall, and of undesirable sound transmission through walls and floors. Some consultants are experts in special kinds of spaces—hospitals, restaurants (and their kitchens), or theaters. Others deal with certain kinds of problems—furniture design, signs and graphic elements, or, particularly when a major collection of artworks is being built up, the selection of works of art. Some large projects may involve almost every one of the specialists and consultants mentioned here, while many small projects may be the work of one designer throughout or may draw on one or two brief sessions with a consultant. Every designer needs to understand these special fields and to know when and where to seek specialized help.

Residential and Contract Design

Interior projects can be divided into two broad classes, each with its own character. Some designers work in both areas, but most choose to concentrate in one field or the other. *Residential* design is concerned with projects that vary from small to medium in size (fig. 18). Even a large apartment or house is within the scope of an individual designer, possibly with an assistant or two. It is easy to take up residential design by working on one's own room, apartment, or house, moving on to work for friends or relatives before becoming fully professional. Residential work tends to be particularly personal, with rapport between designer and client, a shared taste and point of view, vital to success. It is work that calls for patience and a willingness to be involved in detail, often detail so small as to be irritating and troublesome. Many larger firms avoid residential work, finding the problems of client relationships and the level of detail too demanding in relation to the fees that can be charged. This remains an area in which, under favorable conditions, a designer can find opportunities for personal expression in varied and interesting projects.

Contract design, referring to more public spaces for commercial and institutional use, tends to generate larger projects (fig. 15), with clients ranging from individuals to large corporations or institutions. Less personal in their needs and demands, larger organizations are often represented by committees or by various individuals, possibly presenting communication problems to the designer. (The many types of contract design projects are reviewed in more detail in Chapter 13, "Public Interiors.") It is in this kind of work that specialization is most likely to develop, although larger design firms often manage involvement in a varied range of projects. The size of projects, their long duration, and the large fees involved make this kind of work attractive to larger design firms.

For the interior design problems of public spaces, for hotels and motels, for restaurants and offices, schools and hospitals, people have come to realize that there is no alternative to the employment of top professionals from the appropriate design fields. The same attitude—that interior design is a complex endeavor requiring knowledge of its elements and how they fit together—would well serve residential interior design. While hiring the top professional talents is not always economically feasible, it is not necessary to settle for the lowest common denominator or make do with whatever is offered ready-made. Neither is it necessary to spend a great deal of money or follow the advice of the most pretentious magazines on the stand. Putting together comfortable, even beautiful interior spaces takes some effort and deserves some thought and study, but it is not a process out of the reach of anyone who will take the appropriate trouble to learn what is involved.

It is helpful to become aware of all the bad design around us, in order to recognize it, to become critical of it, and finally to reject it, even when it is commercially successful and attractively packaged. A first step toward this goal is to turn away from the bulk of consumer-oriented material, both published and manufactured, in favor of publications and sources directed toward professional designers. Anyone can read professional books and magazines and visit contract showrooms, which present a very different world from the one presented in furniture stores and consumer magazines. Becoming familiar with the books, exhibitions, and literature that interest professional designers and architects soon leads to a growing "feel" for quality in every aspect of design work. The following chapters of this book are concerned with the realities of applying general knowledge to the specifics of actual interior design work. They invite the reader to step over the line from the role of consumer, user, and critic to enter the world of working, creative design.

18

18. An example of residential design: in a New York apartment (1977), Bray-Schaible Design has ingeniously developed a small bedroom area. The clean-lined forms and surfaces make the room appear more spacious and draw into prominence the basket on the right, the art on the wall, and the Mies van der Rohe steel-frame chair. (Photograph: Jaime Ardiles-Arce)

CHAPTER TWO
DESIGN QUALITY

All serious designers aim to achieve excellence in their work. While different designers may represent a variety of approaches and aesthetic attitudes, they share an understanding at some basic level of what excellence is. An excellent design satisfies three essential criteria: it works well, serving the needs and requirements of its users; it is well made of good, appropriate materials; it is aesthetically successful.

DEFINING DESIGN

Before looking more closely at these criteria, it is necessary, first of all, to define what we mean by *design*. This word has so many meanings and is used in so many contexts that it demands clarification. Many people think of it as meaning pattern or decoration, as, for example, a design for wallpaper or printed textiles. Other people associate it only with fashion design and stage design. In engineering, design may deal with sizing structural members, piping, or ducts, while in the fine arts it deals with the way an artist organizes the formal elements of line, shape, color, and texture in a space.

In interior design, industrial design, and architecture, the term describes all of the decisions that determine how a particular object, space, or building will *be*. It can also be described as determination of *form,* with *form* understood to mean every aspect of every quality, including size, shape, material, structure, texture, and color, that makes one particular physical reality different from any other. When we speak of a house, a living room, an office, an automobile, a chair, or a desk, we call to mind an item that contains certain general characteristics and that serves certain useful purposes, but the word tells us nothing of the specifics that make a particular house, living room, office, unique. It is design differences that make one house different from another, one room different from another, and that also allow us to speak of one example as better or worse than another.

EVALUATING DESIGN

Evaluation of design can become very complex. The interior designer usually begins with spaces designed by others, often long ago, possibly for purposes quite different from those the designer must now satisfy. The client may be an owner, a developer, or a corporation creating space to sell to others or to serve users who have no direct relationship with the designer. The elements that make up the interior—its materials, furnishings, and details—are often designed by others, chosen from among the products available from manufacturers who have no awareness of the project in hand. The finished space,

19. *Designer John F. Saladino used a heterogeneous array of materials and textures in the living area of his own apartment. The original architectural details—ceiling moldings and fireplace—were retained; textured painted wall surfaces, various textiles, rugs, mirror, and antique furniture relate well in color and scale. (Photograph: Lizzie Himmel)*

when put into use, may have to serve for years that stretch ahead into times when conditions will change and new generations of users will take over, bringing requirements that may well be different from anything that can be foreseen while design development is in process.

These realities make the interior designer's task more complex than might be suggested by the simple concept of a problem leading to a solution. Nevertheless, the design process can be analazyed in terms of a problem that can be defined and stated with as much clarity and precision as possible. Design proposals can then be viewed as proposed solutions to the stated problem that can be articulated (most often in drawings and models) and evaluated for their success in dealing with the problem.

In order to analyze and evaluate a proposed design, it can be viewed in terms of three closely related qualities: function, structure and materials, and aesthetics.

Function

This is the design world's favorite term to describe the practical purposes that any design is intended to serve. A chair serves as seating support; a living room as a gathering place for varied activities; a dining room as eating space; an office as work space; a shop as the arena for buying and selling; and so on. In order to be a success, any design must support its function. This goes beyond mere success or failure, becoming a matter of a scale of value in which the level of functional service can be related to the level of design quality.

Almost any chair can be sat in, and any room will serve for living or dining in some way. A truly well-designed chair will offer appropriate seating comfort for its intended use. A well-designed room will provide an outstandingly superior setting for its intended function. A well-designed living room, for example, will provide comfortable settings for conversation, solitary reading, music-listening, and TV-watching, as well as a workable setting for entertaining. A dining room will offer space, seating, lighting, and atmosphere suitable to each meal to be taken there, for as few or as many people as may be expected at any one time. An office will provide suitable space for working, equipment, and storage, as well as space to receive visitors and hold small meetings if required. Superior functional performance is the first test of design quality. Failure to function well reflects a larger design failure.

In addition to basic, or *primary,* function, designs must satisfy various secondary functions. Besides providing good seating, for example, a chair should be practical to move, keep clean, repair, and maintain, and its production cost should be appropriate to its intended use. This last issue is so closely

20

20. In an older New York loft building, a huge arched window dominates the space, transforming the exposed sprinkler pipes and plumbing into design accents. The window's shape is echoed by the decorative grid, which informs the patterns and placement of the shelving, rug, and chair. Alan Buchsbaum, designer. (Photograph: © Paul Warchol)

21

linked to the next group of design issues as to leave some uncertainty as to whether it is a functional issue at all. Certainly it ties together matters of function and construction.

Structure and Materials

In order to function, any design must be constructed of specific materials with available techniques of manufacture and workmanship. While closely related to functional issues, quality of materials and constructional techniques can be evaluated separately from functional performance. The choice of materials and workmanship greatly influences an object's durability and its initial and lifetime costs, values separate from *function*. A chair can be comfortable and serviceable (that is, serve its primary function)—at least for a time—even if poorly made of inappropriate materials.

An object's materials and constructional techniques must be appropriate to its intended use. The longest-lasting and most expensive of materials do not best serve every situation. A temporary exhibit will be built very differently from a monumental space expected to endure for generations. A paper cup and a cup of solid gold can be equally well designed, as long as each suits an intended use and is well made.

In an interior, wood plank floors, plastered walls, and simple wood furniture may be appropriate to one set of requirements while marble, granite, leather, and stainless steel may suit

another situation. In each case, excellence requires logical choices and quality workmanship suited to the materials selected.

Aesthetics

In evaluating design, it is easy to focus on functional performance and quality of materials and workmanship. While these are subject to debate—much as people argue over the best make of car—they offer generally understood criteria by which to judge. Aesthetic values, less easy to spell out, are all too often dismissed as "a matter of taste" that cannot be dealt with in any logical way. Teachers and students of design as well as working designers often slip into a belief that design can be evaluated only in terms of its practical aspects, since they cannot explain the aesthetic values at work.

Nonetheless, one can identify levels of aesthetic quality. In the evaluation of design, better is distinguishable from worse, and near-unanimity arises in selecting outstandingly good and bad designs. Such quality distinctions can be made even in the realm of the fine arts, in which the issues of function and workmanship scarcely apply. "Great art" is identified by a wide consensus that includes critics, historians, dealers, collectors, and sensitive viewers with no special qualifications. All of them recognize high quality even in work that may not be appealing to a particular taste or fit any particular definition of "beauty."

21. *In a house in New Mexico, designed by Charles Foreman Johnson, architect, a sculptural, hand-built fireplace is a dominating element that works well with the adobe walls and wooden pole rafters. All of these features have strong* *regional associations—while they might seem awkward or even absurd in other surroundings, they are clearly at home and logical here. The choice of material helps to place a room in a wider context. (Photograph: © 1985 Michael Skott)*

22

Confusion stems from efforts to define aesthetic qualities in terms of *beauty*. The concept of beauty differs with time and place, with purpose and context. An ornate Victorian parlor, an austere modern living room, the interior of a factory or of a primitive hut will all be seen as beautiful or as ugly by various viewers applying different standards. Our definitions of beauty and of ugliness may often be no more than our reactions to certain situations that we either like or dislike, attitudes that may arise from extraneous sources. We find it easy to like what is familiar, what is popular or fashionable, what one has learned to like from family, teachers, or friends, from books, magazines, and advertisements. Almost everyone can remember having had different tastes at some time in the past, tastes that have changed with growth, education, and experience.

The values that are usually called *aesthetic* can be better understood at another, more universally comprehensible level. Those aspects of a design that go beyond the functional and the constructional concern the specific way the design presents itself to the human senses. We use an object to serve some need or want, and we expect its physical structure to support that use. We know about an object through looking at it, handling it, and developing a sensory experience above and beyond its simple use. It is the task of the designer to shape an object so as to communicate to any viewer or user the ideas that define the reality of the object. When these ideas are appropriate and clear and when they are effectively expressed through the mediums at the designer's disposal (form, shape, color, texture, and so on), we *understand* the design at a deep level and feel satisfaction in seeing, handling, and using it.

It is also true that objects can be made useful and sturdy without exhibiting any particular visual quality. It is the unique role of the designer to form designs in such a way that they come to have a meaning beyond their simple physical reality. Viewing them at second hand, in photographs or other illustrations, is one way to test their success. One can develop a certain rapport with a designed object that one has never actually seen if its visual quality is in itself strong enough to provide satisfaction.

Viewing the work of the interior designer in this way gives us a yardstick for measuring excellence. We expect a space to serve its practical purpose well, and we expect it to be well made of suitable materials. We also expect it to give us a sensory experience that will help us to understand its use and its structure as well as offer a range of other ideas about its time, location, and the viewpoints of its designer and owner or client. This is the nature of experiencing a visit to a great

22. The interior of this private Lear jet designed by Herman Miller, Inc., for its own use, is a triumph of design: the severely constricted environment has been made comfortable, even luxurious. Simplicity and the intelligent use of color allow the functional forms of the space and the seating to speak for themselves. (Photograph courtesy Herman Miller, Inc.)

23. In this living room in a Manhattan town house, traditional architectural details provide a congenial background for an eclectic mix of period and contemporary furniture and furnishings. Though somewhat formal, the overall effect is comfortable. Mario Buatta, designer, 1984. (Photograph: Edgar de Evia, courtesy House & Garden)

24

25

24. This bedroom of Morgans Hotel, New York, was designed in 1985 by Andrée Putman. Unlike the overdecorated interiors of many hotel rooms, this space evokes feelings of pleasure and comfort that derive from the elegant simplicity of the materials, color, and functional elements. (Photograph: © Paul Warchol)

25. Margaret Helfand, architect, designed this conference room in the Jennifer Reed clothing showroom complex in Manhattan in 1987. The unusual geometry of the table and wall racks for display are emphasized by the uncluttered setting, which is memorable for its particular quality and charm. (Photograph: © Paul Warchol)

cathedral, a fine château, or other landmark buildings. In the same way, a visit to a more modest office, restaurant, or living room can offer pleasures that go beyond mere practical accommodation. In an ideal world, every space that we enter and use would be designed not only to serve its purpose well but also to offer a visual experience that would be appropriate, satisfying, and even memorable.

DESIGN IN OTHER CONTEXTS

Some confirmation of the validity of these basic design principles can be found by looking at situations outside the worlds of art and professional design. Examples of excellence in design are by no means confined to the works of designers. By examining such examples, we can analyze the qualities that generate satisfaction and try to define the ways in which we perceive excellence.

We can, in fact, begin with design that can develop without human contribution. It is almost a platitude to say that natural things are beautiful. Almost everyone considers trees, flowers,

landscapes, birds, animals, even human beings beautiful. *Design in nature*, while a process that operates very differently from the human design process, only produces objects and settings that work well and satisfy us visually. A second area of design excellence not created by designers is *vernacular design*. This term refers to the products of unsophisticated people working in traditional and familiar ways. Their design arises in direct response to needs rather than from a conscious effort to create an individual object in a special way. A third area, one very much in human control, *technological design* is most often the work of engineers. While engineers use the term *design*, they concentrate on function and structure, giving little or no thought to appearance in their work. Nevertheless, at least some technological design is of outstanding quality.

Natural Design

Nature normally produces its products through processes independent of human control. Inanimate, or inorganic, nature can be described as the result of forces acting on materials in ways that follow natural laws that we have come to understand with increasing precision but whose origins remain unknown. A starry night sky, which, scientifically speaking, is simply a

26

27

28

26. Natural forms have an authority, a rightness, that have inspired design throughout humanity's history. The spiral nebula in Virgo, a vast, unimaginably remote galaxy, is seen here through a powerful telescope. The spiral form is defined by the mathematics of the Fibonacci series. (Photograph: California Institute of Technology, Pasadena, courtesy American Museum of Natural History, New York)

27. The pattern of a snail shell's growth recalls, in miniature, the spiral of the great nebula (fig. 26). This and other natural forms seem to have an almost universal attraction, suggesting that their mathematical basis generates an aesthetic that is intuitively understood. National Museum of Natural History, Washington, D.C. (Photograph: Chip Clark)

28. A staircase in the Codd House on Nantucket, Massachusetts, illustrates the spiral shape adapted to human use. The spiral is repeated as a decorative form on the molding (visible at right). (Photograph: Cortlandt V. D. Hubbard, courtesy Nantucket Historical Trust)

29

30

display of celestial bodies that rush through space and emit light, is universally viewed as beautiful. The Milky Way, the moon, a spiral nebula—all beautiful elements of the night sky—actually mean little to us beyond our recognition of them as visual traces of extremely remote realities. The earth gives us satisfying images closer to our direct experience—the sea, mountains, polar caps, the patterns of rocks, pebbles, sand, cloud forms, and patterns of moving water—events that can be identified and explained by the appropriate sciences.

The evolutionary processes that govern the biological world, or organic nature, have somewhat more kinship to the human design process. Among the great variety of living things, successful forms—in a functional, survival sense—prosper and develop, while less successful variants disappear. This process seems to explain why living things are invariably of excellent design. They are also sources of visual satisfaction, true models for the human design effort. The growth patterns of plant forms, trees, and flowers can be analyzed in terms of geometric and mathematical principles that often parallel patterns in astronomical configurations. Both patterns, organic and inorganic, are responding to the same kinds of physical realities, although on a vastly different scale.

Animal life, from the microscopic forms up to the largest of creatures, is comparably logical and beautiful in design terms. People who object that some living creatures, such as snakes and insects, look ugly are usually simply expressing their fear. Given reassurance against stings, bites, or other forms of attack, one can find design merit in even the most threatening of life forms. Living species change with the passage of time as conditions change. The great prehistoric reptiles, made obsolete by environmental change, can still be appreciated as superb designs for the conditions under which they prospered. It is interesting to note that some animals also produce objects: webs, nests, hives, dams, even lodges. These creations, the result of instinctive drives rather than of conscious planning, are as consistently excellent as the direct biological products of nature.

Vernacular Design

Vernacular design, produced by human beings, has something in common with the processes of organic nature. The objects made by prehistoric and primitive populations, like the organic forms of evolution, emerged through trial and error, and then became *traditional* forms, repeated over generations with minimal change as long as they continued to serve the purposes for which they were developed. Simple tools and weapons, primitive huts and tents, containers of pottery or basketry, and basic woven fabrics are not the design of a

29. A display of beetles in the National Museum of Natural History, Washington, D.C., exhibits an astonishing variety of color and patterned markings. Their purposes—species recognition, camouflage, warning signals—often elude human inquiry, but their beauty is apparent. (Photograph: Chip Clark)

30. Shown here is a detail from a column capital, a feature of the 1986 Saddlery Building in Des Moines, Iowa, by Douglas A. Wells, architect. The forms and color are clearly inspired by natural patterns—of plants, animals, and insects. Compare this design, for example, with the beetles in fig. 29. (Photograph: © 1986 Frederick Charles)

31. In a New York apartment of 1984, Steven Holl created a singular environment of related elements. The table, chairs, rug, wall treatment, and hanging light are all his designs, developed especially for this space. (Photograph: © Paul Warchol)

particular creative person but rather *types* that show up in a particular society with only limited individual variation. These things draw our interest because of the excellence of design they often demonstrate, and because we also find them beautiful in ways that more sophisticated design often has trouble equaling.

Vernacular design is by no means limited to the ancient and primitive worlds. Modern examples surround us in such everyday objects as tools, kitchen implements, bottles, jugs, and jars, sporting and outdoor gear, musical instruments, and the innumerable things for which the question, "Who designed this?" has no answer. The fisherman's dory, the lobster trap, the fireplug, and the telephone pole—all examples of generally excellent vernacular design—like the webs, nests, and hives of the animal world, evolved to fill a specific need without benefit of formal design efforts.

Technological Design

Technology generates design that, while not at all simple or unself-conscious in a technical sense, in aesthetic terms is as

32

33

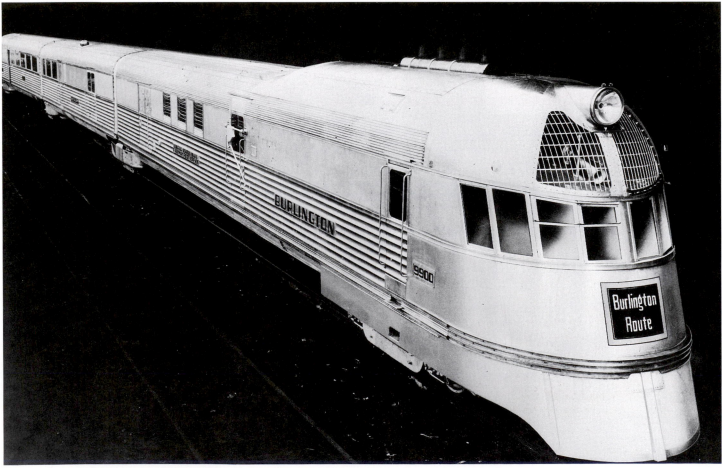

34

32. The traditional vernacular designs of so-called primitive peoples have developed over millennia. These beaded baskets made by the Nevada Paiute tribe are strongly influenced by visual harmonies found in nature. The Denver Art Museum

33. The Zephyr digital clock, designed c. 1933 by Kem Weber for Lawson Time Inc., Pasadena, California, is of brass and copper. Both its name and its shape express the national enthusiasm for technological progress—reflected in such small, everyday products. While streamlining has no functional value in a clock, the recalled form was contemporary in itself (see fig. 34). Collection John P. Axelrod. (Photograph courtesy Alistair Duncan)

34. A diesel-powered passenger train is here clothed in a streamlined, stainless-steel skin, typical of the futuristic aesthetic of the 1930s. The Burlington Zephyr of 1934, built by the Budd Manufacturing Company of Philadelphia, was the first American train to replace the steam-driven "iron horse" with technology and design better suited to the modern age. (Photograph courtesy Burlington Northern Railroad, Denver)

35

36

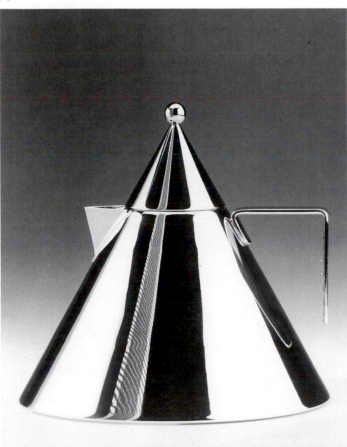

37

38

35, 36. The most familiar instance of technology in the household — the telephone — can take on a wide variety of forms. The two examples illustrated are strikingly different from each other, and both are quite unlike the standard instruments that were, until recently, the universal norm. Parola (fig. 35) has a soft-

rubber exterior that resists cracking and fingerprints. Fausta Cavazza was the designer. (Photograph courtesy Becker Inc.) The shape of Grand Prix (fig. 36), by TeleQuest, is more familiar, yet it, too, is of Space Age inspiration. (Photograph courtesy TeleQuest, Inc.)

37, 38. Today, too, professional designers draw on the pure forms of machine art when developing products for home use. Architect Aldo Rossi, working here as an industrial designer, applied such forms to the design of Il Conico, the kettle in fig. 37, and to La Conica, the home espresso maker in fig. 38. Both are 1982 designs executed in stainless steel; the bottom of the espresso maker is copper-clad. (Photograph courtesy Alessi)

39

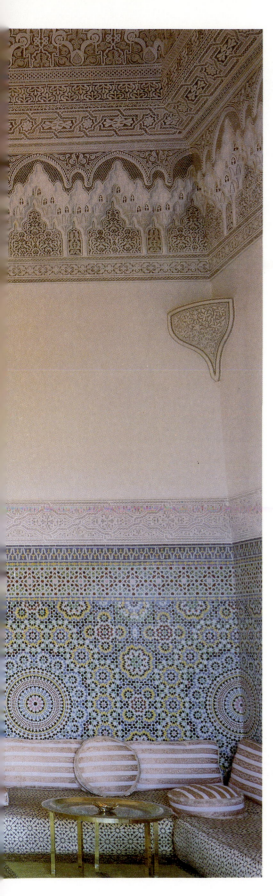

40

natural as the products of nature or vernacular design. Indeed, the term *technological vernacular* is sometimes used to describe the design that has its origin in invention and engineering. The designs of ships, aircraft, bridges, and many kinds of machinery, often deemed excellent, are carefully planned in terms of functional performance and structure but not in terms of aesthetics. In other words, aeronautical engineers, naval architects, designers of turbines, pumps, and printing presses design for performance and do not usually concern themselves with questions of beauty.

Nonetheless, their designs often look beautiful to us. In fact, gears, bearings, propellers, and similar technological objects have been gathered together and displayed in museums under the term *machine art*. We find it hard to believe that the designers of such objects do not take aesthetic considerations into account. We also find it surprising that efforts to improve technological design through the advice of design professionals often do more harm than good.

The design excellence of technological objects comes from the way in which their designs are developed—a way that closely parallels the designs of nature and the vernacular designers. Forms are suggested and guided by functional needs and the practical issues imposed by materials and manufacturing techniques. Each concept, each detail is tested by performance criteria—quite literally in a test laboratory, or in the long-term testing of use—so that better ideas survive while less successful ones fall away.

39. The decorative detail, color, and divan seating point to an Arabic or Moorish locale, while the rich, opulent materials—in contrast with those of the more modest interior shown in fig. 40—indicate a formal function. This living space is in the home of Malcolm Forbes in Morocco. Robert Gerofi, designer. (Photograph: Alain Guillou)

40. The simplicity of modern interior design promotes a kind of relaxed intimacy of its own. In this living room in the resort town of East Hampton on Long Island, New York, white walls and a checkerboard floor act as foils for inviting sofas, stacks of books, and a painting by Jack Ceglic—who also designed the room. (Photograph: © Mary Harty/Peter DeRosa, courtesy House & Garden)

Designers of both buildings and interiors constantly turn to natural, vernacular, and technological design for inspiration and guidance. Their aim is not to imitate or borrow the forms of these designs, although this is not uncommon. Rather, it is to learn how the practical aspects of designing can lead to visual results that express the intentions behind the design process. We expect an interior space to serve its purposes well, that is, to offer comfort and convenience. We expect it to be well made from suitable materials put together with quality manufacturing techniques and workmanship. We also have a right to expect that the space will convey a sense of what it is and what it does and to convey this in a way that is clear and elegant.

A comparison with a written message may be helpful. A badly written paragraph, letter, or newspaper story, even if confusing and ungrammatical, can give accurate information, thus serving its basic purpose of conveying a message. The same content can be expressed in writing that communicates with clarity and ease, even writing that becomes a pleasure to read, or, at best, a form of art that goes far beyond the simple purpose of factual communication.

The old issues of *content* and *form* arise here. In design, purpose and structure make up the *content* of the visual product the designer creates. The *form* in which that content is expressed can be clumsy, confused, inappropriate, and sloppy. It can also be clear, organized, expressive of the design process and its methods, and expressive also of its time and place, its social context, and the ideas of the designer.

ANALYZING EXISTING SPACES

The generalizations offered here become more meaningful when they are applied to actual spaces that can be seen in drawings and photographs or, better still, visited and used. Direct comparison of good examples and bad examples can make theoretical points seem less abstract and more useful in real situations that call for evaluation. It is a helpful exercise to analyze some real interiors, choosing an outstandingly fine example and a distressingly unsatisfactory example in each of several functional categories. A possible list of candidates might include:

A public space (lobby or concourse)
A classroom
An office
A restaurant
A living room
A kitchen

Analysis can then proceed by developing evaluation under the familiar headings of function, materials and structure, and visual expression. Such an analysis might produce something like the following list:

FUNCTION

EXCELLENT EXAMPLE	UNSATISFACTORY EXAMPLE
Size and shape of space well suited to purpose	Size and shape awkward and inconvenient
Placement and choice of furniture support use	Placement and choice of furniture inappropriate
Circulation well planned and convenient	Awkward circulation patterns
Good lighting	Unsatisfactory lighting
Satisfactory acoustical environment	Excessive noise and distraction

MATERIALS AND STRUCTURE

EXCELLENT EXAMPLE	UNSATISFACTORY EXAMPLE
Choice of materials supports functional performance	Materials unsuitable to intended uses
Adequate durability and ease of maintenance	Materials subject to rapid wear and hard to maintain
Workmanship of good quality	Obvious shoddy workmanship
Appropriate cost of construction	Excessive cost of construction
Consideration of safety and environmental conditions	Dangerous and hazardous conditions possible

VISUAL EXPRESSION

EXCELLENT EXAMPLE	UNSATISFACTORY EXAMPLE
Character and atmosphere appropriate to use	Unsuitable atmosphere and visual character
Time and place of design expressed	False or obscure expression of time and place
Character and quality of materials and construction honestly expressed	Materials and structure falsified or obscured
Design intentions clear and strongly developed	Design intention vague or confused

41

Many other observations will probably come to mind under each heading in the presence of an actual example. Similar tests can be applied to the various objects that make up a complete interior—the pieces of furniture, furniture systems, lamps and light fixtures, small accessories, and other individual objects that can each be viewed separately as a *design*.

Although the character of design may vary greatly from place to place and is subject to constant change over the passage of time, an analysis of the sort proposed will serve in every case,

provided that time and place are taken into account. A castle, a palace, a cathedral, an igloo, or a yurt can be evaluated on this basis as logically and reasonably as can the most recent office, apartment, or loft. These standards apply equally to future directions destined to lead to design different from anything we now know. It is the obligation of every designer to work toward the highest levels of excellence that the realities of problems and the available means for problem solutions will permit.

41. *Design of outstanding quality is apparent in this 1985 public interior in the First City Bank of New Orleans. R. Clay Markham, architect; Tom R. Collum, interior designer. (Photograph: © Alan Karchmer. All rights reserved)*

CHAPTER THREE
DESIGN BASICS

Interior design is a complex subject involving many related considerations. These include building structure, functional planning, concern with spatial form in three dimensions, the relationships of one space to another, the placement of solid objects (furniture and accessories) within larger spaces, and effects of color, pattern, texture, and light. As a practical matter, these issues are usually thought about one by one, and they can be studied as separate, individual topics. In designing an interior, however, the aim is always to weave them together in order to create a whole that is more than the sum of its parts.

The term *basic design* indicates a body of ideas about design that are so general, so universal in application as to transcend the special and detailed concerns of design projects. Basic design deals with theories and principles that refer to all aspects of *all* design. Many design schools present basic design in introductory courses (sometimes called *foundation* courses) that explore these basic issues in an abstract way, apart from specific design applications.

An understanding of basic design principles can evolve "from the bottom up," through the experience of working on design projects. However, an introductory study of basics viewed "from the top down," that is, beginning with abstract and general concepts, including line, form, space, balance, rhythm, and harmony, can be useful in developing a framework of thought within which to relate the more everyday realities of design practice. Any hope for a set of "rules" that will guarantee design excellence must be put aside. Design, especially interior design, involves so many variables that these design concepts can be used only to support the more intuitive ways of designing that have served for thousands of years. This chapter presents some of these basic issues as they might be presented in many design schools. (Since a full treatment of color theory is given in Chapter 9, it is dealt with only briefly here.)

DESIGN AND HUMAN PERCEPTION
Visual Perception

The designer's aim is to make the realities of a designed space—its form, materials, furnishings, accessories, and so on—express in an appropriate way a set of ideas that the designer wishes to communicate. Since vision is the primary sense through which the design and the ideas behind it will reach an audience, basic design must be concerned with the field, both scientific and artistic, called *visual perception*. This study explores the ways in which the visual sense works to build a mental understanding of objects, spaces, and total environments through sight. No verbal description can ever

equal the knowledge of reality that comes from actually seeing, although substitute visual images—that is, pictures—can to some extent approach the direct experience. While seeing is such a common experience as to seem to require no explanation, it actually involves many complex processes.

The mind pieces together its understanding of a three-dimensional object from information it receives from both eyes, each of which sends slightly different views. In addition, eye, head, and body movements supply a flow of changing images that, put together, create a mental *model* of the reality. This model can then be held in memory and viewed in the absence of the actual object.

This same process, combined with the physical action of walking, gives us an understanding of space. It is a special quality of space that its experience implies, even requires, movement. We must go *into* a space in order to see it, learn what it is like, and experience its unique qualities. Complex, multispace structures demand that we walk from one space to another, which involves not only motion but also time. Since motion cannot be thought of apart from time, the modern physical concept of space-time becomes useful in designing interiors.

This concept is illustrated by a visit to a large building, a cathedral, a museum, or a concert hall, in which a full exploration of the interior space requires passing from room to room and from one level to another. We understand such a space not as a single entity fixed in time but as a sequence of experiences. As we add each new experience of the space on our progress through it, we substitute memories for the actual experience. The smallest of spatial sequences—a small house, a tiny apartment, even a single room—displays this quality to some degree. In order to truly know and understand any space, we must walk into it, look about in all directions—to all sides, up and down—sit down, move around, and spend some time building up a series of impressions that combine into our final idea of the space.

Visual Impressions

In addition to the understanding of reality that comes with vision and movement, a viewer receives impressions of a more abstract, even emotional character. An object or a place may *look* quiet or lively, cheerful or depressing, solid or vaporous. We learn that a fire or bright sunlight is hot or warm, and so we associate the colors red and orange with heat. We see the sharp edges of tables and boxes and learn that they also feel hard and sharp, while the soft forms of cushions and draped fabric become associated with the sensation of softness. The horizontal surfaces of the sea, a lake, or a meadow connect

42. A complex ceiling construction in architect Marlys Hann's own house in the Catskills, New York, of 1985 generates a dynamic interplay between the triangular shapes and the circular central window. (Photograph: © Paul Warchol)

43

repose with horizontality. The sturdy upright of a tree trunk relates naturally to a sense of solidity and stability. The bright colors of birds and flowers carry associations different from the browns and grays of earth and rocks.

All of these associations are reinforced by the kinetic impressions that we receive from our own bodily positions and movements. We learn that a horizontal position *is* restful, while standing upright promotes attention, formality, even resistance. When running, we lean forward in an aggressive diagonal. While we experience bodily *symmetry* as normal and stable, we can move body parts into *asymmetrical* positions, but we learn to do this in a way that maintains *balance*. A person tilted to one side will fall over unless the body is repositioned to maintain balance or support is found by leaning on or holding on to something.

Man-made designs also contribute to this buildup of interpretive reactions. We see an automobile or airplane that is capable of fast movement, and we come to say that the typical forms *look* fast, even when the object is at rest. When a room

43. Soft and curving shapes connote relaxation and ease in a New York apartment living room designed in 1983 by Juan Montoya. (Photograph: Jaime Ardiles-Arce)

strikes us as cheerful, restful, dignified, or business-like, we may be reacting to memory traces of experiences with rooms that looked a certain way and that turned out to *be* a certain way. It is difficult to say whether this is due to individual characteristics, such as shape, pattern, or color, or whether it comes from a total impression of the sort that the Gestalt school of psychology studies. Basic design begins with a study of the individual elements that go together to form the totality of a *gestalt*.

ELEMENTS OF DESIGN
It is convenient to follow a progression in considering how visual impressions are developed.

Point
As conceived in geometry, a point is simply a location in space having neither dimensions nor substance—an abstract notion difficult to grasp. Two points, however, suggest a beginning and

44

an end and lead to the idea of a connecting line (fig. 47). Points in a random scatter seem meaningless, but a cluster of points in a field of scatter suggests a focus or concentration of interest (fig. 46).

Line

When a point moves through space or when two points are connected, *line* is generated. Line, which may be straight or curved, has length but not breadth. We seem to see lines where

44. In contrast with the interior in fig. 43, this Manhattan loft, with its clean lines, mobile planters, and High Tech exposed plumbing and lighting, uses hard edges and slick surfaces to create an ambience that is both modern and lively. Designed in 1985 by Bromley/ Jacobsen Designs. (Photograph: Jaime Ardiles-Arce)

45

things have edges, where one plane meets another, or where there is a change of color or surface in a plane. Straight lines can be thought of as taking several typical positions:

VERTICAL LINES. These suggest stability and immobility, and, by extension, dignity and permanence. The significance of verticality comes, it seems, from the downward direction of the force of gravity. This force dictates verticals, always perpendicular to all horizontals, as the basic structural support. The vertical columns of a building suggest its solidity and permanence.

45. In this library of a renovated 1920s Texas home, interior designer Mark Hampton created an atmosphere of comfort and luxury by means of warm colors and rich textures. Objects on display range from pre-Columbian pieces to part of a collection of Austrian bird bronzes. The sculpture on the table is a mare and foal by Jim Reno. (Photograph: Feliciano, courtesy House & Garden)

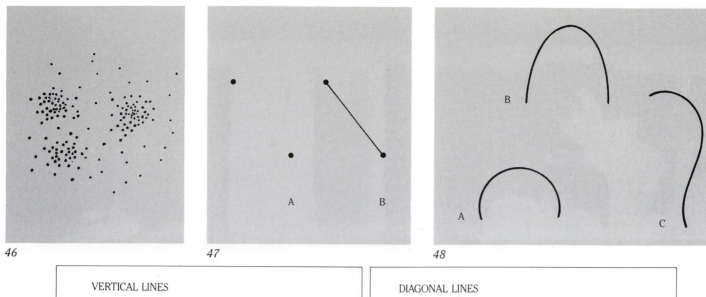

46

47

48

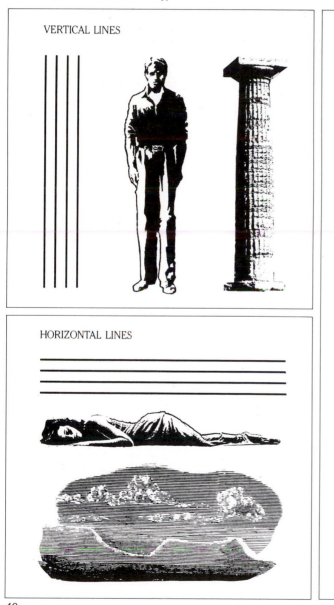

VERTICAL LINES

HORIZONTAL LINES

49

DIAGONAL LINES

46. In a random scatter of points, any cluster becomes a focus of attention. The three clusters here bring to mind the form of a triangle.

47. Any two points will generate a sense of relationship (A), which is mentally translated into a connecting line (B).

48. Curving lines suggest softness and freedom. Segments of circles (A) carry some stability; segments of parabolas (B) and other more complex geometric forms are both freer and more subtle; free curves (C)—curves that are not parts of circles or any other geometric figures—may be flowing, aggressive, or active.

49. Dominant vertical lines contribute to a sense of dignity and solidity. Horizontality relates to feelings of tranquility, calm, and repose. Diagonal forms suggest movement and the dynamic relationship of forces; they promote feelings of activity and motion. In excess, they can be disturbing.

50

HORIZONTAL LINES. These suggest rest and repose. Gravity pulls materials down to a horizontal resting point parallel to the ground in a horizontal line, and earth and sky seem to meet in a horizontal. Human experience of the horizontal reclining position in rest and sleep reinforces these perceptions. Floors and ceilings, normally horizontal, are the surfaces that give spaces their sense of reassuring normality.

OBLIQUE (DIAGONAL OR SLOPING) LINES. These suggest movement, dynamic forces, and activity. Angled lines are always, in a sense, transitional between vertical and horizontal, the positions that gravity tolerates, and are held only through some special means of resistance to gravitational forces. A person leans forward to run, making us associate activity and movement with oblique lines.

While there can be only one horizontal and one vertical direction, oblique lines can take an infinite number of angular slopes. The combination of oblique lines in alternate directions, called a *zigzag*, gives a sense of restless, rapid hyperactivity. It is used to symbolize lightning, electricity, and radio waves. A sloping ceiling or wall makes a space seem active, lively, even possibly disturbing through its implication of movement.

CURVED LINE. The path of a moving point that continually changes its direction gives a curved line. Curving forms occur more often in nature than rectilinear forms, leading us to perceive curvatures as more natural, freer, and more "humane" than straight-lined forms. Circles and segments of circles, having a simple and clear geometric genesis, appear straightforward. More complex curvatures, such as ellipses, parabolas, and hyperbolas, are more varied and more subtle. *Free* curves that have no geometric controls and combinations of curvatures in S shapes or sinuous relationships suggest increasing levels of complexity, subtlety, and softness.

Two-dimensional Forms

A *plane* is a completely flat surface, created by intersecting lines. Planes are *two dimensional,* with length and width, as are plane figures—figures that lie completely in one plane—such as the triangle, square, circle, and so on. Planes also contain irregular or free shapes that conform to no particular geometric definition. The human mind seems to be drawn toward recognition of simple geometric shapes, perhaps because, being perfect forms, they can be held in memory and reproduced with ease. In a scatter of points, the eye will seek out a triangle, square, or circle or find an image with a recognizable form (fig.

50. Horizontal forms evoke a feeling of tranquility in this area of the home of textile designer Jack Lenor Larsen. The sliding screens, which suggest traditional Japanese shoji screens, cover or reveal a collection of porcelains. The floor is of modern Italian ceramic tile; the woven basket chairs are recent reproductions of a 1950 design by the Danish designer Nana Ditzel. (Photograph: Rick Barnes)

51. Strong verticals suggest solidity, formality, and dignity in this living room in the Atlanta, Georgia, home of architect John Portman. John Portman & Associates, designer. (Photograph: Jaime Ardiles-Arce)

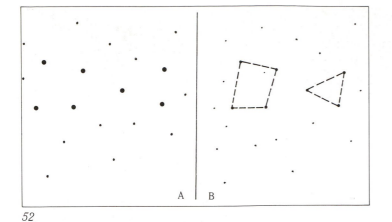

52

52). The constellations of the night sky are images suggested by the relationships of bright stars seen as points. The Big Dipper, for example, is simply an arrangement of bright points that suggests the form of a long-handled cup. Once that grouping is pointed out and named, it becomes easy to locate and recognize amid the vast number of other stars that surround it (fig. 53).

Design makes wide use of our attraction to perfect shapes, whose completeness and stability we find highly satisfying. Imperfect shapes, such as a square with a corner cut off or one irregular side, a circle with a dent, or a shape not fully closed, cause a sense of tension, which may be used to create a more dynamic, unusual design (fig. 54). However, if the "imperfection" is too strong, it leads to outright dissatisfaction and a sense of instability.

More complex forms, such as rectangles of various proportions, other quadrilaterals, polygons, and curved forms, regular and irregular, all have both practical uses and expressive visual qualities of varied sorts.

53

52. In a random scatter of points (A), the mind and eye search out relationships that can be seen as recognizable geometric figures (B).

53. In the random-scatter pattern that stars form in the night sky, the brighter stars seem to form patterns. Once it is pointed out, the Big Dipper becomes a familiar and easily spotted pattern, since its shape suggests a familiar form.

Surfaces, as they occur in reality—rather than in abstract geometry—also have physical attributes, including:

Texture (rough, smooth, matte, glossy, hard, soft)
Value (light, medium, dark)
Color (hue and saturation; see Chapter 9, "Color")
Pattern
Transparency, translucency, or opacity

A surface may be unified, as, for example, a wall painted one color, or it may be subdivided by changes of material, color, or pattern and may also intersect with other surfaces. Transparent and semitransparent surfaces can create complex visual effects, including the spatial illusions resulting from reflections in polished surfaces such as glass and mirror. Surfaces have an almost inevitable relationship with lines since their edges,

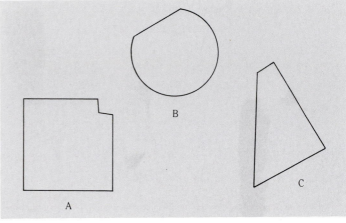

54

boundaries of subdivisions, and intersections are seen as lines. In the fine arts, the mediums of painting, drawing, and printmaking are concerned with two-dimensional surface.

Three-dimensional Forms

Adding depth, or volume, to a two-dimensional form creates a *three-dimensional form*. Furniture, some architectural elements (such as columns or stairs), and buildings are three-dimensional solids. Interior design is particularly concerned with hollow three-dimensional form, or space: rooms or other spaces within buildings, which are the primary element of interior design. Hollow space is articulated by planes of enclosure, that is, floors, walls, ceilings, which separate space inside from space outside and determine the nature of the interior space.

In most interior spaces, the planes of floors, walls, and ceilings are organized in 90-degree, or right-angled, relationships, usually called *rectilinear*, which are considered the

54. Figures that would form a simple geometric shape but for some irregularity are perceived as being defective, and the mind struggles to supply a "correction." Figure A is clearly a square, slightly modified. B is seen as an imperfect circle. C appears as a truncated triangle rather than the irregular quadrangle that it actually is.

55

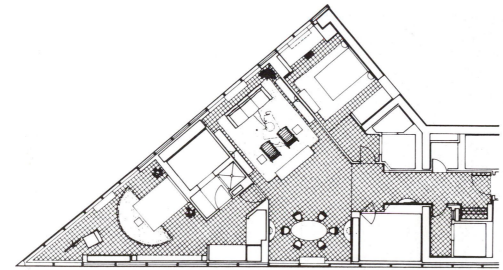

56

55, 56. The diagonal lines and angular and broken shapes of this bedroom (fig. 55) give rise to a sense of nervous activity and motion. The plan (fig. 56) shows the apartment's unusual triangular layout that inspired the room's design. The associations with a ship are intentional: the space is treated as a lookout, with a telescope pointing toward the apex of the triangle. The chair, titled Hell's Angel, is by Patrick Naggar. Andrée Putman designed this 1987 showcase apartment in New York's Metropolitan Tower. (Photograph: © Peter Paige)

57

58

most stable of forms. In fact, such boxlike room forms are so common that they have come to be criticized for their monotony and lack of imagination. Small, boxlike enclosed spaces can suggest confinement and restriction or, on the other hand, privacy and intimacy.

Nonrectilinear three-dimensional room forms can be generated by using non-right-angled relationships for one or more of the enclosing planes, as for example, a sloping ceiling or an angled wall, or by the use of curving planes of enclosure. Curved forms, because they are not so sharply defined by lines, suggest openness and free space. Round or elliptical rooms have a special character, while domes as a ceiling or roof inspire feelings of grandeur and awe by suggesting the infinite openness of the universe. Domes automatically make an internal space special, even monumental, as, for example, the rotundas of many famous buildings.

Complex hollow space can be developed by connecting several simpler forms (as in the design of Gothic and Renaissance churches, whose plans are usually based on connecting quadrilaterals and semicircles); by opening simple spaces into one another with large doorways, open wells, and similar devices; or by providing more than one level in a single space. Stairways, in addition to offering oblique planes, can be designed in complex three-dimensional terms, such as the helix of the popular spiral stair. These are all common ways to

57. *Circular forms imply freeness and sometimes even humor; here, in the Aurora restaurant of 1985 in New York, repeating clusters suggest balls, tops, or, perhaps, soap bubbles. Philip George and Milton Glaser, designers. (Photograph: © Peter Mauss/ESTO)*

58. *The basic geometric rectilinear shapes—the square, rectangle, and triangle—form the basis for most interior design. A top-floor area in a Santa Monica, California, house of 1982 by Robert Yudell, architect, with Charles Jencks juxtaposes all three shapes. (Photograph: Tim Street-Porter)*

60

introduce movement, openness, and variety into a space. Complex spaces can also include areas of intimacy without losing their impression of openness, as, for example, when a lowered ceiling is used over a conversation area that looks out to an open space beyond it.

DESIGN CONCEPTS

In organizing line, surface, and hollow space, a number of other basic concepts will enter into design decisions. Some of these concepts are:

Size

We think of things as large or small in relative terms, in relation to both the human body and other things. A large living room may be much smaller than a large church, but it appears large in relation to an adjacent small entrance hall. Absolute size is usually less important than relative size.

Scale

This term is widely used in design and architecture to describe a rather subtle consideration related to size. It refers to the proper proportion of an object or space to all other objects, to human beings, and to the space to which it belongs. Designers achieve *good scale* by choosing elements that seem to be of an appropriate size for the space they will inhabit; that relate well to human dimensions; and, above all, that look their actual size (fig. 62). Small pieces of furniture often look lost in a large space, while large objects may seem overbearing when crammed into a small room. A large space that appears too small is out of scale. Good scale is indicated when things look so right that the issue does not even come to mind.

Proportion

This concept addresses the relationship of parts of a design to each other and to the whole. Good proportion is a much discussed concept in the arts and in design and is considered a

59. With its curved form and soaring height, a dome lifts a building from the ordinary to the monumental. Many historic religious or governmental interiors have taken advantage of the monumentality of domes; here, for the lobby of the Dow Jones office building in New York (1986), architect Cesar Pelli used a domed space to confer a monumental character on a business purpose. (Photograph: © 1986 Wolfgang Hoyt/ ESTO)

60. A simple space opens into more elaborate adjacent spaces, establishing an intricate set of interrelationships. Certain traditional design elements are repeated—columns and pilasters; the swags of the chandelier, echoed in the carving on the entablature—which, together with the use of color, convey a sense of conservative dignity in this 1986 renovation of a period interior for the Chase Manhattan Bank, New York. John F. Saladino, designer. (Photograph: © Langdon Clay)

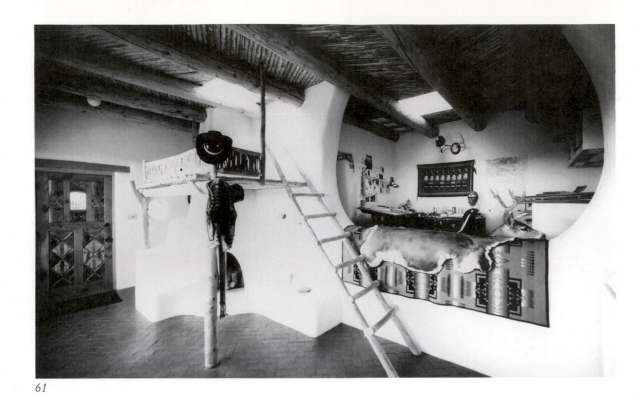

61

key requirement in any aesthetic success. It is not hard to tell if an existing space is well or badly proportioned. In the former case, it looks visually "right"; in the latter case, for example, a room may seem too long and narrow, or an element such as a door, window, or piece of furniture may appear awkwardly placed. Achieving good proportions is less easy than recognizing them, although many efforts have been made to develop systems for doing so.

One approach, using mathematical relationships analogous to the rules of harmony in music, suggests organizing proportions according to geometric ratios of simple whole numbers, such as 1:2, 2:3, 3:4, and 3:5. Many Renaissance architects, including Palladio and Alberti, based their structures on such systems (fig. 63). Other approaches, such as the *Modulor* of Le Corbusier (fig. 67), base dimensional units on human body proportions, such as height and arm reach, and extend these through numerical multiplication into a system for controlling dimensions and their relationships.

The Modulor also makes use of one particular mathematical relationship, often referred to as the *golden ratio* or *golden section* and designated by the Greek letter phi (φ). It has had so much influence on design throughout history as to deserve some special discussion. The terms *golden mean, golden ratio,* and *golden section* all refer to a proportional relationship that satisfies a certain requirement. If one divides a line into two unequal segments so that the ratio of the short segment to the

long segment equals the ratio of the long segment to the total line length (the short segment plus the long segment), this requirement is satisfied. The resulting ratio

$$\frac{.618}{1} = \frac{1}{1.618}$$

is expressed in the irrational number .618... (figs. 64–66).

This proportion can be found in the designs of many famous structures and works of art. Various experiments and comparisons of measurements show a strong preference for the golden ratio among human beings and a high level of occurrence in nature. (See Appendix 6 for a more extended discussion.)

Harmony, Unity, Variety, Contrast

These terms describe concepts with clear bearing on design, although no precise way of defining an "ideal" measure for *harmony* describes the combination of elements and other principles in a way that produces consonance. In order to achieve harmony, all the varied components of an interior, like the notes in a chord, must relate to each other and to the overall theme of the design (fig. 68).

Unity allows the viewer to experience a design as a whole rather than seeing it as a collection of elements. All the parts of

61. A partially enclosing wall with an unusual, horseshoe-shaped opening creates a secluded alcove. John Nieto, an artist, designed this space for his adobe house in New Mexico. (Photograph: © 1985 Michael Skott)

the design will relate so well as to create a unit in which, ideally, nothing can be added, taken away, or altered without changing the totality. Matching or coordinated patterns, closely related colors, and stylistic consistency all lead to harmony and unity, but they also carry the threat of monotony, as in the room in which everything matches everything else in an obsessive way.

Variety and *contrast,* the countervailing qualities of harmony and unity, can relieve monotony, giving the eye a number of different shapes, textures, colors, or details to look at (fig. 70). *Contrast* heightens values through comparison. A light color will seem lighter if placed near a dark color, a large object larger in contrast with something small (fig. 69). In this context, contrast and variety may be viewed as ways to punctuate harmony and unity, heightening the space's overall impact.

Balance

This principle concerns the achievement of a state of equilibrium between forces. We are familiar with balance through our direct experience with gravity, which exerts a force on us that we must counter by maintaining an upright position or using a support that holds us up in a secure relationship. Visually, we find unbalanced relationships tenuous and disturbing, while balanced relationships look normal, at rest, and comfortable (fig. 71).

There are several ways to achieve balance. The most obvious balanced relationships are *symmetrical*, in which the arrangement of forms on one side of an imaginary central dividing line, axis, or plane is the mirror image of the other side. Such bilateral symmetry is characteristic of the human body and the forms of many living creatures. It is thus associated with the beauty of nature. In design, the identical visual weights and the importance of the center create an effect of repose and dignity. A high proportion of historic buildings, interiors, and objects exhibit the symmetrical balance of bilateral organization. Symmetrical balance can be achieved around a larger number of axes as well. *Radial symmetry* establishes balance around a central point, as, for example, the hub of a wheel, with the design elements radiating out like the wheel's spokes (fig. 73).

A more subtle concept, *asymmetrical* balance brings into

62

62. *This Juan Montoya design, in a house in Houston, Texas, emphasizes enclosure and containment in a space with no visible windows. The effect is private and intimate—without a hint of claustrophobia. The low seating accen-tuates the ceiling height and the large painting, creating a scale that stops just short of the monumental—which would be out of place in a private residence. (Photograph: Jaime Ardiles-Arce)*

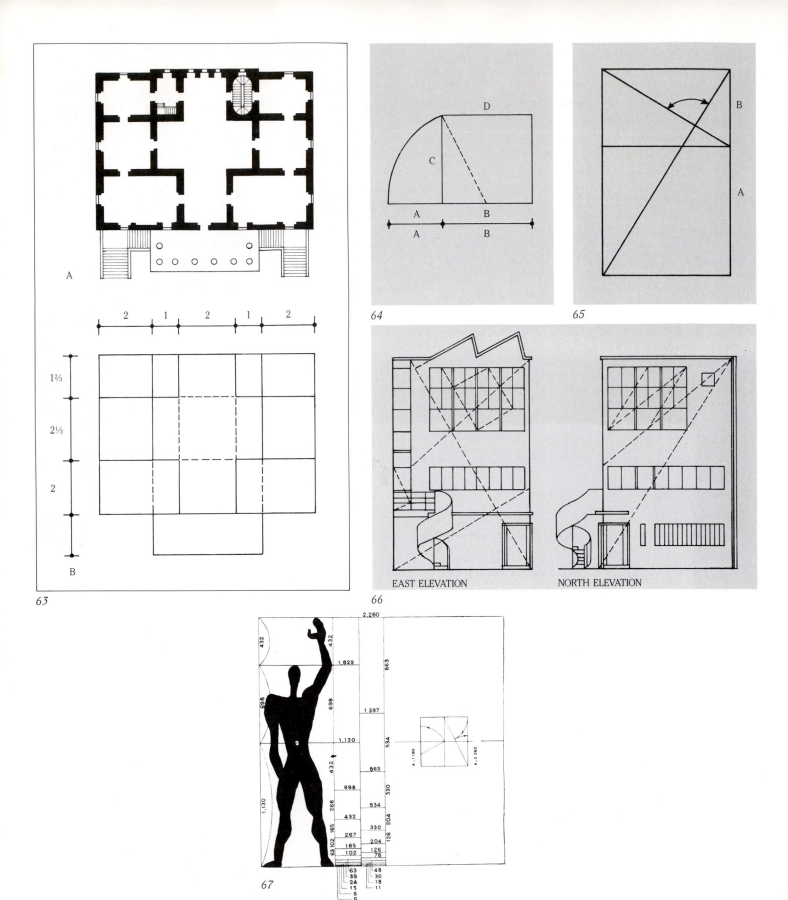

EAST ELEVATION   NORTH ELEVATION

63. Geometric analysis can demonstrate the mathematical basis behind many classical and Renaissance designs. This plan of Palladio's Villa Foscari (La Malcontenta) at Mira (A), when analyzed, turns out to be based on simple arithmetic proportions (B). If the smallest dimensional unit is given a value of 1, the width of the building can be seen to be divided into a rhythmic sequence of 2-1-2-1-2 (making a total of 8 units). The length turns out to total 6 units, divided in the somewhat more complex relationship of 2-2⅓-1⅔. (The relationships can also be expressed in whole numbers by giving the smallest unit the value of 3. The width is then expressed as 6-3-6-3-6, the length as 6-7-5; the totals are then W = 24, L = 18. Reducing these figures to a ratio gives a proportional relationship of $\frac{18}{24} = \frac{6}{8}$ or $\frac{3}{4}$.) Such relationships underlie the relationship of tones that generate musical harmony.

64. In order to divide a line into golden ratio proportions, a dotted line is drawn from the midpoint of side B of the square to the intersection of sides C and D; then an arc is swung downward to the base line. $\frac{A}{B}$ forms a golden ratio.

equilibrium elements that are equivalent but not matching. The principle is demonstrated by a scale of the type in which an object is weighed by moving a weight closer to or farther away from a balance point. A small weight hanging from a long arm will balance a heavy weight placed close to the fulcrum, or balance point (fig. 74). This concept, in which different things of different size or weight seem to come into balance through placement, can also apply to shapes, colors, sizes, and other aspects of objects.

Symmetrical and asymmetrical design are often a product of the architectural structure of a space. For instance, a house with a center hall and rooms of similar size to right and left begins with a built-in symmetrical structure that leads naturally to visual symmetry in its design (fig. 72). Other building plans and room layouts cannot offer symmetry. A room may have windows on one side only, or an entrance located to the left or right of center. In such situations, asymmetry is best accepted and the room brought into aesthetic balance by means other than strict symmetry. Some historic designs used false elements (a dummy door, for example) to force symmetry where it did not occur naturally. This kind of solution rarely works in modern practice.

In addition, symmetry tends to express a sense of formality, dignity, stability, and conservatism. The more the central axis is emphasized, the more strongly these values will be felt—as in many traditional designs for church and temple interiors, courtrooms, throne rooms, and similar ceremonial interiors. A centered fireplace and mantel or a large central window or door

68

69

65. A golden rectangle with a square cut off (A) produces a smaller golden rectangle (B). The diagonals of the larger and smaller rectangles intersect at a right angle.

66. In his design for the Ozenfant house in Paris (1922), Le Corbusier used the golden ratio as the system of regulating lines that formed the basis of his design geometry. This diagram is based on the illustration he used in Towards a New Architecture.

67. Le Corbusier's Modulor is a modern, complex system that uses geometric ratios based on the proportions of the human body to determine the patterns of architectural design.

68. The repetition of square and rectangular patterns, characteristic of the Vienna Secessionist style, endows this hotel breakfast room in the Villa Mozart, Merano, Italy, with a sense of unity and harmony. Designed by the owner. (Photograph: © 1985 Ronny Jacques/ Photo Researchers)

69. In a pre-Revolutionary farmhouse beside the Brandywine River, now the home of Jamie and Phyllis Wyeth, contrasting white and navy blue give the bedroom qualities of crispness, some formality, and a feeling of cool and calm order. Wyeth's painting Wicker hangs over the fireplace; an oil study by Rockwell Kent is above the books between the two French provincial chairs. Designed by the owners. (Photograph: © François Halard, courtesy House & Garden)

70

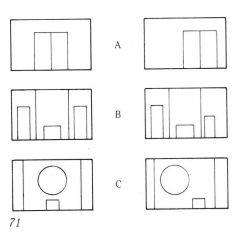

71

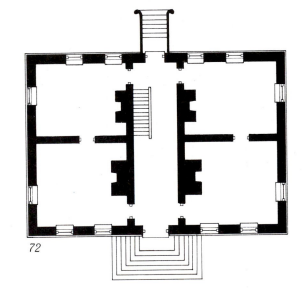

72

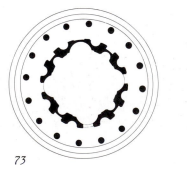

73

74

70. This bedroom in Milan, Italy, combines dramatically diverse styles—antique and modern furniture together with striking modern art within a space of markedly historic character—to achieve both contrast and variety without jarring conflicts. (Photograph: Jaime Ardiles-Arce)

71. Symmetrical balance demands exact equality between two sides of a composition. Slight departures from symmetry suggest some defect or displacement that the mind struggles to correct, creating a tension that may be disturbing or that may be used as an expressive device. A centered doorway seems normal; the same door slightly off-center is disturbing (A). Identical elements on either side of a fireplace are perfectly balanced; a smaller door on the right is

perceived as an error (B). The displacement of the central element in C is similarly distracting.

72. Bilateral (two-sided) symmetry is familiar as the basis for the planning of many buildings, with rooms, windows, and other elements carefully placed on either side of a central axis to create the kind of balanced pattern that occurs in many natural forms, including the human body. This plan of an American Colonial house is a typical example.

73. In radial symmetry, elements are arranged around a central point like the spokes radiating from a wheel, around two or more axes. This plan of Bramante's Tempietto at S. Pietro in Montorio in Rome is radially symmetrical around four axes. Most radially symmetrical plans have two, possibly four, axes of symmetry. Other numbers of axes, even odd numbers such as three or five, are possible, if unusual.

75

76

74. *The concept of asymmetrical balance relates to the physical laws that make it possible for a light weight on a long lever arm (left) to balance a heavier weight on a short lever arm (right).*

75. *The strong bilateral symmetry of this design is accented energetically by the nonsymmetrical pattern of the rug. Steven Holl designed all the furniture for the 1985 renovation of an L-shaped New York apartment. Steven Holl Architects (Steven Holl with Mark Janson and Joseph Fenton), designer. (Photograph: © Paul Warchol)*

76. *In a New York apartment of 1983 by Suzie Frankfurt, designer, the fireplace, mantel, and picture form an emphatic axis, which is balanced by the niche at the left and the arrangement of furniture in an elegantly weighted, asymmetrical relationship. (Photograph: Lizzie Himmel)*

in an otherwise symmetrical room add to the feeling of formality. Asymmetry, in contrast, suggests more openness to change, a more informal and active intention. Many modern buildings and interiors employ asymmetry to express these qualities.

Rhythm *Motion*

Another concept borrowed from music, *rhythm* relates visual elements together in a regular pattern. It can be achieved by *repetition,* whether simple, as in a rhythm such as 1 1 1 1, or more complex, as in *1* 111 *1* 111 *1* 111 *1*. The number 1 might stand for a window opening, a column, or a subdivision in a paneled wall.

The mind enjoys rhythm, and it is an important element in both historic and modern design (fig. 77). The classic architectural *orders* (Doric, Ionic, and Corinthian) are rhythmic systems (see figs. 552–54), while modern modular furniture and structural systems generate rhythmic patterns. The use of rhythm—the choice of small or large units, close together or widely spaced—should be appropriate to the situation. Since repetition can lead to monotony, it must also be balanced against the need for variety.

Emphasis

One of the ways to transmit meaning in design is through emphasis, which ensures that important elements *look* important while minor and trivial elements look subordinate. This is achieved through balancing size, placement, value, color, and selection of materials. A large door centrally placed becomes a point of focus. A brightly colored object in an otherwise quiet space calls attention to itself.

The designer must decide the levels of importance of all the elements that make up an interior and then find a visual expression for each of these levels, from the most important

77

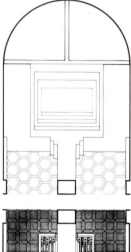
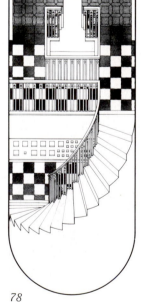

78

77, 78. The repetition of squares of different sizes and in different planes conveys a vigorously rhythmic effect in this New York project (fig. 77). An intriguing study of a stair hall (fig. 78) from the same project demonstrates the same rhythmic effect. Peter L. Gluck and Partners, designer, 1983. (Photograph: © Norman McGrath)

through the less important to the least important. A handsome fireplace mantel centered in one wall of a room is a natural focal point (fig. 79) that is emphasized by placing a fine painting above the mantel. Placing the seating furniture—a sofa and chairs, perhaps—so that it relates to the fireplace while choosing a suitable cover fabric that does not compete with the painting will give the furniture grouping a secondary level of importance. Carpet, ceiling color, and lighting can be treated to appear neutral, almost unnoticeable. Alternatively, a colorful and strongly patterned rug, a strikingly designed seating group, or a spectacular light fixture could be an emphatic focus, in which case the other elements would be deliberately subordinated.

Pattern and Ornament

Smooth surfaces are defined only by their limits, edges, or corners. A patterned surface has visible presence in every part of its extent. The eye focuses on *pattern* and uses it to help measure size and shape, to gain information about material, and to interpret the mood of the design (fig. 80). The fact that pattern is usually repetitious gives it rhythmic qualities on a small scale. Like color—or used in combination with color—pattern can make a surface more or less important or a space seem larger or smaller than it actually is. For example, stripes running vertically make a surface seem narrower and higher, running horizontally, wider and lower.

At the same time, the elements of a pattern can convey messages. Little flowers and regular stripes create very different moods. Geometric squares and naturalistic curves imply different attitudes. In addition to such expressive qualities, pattern has the ability to hide, or at least minimize, soiling and visible traces of damage. Plain surfaces expose every flaw, while pattern tends to camouflage imperfections.

Ornament refers to visual extras unnecessary for practical reasons but added to show off craftsmanship, introduce variety,

79

79. The powerfully axial stepped forms of the chimney breast on the fireplace wall draw the eye irresistibly. The emphatic visual focus organizes the active, varied forms of this Post-modern interior, a living room in the Shulman house in New Jersey, by Michael Graves. (Photograph: © 1982 Peter Aaron/ESTO)

80

and enrich a uniform surface. Ornament played a prominent role in most design of the historical periods. The moldings, eggs and darts, Greek Keys, and similar motifs of classical design, the carved leaves and gargoyles of medieval design clearly express the thinking and the craft skills of their respective eras.

With modern mechanical reproduction, ornament became easier to produce but less meaningful, no longer made by a skilled craftsman for a particular context. The modern movement has often responded by omitting ornament entirely.

(Adolf Loos went so far as to say, "Ornament is a crime.") Still, the gleaming edges of glass, chrome, and marble in the modern interior serve some of the same purposes as applied ornament. Recently, ornament seems to have been rediscovered. It now appears in much contemporary work, often quite brashly and aggressively as an expressive tool (fig. 81).

In all ornamentation, the key to value is the issue of *meaning*. Why is the ornament there? Does it add something or does it merely cover over and confuse? Good ornament emphasizes

80. Strong patterns in drapery, upholstery fabrics, and wall covering pull together to give character and consistency to this living space in a New York town house. Mario Buatta, interior designer, chose the fabric (Georgian Scroll chintz, by J. H. Thorp) to contribute to the effect of a nineteenth-century English town house. (Photograph: Edgar de Evia, courtesy House & Garden)

what is important, draws attention to what is significant, and tells something about the materials and workmanship involved. The molding around a door or window emphasizes that element's size, shape, and position. Moldings at a cornice or baseboard strengthen the line of intersection of walls, floor, and ceiling. A rosette where a light fixture hangs from a ceiling makes the place of hanging more important. The moldings around panels of furniture or room interiors make the size, shape, and pattern of the paneling stronger, clearer, and more decisive. Carved detail on a chair tells us the place and time of its origin, as well as something about the attitudes and crafts skill of its maker. An object that serves a useful function can at the same time become an expressive carrier of a message by the addition of meaningful painted surface designs. Ornament fails or clutters when it has no meaning, is introduced only for show, and has no real relationship with the object or space it adorns. However, when its purpose is genuine and useful, it can be a valuable communicative tool.

All of these techniques have, in the end, the same objective. They are means by which the designer can convey to the audience of users, viewers, even those who know the result only through photographs ideas about the reality of the place that has been designed. Ideas that will be memorable, meaningful, satisfying, and in some way unique to the particular space are the final goal of all design effort.

81

81. The home of architect Charles Jencks and designer Maggie Keswick in England contains this architectural library with unusual, Gothic-accented bookcases. There is a symbolic intent: the bookcases speak of the books' contents using an ornamental vocabulary that refers to specific historic periods. Charles Jencks and Maggie Keswick, designers. (Photograph: © Richard Bryant, courtesy House & Garden)

CHAPTER FOUR
PLANNING

Planning is a primary aspect of interior design. The very term *design* implies planning of a thoughtful and organized nature. Design professionals offer as one of their most important skills the ability to plan, creating spaces that will be practical and comfortable and will serve their intended purposes. Amateurs tend to use available furniture placed according to chance or habit and to rush into choices of new furniture, color, and materials without taking the time to plan methodically. Poor planning—or no planning at all—is probably the most common cause of disappointing interiors. While not as apparent as unsuccessful color or lighting, it is more fundamental to basic performance.

DESIGN DRAWINGS

Although the word *plan* has come to have generalized meaning, it also refers to a particular kind of drawing that is basic to planning. Plans, together with several other types of drawings, are vital to the designer in developing conceptual ideas and communicating them to clients. They provide a means of visualizing and understanding the different ways in which a space can work. In order to be useful, all such drawings must be made *to scale*.

Drawing to Scale

Since architectural spaces are too large to fit on manageable sheets of paper, drawings are made in reduced size with all their parts still in correct proportional relationship. This is *drawing to scale*. A selected dimensional unit, for example, one-quarter inch, is chosen to represent one foot. Multiples and subdivisions of this unit are used to represent all the parts of the actual-size space being drawn. At ¼″ = 1′-0″, the entire space is shown at one-forty-eighth its actual size. The scales most used in interior design are ⅛″ = 1′-0″ (for larger spaces or groups of spaces); ¼″ = 1′-0″ (for rooms and smaller groups of rooms); ¾″, 1″, 1½″, and 3″ = 1′-0″ (for details); and, sometimes, full size (1′-0″ = 1′-0″) for complex details and for some furniture drawings. Scale rulers, including the triangular architect's scale, are graduated in these scales and make it easy to lay out drawings in accurate scale dimensions. Construction drawings give actual numerical dimensions, however, since measuring off scale dimensions cannot be trusted as having enough accuracy for use in building.

Orthographic Projection

In this system, any subject can be shown by three different views that set out its three-dimensional reality on flat paper in a way that permits scale measurement of each view. The views most used to show architectural and interior subjects are the plan, elevation, and section.

PLAN. This is a view from above, looking down, as if a building, room, or rooms have been sliced through horizontally, revealing the floor level and the parts of walls, furniture, and other elements that lie below normal eye level (fig. 89). Also called floor plans or ground plans, plans are similar to maps and are familiar to everyone who has looked at guidebooks, real-estate brochures, and similar materials. In a plan, a space is drawn out to scale with lines representing walls, doors, windows, and columns in their proper relationships. (See Appendix 1, "Architectural Plan Symbols.") A completed interior design plan includes furniture and any other significant elements drawn in their intended locations. The most vital of all architectural and interior drawings, plans usually come first and can convey almost all of the information about a project that needs to be drawn.

ELEVATION. This term describes a view that shows one face (front, side, or rear) of its subject projected onto a vertical plane, as if the face had been transferred onto paper in scale (fig. 89). Exterior elevations of a building resemble a picture of whatever face of the structure is shown. Interior elevations of rooms show one wall surface at a time in scale, usually with whatever furniture or other objects will be on or close to that wall.

SECTION. Sectional drawings show an object, a space, or a building as if it had been sliced through to reveal internal spaces and construction (fig. 89). Two kinds of sections are useful in interior drawings. The first discloses, in addition to the internal spaces and constructions, the hidden structure and materials within the thicknesses of the subject being sectioned (for example, the ducts and wiring placed between walls or above ceilings). A section of a window or a door frame or a cabinet belongs to this category. The other type of section shows the hollow spaces of rooms within a building, making clear their shapes and relationships, without disclosing the composition of thickness. A variation of this type of section (sometimes called a *sectional elevation*) slices the structure so as to reveal the appearance of distant walls or any other elements that would be visible if the near or front wall were removed. Detail sections (often drawn at large scale) are particularly useful in showing how materials are to be put together in actual construction. (See Appendix 4, "Material Indications in Section.")

Perspective Drawing

This technique, familiar in representational art, manipulates line on a two-dimensional surface to show three-dimensional space

82. Situated on a balcony overlooking the bedroom below, this private reading spot in the Atlanta home of architect John Portman affords lofty privacy. John Portman & Associates, designer. (Photograph: Jaime Ardiles-Arce)

83

84

as it actually appears from a given viewpoint, with lines converging toward a point or points on a horizon and objects at a distance drawn smaller than those close up. Since it gives a virtually photographic view, perspective has become a favorite device in interior sketches and formal *presentation drawings* to indicate how a space will look when completed (fig. 90). A fine-arts training usually includes some instruction in perspective, at least at the level of drawing observed space "by eye" as it is seen in perspective. To draw an unbuilt space in perspective, either from orthographic drawings or from imagination, takes a special skill that is usually acquired only with some study and practice. A *measured perspective* can be as accurate as a photograph in depicting a space's actual appearance, and it offers the advantage of showing a space yet to be built—which, of course, a camera cannot do. Elaborate perspective renderings are usually made by specialists who devote all their time to this work. Most interior designers will find an ability to sketch and draw in perspective a valuable skill. Classroom work with a teacher or self-teaching from books are both possible ways to become proficient in perspective drawing. A short summary of the basic technique is provided in Appendix 6.

While all of the types of drawing will be used by the interior designer, the plan is the primary tool of planning. Once a space is built and occupied, we do not see the plan as such, but it controls how well that space serves us. A good plan is basic to the production of a well-designed interior. Seeing a space in

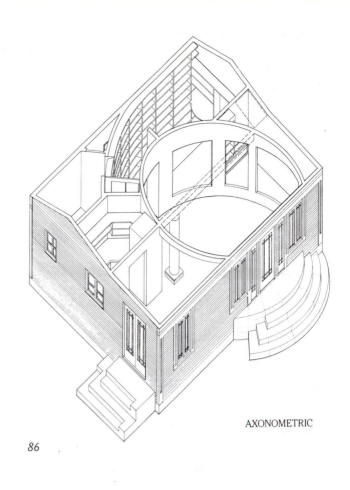

AXONOMETRIC

86

plan on paper makes it easy to analyze the way the built space will perform. Planning makes it possible to try out, study, and revise various possibilities in seeking a satisfactory scheme.

PRELIMINARY STEPS IN PLANNING

Under some conditions one may begin planning freely on blank paper. However, most planning must take account of existing circumstances and other *constraints*, or limitations, such as building code requirements, that restrict what can be done. The interior designer is most often limited by the more or less fixed elements of architecture in the space. This obviously applies when the designer works with an existing space. It also applies when architectural planning has been completed before interior design begins, even when the new construction will provide only an unpartitioned shell.

Ideally, interior design planning should begin along with the architectural planning of fixed elements. This is possible when the interior designer is part of the design process from the beginning. It can also occur when the given architectural space is open and clear, as in lofts and office space rented without

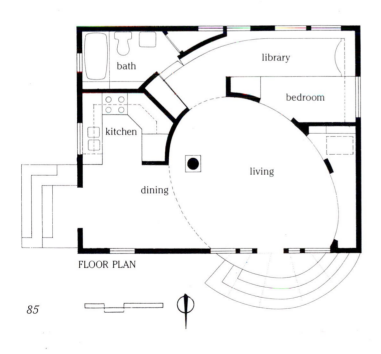

FLOOR PLAN

85

83–86. In this interesting and complex space (figs. 83, 84), ingenious planning has provided for private and semipublic functions within a limited area. A floor plan (fig. 85) helps to understand the design. Such plans are the designer's major tool. In fig. 86, the same plan is axonometrically projected. This type of drawing enables professional—and nonprofessional—designers to picture three-dimensional relationships. The drawing is made to scale for the three axes, height, width, and depth, but with the width and depth drawn at a 45-degree angle to the horizontal. Comparing the plan, the axonometric projection, and photographs of the realized space, one can easily visualize the de-sign and comprehend the concept behind it. Robert Yudell, architect, and Tina Beebe, color consultant, designed the space, in their own home in Santa Monica, California, in 1985. (Photographs: © Henry Bowles, courtesy House & Garden)

87

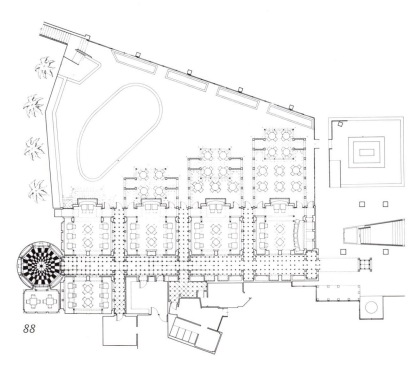

88

87, 88. The plan of a northern Italian town, with its main street, octagonal piazza, and side streets, inspired the architects of an imaginatively conceived hotel restaurant. The vaulted ceiling design is derived from the breakfast room of Sir John Soane's eighteenth-century house in London. Fig. 87 shows one of the "side-street" dining areas of the Cardini restaurant in the Los Angeles Hilton Hotel; its modest scale generates an atmosphere of intimacy. The floor plan (fig. 88) shows the total planning concept. Voorsanger & Mills Associates Architects, designer, 1985. (Photograph: © 1986 Peter Aaron/ESTO)

preexisting partitions. Most houses and apartments are built from plans made before the owner or occupant, much less the interior designer, has any input. By having a house custom-built, the owner can influence the architect or builder and participate in the planning process and can also bring the interior designer into the process.

Selecting Space

A designer can be very helpful before the planning process begins, when a client is looking for space—to rent an office in an office building; to rent or buy an apartment in an apartment house; or to purchase a house. The building or house may be existing or still unbuilt. A client will usually have in mind certain criteria such as general location, size, and cost, but often finds it difficult to choose between alternatives or to evaluate an available possibility. A designer can bring a practiced eye to observe the potential strengths and weaknesses of an available space and offer disinterested advice about how well the given conditions will suit the client's requirements.

The first step is to spell out the client's requirements in a program. The term *program* in the world of architecture and design describes a statement of objectives and requirements that is best written out to form what is sometimes called a *project brief* or *problem statement*. It is axiomatic that a good statement of a problem is basic to finding a good solution. Indeed, the solution to a problem may become almost self-evident once the problem is stated with clarity. Conversely, unclear objectives and uncertainty about requirements typically cause confusion and delays and, all too often, lead to disappointing and unsatisfactory final results.

The program lists, with as much precision as possible, these requirements: the kinds and numbers of spaces to be provided; the relationships of the spaces; any specific needs for equipment, storage, or special furniture; and other specific needs. After the space is selected, this program will form the basis for the new interior design.

Whether the designer accompanies the client on visits to different spaces or evaluates spaces, built or unbuilt, from plans, it is important for the designer to notice and call attention to such things as:

- *WINDOW ORIENTATION IN RELATION TO LIGHT,* at various times of day and in various seasons.
- *OUTLOOK FROM WINDOWS,* for good views or obstruction, including the possibility of future obstruction.
- *QUALITY OF PLAN LAYOUT,* including convenience of spatial shapes and locations. In house and apartment plans, awkward or wasteful spaces often appear. Note potential problems with noise and privacy. Check closets, baths,

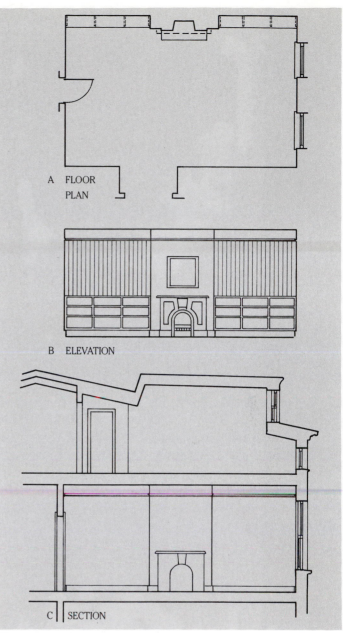

A   FLOOR
     PLAN

B   ELEVATION

C   SECTION

89

and kitchens for adequacy and quality of layout. In apartment, office, and loft buildings, check adequacy of elevators and stairs.

- *POSSIBLE NOISE PROBLEMS,* from elevators or adjacent spaces or from out-of-doors. City street noise and aircraft noise are particularly problematic.
- *ELEMENTS THAT CAN OR SHOULD BE CHANGED: Can walls be added or removed, doors or windows added, eliminated, or changed to improve a space? If closets, kitchens, or baths require change or improvement, will this be possible?*

89. A floor plan (A) is the basis for all planning work. Note the windows (right), door (left), and an opening without a door (bottom). The wall at the top has a central fireplace with bookshelves on either side. The thicknesses of walls do not appear here, but rather in the section (C), which, in this example, *shows the attic space and roof above the room. A drawing like this one would be used if the design were to include a raised ceiling, skylight, balcony, or stair up to the attic. The elevation (B) shows no thicknesses of walls or floors; instead, it includes elements—such as the framed painting over the fireplace, de-* *tails of the mantel, and the bookshelves, as well as indications of a striped wall-covering material—most useful for interior design. A combination of an elevation of this kind with a section gives a sectional elevation, which enables the designer to develop decorative and structural choices simultaneously.*

Designers often note changes that will greatly improve a space at small cost. With an unbuilt structure, a change may be possible at no cost. On the other hand some desirable changes may be very costly or even impossible.

Removing a partition wall, for example, may be relatively easy, but removing a *bearing wall* or column that is part of a building's structure will be difficult and costly, if not impossible. Changes that affect plumbing and ductwork may be easy but will always be costly. They may also be very difficult or impossible where, for example, pipes come from below and continue upward into spaces occupied by other people, preventing the relocation of a bathroom or kitchen.

Legal restrictions relating to safety may rule out certain changes in layout. Window and door locations may be restricted by zoning that regulates exterior appearance. An owner might not permit some changes in rented space. All such issues are best explored before the final selection of a space.

In comparing spaces, the designer may notice that seemingly identical spaces are actually quite different. The same apartment plan, for example, may be better or worse on various floors of a building or with different orientations because of the difference in light and view. In an office building, two plans with the same area may differ in window size and location, in light and view, and in convenience of access from corridors and elevators. Identical houses on opposite sides of a street, because of their orientation, may differ greatly in terms of light, view, and privacy. Clients are often unobservant of such factors, particularly when evaluating space from plans alone, and can benefit greatly from intelligent design advice when making decisions that can be difficult, even frightening, and that often involve large sums of money.

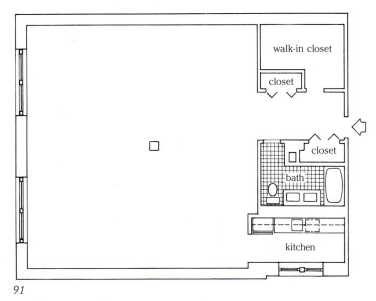

90

90. The architect Frank Lloyd Wright is well known for the beautifully detailed perspective drawings that were produced in his office, often by his own hand. Such a drawing, as, for example, this one of the Larkin Company Administration Building of 1904 in Buffalo, New York, can be as informative as—or more than—a photograph.

91

91. This is the floor plan of a loft space as provided by the rental agent who offered the apartment. The only fixed elements are the kitchen, bathroom, closets, and the single central column.

These, plus the locations of windows and door, are the only design constraints. The final layout can be as open or as intricately subdivided as the new owners and their designer may decide.

92

93

92. Many large loft buildings erected in American cities around the turn of the century have become obsolete for manufacturing and warehouse purposes, and are now often recycled for residential or office use. This space is in the Puck Building of 1885, originally designed by Albert Wagner for the printing presses of a publishing company. The undivided floors, with their large windows, sprinkler systems in place, and vast open areas, will be subdivided for architects, designers, filmmakers, and other commercial purchasers. The lofts are not suitable as homes, because available plumbing cannot serve full bathrooms and kitchens. (Photograph: © Langdon Clay)

93. A huge window wall is necessarily a major element in the design of any space in which it is a feature. Here, the northern exposure—ideal for artists' studios because of the consistent light—and the pleasant view of a public park make this double-height loft space, which houses the studios of both Bray-Schaible Design and designer Joseph Paul D'Urso, particularly attractive. Bray-Schaible Design and Joseph Paul D'Urso, designers, 1978. (Photograph: © 1979 Peter Aaron/ESTO)

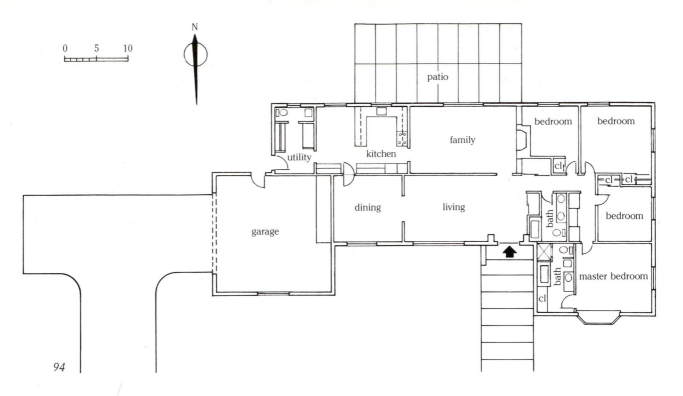

Analyzing and Evaluating Space

Once a space has been selected (or if no selection is required, as when a space in current use is to be altered, renovated, or refurbished), the designer must analyze and evaluate every aspect of it. In this process, it is helpful to categorize elements or characteristics of the space as:

- GOOD *or excellent elements—probably the features that led to the selection or decision to keep the space—that should be retained, emphasized, and exploited in design development.*
- NEUTRAL *qualities that are satisfactory but offer no special merits or attraction.*
- PROBLEMS *and unsatisfactory features that must be altered, eliminated, or at least neutralized or minimized.*

Such attractive features as good daylight or a fine view from windows are easy to recognize and should be exploited. Modern residential and office spaces tend to be largely neutral in character, with smooth floors, walls, and ceilings; windows and doors without ornamental detail; unobtrusive heating and air-conditioning outlets; no fireplaces, molding, paneling, or other special details. Problems sometimes do not present themselves until planning begins—or even after moving in.

Spaces already divided into rooms usually cause more problems than open space. Since houses and apartments are laid out to suit an imagined "typical" occupant or family that may be quite different from the actual one, their plans may well be unsuitable to a particular occupant or have serious faults that would be troublesome under any circumstances. Common problems are:

- SOME OR ALL OF THE ROOMS ARE TOO SMALL. *Kitchens and bathrooms are particularly likely to be skimped.*
- ROOMS RELATE POORLY TO ONE ANOTHER. *For example, the dining room is not adjacent to the kitchen, or the bathroom is poorly placed.*
- ROOMS ARE BADLY SHAPED. *They may be too long and narrow, have awkward notches or cut-off corners, or make furniture placement difficult.*
- CORRIDORS ARE LONG, NARROW, DARK, AND UNPLEASANT. *This not only wastes space, it is usually inconvenient as well.*
- OPENINGS (DOORS AND WINDOWS) ARE BADLY PLACED. *For example, an entrance door opens directly into a major space, or openings are so placed that they take up wall space and make furniture layout difficult.*
- CLOSETS ARE INADEQUATE, BADLY SHAPED, OR POORLY LOCATED.

Once such problems are recognized, it is possible to consider steps that will minimize or eliminate them. Moving a partition or removing it may improve a plan layout and alter room size. Doors can be relocated or blocked up. Some spaces can be enlarged by taking space away from adjacent spaces.

94. *This plan of a suburban house contains a number of serious problems. These include:*

Several major rooms (family room, two bedrooms) and the patio face north—the least desirable orientation.

Major rooms (living, dining, and master bedroom) face the street, resulting in limited privacy and a less-than-ideal outdoor view. Moreover, the prime southern orientation will usu-

ally be blocked by the window treatment required for privacy.

The front door opens directly into the living room, with no vestibule or other transition.

Access from the garage to utility and kitchen areas is only through outdoors, with no convenient access from the garage to the main living spaces.

Living room contains the passage route to dining, kitchen, and family room.

The traffic route to kitchen and patio goes through the family room. Its fireplace is close to this circulation path.

Furniture arrangement in living and family rooms will be difficult due to traffic paths and architectural constraints.

All rooms except the two corner bedrooms lack good cross-ventilation.

All four bedrooms have a partition wall adjacent to another bed-

room, resulting in the loss of acoustical privacy.

Master bedroom closet space (in bath and hall) is poorly planned.

Bay window of master bedroom, apparently added for external effect, is poorly placed in relation to the interior.

Master bath general layout and shower placement are awkward.

Contrast this plan with fig. 95.

A dining room, for example, can often be eliminated and its space given partly to an enlarged kitchen and partly to adjacent living space.

At a more detailed level, poorly placed or awkwardly shaped windows can often be dealt with through drapery or blinds. The appearance of poorly shaped spaces can be improved through choice of wall colors and materials. Color and lighting (each the subject of a subsequent chapter) can make spaces seem larger or smaller, as desired. The size, character, and placement of furniture can help to minimize planning problems. Even a small kitchen or kitchenette can usually be made more workable with suitable choices of equipment and improved layout. Corridors can often be improved through lighting and color and by using them for book storage or a gallery-like display of art.

Collecting all such information about existing conditions or other limitations constitutes the preliminary basis of planning. The designer's main planning tool is a scale plan showing what exists or what is to be built, along with any other data about fixed elements. Such a plan may come from a real-estate firm or architects' drawings. These can be used as a starting point, but an on-site check should be made to ensure their accuracy. Plans provided by real-estate agencies are often small in scale, unclear in details, and inaccurate, at least in minor ways. Building plans may not have been followed exactly, or later changes may not be shown in the plan.

On site with ruler and measuring tape, the designer (or an assistant) should check available plans, obtain heights of ceilings and openings that may not be shown in the plan, note any significant details, and, possibly, take some photographs for reference. If no plans are available, the on-site job becomes larger, requiring careful measurement of the space in question so that accurate plans of existing conditions can be drawn up.

The task of *measuring up* an existing space is often the first assignment given to a junior designer. As a test of accuracy and thoroughness, it is good practice for any beginner. When only one or two rooms are being considered, this is a fairly simple matter. Plans of a whole house or larger building may take considerable time and effort to prepare, but it is vital to have accurate plans before starting design work. The usual procedure is to make a roughly drawn plan on a pad and note down complete dimensions (fig. 103). Back at the drafting board, these are drawn up to scale as a basis for further design work (fig. 104).

PLANNING THE SPACE

Planning can now move to its primary task, the fitting of the project's requirements to the plan.

Programming

If the *program* has not already been prepared in order to select space, it is prepared at this time. (Since the designer usually begins with an existing space to be redesigned, the program is most often prepared at this time.) It may seem unnecessary to prepare a program for a small project (a living room, a kitchen, or an office, for example), but requirements need to be specified, whatever the project size.

When work is being undertaken professionally for a client, a clear program must be developed to ensure that client and designer share a common point of view about their goals. This applies equally to individual clients and to corporations or other

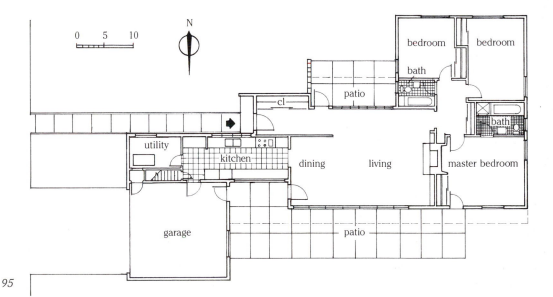

95. This well-planned modern house displays the following desirable features:

The major rooms (living room and master bedroom) face south.
No major rooms face the street (on right).
The main entrance is sheltered, opens into a vestibule, and is close to coat and general-storage closets.
The garage has direct access to the kitchen and utility areas and easy access to the principal living space.
The kitchen follows a logical corridor work-flow plan.
The dining area has direct access to the kitchen and an open, natural relationship to the living space.
The living area is not cut by a major traffic path.
The living spaces and bedrooms all permit reasonable furniture layouts.
All major rooms have good cross-ventilation.
The second bath is accessible to all living spaces and to the smaller bedrooms.
No two bedrooms share a partition wall or a wall with a living area, thus assuring good acoustical isolation and privacy.
Enough closets are provided for each bedroom and for linens and general storage.
At least two outdoor living spaces—patios or terraces—are provided.

A good house plan should offer all, or most, of these advantages.

large organizations. In the latter case, where the designer must deal with and satisfy many people, clear lines of communication become even more important. A committee is always more difficult to deal with than an individual, and clarity of objectives is best determined through agreement on a written statement.

Designers typically begin programming by developing a *general project statement*. This may be no more than a sentence or two outlining the work to be done—its extent and purpose—in the most general terms. They usually follow this by a *survey* organized to collect complete specific details about the clients' requirements. Such a survey will ask such questions as the following: How many people are to be seated in a living room? Will there be books, a piano? Will the kitchen be used by one person or several? Will it be used to prepare only snacks or full dinners for a crowd? Is a dishwasher wanted? a microwave oven? a restaurant range? How is the office to be used? Does it need conference seating, files, a computer? Are there color preferences or other special personal requirements to be taken into consideration? Even when designing for one's own use or for one's own family, it is helpful to note down all such data, in part because the process will raise questions that should be answered before planning begins. In projects accommodating a number of people, each must be interviewed to learn each individual's practical needs, habits of living and work, tastes, and personal preferences. For larger projects it may be neither necessary nor appropriate to interview every person involved. Department heads and a few representative individuals should be able to give data on behalf of the others. It is important to remember, however, that managers' often have mistaken ideas about what their subordinates really need and want. Their information should be cross-checked by conducting some individual interviews.

In addition to ascertaining space and furniture requirements, it is important to collect data on activities and processes, asking such questions as the following: Where is privacy

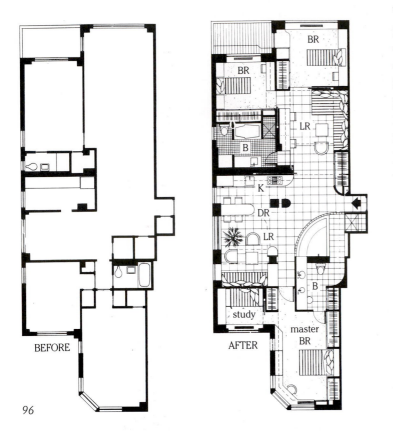

96

97. Knowledgeable replanning was used to customize a space for a particular owner of a Manhattan apartment. The apartment as purchased is shown in the plan at left. As replanned (right), it now provides a two-bedroom suite, a luxury bath, and a living area for two teen-agers (upper portion of plan); common rooms—kitchen, dining, and living area—near the entrance; and a bedroom, study, and luxury bath suite for the parents (lower portion of plan). A curving glass-block wall surrounds the large tub of the master bath, separating it from the living area. Bromley/Jacobsen Designs, designer.

97

98

97, 98. A renovated attic in an older house greatly expands a house's useful space. An attic before (fig. 97) and after (fig. 98) conversion by Bill and Juanita Sharpe in their own home in Grand Rapids, Michigan, 1987. (Photograph: B. Sharpe, courtesy Metropolitan Home Magazine)

99

100

important, and where does interaction occur? Data may be recorded on a simple lined pad or on forms developed for the purpose. It is wise to remind those interviewed that the designer cannot guarantee to satisfy every item on each "wish list"; compromises may be necessary to resolve conflicts and to accommodate budgets. Data must also be collected about

general needs—for example, storage requirements and facilities for group use.

Any program is subject to question and to revision. Testing the program's validity is useful, especially when the designer was not the person who prepared the program. Items may have been included out of habit, questionable assumptions may have

99, 100. A mezzanine level in the Barbizon Hotel served as a visitors' reception area from the 1930s to the 1950s (fig. 99); today, in the Golden Tulip Barbizon Hotel (New York, 1985), the same space is the mezzanine level of La Marée Restaurant, by Judith Stockman & Asso-ciates, interior designers, with Milton Glaser as conceptual director (fig. 100). A fresh and modern feeling replaces the musty flavor of a bygone day. (Photograph of fig. 100: © Langdon Clay)

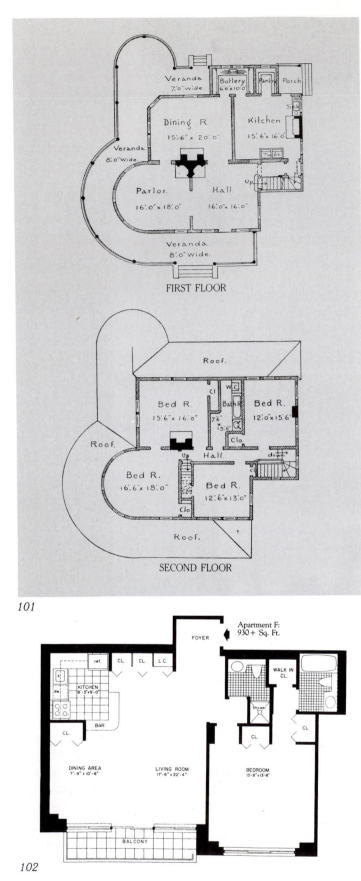

FIRST FLOOR

Veranda 7'-0" wide
Butlery 6'-6"x10'-0"
Pantry
Porch
Dining R. 15'-6" x 20'-0"
Kitchen 15'-6" x 16'-0"
Veranda 8'-0" Wide
Parlor. 16'-0" x 18'-0"
Hall. 16'-0" x 16'-0"
Veranda. 8'-0" Wide.
Up

SECOND FLOOR

Roof.
Bed R. 15'-6" x 16'-0"
Bed R. 12'-0"x15'-6"
Roof.
Bath
Bed R. 16'-6" x 18'-0"
Hall
Bed R. 12'-6" x 13'-0"
Roof.

101

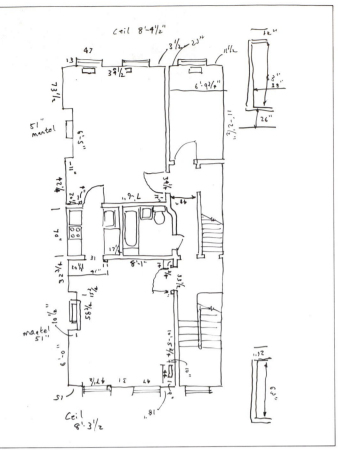

103

Apartment F: 930+ Sq. Ft.

FOYER
ref.
CL. CL. L.C.
KITCHEN 8'-3"x9'-0"
WALK IN CL.
Shower
BAR
CL.
CL.
CL.
DINING AREA 7'-9" x 10'-6"
LIVING ROOM 17'-6" x 22'-4"
BEDROOM 13'-8"x13'-8"
BALCONY

102

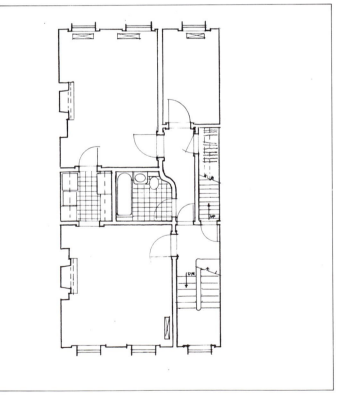

104

101. Older houses in sound condition often make good candidates for conversion—if the projected result is cost-effective. Antiquated kitchens and baths and some room arrangements need replanning in order to adapt the spaces to modern life and to the new occupants' special needs. In this 1890s house, for example, a designer would provide a more modern kitchen layout and additional and better bathroom facilities and better closets and other storage.

102. This apartment plan is typical of those offered in the advertisements of real-estate firms. A designer can help clients evaluate the plans of apartments that they are considering renting or purchasing.

103, 104. Rough, freehand field notes, here on a yellow legal pad (fig. 103), accompany the measuring that precedes the actual interior design. The data collected in the field notes are then organized into a neatly drafted plan drawn to scale (fig. 104). For a small area such as this, the usual scale would be 1/4" = 1'-0". The space is a compact, top-floor apartment in an 1830s Brooklyn, New York, brownstone.

105

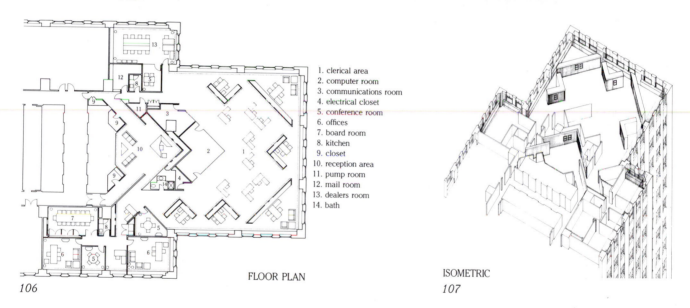

1. clerical area
2. computer room
3. communications room
4. electrical closet
5. conference room
6. offices
7. board room
8. kitchen
9. closet
10. reception area
11. pump room
12. mail room
13. dealers room
14. bath

FLOOR PLAN

106

ISOMETRIC

107

been made. Other elements may have been left out because no one thought about them. Such program testing can take place before planning begins and will often continue throughout the planning process. The designer must also evaluate the program's requirements and ensure that they do not lead to unwise planning. If they do, the issues should be discussed and the program revised.

With simple spaces, the preparation of the program can lead directly to designing (see page 82). In a simple project, the number of rooms and their uses probably have already been

established. The designation of rooms as living room, bedroom, kitchen, and so on rarely comes into question. The designer must still decide whether to combine some rooms (separate living and dining rooms, for example), whether any rooms can or should be made larger or smaller, or whether some room uses should be changed (a bedroom to a study, for example, or even a garage to a new living room), but such changes can usually be kept in mind quite easily. More complex projects, in which many spaces and functions need to be provided, call for several preliminary steps, including the following.

105–7. Imaginative design transformed a neutral area in a modern office building for Banque Bruxelles Lambert, New York, into an interior (fig. 105) with style and wit—the "windows" are inserted elements that mask the structural walls and windows. A floor plan (fig. 106) and an isometric drawing (fig. 107) of the space clearly show the inserted elements. Isometric views show

width and depth to scale at 30- and 60-degree angles. Verticals are drawn at the same scale. An illusion of space similar to that of perspective drawing results, although, because each dimension is equally foreshortened, the isometric view is proportioned differently from a perspective. Emilio Ambasz & Associates, designer, 1984. (Photograph: © Paul Warchol)

Area Assignment

This involves estimating for each space, meaning each function and/or room, an approximate size expressed in square footage. Arriving at appropriate area assignments is partly a matter of common sense and experience, partly a matter of consulting various data handbooks that list commonly accepted area rules for various functions (see Table 1 below). One can work out an appropriate area for a bedroom, for example, by evaluating similar rooms. The minimum size for a bathroom is found in many handbooks. Suggested sizes for offices of various sorts are often listed in tables. Areas for an auditorium, a conference room, or a restaurant can be calculated on the basis of the number of seats to be provided and type of use.

Once footage has been estimated, a list of spaces and their proposed areas, with allowances for circulation spaces, storage, and so on, can be prepared, and the total area added up. Obviously, the aim is to match the total area available fairly closely. If the mismatch is too great, area assignments may have to be adjusted or the space available reconsidered.

TABLE 1. ROOM AREAS IN SQUARE FEET (TYPICAL)

Room	Small	Average	Large
Residential:			
Living room (or space)	150	400	800
Dining room (or space)	75	250	400
Kitchen	50	125	450
Bedroom (master)	120	200	500
Bathroom	30	60	200
Office:			
Executive	250	350	600
Managerial	100	200	250
General office staff	55	100	120
Clerical (minimum)	50	80	100
Circulation space			
(as percent of total)	15%	25%	35%
Hospital room	75	90	125
Hotel/motel room	100	175	400
Auditorium (per person)	6	7.5	9
Restaurant (per person)	7	12	24
Elevator	20	55	120
Garage (one passenger car)	150	200	250

Block Diagramming

In this step, which presumes that area assignment has been made, each area is drawn to scale in the form of a block or a box of arbitrary shape, usually a convenient rectangle, unless a more special shape is called for by the function of the space. A requirement of 4,800 square feet, for example, is drawn as a block of 48 by 100 feet, or perhaps 40 by 120 feet, to scale. All of the blocks representing all of the required spaces make up a chart that gives a clear visual idea of how the space requirements relate in size (fig. 108).

Adjacency Studies

Adjacent means side by side or adjoining. In interior design, the term has been extended to describe a full range of relationships from close to far apart. Rather than describing adjacency needs in terms of yards or feet, the designer usually makes a scale that gives simple numbers or letters to different levels of closeness. Such a scale might be:

> *1 = Adjoining*
> *2 = Near*
> *3 = Medium distant*
> *4 = Far*
> *5 = No contact*

The designer next makes a chart showing all of the spaces to be planned, arranged as in a map mileage chart so that a blank is shown for each relationship of one space to another. This is called a *matrix chart*. For example, a house or apartment made up of

> *LR = Living space*
> *DR = Dining area*
> *K = Kitchen*
> *BR 1 = Bedroom 1*
> *BR 2 = Bedroom 2*
> *B = Bathroom*

would be charted thus:

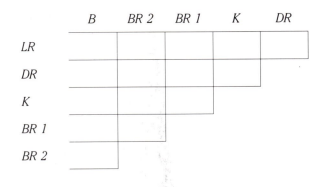

As the designer decides the suitable level of closeness between each pair of spaces, he or she assigns it a corresponding number from the scale and places it in the appropriate box of the chart. The chart above might be completed in this way:

	B	BR 2	BR 1	K	DR
LR	4	4	5	4	2
DR	4	5	5	1	
K	4	5	5		
BR 1	1	3			
BR 2	2				

In such a simple situation, the designer could probably determine the needs for adjacency by common sense and common usage, as well as by asking the intended occupants of the space a few questions, such as: Should bedroom 2 be close to or far from bedroom 1? In more complex problems with many spaces and complicated relationship needs, the designer would take a survey of individuals or key people in various areas, asking them to specify their needs for contact with each other unit in the project. This data may be displayed numerically or with graphic symbols in a matrix chart.

Once this information has been collected, the designer makes a chart combining the block diagram with adjacency data. Lines of different thicknesses represent the levels of adjacency, the broadest line indicating the greatest need for closeness. These lines are drawn to connect the various blocks of space. The designer rearranges the blocks in an effort to make the heaviest lines as short as possible. The result is called a *bubble diagram*, with the blocks shown rounded and connected by link lines representing adjacency needs (figs. 109, 110). Such a

ADJACENCY MATRIX CHART FOR A THREE-BEDROOM HOUSE

	Gar.	Util.	B 2	B 1	BR 3	BR 2	BR 1	K	DR	LR
LR	4	4	2	4	4	4	3	3	1	
DR	5	4	3	5	5	5	5	1		
K	4	5	3	5	5	5	5			
BR 1	5	5	5	1	4	4				
BR 2	5	5	2	5	4					
BR 3	5	5	2	5						
B 1	5	5	5							
B 2	5	4								
Util.	1									
Gar.										

Desired Levels of Adjacency

1 = Adjoining
2 = Near
3 = Medium distant
4 = Far
5 = No contact

LR = Living space
DR = Dining area
K = Kitchen
BR = Bedroom
B = Bathroom
Util. = Utility room
Gar. = Garage

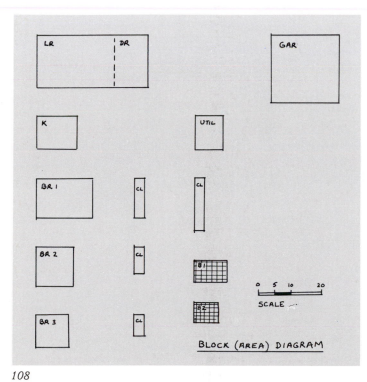

BLOCK (AREA) DIAGRAM

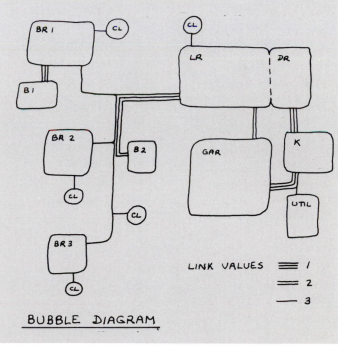

LINK VALUES

BUBBLE DIAGRAM

108

109

108. This block, or area, diagram for a simple, three-bedroom house shows the square footage of the spaces to scale, but the shapes are arbitrary. These diagrams, preliminary planning steps, convert numbers into graphic form.

109. A matrix chart (above) shows the desired relationships among the spaces of the block diagram (fig. 108). The information from the block (area) diagram might next be reorganized into a bubble diagram (below) to show graphically the relationships in the matrix. The term bubble describes the appearance of such plans: when drawn freehand, the shapes are soft and bubble-like. The weight of the lines that represent relationships vary in proportion to the density of traffic; the bubbles are moved about until their arrangement uses the shortest and most direct links possible—with the most important links the shortest of all. When the process is completed, the diagram will suggest an appropriate floor plan.

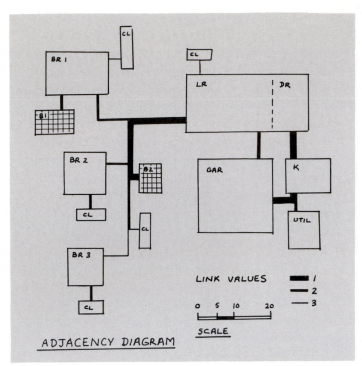

ADJACENCY DIAGRAM

LINK VALUES

SCALE

110

diagram begins to suggest spatial relationships that would be efficient, even though it is not realistically indicative of any actual layout.

While these steps may sound complicated, they are very helpful, even for small projects involving more than two or three spaces. Although it may seem expedient to bypass these steps when planning a house or small office, designers and clients may find that preliminary area and adjacency diagrams clarify the needs and decisions of each and can prevent later problems and misunderstandings. In planning such complex projects as modern hospitals, airports, or large corporate office buildings (figs. 111, 112), they are indispensable. For multistory projects, further diagramming is used to aid *stacking,* that is, locating the elements on various floors.

Designing the Space

Once the program and preliminary diagramming have been prepared, the actual designing begins. In this first phase, commonly known as "making sketches," the usual procedure is to place yellow tracing paper over the plan showing existing

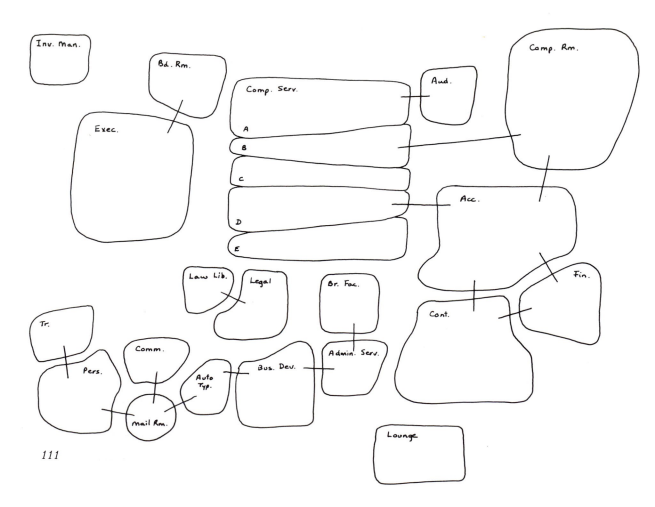

111

110. The bubble diagram (fig. 109 below) is here more carefully drafted as an adjacency diagram, preparatory to discussion and review with the client. The house plan in fig. 95 is derived from this diagram.

111. In contrast to the simpler sketches above, this bubble diagram reflects the complexity of an office project that must incorporate a number of departments with an intricate pattern of relationships. This draft lacks many of the secondary links that have been added to the diagram in fig. 112.

conditions and limitations and sketch out proposals, starting with general space allocations and gradually moving to finer detail (see figs. 134–38). Freehand sketches may be made without a scale base sheet on any medium—on pads or in notebooks, even on the legendary back of an envelope. Preliminary sketching usually begins with floor plans, but sections, elevations, or perspectives can also be used to show developing design ideas on paper. Preliminary design, of course, can also develop mentally, without any drawing, but such design thinking can be hard to hold in memory, and it is often misleading in the way it relates to real spatial limitations. Design ideas are best put on paper as soon as possible so that they can be looked at, compared, and saved as design progresses.

Exactly how the planner arrives at a completed design is difficult to describe. It seems to involve a special talent for visualizing geometric possibilities. The planner looks at the space available and at the information about needs embodied in block diagrams and adjacency charts and derives from this a rough solution, which is sketched out on paper. Then the first proposal is evaluated and improvements suggested. This leads to a next proposal, and a next, and so forth, until a plan emerges that seems to resolve the space allocation problem.

In real situations, this process is modified by any number of pressures that contend with one another for dominance. What elements will be given locations with good daylight and view? What spaces must be close to the point of arrival? How are the conflicting needs of residents, visitors, workers, and other identifiable groups to be reconciled? These concerns, while typical of large and complex problems, come up in small projects as well. How large should the kitchen be when every foot allocated to it must be taken away from some other space? Is an extra bathroom worth its cost in space and in money? What spaces deserve the best light and view? If necessary, rooms can be combined and doors can be moved, closed up, or cut out, but are such steps worth their cost and complication? The planner must consider all these issues while developing a basic plan assigning space locations, sizes, and purposes and positioning walls and openings to achieve a completed project that works well and is visually satisfying.

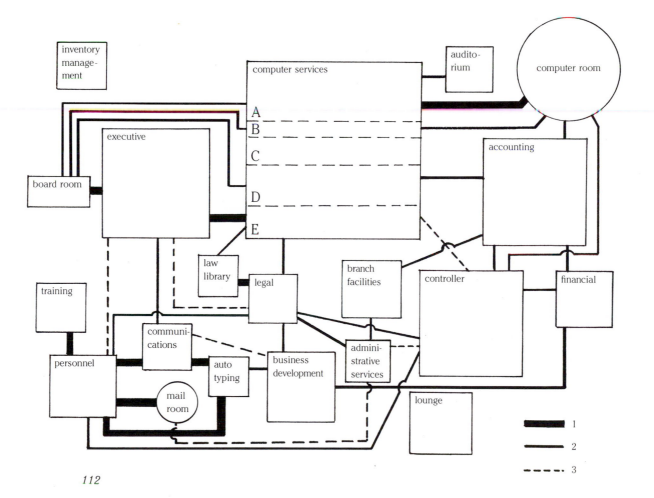

112

112. In this drafted bubble diagram, all projected links have been drawn in with line weights developed from a matrix chart of adjacency requirements. Note that two areas, inventory management and lounge, were found to have no regular business communication with other units. The largest department, computer services, has five internal subdivisions, one of which, C, has no links to any other department, but only to the adjacent subdivisions B and D.

Circulation

A matter that needs special attention in planning, usually called *circulation,* is an aspect of any layout. People using a built space do not stay fixed in unchanging locations. They move about, and the ease and convenience of their movement have a very strong impact on the sense of convenience and comfort that a space provides. When moving from one place to another, a simple and direct route feels better than a roundabout and awkward path. Squeezing through narrow openings and bumping furniture when moving about is unpleasant and irritating. The more frequently a particular line of movement will be followed, the more important it is that the route be direct and ample. A space that will hold a number of people needs routes of movement that interfere as little as possible and that have generous paths. A space serving few people allows more minimal passage that will serve one person at a time.

An *overlay circulation diagram* aids the planner in resolving circulation patterns (fig. 113). In this chart, lines are drawn to show the paths of movement that will be followed most frequently. The planner may vary the line thickness to indicate frequency of movement or the number of people expected to follow a particular path. A circulation diagram makes it easy to spot problems. A good circulation pattern will show short, direct routes, particularly for the most used paths. A problematic pattern will generate a complex and confused circulation diagram, with winding and contorted paths passing through bottleneck points of constriction. When using a built space, one does not ordinarily think about circulation patterns as an abstract concept, but the success of circulation planning will make itself felt in the space's sense of ease and comfort, as compared with other spaces that arouse annoyance and irritation.

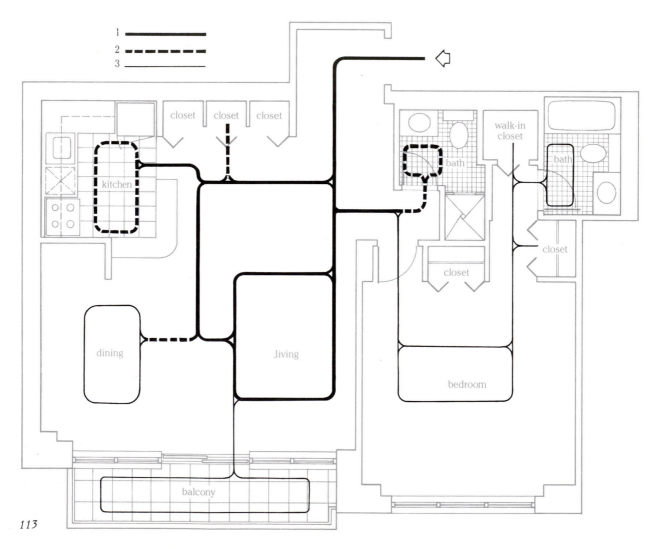

113

113. A circulation diagram drawn over a plan often helps to evaluate the plan's practicality, and can serve for the design of the furniture layout as well. This plan of a rental apartment was provided by a real-estate firm. The projected normal circulation has been diagrammed clearly and neatly, with varied line weights indicating the anticipated level of traffic along each path. A poorly planned layout, by contrast, will exhibit a confused and tangled circulation pattern with many points of overlapping cross-traffic.

Furniture Layout

Furniture layout, a form of detailed planning, usually follows more general space planning, but it is wise to have furniture placement in mind while planning spaces. Most people can come up with examples of rooms almost impossible to furnish because of their basic plan: the bedroom with no wall broad enough to permit placement of a bed; the living room with so many doors and windows that furniture has no place to rest. When an interior design project involves a room or rooms that are not to be changed, planning begins with furniture layout. Wherever it fits in the sequence of planning, furniture layout must follow a pattern comparable to that of space planning.

The first step is to list the furniture required. The designer returns to the program to learn what activities are to take place in the space in question and then decides what furniture clusters will serve those activities. Many other questions arise. What are the needs for storage or for the display of objects? Are there existing pieces of furniture (a treasured antique, perhaps, or a favorite chair or sofa) to be retained? Will any or all existing pieces be appropriate to the new space? Will new built-in units be best for dealing with some furniture needs, such as placement of books, TV and stereo equipment, and kitchen utensils? How many people will use a particular space and how many will need to be seated, both in normal situations and on special occasions? All such questions need to be explored in an effort to arrive at furniture planning decisions that will serve user needs at the best possible levels of satisfaction. A short checklist will often prove useful.

NUMBER OF PEOPLE USING SPACE:
    Normally _____
    Maximum _____
NUMBER TO BE SEATED:
    Upright _____
    Lounge _____
    Reclining _____
TABLES:
    Low _____
    Work _____
    Conference _____
    Dining _____
    To seat (number)
        Normally _____
        Maximum _____
DESKS OR OTHER WORK SURFACES:
    Size(s) _____
STORAGE NEEDS:
    Clothing

    Hanging _____
    Folded _____
Books _____
Records, tapes _____
Dishes, silver, other tableware _____
Other _____
SPECIAL EQUIPMENT AND STORAGE:
    TV, stereo, video cassette recorder _____
    Film/TV projection _____
    Music (instruments such as piano, music stand, printed
        music, and so on) _____
    Bar and serving needs _____
    Files _____
    Typewriter _____
    Computer equipment _____
    Other _____
BEDS:
    Single _____
    Double _____
    Queen _____
    Convertible _____
    Other _____
BATHROOM:
    Standard: _____
        Toilet _____
        Sink _____
        Bathtub _____
    Lavatory _____
    Shower _____
    Bidet _____
    Vanity _____
    Linen storage _____
OTHER REQUIREMENTS:
    Display _____
    Artworks _____
    Hobbies _____
    Plants _____
    Workshop _____
    Miscellaneous _____

In completing such a checklist, additional details about sizes and any other specifics that may be significant should be noted. While many entries may seem obvious, it is surprising how often a methodical review of such a list will discover needs not previously recognized. Like the program and earlier charts, this is another tool to clarify the client's needs and wants and the designer's approach. Using it can avoid future problems and misunderstandings.

114

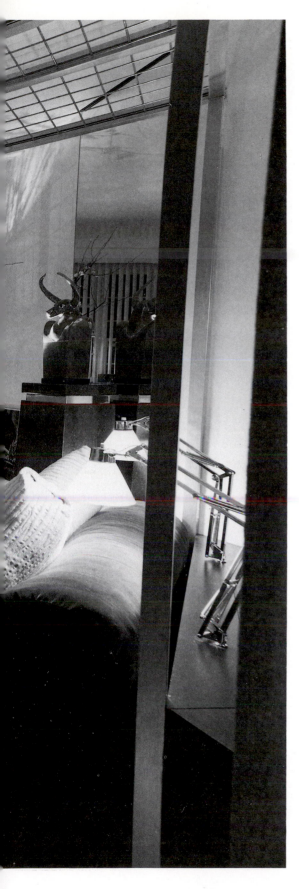

115

With a list of furniture requirements in hand (or in mind), the designer can place the necessary pieces on the floor plan (see fig. 116). The guiding basis for placement must be an understanding of the activities being provided for and a consideration of people's movement into and around the space. The program will list these activities, both everyday and special.

When drawing furniture in plan, it is important to use correct sizes, properly scaled. With practice, it becomes easy to draw furniture to scale without measuring or consulting catalogs for dimensions, but developing this skill takes some effort. Templates with cutouts to scale representing commonly used furniture types in typical shapes and sizes are available for various spaces (home, office, kitchen, and bathroom). While some furniture types are fairly consistent in size (chairs, sofas of given capacity, beds, file cabinets), others vary greatly. Tables and office desks come in a range of sizes and in various shapes. Even pianos range from upright to concert grand.

Exact sizes of existing furniture can be obtained by measurement, of course, while sizes of new furniture are given in manufacturers' catalogs and price lists. A chart of sizes

114. A single, all-purpose room—a New York studio apartment—was developed in such a way as to permit a wide range of functions within the very limited space. Juan Montoya, designer. (Photograph: Jaime Ardiles-Arce)

115. Frank Gehry was the architect for a 1978 renovation of his own 1930s-vintage clapboard house in Santa Monica, California. This living area is organized in a conversation grouping, but books, telephones, and stereo equipment are also at hand. Note the open framing and the seemingly unfinished studs and joists that give the space an almost improvisational quality, typical of Gehry's work. (Photograph: Tim Street-Porter)

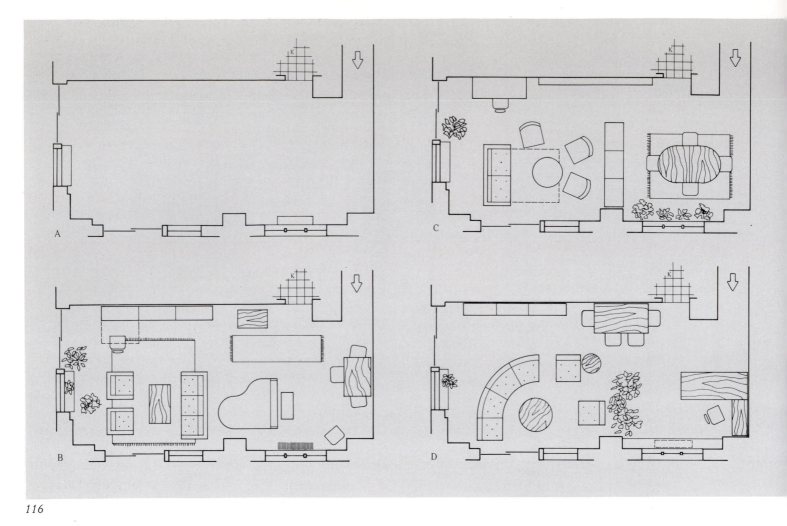

drawn to scale, such as the one provided in Appendix 2, "Furniture Symbols," can be photostated to any desired scale and kept at hand to aid in drawing. It is sometimes suggested to amateur home decorators that they cut out pieces of paper or cardboard, possibly color-coded, at scale sizes, to represent furniture. These can then be moved about on a plan, representing different arrangements. Experienced designers prefer to work with drawing directly, regarding cutouts as an unnecessary planning aid.

The following notes offer some suggestions for furniture planning for the most frequently encountered space functions: *LIVING AREA.* The living area varies widely, from the formal parlor-like space used only for an occasional ceremonial event to the all-purpose space of a studio apartment. In almost every case, the primary uses will call for a furniture grouping suitable to conversation and various types of entertaining. Conversation demands seating that will accommodate an adequate number of people arranged at suitable distances and in comfortable configurations. A sofa on one side of a room and chairs far away on the other side make communication awkward. Distances between 4 and 10 feet are most comfortable for normal conversation. A primary seating group for four to six people is the normal core, usually arranged around a low coffee or cocktail table. Larger numbers of people tend to break up into separate groups. Movable seating works best in such situations.

The same seating will probably serve for music-listening and television-watching, for one person or several, making the location of the TV screen, stereo, and TV controls important. A fireplace, even if it is rarely used, becomes an important focal element. For a while, the television had come to replace the traditional fireplace as a focus of attention in the living space. However, it is becoming increasingly common to relegate the TV to a special viewing area, perhaps in another room, or to conceal it when not in use. Windows with an attractive view offer an alternative focal point. In any case, windows will probably influence furniture layout according to their placement and the amount and intensity of light they admit.

116. *This series of furniture plans shows the same living-dining area planned in several different ways.*

A. *This plan shows the unfurnished space: the entrance is at the upper right, indicated by an arrow; the kitchen access (labeled K) is close to the entrance. Two sets of sliding doors (upper left and lower left) lead to two different terraces.*

B. *The dining table at far right can be opened up to seat as many as six. In the living area, the seating group is placed to relate both to windows and views and to the unit along the upper wall that houses a music system, a bar, and a small drop-front desk. The piano is an obvious visual focal point.*

C. *A room divider is used in this plan to create a separate dining area. The table will seat two to six as placed, and can be extended to seat eight. The convertible sofa is situated so as to be opened easily to become a guest bed. There is a large desk or work table along the upper wall as well as a long shelf upon which to display art.*

D. *In this plan, primary lounge seating is imagined as a curved sectional group with related chairs. The wall unit and dining table are located along the upper wall. A generous home office occupies an area near the entrance, for an occupant who makes major business use of the space during working hours. Wall-to-wall carpet is indicated.*

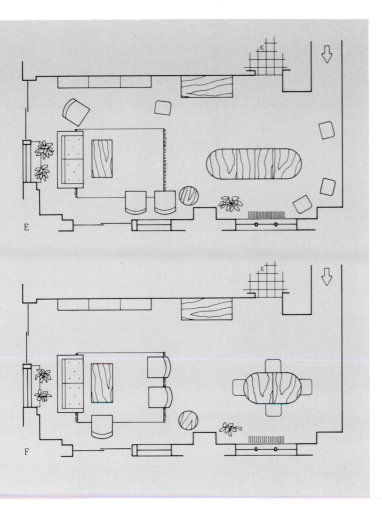

E

F

Many living areas are expected to serve secondary functions as well, for example, as library, office, study, music room, or guest sleeping room. The combined living-dining room demands furniture for the dining function, often a minimal everyday provision that can be expanded for an occasional larger gathering, which leaves more space for the living area's other functions, especially entertaining large numbers of people. Circulation is of special importance at large gatherings, especially if there will be buffet service of food and drink. If normal furniture placement does not allow easy movement, an alternate arrangement should be planned for such occasions (see figs. 116 E, F).

DINING AREA. Whether located in a separate room or in an alcove or other part of a general living space, dining spaces call for a table of suitable size to meet the range from minimum to maximum number of diners to be seated with the appropriate number of chairs available. It is particularly important to leave sufficient space around the table for chairs to be pushed back for access and for serving. Table shape—

rectangular, square, oval, or round—strongly influences the degree of formality that will be associated with dining. Circles and squares, having no obvious head or foot, favor informality, while rectangles and ovals are the norm of formal dining. In the larger or more formal dining room, a buffet, sideboard, or other extra serving surface and provision for storage of dishes and serving pieces may be considered.

FAMILY ROOM. Family rooms—or television rooms, recreation rooms, or playrooms—have become common in larger houses, particularly for families with young or teen-age children. Such an extra room permits the living room to retain some formality and relieves it of an excess of multiple function, as well as giving children their own social space. Its furniture selection depends upon the particular family's habits. Almost all families require TV and stereo system, along with comfortable seating in related locations. Other choices may be recreation equipment and space to store it, table tennis or other game tables, a bar, barbecue cooking provisions, or space for hobby or craft activities. Since family needs change as children grow, highly flexible furniture selections and space planning should permit adjustment as time passes and adapt to alternative functions, such as media room, studio, office, or workshop, after the children have grown up.

BEDROOM. Bedrooms are inevitably planned around the bed or beds they contain. Furniture for sitting, reading, dressing, storage, and other functions may be considered if there is space for it. Many bedrooms will be expected to offer facilities for such quiet or semiprivate purposes as office work, sewing, or hobby activities. Children's rooms need to be planned to adjust to children's changing needs as they grow. Provisions for play, entertaining a friend, study, possibly music and TV, plus storage for clothes and belongings, are essential. Shared rooms need to offer some individual territory to each child. A study, sewing room, or hobby room can often be furnished to serve as a guest room as well.

NONRESIDENTIAL SPACES. Nonresidential spaces are so varied as to make discussion of the furniture planning problems of each type impractical. In general, layout must always begin by considering the primary function and the items needed to support it, with some thought given to secondary functions as well. After the size of the required pieces of furniture and the number of people who will use them regularly or occasionally is determined, placement then proceeds, relating the pieces to the size and shape of the space as well as to the location of fixed elements such as doors, windows, alcoves, or bays. The way people move around within the space while engaged in their customary activities as well as their movement in and out of the space will also guide logical furniture placement.

E. *This is a temporary furniture arrangement for a party where there will be a large number of guests. The dining table has been extended to its maximum length for buffet food service; drinks are on the table near the kitchen entrance. All seating has been pushed close to the walls for easy circulation.*

F. *The same furniture shown in E is here repositioned in a layout for everyday use.*

117

118

117. A dining area in a New York loft was designed by James Terrell, architect, with Peter Kunz as co-designer in 1987. Their guiding intention was to create an environment where "dinner for two was as comfortable as a black-tie party for fifty." The chairs are Ruhlmann-style Art Deco designs in Macassar ebony; the table is a marble top resting on a base of transparent acrylic. (Photograph: Michael Datoli, courtesy Metropolitan Home Magazine)

118. Juan Montoya designed this media room for a New York apartment in 1983. The family enjoys video-viewing and listening to music, and these pastimes determined the formulation of a room that is, in effect, a home theater. Adjustable lighting, the wide screen, and inviting seating make the space particularly effective for its special purpose. (Photograph: Jaime Ardiles-Arce)

119

Many spaces relate closely to residential parallels. A hotel, dormitory, or hospital room functions much like a home bedroom. A private office in an office complex shares some qualities with a library or study. While larger spaces such as restaurants, conference rooms, hotel lobbies, and the public spaces of clubs, airports, and museums do not have direct parallels with residential spaces, the same basic issues arise: furniture planning will be guided by the functions of the space and the furniture; the relation between furniture shapes and the layout of architectural spaces; and the patterns of movement that normal and special usages will generate.

The example of one functional type can serve to suggest the approach to furniture planning for any space. *Private offices* vary greatly in size and intended function. A minimal private office or cubicle may be sized to hold no more than a minimal work surface and a chair. Larger offices usually contain seating for one or more visitors and some extra work and storage provisions. The largest offices have space for both formal and informal meetings and often serve as conference areas. Expressing status level through the amount of space and the size, quantity, and opulence of furniture may be as important as ensuring the office's actual work functions.

Although a desk is usually a key item of office furniture, the term *work surface* better describes the variety of arrangements, whether desk, work counter, table, or other, that may be used to suit particular patterns of work. If windows offer daylight and view, furniture placement should take account of their location. Traditionally, a desk is placed centrally, the office occupant seated behind it and facing the chairs provided for visitors. A low storage unit (called a credenza) is often placed behind and parallel with a desk, giving the user an extra work surface in back as well as storage. A modern variant is the L-arrangement, in which the secondary work-surface unit is placed at one side of the desk to form an L. This layout first emerged to provide a location for a typewriter or other office machines that would keep them off the main desk top but leave them readily at hand. This arrangement satisfies the common desire for a clear desk top by placing gadgets and clutter off to the side, where the user can easily reach them simply by turning.

Many offices are now planned to suit a less formal view of work functions. A work surface may be placed along a wall to accommodate the solitary functions of reading, writing, and telephoning. A table will then provide a focus for meetings and conversations with visitors. Storage drawers, files, and shelves can be grouped at one side of the primary work surface along with space for business machines, often including a computer. Larger offices may have a full lounge seating group and low table, similar to the living room core conversation group, intended for informal and extended meetings.

Offices planned for a particular individual can take account

119. Period moldings, woodwork details, and parquet flooring indicated the selection of traditional furniture, window treatment, and table setting in the dining room of designer John F. Saladino's Connecticut house. Nevertheless, the modern painting by Cy Twombly is at home in the space—since both are based on a classical, spare, clean-lined treatment. (Photograph: © Langdon Clay)

120

of personal work habits and expressions of personality. Offices planned as part of the larger installations serving corporations and other large organizations are usually developed in standardized patterns that recognize the reality of the rate of employee turnover. An office that will serve many occupants over a period of years should require only minor adjustments. *LEVELS OF MOBILITY.* In planning furniture placement, it is customary to draw all furniture in plan using normal or typical locations for pieces that can be easily moved about. It may be helpful to consider, in order, levels of mobility for furniture.

FIXED LOCATION. This includes objects that are to be built-in, such as bookshelves and dressing-room closets, and objects that are impractical to move, such as major kitchen appliances. Some objects that are, strictly speaking, movable may be considered fixed when the

121

120. In this simple, virtually all-white bedroom, the mirrored wall visually doubles the small space. Stephen Shubel was the interior designer for this San Francisco project. (Photograph: John Vaughn, courtesy Metropolitan Home Magazine)

121. Here, a complex space incorporates a bedroom in a renovated older building in Tuscany, Italy. The stairway almost doubles back on itself, as it winds up, in a limited space, to a gallery landing that accommodates a private work area. The stairs continue upward at upper left. The art, furniture, and furnishings are part of an eclectic and personal collection. (Photograph: Jaime Ardiles-Arce)

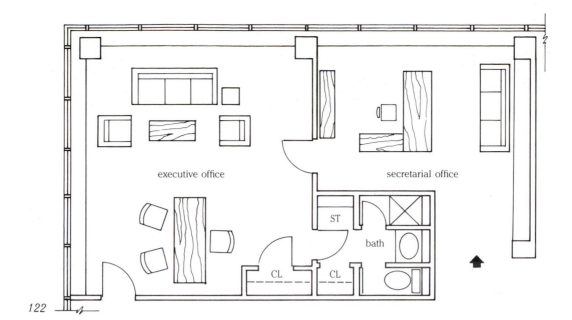

executive office

secretarial office

ST

bath

CL CL

122

123

122. This floor plan shows an executive office suite of a major corporation in a modern New York high-rise. The corner office (at left), designed for a senior executive, includes a desk work area and a spacious, informal conference seating group, as well as closets, storage units, and a private washroom, complete with shower. Primary access is through a secretarial office (at right) that has its own storage wall. The door at lower left provides secondary access.

123. Louis Frye, designer, conceived this executive office in Tech Center, a 1987 office complex in San Diego, California, for its developer's headquarters. Floors of polished marble tiles, glass block for the corridor wall, and shoji screens that soften the intense sunlight together form a pure background for the Bauhaus-inspired furniture, much of it created by Frye for this project. There is an informal seating area (at right) as well as the traditional across-the-desk arrangement. (Photograph: © 1987 William Gullette)

124

space plan permits only one location. This might be true of the bed in a bedroom that has only one wall space that permits bed placement.

SEMIFIXED LOCATION. This refers to furniture that is so large and heavy as to be difficult to move. It is normally kept in a single location. This is often true of a large sofa or sectional seating group, a large storage piece or wall-unit grouping. Although a piano on casters can be shifted about, a fixed location is usual both because of its weight and mass and because there is often only one location that is possible or satisfactory.

MOVABLE FURNITURE. This includes most chairs, tables, and smaller desks, storage units, and lounge furniture. A furniture plan usually shows such furniture in normal locations. Sometimes it is helpful to draw alternate plans to show how furniture can be rearranged for special situations. A living room, for example, may have a normal layout and a planned rearrangement for large parties. A conference room with a center table and surrounding chairs may be converted to a classroom or auditorium plan, with all chairs facing the front of the room.

PORTABLE FURNITURE. This is a special class made up of folding and stacking chairs, folding-leg tables, and furniture on wheels such as tea carts, roll-around files, and projector stands. Typical locations for such furniture and places for storage when not in use need to be considered.

Resolving Conflicts in Planning

Throughout the planning process, whether of extensive spaces or of one room, the designer must always balance conflicting values and requirements that pull in different directions. The designer deals with these by assigning levels of importance to conflicting requirements and finding ways to resolve the

124. This reception area combines inviting, residential qualities—note the open fire, the rugs, the comfortable seating, and the flowers—with the larger scale and dignity of a public institution. Designed by ISD Incorporated for the headquarters of the American Academy of Arts and Sciences in Cambridge, Massachusetts. (Photograph: Jaime Ardiles-Arce, courtesy ISD Incorporated)

conflicts. Typically, the total space available is insufficient to provide ample space for all the various activities the client may wish to pursue. Which activities are to take precedence and which are to be limited? Are there ways to overlap or share activities so that each will be served at an optimum level? A small dining room, for example, might use a large table to serve many guests and permit uncrowded serving space, but the large table may leave limited space for chairs, which will have to be pushed up close to a wall or to adjacent furniture. Generous space for seating and circulation may leave space for only a small and skimpy table. Which value should have priority, or should a compromise be made? What functions in an office space require the best light and view, executive offices used by a few important people or general work space used by many? Is there any compromise that will give maximum advantage to all users of the space?

The most common conflict involves costs. All too often, the list of requirements outruns the available budget. In this case, what features are to be given up? The route of compromise between conflicting values usually appears to be the most reasonable choice, but compromise sometimes results in a situation in which no values are well served and overall mediocrity becomes the norm. In the small dining room mentioned above, a decision to use a medium-sized table may still leave the seating and circulation crowded while making the table inadequate as well. One of the extremes—to provide a generous table at all costs or give up table size entirely in favor of better seating and open space—may well be preferable. Similarly, when it comes to the budget, it is often best to give up some desired feature: to omit a separate dining room, for example, or make do with existing furniture, in order to provide a spacious living room, an all-new kitchen, or a valuable Oriental rug. Ultimately, such decisions rest with the owners, clients, and users, but the designer can aid the decision-making by articulating the choices and by proposing one or more solutions, often in plan form.

At another level, all design involves making choices that imply points of view about what is important and what is not. Although owner, user, or client can contribute to many such decisions, the designer must accept responsibility for making a vast number of small decisions in which the values to be taken into consideration are hardly major enough to be thought about as separate issues. When the sofa is placed here or there, a few inches forward or back, the decision implies some view about the relative importance given to the ways in which the sofa and the space around it are to be used. Every plan is based on innumerable decisions of this sort, and the plan's success reflects the quality of such decisions.

EVALUATING THE PLAN

Effective planning is aided by another special skill that all designers need to develop. This is the ability to visualize in three dimensions what is being drawn out in plan, to imagine a completed space, even though the details have not yet been considered, and to live in that space in the imagination. This skill can be practiced when looking at plans published in books and magazines or plans drawn by others. One can imagine oneself a tiny person existing at the scale of the drawing and enter the space. When actually planning, each proposal can be tested by this kind of mental visit to the place that exists, at this point, only on paper. The aim is to make of the mind something like a moving picture or television camera that makes it possible to see—and to feel and sense in every way—what the built space will be like. In this kind of mental visit to the unbuilt space, the designer can enter, look about, move along the various possible lines of circulation, turn right and left, stop, perhaps sit down where some real occupant of the space might do so. This permits the designer to make a running evaluation of appearance, convenience, and practicality. "How would I like to be here, move thus, sit in this location?" These questions and their answers form a critique of the sketched plan.

In making such a mental visit to a proposed space, a number of points call for special attention. It should become habitual to check these issues as a plan is being drawn, even to consider them when planning ideas are just forming in the mind. Not every issue will apply to every project, but the following lists the more important:

ENTERING. The moment of arrival in a space, the transition from being outside to being inside a house, an apartment, a suite of offices, or a room, is always significant. First impressions are, traditionally, of major importance, and repeated arrivals at the same location only intensify the impression. How does the arriving person move? What does that person see? How are the practicalities (removing coat, placing packages, umbrella, and so on) dealt with? In a home, the impact of the entry is mostly visual and spatial. Everyone knows a house where the front door bursts into the midst of a living space or where there is no convenient place to hang coats. A public space such as an office, shop, or restaurant may require a reception control point, waiting space, or directory information to aid orientation. A cramped waiting room with a tiny wicket window guarding a receptionist is all too familiar a depressing introduction to many professional offices. A handsome, spacious, and suitably furnished reception area suggests, in contrast, a well-organized and confidence-inspiring organization.

126

MOVING INTO DESTINATION SPACE.
This is the next step of experiencing a space. Are there halls, corridors, stairs, elevators, lobbies, doorways to be passed through? How will they look and feel to a first-time visitor, to a regular visitor or user, to a resident or owner? Going down a long, narrow, twisting hall is not the best introduction to a living room, classroom, office, or guest room. While familiarity can blunt the impact, an unpleasant access still leaves a negative impression. Passing through a low, narrow, or dim transition space can be offset by arriving at a large, bright destination space, the contrast heightening the favorable experience of arrival. Most often, direct, simple, and open access, with its implications of ease and welcome, is best.

ARRIVAL AT OBJECTIVE AND ACTIVITY PROVISION THERE. In a living room, where and how does the arriving person greet others, find a place to sit or stand? What is seen as one looks about? Comparable questions can be asked of a dining location, a bedroom, an office, or a shop. Is it possible to move about comfortably? Does the space offer different situations to suit different times, people, moods?

UTILITY SPACES. Kitchens, bathrooms, workshops, and other such spaces need to be planned to make the activities that go on in them as efficient as possible. They also should offer easy movement and a sequence of satisfactory visual impressions. Too often a kitchen planned for strict efficiency turns out to be cramped and inflexible. A workshop need not be less pleasant than a living area in order to be practical.

CIRCULATION. Not simply a matter of abstract planning charts, circulation is a sequence of experiences, visual and kinetic, that can be imagined while studying a plan. It is important to consider the different patterns that may apply to the resident, the visitor, the employee, and other kinds of users, all of whom may use the same space in different ways. In planning a hospital or an airport, the experiences of many

125. In a sedate and traditionally formal entrance hall, Oriental rugs and a crystal chandelier relate to period furniture in a residential setting in Austin, Texas. Kenneth Jorns, designer, 1985. (Photograph: R. Greg Hursley)

126. The dramatic spatial quality of an austerely handsome foyer and stair hall of a house in Uruguay is enhanced by the simplicity of the plank door, plant bench, and slab stair landing. (Photograph: Jaime Ardiles-Arce)

127

different kinds of users, each with different patterns of movement and varied needs, should be traced in order to discover and minimize conflicting patterns.

DAYLIGHT AND VIEW. These need to be thought about when planning. Windowless spaces, while common in many modern buildings, are generally found to present problems. Where will light and view be available, and how can their absence be offset? On the other hand, glare can be unpleasant, and a view, under some circumstances, can be distracting. These situations can be controlled, but wise planning to avoid awkward relationships between people and window areas works best.

DEAD-END LOCATION. While people value freedom of movement within a space, a quality that good, open circulation provides, they also seek out and enjoy cozy spaces at the end of movement paths. Such dead ends, or cul-de-sacs, where no further movement through is possible, may suggest some sort of primitive security or stability. One may, for example, observe people at a party moving on until they reach a location where they must stop. This location, with its feeling of privacy and security, suits certain spaces such as bedrooms, private offices, and bathrooms. Provision of intentionally

planned dead ends is important in serving some of the social inclinations of the space users.

ACOUSTICAL ISSUES. Usually thought of in technical terms of materials and even electronic devices, acoustical issues actually respond best to sound planning. The easiest way to deal with these issues is to place sources of noise as far away as possible from places where quiet will be important. If this cannot be done, barriers of some sort can isolate noise to some extent. In practice, placing a family room with TV as far as possible from bedrooms seems only logical. A wall of closets in between two adjacent bedrooms serving users of different age levels can help to minimize cross talk. In offices, layout can do more to provide *acoustical privacy,* that is, inability to hear conversation from one space to another, than any available materials. The planner, by placing elements so that sound must either travel a long distance or be blocked by natural sound-absorbing barriers, will eliminate the most troublesome acoustical problems (see also Chapter 18, pages 484–87).

SAFETY AND SECURITY. Control of access, surveillance, and safe exit routes, often thought about only after problems appear, are all best dealt with through planning. A few minutes spent imagining various emergency situations (fire, vandalism, theft, and so on) will suggest simple ways to minimize what can otherwise be difficult problems to control. Safety against accidents is also closely related to planning around such elements as glass doors and partitions, steps, stairways, and ramps, and in such high-risk areas as bathrooms. When imagining such problems, the designer should seek to envision the experiences of children, the elderly, and the handicapped (see also Chapter 14, pages 385–86).

All of these points may seem obvious, and thinking about them can—and certainly should—be second nature to the skilled planner, but our everyday observation of the interior spaces we use makes it clear that good planning for all of the building user's needs cannot be taken for granted. Planning is too often viewed as a matter of applying familiar formulas or of staging formal visual effects, whether or not these really serve intended purposes. Consider how many houses have a front door that is seldom or never used, while family and visitors alike go around to the side or back. How much space is given to formal parlor living rooms, used once or twice a year, while normal life is crowded into a family room often located in a dark basement? Public buildings are equally given to main entrances leading to little-used lobbies, while most visitors come from underground subway concourses or parking garages. Good planning avoids all of these absurdities and concentrates on serving real needs with both efficiency and elegance.

127. A broad corridor sweeping through an open office area of the ARCO Chemical Company at Newtown Square, Pennsylvania, seems to invite progress toward a distant destination. Davis, Brody & Associates, designer. (Photograph: Robert Gray, courtesy Davis, Brody & Associates)

128. A quiet and attractive window alcove nestled between storage units makes a cozy dead-end space. Abbie Zabar was the designer for her own house in Nantucket, Massachusetts. (Photograph: © François Halard, courtesy House & Garden)

CASE STUDY 1

OFFICE FLOOR IN A CITY BUILDING
Offices for Wheel-Gersztoff Associates, New York

FORBES-ERGAS DESIGN ASSOC., INC.,
INTERIOR PLANNING AND DESIGN
WHEEL-GERSZTOFF ASSOCIATES, INC.,
LIGHTING CONSULTANTS

A full floor in a Manhattan loft building was developed for a lighting design firm with a staff of sixteen. Because most of the firm's clients are architects or designers, a strong design quality was important, both in order to display the firm's design standards and to demonstrate excellence in lighting design. The flavor of the original building is maintained in the hardwood floors and metal ceiling, which recalls the pressed-metal ceiling characteristic of the period—although this is, in fact, a modern reproduction in cast aluminum. The overall impact of the space is modern and elegant, yet simple and efficient. It serves the partners and staff well, while also signaling an appropriate message to visiting professionals and their clients.

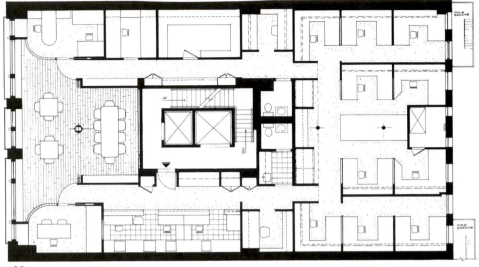

129

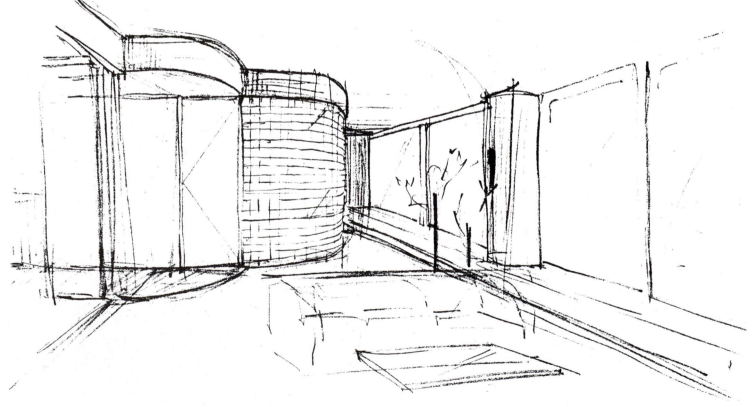

130

129. This plan of the entire floor was intended for presentation to the client. The elevators and stair occupy a central core. The conference area, which can be subdivided by folding partitions as desired, and the partners' offices are at the left; the drafting room, its work stations defined by low screens, is at the right. Note the generous provision for storage, files, and samples in a number of locations.

130. This rough pencil sketch by Susan Forbes is typical of those made during the design process. It depicts the public space at the front of the building, where large windows illuminate a central seating and conference area. The curving glass-block wall defines one of the two identical private offices used by the partners.

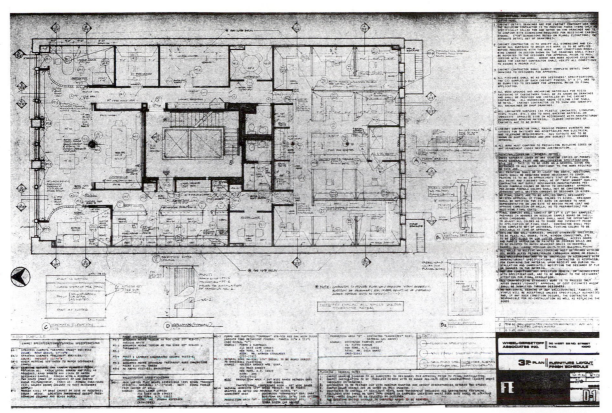

131

132

131. Shown here is a sheet of construction drawings (often called blueprints). These plans include complete details of all the structural tasks to be done, with separate sheets for lighting, air conditioning, and other mechanical work. In this set, the finish schedule, all specifications are found on the plan as well, and an additional sheet includes elevations and sections. The result is a complete information package that will serve both for obtaining estimates and for actual on-site construction.

132. The drafting room incorporates work stations designed and constructed specially for this project. Notice that the lighting has been knowledgeably planned: the general, or ambient, light is projected upward from the storage elements, while task downlighting illuminates counters, and adjustable cantilever lamps can be focused over drafting boards as required. (Photograph: © Norman McGrath)

133

133. The front area that appears in the sketch in fig. 130 is here shown completed; note the metal ceiling. The larger conference area is at the left; folding partitions can close it off. This photograph is taken from one partner's office and looks across to the other private office opposite. Although unobtrusive, the lighting is at the same time practical and pleasant, demonstrating the client firm's expertise in this area. (Photograph: © Norman McGrath)

CASE STUDY 2

DESIGN DEVELOPMENT AS PROCESS
A City Apartment
DESIGN AND DRAWINGS BY NORMAN DIEKMAN

The clients, sponsors of the American craft movement, were a couple who own houses elsewhere and wanted a city base where they could keep and display objects in their collection. They selected this condominium apartment in a Manhattan high-rise primarily for its twenty-fifth-floor location, which provides a flood of afternoon light and spectacular day and nighttime city views from the ample windows.

The design process is traced here in a sequence of drawings, a representative selection from the large number of studies produced in the course of devising concepts and communicating them to the clients for discussion and, ultimately, approval.

Many projects and many designers employ fewer drawings. Norman Diekman is particularly interested in the technique of this medium and in its use as a primary design tool. It is this combination that makes this project an appropriate showcase of creative interior drawing.

134

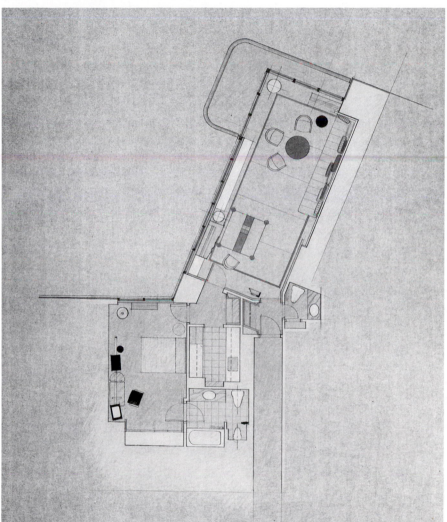

135

134. *The legendary "first sketch on the back of an envelope" is, in practice, not uncommon. These sketches include initial notes made on paper napkins over lunch in a restaurant; the ideas were then developed in the office. They represent the following stages:*

During a lunch meeting with the client, an overall concept emerged (left) that placed the design emphasis upon the light and views that determined the choice of the space. The image of a summer pavilion in the sky takes shape verbally and visually. Another napkin sketch (center), made a few days later, illustrates the treatment of the entrance at an angle where the foyer opens into the living space. A thumbnail perspective sketch (right) captures the space as it will be with afternoon sunlight pouring in. The designer likes to call such a sketch "a Xerox of the mind" — that is, the visual trace of a thought in the course of development.

135. *This complete color plan of the apartment is a study for both designer and client. The background is a black-and-white Ozalid print made from a pencil line drawing on yellow tracing paper showing only the walls and other fixed elements of the plan. A dark print provides the background tone for the drawing with prismacolor and ordinary black pencils, used to indicate furniture and other elements with partially realistic, partially diagrammatic shading.*

The gray background indicates the gray carpet of bedroom and foyer. Yellow is a code color for the existing plasterboard walls and columns; the beige in the living room stands for matting on the wood flooring. The celadon of the chair upholstery and a fabric wall panel was chosen to reflect the copper tones of the roof of a nearby Beaux-Arts hotel tower visible from the windows.

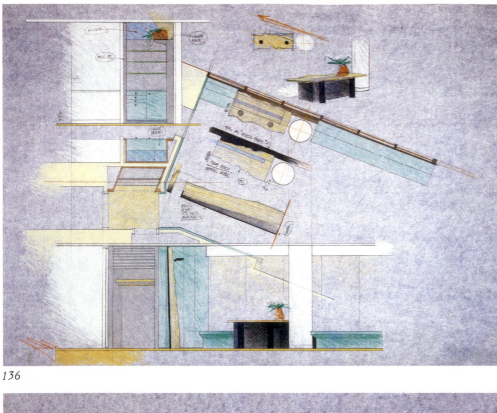

136

137

138

136. After the concept and plan have received general approval, the cost estimates must be addressed. This sheet combines a plan, elevations, and a perspective in order to assemble the requisite details. The lower elevation, the plan above it, and the perspective at upper right focus upon the entrance area, where a console table at the win-dow covers a convector. Note the repeated use of the celadon picked up from the copper roof outside. At the upper left, the proposed bar area is depicted in a mirror elevation, that is, the image would be reversed in a construction drawing. A sheet like this one is in essence a large-scale sketchbook page, a sort of blackboard on which ideas are explored.

137. This perspective drawing focuses on the large table omitted from the study in fig. 138. The table is designed to serve two purposes. For dining, it seats six to eight or can be used for buffet meals; as a display surface, it allows craft objects from the owners' collection to be viewed and studied. A plan of the table appears at the bottom, overlapping the perspective. The designer had originally intended to fill in a nighttime sky and skyline visible through the windows at the right, but decided instead to leave the drawing as it is. As in all creative work, one of the most important skills in drawing and rendering is knowing when to stop!

138. *The theme of a summer pavilion in the sky appears here in fairly precise detail, in a perspective clearly evolved from one of the napkin sketches. The high, curved ceiling suggests vaulting and spreads the afternoon light up and into the space. The daytime view is accurate; another could be drawn as it would be at night to show the space under different lighting conditions.*

Compare the banquette seating and the brown cylindrical wood table here and in the plan view of fig. 135 (at upper right). The square table (fig. 135, below) is omitted here: not yet fully developed as an element, it would appear too distracting.

CHAPTER FIVE
MATERIALS AND ELEMENTS

The *elements* of interior design are the separate parts or components that make up a space. The term comes from the long-used phrase *elements of architecture,* referring to the basic building components—walls, floors, ceilings, columns, doors, windows, and similar items. Every building is made up of *structural* elements, those that actually support the building and enclose it, and *nonstructural* elements, additions that do not affect the building's basic structure. Unless the interior designer participates in the planning of a new building, he or she will find the structural elements fixed in place, and thus difficult or impossible to change or remove. Outside walls, *load-bearing* walls that carry the weight of the roof or ceiling, floors, roofs, and structural columns fit into this category, as do many windows, outside doors, stairways, and other elements that compose the basic architecture of a building. Nonstructural elements, such as interior partition walls, which carry no load, some steps and stairs, doors, and openings, are usually subject to change, addition, or removal, and therefore more likely to be within the control of the interior designer.

All elements are made of materials, such as wood, stone, plaster, paint, and paper. A floor can be stone, brick, wood, or tile, all appropriate to the function of this element. A wall might be built of brick, stone, wood, or plasterboard on studs, but this material may then be covered with plaster, paint, fabric, tile, paneling, or any number of other materials. An important part of interior design work is the selection of suitable materials for the various elements that make up a particular interior space.

A typical interior consists of several elements and a surprising number of materials. It is an interesting exercise to list, for a few familiar spaces, every element and every material, including even the small details of hardware and trim. Such lists may turn out to be much longer than might be expected. Organizing the selection of materials demands knowledge of what is available and an awareness of what is best suited to particular needs and uses. Collecting information about materials, both in memory and in a data file of catalogs, literature, and samples, is a vital part of preparation for interior design work. This chapter offers an introduction to the wide range of possibilities, but cannot begin to cover the vast variety of materials and products currently available. The materials of furniture and textiles, because of their special importance, are covered in separate chapters (6 and 7).

TYPES OF MATERIALS

While all materials originate from natural sources, human needs impose certain levels of modification on materials as they are found in nature.

139. The combination of wide, pine-plank flooring and cedar siding, both inside and out, generates a rustic quality in this ski house in Vail, Colorado, designed by Venturi, Rauch and Scott Brown in 1977. The house is furnished mostly with a collection of Gustav Stickley Mission oak pieces from the turn of the century, with wicker chairs of the same vintage. (Photograph courtesy Venturi, Rauch and Scott Brown)

Natural Materials

These remain unchanged except when they need to be superficially modified for use. The natural materials stone and wood, for example, can be used in their natural forms, but they are usually cut into standard shapes. Quarried stone is most often cut into blocks, in which form it is called ashlar, and trees are cut first into logs, then into boards, or lumber, of standardized forms and sizes.

Processed Materials

These are the result of converting natural materials into special forms for practical use. The natural material clay takes on different properties and uses when fired into brick and tile. Sand and small stones (called aggregate), when bonded together with cement, form concrete, a kind of artificial stone that can be poured in mass, reinforced with embedded steel rods, or made up into blocks similar to cut stone. Wood may be sliced into thin sheets of veneer, and layers of veneer may be glued together to form plywood. All metals require processing to extract them from ore, refine them, and possibly combine them into alloys. Then they are formed into sheets, tubes, rolled sections, castings, or other shapes.

Synthetic Materials

These do not exist in nature but have been brought into being, or manufactured, through artificial processes. Glass is an ancient synthetic made from sand and various other elements fused by heat. Plastics, the most familiar of modern synthetics, are made from various chemicals, most of them derived from petroleum. Synthetics themselves can be combined, leading to the creation of hybrids such as fiberglass.

In practice, many materials result from combinations of these levels of processing. A natural fiber such as wool may be processed through spinning and weaving to make a textile. A core of solid wood may be surfaced with a synthetic plastic laminate. Rolled steel beams or columns may be enclosed in poured concrete and covered in turn with metal lath and plaster, plasterboard, solid wood boards, plywood, tile, or any number of other materials.

BASIC MATERIALS

Although a complete listing of all the materials useful in interiors would be unmanageable, a few primary material groups forming the basis of most building construction and interior finishes are listed in Table 2 on pages 108–9.

TABLE 2. BASIC MATERIALS

Material	Types		Comments
Masonry	Rough stone (field stone, flagstone) Cut stone, or ashlar (limestone, marble, granite, slate) Brick Terra-cotta block	Tile (quarry tile, mosaic, vitreous, ceramic) Gypsum block Concrete block Precast concrete Reinforced concrete Mass concrete	Masonry materials need to be sized and shaped to suit their planned use. Rough stone can be selected to fall within a desired range of size and shape. Cut stone is sized and shaped according to the designer's plans. Brick, tile, and block come in a limited number of standardized sizes and shapes. The shape of poured concrete elements is determined by each design.
Wood	Softwoods (from evergreen trees) such as pine, spruce, fir, cedar, redwood Hardwoods (from the nut, fruit, and other deciduous trees) such as oak, maple, birch, walnut, cherry, poplar, and many more exotic woods	Veneer Plywood (solid core and veneer core) Laminated wood (such as butcher block) Particleboard	Wood is characterized by a lengthwise grain structure, which results from the growth of the tree. Size is limited by the dimensions of available trees of a given species; the dimensions of width and thickness are strictly limited, while lengths of over 16 feet present problems in both availability and handling. Veneer is thin sheet, available only in limited widths and lengths. Plywood and particleboard are made in sheets of standard size, most frequently 4 by 8 feet.
Metals	Steel (structural or *mild*, in various forms such as sheet, rolled sections, and tubing) Stainless steel (in similar forms)	Aluminum (in similar forms as well as in extrusions and castings) Copper, brass, and bronze Alloys for die-casting	Metals other than stainless steel all require finishing to protect them from rust and corrosion. Steel can be painted or plated. Aluminum can be anodized in its natural color or in various other colors. Brass, copper, and bronze can be constantly polished to maintain their natural color, lacquered to avoid polishing, or left to weather to the tones of green that oxidation produces. Chromium plating is a widely used finish for steel and die-cast alloys.
Synthetics	Glass Plastics (in sheet, molded, extruded, and other processed forms)	Manufactured products such as linoleum, resilient floor tile, or Sheet-rock (wallboard)	Glass is available in flat panes or sheets of various thicknesses and sizes. Usually clear, glass can be made in various tints and colors as well. Curved sheets must be made to special order. Tempered glass, of great strength, cannot be cut, so must be made to the desired size and shape. Glass block is glass in hollow, bricklike form. Plastics can take many forms; they appear most often in interiors as flat sheets of clear or tinted acrylic or Lexan, used as an unbreakable substitute for glass, and as thin sheets of melamine laminates, used as a tough surface applied over other materials. It is possible to obtain plastic sheet with bends or curves, but it must usually be ordered from the factory. The most common sheet size is 4 by 8 feet.

Material	Types		Comments

Hybrids and Miscellaneous	Woven fibers
	Leather, cork, rubber
	Rope, cord, netting
	Air-supported
	    membranes
		Paper
		Hardboard,
		    chalkboard, and
		    tack board
		Ceiling tile	

Coatings and Finishes	Paint, varnish, lacquer, stain, enamel	Plastic coatings Plating (of metals)	

Woven fibers, both natural and synthetic, are the materials of carpeting and rugs and of wall-covering materials, including special carpeting and woven sheet material (applied like wallpaper). (See also Chapter 7, which discusses drapery and upholstery textiles.)

Paint, which provides both protection of the underlying material and control of color and gloss, remains the most-used finish. The best traditional paint is based on lead as the pigment and oil as the vehicle. Because of possible health hazards associated with the use of lead, this kind of paint is now outlawed for most uses. Other pigments are substituted, and oil is often replaced by synthetic resins as the vehicle. Paints come in an extensive range of ready-mixed colors, although professional painters often prefer to mix paints to match samples provided by the designer. When this is not possible or desirable, specifying color by selecting a numbered chip in the color system of a particular manufacturer ensures accurate color use. Despite their easily marred surfaces, *flat paints* are generally preferred for walls and ceilings. *Semigloss* is generally used for trim, although *high gloss* (enamel) may also be selected. Gloss paints are usually used in bathroom and kitchen spaces because of their resistance to moisture and staining.

Wood of good appearance may be finished with a clear coating or penetrating finish that permits the grain to show. Staining, which alters the wood's color, is done before the finish is applied. *Varnish* is a traditional clear finish; synthetic (plastic) coatings are now often substituted. Unlike varnish and plastics that develop a surface coating, oil or synthetic *penetrating finishes* soak into wood. These are often preferred where a natural surface appearance is desired. The surface coating *lacquer* (now usually a synthetic) can be clear or of opaque color. It is usually used only where a very high-gloss surface is desired. Even when wood floors are painted with a special floor paint that offers maximum durability, regular repainting will be necessary to maintain good appearance. Clear finishes for wood floors and steps include *shellac,* *penetrating finishes* that require regular refinishing, and, in recent practice, a *polyurethane* synthetic finish of superior durability but of characteristically plastic gloss surface. Wax is frequently used as a protective polish and is occasionally used alone as a finish. It must be regularly reapplied.

Metals can be painted, provided they are carefully cleaned and primed to assure good paint adherence. Brass and bronze are often lacquered to protect and display their natural metallic appearance. Plating and anodizing are alternative ways of finishing metals, as discussed above.

140

140. *A masonry material, marble is much prized for its durability, its ability to take a high polish, and its vast variety of colors and rich patterns of veining. Traditionally a monumental material, marble's hardness, rich appearance, and cool-feeling surface make it an interior decorative material of dignity and for-* *mality. Here, veined marble is used in a matched pattern for a rear wall, as well as for the flooring, column, and plant box. Sawaya/Moroni were the architects for these Fouad Offices in Saudi Arabia, 1983. (Photograph: Jaime Ardiles-Arce)*

TABLE 3. INTERIOR MATERIALS

		Floors	Walls	Columns	Ceilings	Stairs	Doors	Window Frames	Window Treatment	Movable Furniture	Built-in Furniture	Bathroom Fixtures*	Kitchen Fixtures*	Fireplaces	Mantels	Trim	Hardware
WOOD	Soft	[○]	●	●		[○]	●	●		○	●	○	○		●	●	
	Hard	●	○		○	●	○	○		●	○	○	○		○	○	
	Paneling		●				●										
	Plywood	○	●		○	○	●			●	●	●	●				
	Boarding	○	○		○		○										
METALS	Steel: Mild			[●]		[●]	●	●		●	○	○	●	○			●
	Stainless		○							○		○	●				○
	Enameled		○									●	●				
	Iron: Cast			[ ]										○			○
	Enameled											○		○			
	Aluminum: Cast									○					○		○
	Extruded							●		○							
	Bronze																○
	Brass									●							●
	Copper															○	○
	Die-cast																●
MASONRY	Stone: Field stone	[●]	[○]											[○]			
	Limestone		[○]											[○]			
	Travertine	○	○			○				○							
	Marble	●	[●]	[○]		[○]				○		○		○	●		
	Granite	○	[○]			[○]				○		○					
	Slate	●				○				○		○					
	Concrete: Mass	[○]															
	Reinforced	[●]	[○]	●	○	●								[○]			
	Block		[●]											[○]			
	Gypsum: Block		●														
	Brick	○	[●]	[○]		○								[●]	○		
	Tile: Ceramic, vitreous	○	●	○							○	○		○		○	
	Porcelain		○	○													
	Quarry	●				○											
	Mosaic	○	●	○								○	○				
	Terra-cotta		○	○													
	Terrazzo	●				○											

*The word "fixtures" includes plumbing and appliances

		Floors	Walls	Columns	Ceilings	Stairs	Doors	Window Frames	Window Treatment	Movable Furniture	Built-in Furniture	Bathroom Fixtures*	Kitchen Fixtures*	Fireplaces	Mantels	Trim	Hardware
GLASS	Window							●				○					
	Plate							●		●		○					
	Tempered						●	○				○					
	Mirror		○	○	○					○	○	○					
	Block		○														
PLASTIC	Transparent		○					○		○							
	Laminate		○	○			○			●	●	●	●				
	Sheet wall covering		●	●													
	Extrusion					○		●		○	○		○			○	
	Tile	●	○														
TEXTILES	Drapery		○				○		●								
	Upholstery		○							●	●						
	Wall covering		●														
	Carpet	●	○														
FINISHES	Paint	●	●	●	●	○	●	○		○	●				●	●	
	Natural (oil, wax)	●			○		○	○		●	●					○	
	Varnish, shellac	●				○	●	○		●	○				○	●	
	Lacquer						○			○	○					○	
	Wallpaper		●	○	○												
	Plating (metals)																●
MISCELLANEOUS	Partitions: Lath and plaster		●	●	●												
	Partitions: Drywall		●	●	●												
	Partitions: Folding		○														
	Partitions: Movable		○														
	Partitions: Toilet		○														
	Ceiling: Systems				●												
	Ceiling: Acoustic tile				●												
	Flooring: Linoleum	○	○			○							○				
	Flooring: Asphalt tile	●			●												
	Flooring: Vinyl tile	●			●												
	Flooring: Cork	○	○														
	Flooring: Rubber	○															

141

MATERIAL SELECTION

For any given use, a short list of widely accepted materials will usually come to mind, making selection of the specific material for a particular purpose a matter of common usage, personal preference, or habit. Unfortunately, this often leads to unimaginative or cliché selections, to the neglect of less familiar possibilities that may offer real advantages, or, at worst, to downright mistakes, when a chosen material fails to perform as desired. Many of the most common complaints about interior projects relate to materials that fail in one way or another—that break, wear out, attract dirt, prove hard to clean and maintain, or in some other way create problems that could have been avoided.

Evaluating Materials

These problems can be guarded against by using a mental (or actual) checklist in evaluating each choice. Materials are usually chosen to satisfy their primary role—a floor material to be practical to walk on; a window material to admit light; a door material to provide closure. Problems are most likely to arise in connection with *secondary* criteria, which may be overlooked if one focuses on primary function and appearance alone. An otherwise satisfactory floor material may become dangerously slippery when wet; an attractive wall surface may become marred easily and be hard to clean; carpet selected for attractive surface and color may show dirt and wear. It is an important part of the interior designer's work to be alert to

141. Regional traditions lead to design developed around locally available materials. Bamboo is an exotic material in Europe and America, but here in a house near Sanur, Bali, Balinese designer Putu Suarsu makes it the dominant material, giving the space its special *character. The natural materials tile and brick add their warmth to the space. The house dates from 1986; many of the objects are antiques from the Indonesian islands. (Photograph: Tim Street-Porter)*

such issues and to deal with them by learning all of the characteristics of the materials chosen.

The following is a checklist of criteria for material selection:

FUNCTIONAL CRITERIA

Primary: *Suitability to basic utilitarian purpose*

Secondary: *Durability in anticipated use*

               Ease of maintenance, repair, cleaning

               Resistance to damage and vandalism

               Safety characteristics (accidents, fire)

               Acoustical performance

AESTHETIC CRITERIA

   Availability of desired natural or applied colors

   Textures

   Possibilities of pattern

   Visual suitability to intended function

ECONOMIC CRITERIA

   First cost

   Lifetime cost in relation to expected durability and estimated cost of maintenance, cleaning, repair, and future replacement

These matters are interrelated in complex ways, making judgment and selection difficult. For example, the desired appearance may conflict with the material's functional practicality or cost. The relative importance of various criteria will vary with the intended use. Fire safety may be of minor importance in a one-story residence but significant in a high-rise office or hotel. The presence of a sprinkler system can reduce fire safety to an incidental value. The impact of cost will vary with available budget, while lifetime cost will weigh more strongly on a project planned for long use than on one destined to have a shorter span of usefulness. Vandalism, a factor in public spaces in modern cities, rarely impinges on a private home or office. Acoustical qualities may be vital in a concert hall, significant in an office or home, but of little importance in a shopping center. Durability can influence aesthetic values, as some materials wear or age in a way that is visually acceptable (for example, wood, wool, natural leather) while other materials grow unattractive and shabby long before they actually wear out (for example, some carpets of synthetic yarns).

Materials in Their Setting

Along with all the practical matters involved in material selection, some intangibles affect the concept of appropriateness. The impact of climate, regional traditions, and location, for instance, can be a strong influence. Rough white plaster walls, tile floors, and a wood-beamed ceiling suggest a Mediterranean or other semitropical location. Sliding screens, mats on the floor, and austerely simple forms and natural colors

142

143

142. *The gleaming marble of the majestic Ionic columns echoed in the carved fireplace mantel, the hardwood parquet floor, the generous reading tables, and Windsor armchairs all set a tone of dignity consistent with the main reading room of the New York Bar Association library. The building was originally designed by Cyrus L. W. Eidlitz in 1895. James Stewart Polshek and Partners, Architects, were responsible for the 1984 renovation that introduced lively wall colors and modern lighting. (Photograph: © Elliott Kaufman)*

143. *The special aesthetic of the traditional Japanese interior is defined by the use of natural materials left in their own subtle, natural colors. For the Ursanki Tea Ceremony Society of New York (1981), Jeremy P. Lang Architects employed wood, paper-and-wood shoji sliding screens, and woven tatami mats on the floor in simple geometric forms to develop a serene visual harmony with its basis in Japanese aesthetic traditions and philosophy. (Photograph: © Stan Ries, courtesy Jeremy P. Lang Architects)*

144

145

suggest Japan (fig. 143). A country cottage or farmhouse calls for material choices different from those customary for a town house or city apartment. It is possible, of course, to create the look of a Mediterranean villa in a northern city high-rise or a Scandinavian modern space in California or Mexico City, but such unexpected concepts raise questions about their suitability.

There are also traditional usages for certain spaces in relation to their materials. Dark wood paneling, with its air of sober formality, has often been adopted for a conservative board room or law office or for the library in a rather formal home; for the same reasons it would seem out of place in a children's playroom or a fast-food restaurant. Glittering materials (brass, mirrors, crystal) suggest a casino, an opera house, or a shopping center; in a library, a hospital, or a country cottage they would seem inappropriate and absurd.

It is a useful exercise to develop material selection (and color choices, since the color of materials will influence the color scheme; see Chapter 9, "Color") for various kinds of spaces without reference to actual design. In the process, ideas about what is appropriate will emerge quite strongly. A list for this experiment might include:

A living room in a country house in Maine
The board room of a major corporation
A small kitchen in a city apartment
A hospital patient's room in a small Southern city
A Japanese restaurant
An office for an executive of a cosmetics firm
A bedroom for a young child
An IRS tax-audit service office
A fashion boutique

Many others may come to mind as a device for demonstrating the visual impact of material selection. While it is important to avoid cliché material choices, total disregard for widely accepted traditions of usage tends to lead to bizarre results.

Genuine versus Imitation

The idea that materials should be what they appear to be has wide acceptance as a basic value in design. Some designers even insist that *all* materials be used only in their own natural color; they develop color schemes through choosing materials with their natural colors in mind. This may be problematic in the case of synthetics. Plastic laminate, for example, can hardly be said to have a "natural" color; its use requires acceptance of an artificial color and perhaps of texture or pattern as well.

Most designers prefer to avoid materials that attempt to imitate some other material in an artificial way. Fake materials tend to degrade the quality of the space where they are used.

Unfortunately, many modern materials are made with the specific purpose of mimicking some other, usually superior (and more expensive) material. Linoleum can be had in patterns that imitate tile, wood boards, parquet, or marble. Wallpaper can be found that imitates wood boards, marble, tile, or brick. Some plastic sheeting is embossed to imitate the texture and mortar joints of brickwork. Imitation wood beams of plastic can be glued to ceilings to suggest structure that does not exist. Serious design work of good quality rejects all such imitations as cheap, shoddy, and generally of such poor appearance as to fool no one.

Every designer has to make decisions about where to draw the line on the issue of imitations. Is a plastic laminate that imitates a wood veneer satisfactory as a table- or desk-top material? Are paper-thin wood tiles that imitate parquet acceptable since they really *are* made of wood? Is a plastic material that imitates leather a satisfactory alternative to the real thing? What about false wormholes in the *distressed* finishes applied to some antique reproductions? Such questions may have to be decided on a case-by-case basis, but it generally makes sense to minimize or avoid imitations wherever possible.

Some imitations can be seen in another light. We know that painted imitations of marble were often used in Baroque churches, and that Early American floors were sometimes painted in patterns to suggest tiles. The aim in these instances, however, was not so much to deceive as to elicit delight in the maker's skill, as, for example, is the case with *trompe l'oeil* painting and the art of theatrical scene painters.

If plastic is to replace leather, a plain surface or texture is preferable to one that tries to mimic pigskin or elephant hide. Laminates come in plain colors and in patterns that are purely geometric rather than imitative. Plastic butcher block or knotty pine, linoleum marble or flagstone, simulated brick and tile, fake fireplaces, and plastic plants are among the absurdities that have no place in a well-designed interior.

On the other hand, the changing of color through dyeing (of textiles, carpets, and similar elements) and the changing of a surface through materials such as paint and wallpaper have come to be widely accepted. Most surface materials have appearance characteristics that make it clear that they *are* surface. A tiled wall does not suggest that the wall is tile all the way through. Wood paneling looks very different from structural woodwork. Even stone used as a surface material (in large, thin sheets) looks quite different from the smaller blocks of actual stone construction. The idea that structural and surface materials *should* look different has been a recognized design principle for many years.

144, 145. Decorative painter Richard Gillette has called his Manhattan loft "a tribute to the last days of Tribeca." An extraordinary diversity of materials and finishes gives the space in an old commercial building a unique quality (fig. 144). The floor is inlaid marble and painted plywood. Other materials include cast and wrought iron, glass, pottery, carved and painted wood, and various textiles. The uncurtained windows can be covered with shutters. The exposed brick wall with its brick arch bears seemingly ancient bits of painting, which were actually done by the artist-occupant. In the kitchen detail (fig. 145), he used the technique of trompe l'oeil, which describes a superrealistic style of painting intended, literally, "to fool the eye" of the viewer. What is real and what is art merge in an intriguing confusion. (Photographs: Bruce Wolf, courtesy House & Garden)

MATERIALS IN RELATION TO ELEMENTS

Each element, whether structural or nonstructural, is composed of one or more materials. As previously mentioned, the structural elements in a space are usually the result of architectural decisions over which the designer has little control. However, since elements can be modified through surface treatment, which can make drastic changes in appearance, the designer has a wide range of choices:

LEAVE MATERIAL EXPOSED in its natural, unfinished state or, if already covered, uncover to expose it. (Brick, stone, wood, even concrete are often used in this way.)

TREAT EXPOSED, NATURAL MATERIALS with a finish chosen to preserve their natural appearance while protecting against wear and dirt. In practice, such natural finishes will change the color and appearance of the material to some degree, usually darkening the color somewhat. (Typical finishes of this kind are wax, oil, and various clear varnishes and lacquers.)

COAT EXPOSED MATERIALS with a finish that covers and seals the surface and hides it with a colored pigment (usually paint). Even when the color is changed, the texture of the material shows—that is, a red brick wall painted white (or any other color) still looks like brick. Paint tends to hide construction details, such as mortar joints, and may change texture.

COMPLETELY COVER OVER MATERIALS with a layer of a second covering material. (Examples are wood veneered or covered with plastic laminate; wallpaper or plastic sheet material on walls; carpeting on a floor.)

In many situations, a basic, often structural material is hidden by another structural layer. Such a covering layer of material may then be finished with still another

146

146. In this ranch house near Cody, Wyoming, built in the 1920s, exposed structural materials—wood beams, log walls, a stone fireplace and chimney—and rustic furniture work together with timber-wolf pelts, cowhides, and Navaho rugs to create a regional tone in keeping with the location and style of the house. (Photograph: Copyright © 1985 Michael Skott)

coating. (In a wooden house, the wood studs and joists of wall, ceiling, and roof construction are usually covered by lath and plaster or, in modern practice, plasterboard, which is then finished with another material such as paint. Steel structural columns are wrapped with an insulating material for fire protection, which is in turn covered by a material chosen for its finished appearance.)

The following survey gives the most common materials and finishes for each major interior element, with some notes on bases for selection.

WALLS
Load-Bearing Walls

Since they support floors and roofs, load-bearing walls must be of considerable structural strength. Their material has usually been determined by the architectural design of a building. The primary material, often covered and concealed by finish materials, can be an important interior element when left exposed. Common examples are:

- *BRICK. Exposed or painted.*
- *CONCRETE BLOCK. Exposed or painted. It is usually left exposed only in utilitarian spaces such as garages or basements.*
- *CONCRETE. Mass or reinforced.*
- *STONE. Available in varied colors and textures. Field stone (fig. 147), laid up, or constructed, in a variety of ways from very rough to more regularly patterned courses, or layers. Ashlar, or neatly cut stone, is often used in monumental architectural spaces.*
- *WOOD. Large frame members and planking of post and beam construction, exposed or finished (see fig. 139). Most common carpenter-built construction is usually concealed.*

147

147. The wall and fireplace here are of rough-cut limestone. The exposed stonework in this 1849 house in Castroville, Texas, establishes an informal, rustic quality. (Photograph: Copyright © 1985 Michael Skott)

Partition Walls

Partition walls (or simply partitions) typically have an inner, hidden support structure and an outer surface, which, in turn, may be covered with a surface finish. The same combination of materials that makes up a partition is often used to line (thus concealing) bearing wall materials (see fig. 661).

WOOD STUDS. Wood strips, usually 2-by-4-inch studs spaced 16 inches apart, are the most common partition structure in nonfireproof construction. They provide space for pipes, wiring, and ducts. Where drainpipes are to be run within a partition, 2-by-6-inch studs are used. A double wall with two separate sets of studs can improve acoustical isolation between spaces.

METAL STUDS. Steel studs are used in place of wood to offer improved fire-resistance while still providing hollow space within a partition's thickness for pipes, ducts, and wiring.

GYPSUM BLOCK. This light masonry material, used only in partition-wall construction, gives superior fire-resistance and acoustical control and provides a sturdy surface for plaster or other surface treatment.

CONCRETE BLOCK. (Usually cinder-concrete block.) A masonry block even heavier and more solid than gypsum block, it is used for spaces that need particularly good isolation, such as fire stairs, elevator shafts, machinery rooms.

148

148. *Office partitions of several heights and with stepped profiles give various levels of privacy in these offices designed by Gensler and Associates/Architects for the Computer Systems Development Facility of the Crocker National Bank in San Francisco in 1982. The partition units are of conventional drywall construction. Glass panels can be added to make a full wall, providing additional privacy. (Photograph: Jaime Ardiles-Arce)*

149

LATH AND PLASTER. The traditional partition surface of older construction is wood lath supporting a covering of plaster applied by hand, wet, in several coats. More modern lath may be a perforated gypsum board, or an expanded metal mesh. Metal lath is usually used over metal studs to provide good fire-resistance. Lath and plaster may be used to line bearing walls as well. Plaster may be applied directly (without lath) to gypsum or concrete block. High labor costs and slow drying time have tended to discourage the use of plaster walls.

DRYWALL. This is the term given to the most common alternative to stud and plaster partition construction (fig. 148). Studs (wood or metal) are covered with sheets, usually 4 by 8 feet, of plasterboard, a factory-made sheet composed of gypsum plaster sandwiched between sheets of a special heavy paper. This wallboard can be cut and nailed in place quickly and easily. Joints are covered with a special tape and both joints and nailheads are covered with a plaster-like compound, producing a fairly smooth wall. Drywall partitions often show some bulges or waves, and the marks of joints and nailheads may also show up. Cracking is, however, less likely than in lath and plaster surfaces.

MOVABLE PARTITIONS. These are factory-made products available as complete systems that incorporate doors, glass panels, and, usually, provision for wiring. The prefabricated elements can be taken apart and reused in new locations and arrangements as necessary. Metal or metal and glass are the most usual materials. Movable partitions are most widely used in office installations (fig. 149).

FOLDING PARTITIONS. Also factory-made products, these use panels or accordion-folding elements that slide on ceiling or floor and ceiling tracks to make it possible to combine or separate adjacent spaces at will. Both appearance and acoustical performance of folding partitions tend to be problematic, but their use is common where a special functional need requires this kind of flexibility, as in making dining or conference rooms larger or smaller to suit the needs of various groups.

149. Privacy in open-plan offices can be achieved as needed by means of flexible office-partition systems. The solid, opaque, and clear-glass panels of this partition are part of a system that includes furniture designed by William Stumpf for Herman Miller. (Photograph: Peter Kiar, 1985, courtesy Herman Miller, Inc.)

150

151

152

TOILET PARTITIONS. Another factory-made system product, these provide panels and doors for the stalls and screen elements used in public toilet facilities. Metal with baked enamel finish is the most usual material, although slate and marble were once common and are still used occasionally.

GLASS. In addition to its use in movable partitioning (fig. 152), glass can be used with wood or metal framing to create walls that offer transparency or translucency in varying degrees. Glass is available in a wide range of colors and textures and in shatterproof form. Glass partitions can also be built up of *glass block*, a masonry-like material providing translucency and a unique appearance (figs. 150, 151, 153).

150. Large-scale glass block is used in this restaurant for an internal screen— partition wall. The area beyond can be seen, but the ripple texture of the block distorts the visual image in a way that adds interest to the sense of space. The 72 Market Street restaurant in Venice, California, is a 1983 design by Michael Rotondi and Thom Mayne of Morphosis. (Photograph: Tim Street-Porter)

151. Glass blocks are produced in a variety of sizes, shapes, and textured patterns. Their hollow construction makes them good insulators; they block vision but admit light and generate interesting patterns. (Photograph courtesy Pittsburgh Corning Corporation)

152. Sliding glass doors can convert a space from an open garden pavilion into an enclosed room. A new owner required that an existing (1955) house by the famous architect Mies van der Rohe be expanded to provide entertaining and guest rooms. Peter L. Gluck and Partners, architects for the 1981 proj-ect, left the original house untouched, adding instead a two-pavilion complex adjacent to the original building. In his Tugendhat house of 1930 in Brno, Czechoslovakia, Mies himself set the precedent for entire walls of sliding doors. (Photograph: © Paul Warchol)

153

154

Wall Finishes

Surface or finishing materials applied to bearing walls or partitions usually become important ingredients of any completed interior. Because many of these finishes can be renewed and changed with ease and at modest cost, they are particularly adaptable to frequent redecoration schemes.

PAINT. This is probably the most widely used of wall (and ceiling) finishes. An infinite range of color possibilities and some variety in available texture along with low cost and easy renewal make paint endlessly adaptable. Top-quality paints justify their extra cost because of their ease of application and durability. Better paints offer a wide choice of ready-mixed or custom-mixed colors. Special colors can be mixed on the job by skilled painters.

WALLPAPER. This surface material offers a vast variety of textures, patterns, and imagery, making it a popular alternative to paint. Wallpaper was widely used during some historic periods, and reproductions of many excellent historic designs continue to be available (fig. 155). Color and pattern coordination with printed textiles is offered by some manufacturers. Intelligent use of wallpaper can avoid some of the mistakes of unsuitable use and inferior patterns that have sometimes given this material a bad reputation with modern interior designers.

WOOD. Paneling, whether in designs using elaborate moldings and joinery or in simple flush designs, is a valued wall surface treatment (fig. 156). It usually suggests opulence and luxury. Traditional paneling is assembled from rails and panels of solid wood. Plywood is often used for modern paneling, but simulating traditional designs by applying moldings to plywood leads to unfortunate visual results. The simple paneling of solid boards, tongue-and-grooved together or with moldings or reveals at joint lines, is also in wide use. Prefinished paneling tends to be of poor appearance, particularly in the very inexpensive forms often used by home craftsmen. Simulated wood finishes are particularly objectionable, and knotty pine, whether genuine or simulated, has been so overused as to become a cliché.

Natural finishes or stains that show the grain of the wood are most often used for paneling, but paint finishes are also appropriate and have been widely used in traditional interior design.

TILE. A vast variety of tiles, from tiny mosaic to large squares and rectangles, in many colors, textures, patterns, and materials, can be used as wall surface treatments. Tile is particularly suited to wet, humid locations with water splash and steam, typically, kitchens, bathrooms, areas around pools, and similar spaces. Decorated and painted tiles can approach an art form. Spanish or Dutch painted tiles suggest specific periods and countries; at their best, they are objects of collectors' interest.

MIRROR. This special form of glass has a particular interest as a wall material because of its ability to create the illusion of increased space. Floor-to-ceiling and wall-to-wall

153. Glass block, developed and much used in the 1930s but subsequently neglected, has been rediscovered in recent years. Here it forms an outside wall of an East Hampton, Long Island, residence of 1979 designed by Gwathmey Siegel & Associates, architects. The blocks admit light while assuring privacy and good thermal insulation. (Photograph: © Norman McGrath)

154. Large areas of mirror visually repeat an interior, effectively doubling its space. This high, narrow room appears more spacious than it is, with the glass-block wall and marble-topped desk extending into their mirrored doubles. Gwathmey Siegel & Associates were the architects for this 1981 executive office for the Evans Partnership, Montvale, New Jersey. (Photograph courtesy Gwathmey Siegel & Associates)

155. This 1881 design by William Morris, the founder of the British Arts and Crafts Movement, has been reproduced for contemporary use. The design, called St. James, was originally developed by Morris & Co. for the redecoration of the Throne and the Wellington rooms of St. James's Palace in London. (Photograph courtesy Bradbury & Bradbury Wallpapers)

156. Interior designer Mark Hampton has made modern use of dark wood paneling in the library of a brownstone apartment in 1985. The contrast between the colorful Oriental rug and upholstery and drapery fabrics and the dark wood dispels any hint of heaviness or gloom. (Photograph: Robert Levin)

mirror doubles space visually (fig. 154). Parallel mirrors placed opposite generate an illusion of endlessly continuing space. Tinted, *antique,* and small squared mirrors generate other visual effects. As mirror has been overused and misused, its selection should be considered carefully.

P L A S T I C . Vinyl and other plastic sheet materials are in wide use as wall coverings, both for their ability to resist damage and for the variety of color and textural patterns they offer. Many plastic wall coverings simulate other materials such as grass cloth, canvas, suede, even metals. Once damaged, plastic materials are more difficult to repair than painted surfaces.

F A B R I C . A traditional material for wall covering, fabric offers a fine variety of colors and textures. Silks, satins, and brocades were often used in luxurious interiors of traditional design. Simple canvas can be used as a base for paint, providing a reinforced wall surface and a subtle texture. Genuine grass cloths and varieties of burlap, although now widely imitated in plastic, remain fine wall covering possibilities.

S T O N E . Although usually thought of as a structural material, stone in thin sheets is a possible wall covering. Marbles in varied colors and veining patterns are particularly appealing. Travertine, either filled or with an open, porous texture, is often used as a wall surface in monumental spaces.

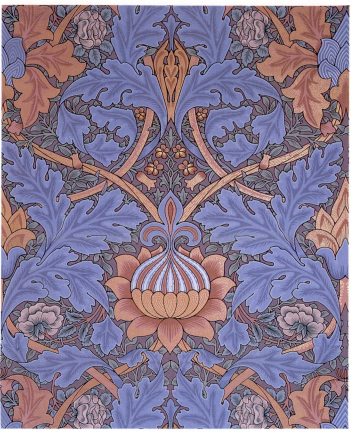

. 155

156

157

DOORS

Walls require openings for access. Doorways provide access to a space, and doors control access. Door frame and door, usually thought of as a unit, are often manufactured and sold together. The selection and specification of a door can be more complex than might be expected. In addition to the door itself and its frame, the designer must choose a knob, a lock, and hinges. Optional items include the saddle (threshold), push and kick plates, closer, panic bolt, alarm gear, and other items that may affect fire safety, security, and performance.

Door Materials

Most doors are made of the following materials:

WOOD. Doors may be of panel construction (composed of *stiles,* or vertical members, and *rails,* or horizontal members, into which are inserted thinner panels) or *flush* (that is, smooth of surface and seemingly of one piece). Flush doors may be of solid (heavy) or hollow-core (lighter) construction. Surfaces may be of genuine wood veneer or the more durable plastic laminate. They may be finished with stain (leaving the natural look of wood) or paint. It is possible to design wood doors of unusual shape, size, or surface design. Where heavy two-way traffic is anticipated, a small glass window in an otherwise

solid door is often introduced to discourage collisions.

METAL. Metal doors, usually of hollow steel construction with a solid fiber infill, are sturdy and have been rated for fire safety. Finish may be paint or plastic laminate.

GLASS. Glass doors are usually framed in wood or metal (fig. 161), although frameless tempered glass doors are also widely used (these require safety precautions; see Chapter 14, page 385). Glass may be colored or patterned, frames may be simple or decorative in design.

Door Types

Special types of doors (fig. 160), which may be of any appropriate materials, include:

DOUBLE DOORS (fig. 157).

SWINGING DOORS. Hinged doors swinging inward or outward or in both directions (fig. 159).

SLIDING DOORS. These avoid the space-consuming outward swing of a hinged door. A single sliding door requires a *pocket,* or hollow space in the thickness of the adjacent wall, to slide into. Paired sliding doors (or a grouping of more than two) can slide over one another. While this requires no pocket, it limits the opening to 50 percent of the

157, 158. A conference–dining area located at a corner between two adjacent executive offices (fig. 157) is accessible to both through double, hinged doors (one is visible at left), while blinds over the glass partition safeguard each office's privacy. In the plan of the space

(fig. 158), the conference–dining area is at the upper right corner; the adjacent executive offices are below it and to its left. Charles Kratka Associates designed the offices for Times Mirror, New York, in 1984. (Photograph: Jon Naar, courtesy Charles Kratka Associates)

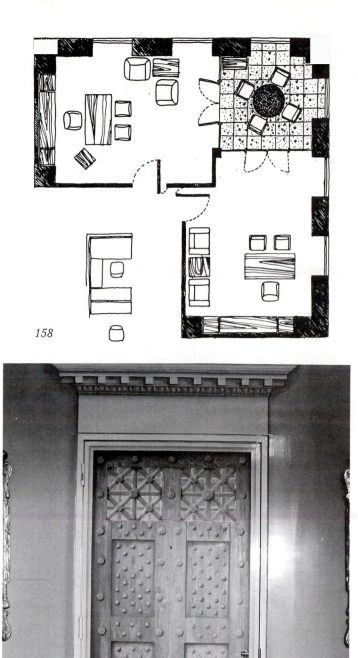

158

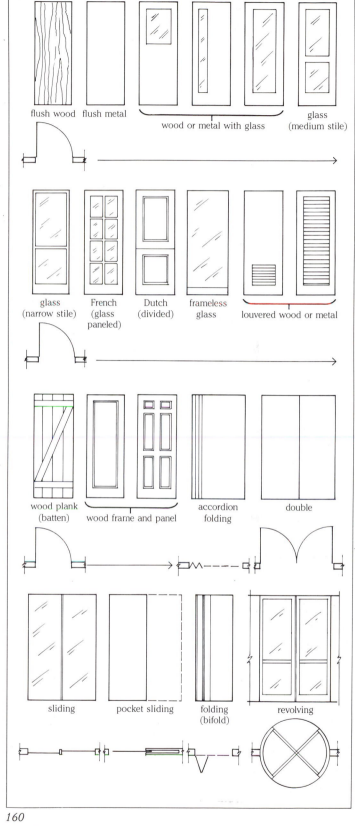

DOOR TYPES

flush wood   flush metal   wood or metal with glass   glass (medium stile)

glass (narrow stile)   French (glass paneled)   Dutch (divided)   frameless glass   louvered wood or metal

wood plank (batten)   wood frame and panel   accordion folding   double

sliding   pocket sliding   folding (bifold)   revolving

159

159. This medieval, nail-studded door is, in fact, a fantastically successful trompe l'oeil *done on an ordinary, plain panel. David Fisch was the artist. (Photograph: © Jeff Blechman)*

160

160. Various types of commonly used doors, including solid, all-glass, and partial-glass types, are shown in elevation above, with the architectural plan symbols that represent them below.

161

161. This Spanish-style California
house of the 1920s was renovated by
designers Sussman & Prejza in 1986 for
their own use. The steel-framed window
and French doors now boast red-painted
frames that pleasantly modulate the
view into the garden beyond. Related
color in the floor, upholstery fabric, accessories, and the window and painting
on the right unify the space. (Photograph: Tim Street-Porter)

162

total width. Such doors run on tracks that place the alternate doors in different planes. Special hardware permits setting paired sliding doors flush when closed and then angles the tracks slightly to allow the doors to slide. Aluminum-framed sliding doors are popular for outside window-door uses. Sliding *shoji* screens, adapted from traditional Japanese practice, can be considered a form of sliding door that permits a flexible subdivision of space.

FRENCH DOORS. Actually long casement windows that extend to floor level, these are simply double, hinged doors of framed glass.

LOUVERED (OR JALOUSIE) DOORS. Usually made of wood, these permit air circulation. They have become popular for closets that require some ventilation.

ACCORDION FOLDING DOORS. A kind of compromise between swinging and sliding doors, they permit full opening but when open do not project into adjacent space as far as conventional swinging doors do.

REVOLVING DOORS. Widely used to control drafts and loss of heat at entrances that handle large numbers of people, they are usually standardized factory-made products, but come in many different designs and with varied details.

GATES. These may be regarded as a special type of door. They come hinged or sliding and of various materials and designs. Special forms of roll-up and sliding gates, available for security closure, are often used in addition to more conventional door types.

162. Levelor vertical blinds are used in the 1980 guest bedroom of a Coconut Grove, Florida, apartment. The designer, Juan Montoya, explained that the blinds "were used to create blades of light and shadows at night." The construction of the Italian beds allows the slipcovers to be easily removed for cleaning. The chair is a replica of the deck chair used on the French liner Normandie of the 1930s. (Photograph: Norman McGrath, courtesy Juan Montoya)

163

WINDOWS

An important element in basic architectural design, windows are also important elements in the interiors that they serve. Since windows greatly influence the nature of an interior, designers often change or replace them as part of their design schemes. This alteration concerns both the window itself and the *window treatment,* any additions to the window, such as shades or curtains, that can modify both the appearance and the function of the actual window.

Glass is obviously the primary window material, in the form of *window* (thin) or *plate* (thicker) glass, clear or patterned or *obscure* (not transparent). Virtually unbreakable Lexan plastic has come into use as a glass substitute where breakage is a major problem.

Window Types

Types of windows can best be classified according to how they are framed to hold glass (fig. 165).

FIXED GLAZING WINDOWS. Fixed into place, these cannot be opened. They require only simple frames and are widely used where opening capability is not required, as with shopwindows and windows of air-conditioned spaces, or in combination with windows that open. Fixed glazing requires consideration of means for cleaning, of impact on fire safety (access and escape), and of provision for alternative ventilation in the event of mechanical ventilation system failure.

DOUBLE-HUNG WINDOWS. This type uses the most familiar sash, two up-and-down sliding units giving a 50 percent opening in any combination of top and/or bottom.

163. The unusual silhouette of a large window with arched top, vertical sash, and smaller, stepped sash on either side lends a unique accent to a bedroom in a house by Tigerman Fugman McCurry Architects. (Photograph: Howard N. Kaplan, © HNK Architectural Photography)

CASEMENT WINDOWS. These swing outward or inward like small doors and most often appear in pairs. *French windows* (listed above as doors) are casement windows that extend to floor level (fig. 164).

AWNING AND PROJECTED WINDOWS. These have framed units hinged horizontally to swing in or out in various configurations.

JALOUSIE WINDOWS. A special form of awning window, these use many small hinged louvers of glass.

SLIDING WINDOWS. These move sideways on top and bottom tracks. Floor-to-ceiling versions opening to the outdoors are widely used.

All of these window types may use frames of wood, steel, or aluminum. Double-hung and casement windows may use large panes of glass filling each movable unit or have a number of smaller panes set into small frame members called *muntins*. The pattern of windowpanes has a strong impact on the visual effect of windows and can suggest a particular style or period of design. For example, the small panes of Colonial windows are very different from the plate glass of Victorian windows.

Window Treatment

Window treatment (fig. 166) serves a variety of purposes, including:

> *Control of excessive light, sun, and glare*
> *Screening of the blank nighttime "black-glass" effect of exposed windows*
> *Limitation of heat gain from summer sun*
> *Limitation of winter heat loss to cold glass surface*
> *Screening of indifferent or unpleasant view*
> *Screening for privacy of occupants*
> *Hiding or modification of unsatisfactory window shape, location, or detail design*
> *Improvement of bare or unfinished-looking window opening*
> *Introduction of desired color and texture*

Most window treatment calls for adjustability to deal with night and day, summer and winter, and changing conditions of use. A wide variety of blinds, shutters, curtains, and drapery techniques have been developed to deal with these problems. Some of the most useful include:

164

164. In this 1870s residence in Remsenberg, New York, renovated by Hagmann Mitchell Architects in 1985, French doors flank an alcove with double-hung windows on either side of a central, fixed-glass window surmounted by a small lunette window. The bench, side chairs, and table in the alcove are all Biedermeier. The upholstered chairs at the left are Villa Gallia designs by Josef Hoffmann from about 1913. The rugs are contemporary, washed Tibetan. (Photograph: © 1985 Frederick Charles)

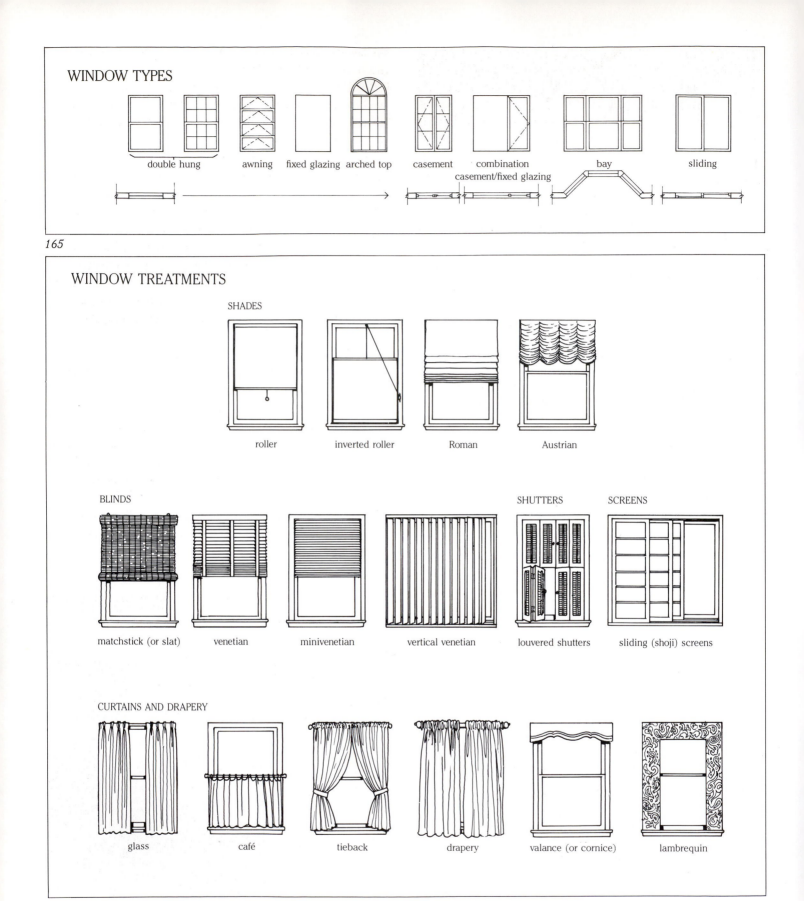

WINDOW TYPES

double hung   awning   fixed glazing   arched top   casement   combination casement/fixed glazing   bay   sliding

165

WINDOW TREATMENTS

SHADES

roller   inverted roller   Roman   Austrian

BLINDS

matchstick (or slat)   venetian   minivenetian   vertical venetian

SHUTTERS

louvered shutters

SCREENS

sliding (shoji) screens

CURTAINS AND DRAPERY

glass   café   tieback   drapery   valance (or cornice)   lambrequin

166

165. Various types of windows are shown in elevation above, with the architectural plan symbols that represent them below.

166. Various types of commonly used window treatments, both hard and soft.

167

ROLLER BLINDS (OR SHADES). A piece
of cloth or heavy paper on a spring roller, these usually pull
down from the top. Variations exist that pull up from the bottom
or that have a roller suspended by pulleys, permitting any
desired opening, top or bottom. Special roller blinds effectively
black out light, making them a good choice for spaces used for
slide or film projection or where daytime darkening of a
bedroom is desired.

ROMAN AND AUSTRIAN BLINDS. These
types, which pull up with a cord into accordion folds, are
particularly suited to some traditional interiors.

MATCHSTICK OR SLAT BLINDS. Blinds of
thin bamboo or wood strips, they pull up by cord into a roll
and make a somewhat informal, as well as inexpensive, simple
window treatment (fig. 167).

THERMAL SHADES. Special energy-saving shade
materials use plastic sheet or special weaves to provide sun
control through tiny microlouvers. Mechanized systems use
motors to raise and lower blinds in response to conditions
measured by light- or heat-sensitive sensors.

HORIZONTAL VENETIAN BLINDS. These
familiar and useful controls of light and view come with slats of
wood, plastic, or aluminum in a wide variety of colors and
finishes. Heat- and light-limiting/conducting materials can be
added as an energy-conservation measure. Contemporary design

167. The steel-framed casement windows of this bedroom have roll-up bamboo slat blinds for light control and privacy. Such blinds with very thin slats are
called matchstick blinds. The room is a
1977 interior by Frank Gehry, architect, in his own home in Cheviot Hills,
California. The overall character of the
building—a remodeled 1940s bun-
galow—suggests the influence of Japanese design. (Photograph: © 1986
Tim Street-Porter)

has favored blinds with very narrow slats (about ⅝ inch), which
give a particularly neat look.

VERTICAL VENETIAN BLINDS. Widely
used in modern interiors, these blinds pull to the side (fig. 162).
Their louvers come in various widths, materials, and colors.

DRAPERY. This refers to loosely hung fabric, usually
heavy and opaque, that can cover an entire window or extend
from floor to ceiling or wall to wall. A vast range of fabrics can
be used, and various fabrics in combination with linings can
provide any desired degree of light and privacy control. Sheer
fabrics permit light transmission and some degree of see-
through vision. Several layers of drapery make different levels of
light and view control possible. Since drapery introduces
textiles at window openings, it offers color, pattern, and various
kinds of trim, making possible a great variety of aesthetic
effects (figs. 168, 169). (See Appendix 7, "Estimating Material
Requirements.")

CURTAINS. A more modest form of drapery, curtains
are usually placed within the window frame, possibly attached
to the actual window sash (fig. 170). Simple sash, café, lace,
and net curtains offer limited light and vision control, often in
ways appropriate to particular historical stylistic treatments.

SHUTTERS. Often also called blinds, these come solid
or louvered and appear in many traditional interiors (fig. 171).
They can be used alone or in combination with shades,
curtains, or drapery.

SHOJI SCREENS. Screen panels sliding on tracks
not only function as shades but also give the window area a
special character.

168

168. Simple swags of drapery frame
windows and introduce overtones of
opulence and tradition into an otherwise
simple, even austere space. Robinson
Mills & Williams of San Francisco were
the designers for San Francisco's Fair-
mont Hotel. (Photograph: Nick Merrick,
Hedrich-Blessing)

169

170

171

169. Photographer Chris Mead conceived this ultrasimple window treatment for his own Long Island, New York, home. A rectangle of canvas, used as a shade, is simply buttoned up to admit light. (Photograph: © Chris Mead)

170. Mario Buatta designed this elaborately festooned window treatment for a Kips Bay Show House of 1987 in New York. Formal and highly decorative, but of questionable utility, its purpose is to draw attention to the rich fabric used. (Photograph: © Robert Levin, appeared in the New York Times, April 30, 1987)

171. Traditional shutters with adjustable slats, a favorite tropical window treatment, are used in a 1760 house on Martinique. The four-poster beds are equipped with mosquito netting that doubles as ceiling-suspended canopies. Note the tile floor, with its small and simple rugs. (Photograph: Gilles de Chabaneix)

METAL CHAIN DRAPERY. A recent development, links or beads in long strands provide some degree of security protection in the event of glass breakage.

COLUMNS

Totally bearing-wall structures, including most houses and small buildings, do not require columns. In large modern buildings with frames of iron, steel, or concrete, structural columns that carry the building's weight often stand free in interior spaces. They can be hidden by partitioning, but the large open spaces of stores, offices, lofts, and similar large interiors often leave them exposed.

Columns in older buildings often make use of decorative motifs from historic architecture. Whether plain or decorative, columns invite various treatments, ranging from simply painting the exposed column to wrapping it with materials that cover the original, changing its form and providing it with a surface of any desired materials, textures, and colors.

Steel columns, most often tubular or of H-shaped cross section, may be exposed only in buildings where strict fire-protection rules do not apply. Otherwise, they must be enclosed in insulating materials, which gives them a simple boxlike appearance similar to that of concrete columns. Wood columns (or *posts*) and brick piers also have simple rectangular or square shapes. Their surfaces may be left exposed or covered or wrapped as desired. Many of the techniques for wall treatment apply to columns as well, including paint, wallpaper, wood paneling, metal sheathing, and combinations of such treatments. Columns are sometimes covered with mirror to minimize their visible impact, although the resulting glitter may make the column appear *more* rather than less important.

FLOORS

Along with ceilings, these elements of the interior represent the largest shares of area. Since a space's users come in direct contact with floors, they are usually far more important than ceilings as major design elements. Floors are ordinarily flat, but may include level changes created by raising a false floor in some areas or by depressing floor areas as a part of basic construction. This has been an accepted way to provide a sense of separation between spaces and to introduce spatial variety for aesthetic reasons.

Changing the floor level can present problems, however. A

172

172. A 97-foot-long loft space, now a residence in a reinforced-concrete loft building, gains a special quality from the gargantuan mushroom columns. The columns, typical of warehouse construction, have bush-hammered surfaces that exaggerate their integral tex- ture. The blue panel leaning against the wall at the right is an acrylic plank sculpture by John McCracken. Frederick Fisher and Eric Orr were the architects for this Los Angeles project. (Photograph: © Timothy Hursley, courtesy House & Garden)

dropped area will reduce the height of the space below and is therefore usually practical only in new construction or in total renovation. In the latter case, it is also likely to be costly, since the old floor must be removed and replaced at the lowered level. A raised area is less problematic, since it requires only the building of a false raised floor on top of the existing floor. There must be sufficient ceiling height to give satisfactory headroom after the raised level is in place.

All floor level changes require steps or ramps at access points, making them potential accident spots. Small level changes of one or two steps, because they are easy to overlook, cause the most accidents. These should be avoided in public spaces and wherever crowds of people gather. Railings, edge markings, lights, and similar devices at level changes and at edges of raised floor areas offer some protection from accidents.

Floor Materials

Most floors are composed of a basic structural material such as wood or concrete, which may be left exposed, treated, or totally covered with a special flooring material. Some heavy flooring materials, such as stone, brick, terrazzo, and ceramic tile, are suitable only to ground-level locations or over heavy subfloors, such as concrete. Lighter floor materials may be considered in almost any location, with selection determined by functional and aesthetic considerations. Widely used flooring materials are:

CONCRETE. This is the basic structural material of floors in most modern buildings, including the *slab on grade* ground floors of many houses. Bare concrete can be troweled to a smooth surface, but is still generally regarded as acceptable only in utility spaces. Concrete floors are usually surfaced with one of the floor coverings or other treatments listed below.

173

173. The massively scaled flagstone flooring, part of Marcel Breuer's original design for his 1967–69 house in Lawrence, New York, dominates and stabilizes the space. The more recent (1981–83) interior design, by Juan Montoya, uses African urns and a coffee table of Montoya's own design. (Photograph: Peter Vitale, courtesy Juan Montoya)

174

MASONRY MATERIALS. These are widely used to give floors a hard and durable surface. These materials are usually laid over concrete or another subfloor that provides structural support. Typical materials include brick (fig. 174), slate, flagstone (fig. 173), marble (including travertine), and granite.

TERRAZZO. A special form of masonry floor surface, it uses marble chips mixed into a cement mortar (fig. 175). The mix is then ground and polished to a smooth surface after setting. Metal divider strips subdivide areas to discourage cracks and to create patterns or designs. A wide variety of color and textural effects is possible.

WOOD. A widely used flooring material, wood may be used as the basic construction and left exposed; as a subfloor and covered with another material; or as a surface material applied over a subfloor. Although not very durable, softwoods are often used for simple board floors, including the admired wide-board floors of old buildings, and can be painted or finished to expose natural color and texture (see fig. 139).

Hardwood floors may be simple strips of maple or birch or tongue-and-grooved strips made up for the purpose, most often of maple or oak. Parquet flooring is composed of small blocks of hardwood fitted together in patterns, often using woods of two or more contrasting colors.

174. Brick steps and flooring were used in a poolhouse in Greenwich, Connecticut, designed by Robert A. M. Stern and John S. Hagmann, Architects (1973–74). Brick is an ideal material here, providing the desired water-resistance and nonskid property as well as a pleasant warmth of color and texture. (Photograph: Ed Stoecklein, courtesy Robert A. M. Stern Architects)

Factory-made units of parquet make it possible to lay a parquet floor in a manner similar to tile. Thin, prefinished wood floor tiles simulate parquet with somewhat limited success.

TILE. A flooring material with a long history of acceptance, tile is particularly suited to use in kitchens, bathrooms, near pools, and in other locations where water will often be present. Besides being waterproof, its hard surface promotes good sanitation.

Tiles of baked clay, such as the popular quarry tile, are similar to masonry materials and require a sturdy subfloor. Ceramic tile, in various sizes, shapes, colors, and textures, permits a great variety of color and pattern treatments (fig. 178). Very small tile, usually called *mosaic tile,* promotes textural and patterned effects.

Floor Coverings

Floor coverings are laid over a structural floor of concrete, wood, or other material. Wall-to-wall coverings can be used over a subfloor of unfinished appearance, while rugs that occupy less than a total floor area require a subfloor of finished appearance. The most-used floor coverings are:

PAINT. Usable over concrete or wood with an endless variety of color and patterns, paint wears rapidly and must be renewed regularly. It is therefore a poor choice where heavy traffic and usage are anticipated.

RESILIENT FLOORING. This is the term for a variety of manufactured products available in sheet form or in tiles, usually in squares of 9 or 12 inches. The common resilient materials are linoleum, asphalt and asphalt-asbestos mixtures, vinyl plastic, cork, and rubber. An extensive variety of color and pattern choices is available, and designs can be created with arrangements of tiles or with inlay strips in sheet-flooring installations.

WOVEN SOFT FLOOR COVERINGS. Various types of matting, rugs, and carpeting, these are special types of textiles and are made in a bewildering variety of weaves, fibers, colors, and textures.

The term *rug* describes a movable unit of carpet, usually smaller than the room in which it is used. *Area rugs* are often used to help group items of furniture within a larger space, thus defining an area for conversation, dining, or other activities. Rugs are made in a great range of sizes from very small (often called *mats*) up to room size. Many popular types of rugs come from particular regions and are made in locally characteristic styles and colors.

Oriental rugs are handmade in various regions of the Near and Far East. Antique and *fine,* or high-quality, Orientals can be very costly; museum-quality examples are viewed, and priced, as works of fine art (fig. 177). The names of various types refer to the place of origin and to pattern. Full knowledge of types, quality, and value of Oriental rugs involves extensive study, but a basic ability to recognize quality can be developed through examination of examples in museums and in the displays of recognized dealers and auction galleries.

Genuine Oriental rugs are handmade in the slow and painstaking process of knotting. A warp is stretched on a loom, the weft threads are woven across at the starting end, and then the yarn tufts that give the rug its pattern and color are inserted and knotted to the warp, one knot at a time. After each row of knots, from one to four weft strands are woven through to build up the rug base before the next row of knots is begun. These knots are visible on the rug's underside and can be counted. Generally, the more knots per square inch, the finer the rug. In a fine rug, there may be as many as 800 knots per square inch—in a 9-by-12-foot rug, 12,441,600 knots! A skilled weaver can tie something like 12,000 knots per day, but even at this rate, such

175

175. The Memphis influence is evident in this Esprit shop in Cologne, West Germany, by Sottsass Associati, directed by Memphis leader Ettore Sottsass. Large silicone-joined terrazzo tiles are used for walls as well as for the floor. (Photograph: Aldo Ballo)

176

a rug represents about one thousand days of handwork of a highly skilled kind. Oriental patterns are sometimes printed on factory-made rugs, producing a reproduction, usually of inferior quality, which should be clearly distinguished from genuine Orientals.

The Indian *dhurrie* is an inexpensive modern rug type available in simple stripes and patterns and in varied and excellent colors.

Scatter rugs are small units used over other floor materials such as wood, tile, or even carpet. Many types are available in a range of sizes, extending up to area or near-room dimensions. Familiar types include hooked and braided rugs, rya rugs made in Scandinavia, modern handweaves, and rag rugs.

Carpet is the term for floor covering made in continuous rolls, with widths from as little as 27 inches up to *broadlooms* as wide as 18 feet. Modern carpeting is factory-made, and

176. In the home of Charles Moore in Los Angeles, California, designed in 1978 by his firm, Moore Ruble Yudell Architects & Planners, antique Oriental rugs and plants soften the modern living space. The ceramic-tile floor can be seen continuing into the garden beyond the sliding glass doors. (Photograph: © 1981 Glen Allison)

177

is widely used *wall-to-wall* over a floor that need not be of finished appearance. Carpet is made from a number of fibers, both natural and synthetic, and with a variety of constructions or weaves. Color and pattern possibilities are almost unlimited, with a wide range of quality and price. The soft texture, feel, and appearance of carpeted floors, their acoustical effectiveness in absorbing sound, and their relative ease of cleaning and maintenance have made them very popular for residential, office, and commercial spaces. Even schoolrooms, hospital rooms, and bathrooms, traditionally thought unsuitable spaces for carpeting, are now often carpeted.

The disadvantages of most older types of carpeting have to do with their absorbent and hard to clean surfaces, which hold spots and odors and form an unsanitary harbor for the growth of bacteria. Modern synthetic fibers and carpet constructions minimize these problems; they can be maintained by simple vacuum cleaning, quite as effective as the washing and waxing

required by hard-surface floor coverings and less costly. The ability of carpet to minimize noise from footsteps and furniture movement together with its absorption of sound from other sources makes it an asset in the acoustical ambience of hospitals and schoolrooms. Where sanitation, soiling, and moisture are significant problems, only carpet specially developed for such service should be specified. (See Appendix 7, "Estimating Material Requirements.")

Carpet tile (also called carpet squares) is a recent development in which carpet is made and laid in small units of one to two feet square rather than in wide rolls. Easy replacement of damaged areas, access to underfloor wiring where it is in use, and the possibility of a pleasant tilelike visual pattern are among the reasons for selecting carpet tile. Both glued-down and loose-laid types are in current use.

Underlayment, or cushion, is suggested for use with many carpet types. Special-purpose materials provide additional softness, help to protect and thus extend carpet life, and facilitate the removal of the carpet itself for relocation or replacement. Various types, made from natural fibers or from rubber, exist. Advice of the carpet manufacturer or supplier about choice of underlay or padding is usually a sound guide to selection.

Table 4 on pages 140–41 is a guide to the great variety of fibers, constructions, and other characteristics in current use.

Carpet selection presents a complex problem in which cost and durability must be balanced against one another and related to aesthetic decisions about color, pattern, and texture. The high cost of wool as a fiber has encouraged the acceptance of synthetic fibers, with new forms constantly appearing. New fibers have not had a chance to demonstrate durability over time, but the performance of synthetics has been, to date, disappointing in terms of wear, resistance, ease of cleaning, and the ways in which appearance changes with use. Fire-safety issues also are a cause for concern with many synthetics. In evaluating costs, it is wise to consider life-span cost, including maintenance and repair cost along with estimated durability, before accepting substitutes for wool on the basis of assumed economy. For large projects, laboratory and use testing is advisable before specifying a particular carpet.

ACCESS FLOORING. This is a new kind of raised floor system often used in modern office design. It involves lift-out floor panels supported by an understructure (see fig. 665). The purpose is to provide an underfloor space for wiring and, in some cases, for air and water supply, providing easy access for changes and repairs. Access flooring is most often used in computer rooms and office spaces where the use of computers and other electronic devices will be extensive.

177. *Oriental rugs come in a vast range of colors and patterns and can harmonize well with either traditional or modern interiors. They are most often used as floor coverings, but fine examples are sometimes wall-hung as tapestries, both to protect them from wear and to display their pattern unencumbered by furniture. This example, an all-wool antique Kazak carpet of circa 1880, was handmade in the Caucasus (USSR). (Photograph courtesy Fred Moheban Rug Co., New York)*

178. *The artist Miriam Wosk used tiles in dazzling colors and patterns suggesting rugs in the floors and stairs for her home in Beverly Hills, California. The interior design is largely her own; the space, a penthouse renovated by Frank Gehry, was built onto the roof of an older building. (Photograph: © Grant Mudford, courtesy* House & Garden*)*

TABLE 4. CARPETS

Carpet and Rug Fibers

FIBER		CHARACTERISTICS
NATURAL:	Cotton	Soft fiber with limited durability. Inexpensive and often used for informal area or scatter rugs. Often dyed in strong colors, as in Indian *dhurries*.
	Wool	Best-quality natural fiber. Excellent texture and appearance. Good resistance to soil and wear, appearance survives wear well. Dyes well in wide range of colors. Expensive, standard for top-quality carpeting.
	Cellulosics	Hemp, jute, sisal, various grasses. Generally used for informal matting of natural color and texture. Fair to poor durability and resistance to wear and soiling. Inexpensive.
SYNTHETIC:	Acrylics	Warm, soft textures imitative of wool. Good resistance to soil and wear. Color and texture may be harsh and glossy. Pile subject to crushing. Moderate price.
	Nylon	Most-used fiber for commercial carpet. May be dull to glossy with good color range. Best moderate-price alternative to wool. Resistant to mold and mildew. Static-resistant treatments available where required.
	Olefin	Limited color and pattern, some gloss, waxy texture. Water-resistant. Good soil-resistance.
	Polyester	Good resilience and texture, soft quality resembling wool. Good soil- and wear-resistance, wide color range. Some crushing possible with wear.
BLENDS:		A wide variety of blends combining wool with synthetics or different synthetic fibers is available. The aim is to obtain the best qualities of each fiber while arriving at moderate costs. Wool and nylon and acrylic-nylon blends are most widely used.

Carpet Textures

TEXTURE		CHARACTERISTICS
CUT PILE:	Plush or velvet	Dense pile with surface cut at level height (usually less than one inch). Smooth, velvet-like surface of luxurious appearance. Wears well under moderate traffic.
	Saxony	Similar to plush but with two or more yarns twisted together to form pile tufts more distinguishable in the surface texture. Pile may be deep but less dense than in high-quality plush or velvet. Medium wear characteristics.
	Frieze	Similar to plush but with tightly twisted yarns forming a strongly textured pile with a pebbly appearance. The tight yarn twist generates good wear-resistance, making it suitable for heavy traffic areas.
LOOP PILE:	Level loop	Uncut loop pile with uniform height loop. When made with quality yarn in high density, this is the most durable and wear-resistant carpet. Suitable to public spaces and other heavy-service contract applications and for home use where heavy use is anticipated (as in kitchens, baths, family or recreation rooms).
	Multilevel loop	Uncut loop pile with loop of varied heights, producing a random or patterned (sculptured) surface.
	Tweed	Uncut loops, larger and with less density than level loop, producing a rougher, more informal or tweedy texture. Usually a lower-cost and less durable carpet type. Yarn tufts of different colors are often mixed to form a pattern.

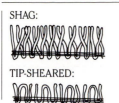

SHAG:	A term for carpet with a very long (over one inch) pile loop (usually cut, but may be uncut or mixed) and with low density, so that the pile lies on its side to give a rough, shaggy appearance. Not suitable for heavy wear applications.
TIP-SHEARED:	Mixed cut and uncut pile loops, also called random-sheared. Various textures and patterns are possible. Usually of medium wear qualities.

Carpet Constructions

CONSTRUCTION		CHARACTERISTICS
WOVEN:	*Wilton*	Woven on a Jacquard loom, permitting up to five or six colors in a pattern design. Top-quality construction, particularly when woven of worsted yarn. Density (and quality) are defined by the number of warp lines per inch, called the *pitch*. Older Wilton was woven on a 27-inch loom with 256 warp lines, called *full pitch*. Warp lines (rows or *wires* per inch) may vary from 13 for top quality to 8 for medium quality. Cut pile is normal. A Wilton with an uncut pile may be called a *Brussels carpet*. Broadloom widths have been produced.
	Axminster	An industrial weaving technique (now obsolescent) permitting great variety in color and pattern, with some similarity to hand weaves. Quality is defined by the weft count, given in rows to the inch. The range is from 11 rows (top quality) to 5 rows (lower quality) per inch. Widths up to 12 feet (broadloom) have been produced.
	Velvet	Normally a cut-pile carpet industrially produced in varied color and pattern. (A similar uncut pile weave is called *tapestry*.) Quality is similar to Axminster, inferior to Wilton weaves.
TUFTED:		This is now the most widely produced type of carpet. Industrially produced in broadloom widths with yarn pushed up through a backing to form tuft loops, which may be cut or left uncut. A latex backing may be added to secure the tufts. The density of the yarn and the height of the pile influence appearance and durability.
NEEDLEPUNCHED AND NEEDLEBONDED:		A manufacturing technique using hooked needles to insert fibers into backing. First developed for production of kitchen, bath, and outdoor carpeting of polypropylene fiber, now also used for general-purpose carpet.
KNITTED:		Construction superior to tufting in durability, but inferior to weaving. Multiple needles knit pile and backing together, usually with an added latex backing. Loop pile in solid color or tweed is most common.
FLOCKED:		Short fibers are stood on end electrostatically and adhered to a backing. Surface resembles a cut-pile velvet. Patterns may be printed on flocked carpet. An economy construction producing carpet of inferior wearing qualities.
HANDMADE:	*Knotted or tied*	The construction of Oriental and American Indian rugs, in which the yarn is tied into a woven backing with individual knots. Up to 800 knots per square inch are used in high-quality Orientals. The ends of knots may be cut off to form a pile, or the surface may be formed of knots, giving a flat, durable surface.
	Woven without knots	Kilims and Soumaks are fine Oriental weaves hand-woven without knotting. Kilims are thin and light but durable. The Soumak adds a third element to the warp and weft and forms a smooth surface. Soumaks are also sometimes called Cashmeres.
	Hooked	Tufts of yarn are pushed through a woven backing to form a pattern or pictorial design. A traditional craft technique producing durable rugs or mats, usually of traditional design types.
	Braided	Developed as a means of using discarded fabric remnants by braiding narrow strips together into strips that can be sewn into rugs or mats. Often called *rag rugs*. A traditional handcraft technique capable of producing work of lively color and charm. Commercially produced imitations are also available.

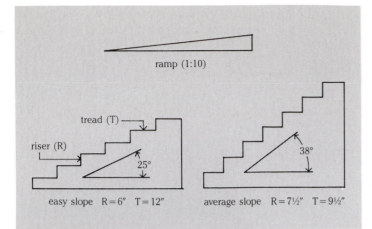

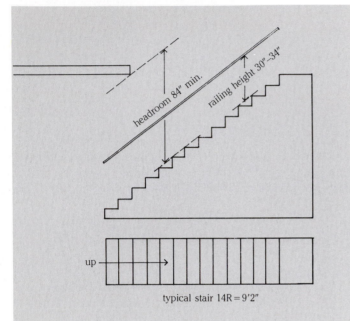

179

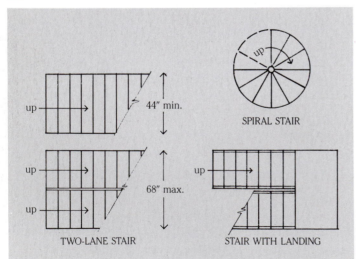

180

STEPS AND STAIRWAYS

These elements can be considered a special form of flooring, since they make use of many of the same materials and surface finish techniques. Stairways may be constructed from wood, concrete, or steel, in accordance with the overall structure of the building in question. Steel stairs may have treads of cement or composition, and exposed surfaces can be covered and finished to suit the intended use. Many steel stairs are factory-made and supplied in prefabricated form for installation on site. Spiral stairs, a favorite for fitting a stair into a limited space, are also available in prefabricated form.

Designing Stairways

Where new steps or stairs are to be constructed, it is necessary to observe the basic dimensional limitations that control the convenience and safety of all stairs. A step is made up of a riser (the vertical surface between stepping surfaces) and a tread (the horizontal step surface). The riser and tread dimensions together establish the slope of the stair and, therefore, the ease

181

182

179. Slopes and riser and tread dimensions for a ramp and typical stairways are given here.

180. Railing height and headroom clearance for a typical stairway are shown.

181. These drawings represent architectural symbols for several stairway examples.

182. A handsome staircase becomes a striking design feature in an East Hampton, Long Island, house of 1975–76 designed by Robert A. M. Stern Architects. The steps that actually bear traffic are carpeted, while the uncarpeted lower steps are used to display plants. The tubular railings are of polished metal. (Photographer: Ed Stoecklein, courtesy Robert A. M. Stern Architects)

183. Spiral stairs, in spite of their imperfect safety record, continue to be popular, both for their compact dimensions and for their interesting—sometimes spectacular—appearance. This decorative spiral rises from the corner of the living room of a Chicago duplex apartment to the gallery above. Richard Himmel, designer. (Photograph: Feliciano, courtesy House & Garden)

and convenience of its use. Riser height should fall within a range of 6 to 9 inches, 7 inches being desirable.

Since all risers in a flight (or *run*) of stairs must be equal, the exact riser height is determined by dividing the total level change into equal units.

For example:

Given a level change of 9'8" (116") and trying to get a riser height close to 7", divide 7 into 116:

$$\frac{116}{7} = 16.57$$

Since the number of risers must be a whole number, either 16 or 17 risers might be selected:

$$\frac{116}{16} = 7.25 \text{ and } \frac{116}{17} = 6.82$$

This gives the choice of a riser 6.82" high or 7.25" high. The lower riser will yield a stair that is easier to climb. The 7.25" riser will produce a slightly steeper stair, but it will take up less space because the fewer risers will require fewer treads.

The number of treads is always one less than the number of risers, since the topmost riser requires no tread.

Tread dimension is determined in relation to riser dimension. Old rules of thumb for this relationship (which are still in general use) are:

Riser plus tread should equal 17 to 17½ inches.

Riser multiplied by tread should fall between 70 and 75 inches.

In the example above, if a 7.25-inch riser had been chosen:

$$17 - 7.25 = 9.75 \text{ and } 17.5 - 7.25 = 10.25$$

$$\frac{70}{7.25} = 9.66 \text{ and } \frac{75}{7.25} = 10.34$$

Applying the first rule yields a tread dimension between 9¾" and 10¼", while the second rule gives between 9.66" and 10.34". Averaging this out, a tread of 10" (a comfortable tread length) might be selected. The total length of the run of stairs, or the amount of space the stairway will actually use, would then be 16 (the number of risers) minus 1, or 15 (the number of treads) times 10", or 150" (12'6"). Treads are often designed to overhang the riser below with a projection called a *nosing*. This overhang dimension is not considered in calculating stair dimensions.

Having established the slope of a stair through tread and riser calculation, the width must be established and the overhead clearance worked out. One person using a stairway needs a width of at least 26 inches; a stairway permitting two users to pass needs at least 44 inches, although a wider dimension up to 68 inches is more comfortable. Stairways wider than this must be subdivided by railings so that every user has a rail to grip.

Headroom calls for at least 84 inches of clearance. The length of a stairwell, or the floor opening through which a stair passes, is determined by the line of headroom as it passes through the structure of the floor above.

All stairways need railings. Stairways that are open at the side require some form of rails or banisters that prevent anyone from falling. Rail or baluster elements should be carefully spaced so that young children can neither slip through and fall nor catch their head between elements. Long runs of more than 20 to 24 risers should be broken up into shorter runs with landings. *Winders,* the wedge-shaped treads used in curving stairs, have such a bad record in causing accidents that they are best avoided, especially in public spaces. Objects of breakable materials such as glass and mirror should not be placed close to stairs, and materials that can be slippery, in normal circumstances or when wet, should not be used on or near stairs. Nonslip nosings and tread materials can minimize the risk of slipping.

CEILINGS

Inevitably, ceilings form an important aspect of all interiors, at least in terms of square footage. Many ceilings are simply blank, neutral areas, often, like the sky out-of-doors, providing a simple overhead for more complex elements at eye level and

184

184. Skylight panels set into the ceiling and roof of this California house allow light into a loft sleeping area, thus providing light while preserving privacy. Brian A. Murphy, designer. (Photograph: Tim Street-Porter)

185

below. However, thought and design effort may make the ceiling a more active part of an interior.

A simple and basic issue in ceiling design involves the decision to keep a ceiling as a single plane or to introduce lowered areas (usually called *soffits*) in portions of a space to contrast with areas of full height. The term *cove* is often used for a curved transition from wall to ceiling or for a curved profile where a lowered ceiling makes a transition to a higher ceiling level. A cove is often formed in a pocket-like profile, providing a space where *cove lighting* strips can be concealed

to form a source of indirect lighting. Ceiling planes can also slope at an angle, as seen in many attic spaces and spaces with dormer windows. The term *cathedral ceiling* is a rather misleading designation for ceilings that are high and introduce sloping surfaces.

The ceiling plane establishes the height of a space and therefore its volumetric proportions. A maximum height is usually established by structure, but a lower ceiling, called hung or *furred,* can be introduced down to whatever level may be considered minimum headroom (8 feet 2 inches is a

185. The entire ceiling of a kitchen has here been turned into a skylight. Cooking thus becomes an almost out-door activity, particularly pleasant in the southern California climate. Frank Gehry was the architect for this Los Angeles project. (Photograph: © 1986 Tim Street-Porter)

186

187

186, 187. In converting a large mansion-like town house in New York into a group of medical offices, the interior designer John F. Saladino retained the ornamented plaster ceilings. The 1986 waiting-room interiors display a compatible, traditional, and rich character—in dramatic contrast to the usual drabness of doctors' offices. (Photograph: Peter Vitale)

commonly accepted minimum, although heights as low as 7 feet 2 inches will not create any physical problem). In setting ceiling height, it is often necessary to consider what is to be placed above the ceiling, since the space between ceiling and structure is commonly used to house ducts, wiring, and plumbing (including sprinkler pipes, when they are used), while many architectural lighting fixtures are recessed up into the *plenum,* or cavity above the ceiling. Dimensional clearances must be sufficient to avoid any interference between these elements and any structural elements, such as beams and girders, present.

The visible ceiling surface may be smooth and blank, but it may also be studded with such functional elements as lighting fixtures, air-conditioning outlet louvers, sprinkler heads, and audio loudspeakers. It may also take on the functional demands for specific acoustical performance. Ceilings of open louvers, slats, or *egg-crate* create a visual overhead plane while permitting easy access to ducts, sprinklers, and other functional elements, for economic or technical reasons. Another approach, which finds particular favor in interiors of High Tech character, is to expose all piping, ducts, and other technical elements, possibly painting them with strong colors to make them decorative features rather than offensive necessities to be hidden (see Chapter 18, "Technical Issues").

For purely visual reasons, a ceiling may be ornamented with peripheral moldings, one or more decorative rosettes, or even rich sculptural and painted decoration, as in many historic interiors. Structural elements such as beams may be exposed and, in turn, decorated. Coffered ceilings (with a waffle-like pattern of squares) and the varied and often complex patterns of vaulting, domes, and modern shell structures all form alternative kinds of ceilings. In spaces under the roof level of a building, skylights can be introduced into ceiling design for both practical and visual reasons.

Ceiling Materials

A listing of widely used ceiling materials includes:

PLASTER. A primary traditional material, this is applied wet on lath to achieve both plain and decorated ceilings (figs. 186, 187). Plaster moldings and trim are important elements in many historic interiors. As with walls, the scarcity and high cost of the plasterer's skilled labor combined with the plaster's slow drying time discourage its use in modern practice. Moldings of wood or plastic are now sometimes used to patch, repair, or simulate the decorative elements characteristic of plaster. Paint and wallpaper are common finishes.

SHEETROCK OR WALLBOARD. This is now the most common inexpensive material for plain, smooth

188

ceilings similar in appearance to plaster. Its treatment is similar to the same material on walls.

WOOD. This appears as a ceiling material when the beams or joists and planks of wood construction are left exposed. Natural or painted finishes are possible. Wood paneling similar to wall paneling is occasionally used in more traditional interiors (fig. 188). An unusual but effective ceiling results from the use of narrow tongue-and-grooved boards of the sort supplied for hardwood flooring, normally used with a natural finish.

ACOUSTICAL CEILING MATERIALS. Special ceiling tile and panels of pressed paper, fiber, and mineral composition have holes or pores that trap and absorb unwanted sound (fig. 189). Small tiles (usually one foot square) may have clearly visible round holes or a less noticeable texture of pores suggestive of travertine stone. Bevel-joint lines accentuate the pattern of tiles; flush joints are less visible and suggest a smooth ceiling plane. Similar materials are also made in larger panels (commonly 2 by 4 feet) for use with a system of support structure that can coordinate with lighting fixtures and HVAC (heat, ventilation, and air conditioning) outlets on the same dimensional module.

CEILING SYSTEMS. Panel materials (usually with

188. The Social Saloon in the transpacific paddlewheel steamship China, designed and built by William H. Webb in New York in 1867, displays an elaborate, gilded ceiling. The skillful woodwork of ships' joiners and the rich decorative carving seen here were typical of the interiors of nineteenth-century passenger ships. This relic of what is said to have been the largest wooden ship ever built has been restored (1986) and is now preserved by the Belvedere-Tiburon Landmarks Society in California. (Photograph: Philip L. Molten)

189

190

189. *Acoustical ceilings absorb noise in spaces where sound may otherwise reach disturbing levels. In the Merchant & Main Bar & Grill in Vacaville, California, the designers James and Robert Tooke used a system ceiling: a grid of metal supports holds squares of sound-absorbent material, which reduces restaurant noise generated by hard, sound-reflective surfaces to a comfortable level. (Photograph courtesy Chicago Metallic Corporation)*

190. *A complex ceiling design uses stepped, recessed panels to create a decorative pattern that incorporates lighting fixtures and air-conditioning supply diffusers. The interior is the Diane von Furstenberg store in New York designed in 1984 by Michael Graves, architect. (Photograph courtesy Michael Graves)*

acoustical value), supporting structure, which may be visible or hidden, and, often, lighting and HVAC elements are all integrated into a factory-made product system. It may include visually striking elements such as coffers or other forms. Such integrated systems most often find use in office and other contract or commercial interiors (fig. 190).

METAL CEILINGS. Some systems use spaced metal strips with the intervals open to the acoustical material above. Metals such as stainless steel, aluminum, copper, or bronze also find occasional use as surface materials for ceilings. Pressed-metal ceilings (erroneously called *tin* ceilings), once popular Victorian elements, have now been rediscovered.

GLASS. The usual material for skylights, glass is normally set in a framing of wood or metal (fig. 185). As skylighting expands to become a total ceiling, it is possible to speak of a glass ceiling—a feature of some famous architectural structures. Glass, mirror, or a plastic substitute as a ceiling material can create spectacular and startling visual effects.

MISCELLANEOUS ELEMENTS

Of the surprising number of components in an interior, many may seem minor or incidental, but each calls for design attention in terms of material selection and specification. The following is a very condensed list of such elements with some notes on the material selection issues that they involve.

BUILT-IN ELEMENTS. As these usually function as furniture pieces, they are discussed in Chapter 6. Wood, both solid and plywood, is the most commonly used material. Where toughness and durability are of primary importance, plastic laminate is frequently employed as a surface material.

FIREPLACES AND HEATING STOVES. Although more or less obsolescent in a functional sense, fireplaces are still widely valued and used for aesthetic and nostalgic reasons. The materials and designs of fireplaces and hearths, mantels, and accessories (fig. 191) remain a significant aspect of both traditional and modern interior design. Since the public has become concerned with energy conservation, heating stoves have been rediscovered as economical heating devices and as objects with strong aesthetic appeal. A wide variety of both traditional and modern designs is available.

TRIM. This is a general term for moldings, cornices, reveals, baseboards, nosings, wainscots, railings, and similar elements used for functional and/or aesthetic reasons. Wood, metals, and plastics are all common materials for elements of trim, which usually are ordered from catalogs but can be custom-designed to fill a particular need.

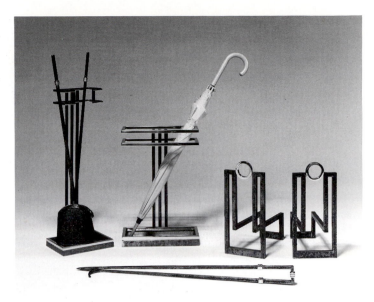

191

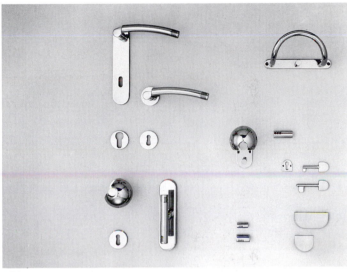

192

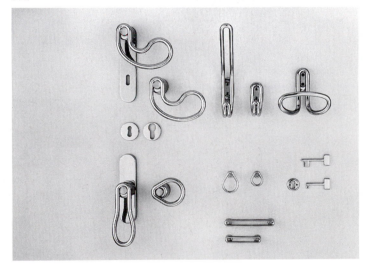

193

191. An umbrella stand, fireplace tools and tool holder, and andirons of strongly geometric features, in lacquered and distressed iron with mirror-polished brass accents, make handsome accessories for any modern interior. Designed by Matthew Smyth Accessories and produced by LCS (Luten Clarey Stern Inc). (Photograph: © 1986 Dan Cornish/ESTO)

192, 193. Serie Otto G hardware by Italian designer Vittorio Gregotti (fig. 192) and Serie Otto A hardware by Italian designer Gae Aulenti (fig. 193) include door hardware and coat hooks in cast brass, chromium, or nerox plate, which present excellent design alternatives to the bland, largely banal hardware in common use. Because they are in daily use, these objects—usually considered minor design details—have significant influence. (Photograph courtesy Fusital)

HARDWARE. This is an important part of every interior. It is customary to distinguish between *builders'* and *cabinet* hardware. Builders' hardware includes doorknobs, hinges, latches, locksets, and similar items used on architectural elements (figs. 192, 193). Cabinet hardware includes the hinges, latches, pulls, and many minor devices that are part of furniture and built-in components. The design, materials, and finish of hardware elements form important details of the interior design. Components of fine quality and aesthetic merit are available, but it takes some effort to seek them out and assure their use.

SIGNS AND GRAPHICS. Residential interiors may need no more than a house number or nameplate, but many contract interiors require a large number of directional and identification signs, exit signs (fig. 194), and sometimes sign elements that relate to advertising and display. If left unplanned, these elements can grow chaotic and be distracting. A list of requested sign elements should be drawn up for every project and a careful effort made to design and coordinate their use. A number of sign systems offer materials of high design quality.

MECHANICAL SYSTEMS. HVAC, electrical, and plumbing systems introduce visible elements, such as air louvers, grilles and convectors, switches and outlets, filters and plumbing accessories, which need to be carefully chosen. At worst, these necessities can be unpleasant intrusions into designed space, while at best they can become fine details that enhance the total quality of a completed interior.

SAFETY AND SECURITY EQUIPMENT. Like the visual elements of mechanical systems, fire-alarm boxes, extinguishers, hose cabinets, panic bolts, TV scanners, and similar equipment too often look like afterthoughts and clutter the spaces where they are required. Planned locations and equipment selection are an interior design responsibility.

VERTICAL TRANSPORTATION. Elevators and escalators (fig. 195) are part of many large-scale interior projects. These elements are generally factory-made and standardized, but there is a wide choice of standard and custom designs for elevator doors and cab interiors and for the external parts of escalators. Elevator call buttons, control buttons, and location indicators can become significant design details.

194

194. Graphics—typography and layout—for signs has become a specialized phase of design detail called signage. This section of a New York subway station, the 53rd Street concourse, was designed by Beyer Blinder Belle in 1984. The sign, produced by Whippany Park, is clear and decisive and provides a striking visual accent. (Photograph: © 1985 Frederick Charles)

195. These escalators add a dynamic visual element to the vast, dramatic atrium in the Hong Kong Bank, a 1986 project of the British architectural firm Norman Foster Associates. (Photograph: © Richard Bryant)

FURNITURE

With the exception of certain monumental spaces such as lobbies, circulation areas, and ceremonial interiors, almost all interiors require furniture. For most users, it is the furniture that makes the architectural space into a useful and personal place where human activities can take place with comfort and convenience. Human beings, especially the populations of the Western, developed countries, have come to regard furniture as a virtual necessity for almost every activity. We use chairs, tables, and desks for working; chairs and tables for dining; chairs and sofas for conversation and watching television. Sleeping has become synonymous with going to *bed*. We store our possessions in chests, cabinets, and on shelves. Even such special-purpose objects as television receivers, stereo equipment, and some musical instruments turn into pieces of furniture.

It is not surprising, then, that most people think of an interior as the sum of its furnishings. The process of moving into a house, apartment, or other space turns out to be primarily a matter of placing furniture. No one considers a space occupied until this process has been carried out. The completed interior's visual character and comfort are largely derived from the furniture within it.

For the designer, therefore, the selection—and in some cases the designing—of furniture is a key activity. While it may come to seem simple and almost routine, it is actually based on a considerable fund of knowledge combined with much complex decision-making. All furniture types exist in an almost infinite variety of materials, constructions, sizes, and styles. Choosing intelligently among them demands studying the characteristics of each material, the different construction techniques, styles, and finishes. Each of these factors must be balanced against the others when making a decision about a furniture piece for a particular context, which usually imposes a set of constraints about size, appropriateness, durability, and ease of maintenance.

PRELIMINARY FURNITURE DECISIONS

In a typical design project, planning takes place before furniture selection is considered. One plans with function in mind and indicates furniture in a generalized way, using average sizes and forms to designate desk, table, chair, sofa, bed, and so on. Templates with such average size forms cut out at various scales help the beginning designer with this task. Most experienced designers become adept at drawing the plan forms of familiar furniture pieces at the commonly used scales without help from templates or even reference to a scale.

196. A child's bedroom is furnished with a sleigh bedstead, draperies, pillows, sheets, and blankets that create an overall effect of storybook snug comfort. The window treatment, rug, wicker chair, and flowers all add to the ambience of romantic charm. Carol Helms, designer. (Photograph: Bill Helms, courtesy Metropolitan Home *Magazine)*

BUILT-IN VERSUS MOVABLE FURNITURE. Some furniture types that impose constraints at the planning stage must be considered beforehand. This is the time to make decisions about built-in versus movable furniture. Built-ins tend to be neat and efficient, to save space, and to contribute to a modern look. In addition, they may be the most economical way to provide certain functions, such as the storage of books or quantities of other objects. In rented spaces or where long-term occupancy is uncertain for other reasons, movable furniture has, of course, the advantage of being readily transportable to a new location. It also permits easy rearrangement as needs change, or simply to satisfy the desire for change for its own sake. Certain functions, those of dining chairs, for example, almost require mobility (although fixed booth seating and banquettes are not uncommon in restaurants).

SYSTEMS FURNITURE. The use of what has come to be called *systems furniture* should also be considered in advance of planning. The systems developed largely for office use consist of elements linked together in clusters. Some of the elements provide spatial subdivision in addition to their primary functions. Each available system has its own dimensional characteristics and may influence plan layout by favoring certain arrangements or making others impractical or impossible.

REUSING FURNITURE. Whether or not to reuse existing furniture is a third decision to be made before planning begins. This decision may be based on reasons of economy or on a client's desire to retain well-liked or treasured pieces. In residential design, it is probably more common to reuse at least some existing furniture than to start out with everything new. The designer typically inventories and measures existing furniture, noting down which pieces *must* be reused and which might be considered for reuse as design develops. New furniture specifically chosen falls into a similar category. A desired seating group, a new grand piano must be planned for as if they already were on hand.

SELECTING FURNITURE

With these decisions made and a basic plan of the interior space completed, furniture selection can begin. Another decision—which may apply to an entire project, or be taken on a piece-by-piece basis—then confronts the designer. Should any furniture for the project be custom-designed and -built, or should it be purchased ready-made from shops, showrooms, catalogs, galleries, and dealers? The pros and cons of these two approaches deserve some discussion.

1,97

Specially Designed Furniture

This can be tailored to suit the precise needs and desires of users and can give an interior a unique visual quality. On the other hand, it involves some element of risk; if the finished product turns out to be unsatisfactory in some way, it may be difficult and expensive to change or replace.

In general, special furniture is likely to be more expensive than standard, available products, not only more expensive to produce but also more expensive in terms of design time. Designing a piece of furniture is a major project that cannot be dealt with in a few minutes or hours. Built-in furniture, almost by definition, is specially designed. Simple shelving presents no problem to the designer, carpenter, or cabinetmaker. More complex cabinetry, such as dressing-room fittings, a room divider, or special kitchen or bathroom cabinets, can range from fairly simple to extremely complex and costly.

The process usually begins with simple sketches, moves to drafted elevations and cross sections, and finally to construction drawings for the shop or cabinetmaker that will build the piece or pieces. Scale models are helpful to the design process; even full-size mock-ups are often made before going ahead with a special design. Designing seating is very demanding; chairs in particular have gained a reputation as being difficult to design. The challenge they pose may explain why the design of a special chair has come to be regarded as the signature of a master designer. The designing of a chair proceeds as described above, except that a full-size mock-up or prototype that can actually be sat in is almost essential in order to test for comfort, strength, and stability.

Many fine historic interiors are largely furnished with specially designed elements. An Adam brothers room, an Art Nouveau interior, a Frank Lloyd Wright house can hardly be separated from the special furniture that they contain (see figs. 581, 595, and 606). Many designs now in production originated as "specials" for a particular project. Most of these date from times when fine craft labor was cheaper and more available and budgets more generous than today. The modern tendency is to avoid special furniture design except for simple built-ins or an occasional single piece when no acceptable stock alternative is available. Economic pressures and clients' desire to see a sample before making a decision are probably equal factors in limiting the development of special designs.

Specially designed furniture also includes handcrafted furniture by artisans and furniture by artists (see page 186).

Ready-made Furniture

This can include fine antiques, simpler old furniture, modern furniture that has become *collectible*, and any other furniture

197. A complex grouping of built-in furniture, including bookshelves, table surfaces, and seating, accents the bridgelike architecture of a vacation house in Ontario, Canada. Jim Strasman, designer, 1983. (Photograph: © O. Baitz, Inc., courtesy House & Garden*)*

that is already a valued possession for reuse. However, most selections will be made from furniture in regular production. It can be inspected in a shop, store, or showroom. Manufacturers' catalogs illustrate available pieces and give fairly complete data on dimensions, construction, and available finishes, and often include suggestions about planning and layout as well. Production furniture comes in a wide range of quality and price levels and in a vast variety of styles.

Using a reputable manufacturer and dealer offers some assurance of quality and of repairs, service, and replacements over a period of time. The possibility of both viewing and "trying out" an actual sample in shop or showroom before making a purchase can safeguard against unhappy surprises, giving both designer and client or user security about a decision that can involve large expenditures.

In exchange for these advantages, one gives up having furniture exactly fitted to specific needs and accepts the closest available standard solution. One must also accept seeing the same designs in other places, in some cases to the point of boredom with what may become a current cliché. Manufacturers do their best to minimize monotony by offering a maximum variety of designs, optional details, and finishes.

Criteria for Choosing Furniture

The primary issue in choosing appropriate furniture, whatever its source, is *quality*. It is an unfortunate fact that the most widely available furniture tends to be mediocre; badly designed and poorly made, it is intended to sell quickly and serve briefly before being discarded, either because it goes out of style or it physically disintegrates. Furniture only a few years old can be observed in trash piles almost every day, while good furniture can last for a very long time, as demonstrated by antiques still

198

198. In Miss Cranston's "The Willow" tearooms in Glasgow (1904), Charles Rennie Mackintosh created these unique ladder-back chairs as part of his overall design scheme (including the stained-glass windows and every other detail of the project). Today they are viewed as historic masterpieces of their time and place. (Photograph: T. & R. Annan, Glasgow)

199

serviceable after hundreds of years. Evaluating furniture quality involves several issues, many easy to evaluate, others more difficult. The primary issues are the same that apply to the evaluation of all design—function, structure and materials, and aesthetics (see Chapter 3, "Design Basics")—but with more particular bearing.

Function relates to the furniture's purpose. Almost all furniture has a practical use, and good furniture serves that use effectively and reliably. Different uses call for specific qualities and characteristics. For example, storage furniture must be sized to hold whatever it will contain efficiently and conveniently, and its drawers and doors must work well and continue to work well over years of use. Chairs and other seating and reclining furniture must fulfill the requirement of providing comfort.

Structure and materials concern how the furniture is made.

200

199. Designed at the height of the Art Deco era (1926–31), Jacques-Emile Ruhlmann's aptly named Elephant Noir chair offers comfort—and a touch of humor. It is now a collector's item. (Photograph: © Editions du Regard, Paris, 1983)

200. Gwathmey Siegel & Associates, architects, brought together a pair of Ruhlmann Elephant Noir chairs, contemporary sofas in a related design, and a Josef Hoffmann Vienna Secession screen—an extraordinary mix of objects from diverse times and places—in an East Hampton, New York, interior of 1979. (Photograph: © Norman McGrath, courtesy Gwathmey Siegel & Associates)

Good furniture is well made of appropriate materials. Examining the broken furniture left on garbage heaps reveals slick or showy finishes covering flimsy materials and slipshod construction. Since inexpensive furniture of good quality exists, it is clear that the poor quality of such materials and construction stems only partly from an effort to maintain low prices. The difference lies in the maker's awareness of and attention to the kind of construction the furniture calls for and an effort to use affordable materials honestly and to their best advantage.

Aesthetic success is probably the hardest element of furniture quality to evaluate. Furniture that is well designed in terms of function, structure, *and* the expressive qualities that we call aesthetic generally has a long life and gives high levels of satisfaction over that long life. Exactly what aesthetic excellence is remains a matter of disagreement and discussion. To say that furniture should be beautiful seems an easy way of setting a standard, but beauty means different things to different people, in different contexts, and at different times. Many of the greatly valued classics designed a few years ago may not seem beautiful to most people. Designs of the Victorian era considered monstrosities only a few years ago are now valued by collectors. Too often, what people call beauty is a matter of superficial appeal.

A better way to define the aesthetic characteristics of quality furniture is through the strong expression of concepts that were significant when and where the design was developed. Clear expression of functional and structural intent along with a kind of "spirit of the time" seems to make for furniture design that is lasting and satisfying. Stickley Craftsman furniture of the late Victorian era, angular De Stijl designs by Gerrit Rietveld from the 1920s and 1930s, Bauhaus tubular designs by Marcel Breuer all possess an integrity that makes them just as worthwhile as Georgian Chippendale, Colonial Windsor chairs, or Shaker rockers. Any number of current fashions of the intervening years have become dated and worthless because they lack any comparable integrity of ideas.

Leaving aside aesthetic questions, the more tangible issues of function and construction can be examined in greater detail.

FUNCTION

The usefulness of a piece of furniture relates to its size, shape, and details in fairly clear ways. The functional values of some special-purpose furniture types are described by their names: tea carts, typewriter stands, mobile files, cribs and highchairs, wheelchairs, outdoor furniture. They are available in considerable variety and tend to be closely suited to their particular function. Other furniture types have so many variables that they can be studied individually.

201

201. Thanks to its timeless aesthetic quality, Craftsman furniture of the early 1900s, designed and produced by Gustav Stickley, is harmoniously at home in this contemporary Los Angeles interior. Barton Phelps, designer. (Photograph: David Zanzinger)

202

203

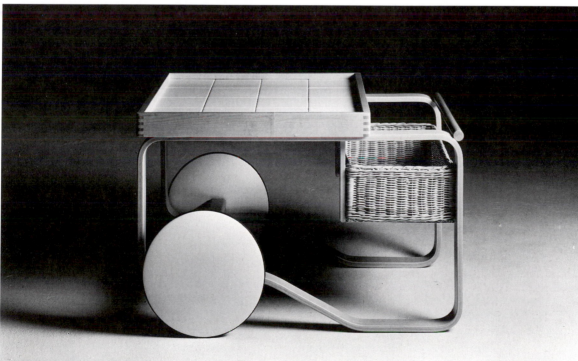

204

202. An American Colonial Windsor chair designed and made by J. M. Hasbrouck in the eighteenth century exhibits an ingenious arrangement of thin hardwood turnings, here, of maple and hickory. The result is a remarkably strong structure with a minimum of material and weight—and a clear, pleasing design that does not date. 36¼ × 22¼ × 22¼". The Art Institute of Chicago. Gift of Emily Crane Chadbourne

203. Gerrit Rietveld's "Red and Blue" chair, a design of 1917, is an emblem of the De Stijl movement. Of solid wood and plywood, the frame elements are all painted black—except for the ends, which are bright yellow. The blue-painted seat is of plywood, as is the red-painted back. A modern reproduction is available from Atelier International, Ltd., a ⅙-full-size scale model, in kit form, from the Museum of Modern Art, New York. 34½ × 26½ × 26½". The Museum of Modern Art, New York. Gift of Philip Johnson

204. The Finnish architect Alvar Aalto designed this tea trolley in 1936. The frame is of molded, laminated birch wood, the top tray has a linoleum tile surface, and the basket is of woven wickerwork. The strong visual impact of this special-purpose piece has made it famous in its time—and it is still manufactured today, by Artek in Finland. 35½ × 23⅝ × 25½".

Tables

A table needs to be of a size and shape appropriate to its use. How many people are to sit around it, giving each person 24 to 30 inches of edge space? Is the standard height of 29 to 30 inches appropriate or is a lower height (as low as 25 inches) better for certain uses, such as typing? How do square, rectangular, round, or other shapes relate to use and to the space where the table will go? Are legs or other supports arranged for good stability without interference with users' legs or knees? Is expansion or folding desirable and/or practical for the intended use? Is the top surface serviceable and of suitable color and texture? Is it practical to maintain?

Since tables are made in great variety, the selection of an appropriate design for a particular use involves considering a number of factors. Table 5 below includes most of the available alternatives, with some criteria for selection.

TABLE 5. TABLE SELECTION

Function	Dining Conference Coffee/cocktail Side/end Bedside	Special purpose (typewriter, projector, TV, and so on) Mobile	
Shape	Rectangular Square Round Racetrack (rectangular with semicircular ends)	Boat-shape (curving sides with straight ends) Elliptical, or oval Hexagonal Irregular, or free-form	
Support structure (base)	Four legs, at or near the corners Three legs (note possible instability)	Center pedestal Two or more pedestals Trestle Complex structure	In addition to dimensions, it is important to consider leg or base locations in determining comfortable seating patterns at a table. Besides making sure that chair seats fit under the table edge, the designer must verify that occupants can sit without their knees or legs coming in contact with the table legs or base.
Height	Coffee: 12″–18″ (15″ average) Low conference/ dining: 25″–28″	Standard conference/ dining: 29″–30″ End/bedside: 15″–26″	Wheelchair access to tables presents a problem. Wheelchair arms require a clearance of 29″–30″ under a table top. This forces a height of 30″–32″, too high for other users. It appears best to set a top height of 29″–30″ and to expect that wheelchair occupants can remove their chair arms when drawing up to a table.

Surface dimensions (width by length)	Coffee: 15″–24″ × 30″–60″; 24″–60″ round
	Conference/dining: 24″–30″ edge per seated person
	  Seating 2: 24″–30″ square or round
	      24″ × 30″ rectangular
	  Seating 4: 30″–42″ square
	      36″–42″ round
	      48″–54″ × 30″–40″ rectangular
	  Seating 6: 40″ × 48″–54″ rectangular
	      42″–48″ round
	  Larger: allow 24″–30″ edge per person
			When determining table sizes, it is important to consider clearances for chairs both when they are occupied and when they are moved away from the table for access. Distances to walls and other tables and suitable circulation space for access and service may be factors of importance.
			
			In restaurants, the size and spacing of tables affect the character and atmosphere of the space. Extreme crowding is, oddly enough, desirable in some situations (city nightclubs, for example), while generous table sizes and spaces may convey a sense of luxury in other circumstances.

Surface material	Solid wood. This is subject to warping and splitting Plywood or other core with wood veneer or plastic laminate surface	Glass Marble, slate, tile
Base material	Wood Steel	Aluminum
Edge treatment	Shape: thickness, square, half-round, irregular curve Corner: square, radius (curved)	Material: *self* (same material as top surface), veneer, solid wood, metal edging, plastic edging
Special functions	Stacking, nesting Extension: inserted leaf or leaves, contained (fold-out) leaf	Drop leaf (with pull-out or swing-out supports) Gateleg (with extra leg that swings out to support leaf)

205

206

205. The Tippy Jackson is an ingenious folding table that is decorative both set up and collapsed. The three curved, tubular-steel legs, each carrying a support post, pivot outward from a central hub to open into a stable triangular base. The top is of sheet steel. The design, by Philippe Starck, suggests both Bauhaus and Art Deco influences. (Photograph courtesy Furniture of the Twentieth Century, New York)

206. Cini Boeri's Shadow table is in fact a table system. The steel base supports sections of clear glass sandblasted around the perimeter to give a frosted texture. The translucent lower glass shelf is etched. Surfaces of different sizes and shapes—square, rectangular, or with rounded ends—can adapt the table to various purposes. Smaller sizes, for example, are suitable for use as desks or dining tables, while longer versions serve well as conference or board-room tables. A smaller, low version makes a coffee table. 28¼ × 94½ × 55⅛". (Photograph courtesy Cadsana)

208

209

207. These restaurant tables were designed for the Los Angeles restaurant Rebecca by its architect, Frank Gehry. Note the extensive use of copper in the bar area in the background. (Photograph: Tim Street-Porter)

208. Chairs by Vico Magistretti (in the foreground) make dramatic gestures that echo those of Robert Longo's wall piece and contrast with the more sedate forms of the 1950s-vintage Diamond wire chair by Harry Bertoia, visible to the right of the fireplace. Art and furniture-as-art give the room, in a renovated 1950s California house, its character. Brian A. Murphy, designer. (Photograph: © 1986 Tim Street-Porter)

209. A small table by Bruce Tomb and John Randolph comprises an unpolished ¾-inch-thick glass top on a sandblasted-steel frame supported by four legs of rough, stonelike poured concrete. A larger version is available as a conference table. (Photograph: © Paul Warchol)

Desks

Desks can be evaluated with a list of questions similar to those for tables, plus questions about storage needs. Does the desk require a file drawer? surface space for a typewriter? space for a computer with keyboard and monitor? Desk requirements for office uses can become complex and quite specific, leading to *work stations* that go beyond a simple desk to become a complete multipurpose working-space unit (see pages 172–73).

Seating Furniture

Seating furniture presents complex problems that are often not well understood.

SEATING COMFORT. It is a truism that a chair should be comfortable, but comfort is, in practice, a very variable thing. One can be comfortable seated on a bicycle or tractor seat, on a picnic bench, or even on a rock. A hard stool is ideal for certain intermittent uses, a contoured chaise for others. The problem is further complicated by the reality that human beings vary greatly in size and shape. If shoes were made in one size only to suit all wearers, a great many people would have uncomfortable feet. Yet chairs (with certain exceptions) are produced in one size for all.

Several issues enter into the consideration of comfort in seating furniture:

- *WHAT KIND OF COMFORT IS DESIRED FOR A PARTICULAR USE? An upright seating posture is best suited to dining and desk work. Lounge seating, in a semireclining position, is a modern concept not recognized in historic furniture. It can range from the slightly lowered and back-tilted posture now preferred for reading, conversation, and the long-term seating in transport vehicles to a near-fully reclined position suited to rest or even sleep. Reclining seating supports a prone or near-prone position. No single seat can provide for all of these needs, although adjustability can introduce a range of suitability to varied seating postures.*

- *HOW WILL THE VARIATION IN HUMAN BODY DIMENSIONS BE ACCOMMODATED? A chair intended for one particular user can, of course, be selected with that person's requirements in mind, but most chairs and other seating are intended for anyone. Having a different dining chair for each member of a family—not to speak of every guest—would be absurd. In practice, this means making several compromises that, taken together, provide acceptable*

210

210. The desk and storage units in this modern executive office are from a complete system designed by Bruce Hannah in 1980 for Knoll International. The chairs are classics by Mies van der Rohe. (Photograph courtesy Knoll International)

211

comfort for most. The "average person" charted from
statistics on the general population is in actuality quite
rare, but a very large proportion of the population comes
fairly close to this theoretical average.

By designing seating with dimensions that favor small
users but will not trouble larger users (a shallow seat, for
example, is not a problem to people with long legs while
a deep seat is not suited to the short-legged), it is
possible to arrive at seating dimensions that will suit all
but the very largest and smallest users reasonably well.
Some seating that will be used by one occupant for long
periods of time, such as an office desk chair or an

airplane pilot's seat, needs to be adjustable so that the
key dimensions can be set to fit the actual occupant
rather than an assumed average person.

• WHAT ARE THE PHYSIOLOGICAL REQUIREMENTS? Comfort is
too often judged on the basis of a quickly formed first
impression. This tends to favor the softness of thick
padding and deep cushions. Actually, the body is better
accommodated by firm support at certain key points
where weight is transferred and limited softness at other
locations. The pleasant sensation of "sinking into" a soft
seat soon leads to unexpected discomfort—the feet fall
asleep and the sitter becomes restless—and can

211. Rattan furniture of the 1930s displays traditional manufacturing techniques. The material is particularly
suited to informal, outdoor-related
rooms, like this windowed living space
in River Oaks, Texas, by Mark
Hampton, designer. The fabrics are by
Brunschwig & Fils. (Photograph: Feliciano, courtesy House & Garden)

212

213

215

214

216

212. *The Eames lounge chair (with ottoman) of 1956 is probably the most famous—and most imitated—of all the Eames' designs, perhaps because it is a modern design that offers lasting comfort as well as excellent form. Molded rosewood plywood units holding fitted leather cushions are supported by a cast-aluminum base. Lounge chair 33⅜ × 32½ × 32¾", ottoman 15 × 26 × 21". (Photograph courtesy Herman Miller, Inc., Archives)*

213. *These modern upholstered chairs are part of a complete group, Tentazione, by Italian industrial designer Mario Bellini. (Photograph courtesy Atelier International, Ltd.)*

214. *This elegant, lightweight stacking chair, the Handkerchief chair of 1985 by Vignelli Design, has a seat-and-back shell of molded plastic supported by a steel frame. It is available with or without arms, and with or without an upholstered pad. (Photograph: Mikio Sekita, courtesy Knoll International)*

215. *This drawing of a modern, ergonomic office chair shows the features and adjustments that maximize seating comfort and physiological benefits. The tilt articulation of seat and back are synchronized; the contours distribute the user's weight; the seat angle can be modified, then locked at any desired angle; and the seat itself can be raised or lowered. The chair swivels and rolls on a five-caster base. (Courtesy Steelcase, Inc.)*

217

218

219

contribute to physiological problems. Long periods of sitting in chairs designed without regard for physical needs can give rise to back ailments and may contribute to such major physical problems as varicose veins and heart and circulatory ailments.

In recent years, various seating designs described as ergonomic, *that is, suited to human body mechanics,* have appeared (fig. 215). Seating that is truly ergonomic, whether or not so described, will provide comfort in long-term use and will minimize physiological damage that poor seating postures can cause. Many traditional designs from simple wood stools to old-fashioned rockers are ergonomically successful, while much "luxury" seating is far less satisfactory.

In selecting seating furniture, then, appropriate comfort along with the best possible ergonomic performance are the primary considerations. Suitable size and shape for a particular use follow.

SEATING TYPES. Seating products are available that offer a wide variety of special-purpose features, such as rolling, swiveling, tilting or reclining, stacking, folding, and even conversion to other use—most often in the familiar *convertible* that makes up into a bed.

Multiple seating has developed a terminology of its own that can be confusing. *Sofa* is the generic term; *two-seater* and *three-seater* are self-explanatory. *Love seat* is a charming synonym for two-seater. As most sofas have arms, *armless* is used to designate the occasional exception. Other terms sometimes used include *Chesterfield* for an overstuffed sofa with padded arms; *Lawson* for sofas with arms lower than the back; *tuxedo* for sofas with arms the same height as the back.

Modular seating refers to the sectionals that appeared in the 1930s and continue to be popular. These are single units that come armless, with a single arm at right or at left, and as corner units. Several can be assembled in a variety of ways, including straight or angled sofa-like groupings (fig. 220); they can be rearranged to suit changing needs or locations. The term *modular* is also used for modern seating systems with a continuous base structure that supports individual seat sections. Arms, corner units, even end-table elements or planters may be added to the basic unit to make up groupings uniquely planned for a particular location. Some modular systems use units less than one seat in width and include tapered units, enabling the formation of curves, circular shapes, and S-shaped groupings. Large modular seating assemblies are particularly useful in public spaces such as lobbies and lounges that call for a large number of seating spaces (fig. 219).

216. *The folding Willow piece X-chair, a refined version of the familiar director's chair of Hollywood movie production fame, is now in wide use as a convenient portable armchair. Here, two examples flank an altar table in a San Francisco town house, an unusually formal use for a usually informal chair. Designed by the owners. (Photograph: Russell MacMasters, courtesy the McGuire Company)*

217. *This love seat was handmade of willow, or twig, in a traditional method of simple furniture-making that continues today. It is particularly suited to rural, informal settings. (Photograph courtesy La Lune Willow Collection)*

218. *Jay Spectre designed this Steamer chaise. Its massive proportions recall the streamlined forms of Art Deco, once more a popular vocabulary of forms. (Photograph courtesy Century Furniture)*

219. *This type of modular seating is suitable to public spaces, particularly those outdoors. Mounted on a tubular steel support, the contoured, ergonomically designed seats can be grouped as desired with table tops, planters, trash receptacles, and other elements, in straight-line or curved combinations. The metal parts are coated with weather-resistant polyester. (Photograph courtesy Landscape Forms, Kalamazoo, Michigan)*

220

220. Sectional, or modular, units—seats, arm ends, and corners—can be arranged into many configurations for flexible multiple seating. The Dallas room illustrated was designed by Byron Craig. (Photograph: Rick Patrick, courtesy Southern Accents *magazine*)

Sleeping Furniture

Furniture for sleeping can range from simple pads placed on the floor through futons and platform beds to elaborate bedsteads with head- and footboards and auxiliary elements such as bedside stands, lamps, and electronic controls and gadgets. A mattress on a spring unit, varying in size from a narrow single up to roomy king-size, mounted on a scarcely visible metal base has become a near-standard form of bed. The platform bed (mattress or mattress and box spring on a boxlike base) has become a popular alternative. As with seating, comfort and physiological serviceability are complex issues that require research and thought. In general, harder beds are probably better than softer, which can cause or aggravate back problems, and simple systems of construction are likely to be more durable than complex inner- and box-spring systems. Such innovative approaches as air-inflated and water-filled beds have not had a very good record of success in continued use. Foam mattresses, on the other hand, which came into wide use with platform beds, continue to be popular.

In spite of the variety of beds available, the differences between them are mostly superficial. There is probably less variety of basic design in sleeping furniture than in any other furniture type.

Convertible sofabeds are a widely used solution to the furniture problems presented by a one-room apartment or studio. Seeing that the designers of such furniture must always compromise the needs of the two functions, it is surprising how well such products, at their best, serve the conflicting needs. They must, of course, be evaluated for both uses. Fold-up or wall beds, once also a popular solution to the space problem, seem to have been largely displaced by improved convertibles, although they have recently become available in a variety of styles and systems.

Other types of sleeping furniture include the loft bed, that is, a bed on a raised platform that frees the space beneath it for other use; the bunk bed, particularly adaptable to children's rooms; and the trundle bed, which is an extra bed hidden under a larger bed.

Storage Furniture

Storage furniture is logically selected to suit the kind and quantity of materials to be stored. Open shelves and various cabinets with hinged or sliding doors and arrangements of drawers in many sizes and shapes are available in various combinations to suit specific needs. *Storage systems* offer standard related components that can be grouped together to suit a particular set of storage needs.

Modern storage systems often incorporate elements to serve

221

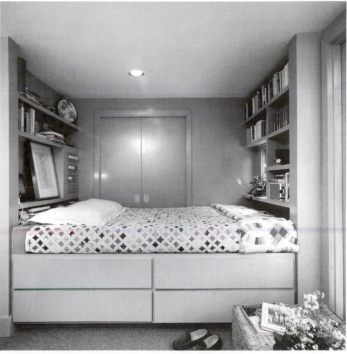

222

223

221. This bed, headboard, and night table make up a unit called Variations, by Peter Maly of Germany for Ligne Roset. The sleek, floating profile is characteristic of modern sleeping-furniture design. (Photograph courtesy Roset USA Corp.)

222. A built-in platform bed atop storage drawers is an element in a compact sleeping and study alcove. The 1979 design is by Moore Ruble Yudell Architects & Planners for the Rodes house in Brentwood, California. (Photograph: © 1986 Tim Street-Porter)

223. This unit, Flou-flou, by De Pas, D'Urbino, Lomazzi, designers, is actually a convertible sofabed. The Dacron-filled, quilted-overlay cushioning is removed to give access to the foldout bed underneath. (Photograph courtesy Roset USA Corp.)

225

226

227

224, 225. In the designer's own home in Guilford, Connecticut, Warren Platner has used built-in furniture extensively. Shelves and seating line the hallway (fig. 224), while glass shelves store books in the landing space (fig. 225). The 1971 house is by Warren Platner Associates Architects. (Photograph: © Ezra Stoller/ESTO)

226. A console (six-drawer cabinet) designed in 1933 by Louis Süe is typical of the 1930s modern style, now usually called Art Deco. It is of burl ash veneer with an aluminum structure. 35 × 55½ × 25½". (Photograph courtesy Christie's, New York)

227. Storage units, a desk, and a chair display the characteristic whimsicality of Memphis design. The Donar Collection, in wood, is an early-1980s project by Italian designer Ettore Sottsass. (Photograph courtesy Furniture of the Twentieth Century)

228

229

other special purposes, such as desk use, the service of food or drinks, or housing for TV and other electronic devices. Storage can also offer possibilities for display, either for ease in locating specific items, as with open bookshelves, or simply to offer protection while making collections of objects of interest or beauty visible.

Modular or *system* storage furniture is particularly well suited to making up storage walls and room dividers. The former are assemblies of connected storage components that fit from floor to ceiling, often using a custom-fitted insert at the top. They serve the function of a partition wall while providing storage accessible from one or both sides. A storage wall may separate adjacent living and dining spaces, two territorial areas in a shared children's bedroom, or two adjacent office spaces. Room dividers serve similar uses, but do not extend to the ceiling nor, in most cases, from wall to wall. They divide a large room into two sections while preserving its sense of unity and providing storage at the same time. Dividing living and dining spaces is one of the most common uses of a room divider. The living side can accommodate books, records, TV, and stereo equipment, while the dining side can hold dishes, glassware, silver, and linens. (See also Chapter 11, "Kitchens, Bathrooms, Storage.")

Contract Design Furniture

Contract design calls for many specialized types of furniture designed to satisfy specific needs. There are special lines of

furniture tailored to the requirements of hospitals and health-care facilities, offices, libraries, hotels and motels, restaurants, theaters and auditoriums, and retail shops, to name a few of those most widely available. Among these, the most highly specialized types, such as hospital and laboratory equipment, need only be noted here as areas served by product lines developed to fill such needs.

Other contract furniture products have more varied uses. Theater seats, for example, may also be used in school and college auditoriums and lecture halls. Stacking chairs may be specified for auditoriums, ballrooms, lecture rooms, cafeterias and dining rooms, conference rooms—wherever changing uses call for closely spaced seating at times and clear space at other times. Restaurants demand special tables, attractive and durable when table tops are left exposed, simple and unobtrusive when tablecloths will virtually conceal whatever is beneath. Banquette seating may be a standard product or may be built to order.

Office furniture has become a very important specialty as office work has become a major part of modern working life. The simple desk and chair continue in wide use, but systems furniture has come more and more to replace the free-standing desk with a complex of work surfaces, screen panels, and storage units that serve as partitioning as well (fig. 228). The *work station* is supplanting the conventional office room, occupying less space while, at best, providing better function (fig. 234). The typical office workday of long hours spent sitting

228. An example of contract systems furniture is this modern office installation. A desk and work station double as partitioning in an open-plan office. The table in the foreground can serve as an auxiliary work surface or a small conference table, as needed. (Photograph courtesy Haworth, Inc.)

229. Mobile file and storage pedestals for contract use roll on large casters that enable them to be placed easily beneath a table-desk, or in any other convenient spot. 24 × 16 × 22". (Photograph courtesy Howe Furniture Corporation)

230. Several types of joints are illustrated here. A dowel joint (A) is pictured here. Dowels are wood pins glued into bored holes to position parts and reinforce glued joints. The ends of dowels are sometimes exposed, but are shown here blind, that is, concealed. B gives an example of a dovetail joint. Hand-cut

with a dovetail saw and chisel and left exposed, these joints are often found as decorative details in crafted furniture, both antique and modern. Machine-cut dovetails, however, are frequently used in modern furniture construction. C shows a handcrafted blind dovetail joint.

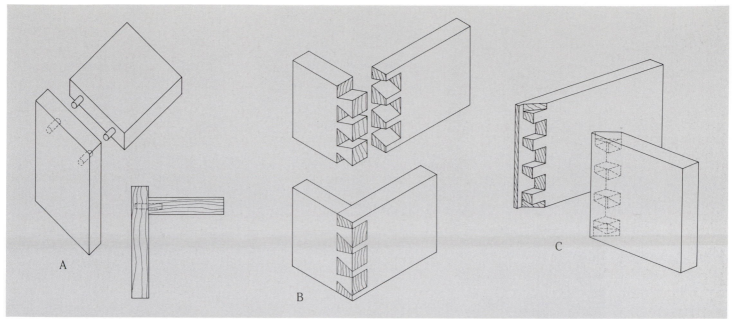

230

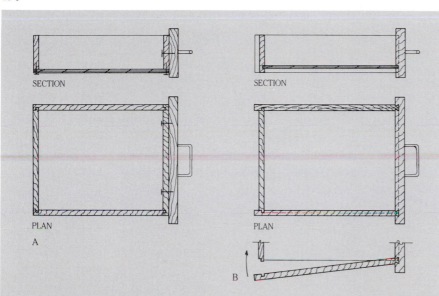

231

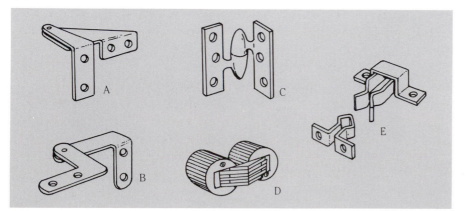

232

233

231. This diagram gives two different drawer constructions. (A) shows an economical construction of inferior quality. The drawer bottom is glued and nailed or stapled to the sides and back of the drawer and to an inner front. The front is attached to the inner front with glue and nails or screws. (B) is a superior construction. The sides are attached to the front with through dovetails, that is, the sides are slid upward into dovetail grooves in the drawer front. The bottom is then inserted into grooves in the front and sides, and a back is added, trapping the bottom in a groove by slightly spreading the sides as the bottom is slipped into place. The sides are then pressed together, locking in the back.

232. Some typical furniture hardware is pictured here:
A. A pivot hinge.
B. A pivot hinge, offset for attachment to the top edge of a door.
C. A hinge with an exposed pivot housing—called an "olive knuckle butt."
D. A fully concealed hinge mounted into drilled holes.
E. A spring-clip catch for a door.

233. Sliding door hardware is pictured here. In A, a fiber strip acts as a lower track; a nylon antifriction block slides along the strip, while a top guide slides within a groove cut in the upper surface. B shows extruded aluminum or plastic track for a sliding glass, plywood, or pressboard door.

234

235

in a chair has led to the development of ergonomic chairs offering improved comfort and physiological impact through shape, dimension, and adjustments that minimize muscular stress. Conventional file cabinets have been augmented by lateral files (in which the filed material is stored side by side instead of front to back) and special equipment for microfile materials. Computers require special stands and tables for their keyboards, screens, and printers, all of these connected by wires and cables that must be accommodated in suitable furniture units.

Other contract uses require special versions of ordinary home furniture. Motel and hotel furniture, drawer chests, desks, beds, and bedside tables differ from home equivalents only in having more durable surface finishes, heavy-duty mattresses, and sturdy casters on the bed frames to facilitate movement for bed-making. Chairs for restaurant service need to be strong and to have spot-resistant cover fabrics. Public lounge furniture is similar to living room furniture except that it, too, demands extra sturdiness and wear-resistant properties. On the other hand, transportation seating (for buses, trains, and airplanes) is of a very special type that must meet exacting performance and safety standards.

The interior designer confronting a specialized contract assignment for the first time will usually need to spend some time visiting special furniture showrooms, talking with salespeople in the field, and collecting a library of current catalogs devoted to suitable furniture products. Some industry manufacturers' associations have established quality standards that are an aid in evaluating available products. The Architectural Woodwork Institute (AWI), for example, produces a quality standards manual that defines three levels of quality, designated as *economy, custom,* and *premium,* in detailed specifications. Although meant for built-in woodwork, the same standards are useful in evaluating any wood furniture. BIFMA (Business and Institutional Furniture Manufacturers Association) has published similar standards for performance tests to be used by its member firms.

MATERIALS AND CONSTRUCTION

Quality of materials and workmanship in furniture construction has a major impact on both its durability and its proper use. Furniture is made in many ways from a great variety of materials. Generally, the details of construction are at least partially concealed in the finished product. The reputation of a particular manufacturer, published specifications (when available), and price are all clues to quality construction.

Well-made furniture need not be expensive, but cheap duplicates of quality products are almost certainly the result of some skimping on materials or quality details. When evaluated over its useful life, quality furniture is often a better bargain than cheap substitutes. An inexpensive dinette table that must be replaced in five years may, over the long run, end up costing more than a high-priced table that will still be serviceable (and perhaps more valuable) after a hundred years.

The examination of an actual sample, along with some simple testing in the form of shaking, bouncing, pushing, and pulling (particularly if done in comparison with several similar objects), can give some idea of constructional quality. Good furniture is not weak, fragile, or shaky when new and will not develop weaknesses with normal use over long periods of time.

Just how sturdy a piece of furniture needs to be depends on its intended use. Many fine antiques that have held up over centuries are actually quite delicate, but they have been used, as intended, only under conditions that do not impose too much rough usage. In general, home furniture need not be as rugged as furniture used in institutional and public spaces. Delicate materials and finishes can survive in private living spaces or in executive offices better than in hotel rooms, dormitories, or where young children will be regular users. Whatever its intended use, good furniture is characterized by good materials, workmanship, and finishes at an appropriate level of durability.

Although a variety of materials is used for specific details, the primary structure of most furniture is based on three families of materials, used alone or in combination. Each material family has its own constructional characteristics.

Wood

Still the most-used furniture material, wood was almost the only material of most historic furniture (see Table 6 on page 177). *SOLID WOOD.* The *softwoods* that come from evergreen trees (pine, spruce, fir, cedar, redwood) are the common, easily worked materials of carpentry. They serve well for simple utility furniture and show up in older country tables and chests. They are generally not considered suitable for fine furniture that will hold up well and take attractive finishes. The *hardwoods* of nut, fruit, and other deciduous trees, such as birch, maple, oak, walnut, and more exotic woods such as cherry, elm, or rosewood, are the materials of good cabinetry. Today, as in much traditional cabinetwork, such solid woods are used for chair frames, table bases, and cabinet legs, although wide surfaces are more often not solid but veneered. *VENEER.* Veneer is a very thin slice (usually 1/28 inch) of a fine solid wood. It is glued to a *core,* which may be a solid wood of lesser quality, a number of layers of thicker veneer, or,

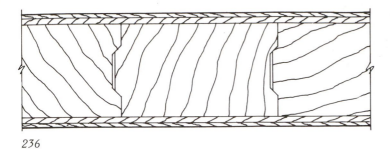

236

in modern practice, *particleboard*. The last is a manufactured board made from chips and sawdust, the scrap of woodworking, held together with a resin adhesive. It is, of course, wood, and very stable against warping, shrinking, or cracking. It is often assumed that veneer is a cheap substitute for solid wood, but this is not its primary reason for being. Solid wood in wide boards will warp and crack with changes in temperature and humidity, a problem that veneer circumvents. A core of solid wood is first covered with a utility veneer, its grain running at right angles to the grain of the core. *Face veneer*, which appears on the surface, is glued on top of the underlayer (called *cross-banding*), its grain running the other way (fig. 236). Such a sandwich is far more stable than any solid wood; as an incidental benefit, it contributes to the conservation of the fine wood used for the face veneer. Cross-banding is not needed on plywood (veneer) cores or on cores of particleboard. In modern practice, plastic laminates are often used as a surface material over a core where an especially tough and durable surface is required.

PLYWOOD. Plywood, most familiar as a basic construction material, is a number of layers of thin veneer laminated together with the grain of each layer running at right angles to the grain of the layers above and below it. Fir plywood is widely used in carpentry, but it is not generally acceptable for furniture construction uses. The outer surfaces of veneer plywood may be of better-grade woods, but rather than applying good veneer to a plywood core most furniture uses solid wood or particleboard cores. An exception arises because it is possible to make plywood in forms other than flat sheets by placing the layers of veneer in a mold while the adhesive between the layers is still wet and applying pressure (in a

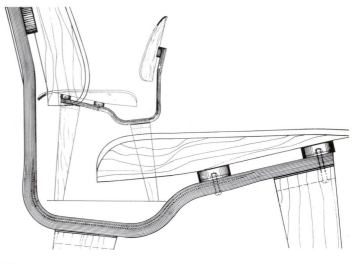

238

press) while the glue is setting. The resulting plywood will take the form of the mold, usually curved, to produce parts (seat, backs, or legs) of furniture, or even, in some cases, whole chairs or bench sections. The term *bent plywood* is often used to describe this process, but it is a misleading term, since flat plywood is not and cannot be bent; it is more properly called molded. A number of famous and highly successful modern designs use this process (figs. 237, 238).

BENTWOOD. Bentwood is the term for a different process, in which thin strips of solid wood, usually a European beech, are put in a pressure chamber and softened with steam. The strips are then bent around molds or forms and clamped in place until they cool and dry out, when the bent shape becomes permanent. Chairs and other objects can be designed to be made up as assemblies of a number of bentwood parts. Several designs developed near the end of the nineteenth century, when the process was invented, have become classics, collected in their original forms and still produced currently (fig. 239). At its

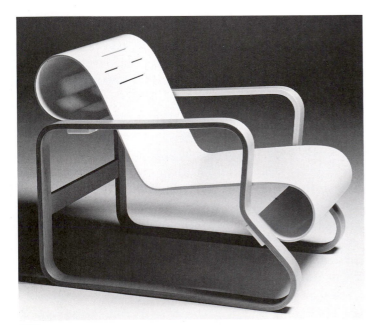

237

236. *Illustrated here is a cross-section of a veneer panel, a common element of modern wood furniture. The panel is made up of a central core—either solid wood or particleboard—with layers of veneer on either side of the core, the grain running crosswise. (This layer, called cross-banding, is often omitted with a particleboard core, because the uniform structure of the grainless material is almost immune to splitting and*

shrinking.) The layers on either side of the core must be of the same wood to prevent warping. The outer surface, or face veneer, makes up the final, outer layer. If the face veneer is to be concealed inside or under a unit, it may be a wood of inferior appearance. Otherwise, a first-quality veneer will be used, giving the finished product its external appearance.

237. *This armchair by Alvar Aalto represents an early (1930–33)—and famous—use of molded plywood for a chair's side frames, seat, and back. These parts are often described as being of bent plywood, but the term is misleading, because the material cannot be bent after manufacture. $31\frac{1}{4} \times 23\frac{3}{8} \times 24\frac{7}{8}$". (Photograph courtesy Artek)*

238. *This molded-plywood chair, part of a related group, was developed by Charles Eames, in association with Ray Eames, in 1946. Rubber shock mounts attach the seat and back units to the structural frame. This chair remains among the most admired of American post–World War II furniture designs. (Drawing courtesy Charles and Ray Eames)*

TABLE 6. CHARACTERISTICS OF THE MOST-USED FURNITURE WOODS

A large part of the wood visible in modern furniture is *plywood,* in which only the outermost thin layer of veneer is of the species named. In this case, the only significant characteristics are the color and finish surface of the face veneer. Where *solid* wood is used, as in legs, rails, and stretchers, other characteristics are also significant. Woods rarely used as solids but commonly used as decorative veneers are not included in this list.

Species	Typical Color	Relative Cost	Current Availability	Typical Uses and Special Characteristics
HARDWOODS				
Birch	Light beige-tan to near-white	Medium	Good	Hard, strong, compact grain, works and finishes well, generally useful in all furniture applications.
Cherry	Reddish-brown	High	Limited	Works and finishes well, well suited to handcrafting.
Ebony	Brown with near-black grain	High	Limited	Dense and heavy wood with striking grain pattern. Often stained black.
Mahogany	Reddish-brown to red	Medium	Good	Relatively soft, easy to work and finish. Typically red color often deepened with stain.
Maple	Light beige-tan	Medium	Good	Similar to birch (see above), with which it is sometimes combined in one product.
Oak	Light grayish-brown	Medium to high	Good	Hard and strong with marked, coarse grain. Often stained to darker browns.
Poplar	Light tan with pink and greenish streaks	Low	Good	Soft and easy to work. Color and grain not attractive. Much used for hidden parts and panel cores.
Rosewood	Deep red with black graining	High	Very limited	Striking and highly decorative appearance. Most used as veneer, often in matched patterning.
Teak	Warm, light brown	Medium to high	Fair	Close, uniform grain, easily workable. High oil content makes oil finishes desirable.
Walnut	Grayish-brown	Medium to high	Fair to good	Strong, consistent grain and good appearance. Suitable to general furniture uses in solids and veneers. Medium-dark color often further darkened with stains.
SOFTWOODS				
Cedar	Orange to red	Low	Good	Occasionally used in furniture, most often as storage lining because of its pleasant (and moth-repellent) aromatic odor.
Pine (white)	Clear, near-white	Medium	Limited	Soft, even grain and easy workability suited to handcrafting. Limited strength.
Pine (yellow)	Tan, orange to yellow	Low	Excellent	Soft, grainy, and difficult to finish well. Primarily for carpentry. Limited use, low cost, roughly worked applications.
Redwood	Reddish-brown	Low	Excellent	Natural oil content makes it usable outdoors without a finish. Soft and easy to work. Limited strength.

239

best, bentwood furniture is light and strong, relatively inexpensive, and original and handsome in design. In America, where suitable wood for bending is not easily available, this technique has not been developed extensively, although it is used to produce the curved back rims of some Windsor chairs and other curved chair parts.

Most curved parts in wooden furniture are cut out in curved form from wider planks by *bandsawing*. Because a single strip of wood with the grain running through it is fragile, the curvature must be limited or the part must be made up of

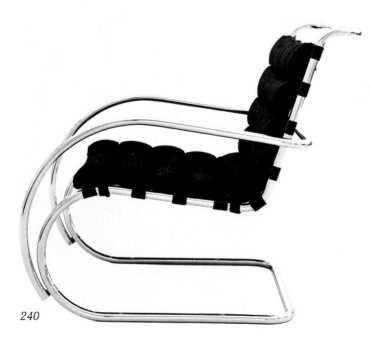

240

several pieces carefully joined. Grain must run close to parallel with the direction of curvature to avoid a weak point subject to easy breakage.

EVALUATING CONSTRUCTION. The quality of wood construction can be evaluated by inspecting the joints of solid parts and, in cabinet furniture, by observing the joinery of drawers and hidden parts inside, at backs, and underneath the body of a unit. There should be no visible nails or staples, no dripping glue, no bottoms or backs of thin cardboard-like fiber. Drawers should fit and slide well; catches, latches, and pulls should be of good quality and work well. Drawers should have neat and strong joints at all their corners and should withstand tugging and pulling in any direction.

The edges of doors and drawers (including bottom edges) reveal the construction of their panels—whether they are solid or veneered; if veneered, the nature of the core, layers, and veneer; the character of the machining—and give an idea of the piece's overall quality. Finishes are also a major clue to construction quality. Penetrating oil *(natural)* finishes hold up well and are easy to repair and maintain; they are satisfactory only when applied on good wood construction. Synthetic lacquers are used to produce a hard, smooth finish of high quality. The wood is usually first filled with a wood-filler paste to close the open-grain structure; then several thin coats of lacquer are applied. Poor-quality wood furniture depends heavily on finish to hide what lies below. Beware of strongly toned stained finishes, finishes with shaded color tone or with simulated grain or patina effects. Plastic parts that attempt to simulate wood are a sure sign of cheap and shoddy construction.

A possible exception to this last rule is the use of plastic laminate surfaces in simulated wood-grain patterns. Although generally frowned on by designers, wood-grained plastic tops have come to be widely used in office desks and in institutional furniture, where their resistance to damage outweighs their questionable appearance. There is a range of quality in laminates; the use of a good (that is, highly realistic-appearing) laminate indicates good overall quality. Cheap laminates look like a bad color photograph of wood. Their use signals corner-cutting throughout. A magnifying glass is helpful in looking at laminate, although the general impression it gives from a distance is also a trustworthy indicator of quality.

Metal

As a furniture material, metal appears in parts (legs, frames, and table bases) and as a primary material for office furniture, kitchen cabinetry, utility shelving, and in some other products as well. Steel, in the form of rods, tubing, and sheets, is the

239. *True bentwood construction uses lengths of solid wood, which are first softened by steam heat and pressure, then bent around molds, where they cool and dry, taking the forms of the molds. This famous rocking chair of 1860 is one of the best known of Austrian Gebruder Thonet's many products. The chair is of bent beechwood with caned seat and back. Height 37½". The Museum of Modern Art, New York. Gift of Café Nicholson*

240. *This Mies van der Rohe armchair was first produced in 1970, although the design concept dates from the late 1920s or early 1930s. The frame is of tubular stainless steel with a polished finish; the upholstery is a channeled-foam cushion resting on straps of saddle leather. 33 × 23⅝ × 35¼". (Photograph courtesy Knoll International)*

241

241. A table-and-chair group designed
by Margaret Helfand, architect, makes a
striking visual accent in the Jennifer
Reed showroom in Manhattan, 1987.
The table base is composed of steel
plates that have been finished by grind-
ing, producing a textural pattern. The
same material and finish were used for
the wall and shelves behind the table.
(Photograph: © Paul Warchol)

most used metal. Aluminum appears in tubes and formed sections such as angles, channels, and Ts and as a material for cast legs, frames, and small parts. Alloys are used for the casting of small metal parts such as pulls and other hardware elements.

As steel is subject to rusting, it must be finished either by painting or by plating, usually with chrome plating, which can be polished or finished to a frostier *(satin)* surface. Stainless steel requires no finish but is hard to work and therefore expensive and suitable only for certain designs. Aluminum is much less strong than steel and is costly relative to its strength. While it does not rust, it requires a finish called *anodizing* to prevent its gradual corrosion, which forms a gray oxide seen on much used kitchen pots and pans. Anodizing may be done with color or aluminum can be finished with various types of paints and coatings.

Metal office furniture and utility files, cabinets, and shelving are made of steel sheet. The sheets are cut and then bent to form box shapes or, with bent flanges, shelves or tops. Parts are welded together to make up complete units. The gauge of metal used is a significant factor determining quality. Thin sheet metal can be dented easily and may cause drumming noises, a sign of flimsiness. Flat sheet metal should not "oil can" (pop in and out) and should be difficult to dent with anything less than a hammer blow. It should be impossible to put a bend or kink in

any metal part through any stress of normal use. The forming of bent flanges contributes to structural sturdiness; quality sheet-metal furniture often uses nested, doubled-up box forms to produce panels of great strength. Hollow cavity spaces in sheet-metal furniture need to be filled with inert fiber panels to deaden drumming noises and resist denting.

In all metal furniture, the connections are crucial. Joints may be welded or mechanical, that is, held together with screws, nuts and bolts, or other fasteners. Pushing, pulling, bouncing, and shaking with particular attention to joints will give a good idea of sturdiness. Metal tubes and other thin sections, even when amply strong to resist breakage, may be springy. In a chair this may be pleasant; in a desk or shelf unit excessive springiness can be annoying.

Good finishes not only attest to general quality, they also resist rust, corrosion, and damage. Look for chipped paint at edges and corners; if circumstances permit, try to chip a corner or edge in some hidden location (the bottom rear of a drawer, for example). Chrome-plated finishes are harder to evaluate, since even the poorest-quality chrome looks bright and resists damage when new. However, after a short time, poor chrome plate permits rust to form, which eventually damages the plating. The best assurance of quality plating comes through the written specifications offered by reputable manufacturers.

In evaluating metal furniture, some consideration should be

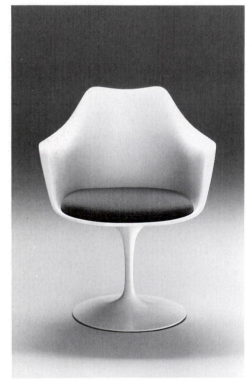

242

243

244

242. Eero Saarinen designed this grace-ful pedestal-base armchair in 1956. The shell of molded plastic, reinforced with fiberglass, is supported by a cast-aluminum base. The shell has a lacquer finish, the base a finish of fused epoxy plastic. The removable cushion is of foram foam. 32 × 26 × 23½". (Photo-graph courtesy Knoll International)

243. Danish furniture designer Verner Panton took full advantage of molded plastic's malleability in this flowing, strikingly sculptural stacking chair, made as a single unit (1959–60). 32⅝ × 19¼ × 23½". (Photograph cour-tesy Herman Miller Archives)

244. The Wiggle dining chair (1971–72) by Frank Gehry, architect and de-signer, is made of the pressed corrugated cardboard used for shipping cartons. When laminated and pressed in many sheets, the material develops surprising strength. 34 × 15 × 23". (Photograph courtesy Max Protetch Gallery, New York)

given to the demands the intended use will present. Folding outdoor or camp furniture, intentionally lightweight and built for limited use, cannot be expected to have the toughness and durability that heavier construction can offer. Office furniture, built for a long life of hard use, will stand up against considerable abuse, and consequently will be heavy and correspondingly expensive.

Plastics

A relatively new material for furniture construction, plastics come in so many different varieties that generalization becomes difficult. Price increases of recent years (most plastics are petroleum-based substances) have somewhat set back earlier expectations that plastics would become the primary material for furniture-making. Still, many modern designs use plastic parts, and certain plastics are widely used for special applications. Its most visible application in furniture is probably as sheet laminate, used as a tough surface material (see above under wood furniture).

PLASTIC LAMINATES. Laminates are composed of layers of heavy paper impregnated with melamine resin. Plain colors, patterns, and imitations of wood grain are common surface finishes. The thickness of the laminate shows as dark brown or black at the edges unless they are trimmed in some way. Some recently developed laminates, of uniform color throughout their thickness, do not create edge-appearance problems.

ACRYLICS. Acrylics (such as Plexiglas or Lucite, to mention two well-known trade names) resemble glass in their transparency. They also can be made translucent and colored. While less subject to breakage than glass, they scratch more easily and attract dust and lint with static electrical charges. Acrylics can be bent and molded into curved shapes and are used mostly to make transparent parts and occasionally entire pieces of furniture.

MOLDED PLASTICS. Molded plastics, such as styrene, polyethylene, nylon, and vinyl, are often made into small parts for special purposes such as glides, rollers, edge trim, and drawer pulls. The only other plastic sufficiently strong and moderate enough in cost to be usable for major furniture parts is *fiberglass*, a hybrid material in which glass fibers are embedded in a molded polyester resin. It is commonly used to make custom auto-body parts and small boat hulls. Fiberglass chair shells can be molded to body conforming shapes that are very strong and durable when well designed. The plastic may be exposed, painted, or covered with upholstery padding. Fiberglass chair shells can be tested for strength with deliberate rough handling, in testing machines, and through observation of chairs in regular use. The sight of broken plastic shells is common in public spaces, which impose the harsh tests of

245

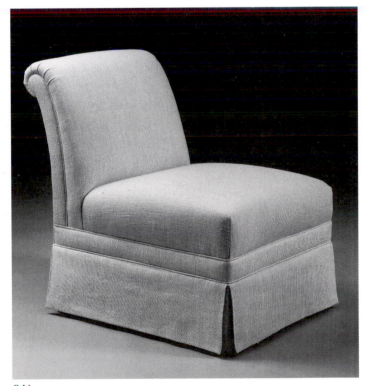

246

245, 246. Simple and timeless examples of conventional upholstery, the Mayfair Looseback Chair (fig. 245) and the related slipper chair (fig. 246) offer excellent comfort in neutral styles that can be adapted to many different situations. (Photographs courtesy Brunschwig & Fils)

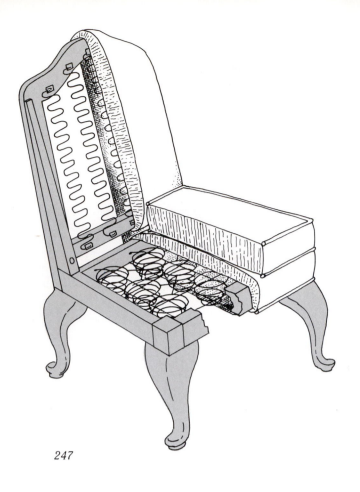

247

heavy use and, sometimes, deliberate vandalism. Chair shells made of plastic softer than fiberglass, used in many designs, cannot be expected to stand up to this kind of heavy usage.

A fair test of any plastic chair is to kneel in the seat and try to tear loose the back by pushing back and pulling forward. Also, test leg or base connections to the chair body; they should be unbreakable in any reasonable form of rough treatment.

FOAMED PLASTICS. Foamed plastics have become favorite materials for cushions, mattresses, and padding in upholstery. Foam takes the form of slabs, thin sheets, or molded parts shaped into cushions or fitted to entire chair forms. Upholstery foams vary greatly in degrees of softness, durability, and resistance to fire. Poor quality foams do not hold up well, and some foams produce toxic fumes when burning. The quality of foams can only be verified through manufacturers' specifications and guarantees, since testing calls for laboratory techniques.

Plastic foams can also be made stiff enough to be called rigid. Combinations of soft and rigid foam are used in some modern upholstery, either alone or with embedded frames of wood or metal or with bracing panels of wood, metal, other

247. *This diagram illustrates the construction of conventional upholstered seating as it is now most commonly produced. Coil springs are used for the seat, while the more economical modern alternative, sinuous—No-Sag—springing is used for the back. Rubberized hair or foam has generally replaced the traditional cotton felt and horsehair cushion stuffing.*

plastics, or fiber. Evaluating such hybrid plastic furniture is somewhat difficult, since the construction is concealed in the finished product. Testing for comfort, durability against hard use, and similar characteristics can be done fairly easily by sitting in each piece, moving in it, and deliberately trying to break it. Durability in service over a long period can be tested only by the product's service record, so any new construction material should be approached with caution.

Given a structural framework of a stronger material, such as wood or metal, rigid foam, with a plastic surface finish, can also be used as the primary material of storage furniture. This technique is currently used to create mass-produced furniture of minimal quality with surfaces colored to simulate wood. Its potential for use in well-designed furniture of higher quality will probably be developed eventually.

Upholstery

This is a technique using a variety of materials to create softness in seating and reclining furniture. Upholstery can range from a thin pad added to a hard seating surface to a complex construction that provides excellent comfort. Since a covering of fabric, leather, or plastic usually conceals all upholstery construction, its techniques and quality are hard to evaluate. Inspecting an upholstered unit before it is covered or watching the upholsterer at work in the shop are the best ways to become acquainted with upholstery techniques.

Traditional upholstery, still used in many quality products, begins with a frame, sturdily made in hardwood, with strong joints (fig. 247). This establishes the outer form of the finished unit. The open bottom is laced with an over-and-under weave of heavy webbing. Onto this, a number of coil springs (16 to 25 per seat) are tied and sewn to be pulled down into a partially compressed position. Canvas is placed over the springs and a cushion added on top. The cushion may be a removable unit or sewn down in place. The back is similarly treated, often without the coil springs. Padding is placed on arms and edges, and the whole is covered with the material that will be visible in the finished product. (See Appendix 7, "Estimating Material Requirements.")

Traditional upholstery, which depends on skilled labor, is slow and costly to produce. Most modern variations stem from efforts to reduce this labor cost. For example, flat, sinuous springs or elastic webbing often take the place of coil springs. Plastic foam (discussed above) may replace older cushioning materials, such as down, felt, or cotton, or various grades of foam may make up the entire upholstery construction. The resulting comfort can be evaluated by direct trial. Durability is, again, harder to evaluate. Upholstered furniture made with good

248

workmanship using good materials can have a long life, but upholstery using shortcut methods and cheap materials can be a doubtful economy, leading to the dismembered examples so often seen discarded after a short life. The reputation of a particular manufacturer is again the best guide to quality.

FURNITURE DESIGN

Furniture design tends to follow the trends in architectural and interior design. Historically, a furniture style displays both the general concept and specific details of its own period. The furniture of the Middle Ages exhibits Gothic details, that of the Renaissance elements from classical antiquity. Typical Victorian furniture has a vertical proportion and elaborate and fussy details, while modern furniture generally appears simple in both form and detail.

The terminology of furniture styles can be confusing, as some terms referring to historic periods and other terms describing an approach to design are used in ways that overlap. The modern habit of reproducing furniture designs from the past generates some of this confusion. The term *Colonial*, for example,

249

248. This Victorian tête-à-tête is an American antique piece of circa 1850. The frame is of rosewood, elaborately carved, in keeping with the taste of the time. 44½ × 52 × 43". The Metropolitan Museum of Art, New York. Gift of Mrs. Charles Reginald Leonard, 1957, in memory of Edgar Welch Leonard, Robert Jarvis Leonard, and Charles Reginald Leonard

249. A Queen Anne–style antique wing chair of circa 1725, in walnut and maple, is a product of a New England shop. The cover fabric is the original needlepoint. 46¾ × 31½". The Metropolitan Museum of Art, New York. Gift of Mrs. J. Insley Blair, 1950

250

describes both actual antiques from the Colonial era and modern reproductions of Colonial designs. *Modern* logically means nothing more than recently produced, but the term has come to designate a particular style as well. Sorting out this tangle demands careful use of the terms discussed below.

Antique Furniture

This term refers only to furniture made over a hundred years ago (according to the definition used by U.S. Customs) in the particular style then current. Dealers and galleries that deal in antique furniture usually reserve the term for examples of good quality, often called fine antiques. As the years go by, old furniture that was once scorned often comes to be appreciated and valued.

Country antiques can still be found at reasonable prices, and good antiques are sometimes, surprisingly, no more expensive than reproductions. Truly fine antiques, considered to be of museum quality, have become very costly; they are selected and bought as much for their investment potential as for their use as furniture. These should only be purchased from reputable dealers, galleries, or auction houses.

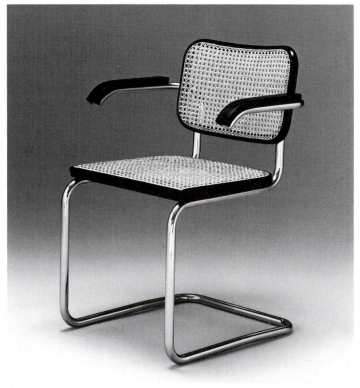

251

250. A classic modern sofa of 1928 by Le Corbusier is part of a group that includes an armchair, an extended, or wide, armchair, and a love seat. Polished-steel tubing supports rubber straps with surrounding steel springs for the seat and back, which hold the inserted seat, back, and arm cushions. In modern production, the cushions are of polyurethane foam, latex, and rubberized cocoa fibers, and are covered in fabric, vinyl, or leather. 28⅞ × 61⅛ × 24¾". (Photograph courtesy Carsina)

251. The Cesca armchair, a famous classic modern design of 1925 by Marcel Breuer, is usually considered the first tubular-steel chair. It is said that, on a visit to a bicycle factory, Breuer was impressed with the possibilities of using steel tubing, a strong, economical, and easily manufactured structural material, for furniture. The photograph shows a modern (1968) reproduction currently available. The seat and back frames and arm pads are of hardwood, the seat and back surfaces of handwoven or machine-made caning. 31¾ × 22⅝ × 21⅝". (Photograph courtesy Knoll International)

252

Many excellent designs made less than a hundred years ago may be highly valued and sought after. These are generally covered by the term *collectibles*, which also applies to a great variety of old objects including both very costly one-of-a-kind pieces and inexpensive mass-produced items.

Reproductions of Antiques and Collectibles

These recently made objects reproduce the design of antique originals, more or less accurately. Good reproductions are extremely accurate copies of particular examples of fine antiques. Makers sometimes go so far as to create finishes (called distressed in the trade) that imitate the effects of wear, down to such details as false wormholes.

Many designers frown on the use of reproductions, regarding them as a form of fakery that is dishonest when it truly deceives, foolish when it fails to deceive. Designer and client must judge this issue according to a particular context. For example, reproduction captain's chairs in a restaurant designed in a particular style may seem easier to accept than a brand-new imitation Chippendale breakfront in a living room.

253

252. The Stuart sofa, an example of contemporary-style furniture, is in current production but has no characteristics of the modern, or forward-looking, style. On the other hand, it imitates no particular historic period. It is simply graceful and comfortable in appearance and in performance. (Photograph courtesy Brunschwig & Fils)

253. In this rocking chair, a 1975 handcrafted piece, Sam Maloof of Alta Loma, California, displays both a woodworker's skill and a designer's sensitivity. The result is an object that is both useful and beautiful. Walnut, $45 \times 27\frac{3}{4} \times 46$". Museum of Fine Arts, Boston. Purchased through funds from the National Endowment for the Arts and the Gillette Corporation

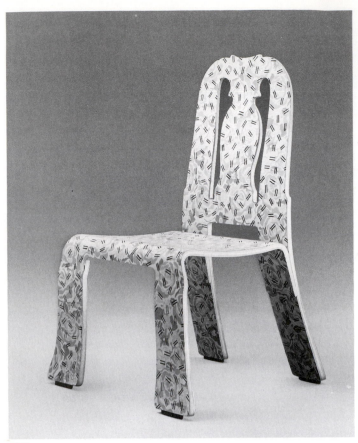

254

Whatever may be said of quality reproductions, bad reproductions, often called imitations, which are far more common, are an insult to any sensitive observer. Crude designs labeled "Colonial maple," television cabinets of baroque design reproduced in plastic, and the furniture of nonexistent "periods" such as "Mediterranean" are unacceptable for use in interiors of any genuine design quality.

Modern

Logically, this should mean anything new or recent, but it has come to refer to design that is new in concept, particularly the design of the twentieth century related to modern art and committed to simplicity, functional performance, and technology. More specifically, it identifies the stylistic directions (also called *International Style*) exemplified by the Bauhaus. Increasingly, we hear the terms *early modern* (1900 to the 1920s or 1930s) and *classic modern* (for certain famous designs that have lasted for many years) to distinguish them from truly recent designs.

Modern furniture (that is, new in concept) has come to be widely used in commercial, institutional, and office interiors. Its residential design use in the United States is still limited to

254. Although he disavows the term, the designs of Robert Venturi are widely viewed as Post-modernist expressions. This molded-plywood chair is cut out so as to suggest a traditional style—it is called the Queen Anne chair—and is shown here with a surface decorative pattern called Grandmother. 37⅜ × 25½ × 23¼". (Photograph courtesy Knoll International)

professionals in the design fields and a small public with an aesthetic and intellectual interest in modern art and architecture. After decades of being exposed to it, however, the general public has become increasingly accepting of modern design, as evidenced by the products illustrated in consumer magazines and sold in retail furniture stores.

Contemporary

This simply means "of or in the style of the present or recent times." It should be an umbrella term to refer to whatever is being made now, but it is generally used to refer to designs that, on the one hand, do not reproduce antiques, and on the other, do not belong to the category known as *modern*. In the furniture trade, it usually means a current design with no strong stylistic character, furniture that can blend in with almost anything else. The term *transitional,* also sometimes used, is misleading since such designs are not truly between any two identifiable stylistic directions.

Post-modern

As a term and a design concept, Post-modern is still so new that its exact meaning has yet to be defined. It refers to whatever design trends follow the modern style discussed above, but so far the new directions explored by designers have led to separate paths rather than a coherent center. More specifically, Post-modern refers to the recent design trend that rejects the strictly functional and logical criteria of the modern movement in order to introduce elements of whimsy, variety, and, at times, absurdity. References to historical precedents in a contemporary vocabulary or context are not uncommon.

Craft and Art Furniture

Recent years have seen an upsurge in interest in handcrafted furniture designed and made by craftsmen, either by hand or with limited shop equipment (fig. 253). Their furniture displays a wide range of construction and design. Of course, even the finest craft skills do not assure good design skills. At its best, craft furniture is both useful and interesting, and may take on some of the qualities of an individual work of art as well.

This latter quality comes to the fore when artists choose to make objects of furniture vehicles for artistic creativity (figs. 257–60). The level of usefulness varies, as does the quality of the artistic expression involved. While furniture as art is generally costly and often individualistic to the point of eccentricity, it opens up a relatively new and adventurous channel of artistic expression for the interior.

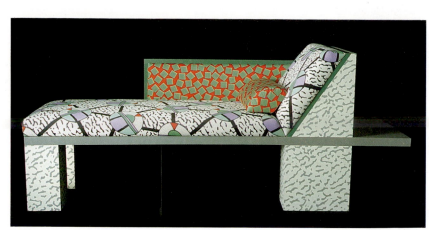

255

256

257

255. Nathalie du Pasquier's Royal couch of 1983 is a classic example of the Memphis orientation. The surfaces are of plastic laminate in various patterns; the cotton fabric that covers the cushion and armrest is a design by George J. Sowden. 37 × 78 × 29¼". (Photograph courtesy Memphis/Milano)

256. A dressing table designed by Michael Graves in 1981 for Memphis evidences the relationship between Postmodernism and the Memphis style. Its fantastic and curious forms suggest the directions taken by Post-modern architects—Graves among them—in buildings that exchange restraint and logic for a freer, more expressive style. The Memphis aesthetic closely parallels the experimentalism and whimsy of Postmodernism. (Photograph: Scott Hyde, courtesy Michael Graves)

257. Furniture is sometimes customdesigned for a specific space by artists or sculptors whose interest in expressive form transcends the merely utilitarian. These tables and chairs, designed by artist and designer Lisa Lombardi, are fantastic elaborations of vegetable motifs. The interior in Santa Monica, California, was designed by Brian A. Murphy. (Photograph: © 1986 Tim Street-Porter)

259

258

260

258–60. Furniture-as-art often takes fantastic forms that are only structurally related to a piece's functional purpose. Figs. 258 and 260, although of different design, share an extraordinary visual power. They were both designed by Milanese designer Piero Fornasetti. Fig. 259, a spidery side chair of scrap metal, is by English designer Tom Dixon. (Photographs: Eric Himmel, courtesy Paul Smith, New York)

TABLE 7. FURNITURE SELECTION CHECKLIST

Furniture selection is based on the familiar design criteria of *function, structure and materials,* and *aesthetics* (or appearance). The intelligent evaluation of available products will normally be based on the following issues:

Function

WHAT IS THE BASIC PURPOSE OF THE UNIT?

Is it a table, desk, chair, sofa, bed, storage unit?

WHAT IS THE UNIT'S SPECIFIC FUNCTION?

Is it a chair for dining, desk use, or lounging? How many people are to be seated on a sofa? How many people, minimum and maximum, are to sit at a table? Is a desk for office or home use, and what must it accommodate and store? What objects will be stored in cabinets, or on shelves, and how much are the storage units expected to hold?

WHAT SIZE IS REQUIRED?

This is determined partly by function and partly by available space. What are the clearance dimensions for delivery? (Will it fit through the door to the building, elevator, house, apartment?)

Structure and Materials

WHAT LEVEL OF STRENGTH DOES THE INTENDED USE REQUIRE?

Are materials strong enough and the size sufficient to preclude weakness or breakage? How strong are the joints? Tests include:

Loading for intended use. Do shelves sag, do sofas or beds wobble? Extraordinary stress-resistance. Test for extremes of use, such as moving, dropping, and tipping back a chair.

WHAT IS THE QUALITY OF MATERIALS?

What is the thickness of plywood and solid wood? the surface material and finish? the gauge (thickness) of metal parts? Inspect edges, backs, undersurfaces. Check available written specifications for the quality of hidden elements (as in upholstery).

WHAT IS THE FINISH?

Check the appearance and durability of exposed surfaces. Durability may require testing or checking specifications. Check the scratch- and impact-resistance of surfaces, the rust- and corrosion-resistance of metals, the longevity of plastics exposed to sunlight and air pollutants. Abrasion-resistance and ease of cleaning are important characteristics of cover fabrics and other materials (such as leather and plastics).

IS THE UNIT DURABLE?

Overall, this factor is a product of the factors discussed above. For demanding situations (such as use in public spaces and institutions), *testing to failure* (until the product breaks or falls apart) is the best measure of life expectancy. In more general use, the criteria listed above in combination with the reputation of a particular product and its manufacturer provide an adequate standard. Guarantees and warranties may be something of a guide, although failure most often occurs after years of use. Appropriate standards for durability must also be measured against cost (see below).

Design

ARE THE STYLE AND CHARACTER APPROPRIATE BOTH TO THE UNIT'S INTENDED USE AND TO THE OVERALL DESIGN APPROACH DEVELOPED FOR THE SPACE IN QUESTION?

Period styles have obvious characteristics, such as ostentation, rich elaboration, formality, rustic simplicity, even crudity, which must blend in with or work well with their surroundings. Contemporary design must be evaluated in terms of scale, proportion, and other, more subjective qualities. Even in modern design, a particular approach may seem more or less conservative, avant-garde, playful, or dignified.

DOES THE UNIT POSSESS AESTHETIC MERIT?

This is the most problematic of criteria, since individual values vary so widely. Still, classics that have wide acceptance can be identified. The reputations of individual designers and manufacturers and the opinions of critics and museum curators offer some basis for evaluation more objective than personal opinion alone.

Cost

WHAT IS ITS COST IN RELATION TO THE AVAILABLE BUDGET?

Few projects are totally free of budget limitations. Decisions on how to apportion budgets can be difficult, but they must be made. Inexpensive items of fine quality and excellent design might be used in some locations to make budget available for some selected items of higher cost.

WHAT IS ITS LIFETIME COST?

First cost is only one aspect of a unit's true cost. Lifetime cost includes first cost *plus* the cost of maintenance, energy consumed, cost of disposal, and cost of replacement. These factors must be considered in arriving at realistic comparisons between products at varied price levels. Costly items with a long life expectancy may be more economical than inexpensive products that will need early replacement. Still, available funds will limit the range of products that can be considered.

CHAPTER SEVEN
TEXTILES

Among the many materials that contribute to the design of a complete interior, textile fabrics have a particularly important role. They introduce a sense of softness, curvature, and flexibility into a space, making a hard- or bare-looking room seem soft, comfortable, and humane. With their vast range of colors, textures, and qualities, they offer unlimited design possibilities.

Fabrics most often appear in interiors as upholstery cover materials for chairs, sofas, cushions, as bed and table covers, and in window treatment, usually called by the traditional term *drapery*. Lesser uses include curtains in locations other than windows (at door openings, for example) and as wall-covering material. Textiles for interior use are usually divided into two basic groups, upholstery and drapery, with some belonging to both. These are identified in Table 8 on pages 192–193. (Carpets and rugs, although technically textiles, have been grouped in Chapter 5 with other floor-covering materials.)

In comparison with the basic construction materials (stone, brick, wood, or plaster) that are likely to line a raw space, textiles are less lasting. While this may appear to be a disadvantage, it turns out to be a major reason for textiles' significance to the interior. Since, like paint, they require periodic renewal and are easy to change, they regularly provide an opportunity to do over a space with new color and texture. Indeed, the phrase "to redecorate" implies new paint and new fabrics as the primary means of renewal.

It is probably because of this sense of textiles' impermanence that designers feel free to be somewhat adventurous in their choice of fabric colors, textures, and patterns. This in turn has encouraged designers and manufacturers of textiles to offer a tremendous variety. Fabric design has a close relationship to the world of fashion and shares its constant search for newness and change. Some fabrics, particularly prints and other patterned fabrics, enjoy a brief popularity and then disappear because they come to look dated and out of style. Textile lines reflect changing tastes in terms of color and weave as well. On the other hand, certain basic fabrics will always be available, and any color can be produced on special order, even if color lines change. Fabric selections should always be made after a fresh review of what is currently available.

SELECTING TEXTILES

The selection of textiles often ranks with the choice of furniture, floor coverings, and paint colors as a key element in the designer's contribution to a design project. Textile selection may seem deceptively simple—a matter of casually choosing some attractive colors and textures—but the subject is actually complex and merits more careful attention. For this reason, textiles occupy a full chapter in this book, while other materials are dealt with in the context of their use or together in Chapter 5.

Color

It is most practical to make fabric selections while the color scheme is being developed. This can be approached in two ways. One way is to select approximate colors for the fabric, using colored papers or any other color medium to represent the desired fabric color, while leaving the selection of the actual material to a later time (when visiting various showrooms, for example). However, this creates an extra step when the process can be dealt with all at once. (It is also often difficult to locate a close match for a sample in a particular kind of fabric.) The other approach, to make a final fabric selection when developing a color scheme, saves the extra step but presents other difficulties. It requires having on hand a library of samples large enough to include almost anything that might be desired. Large design firms usually maintain large files of samples from the manufacturers they most favor, but the individual designer will probably have a much more limited selection on hand.

Dealing with this problem requires building up a sample file large enough to contain at least a few examples of almost anything that may be needed. This involves visiting the showrooms of textile manufacturers in major cities to collect samples. A list of the best-known sources for decorator fabrics can be compiled from advertisements in design magazines. Many furniture manufacturers are also textile distributors, not only providing fabrics for their own products but for general use as well, often offering drapery in addition to upholstery fabrics. Some will provide complete sample swatch sets on request or at a small charge.

The designer can usually tell quickly from a showroom visit if it is a source of strong interest. After making a selection of fabrics according to color and other qualities, the designer may request sample swatches, which can be put on file for reference when a scheme is being planned. Swatches, usually small (three or four inches square), are attached to a card identifying the manufacturer and pattern number and giving other data such as width, fiber content, and price (fig. 263). While small samples give a poor indication of the appearance of large-scale patterns and prints, and may even misrepresent basic colors and textures, the swatch remains a primary selection tool because of its convenience, availability, and low cost. Manufacturers will loan out samples of a square yard, called a *memo square*, of prints and larger patterns. If the scale of the project or the fabric's intended use warrants it, memo squares can be purchased.

261. Many historic interiors, particularly residential interiors, use textiles extensively, thereby generating a sense of both comfort and opulence. In the English great house of Chatsworth in Derbyshire (William Talman, architect, 1687–96), Carr of York decorated this Blue Drawing Room in the 1770s with brocade-covered walls. The rug and upholstery fabrics are more modern, but perpetuate the original spirit of the room. The large painting is Sargent's portrait of the Acheson Sisters. (Photograph: © James Pipkin)

TABLE 8. TEXTILES IN GENERAL USE IN INTERIORS

FABRIC NAME	FIBER(S)	WEIGHT	WEAVE OR CONSTRUCTION	DESCRIPTIVE NOTES	USES
Batik				Term refers to use of resist-dyeing technique to generate color patterns.	D, (U)
Batiste	C, Syn.	T	Plain	Lightweight; usually light colors, often printed.	C, D
Broadcloth	C, S, W, Syn.	M	Plain or twill	Used for tablecloths, bedspreads, drapery.	D
Brocade	S, Syn.	M	Jacquard	Usually patterned with raised relief design.	U
Burlap	Jute, hemp	L	Plain	Coarse utility fabric. Occasionally used as drapery. Natural tan color, can be dyed.	(D)
Calico	C	L	Plain	Inexpensive, usually printed.	C
Canvas	C, L	M	Plain	Strong, utilitarian fabric. Suitable to outdoor uses, awnings, upholstery.	U
Casement cloth	Various	T	Plain, twill, or leno	Many fibers and weaves; for use as lightweight curtain material.	C
Chambray	C, L	L	Plain	Smooth surface with frosty appearance in various colors.	D
Cheesecloth	C	S	Plain	Very thin utility fabric sometimes used for curtains.	C
Chintz	C	L	Plain	Usually printed and with glazed (glossy) surface.	C, D, (U)
Corduroy	C, Syn.	H	Pile	Pile in ridged textures of wales or ribs.	U
Crash	Various	M	Plain	Rough texture developed from irregular yarns.	D
Cretonne	C	M	Plain or twill	Usually printed in strong patterns. Not glazed.	D, U
Damask	C, S	M	Combination	Jacquard patterns combining two weaves.	U
Denim	C	M	Twill	Inexpensive cotton utility fabric. May have small woven pattern.	U
Dimity	C	L	Plain	Lightweight cotton with a raised warp, giving it a striped effect.	C, D
Drill	C	M	Twill	Sturdy cotton with diagonal twill weave. Normal color gray, but is also dyed.	U
Duck	C	M	Plain	Sturdy utility cotton.	U
Felt	W, Syn.	M–H	Nonwoven	Made by pressing fibers together instead of weaving. Used for table and wall coverings. Cut edges require no hemming. Bright colors available.	(D)*
Fiberglass	Glass	T–M	Various	Glass fibers made into yarn and woven in various weights. Fireproof. Poor abrasion-resistance.	C, D
Gingham	C, Syn.	L	Plain	Woven from dyed yarns, often in stripes, checks, and plaids. Sturdy; launders well.	D, U
Grass cloth	Jute, hemp, etc.	M	Plain	Woven from grass or similar fibers. Often on paper or plastic backing.	W
Homespun	C, W	L–M	Plain	Coarse yarns in textured weave suggesting hand weaving.	D, U
Hopsacking	C, Syn.	M	Plain	Heavy, coarse, open weave. Durable and economical.	U
Jaspé cloth	Various	L–M	Plain	Sturdy fabric with woven textural striped effect in muted colors.	U
Jersey	W, Syn.	M	Knitted	Knitted with resulting elastic, stretch quality.	(U)
Leather	Animal hide	H	Nontextile	Animal hide finished (and often dyed) for use as upholstery cover, table top surface, and so on.	U
Linen	L	L–M	Plain	Any fabric woven of linen (flax) fiber. Typically smooth, hard surface. Commonly used for tablecloths.	(D), (U)
Marquisette	C, S, Syn.	S	Leno	Light, sheer, or open weave. Sometimes printed or dyed in light colors.	C, D
Matelassé	C	H	Jacquard	Double cloth with quilted or puckered surface patterning.	D, U
Mohair	Goat hair	M	Twill or pile	Goat hair (often mixed with cotton or wool). Sturdy and durable. May have a woven pattern.	U
Moire	S, Syn.	L	Plain	Watered textural effect achieved by special finishing.	D
Monk's cloth	C, jute, hemp + C	M	Plain or basket	Coarse and heavy. Usually used in its natural gray color.	(D), (U)
Muslin	C	T	Plain	Lightweight utility cloth. Economical, often used as under layer for upholstery cover.	C

FABRIC NAME	FIBER(S)	WEIGHT	WEAVE OR CONSTRUCTION	DESCRIPTIVE NOTES	USES
Needlepoint	W over backing	H	Hand embroidery or Jacquard	Hand embroidery over canvas or net. Also simulated with Jacquard weave.	U
Net	Rayon or other	S	Plain	Very open (lace) construction. Provides see-through drapery appearance. Many patterns.	C, D
Organdy	C	S	Plain	Crisp cotton sheer. Varied colors, also prints. Primary use in curtains and drapery.	C, D
Osnaburg	C	T	Plain	Strong and durable coarse cotton weave. Often used in its natural color but also dyed or printed.	C, D, (U)
Oxford cloth	C	M	Plain, basket, or twill	Often in stripes or checks. A popular shirt and dress material, also usable for curtains.	C, D
Plastic sheet and film	Plastic	H	Nonwoven	Vinyl or PVC, unbacked or cloth-backed for use as wall covering or as upholstery cover (simulating leather).	U, W
Plush	W (mohair), Syn.	H	Pile	Cut pile like velvet but with a deeper pile.	U
Pongee	S	T	Plain	Wild silk with irregular texture. Also imitated in cotton and synthetics. Subject to shrinkage.	C, D
Poplin	C	L	Plain	Lightweight fabric with small-scale ribbing.	C, D
Sailcloth	C	M	Plain	Sturdy utility fabric. Suitable to outdoor use.	U, (D)
Sateen	C	L	Satin	Sturdy, glossy surface, similar to satin. Often used as lining for drapery.	D, U
Satin	S, Syn.	L	Satin	Smooth, glossy, rich silk. Often used for luxury draperies.	D, (U)
Seersucker	C, Syn.	L	Plain	Light material with a characteristic ribbed surface in various widths of ribbing. Primarily used in apparel.	
Serge	W	M	Twill	Tough, closely woven material primarily used for suiting.	(U)
Shantung	S, Syn.	L	Plain	A heavy grade of pongee. Also imitated in other fibers.	D
Swiss muslin (dotted)	C	S	Plain	Fine sheer, usually in dotted pattern known as *dotted swiss*.	C, (D)
Taffeta	S, W, C, Syn.	L–M	Plain	Silky, papery smooth surface, usually with a fine ribbing.	C, D, (U)
Tapestry	W, C, L	H	Jacquard or hand	Hand-woven, usually pictorial, wall hanging or modern Jacquard weave in imitation of handmade tapestry. Usually strongly patterned.	U, (D), (W)
Terry cloth	C, L	M	Pile	Uncut loop pile surface. Much used for toweling, occasionally for bedspreads or drapery.	(D)
Ticking	C, L	M	Twill or satin	Usually light with characteristic stripe. Widely used as mattress covering.	(U)
Tweed	W and various	H	Plain, twill, or herringbone	Usually a 2-up and 2-down twill in solid color, mixtures, stripes, and checks. Much used for suiting.	U
Velour	Various	H	Velvet pile	Durable cut-pile fabric.	U
Velvet	Various	H	Velvet pile	Cut or uncut loop pile. Rich and luxurious appearance, particularly in silk. Shows wear readily.	U, (D)
Velveteen	C, Syn.	H	Velvet pile	Cotton or synthetic fibers in velvet-type pile weave. Stronger and more durable than actual velvet, but less luxurious in appearance.	U, (D)
Voile	C, S, W, Syn.	S	Plain	Open, sheer drapery material. Varied colors and patterns.	C, D

SYMBOLS
Weight:
S = sheer, very thin, T = sheer, thin, L = light, M = medium, H = heavy.

Fiber:
C = cotton, L = linen (flax), S = silk, Syn. = synthetics; W = wool.

Use:
C = curtains, D = drapery, U = upholstery, W = wall covering. Enclosure in parentheses indicates secondary (unusual or rare) use.

*Felt is used in special applications such as drawer linings and, occasionally, for wall covering.

262

263

262. *Small swatches of fabric and larger pieces—called memo squares—are here spread out, along with samples of woods, carpet, marble, tiles, and paint colors. Decorators work with similar selections drawn from large files, in order to develop total, coordinated interiors. (Photograph: George Hein)*

263. *A panoply of swatches shows the color ways, or ranges of color, available in various weaves and fibers. Here, a portion of the color way includes, from left to right, cotton velvet, silk, linen, and cotton. Small samples are ideal for filing; larger samples are often requested when decorators make their final selections of the textiles that will be part of the overall color scheme. (Photograph: George Hein)*

264

Since color is usually the starting point in selection, most designers file samples by color, although they can also be filed under such categories as manufacturer, fiber, or appropriate use. Drapery and upholstery textiles are often filed along with other upholstery cover materials (such as leathers and simulated leathers) and sometimes with other decorative materials such as plastic wall coverings, window shade and blind materials, and wallpapers. (Because of their greater bulk, carpets and rugs are usually filed separately.) It is often convenient to file favorite fabrics in duplicate so that a file record will remain when a sample is removed for use in planning a color scheme. For a complete color scheme, fabric swatches are grouped with other material samples (fig. 262).

It often turns out that an ideal choice is not on file. When this happens, something close to it can be chosen and marked as a stand-in until another visit to showrooms can be made. In any case, it is a good idea to make frequent showroom visits. They enable the designer to keep up with new patterns as they are introduced and to discuss needs or questions about particular fabrics with the sales staff. Such visits present no problems to residents of major cities. Designers working in small towns or cities routinely plan a visit to a major market center at least

265

264. A group of richly decorative cotton fabrics in designs of traditional character is displayed here. (Photograph courtesy Fortuny Fabrics)

265. These contemporary fabrics are printed with white on a natural (beige-tan) linen/cotton blend. The strictly geometric patterns are typically modern; the flower designs introduce a touch of nostalgia. (Photograph courtesy Hinson & Company)

once a year. Otherwise, less centrally located professionals avail themselves of the services of dealers and traveling representatives who carry several manufacturers' products.

Other Factors

In selecting a fabric, color is only one significant element among many, including durability, resistance to dirt, textural qualities, and, of course, price. A checklist of criteria for fabric selection will include the following items, not necessarily in order of importance:

> *Suitability of weight, weave, and texture to intended use*
> *Color (or colors)*
> *Durability, including the basic life of the fiber; resistance to wear, dirt, and spotting; ease of cleaning; and, where applicable, ease of repair*
> *Possibility of shrinking or stretching*
> *Ease of working (sewing) into form for intended use*
> *Color-fading characteristics*
> *Fire-resistance*
> *Price*

The importance of these issues will vary with the intended use. Resistance to fading is vital for curtains at a sunny window, fire-resistance in offices and public places such as restaurants, theaters, or airplane interiors. Price is a more complex issue than it may seem. The initial cost of fabric yardage tells nothing about the fabric's lifetime cost, which takes into account its durability, cleaning costs, and replacement cost. (This last becomes important with frequent redecoration.) The cost of drapery and upholstery includes the work of making up curtains or covers plus the cost of additional materials such as linings and hardware. (These costs generally do not depend on the type of fabric chosen.) A better fabric at a higher price may be more economical, in the long run, than a cheap material with a short life. However, if the user plans to change fabric frequently, this may not apply. Such intangibles as user satisfaction and aesthetic qualities are important criteria that cannot be priced.

Many fabrics offered for institutional, office, and commercial use have been tested for such things as wear and fire-resistance, and this data can help the designer to select wisely.* However, no such data exist for many other fabrics. In this case, the designer must rely on experience and observation of fabrics in use and on the advice of manufacturers' sales staff. This may, of course, be biased, but reputable suppliers of textiles will

---

*Certified test results for local, county, and state fire codes are routinely supplied by textile suppliers. These tests have been conducted in accordance with specific code requirements by independent certified laboratories.

usually try to give good information about suitability for a given use. They have a stake in satisfying specifiers (the people who select or order fabric) and end-users (clients or actual users) and will try to prevent such problems as a fragile fabric being specified for a heavy-duty use; unexpected fading or shrinkage; or selection of a fabric that does not clean well.

FABRIC TYPES AND CONSTRUCTIONS

Knowledge of fabric materials and construction is an important aid in making good fabric choices. This subject becomes constantly more complex as new fibers and manufacturing techniques are developed. The basic information provided here can serve as a point of departure for developing a knowledge of textile technology.

The common names of fabrics—for example, wool, satin, Dacron—are more confusing than helpful since they refer variously to fiber (wool), construction or weave (satin), or even, in some cases, trade names (Dacron). In order to look at fabrics in a systematic way, any given example is best considered in terms of:

> *Fiber or fibers*
> *Yarn or yarns*
> *Construction (weave or other type)*
> *Finish*
> *Dye or print*
> *Special characteristics (if any)*

The following summary is a condensed (and by no means complete) listing of the most frequently encountered possibilities within each of these characteristics.

Fiber

Fiber refers to the basic material from which the cloth is made. It often gives its name to the fabric or to a whole range of fabrics made from that particular fiber. The list of natural fibers in traditional use is fairly short, but modern invention has added many man-made fibers, while the possibilities of combining fibers have become limitless. The most widely used fibers can be grouped into a few categories (see Table 9 on page 198).

Yarn

Yarn is the term for the long, continuous strands or threads made from fiber to prepare it for construction into fabric by such common techniques as weaving or knitting. The yarns themselves can be of various constructions (fig. 266); those most frequently encountered include:

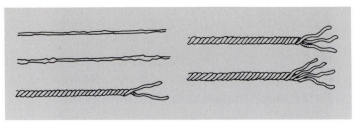

266

MONOFILAMENT. This means a single strand of material, all of the same substance. The most familiar monofilament yarns are those extruded from a plastic (like the much-used fishing lines) and those made by slitting flat plastic sheet. Horsehair can be considered a natural monofilament yarn.

MULTIFILAMENTS. Several monofilament yarns twisted or plied together make a single multifilament yarn. Multifilaments may be used alone or may be spun with other synthetic or natural fibers.

SPUN YARNS. Using a traditional technique, a continuous strand is made from the short natural fibers such as cotton and wool. Hand spinning is the ancient way of making such yarns. Spinning machines that took over this function were among the first important inventions of the Industrial Revolution. Synthetic multifilaments cut into short lengths have been blended with natural fibers in an attempt to combine the best qualities of both fiber types.

TWISTED YARN. Spun yarn may be twisted, which increases the strength of the yarn. The tightness of the twist influences the fabric's texture and appearance.

PLIED YARNS. Several yarn strands wound together increase thickness and strength and produce varied textures and appearance. Multiple strands may be plied together. Using strands of more than one color creates special visual effects.

SLUB YARN. Irregular in diameter, slub yarn may be produced either by spinning yarns that have not been combed or by mechanically introducing deliberate irregularities. It gives the fabric a special texture.

STRETCH YARNS. These return to their original length after stretching. They may be constructed with the fiber wrapped around a stretchable core (of latex or similar material) or may be the result of new processes in which synthetic fibers are crimped, giving them a springy, coil form. Fabrics made from stretch yarns, used widely in apparel, are useful in certain upholstery applications.

Construction

Construction refers to the way in which fiber is made into a cloth or textile. The most familiar constructions use yarn as a basic element, but constructions that do not require fiber in yarn form also exist. A list of the most used fabric constructions follows.

FELT. Fibers, usually wool, that have not been made into yarn can be worked together through pressure, heat, chemical reaction, or other means to produce a homogeneous sheet of tangled-together fiber strands called batting. Some synthetic fibers can be felted with the aid of an adhesive.

FILMS. Synthetic materials such as the plastics polyester and PVC can be made into a continuous sheet, familiar in such uses as shower curtains. Films may be laminated over woven fabric to produce plastic sheeting that can be cut and sewn with ease. Plastic wall-covering materials and imitation leathers are often of this construction.

WOVEN FABRICS. The dominant type of textile, these come in a variety of constructions (fig. 270). Most are of the sort called *two-element* weaves, constructed with the familiar technique of the over-and-under interlacing of a lengthwise *warp* and the horizontal *weft*, or *filling.* The strands are normally at right angles, with construction taking place on the weaver's equipment, a loom. The loom holds the warp strands in place and provides a way of lifting some (often alternate) warp strands to open a *shed,* or space, through which the weft strands can be passed, one strand at a time. In hand weaving, the weaver passes the weft strands through the shed, while power looms do this mechanically. Variations in the

267

266. From upper left, the following yarn constructions are pictured: monofilament, one-ply, two-ply, three-ply (upper right), and multiple, or cable, ply.

267. A complex fabric woven in Ireland, Academia by Jack Lenor Larsen, is suitable for both upholstery and drapery. The recessed squares are of platinum-colored metallic yarn with a surround of natural-color worsted in a double-twill weave. The fabric can be coordinated with a related design in a Wilton-weave carpet. (Photograph courtesy Jack Lenor Larsen, Inc.)

Natural Fibers

IN WIDE USE

WOOL. This is sheared from sheep and processed to various levels of refinement. It comes in only a few natural colors, although it can be dyed. Its performance characteristics are generally excellent.

MOHAIR. This is a goat's hair usually considered a wool.

COTTON. A plant fiber. Under many names, cottons are widely used utility and decorative fabrics.

SILK. Unwound from the cocoon of the silkworm moth, this luxury fiber, while somewhat costly and fragile, is valued for its unique appearance.

LINEN. A plant fiber produced from flax, it provides strong yarns with a characteristic smooth appearance.

IN LIMITED USE

JUTE. A plant fiber of coarse and rough character. Burlap is the most useful product.

HORSEHAIR. A strong, smooth cloth is made from this fiber. It has had significant use as an upholstery cover in traditional design.

CASHMERE. A delicate wool generally too costly and fragile for interior use.

CAMEL'S HAIR. Another fine wool too costly for extensive interior use.

GRASS AND PALM FIBERS. Woven grass cloths are not uncommon as wall-covering materials.

Artificial (Man-made) Fibers

FROM NATURAL (CELLULOSE) POLYMER

ACETATE. A common economy substitute for various natural fibers, acetate is versatile and inexpensive.

RAYON. Viscose rayon is the type in widest use. One of the most-used economy substitutes for natural fibers, rayon can be processed to resemble many fibers. It has recently been largely displaced in quality fabrics by other synthetics.

FROM SYNTHETIC POLYMERS

ACRYLICS. Wool-like fibers. Modacrylics are so named because they have been chemically modified to offer good flame-resistance. Trade names include (unmodified) Acrilan, Orlon, Verel, Sef, Zefran, and Dynel (which also comes modified).

OLEFIN. This includes the varieties polyethylene and polypropylene. A very light fiber, Olefin particularly resembles wool. Herculon is a trade name.

POLYESTERS. A light fiber, polyester is often blended with natural fibers. Dacron, Fortrel, and Kodel are trade names.

POLYAMIDE (NYLON). One of the first and most useful synthetics, nylon has high strength and good elasticity. Many types are now available. It is frequently used in blends. Antron and Cordura are familiar trade names.

PVC (POLYVINYL CHLORIDE). Familiar under the trade name Saran, it is made into both a yarn and a sheet. Yarns are also made by slitting film. A heat-sensitive fiber, it is suitable for heat-sealing.

POLYURETHANE. A highly elastic fiber, this is used for stretch fabrics such as Spandex.

Fiber Blends

Two or more fibers are combined in one yarn in order to maximize the strengths and minimize the weaknesses of its component fibers. For example, natural and artificial fibers may be combined to retain the texture and appearance of the natural yarn while gaining the wrinkle- and dirt-resistance and durability of the synthetic.

Dacron and cotton, wool and nylon are useful blends. The different fibers may be spun together into a single yarn or several separate and different yarns may be woven together. More than two fibers may be combined in complex blends, as for example, a blended yarn woven together with a yarn of a third fiber.

Mineral Fibers

These are technically natural but of nonorganic origins.

ASBESTOS. Formerly valued for its fire-resistance, it has largely dropped out of use because it presents health hazards.

METALS. In the form of thin strands, copper, gold, silver, and stainless steel can be used as a fiber, usually in combination with other fibers. Lurex is a trade name for plastic-coated metal strands. Imitation metallics are made by coating a plastic with a metallic finish.

GLASS. Fiberglas (trade name), or fiberglass, is a thin spun strand of glass. It is resistant to fire and moisture but with flexing the fibers tend to break and shed.

268. Fabric-covered walls, an Oriental rug, and coordinated material for upholstery and drapery create a soft and hospitable effect in this sitting room in a Pennsylvania house, typical of traditional interiors at their best. Irvine & Fleming, Inc., designer. (Photograph courtesy Irvine & Fleming, Inc.)

269. Handmade quilts such as this are among the finest products of American vernacular craft. Scraps of fabric are cut, assembled, and quilted, following one of a myriad of time-honored patterns; the result is both unique and traditional. The quilt here covers a four-poster bed of c. 1850, in a 1949 cottage in Castroville, Texas. (Photograph: © 1985 Michael Skott)

268

269

TABLE 10. TEXTILES

Textile Fibers

FIBER		TRADE NAMES	CHARACTERISTICS	COMMON USES
NATURAL: Plant Origins	*Cotton*		Versatile, widely used, economical. Soils easily. Special treatments and fiber blends provide improved service characteristics.	C, D, U, R, L, S
	Linen (flax)		Smooth texture with slight gloss. Soils and wrinkles easily. Insect-resistant. Washes well. *Sanforizing* treatment will limit shrinkage.	C, D, U, R, L
Animal Origins	*Silk*		Unique texture and surface gloss. Luxurious appearance. Damaged by exposure to sunlight. Good resistance to soiling.	D, U, R
	Wool Also: Mohair Camel's hair		Versatile, high-quality fiber. Good soil- and spot-resistance. Cleans well. Subject to moth damage. Special treatments and blends with synthetics improve service characteristics.	D, U, R, B, S
Mineral Origins	*Glass*	Fiberglass PPG Fiberglass	Strands of glass flexible enough to be spun into yarn and woven. Noninflammable. Poor resistance to abrasion. Troublesome to sew.	C, D
	Metals	Lurex Metlon	Stainless steel, aluminum, silver, and gold in thin strands or coated on or with plastic to provide a decorative accent. Conductive metal strands may be woven into rugs to eliminate static buildup.	D, R
SYNTHETIC:	*Acetate*	Acele Avisco Celanese Chromspun Estron	Economical. Poor resistance to sunlight. Fair soil-resistance.	C, D, U, R, S
	Acrylic	Acrilan Creslan Orlon Zefran	Wool-like qualities. Washes and dry-cleans well.	C, U, R, B
	Modacrylic	Dynel Verel	Similar to acrylics but better stain-resistance. Texture suited to synthetic furs and some rugs. Flame-retardant.	D, U, R, B
	Nylon	A.C.E. Antron Cordura	Silklike, elastic texture. Excellent in fiber blends. Poor resistance to sunlight. Widely used in carpeting. High tensile strength.	U, R, S
	Olefin (polypropylene)	Herculon Vectra	Wool-like texture, light in weight, good heat insulator. Soil-resistant.	U, R, B
	Polyester	Dacron Fortrel Trevira	Silk- or wool-like. Soils easily but washes well. Used in blends. Dacron used as synthetic substitute for down in cushions and upholstery. Dimensionally stable.	C, D, U, R
	Rayon	Avril Enka Zantrel	Economical substitute for cotton or silk. Texture may be glossy or dull; drapes well. Swells when wet. Modifying treatments that improve its appearance qualities are available. Widely used for low-cost apparel, curtains, table linens.	C, D, U, R, L, B, S
	Triacetate	Arnel	Drapes and washes well, retains press.	C, D
NONFIBROUS: (Textile alternatives)	*Leather*		Animal hides tanned and processed in natural and dyed colors. Textures include suede (matte) and patent leather (high gloss). Sold not by the yard but by the hide. May crack and decay unless carefully maintained.	U, (W)
	Plastic Vinyl PVC	Naugahyde Saran	Plastic sheet is usable as curtain (shower curtain) material and as wall covering. Fabric backing improves strength for use as wall covering and for upholstery as a leather substitute. Wide range of colors and surface textures.	C, U, W

USE LETTER CODE
C = curtains, D = drapery, U = upholstery, R = rugs, L = linens (table), B = blankets, S = bedspreads, W = wall covering, (W) = occasionally used as wall covering.

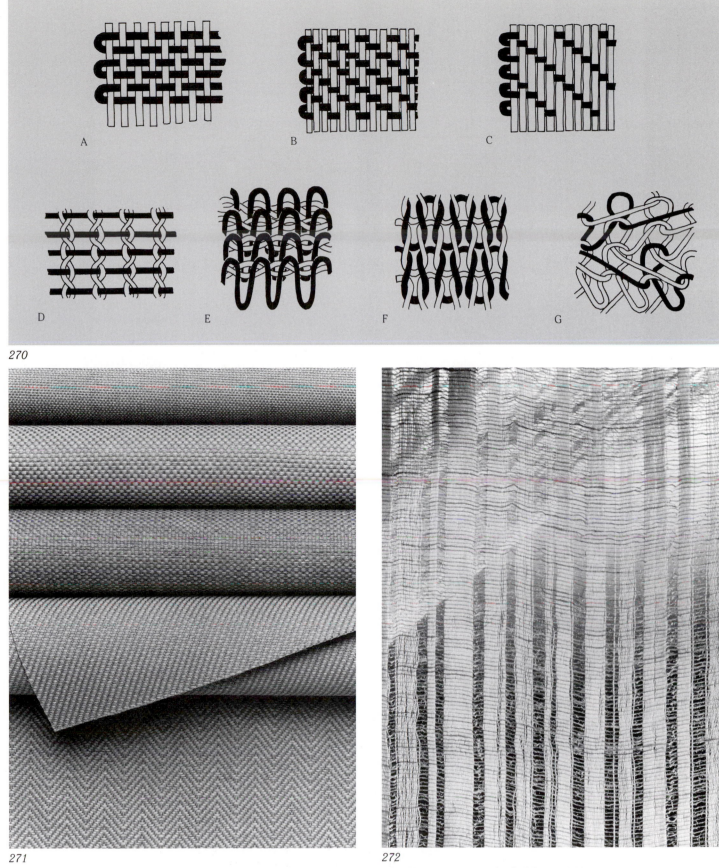

270

271

272

270. The following weaves are illustrated: plain (A), twill (B), satin (C), leno (D), and pile (E). The last two show weft-knit (F) and warp-knit (G) constructions.

271. This wall covering of polyolefin, a synthetic textile, has been made into a plasticized sheet for excellent stain-resistance and easy maintenance. The weaves illustrated are, from top to bottom, plain weave, two plain basket weaves, a twill, and a herringbone twill. The product is called Tek-Wall. (Photograph courtesy Maharam Fabrics)

272. The fine, open casement-weave fabric lends itself well to use as curtains or draperies. This one is made from Egyptian cotton, goat hair, and a gold guimpe. (Photograph courtesy Jack Lenor Larsen, Inc.)

arrangement of over-and-under strands and in yarn texture and color make possible a vast variety of patterns in woven fabrics.

Weaves may be of two, three, or four elements, each element being a particular kind of yarn. Two-element weaves are the most common, the warp and weft each forming one element. In *three-element weaves,* an additional yarn element is added to either the warp or weft. *Four-element weaves* may be constructed with three warps and one weft, but most are *double cloths* made up of two warps and two wefts. Within each of these weave types, the pattern of over-and-under interlacing of the elements can vary. The name of a cloth refers both to the number of elements and the pattern of weave. Weave patterns are described as *plain, twill,* or *satin.*

Plain weave is the simple and familiar over-and-under interlace. A one (warp thread)-to-one (weft thread) interlace produces gingham, taffeta, monk's cloth, and muslin. A two-and-two interlace (or *basket weave*) is characteristic of canvas and duck, while sailcloth employs a one-to-two relationship. All of these are two-element weaves. Adding a third element produces brocades and the *pile weaves,* which include the cut piles—plush, velour, and velvet—and the uncut piles—terry cloth and velveteen. In pile weaves, the third element projects above the plane of the basic weave, forming loops. These are the uncut piles. When the loops are cut, leaving individual standing strands of yarn, the typically velvety fuzzy surface of the cut piles results. Corduroy is also a three-element plain weave. Four-element construction in double plain weave produces *double cloths,* which are, in effect, two separate cloths woven at the same time and held together by strands that intermittently cross from one surface to the other. The two faces may have different patterns and colors. *Matelassé* combines single and double cloths with doubled areas stuffed to produce a quilted appearance.

Twill weave is produced by passing weft strands over one or more and under one or more warp strands in a shifting sequence to produce an appearance of diagonal pattern. Two-element twills include cheviot, denim, drill, gabardine, herringbone, and houndstooth. Three-element twill brocades and velvets and four-element double twill can be produced.

Satin weave describes a construction in which the warp is carried over four, five, or six weft strands and under one in a staggered pattern that avoids the diagonal patterning of twills. Satin, sateen, and damask are cloths of satin weave.

The term *Jacquard weaving* refers to a mechanical method of controlling a power loom in order to produce woven pattern by means of cards, similar to the punched computer card, that

274

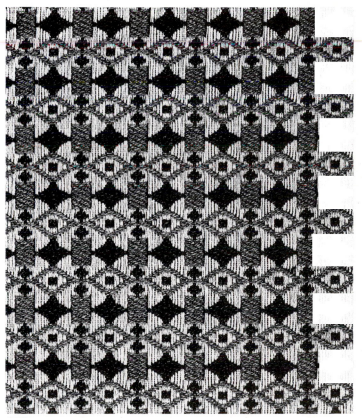

275

273. A blue Thai batik is used here as a tablecloth and for chair-cushion covers in the Paris home of the fashion designer Kenzo Takada. The textile; the French chairs and chandelier; the prints of Egyptian architectural subjects; and the plants, flowers, and ceramic accessories transform a simple room into a unique and personalized environment. (Photograph: © Jacques Dirand, courtesy House & Garden)

274, 275. The contributions of Vienna Secessionist Josef Hoffmann (see Chapter 16, page 439) to the Wiener Werkstätte craft shops retain a surprisingly contemporary look. Designed in 1908, but once again in production, these are his Zickzack (fig. 274) and Orlick (fig. 275) fabrics, both viscose, or rayon, and cotton weaves. (Photographs courtesy Bachausen, Vienna)

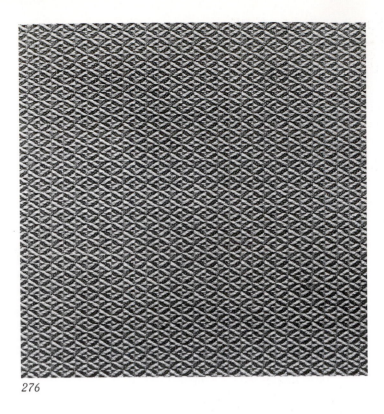

276

control the interlace of strands. Brocades, damasks, velvets, *tapestry weaves,* and matelassés are often Jacquard-woven.

OTHER CONSTRUCTIONS. Another fabric construction in current use is *knitting,* which is not a weave using warp and weft but a kind of knotting technique in which a single strand is looped or threaded together, in the way hobby knitters make scarves, sweaters, and laces, but now usually produced on complex modern knitting machines. Knits may be of either single- or two-element construction.

Malimo is a modern fabric construction in which many weft strands are laid across the warp and anchored down by a stitch of a third yarn element mechanically knitted into place. *Leno,* or *marquisette,* is a variation on plain weave in which pairs of warp threads cross between strands of weft to discourage the individual strands from slipping. The technique is often used to create open, casement, or drapery fabrics of good strength.

Finishing

The term refers to the various processes that follow basic fabric construction to prepare the textile for use. Many finishing processes, such as boiling, carbonizing with acid, shearing, calendering (pressing between rollers), and fulling (a controlled shrinking), are parts of production that need not concern the designer. Glazing polishes a cloth surface, familiar in the glazed cottons such as chintz. Various finishing processes promise resistance to wrinkling, soil-repellency, and mothproofing.

276. This fabric, Saranac, is a cotton Jacquard woven in Belgium. The pattern is based on fabrics seen in old photographs of an Adirondack vacation house and is part of a collection called, appropriately, Adirondack. (Photograph courtesy Gretchen Bellinger Inc)

Widely advertised treatments with trade names such as Scotchgard and Zepel aid in resisting soiling, while other treatments tend to repel water. In recent years, various finishing processes have been developed to aid fire-resistance through a chemical treatment that discourages the spread of flames. Antistatic treatments that reduce the buildup of electrical charge that occurs with some synthetic fabrics have also been developed. The availability of such finishing processes is generally clearly recorded and explained in manufacturers' specifications and advertising. Backcoating of upholstery fabrics with acrylic latex reduces seam slippage and generally improves abrasion resistance and dimensional stability.

Table 11. Textile Finishes (Processes and Trade Names)

Fireproofing Fiber or chemical treatment providing noninflammability.

Fire-retardant Chemical treatment to resist ignition and retard flame spread.

Flame-resistant Chemical treatment to resist ignition.

Glazing Surface-coating treatment to give high-gloss surface (often used for chintz or cretonne).

Mercerization Chemical process used only on cotton to improve strength and luster.

Mildew-resistant Chemical process to resist development of mildew, mold, and fungus growth.

Moth-repellent Chemical process to resist moth damage.

Preshrunk Treated to limit shrinkage when wetted.

Sanforized A particular preshrinking process limiting shrinkage to 1 percent or less.

Scotchgard The trade name for a chemical process to make textiles resistant to stains.

Soil-release finish Chemical process making textiles resistant to soiling.

Zelan The trade name for a process to make cotton and rayon water-repellent.

Zepel The trade name for a process to increase stain-resistance of textiles.

Color

DYEING. This is a primary means of introducing color in fabric, which otherwise has generally neutral gray or grayish tones. (In the trade, *greige goods* refers to undyed and/or unfinished fabrics.) Piece dyeing of woven textiles is a finishing process that produces a solid color. Dyeing yarns before weaving them permits color variation and pattern when variously colored yarn strands are woven together. Traditionally, dyes were made from various natural sources, most of which produce soft colors or colors that tend to be pleasant and harmonious even when more intense. Modern chemically

277

manufactured dyes produce a much wider range of colors and color brightness, but tend to be harsher and more garish. Since natural (undyed) yarns and natural dyestuffs rarely produce objectionable effects, they contribute greatly to the excellence of so many traditional woven materials.

Dyed materials are subject to fading from the effects of sun and other light and to fading and running in washing and cleaning. The *fastness,* or lasting quality, of dye color is a significant issue that needs to be tested or checked when making fabric selections. Some fading, running, and deterioration through wear is inevitable. These effects are least noticeable when colors are soft rather than bright, patterns are subtle rather than harsh, and textures are rough or coarse rather than smooth. Medium tones are less likely to show fading and wear than very light or very dark shades. However, if a fragile textile subject to rapid wear or fading also has a unique appearance, its use may be justified.

PRINTING. Printing onto a fabric is another widely used way to add color and pattern to textiles. Traditional techniques include *resist printing,* in which a wax or starch applied to the fabric blocks coloring when the cloth is dipped in dye. Afterward, the resist material is washed out. It may be reapplied and the cloth dipped again, and so on, to create complex patterns with several colors. This is the technique of *batik,* a well-known craft process (fig. 273). *Block printing,* in which individual wood blocks are coated with color and applied to the cloth, was once an important fabric-printing method in Europe. Its dependence on skilled handwork and the development of modern mechanized printing methods have rendered it generally obsolete in the industrialized world.

Roller printing involves mechanization similar to that of modern printing on paper. Rollers with the pattern for the fabric design embossed onto it are made, one for each color. As the cloth is passed under each roller in turn, the roller prints its color in the proper pattern onto it. The design will repeat on a dimension equal to the circumference of the roller. Fine detail and shading similar to that of imagery printed on paper are possible with roller printing. Although a modern mechanical technique, this method is also passing out of use in favor of screen printing.

In *screen printing,* as in silk-screen printing on paper, a screen of finely woven fabric is used for each color. The screen

277. This is a handsome printed chintz, a traditional fabric still in wide use, particularly for draperies, curtains, and upholstery. (Courtesy Brunschwig & Fils)

has blocked-out areas where the color is not to appear. Color is squeezed through the unblocked portions of the screen onto the fabric being printed. Printing may be done by hand, with fabric placed on a flat table; mechanically, onto flat fabric; or with a rotary technique, in which the screens are in roller form, the fabric rolling past printing cylinders for each color required. This is a fast and economical technique for quantity production.

Print design has developed in relation to changing historic styles. Today, many traditional designs are still available, in their original or adapted forms. Floral prints and prints incorporating many kinds of imagery abound. Modern print design includes more geometric and abstract patterns, along with new versions of more representational imagery.

A single design can be varied by altering the colors chosen, by adding or omitting certain color elements, and by changing scale through enlargement or reduction. A print design, usually limited in area, is extended to cover an unlimited yardage through *repeats* of the same design. These are generally planned so that the match line, where one repeat ends and the next begins, is unnoticeable. Print designs have come under copyright protection in order to cut down on the piracy, or imitation, of designs by manufacturers unwilling to pay the expenses and take the risks of commissioning new designs.

Special Characteristics

Various specialized forms of textiles also deserve note. These include *embroidery*, familiar as a handwork technique but now mechanically produced, and *quilting*, also best known as a craft technique for layering together several fabrics, possibly with a filling between layers (fig. 269). Mechanical techniques for quilting are in current use. *Tufted fabrics* are made on a cloth base with tufts of fiber needled through the base and anchored on the back with a coating.

In *coated fabrics*, a surface material is spread over a woven base, as in oilcloth. Coating is now used to make plastic upholstery materials, which often simulate leather or some other material. These offer good durability at low cost. Coated fabrics have also come into wide use as wall-covering materials more durable than paint or paper and available in a range of textures, in imitation of materials like grass cloth, wood, or even metals or of original design and texture.

The vast variety of materials and manufacturing techniques used in making textiles and the complex terminology used in describing fabrics can seem intimidating and confusing. By checking manufacturers' suggestions and directly assessing such qualities as texture, weight (density), and feel (or *hand,* as

this quality is called in the textile trades), the designer can find a range of fabrics appropriate to the intended use. These choices can be further narrowed down by balancing the fabric's aesthetic qualities of appearance, such as color, pattern, and texture, against its practical qualities, such as durability, strength, and colorfastness, and against its price.

While a detailed knowledge of fibers and weaves is not essential to interior design, the designer who wishes to become an intelligent specifier will learn as much as possible about textile technology. It can be an interesting exercise (which can become a useful habit) to take small cuttings of fabrics and pull out the woven strands to identify the fibers and yarns and determine the weave or other construction used. To make a systematic study, the cutting can be attached to an index card and full information entered on the card. For example:

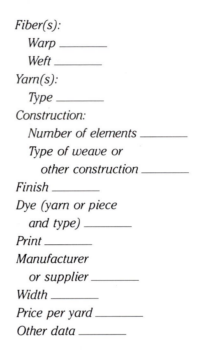

Fiber(s):
  Warp _____
  Weft _____
Yarn(s):
  Type _____
Construction:
  Number of elements _____
  Type of weave or
    other construction _____
Finish _____
Dye (yarn or piece
  and type) _____
Print _____
Manufacturer
  or supplier _____
Width _____
Price per yard _____
Other data _____

The tags that manufacturers attach to samples give some of this information (the name and number of the fabric, width, fibers, finish, and, sometimes, price); further information must come from inspecting the fabric and questioning knowledgeable salespeople who represent the manufacturer.

Although by no means complete, the listing of fabric names provided here in Table 10 on page 200, together with their classification by weight and with notes on their typical uses, can be helpful in clearing some of the confusion associated with textile identification. It can also provide a basis for classification as one builds up a collection of sample swatches of the materials that will be under consideration for actual interior design projects.

278

279

278, 279. Tones and textures inspired
by comic books and incorporated into
the Pop Art of recent years have found
their way into the Memphis design
movement in Italy. The harsh—even
shocking—forms and colors challenge
the established decorative aesthetic. Tri-
angolo (fig. 278), by George J. Sowden,
and Cerchio (fig. 279), by Nathalie du
Pasquier, are both printed cottons produced by Rainbow, Milan, 1983. (Photograph courtesy Memphis/Milano)

CHAPTER EIGHT
LIGHTING

Vision is the sense we find the most useful—in learning about our living spaces, in moving around those spaces and locating objects we need for our comfort or use, and in forming the mental images, impressions, and emotions that make those spaces understandable and memorable—and vision is dependent on light. Because we cannot see in the dark, and because electricity is so readily available, we have come to take it for granted that interior spaces will be lighted. It is not surprising, then, that lighting is one of the most important aspects of successful interior design. Good lighting supports convenience, comfort, and favorable emotional reactions. Improving the lighting of a space can be more effective than any other single factor in increasing overall sense of satisfaction. Bad lighting hampers utility and produces depression and displeasure with the space, making an otherwise attractive room dismal and ugly.

Stage designers are well aware that the lighting of a set can do more than anything else to establish a mood, focus attention, even create illusions. In addition, lighting is easy to control and, in comparison with solid materials such as walls, furniture, or carpets, highly economical. It is all too common to plan an interior in terms of such substantial elements and treat lighting as an afterthought, to be provided by routinely chosen fixtures and lamps. Intelligent interior design recognizes lighting's ability to influence the way in which occupants see a space and considers lighting a primary means of giving a space special character.

A glaring light bulb or two actually gives enough light to see clearly, but such light is painfully unflattering to the space, its contents, and its occupants. Its uniform level and unconsidered placement reveal every defect and show everything equally, offering no variety or subtlety. A room considered ugly almost always turns out to be badly lit. Switching off a glaring ceiling light and substituting a few well-chosen and well-placed lamps or fixtures can make a startling, instantaneous improvement, often at very little cost.

Good lighting can achieve the following effects:

- *SET A DESIRED MOOD OR ATMOSPHERE. Dim light usually makes a space seem intimate and cozy, bright light business-like and energetic. Restaurant designers and managers are well aware that bright, even light encourages quick turnover in a fast-food outlet but that it works against a mood of leisure and comfort.*
- *DIRECT OR CONCENTRATE ATTENTION. Brightly lit areas within an otherwise dim space draw visual focus. Strong light on a dining table within a generally dimmer room renders table settings, food, and drink more attractive. A brightly lit wall or spotlights clearly display artwork. A*

good light at a desk, with the surround at a lower light level, helps to concentrate attention on work. Merchandise on display under strong spotlights draws attention in a showroom or store.*

- *CONTROL SHADING AND SHADOW TO AID THE VIEWER IN SEEING FORM AND TEXTURE. Diffuse, even light tends to flatten objects. Sharp shadows emphasize forms, and strong cross light coming from one side brings out texture. These effects are obvious outdoors—the light of a bright and sunny day makes objects seem sharp and crisp, while a cloudy sky, with its more even light, suggests a dullness that can set a somber, even depressing tone.*
- *EMPHASIZE OR MODIFY SPATIAL PERCEPTION. A dark ceiling appears lower, even oppressive, while a brighter ceiling can seem to float upward, almost like the sky. Bright windows draw attention to their size and shape. Using blinds or curtains to diminish their brightness makes them less important; lighting other areas more strongly makes them almost unnoticeable.*

Until modern times, daylight was the primary source of light everywhere; the design of buildings had to take into account the lighting of interiors through windows and such alternatives as skylights. Auxiliary light came from open fires, candles, and the various types of lamps developed over the years. Simple in nature, these gave a limited amount and quality of light and were difficult to control. Electric light can be so efficient and effective that it has taken over all night lighting service and has become the primary source of light in many spaces. Windowless spaces—even buildings—in which daylight is insignificant have become common, especially in large stores and offices. Artificial light again becomes primary in homes, where most people spend much of their time after dark. Since we now so rarely experience daylight as an important source of lighting, we may even overlook it.

Modern electric light can be produced by a variety of sources (incandescent, fluorescent, and so on), each quite different from the others. Portable lamps and fixed lighting fixtures give a wide range of control over the location, intensity, and quality of lighting output. Daylight is also subject to control from a variety of kinds of window glazing and window treatments, such as blinds, shades, and curtains. Since light is a form of basic energy, lighting interacts with heating and air conditioning in a way that can be quite complex.

With so many options, lighting has become a complicated subject that can be studied from a technical point of view. At the same time, it is something of an art and involves creative thinking and imagination. Illuminating engineers and

280. A group of the popular Tizio cantilever, adjustable desk lamps designed by Richard Sapper are displayed in the New York showroom of Artemide Inc., an importer of Italian lighting elements. The showroom was designed by Massimo Vignelli. (Photograph: © Paul Warchol)

professional lighting consultants, specialists in these matters, are often employed to assist in interior design projects in which lighting will be both important and complex. Every interior designer needs to have a basic understanding of lighting issues, in order to deal with simpler situations directly as well as to work well with lighting specialists when they are involved in a project.

VISION AND LIGHTING

It is an unfortunate reality that bad lighting is all too common. It may result from simple carelessness or indifference, but it can also come about in planned situations, even when handbook recommendations or manufacturers' advice is followed. The design of lighting is too often limited to providing a high level of light, with the assumption that this will take care of all users' needs. However, seeing depends on many additional factors—shading and shadow, limitation of brightness contrast, color quality—that, along with level of intensity, make seeing easy and satisfying. To understand the complexities of these issues, it is necessary to consider the basics of human vision, the sense that lighting is, after all, intended to serve.

Almost everyone has at some time studied, at least briefly, the physiology of the human eye and can recall something of its mechanism (fig. 283). The familiar analogy with a simple camera still serves to explain it. The eye itself is the dark chamber comparable to the box or bellows of the camera; the retina at the back of the eye is the light-sensitive surface comparable to the film or plate of photography. The pupil of the eye is a lens that can change focus to form a sharp image on

281

281. Daylight, ambient light from hanging overhead fixtures, and task lighting from table-mounted lamps work together in a barrel-vaulted former assembly hall, now the Kaskel Library, of the Hackley School in Tarrytown, New York. This conversion project won a lighting award in 1986 for its designers, Keith Kroeger Associates, architects, with Cline Bettridge Bernstein, lighting consultants. (Photograph: Adam Bartos, courtesy Keith Kroeger Associates)

282

the retina of objects near or far away. The retinal image is transmitted through the optic nerve to the brain, which interprets the image to create the mental picture that we see. The image is, of course, in color, and it is in sharp focus only at its center. Through movements of the eyeball, head, and body, the eye scans the scene before it and builds up a mental image that includes a wider, more sharply focused field of view than the eye itself can generate at a given moment.

As it focuses on individual objects, what the eye sees depends on the kind and quality of light available. Light bouncing off objects reflects back to the eye variations in brightness and color that correspond in a complex geometric way with the size, shape, distance, color, and texture of those objects. This creates on the retina the picture in perspective that we learn to understand as being the appearance of whatever we look at.

282. In the social context of residential and restaurant settings, candlelight still generates a special, intimate aura as no other light source can. This dining area in a New York apartment is by John F. Saladino, designer. (Photograph: © Peter Vitale)

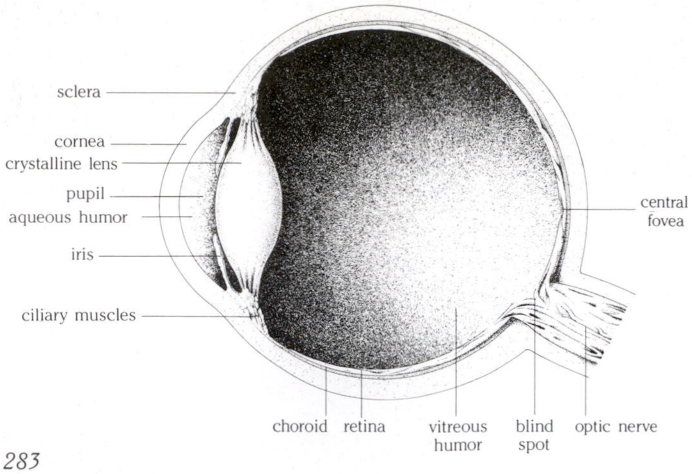
sclera
cornea
crystalline lens
pupil
aqueous humor
iris
ciliary muscles
choroid
retina
vitreous humor
blind spot
optic nerve
central fovea

283

Considerations for Good Lighting

The goals of lighting are to promote good visibility and to generate qualities of atmosphere, the aesthetic and emotional impressions that convey a mood appropriate to the space in question. These goals may be in conflict, as in the restaurant where the dim "candlelight mood" lighting creates a pleasant atmosphere but makes it difficult or impossible to read the menu or cut the steak. Many spaces demand that lighting deal with varied tasks and moods. A living room may be used for reading, cleaning, conversation, TV-watching, and a range of other occupations. No single lighting setup will answer each of these activities. Therefore, means of varying the lighting must be found. For every task and every situation, the following issues must be faced:

LIGHT LEVEL. This is the simple quantity of light at a task, which is easily measured. The eye, which developed through millions of years as a device to aid adaptation to the totally natural environment, is equipped to adjust to the extremes presented by natural light, from the brilliant noonday sun to dim starlight or less. Two devices deal with this adjustment. One is the iris, the ring around the pupil that gives the eye its distinctive color. According to the brightness of the scene viewed, the iris automatically enlarges or contracts to admit more or less light, exactly as the iris of a camera does.

A second level of control, in the retina–optic nerve–brain system, is called accommodation. Over a period of minutes, it becomes possible to see better in dim light (as in a darkened auditorium) or to adjust to beach or snow brightness. Together, the adjustments of the iris and accommodation make possible satisfactory seeing through a surprisingly wide range of

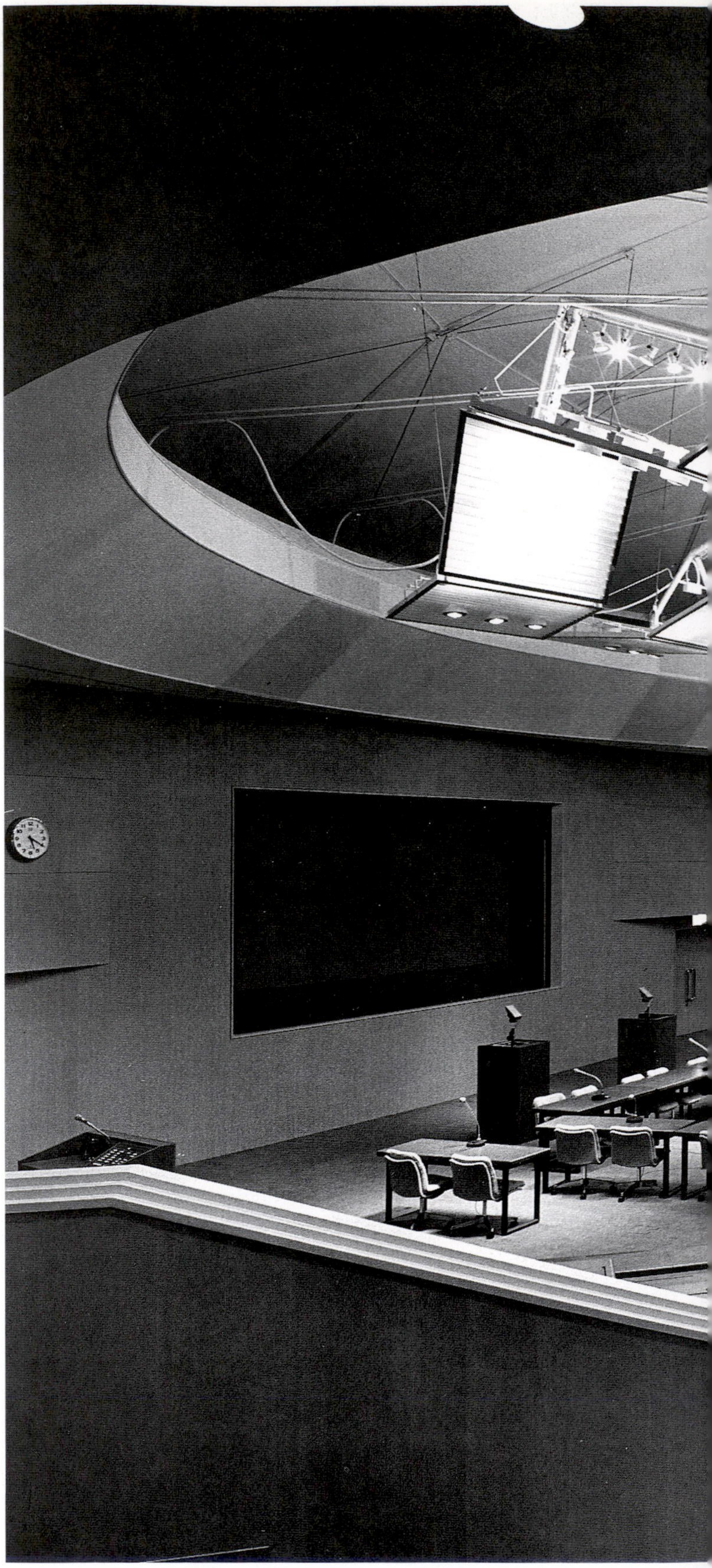

284

283. The human eye is the receptor that all lighting is designed to serve. The iris varies the size of the pupil, controlling the amount of light that reaches the retina, thereby enabling the eye to adjust to a wide range of conditions. The cross-sectional drawing is by Giorgio Brunelli. From Theory and Use of Color *by Luigina De Grandis*

284. Imaginative lighting brightens a windowless auditorium. Jointed panels of acrylic plastic diffuse light from bulbs set along a track; the result is a soft, overall illumination. A motor lowers the tracks for relamping. Hidetoshi Ohno, architect, principal of A.P.L. Sogokei-kaku Jimusho of Tokyo, designed the lighting; Endo Planning provided the interior design. The space is the International Conference Hall of YKK 50 of the Yoshida Kogyo Company, Kurobe, Japan. (Photograph: Taisuke Ogawa)

conditions. Therefore, light level is actually less important than many other factors. Still, one candle cannot provide sufficient light for reading, while too much light may create glare and will certainly cost more than necessary. Since older people and people with vision problems need more light for a given task than others, it has become customary to provide an ample light level for reading, writing, sewing, drafting, or other demanding seeing tasks. A generous excess of light is appropriate for such tasks as industrial inspection, medical examination, or surgery.

CONTROL OF BRIGHTNESS CONTRAST AND GLARE. The adjustments of the iris and retina–optic nerve–brain system cannot deal with a visual field that includes bright and dim areas that both demand attention, as when trying to read while facing a bright window. The iris of the eye struggles to open up to aid seeing the book but is forced to close down to control the bright window light. Tired eye muscles and difficulty in seeing inevitably result. Such excessive brightness contrast is one of the most troublesome of lighting situations.

When the difference between the brightest and dimmest points within a visual field is not extreme, the eye need not struggle to find a compromise adjustment. This entails shading direct sources of light, such as unshielded bulbs, fluorescent tubes, or windows letting in bright sunlight; avoiding dark backgrounds behind bright objects (desk and table tops and floors are frequent offenders); and providing *fill light* to keep less lighted background areas from contrasting with bright visual areas.

Excessive brightness, called *glare*, comes from such familiar situations as an unshaded ceiling light bulb or from ceiling-mounted fluorescent light fixtures that form bright spots in an otherwise dim ceiling. Both situations are common because they provide a high level of light economically.

One special form of glare, called *veiling reflection*, comes from looking at somewhat glossy material placed so as to reflect a source of illumination, such as a window or light bulb. A person reading print on glossy paper will move the paper around in an effort to find a position that kills the glare. Special efforts to deal with this problem (discussed on page 238) are called for wherever reading, writing, or other close seeing will take place for an extended time.

CONTRAST AND DIFFUSION. Shade and shadow emphasize form but conceal detail in the shaded areas. Light that comes from a concentrated source, or point source, tends to create strong shade and shadow, while diffused light tends to diminish or block out shading. The sun, a point source, casts strong shadows that make objects look crisp and sharp. A cloudy sky gives a soft, diffuse light that reveals detail in shade but may seem dull or depressing in mood. Actually, sunny daylight is a mixture of point-source direct sun and diffuse light from the sky. A pure point source, such as a theater or photo spotlight, accents form by creating even sharper shadows, but its light may seem harsh.

High-contrast point-source lighting draws attention and accents form and texture. Diffuse light promotes good general vision but may seem drab and characterless. The absence of shadows can make some tasks harder because shadows aid three-dimensional depth perception. When writing or drawing, the shadow of pen or pencil as it is lifted and lowered aids in seeing and control. For most situations, a suitable mix of point-source and diffused light will serve best.

ECONOMIC ISSUES. Daylight is free, but windows and skylights are not. Moreover, windows and skylights admit summer heat and allow winter heat to escape, effects which must be offset with mechanical equipment that is costly to provide and operate. Artificial light requires the purchase of lamps, fixtures, and wiring as well as the ongoing cost of maintenance, replacing bulbs and tubes, and power. In addition, the heat generated by lighting calls for additional summer air conditioning, which is rarely balanced by comparable savings in winter heating. This is usually a minor factor in residential lighting design but a major concern in stores, offices, and factories, where artificial light is required on a near full-time basis. Given the present high cost of energy, it becomes important to design lighting that offers the best possible results with the minimum first cost and operational expenses.

DAYLIGHT

In recent years there has been a tendency to ignore daylight as a significant source of illumination. Although it costs nothing, it varies with the season, weather, and time of day, and it requires building design that places windows (or skylights) to make light available where needed. Still, in many ways, daylight remains the most attractive form of illumination. It is the lighting for which the eye was developed, and its variability actually helps to make it pleasant and satisfying. Interior designers often seem to neglect the possibilities of using daylight, first, because they take windows for granted as a given condition of interior space, and secondly, because they think of windows as elements to be "treated" in some decorative way rather than made functionally useful.

Admitting Daylight

The nature of daylight in the interior is determined by the architecture of the space, as well as by the location and

285. Besides admitting an appreciable amount of sunlight, this window wall establishes a spectacular presence in a residential space. A duplex apartment designed by Richard Himmel, Chicago. (Photograph: Feliciano, courtesy House & Garden*)*

286

orientation of the building. It is worthwhile to study those given circumstances and to consider how they might be exploited to make the best use of natural lighting. Windows vary in size and shape, in details of framing and opening. Latitude and climate affect the light they admit, as do external shading (through overhangs, sunshades, awnings, nearby trees, and buildings). Skylights, encountered less often in existing buildings, are subject to some of the same variables. Where the space under consideration is already built, it is wise to observe and make note of the way windows perform—in what direction they face, their height and position, what view and shading they offer, and, incidentally, if they present problems with noise, heat loss or gain, or privacy. Where design work concerns a space not yet built or undergoing a major renovation, the same issues must be considered based on the facts available from drawings and on-site observation.

Windows can be changed—blocked up if badly placed, enlarged, combined, or reshaped—although this is likely to be a costly step. The effect of any changes on the exterior of the building must, of course, be considered, and permission obtained when the building owner is not the tenant of the space. Major changes in windows may require the help of an architect to deal with structural details and any applicable building code limitations. In general, changing frames or glazing within a window opening is fairly simple, as is cutting down a small window to make it larger (or into a door).

Cutting an opening for a new window of moderate size is also usually fairly simple. Large windows present more problems because the new opening requires supporting structure above it. Combining several windows, greatly enlarging a window in width, or making an entire window wall, while costly, may be worth considering. Modern architecture has favored large windows not only for stylistic reasons but also because they give more light, of a more uniform quality, to spaces within (fig. 285). Small windows tend to be bright spots in a dark wall while a full window wall floods a space with even light.

286. In the living space of a renovated carriage house in Saratoga Springs, New York, cheerful natural light serves as the primary light source during the day, and table lamps illuminate the space after dark. Richard Lowell Neas, designer, 1984. (Photograph: © François Halard, courtesy House & Garden*)*

Skylights, too, can be removed, relocated, enlarged, or introduced where they did not previously exist, provided, of course, that the space in question faces the sky. For both skylights and windows, problems with heat loss and gain can be controlled by multiple glazing, heat-controlling glass, and, most effective of all, consideration of orientation.

Controlling Daylight

MULTIPLE GLAZING. Multiple glazing uses two, sometimes three, sheets of glass factory-assembled into a sandwich. The dead-air spaces between the layers minimize heat loss, much as storm windows work. Special glass tinted to filter out heat energy while permitting most light to pass through can be obtained. While multiple glazing defends against winter cold, light-controlling glass minimizes summer heat gain. A good orientation—ideally, facing south, with appropriate exterior sun shading—makes a difference in both summer and winter. Unfortunately for interior designers, these matters usually lie beyond the normal areas of interior design concern. Nevertheless, the impact of orientation merits thought and attention, as it influences both newly planned and existing situations.

ORIENTATION. The pattern of the sun's movement is determined by latitude and season. In the Temperate Zone of the Northern Hemisphere, the sun appears to travel across the sky each day from east to west in a path south of the zenith; the farther north the location, the lower the path for a given date. The altitude of this path changes with the seasons, being lowest in winter, highest in summer. These natural laws influence the way in which daylight penetrates interior space (fig. 287). Openings facing north, which never admit direct sun, generally receive cool but consistent light from the north sky, the traditional north light of the artist's studio. East-facing windows admit strong sunlight early in the morning and lose the sun sometime before noon. West-facing windows receive later afternoon sun, sometimes too much sun on summer

afternoons. South orientation has the advantage of receiving sun consistently for most of the day, at an angle that changes with the season. In winter, the low sun angle gives maximum heat and light, while in the summer the high angle reduces the sun's penetration. Careful planning of sun shading can control sun penetration precisely, a technique used as a basis for the design of solar houses that exploit the sun's energy to a maximum. Since sunlight is not available on cloudy days, only north-facing openings can offer consistent lighting. A south orientation is generally considered the most favorable in terms of light, pleasantness, and controllability.

Given a particular orientation and opening of known size, shape, and location, it is possible to predict the light patterns in summer and winter, at different times of day, and on sunny or dark days. This information will aid in determining window treatments, artificial light backup, and, sometimes, furniture placement and color schemes.

WINDOW TREATMENTS. While windows can provide excellent light, direct sun can be a problem and must be controlled. With east or west orientations, early morning or late afternoon conditions always call for sun control. Shades or blinds, with or without curtains, offer fully controllable adjustability, which curtains alone cannot give. (See Chapter 5, pages 129–33, for a full discussion of window treatment.) Using daylight requires artificial backup light, even in spaces used by day only, for dark days and winter afternoons. For spaces used at night, the artificial lighting planned for that use will usually serve as the daytime backup.

When placing furniture, it is important to keep bright windows out of the field of vision of a person doing any task involving close work, such as reading, sewing, or desk work. Seating for visual tasks with the back to the window can also cause problems because of the shadow cast forward. Thus, the traditional "light coming from over the left shoulder" remains ideal, although light from the right is also satisfactory for most tasks, and best for left-handed people.

ARTIFICIAL LIGHT

Barring remote wilderness cabins and atmospheric candle-lit restaurants, artificial light in the modern world means electric light. Since Thomas Edison introduced his pioneer invention, a wide variety of electric light sources and lighting devices has been developed, making electric light marvelously useful and controllable. To the designer, artificial light has the potential advantage of being totally controllable in terms of brightness, color, placement, and quality. For these reasons it is actually preferred in many situations (for example, restaurants, stores,

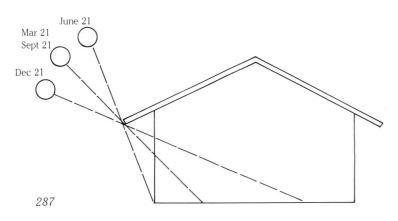

287. In the temperate zones, the sun's path across the sky is low in winter, high in summer. Properly shaded, southern exposure admits the light and warmth of deep winter sun but blocks the strong summer sun—thereby reducing air-conditioning costs.

showrooms, and exhibition spaces). At its best, it can compete favorably with daylight when used in offices, residential spaces, and many special-purpose spaces such as classrooms, lobbies and lounges, waiting rooms, and many utility and work spaces.

PLANNING LIGHTING

Planning lighting for an interior normally means planning the artificial electric lighting. Since daylight is at best a part-time source of lighting, artificial light is generally planned to do a total job.

Many people tolerate lighting planned on a hit-or-miss basis, following habitual routines—they accept a central ceiling fixture in each room and plug an occasional lamp into some convenience outlet. Good results are hardly to be expected from this approach. Good lighting for a given space depends on careful planning, starting with an analysis of needs, followed by the intelligent selection of lighting devices to suit those needs, and ending with fixture spacing and location to achieve the lighting levels and effects desired. Observing lighting installations in use, both good and bad, will build up a memory stock of examples to follow and errors to avoid. Typical planning steps are:

- *DEFINE THE GENERAL AIMS IN TERMS OF CHARACTER AND ATMOSPHERE. Is the space to be business-like, efficient, restful, cozy?*

- *CONSIDER THE SPECIFIC PURPOSES FOR WHICH LIGHTING IS REQUIRED. Is the space used for working, dining, reading, watching television? Does it combine several purposes, necessitating varied or changeable lighting? Most people want their living spaces to be pleasant and relaxing, but they also demand good light for reading or writing as well as efficient light for cleaning. A store must use lighting to set a tone suitable to its style and quality level and, at the same time, to flatter and feature merchandise.*

- *ASCERTAIN THE INTENSITY LEVELS FOR PROPER VISION AND BALANCE THESE AGAINST ENERGY AND FIRST-INSTALLATION COSTS AND OTHER FACTORS TO DECIDE ON LIGHTING TYPE. Efficiency plays a major role in determining lamp type and fixture location, particularly in large installations. For example, the efficiency of fluorescent light favors its use in factories and other large spaces requiring bright light. However, it is important to plan carefully to avoid the visual and psychological problems associated with its use.*

- *SELECT FIXTURES BASED ON GENERAL AIMS AND SPECIFIC NEEDS. Once a decision is made to have brightness in one place, subtlety in another, variety for stimulation, or*

uniformity for efficiency, actual products should be chosen to create those effects, such as ceiling lights fixed in place for general illumination, indirect lighting for softness, concentrated spot lighting for emphasis and variety, and portable lamps for local accent and easy individual control.

- *PLACE FIXTURES. This can be dealt with on an ad hoc (improvisational) basis in typical residential projects and similar situations where variety and atmosphere outweigh efficiency. In most larger projects, such as offices, restaurants, and stores, placement is determined by calculation, using formulas that yield the desired light levels along with the satisfactory quality of light.*

Lighting is usually planned on overlay sheets placed over floor plans. A *reflected ceiling plan* is the usual final drawing in which most lighting is indicated, although portable lamps are indicated on furniture plans. Although they detail the specifics of lighting location, plans and drawings give no idea of the *visual effect* of lighting. This remains an aspect of interior design almost impossible to present visually in advance of actual installation. Recent efforts to develop computer programs that will produce visual images—actual pictures illustrating a space as illuminated by a particular lighting installation—have met with some success, and they may eventually become widely available. At present, the informed imagination of the designer is the only generally useful means for planning and predicting how lighting will really look.

LIGHTING NEEDS

The first step in making a lighting plan is an orderly assessment of lighting needs. These will normally fall into three categories:

1. Light for specific visual functions, now often called task lighting. *This means providing adequate and suitable light for every activity that depends on good vision. The typical tasks that call for special light are:*

    Reading
    Writing
    Sewing
    Drafting
    Food preparation and cooking
    Eating
    Dressing
    Washing, shaving, and makeup
plus any number of special tasks that may arise in a particular home environment (music practice, for example), in work places such as offices, factories, and hospitals, or in such special-purpose interiors as theaters,

288

museums, galleries, gymnasiums, or pools.

2. In addition to lighting for specific tasks, good lighting calls for general lighting, *which provides a comfortable level of light for finding one's way around a space, locating objects, and seeing people and objects. This general or background lighting, often called* ambient light, *should be strong enough to avoid excessive brightness contrast between it and bright task lighting.*

3. Special lighting *focuses attention on specific objects or areas and generates variety and contrast to make a space lively and interesting, even to add aesthetic impact. Attention is always drawn to brightly lit areas and objects, a phenomenon exploited in store and showroom display lighting. This is often called* accent lighting, *to describe the strong light concentrated on a painting, a display of objects, or simply on a wall.*

Once the kinds of light needed in various locations have been identified, it is helpful to gain an idea of the desired light levels. Lighting measurements are based on a unit called a candlepower, the amount of light given by a standard candle of controlled size and composition. The level of light delivered to a surface one foot away from such a standard candle is designated as one footcandle. Light meters measure light levels in terms of this unit. A laboratory light meter gives very precise readings but is an expensive device. Many photographic exposure meters measure footcandles with sufficient accuracy for most practical purposes.*

The meter known as the Sekonic Studio Deluxe Model L-398 is particularly suitable for use as a footcandle meter; it is an excellent exposure meter as well.

288. Strong task lighting above work surfaces and a much lower level of ambient (general) light provide comfortable visual conditions at minimal energy cost. These New York University library study carrels are by Voorsanger & Mills Associates Architects. (Photograph: © 1983 Peter Aaron/ESTO)

289

289, 290. In the restaurant Caffe Roma in New York (fig. 289), a strip of theatrical border lights in four colors is mounted below the exposed, painted brick wall. A cross-fading system is programmed to increase and decrease pairs of the four colors randomly at five- to ten-minute intervals, producing subtle, constantly changing color effects. An axonometric drawing of Caffe Roma (fig. 290) shows the illuminated wall above and behind the banquette seating at top. Haverson/Rockwell Architects; Gepy Mariani, designer, 1986. (Photograph: © Mark Ross, 1986)

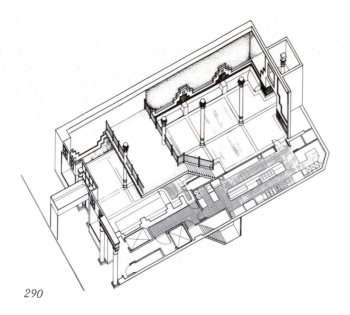

290

Tables of recommended illumination levels for various purposes appear in lighting handbooks. For many years, recommendations have tended to move upward, but, in view of rising energy costs, recent reevaluation has led to lower light level recommendations, with the increasing understanding that other factors may be more important than the simple intensity of lighting.

Carrying a light meter to measure the footcandle level in familiar situations leads to the surprising conclusion that a very wide range of levels can be acceptable for many tasks. One can see reasonably well with as little as a footcandle level of 5, although somewhat more will help with demanding tasks (reading fine print or sewing on dark materials, for example). At the other extreme, full daylight can reach levels of 6,000 foot-candles without causing discomfort. A table such as the following should, therefore, be regarded as no more than a general guide or suggestion:

TASK	RECOMMENDED FOOTCANDLE LEVEL
Movie theater (during picture)	1
Passages and storage areas	5
Stairways, shipping areas, TV-watching	10
Cooking, washing, cleaning, playing games	10–20
Intermittent reading or writing	20
Reading fine type (for example, a newspaper)	25
Typing, bookkeeping, switchboard operation	30
Prolonged reading, study, business-machine operation, close work	50
Drafting	50–100
Sewing black thread on black	500
Surgery	2,000

A particular light source, that is, a lamp of a certain wattage, has a light output measured in lumens. The lumen is the unit of light that will deliver a level of one footcandle to a surface one foot square at a distance of one foot. Illumination level varies with the distance from a light source, in accordance with the inverse square law familiar in many physics experiments. A light source that delivers 20 footcandles to a surface two feet away, when moved to a distance of one foot, will deliver not twice as much light, as might be expected, but four times as much, or 80 footcandles. When moved further away, to four feet, illumination will fall to one-quarter the level, or 5 footcandles (fig. 291). In practice, the illumination level delivered by a particular source will also be influenced by its age and cleanness, by the design of the fixture used, and by the characteristics of the space where it is located. White or light-color surfaces nearby reflect and conserve light; dark surfaces or open space do not.

The selection of lighting devices involves several decisions, all of which entail choosing among a vast range of possibilities. The basic light source—called the *bulb* or *tube* by laymen but known professionally as the *lamp*, the term that will be used here—may be any one of a number of types, including incandescent, fluorescent, and high-intensity discharge, or HID. It may be mounted in any one of a wide variety of fixtures, which may be located and spaced in many different ways. Controlling intensity, contrast, glare, and visual effect while juggling these variables in combination can become quite complex.

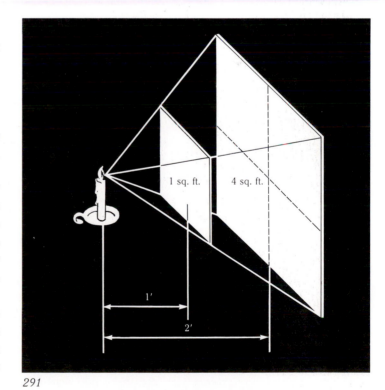

291

291. This diagram illustrates the inverse square law; the light of one candle falls on one square foot at a distance of one foot, but from two feet away, the same pyramid of light falls on four square feet—providing one-quarter the intensity of light.

LIGHTING SOURCES

Selecting lighting devices begins with consideration of the type of light source, the lamp to be used (fig. 292). The most familiar sources are the incandescent bulb and the fluorescent tube, both in wide general use, both available in a great variety of sizes, shapes, and types. In recent years, several other sources, less familiar to the general public but increasingly used in architectural lighting, have become available, in bulbs or tubes and in portable lamps. These sources include cold cathode, neon, and, particularly useful, the family of sources call HID, or high-intensity discharge lamps. Each of the basic source types has its own set of advantages and disadvantages. These can be summarized as follows:

Incandescent Light

Incandescent lamps, invented by Thomas Edison, are the oldest and most familiar of sources. Incandescent light is by nature a point or near-point source, which tends to cast sharp shadows and form bright highlights. This characteristic can be modified to offer some diffusion, by frosting the lamps, by using certain shapes such as the T or tubular form, or by employing various shades or fixtures. Like sunlight, candlelight, or oil-lamp light, incandescent light has a continuous spectrum that includes all colors of light to form a white. However, the white of incandescent light contains more red and yellow and less green and blue than daylight, making it much warmer. This warm color tends to be attractive, flattering to human coloring, and suggestive of coziness and comfort (see fig. 1).

Incandescent light can be made to serve virtually all lighting needs, but it presents economic problems. It uses much of the electrical energy it consumes to produce heat as an unwanted by-product of light. This makes it costly in terms of power consumption per lumen produced and can also create an extra load on summer air conditioning. As a result, it is rarely used in factories, office buildings, and other structures that require large amounts of electricity. Smaller users need not be as concerned with economic factors, so incandescent light is a general favorite for most home uses. It is also widely used in places that

benefit from its point-source characteristic, as in store displays, where it is flattering to merchandise; in restaurants, where it renders both people and food maximally attractive; and in other locations where aesthetic considerations take precedence over economics.

Tungsten-halogen lamps are a recently introduced, special type of incandescent lamp that gives a higher light output than standard incandescents for a given wattage. They are made in several forms (bulbs, tubes, and mushroom-shaped reflector types) and are generally very compact in relation to their output. They operate at high temperatures and therefore usually use a quartz (heat-resistant) glass envelope. Because of their high heat output, their need for protective shielding to guard against possible injury in case of breakage, and the unusual size and shape of the lamp envelopes, halogen lamps are generally not interchangeable with standard types and require a specially designed fixture, or lamp holder.

Fluorescent Light

Fluorescent lighting, developed in the 1930s for general use, is a highly economical alternative to incandescent light. Its power consumption for a given light output, at about one-third to one-quarter that of incandescent lamps, soon pays off the higher cost of the lamps and their fixtures to produce major economies. This has made fluorescent lighting the norm for factories, offices, and classrooms and for restaurants and stores that strive for lower operating costs.

The typical fluorescent lamp is a long tube and therefore gives off diffuse, shadowless light. While this promotes good general vision, it makes certain kinds of detail harder to see and tends to create a bland and monotonous lighting effect, rather like outdoor light on a cloudy day.

Fluorescent light has another troublesome characteristic, its color quality, which does not receive as much attention as it deserves. Part of the light from a fluorescent tube is full-spectrum light, that is, light with all colors present. However, this is true only of the portion of light output that comes from

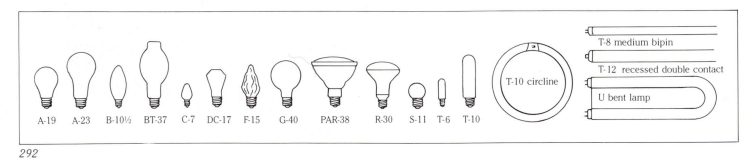

292

292. Light bulbs and tubes (both called lamps in the industry) are available in a variety of sizes and shapes. In the standard industry designation, letter indicates shape, the following number indicates size (diameter, in eighths of an inch).

293

294

293. Fluorescent light diffused by plastic sheeting creates a luminous ceiling that provides even, almost shadowless illumination. The Manufacturers Hanover Trust Company Building, New York, is a 1954 project by Skidmore, Owings & Merrill, architects. (Photograph: © 1954 Ezra Stoller/ESTO)

294. Lighting is the dominant element in Batons in New York. The name of the restaurant is taken from the shape of the fluorescent tubes, which suggest giant swizzle sticks. They can be moved from side to side and from front to back, like mobiles. Sam Lopata, designer, 1985. (Photograph: © Peter Paige)

the glowing phosphors on the inside of the tube that fluoresce to give the source its name. The gases in the tube (mercury vapor, xenon, and others) emit light of a single, pure, one-frequency-number color. When viewed with a laboratory instrument called a spectroscope, this can be seen clearly as a dim rainbow band with superimposed brilliant lines of sharp color. While giving the illusion of normal white light, this spectrum does odd things to color perception, distorting the natural coloring of many objects. This makes fluorescent light aesthetically unpleasant—and possibly the source of various physiological discomforts.*

This problem has been addressed by introducing fluorescent tubes in a great variety of white colors, such as *warm white* and *deluxe warm white,* some of which certainly improve color rendition. Unfortunately, when fixtures are relamped, there is no guarantee that maintenance staff will trouble to use a particular color tube. Most often, they install the basic daylight tube, which is the cheapest, most widely available, and least desirable tube, generating the cold, blue-greenish "daylight" that makes people and objects take on an unattractive color cast.

Fluorescent lamps require a transformer, or ballast, and a special starting device, normally incorporated into the fixture. These present an additional first cost and maintenance expense.

In spite of these problems, the economic advantages of fluorescent light keep it in general use. Where it must be used for economic reasons, lamping with tubes of improved color characteristics, selecting good fixtures (which means avoiding the least expensive tube and fixture), and, whenever possible, mixing its use with incandescent light or daylight will help to make fluorescent light a more satisfactory choice.

HID LIGHT. HID (high-intensity discharge) lighting is a recent development that combines some of the advantages of incandescent and fluorescent light. The lamps, of bulb shape, give point or near-point light; the economy of operation is excellent; and it offers lamp types with desirable color characteristics—not, however, full- or continuous-spectrum light. First cost is high for both lamp and fixture, the latter of a special type, with a bulky and expensive transformer. HID lights have a slow starting characteristic, coming up to full light output only gradually over some minutes.

HID lighting is now in extensive use in public spaces, as an ambient (general or background) light source in offices, where it is often installed in special upward-directed fixtures to provide indirect light reflected from the ceiling, and in portable lamps and uplight fixtures for home and other general uses.

Other Lighting Sources

NEON. These tubes, familiar in illuminated signs, are available in a full range of colors, including several tones of white. The thin neon tube can be bent to any shape, including decorative and fanciful forms. Although its tube life is very long (many years), a transformer is required. Neon is limited mainly by a low efficiency (output in lumens per watt); it is usually only considered for special, decorative applications.

COLD CATHODE. Cold cathode lighting is somewhat similar to neon, using a thin tube bent to desired forms. Because it is permanently installed, it is sometimes useful in such special situations as indirect lighting coves (pockets in which the light source is hidden) of irregular shape. It has the same efficiency characteristics as neon.

MERCURY AND SODIUM. These lights of the gaseous discharge family are highly efficient in terms of lumens produced per watt of current consumed, but their one-color light (bluish for mercury, orange for sodium) makes them unsuitable for general use. They are often used for street and highway lighting, and mercury lamps have been used in industrial plants.

Color Characteristics of Artificial Lighting

Comparing the color characteristics of the many types of artificial light with one another and with natural light is difficult because of the discontinuous, line-spectrum components of fluorescent and HID sources. A continuous-spectrum light includes all wavelengths (that is, all colors) visible to the eye. When passed through a prism, this light is broken up into its separate wavelengths into a rainbow with all colors present (fig. 295). A discontinuous spectrum includes only certain wavelengths, possibly a single color (for example, red neon) or a number of colors that together give an impression of white light. Such light passed through a prism turns out to consist of sharp lines of intense color. Mercury vapor and sodium lights have a discontinuous spectrum. Fluorescent and HID lights combine the two types of spectra (fig. 296); daylight and incandescent light have continuous spectra.

Continuous-spectrum light (daylight, incandescent light) can be compared in terms of their warmth or coolness quite readily. To make this comparison orderly and consistent, the concept of color temperature, expressed in degrees Kelvin (°K), or, in

---

Although full research into the matter is not available, preliminary reports suggest that the physiological consequences of deprivation of full-spectrum light for extended periods is more extensive and more serious, both physically and psychologically, than is generally supposed. Special full-spectrum fluorescent light sources are now available and may come into more general use in the future.

recent terminology, simply kelvins (K), is used. High K numbers indicate cool light, low numbers warm.

In order to deal with fluorescent and other discontinuous-spectrum sources, an equivalent color temperature figure is used, that is, a number describing a continuous-spectrum light that *appears* to match the discontinuous source in question. It must be remembered that although the apparent color may match, the effect of discontinuous light on color matching and on vision can be quite different from that of its similar continuous-spectrum source. Color temperatures of some common light sources are:

SOURCE	CORRELATED COLOR TEMPERATURE IN KELVINS
Clear blue sky	25,000–12,000
Hazy blue sky	9,000
Overcast sky	7,500
Daylight fluorescent	6,500
Cool-white fluorescent	4,200
Metal halide (HID)	4,200–3,900
Mercury vapor	3,900–3,300
High-pressure sodium	3,100–2,100
Warm-white fluorescent	3,000
Incandescent 1,000 watts	3,000
Tungsten-halogen	3,000
Incandescent 150 watts	2,800
Incandescent 60 watts	2,790

The values given are averages. Different brand sources of similar types may vary somewhat. The term *deluxe* is used for modified versions of certain fluorescent and HID types to indicate altered (improved) color rendition. Color temperature shifts as lamps age; new lamps are cooler, aged lamps warmer than average

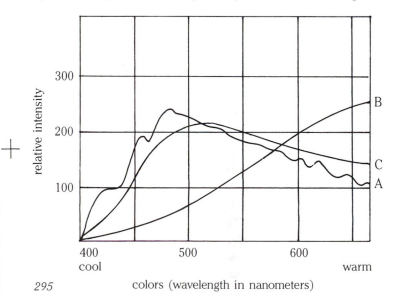

295

colors (wavelength in nanometers)

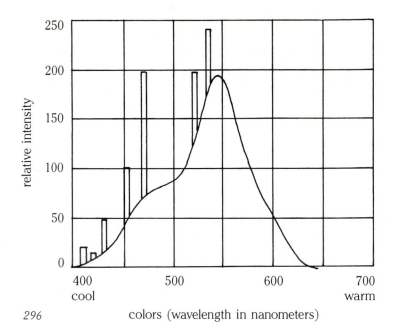

296

colors (wavelength in nanometers)

values. The use of a dimmer always shifts color toward warmer (lower kelvin number) values.

Lamps are usually rated by the manufacturer in kelvins with a number that appears in manufacturers' literature and, often, on the actual lamp carton. For comparison purposes, lighting engineers have agreed to a "standard daylight" of 4,870 K. Mixtures of light from various sources will, of course, have a color temperature between those of the sources resulting from the relative intensity of the types of light making up the mix.

Economic Issues of Lighting

In considering the economic impact of the selection of a light source, some fairly complex issues must be faced. They include:

> First cost of fixtures and lamps (manufacturer's list price).
> Cost of fixture installation and wiring (electrical contractor's estimate).
> Cost of maintenance, repair, and cleaning over its useful life.*
> Cost of relamping over its useful life.*
> Current consumption at an estimated cost over its useful life.*
> Additional cost of air conditioning (first cost and operational cost over its useful life) to offset heat production of lighting.*
> Savings (if any) in heating cost resulting from heat production of lighting over its useful life.*

*This item can only be estimated, since future costs of energy, products, and labor may change (probably upward).

295. This chart graphically displays the wavelengths of the colors of various full-spectrum light sources. Both sunlight (A) and incandescent light (B) contain all colors, forming a continuous spectrum. The red, orange, and yellow, or warm-color, wavelengths are somewhat stronger in B than in A, and this accounts for the noticeably warmer quality of incandescent light. A special "full-spectrum" fluorescent called Vitalite (C) includes invisible as well as visible wavelengths and approaches the color balance of daylight.

296. This chart of fluorescent-light spectra shows that this source includes both a continuous-spectrum component—similar to that of incandescent light—and discontinuous components. The continuous spectrum is generated by the glowing phosphors on the fluorescent tube, the discontinuous spikes by gases in the tube that produce pure color light at certain wavelengths. The resulting mix appears as white light but is quite different from sunlight in its makeup—and in its effects.

297

Since maintenance and lifetime costs, among other factors, can only be estimated, no exact comparative figures can be produced. Nevertheless, comparing various systems can be helpful in making decisions about large installations, in which even small differences, over a period of time, can have a major impact. Systems are often compared on the basis of a simple calculation dealing only with energy consumption. The total wattage of a planned lighting system is simply divided by the floor area to be lighted:

$$\frac{Total\ wattage\ of\ lighting}{Floor\ area\ in\ square\ feet} = Watts\ per\ square\ foot$$

For example:

$$\frac{6,900\ watts\ (or\ 6.9\ kilowatts)}{3,000\ square\ feet} = 2.3\ watts\ per\ square\ foot$$

The resulting figure is a good index of the efficiency of the planned installation. In many areas, building codes now try to reduce energy-wasteful lighting practice by setting a maximum watts-per-square-foot average permitted in new installations. Efficiencies of 3 watts per square foot are considered reasonable; some highly efficient installations achieve levels as low as 2 or even 1.5 watts per square foot.

The carton in which lamps are shipped carries information, not only on wattage but also on average lumen output (how much light is produced) and average life of the lamp. These are all factors in the economic performance of a particular lamp, whatever its type. Certain types of lamp, such as soft-white or long-life, while offering special features, are uneconomical compared to standard lamps. For example, a standard 60-watt lamp delivers 870 lumens over an average life of 1,000 hours, or

297. Neon lighting in the Beverly Hills Bar & Grill (previously the Heartthrob Cafe) evokes the nostalgic charm of a 1950s diner or luncheonette. The award-winning Philadelphia restaurant was designed by architect Edwin B. Bronstein of Bartley Bronstein Long Mirenda with the lighting design firm Grenald Associates in 1986. (Photograph: © Tom Bernard)

870,000 lumen-hours. A 60-watt long-life lamp delivers 740 lumens over 2,500 hours, or 1,850,000 lumen-hours. If the cost of the standard lamp is thirty-eight cents and that of the long-life eighty-five cents, one penny buys 22,895 lumen-hours from the standard lamp but only 21,765 lumen-hours from the long-life.

Lamps of different wattage also differ in economic performance. The standard 60-watt lamp with its lifetime output of 870,000 lumen-hours may be compared with a standard 100-watt lamp having an output of 1,750 lumens and a life of 750 hours, for a total lifetime output of 1,312,500 lumen-hours. Both lamps cost the same, but the 100-watt lamp consumes 66 percent more electricity. The 100-watt lamp therefore delivers 13,125 lumen-hours per watt, while the 60-watt lamp delivers 870,000 divided by 60, or 14,500 lumen-hours per watt. The impact of such calculations depends on local energy costs. The few lamps used in a typical home make such differences insignificant for residential installation, but they become important in large installations using many lamps.

FIXTURE SELECTION

Once the light source is selected, the next logical step is selecting fixtures. Many fixtures will take a variety of lamps, so the selection depends primarily on the type or types of lighting desired for a particular space. For example, a living space combining such activities as conversation and reading may need both soft, indirect general light and good task lighting, to which may be added spot lighting to display art and provide variety. A torchère (a type of floor lamp) can provide indirect uplight; a couple of well-placed lamps give good light for reading or other tasks requiring good light, as well as throwing light upward for more general light; and track lighting emphasizes artwork and rounds off the lighting scheme. Since many different fixtures will work in any specific situation, other factors, including cost, the look desired, and maintenance, then enter the decision-making process.

All lighting devices fall into one of two classes, *architectural* or *portable*.

Architectural Lighting

Architectural lighting is fixed in place through fixtures built into the structure of the building, often recessed or more or less concealed (fig. 298). Portable lighting includes lamps and other movable lighting devices that are plugged into outlets and can be moved about, removed, and replaced at will.

The lighting of public spaces, factories, and offices is primarily architectural. Residential lighting may combine both types but tends to emphasize portable lighting. The built-in lighting provided in most houses and apartments is of such poor quality and so badly located that it is best replaced, removed, or ignored. Replacement in an existing space can be difficult and expensive. Good architectural lighting is usually planned in advance and installed as a space is built or renovated.

Portable Lighting

The variety of lamps (portable lighting devices) and fixtures available from the many manufacturers of lighting equipment is considerable, and selection can often be a confusing matter. A high proportion of the lamps and fixtures displayed in lighting stores and other retail outlets are of poor design and shoddy construction. Manufacturers of better lighting equipment maintain showrooms in major cities and produce catalogs and data sheets describing their products and giving accurate technical data. Most designers and architects build up a file of data from preferred manufacturers and use the information when they plan lighting.

Types of Light Produced

There are several ways to classify lighting devices. In addition to size, wattage, type of light source, type of mounting (or portability), and appearance, a classification can be made on the basis of the way in which light is delivered. Luminaires (as fixtures are called in technical terms) and lamps all deliver light in one or a combination of the following ways:

- Concentrating, *or beaming, usually from a point source:*
  Up
  Down
  Both up and down
  In any direction (adjustable)
- Diffusing, *so as to scatter light in many directions:*
  Up
  Down
  Both up and down
  In many or all directions

An incandescent reflector spot, flood, or downlight produces a concentrated beam of light. A frosted globe delivers diffused light in all directions. A typical table lamp produces a complex mix of concentrated light from the actual light bulb, somewhat diffused light from the lamp shade, and upward-directed light, which is reflected from the ceiling to become diffused indirect light. Such mixtures tend to create the most satisfactory kinds of lighting, the direct light providing strong illumination for

298

298. The recessed ceiling lights used in this auditorium are an example of the most popular of architectural, or built-in, incandescent light fixtures. The room was designed by the Space Design Group for the corporate headquarters of the International Paper Company in New York. (Photograph courtesy the Space Design Group)

tasks and sharp shadows and highlights that aid clear vision, while the indirect diffused light fills in surrounding areas and prevents excessive brightness contrast. This mixture also most nearly duplicates the light of a sunny day, in which direct sunlight combines with diffuse reflection from the sky and clouds.

Many lamps and light fixtures, including some of handsome appearance, are designed so as to form a bright spot. Such fixtures—small globes, bare lamps or tubes, or ceiling fixtures with diffusing surfaces that show up as bright panels—almost always create excessive brightness contrast, causing vision problems even when ample light is present (see page 214). Bare bulbs in ceiling sockets and inferior fluorescent ceiling fixtures are notorious sources of such problems. In general, except for occasional decorative uses, avoid fixtures that leave the bare lamp or tube open to direct vision, as well as fixtures with shades or diffusers that themselves form spots of great brightness in a normal field of vision.

Arranging indirect lighting by beaming all light upward avoids this problem totally, but this gives a light that often seems bland and unattractive in its overall shadowless quality. It also tends to be inefficient, because of the light loss resulting from the round trip light must make—up from the fixture and back downward—and from a degree of absorption by the ceiling surface, which, even if painted a pure white, will always absorb some part of the light.

The following is a summary of the types of lamps and fixtures in most general use (fig. 299).

LAMPS AND LIGHTING FIXTURES

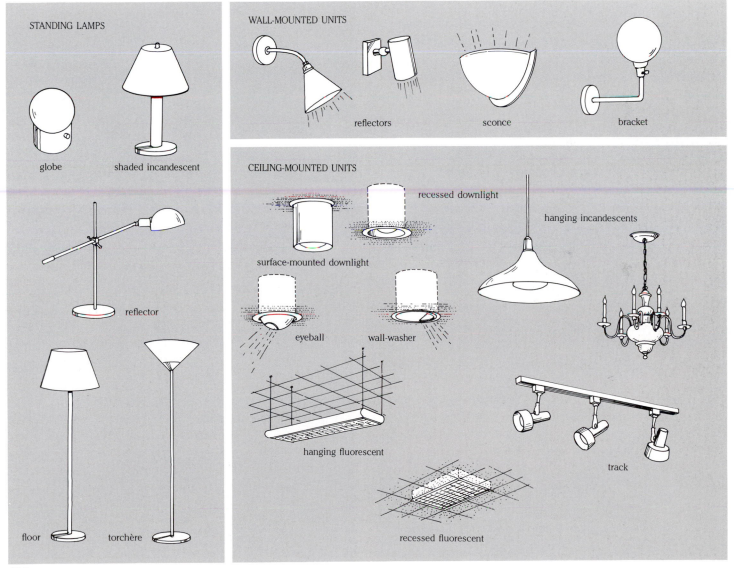

STANDING LAMPS

globe

shaded incandescent

reflector

floor

torchère

WALL-MOUNTED UNITS

reflectors

sconce

bracket

CEILING-MOUNTED UNITS

surface-mounted downlight

recessed downlight

eyeball

wall-washer

hanging incandescents

hanging fluorescent

recessed fluorescent

track

299

299. Light fixture types in general use are shown here. Standing types are at left; wall-mounted fixtures are given above right; and ceiling-mounted fixtures appear below right.

Floor, Table, and Desk Lamps

SHADED INCANDESCENT LAMPS.
These are probably the most familiar and useful of lamp types
(figs. 300, 302–304). The bulb or bulbs are surrounded by a
shade, which reduces glare but disperses *direct light* both
upward and downward. Such lamps, while often of ornate and
objectionable design, deliver excellent lighting. Well-designed
versions are hard to find but very useful.

GLOBE LAMPS. In these, the shade is replaced by a
frosted glass or paper sphere, which reduces the brightness of
the enclosed incandescent bulb and delivers *diffuse light* (fig.
305). Such lamps, while often of good appearance, tend to form
a spot of glare and to deliver unattractive flat lighting. Versions
that combine globe and directional shading are hard to find but
very useful.

REFLECTOR LAMPS. These enclose a regular or
reflector incandescent (type R) bulb in an opaque reflector,
which directs light in one direction, usually with adjustability
(figs. 306, 307). These make good *reading or work lights* but
can produce excessive brightness contrast unless fill light is
provided from some other source. Small versions make good
bedside reading lights.

300

300. This table lamp by Ron Rezek
Lighting & Furniture is named Zink—a
reference to the zinc-galvanized steel
that gives it its characteristic look of raw
metal. The light source is a standard
incandescent lamp. (Photograph courtesy Ron Rezek Lighting & Furniture)

301

301. In Tokyo's Hanajuban Restaurant,
sconces are used in combination with
table uplights and ceiling-mounted lighting, creating a well-lit but soft effect.
K.I.D. Associates Co., Ltd., designer.
(Photograph: Yoshio Shiratori)

304

302

305

303

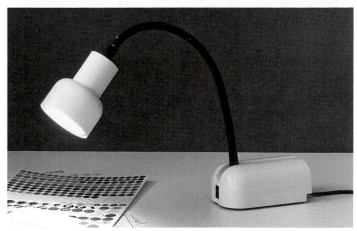

306

302. A classic shaded table lamp in modern form, the Dropp lamp is made in Sweden. The base is of polished brass, the shade is a textile on a wire frame. (Photograph courtesy Lighting International, Hollis, New Hampshire)

303. A table lamp in contrasting metals has a shade of metal mesh with a frosted-glass insert. A 300-watt halogen lamp is the light source, and there is a full-range dimmer. Robert Sonneman, designer. (Photograph courtesy George Kovacs Lighting, Inc.)

304. The Sensu table lamp of anodized aluminum, by Sean Corcorran and Jorge Freyer, designers, incorporates contemporary technology: an infrared sensor activates the lamp, moving the shade up when the light goes on and down when the light goes off. (Photograph: George Hein, courtesy Sointu, New York)

305. The shade of this small table lamp is a luminous glass globe lighted by the incandescent lamp (bulb) within. The design, Onfale-Onfale Piccolo, is by Luciano Vistosi. (Photograph courtesy Artemide Inc.)

306. The fully adjustable Tholos Studio reflector lamp, by Ernesto Gismondi, is well suited to desk-top or other task-lighting applications. (Photograph courtesy Artemide Inc.)

307

308

309

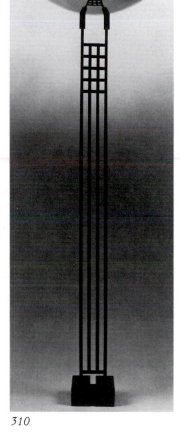

310

UPLIGHTS, OR TORCHERES. These are usually floor lamps that aim all light output upward to provide *indirect, general lighting* (figs. 308–10). The source of light is usually incandescent, but HID or halogen versions are increasingly popular. Floor lamps combining uplight and shaded reading light have been favorites for many years. Small can lights that rest on the floor and direct louver-shaded light upward to walls and ceilings are also compact and useful. Uplight is also provided by powerful floor-standing tubular, or kiosk, units for ambient (general) lighting in office and public spaces.

307. *An adjustable table or desk lamp, Condor is suited to task-lighting applications. Hans von Klier, designer. (Photograph courtesy Bilumen Lighting Ltd.)*

308. *Luciano Vistosi's floor lamp is clearly related to the small table lamps illustrated in fig. 305. Onfale Floor is 71 inches high and provides uplight as well as diffuse downlight from the frosted-glass reflector. (Photograph courtesy Artemide Inc.)*

309. *Three floor-standing uplights by Ron Rezek are here used in a living space of a Santa Monica, California, house designed by Brian A. Murphy (see fig. 4 for another view of this interior). (Photograph: © Tim Street-Porter, courtesy House & Garden)*

310. *This sculptural floor lamp, a design by Robert Sonneman, directs all light upward for indirect illumination. A 400-watt halogen lamp is used with a full-range dimmer. (Photograph courtesy George Kovacs Lighting, Inc.)*

311

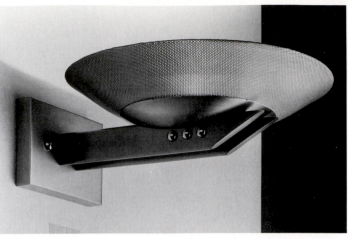

313

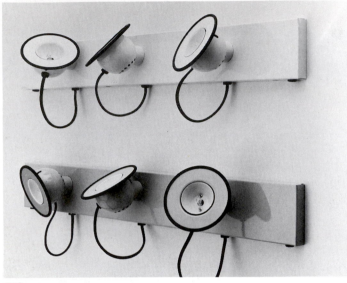

312

314

Wall-mounted Units

WALL BRACKETS. Units that use bare lamps (bulbs or tubes) or unshaded globes for *direct light,* these were once widely popular, often in simulated candle form, and are now less used. Simple versions are useful in corridors or at stairs and in bathrooms and dressing rooms (fig. 311). Shaded versions, still available, have fallen into disuse.

WALL-MOUNTED REFLECTOR LAMPS. These are similar to the floor and table versions discussed above. Many have swivel or gooseneck mountings, which provide adjustability for *display lighting* and for *reading and bed lamps* (fig. 312).

WALL-MOUNTED UPLIGHTS. Often called sconces, these serve the same purposes as floor uplights in fixed locations, providing *indirect, general light* (figs. 313–15). Popular in the 1930s, units of this type have recently gained new popularity.

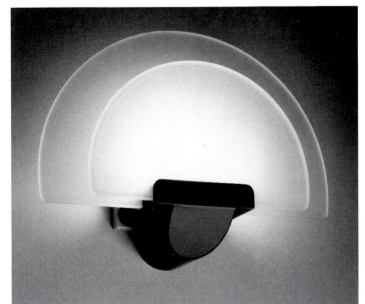

315

311. A wall-mounted globe lamp, the Aggregato adjustable spot lamp was designed by Enzo Mari and Giancarlo Fassina. (Photograph courtesy Artemide Inc.)

312. Gae Aulenti designed the Minibox swiveling wall lamps with built-in transformer. Low-voltage reflector lamps are held in place by magnets. (Photograph courtesy Stilnovo)

313. A wall-mounted uplight, or sconce, by Robert Sonneman, has a metal-mesh reflector with a frosted-glass insert. It uses a 200-watt halogen lamp. (Photograph courtesy George Kovacs Lighting, Inc.)

314. A three-tiered sconce. (Photograph courtesy Trakliting, Inc.)

315. The front panel of Diva, a sconce by architect and designer Ezio Didone, is a semicircle of frosted, patterned glass in white or rose. The second, larger semicircle is of unpatterned white glass, both panels providing diffuse light. A textured, white, enameled-aluminum backplate reflects the light directly from the source, a 100-watt incandescent lamp. (Photograph courtesy Atelier International Lighting)

316. Custom-designed, hanging incandescent lighting units illuminate the lobby of the corporate headquarters of Procter & Gamble in Cincinnati. Kohn Pedersen Fox were the architects in 1985. (Photograph: © 1985 Peter Aaron/ESTO)

317

318

317. A specially designed lighting fixture becomes a focal point in this guest dining room for YKK 50 of the Yoshida Kogyo Company, Kurobe, Japan. The fixture, designed by Hidetoshi Ohno, who also designed the space, has a painted steel frame with insert of mother-of-pearl shell. The cupboard and dining table were designed by Kazuko Fujie. (Photograph: Taisuke Ogawa)

318. The suspended fluorescent lighting in the New York University Midtown Center in New York has been incorporated into the ceiling. The painting on the end wall is by Richard Haas. Voorsanger & Mills Associates Architects, designer, 1980. (Photograph: © Nathaniel Lieberman)

Ceiling Units

DOWNLIGHTS. These cans housing an incandescent lamp, usually with a lens or shade to prevent direct glare, are among the most widely used of incandescent architectural lighting devices to give *general light.* They may be recessed, surface-mounted, or hung on a stem. HID versions are coming into use for large spaces with high ceilings.

EYEBALL AND WALL-WASHER ADJUSTABLE UNITS. These are similar to downlights but offer *direct light* that can be *adjusted* to any desired angle (fig. 319). Wall-washers direct light from ceiling level to an adjacent wall to "wash" it with light.

HANGING FIXTURES, OR CHANDELIERS. These widely used fixture types may imitate historic designs or take contemporary forms (figs. 316, 317, 320). They provide *general light,* which may be directed up, down, or both. Various types of globes and shades are used, and height adjustability is sometimes provided. Versions for residential use are usually incandescent. Fluorescent versions are often used for office and store lighting. Ugly and fussy versions abound, but excellent designs of this type are also available.

SURFACE-MOUNTED AND RECESSED LUMINAIRES. These are among the most widely used of architectural *general lighting* devices, usually in fluorescent versions (fig. 318). By spacing according to systematic calculation (see pages 238–40), predictable levels of consistent light can be delivered at work-surface levels. Unfortunately, low-cost versions of such fixtures are responsible for the glaring ceiling light all too common in offices, factories, and shops. Glare control requires the use of lenses or louvers that cut off glare at normal viewing angles, making the fixtures appear no brighter than the surrounding ceiling surfaces. Louvers of parabolic cross section do this with a minimum of light loss.

TRACK LIGHTING. This system uses an electrical track that can be ceiling-mounted or hung (fig. 321). Many different types of *adjustable* lighting units, which give both *general and spot lighting,* can be plugged in where desired and moved about as needed. This system is particularly useful for display and gallery lighting (fig. 323), and has come into increasing residential use.

Built-in Lighting

COVE LIGHTING. This requires a cove, or pocket, built into the ceiling (or, sometimes, wall) construction. Light units, usually fluorescent or cold cathode, are concealed in the cove and provide *indirect light.*

319

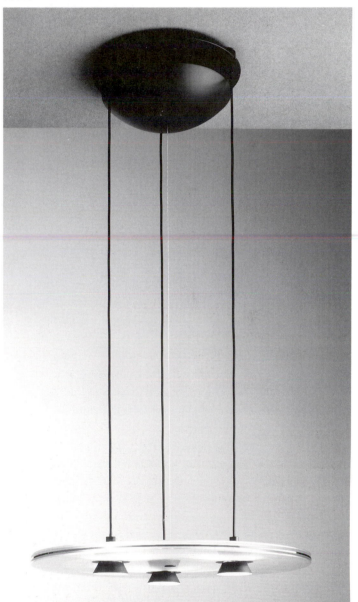

320

319. A ceiling-mounted, adjustable, recessed eyeball fixture permits the lighting to be directed as desired. (Photograph courtesy Lightolier, Inc.)

320. Aurora, a hanging fixture by Perry A. King/Santiago Miranda of 1986, uses three 50-watt, 12-volt quartz-halogen lamps in reflectors. The light output is a combination of direct downlight and diffused light from the large, textured-glass disc. (Photograph courtesy Atelier International Lighting)

LUMINOUS CEILINGS. A false ceiling of louvers or diffusing glass or plastic forms the entire ceiling, with lighting units, usually fluorescent tubes, mounted in the space above. An overall *diffused, shadowless light* results. This form of lighting became popular in the 1950s but has declined in acceptance in recent years. Cleaning of the ceiling louver or diffusing material is a problem, and the even, shadowless light the system gives has proven less satisfactory than originally hoped.

INTEGRATED CEILING SYSTEMS. These systems incorporate *general lighting,* acoustical treatment, and usually air-conditioning supply into their structures (fig. 324). Such systems may be unique to a particular installation, designed by the architect or interior designer, or a manufactured standard product. Use is most common in offices, public spaces, and other large institutional spaces.

Miscellaneous Types

Although the following lighting types belong to one of the groups listed above, they are singled out here for their special characteristics.

CLIP-ON PHOTO LIGHTS. These are a very economical form of incandescent fixture, giving *general and spot lighting,* fully *adjustable* and available with many different types of reflector (fig. 322). They have become a favorite ad hoc, low-cost solution to many residential lighting needs.

LUXO LAMPS. These are a familiar form of cantilever, *adjustable desk lamp,* available in many colors, base types, reflector types, and sizes. Like photo lamps, they have become a popular, inexpensive solution to many home and some office lighting problems. More costly adjustable cantilever lamps of similar function are also available in a variety of excellent designs (see fig. 280).

ANTIQUE REPRODUCTIONS. Many lamps and fixtures are made in more or less convincing imitation of older lighting devices. These are widely used in interiors of traditional design. Since candles, oil, and gas produced light levels far below modern expectations, and since these sources were totally different in size and shape from electric bulbs and tubes, simulation of traditional types is not usually very satisfactory. For stage or museum display use, reproductions of historic lighting types are available with special bulbs that simulate the historic sources. However, these are equally unsatisfactory; far from providing a good imitation of candlelight or gaslight, electric light, when dimmed and given a synthetic flickering effect, merely looks false and unnatural. In historic interiors where modern lighting may seem intrusive, concealed lighting is usually the best solution.

TASK-AMBIENT LIGHTING. This term describes a recently developed system of office lighting that does not use bright general lighting. Instead, *ambient light* from ceiling fixtures or uplighting units provides a low lighting level, adequate for circulation needs and to prevent dark pockets. *Task lighting* at each desk or work station gives a normal light level for the actual work area only (see fig. 288). Since no light is wasted lighting passages, empty spaces, and tops of heads, this approach can deliver a very high level of efficiency in terms of watts per square foot required.

A problem may arise where a task light tube is placed across the edge opposite the seated person at the desk or work surface. This creates a viewing angle from the seated person to papers and other work materials that matches the angle at which light falls on these materials, making for veiling reflections that obscure details of print and writing. Installing special prismatic lenses below the lighting tubes or changing the location of the fixtures (usually to one or both sides of the viewer) will reduce or eliminate this problem.

FIXTURE PLACEMENT AND LOCATION

In small projects, placement can proceed on a case-by-case basis. Lights for special purposes, such as reading and dining, and lights to give general illumination can be placed according to local needs.

CALCULATING PLACEMENT AND LOCATION. More complex projects use formulas to determine placement and location. It is possible to calculate the level of illumination that a proposed installation of light fixtures of a known type and spacing will give. The same formulas can, in reverse, suggest the number and spacing of fixtures needed to produce a desired level of illumination. The relationship basic to all such calculations is:

$$\frac{\text{Illumination}}{\text{(in footcandles)}} = \frac{\text{lumens supplied}}{\text{area in square feet to be lighted}} \quad \frac{\text{(lumens per watt} \times \text{wattage)}}{}$$

The approximate lumen output of various lamp types is given below:

TYPE OF LAMP	LUMENS PER WATT OUTPUT
Incandescent	20
Mercury	50
Fluorescent	80
HID	85

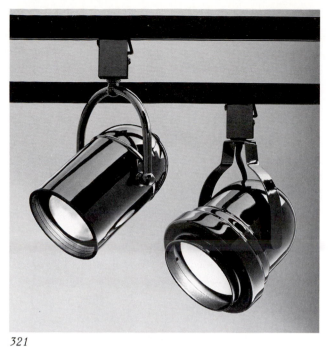

321

322

323

321. Track lighting allows fixtures of many different types to be placed anywhere along tracks that also bear the power line. The two incandescent units illustrated are Manhattan (left), a design of about 1972, and Europa (right) of about 1970. (Photograph courtesy Trakliting, Inc.)

322. Clamp-on, pipe-supported, adjustable, reflector incandescent lights, originally developed for theaters and photographic studios to give strong, concentrated light, are now often adapted to more general interior and architectural use. Oreste RE is a design of Ernesto Gismondi. (Photograph courtesy Artemide Inc.)

323. Track lighting is ideal for illumination in museums, where it can be almost endlessly adapted to changing exhibits. Shown here is the North Gallery of architect Louis Kahn's Kimbell Art Museum in Fort Worth, Texas, 1984.

For example, to arrive at 60 footcandles throughout an area of 6,000 square feet with fluorescent light:

$$60\ footcandles = \frac{80 \times required\ wattage}{6,000\ square\ feet}$$

or

$$60 = \frac{80 \times wattage}{6,000}$$

giving

$$4,500 = wattage\ required$$

The wattage could be provided, for example, by 112 40-watt tubes installed in 28 four-tube fixtures placed at regular intervals to provide even coverage of illumination in the space.

This calculation is, however, oversimplified, since it takes no account of the design of the fixture used, its state of cleanness as time passes, nor of the characteristics of the space, such as its shape and paint color tones, that will affect the lighting to be installed. These factors are taken into account through two steps:

1. The arbitrary lumen-per-watt figure given above is replaced by a figure given in the manufacturer's specifications for the particular fixture selected for use.
2. This figure is multiplied by a coefficient of utilization (CU), also obtained from manufacturer's literature, which takes account of the size and shape of the space and the reflective values of wall and ceiling surfaces. This CU can be further modified by factors to take into account the lamp depreciation (the average dimming of the lamp over its useful life) and a factor for dirt depreciation to allow for dimming caused by dirt buildup.

The restated formula becomes:

$$Footcandles\ delivered = \frac{lumen\ output \times CU \times lamp\ depreciation \times dirt\ depreciation}{area\ in\ square\ feet}$$

This formula can be used to find out the illumination level that a proposed layout of a given fixture will provide or to determine the number of fixtures of given wattage that will be required to deliver a desired light level.

For example, suppose that a level of 75 footcandles is desired in a space having an area of 8,000 square feet. The fixture chosen uses four 40-watt fluorescent tubes with a lumen output of 3,200 per lamp (tube). The manufacturer's literature gives the following data:

CU for the space in question   *.56*
Lamp depreciation   *.80*
Dirt depreciation   *.75*

The formula can now be used to find the area that one fixture will light satisfactorily:

$$75 = \frac{(3,200 \times 4) \times .56 \times .80 \times .75}{area\ in\ square\ feet}$$

This gives an area of 57.34 square feet covered by each fixture. The total area would then require:

$$\frac{8,000}{57.34} = 139.52\ or,\ rounding\ off,\ 140\ fixtures$$

These might be arranged in ten rows of fourteen fixtures, five rows of twenty-eight fixtures, or a different layout suited to the shape of the space. Calculation of this sort is most useful in planning the overall lighting of offices, factories, classrooms, or similar uniformly lighted spaces. Simpler calculation of the same kind can predict the illumination level to be expected from a single lamp or light fixture.

With architectural lighting, the anticipated level of illumination, or brightness, can be calculated quite accurately. This cannot easily be done with portable lighting, since lamps may be moved and wattages changed and since an even illumination level is not usually sought. In residential and other less formal spaces, experience (which can be aided by the use of a light meter) rather than calculation usually guides the placement of lighting.

SWITCHES. It should be remembered that any lighting installation will require switching to provide control from convenient locations. This can be provided by switches at individual fixtures, multiple switches for a single fixture, switching from remote locations or central panels, or, in special cases, multiple switching or switching controlled by clock or light sensors. Switching controlled by sound- or heat-sensitive *proximity* switches, recently developed, turns lighting on when people are present and turns power off when people leave.

Light switches are normally provided at the entry to each room or space. A space that can be entered from two or more directions calls for multiple (upstairs-downstairs) switching. Convenience outlets along walls should be spaced so that an outlet is always available within 6 feet. Wall switches are routinely placed at a height of 50 inches, outlets at 12 inches from the floor. Although they are minor elements, switches, switch plates, and outlet plates should be selected by the interior designer to complement the design of the space, not left to the whim of the electrician, who merely installs what he has on hand, regardless of its design appropriateness.

DIMMERS. Dimmers, a further modification of switching, permit a range of light levels from very low up to the

324

maximum available, and provide them in a smooth transition. When incandescent lights are dimmed, they become warmer in color. This effect of coziness is favored in residential spaces and in dining areas generally. Automatic dimmers can alter light levels gradually, in response to time, outside light levels, or an arbitrary program.

The complexity of lighting as a technical matter and the constantly increasing variety of lighting sources and devices may tempt the interior designer to turn over all lighting problems to a specialized consultant. It should be remembered that the consultant, however expert, is primarily a technical aid. It remains for the designer to suggest the character, atmosphere, and visual effects desired. The more knowledgeable the designer is about technical issues, the easier it will be to communicate with a consultant, and the greater the probability of a satisfactory result. For modest projects that cannot include the services of a consultant, the designer must accept full responsibility for planning lighting that will balance technical performance with pleasant visual impact.

324. An integrated, factory-made ceiling system, Metalinear combines acoustical treatment, air-conditioning distribution, and lighting. (Photograph courtesy Armstrong World Industries' Architectural Building Products Division)

CHAPTER NINE

COLOR

Among all the aspects of interior design, color is one of the most important—perhaps *the* most important element. A successful interior invariably includes color that creates a strong and satisfying impression. Badly chosen color will make any space, however well planned otherwise, seem unpleasant. Unsatisfactory color is probably the most common source of failure in interior design. The depressing effect of "institutional green" in offices, hospital rooms, and classrooms is well known. Harsh, random, and clashing color is commonplace in living rooms in which rugs, paint colors, and furniture have been brought together by chance or by separate purchases without thought for color relationships. A room with a rosy red rug, pea-green walls, blue-and-yellow striped curtains, a brown leather sofa, and a yellow-and-orange flower print hanging on the wall offers a great deal of color, but it is more likely to disturb than to please.

Changing the color scheme is one of the easiest ways to improve a space. Even if one existing color element is retained, the intelligent selection of new colors for other items will often transform an unattractive space into something much more agreeable. In the room described above, white or beige paint for the walls and new curtains in related, subtle tones might make the rug, sofa, and flower print acceptable by bringing all of the colors present into a better relationship. Color is an important design tool as well as a major element of the designed space. An aspect of color that does not get much attention is its ability to affect space visually. Color can make a small space look larger or can camouflage bad proportions.

Color planning involves complex issues that require some study in order to master good color use. Color planning has, moreover, become surrounded by a certain mystique—beliefs that stand in the way of dealing with color directly and successfully. Too many people, including otherwise competent teachers of design, assert that color cannot be taught, that skill in using color is an inborn talent possessed by only a few people. Others suggest that it cannot be taught systematically, that learning to use color can be managed only through experience.

Neither of these views matches reality. Certainly it is true that some people seem to have a special sensitivity to color and that its use is easier for them than for others, and no one can doubt that experience is helpful in developing color usage skills. It is equally certain that the study of color can make what at first seems confusing and mysterious become clear and understandable. While there are no absolute rules that govern color use, accumulated experience has led to a variety of suggestions that anyone can follow to arrive at good color

schemes that will be comfortable, satisfying, stimulating, even exciting.

Our ability to see color, besides being useful, gives us a tremendous amount of pleasure. People who disclaim any artistic interests appreciate the colors of flowers and trees, water and sky, and the human uses of color in costume, graphic materials, architecture, and interior design. Even those with the physical problem known as color blindness (which causes confusion only between certain pairs of colors) are not prevented from enjoying color. Color blindness is not even a significant handicap in working with color. A designer with this condition can easily compensate by using name identification of the problem colors. Otherwise, color work is no different than it is for those with fully normal color vision. Working with color is almost universally enjoyed. Putting together a color scheme is probably the most pleasurable aspect of design work. Developing skill in using colors begins with the study of color systems, which are based on the scientific principles of light and color.

LIGHT AND COLOR

Human vision depends on the presence of light, and the effect of color results from some special properties of light. Light is a form of radiant energy. The eye distinguishes different wavelengths of the radiant energy, or light, and interprets them, in the brain, as different colors. Light energy at the extremes of wavelength—infrared at the long end and ultraviolet at the short end—becomes invisible.

THE COLOR SPECTRUM. Daylight, or white light, is a random mixture of light of all wavelengths. (Artificial light that appears to match the color of daylight is also called white light, although it usually has a somewhat different color makeup.) When white light passes through a glass prism, its different wavelengths become sorted into colors, creating the familiar rainbow, or spectrum, arranged according to wavelength (fig. 326). The longest is red, followed by orange, yellow, green, blue, violet. Their measure in nanometers (formerly designated millimicron), or one-millionth of a millimeter, is generally assigned as follows:

Red	*700–650 nanometers*
Orange	*640–590 nanometers*
Yellow	*580–550 nanometers*
Green	*530–490 nanometers*
Blue	*480–450 nanometers*
Violet	*440–390 nanometers*

325. In a well-designed interior, color relationships are fundamental in establishing an ambience of comfort, welcome, and well-being. The tints chosen for this hallway of a classic New York duplex apartment, although restrained, are a major factor in the success of its design. Robert A. M. Stern Architects, designer, 1980–82. (Photograph: Jaime Ardiles-Arce)

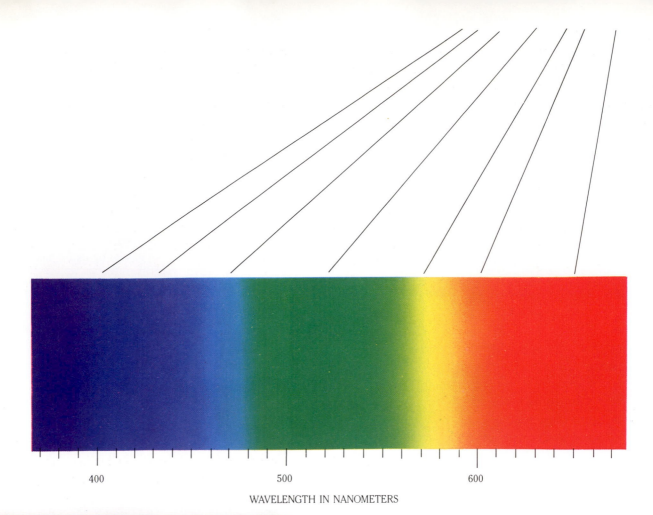

326

WAVELENGTH IN NANOMETERS

327

The various wavelengths of daylight are not always balanced. At dawn or sunset, daylight tends to be short of blue-green components, thus appearing reddish. Incandescent lamps share this characteristic. On cloudy days, daylight is weak in red-orange, so it appears bluish. In such situations, the brain introduces a compensatory bias. The mind soon adjusts to the varying tints of daylight and the quite different color content of artificial light sources (firelight, candlelight, incandescent, or fluorescent light), quickly accepting them as "normal," so that colors appear quite recognizable under any of these different kinds of light.

ADDITIVE COLOR. Colored light, produced by filtering white light so that only one color can pass through the filter (a colored glass or gelatin), makes normal color vision inoperative: everything appears as a tone of the colored light. For example, in pure red light, white and red objects appear bright red, green objects almost black, and other colors as intermediate tones of red. Colored light is used in stage lighting and sometimes in lighting displays but rarely in lighting interiors, since it distorts real color and the single color soon becomes irritating and monotonous.

326. When white light passes through a prism, it is broken up into a spectrum, or a rainbow of colors—red, orange, yellow, green, blue, and violet—their order determined by the wavelengths of the radiant energy they represent. From Theory and Use of Color *by Luigina De Grandis*

327. Additive color is the term used to describe the mixing of colored light. The primary colors of light are red, green, and blue. Yellow results, as demonstrated here, by adding red and green light. All three primaries combine to form white light.

Color mixing of light, used mostly in the theater, is called *additive* color, because mixtures are obtained by adding together the wavelengths that represent the three colors considered *primary* since they cannot be made up by mixing other colors (fig. 327). Any other color can be produced by mixing the three additive primaries—red, blue, and green (yellow is produced by adding red and green). All three produce white or normal light.

SUBTRACTIVE COLOR. In interior design (as in painting, printing, and any other situation using pigments and dyes as the colorants), one is usually working with *subtractive* color. That is, the object or material absorbs, or subtracts, all the colors of light *except* the color of the object, which is the color we see. A red object is actually one that absorbs all colors but red and reflects back only red light. If we mix two colors, for example red and yellow, as paint or pigment, the red pigment is subtracting all but red light reflection, the yellow all but yellow, so that the mixture reflects back some red and some yellow, producing the visual impression of orange color.

THE COLOR WHEEL. When dealing with subtractive color, the colors that cannot be produced through mixing turn out to be red, yellow, and blue. Given these three *primaries* (fig. 328), any other color can be produced by mixture. On the color spectrum, the band of colors arranged according to wavelength, the primaries alternate with *secondaries*, which can be mixed from the primaries that are their neighbors on either side. The spectrum begins with red. Its neighbor, orange, results from mixing red with the next color of the spectrum, the primary yellow. Yellow is followed by green, a secondary made from yellow and blue, the next primary. The visible spectrum ends with violet (or purple), a secondary that can be made by mixing blue with red, the color at the beginning of the rainbow band.

This has led to arranging the band in a circle, so that its end meets its beginning. In the resulting *color wheel* (fig. 329), the primaries and secondaries are equally spaced, with each secondary between the two primaries that can be mixed to create it. This wheel arrangement is the basis for each of the various color systems that organize the confusing realities of color into an understandable entity.

COLOR SYSTEMS

Color systems are extremely helpful in any discussion of color because they clarify the confused terminology used in everyday conversation about color and suggest organized ways of arriving at visually satisfying color schemes.

Once ordinary color names go beyond the primaries and secondaries, they become more and more imprecise. Modifiers such as light, bright, deep, dull, and dark are used in various

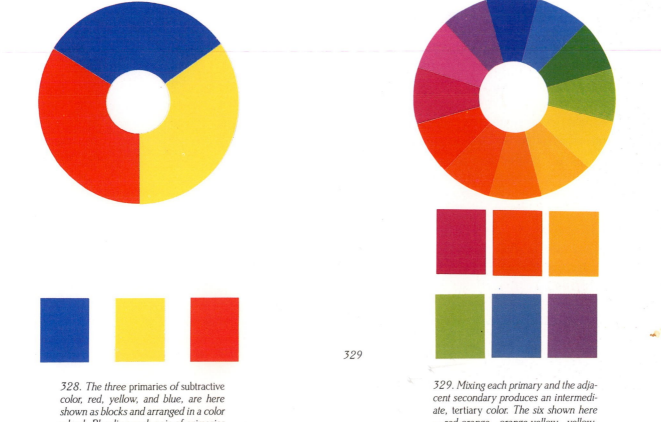

328

329

328. The three primaries of subtractive color, red, yellow, and blue, are here shown as blocks and arranged in a color wheel. Blending each pair of primaries generates the secondaries, orange, green, and violet. When each of these is placed between the pair of primaries that creates it, the six-color wheel results—the spectrum in its natural order.

329. Mixing each primary and the adjacent secondary produces an intermediate, tertiary color. The six shown here —red-orange, orange-yellow, yellow-green, green-blue, blue-violet, and violet-red—make up a spectrum-like band, but one that has shifted slightly from the primary-secondary position. When the tertiaries are placed between their components, a twelve-color wheel results.

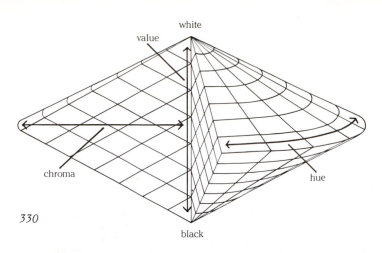

330

and confusing ways, and many color names, such as tan or buff, suggest a wide range of color tones. Color names drawn from real objects are equally imprecise. Just what color is rose, cream, or sky-blue? Manufacturers of paints, textiles, and other materials deepen the confusion by designating their products with such names as flame, champagne, and colonial blue, which defy precise identification.

Efforts to understand color in a systematic way go back at least as far as Goethe's study of 1810. Modern systems vary somewhat in detail, but each provides an organized way to arrange and name colors. The best-known systems are those developed by Wilhelm Ostwald (1853–1932; fig. 330) and Albert Munsell (1858–1918) and the modern OSA-UCS* (1974), a modification of the Munsell system introducing some improvements of primarily technical interest. The Munsell system, widely used in dealing with colors produced by dyes and pigments, is the system most widely accepted in interior design work and forms the basis for the following discussion.

The Munsell Color System

In the Munsell system, any color is described in terms of three attributes. By noting these three qualities according to a standardized system, any color can be exactly described and specified. Understanding the three dimensions of color is the key to dealing with color problems in an organized way.

HUE. The first (and most obvious) characteristic of a color is its position in the spectrum, the quality that gives it its basic name. In the Munsell system, this is called *hue,* and it is designated by a letter identification. Munsell chose to recognize *five* basic hues, a decision that goes against the normal understanding of primaries and secondaries. In practice, the Munsell system is usually modified to use six hues, three primaries and three secondaries, which can be identified by the

letters R, O, Y, G, B, V (red, orange, yellow, green, blue, violet). Intermediate hues between these six are then identified by two-letter combinations, for example, RO for red-orange, OY for orange-yellow, and so on. These hues are often called *tertiaries.* Still finer gradations of hue *(quaternaries)* can be inserted between the first twelve with three-letter designations (OOY, OYY, YYG, and so on). This subdivision can be continued indefinitely.

VALUE. The second characteristic of any color is its lightness or darkness, called its *value.* The value of a color depends upon the amount of light it reflects (lighter) or absorbs (darker). Adding white, which reflects all light, lightens a color without changing its hue; similarly, adding black, which absorbs all light, darkens a color without changing its hue. Munsell measures value by means of a scale of tones ranging from light to dark (fig. 332). White, placed at the top of the scale, is designated 10, black, at the bottom, is designated 0. The value scale between them has nine equal steps of grays ranging from dark to light. The value of any color can be found by matching its lightness or darkness with one of the steps of gray. In mixing color, a sample of a particular hue can be moved upward on the value scale by adding white or downward by adding black. Light values, above the middle of the scale, or 6 through 9, are called *tints,* dark values, below the middle, or 1 through 4, are *shades* (fig. 333).

Values strongly affect the perception of a color. The same color, or hue, placed at opposite ends of the value scale has greatly different effects. For example, the lightest tint of violet, often called lavender, is a delicate, light color that might be used in a summer home. Its darkest shade is a very deep purple that would appear heavy and oppressive in the same setting.

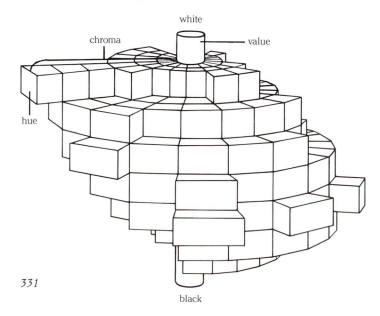

331

OSA-UCS stands for Optical Society of America, Uniform Color Scales.

330. In the Ostwald system, a central axis is a scale of grays, from white at the top to black at the bottom. A color wheel is arranged around it with each hue's maximum chroma, or saturation, at the circumference. The hues become gradually less saturated as they near the central axis, where they reach neutral gray. Above and below the wheel the hues parallel the gray value scale, upward for tints, downward for shades, in disklike steps. These circles become smaller as the number of steps to maximum saturation decreases toward the upper and lower points. When all the possible colors are placed, forming a geometric solid, the result is a symmetrical figure—a pair of identical cones meeting at the center plane. (Courtesy U.S. Department of Agriculture)

331. The color solid developed in the Munsell system, as in the Ostwald system, has a gray scale as its central axis and hues arranged in a wheel. Munsell, however, recognized the fact that different hues reach maximum chroma at different levels of value between black and white, and that some hues permit more steps of chroma variation (from maximum to gray) than others. Steps of difference in chroma and in value are kept constant in each Munsell scale; as a result, when all colors are arranged in a solid, the figure produced is not geometrically regular but uneven, or lumpy. Yellow reaches maximum chroma high up in the solid, while red, violet, and blue reach their greatest chroma nearer the bottom. The Munsell system is particularly useful in design, allowing color samples to be designated by precise letter and number codes.

TINTS

SHADES

333

332

334

In the Munsell system, the value number of a color follows the hue designation. For example, YG/7 is a yellow-green with a value matching step 7 of the gray scale.

C H R O M A . The third aspect of color is its intensity or purity, called its *chroma* in the Munsell system. *Saturation* is also a commonly used term for this quality. Steps of chroma are numbered up to 14, from low chroma to maximum chroma, although different hues reach maximum chroma at different step numbers (fig. 334). Maximum chroma signifies a particular hue in its purest form. Adding the hue opposite to it on the color wheel lowers the chroma, making the color less pure and intense. Mixing equal amounts of the colors opposite to one another on the wheel produces a neutral gray, identified as chroma 1. The intensity of a color usually affects its value as well. In Munsell's notation of colors, the chroma number comes last. Thus, YG/7/4 indicates a yellow-green hue at a value of 7 and chroma of 4.

T H E   C O L O R   S O L I D . Arranging colors using the gray value scale, which is neutral, as a central axis, the circular arrangement of hues as a ring with the axis at its center, and all possible steps of chroma connecting the axis (low chroma)

with the hue on the rim of the wheel (high chroma) like spokes gives a three-dimensional cluster, or *color solid*, with every color in a logical place (fig. 331). Because various hues reach maximum chroma at different value levels, the Munsell color solid does not form a neat sphere or any other perfect geometric shape. Yellow, for example, becomes most intense at a high-value level, blue and red at a lower value. The color solid is therefore somewhat irregular and lumpy. Some color systems force a perfectly symmetrical color solid by imposing different ways of spacing and annotating actual color specimens.

Complementary Colors

In practice, it is most useful simply to bear in mind the concepts of value and chroma while working with a color wheel that places the strongest possible chroma of each hue in the rainbow-order ring. In this arrangement, each hue will be found to be directly opposite (across in a straight line from) a hue that we think of as opposite in character: red across from green, orange from blue, yellow from violet. Thus each primary stands across from a secondary made up by mixing the two other primaries. Such opposite colors are called *complementary*.

332. The gray scale of values from white to black in ten tones (A) is shown adjacent to a value scale of reds (B), with the clear primary near the center. Adding white, to produce the lighter tints, or gray or a complementary, to produce darker shades, reduces the chroma of the pure color. The equivalent gray tone is shown adjacent to each color tone. It is not possible to produce a tint as light as pure white or a shade as dark as solid black.

333. When tints and shades become discernibly different from the pure colors on which they are based, they are given new names. Pink, cream, and beige (above) are tints of red, yellow, and orange. The shades (below) may be called tan, olive, and taupe. They are derived from yellow, green, and orange.

334. Here, a scale of chroma moves in seven steps from the fully saturated pure color to a least saturated neutral, while maintaining the entire scale at a constant value.

335

335. Subtle, mostly cool pastel colors
define the character of designer John F.
Saladino's own apartment in New York.
(Photograph: Lizzie Himmel)

Mixing two complementaries—in effect, adding together the three primaries—results, in the subtractive color of dyes and pigments, in a neutral gray. (In reality, the actual color may be a brownish or bluish neutral rather than the theoretical neutral gray of the color systems.)

Warm and Cool Colors

Looking at the color wheel, we see that the circle is divided through its center into two families of color that make a strongly different impression. Red, orange, and yellow are described as *warm* colors, green, blue, and violet as *cool*. A clear mental association between the colors themselves and the temperature sensations of hot and cold has been established. Warm colors actually seem to raise the apparent room temperature, making spaces feel cozy and pleasant indoors in winter, while cool colors provide relief on a hot day or in a warm climate. Notice that a complementary pair is always made up of one warm and one cool color.

Neutral grays, black, and white are neutral in relation to the warm-cool range, as one might expect from their position as the central axis of the Munsell color solid. Tints and shades close to neutral, located near but not at the axis, can be spoken of as warm or cool according to which side of the color wheel they lie on. They are sometimes hard to identify in terms of hue, partly because we use different color names for colors of low values and low chroma. A dark red or orange of low chroma will usually be called a shade of brown. A blue in a similar position in the color solid will be seen as a cool gray. Colors with names such as tan, olive drab, or taupe at the darker end of the scale or pink, cream, or beige at the light end are examples of hues given new names when of low chroma and either high or low value.

PSYCHOLOGICAL IMPACT OF COLORS

It is widely recognized that colors have a strong impact on human moods and emotions. Even some physical sensations can be modified by the presence of colors. However, the exact nature of these influences is not well understood, and the confusion is compounded by the complex ways in which color interacts with spatial perception as well as the ways in which colors influence each other.

It is generally agreed that warm colors convey a sensation of warmth, both physical and emotional. Well-documented cases demonstrate that complaints about inadequate heat have been silenced by a change of color scheme, with no change of actual air temperature. The idea of a cozy room is strongly identified with the use of warm color and warm lighting that emphasizes the warmth of the colors present (see fig. 342). In contrast, cool colors suggest formality and reserve and communicate a sense of physical coolness as well (see fig. 339).

Many attempts have been made to identify the impact of the various hues, but it cannot be ascertained whether these reactions are innate or cultural. For example, death and mourning are associated with the color black in Western traditions, whereas in China and other Oriental civilizations the color of death is white. The response may also differ according to the context. Red is commonly associated with danger and the meaning *stop*, yet it is used for exit signs that indicate a route out of danger to safety. A color that may communicate excitement of a pleasurable sort in one context may be irritating in another; a hue that is calm and soothing under one set of circumstances may be depressing in another. With these cautions in mind, it may be useful to review the generally accepted associations for the various hues:

Reds are seen as warm, even hot, exciting, and stimulating. They are associated with tension and danger (heat and fire). Limited amounts of red can augment and balance blues and greens in a color scheme, adding life and cheer. Strong reds and greens together in large areas can generate unpleasant tensions.

Oranges share the qualities of reds to a slightly reduced extent. Small areas of red-orange are a useful, stimulating modifier in otherwise neutral or cool color schemes.

Yellows, the mildest of the warm colors, are usually associated with cheerfulness, even humor (in theater lighting, it is traditional to use yellow for comedy scenes). They give a strong effect of brightness while suggesting less tension than reds and oranges. Yellow tints (creams and beiges) are known as safe colors, with no negative implications, but their overuse subjects them to insipidity.

Greens are the cool colors closest to warm. They have become a favorite for balanced color schemes seeking to be calm and restful, peaceful and constructive, associations stemming from green as the color of grass and leaves. The color theorists of the 1930s so successfully promoted green as the best color for offices, classrooms, and hospital interiors that its overuse has made "institutional green" an objectionable cliché. However, green remains a good color to impart serenity, especially when used with limited areas of red or red-orange to counter any sense of drabness.

Blues are the coolest of the cool colors, suggesting rest and repose, calm and dignity. Overused or in too strong a chroma, blues can generate depression and gloom, as evident in the phrase "to have the blues." Intense blue in small areas can be a helpful accent in warm and warm-neutral color schemes.

Violets, along with their stronger versions called purples, have a reputation as problematic and unsafe colors. At the borderline between cool and warm, they seem to convey uncertainty (in contrast to borderline green, which communicates strength from both families). Violets are often seen as artistic, suggesting subtlety and sensitivity, but at the risk of conveying ambiguity. Purples even more strongly intimate tension and depression, although they also project dignity (the "royal" purple). Violets can be highly expressive but must be used with caution.

Neutral colors—grays, more or less warm, cool, or exactly neutral, as well as browns and tans—tend to convey, in milder form, the impressions of the hues that they contain in dilute form. The truly neutral grays make good background colors, easy to live with over long periods. However, they are subject to dullness and an impression of monotony. When used with limited areas of more chromatic color, grays can be very useful. Browns and tans, which are actually somewhat neutralized reds and yellows, have a traditional association with a snug, clubby atmosphere. They appear homelike in their milder tones, masculine in their heavier values.

Whites and near-whites suggest clarity, openness, and brightness. White is always a safe color and can be used in large areas to highly satisfactory effect if offset with small areas of chromatic color. The association with cleanliness and sanitation is an obvious one. All-white schemes can seem forced and empty, but whites used with appropriate accents imply modernity and high style, perhaps in part because whites were so widely used by early modernist designers.

Black is a powerful accent color, depressing if used to excess. It suggests weight, dignity, formality, and solemnity. Extensive use of black is best limited to spaces occupied for brief periods of time (elevator cabs, vestibules, bathrooms). As dark grays share some of these qualities to a reduced degree, they can be used more safely where strong, dark accents are required.

While these generalizations seem to have considerable value, it must be remembered that colors are rarely used alone and that colors used together interact in ways that are very complex. One cannot simply mix a bit of red for excitement, some black for dignity, and some green for calm and expect to achieve a scheme with all of those qualities. Almost any color can work in certain situations, and almost any combination can be successful, given balanced relationships of hue, chroma, and value and sound choices of location, area, texture, and other variables. In practice, all of the systematic knowledge of color reviewed above is best absorbed as background for creative work that proceeds in ways that have no dependence on formula or routine.

336

336. Bold colors—contrasting in both value and hue—create an atmosphere that is vibrant, active, even aggressive, a strikingly different approach from the subdued relationships illustrated in figs. 325 and 335. Frank Gehry, architect, remodeled the Los Angeles home of artist Miriam Wosk, who created the interior design. (Photograph: © Grant Mudford, courtesy House & Garden)

COLOR SCHEMES

The concept of *color harmony* is one of the keys to understanding the theory that lies behind the development of various color schemes. This concept has its origins in a comparison of colors with musical tones. It is well known that certain musical notes sound well together, while others make a discordant or clashing sound. There is a basis for this in the physics of sound, which explains the reasons for harmonious chords in music. While the physical basis of color harmony is not so easily explained, it is commonly observed that some colors clash in a harsh relationship while other combinations, whether soothing or exciting, subtle or aggressive, are pleasant.

Planned color schemes can be classified into a number of types, regardless of the actual hues used or whether warm or cool colors dominate. These types are discussed here in order of complexity, beginning with the simplest. Not unexpectedly, this parallels the order of difficulty involved in producing a successful scheme. The most complex and difficult types can be extremely beautiful, but putting them into practical use takes more experience and skill (or perhaps special talent) than working with the simpler types of scheme.

Monotone (Neutral) Color Schemes

These use a single color of low chroma in one value or a very limited range of values (fig. 337). Typical colors used are grays, tans, and tinted whites. It is almost impossible for such a scheme to fail through harsh or clashing effect, but monotony— as the name suggests—is a risk. Monotone schemes are ideal for situations where strong color will enter in some transitory way—in the costumes of occupants, the display of colorful art or merchandise, or the dramatic views through large windows. In practice, the monotone scheme is often modified by the introduction of some stronger color in minor accent elements. A strictly monotone scheme can seem somewhat forced, as in the case of the all-white room, which has become something of a decorative cliché. All-beige or almost all-beige schemes are very safe and, if monotony is relieved by some changing element not strictly a part of the scheme, can be fully satisfactory.

Monochromatic Color Schemes

Similar to monotone schemes, these use a wider range of chroma and value in a single hue (fig. 338). The familiar ideas of a red room or blue room exemplify schemes of this type. Such schemes also can be developed using the natural colors of materials that fall in a narrow range, such as red-orange tones ranging down through browns and tans, all of the same hue. Like monotone schemes (which may be considered a special

case of monochromaticity), these schemes tend to be easy, since harsh clashes are almost impossible. Monochromatic schemes likewise risk monotony or a certain artificiality.

The latter problems arise when every item—carpet, walls, furniture, curtains—is given a strong version of the chosen hue, such as a particular blue. Rooms with a single strong color can be dramatic and often look good in photographs, but they can be hard to live with over an extended period of time. Such schemes may work best for spaces, such as bathrooms or elevators, that people occupy only briefly.

Analogous Color Schemes

These schemes achieve harmony by using hues that are close together on the color wheel (fig. 339). The typical analogous scheme uses one primary or one secondary plus the hues adjacent to it on either side. Two examples are blue with its neighbors blue-green and blue-violet and green plus blue-green and yellow-green. An adjacent primary and secondary plus the tertiary hues between them (blue and green plus the blue-greens between them, for example) also generate an analogous scheme. In each case, the hues included fall within a segment of the color wheel that spans no more than about 90 degrees. As long as hue is restricted to one-quarter of the wheel, a range of varied value and chroma may be used.

Once again, because of its restriction, the analogous scheme virtually guarantees harmony. Because of its greater color range, monotony is less of a hazard than with monotone and monochromatic schemes. Complementaries from across the color wheel are often introduced as accent colors; however, if these become important elements in the scheme, it is no longer truly analogous but a species of complementary scheme.

Complementary Color Schemes

As the name implies, these schemes use contrasting hues from opposite sides of the color wheel: reds with greens, oranges with blues, yellows with violets (fig. 342). The basic hues may be more subtle intermediate colors rather than primary or secondary colors, as long as they face each other across the wheel. Complementary schemes, which tend to seem bright and balanced, are generally well liked when skillfully assembled. The danger in complementary schemes is that they may become overbright, even garish. Flags, sports costumes, display advertising, and some stage design make good use of such sharply contrasting complementaries, but interiors in strong bright reds and greens or blues and oranges will appear unpleasantly harsh, tiring, even ugly.

Successful complementary schemes usually use a color of low chroma and either high or low value (tints or shades) from

337. In their "Thematic House" bedroom, Charles Jencks, architect, and his wife, Maggie Keswick, designer, have restricted color to a monotone except for a few small accents. The result is that attention is focused on the symbolic motif of this "Foursquare Room"—repeated in ornamental details in the design of the ceiling, mirrors, lighting elements, and the four-poster bed. Although the color is limited to tones close to ivory white, the effect is still richly colorful. The house is in London. (Photograph: © Richard Bryant, courtesy House & Garden)

338. In this weekend house on Long Island, New York, designed by architects Tod Williams and William McAnulty, the color scheme of the main living space is largely monochromatic, in values of bluish-grays. The rose tone of the chair upholstery and of the coffee table pedestal provides an accent. (Photograph: Oberto Gili, courtesy House & Garden)

337

338

339

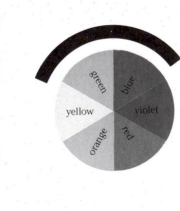

340

341

one side of the wheel to cover large areas and stronger colors from the opposite side of the wheel for smaller areas. Neutralizing each color by adding the complementary to it helps to unify complementary schemes. For example, a room might have floor and wall areas of a light green, grayed (reduced in chroma) by the addition of red. Some objects, perhaps upholstered furniture, would display the complementary red in strong but not full chroma, reduced by a small addition of green.

Complementary schemes are more difficult to plan than the simpler scheme types discussed above, especially if one considers the range of variations on basic complementary color. It is possible to widen the band of hues used on either one or both sides of the color wheel while still maintaining a

339. The color scheme for this living space in a Lake Tahoe residence is described as analogous, as the colors used are adjacent in the spectrum—primarily a range of blue and its neighbor green, the green reaching over to its other neighbor, yellow, in the yellow-tans of the wood and rush chairs, stools, and wooden wall finish. It is also, by virtue of the dominant blues and greens, a cool scheme, suitable to a hot climate. Michael Taylor, designer. (Photograph: Timothy Hursley, © The Arkansas Office, courtesy House & Garden)

340, 341. The strongly chromatic colors in the scheme illustrated in fig. 339 are all blues and greens; the more neutral tones are tans and beiges, that is, desaturated yellows. The chart (fig. 340) thus shows a range from blue-gray through blue and green to yellow. When charted on a color wheel (fig. 341), all tones are adjacent, staying within one-third of the full spectrum.

342

complementary balance. Both red and the adjacent red-violet on one side of the wheel might be used with the slightly yellowed green opposite or with a range in the yellow-green to green band. Once again, such schemes require care and subtlety to avoid garishness.

A further variant of complementary schemes, sometimes classified as a totally different type, is the *split-complementary scheme*. In this scheme, a hue on one side of the wheel is used with the two hues that fall on either side of the directly opposite complementary. With red, for example, both yellow-green and blue-green could be used, omitting the true green between them (hence the term *split*). This scheme also works best using lower levels of chroma for the hues from one side of the wheel in larger areas and more intense color from the other side of

343

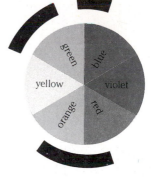

344

342. Complementary colors were chosen by Mrs. Henry Parish II, designer with the firm of Parish-Hadley, for her own home in New York. Such schemes are rich in color and, when warm tones dominate—as they do here—endow a room with an inviting, comfortable charm. (Photograph: Oberto Gili, courtesy House & Garden)

343, 344. The strong orange and yellow tones that compel one's attention in the space shown in fig. 342 are balanced by smaller areas of color from the opposite side of the wheel, making a complementary scheme. The color chart (fig. 343) demonstrates that the greens of the painted panels, however, are close to yellow, while those of the

plants—a significant element in this scheme—are closer to blue; the result is a split complementary scheme. The dark brown wood finishes may seem to fall outside the main color range, but they are, in fact, very deep tones of orange. On the wheel chart (fig. 344), the split tones are slightly shifted from a position exactly opposite one another.

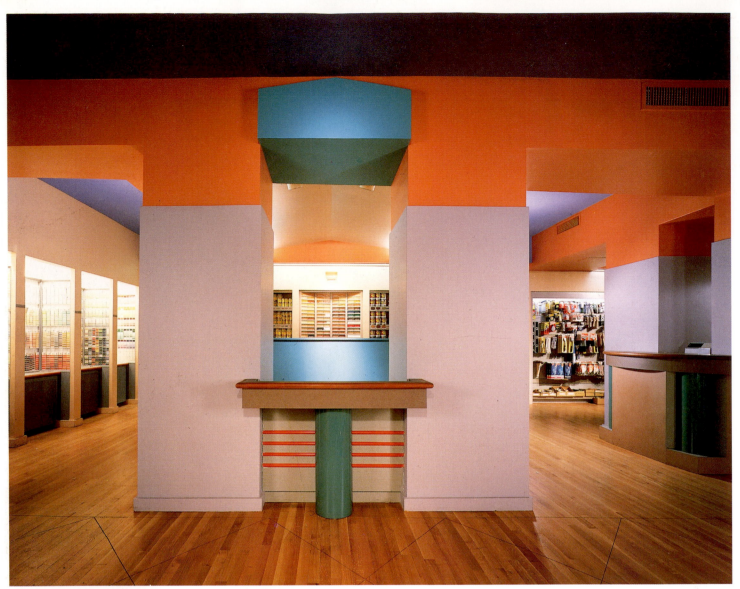

345

346

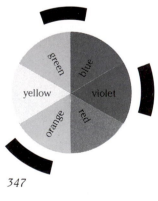

347

the wheel in smaller areas and accents. Effective split-complementary schemes look lively and colorful. They make a subtler and more varied impression than simple complementary schemes.

Triad Color Schemes

Choosing three hues approximately equidistant from one another on the color wheel—for example, red, yellow, and blue; orange, green, and violet; or slightly shifted versions of these combinations—creates triad schemes (fig. 345). These are the most difficult of all the color schemes discussed so far, and the most likely to slip into harshness and confusion. Successful triad schemes generally employ reduced intensities of all hues

345. A triad scheme uses chromatic colors that are more or less equally spaced around the color wheel. The most common, or major, triad is red, yellow, and blue (see fig. 514). Shown here is a minor triad, made up of the secondaries, orange, green, and violet. Because they are based on saturated

hues, triad schemes tend to have great impact—so it is not surprising to find this example in the showroom of a paint company, Janovic Plaza in New York. Voorsanger & Mills Associates Architects, designer. (Photograph: © 1982 Peter Aaron/ESTO)

346, 347. The triad scheme in fig. 345 is illustrated here in chart form (fig. 346). A neutral color acts as background for the triad. The three secondaries that make up the dominant chromatic colors are about equally spaced on the color wheel (fig. 347).

348

or all but one hue. Triad color is often used in small areas in an otherwise mostly neutral scheme. An interior following this scheme might have mostly white surfaces, with flooring in one hue of the triad at reduced value and chroma plus accents in the other two hues of the triad.

Tetrad Color Schemes

These use four hues equally spaced around the color wheel (fig. 348). The comments offered for triad schemes are even more strongly applicable to tetrad color. Examples are, in practice, fairly rare, but, difficult though they may be to produce, lively and satisfactory schemes of this type remain a possibility.

349

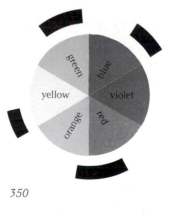

350

348. A tetrad *color scheme* is composed of four hues equally spaced around the color wheel. In this living area in a Houston home, built c. 1919–21 by Harrie T. Lindeberg, Mark Hampton has used a subtle tetrad scheme in a 1983 remodeling to generate a feeling of ease in familiar, traditional terms. (Photograph: Feliciano, courtesy House & Garden)

349, 350. Although the color tones are muted, the four hues that form a tetrad scheme are distinct here (fig. 349). The greens of the upholstery and the blue of the rug are prominent values. The red and pink of the sofa and the browns of the wood finishes represent the third hue, while the creamy yellow lampshades and the beige-tan of the painted wall surfaces complete the tetrad. The tetrad color scheme diagrammed on a color wheel (fig. 350) shows the four hues at even intervals around the circle.

352

SPECIAL COLOR EFFECTS

A number of circumstances alter the appearance of color. In the theoretical consideration of color schemes, all colors are thought of as uniform, solid, and flat (nonglossy). In practice, real materials have characteristics that modify the way color is seen. A glossy finish often alters the apparent color of an object due to its high reflectance. Light reflected from its surface tends to dilute and weaken the visible color, while adjacent colors (such as floor color) reflected on it may actually cause a shift in its apparent hue.

Effects of Texture, Pattern, and Metallic Materials

TEXTURE. Textured surfaces alter apparent color by introducing shadow or gloss at a microscale. Under a microscope, the texture may be seen as tiny hills and valleys, a series of pores, pits, flakes, shreds, or slivers that may have gloss surfaces or may cast shadows or do both. The color seen is then the color of the material modified by these textural elements. Due to these effects, many textured materials will shift color when observed at different angles or when rubbed or

351. Used together, strong red and blue suggest excitement and activity in this house in Mexico designed by George Woo, architect. (Photograph: © Balthazar Korab, courtesy House & Garden)

352. The original pressed-metal (or tin) ceiling in this loft inspired the use of the same material as a new wall surface. Like the polished floor, the metal reflects and extends the rather limited chromatic range in the converted residential space, a musician's home. Preston Phillips was the architect. (Photograph: © Peter Aaron/ESTO, courtesy House & Garden)

stroked in one direction or another. Suede, many solid-color carpets, and textiles exhibit the latter effect. Even wood, if it is left unfinished or is finished to preserve its natural color and texture, may change color according to the angle of view and the angle of lighting. Textiles and carpets with strong texture shift the visual appearance of the actual dye color in ways that are hard to predict. Textures of surfaces (plaster, brick, stone) can alter the appearance of paint color. In order to take texture into account, color effects should be judged from actual samples of the material to be used.

PATTERN. Color also appears in patterns, from the slight pattern of some woven fabrics up to the large-scale, highly visible designs of some printed textiles and wallpapers. When viewed at a distance, small-scale patterns appear as a solid color, the result of visually mixing the colors that make up the pattern. Larger patterns should be categorized as sets of colors grouped together, each component having a separate identity.

METALLIC MATERIALS. Metallic materials show color in a way that can be confusing. Polished metals act as a mirror, reflecting adjacent colors. The white metals — namely, silver, stainless steel, aluminum, and chromium — reflect colors back with little change. Brass, gold, copper, and other colorful metals act much as a tinted mirror, tinting the adjacent colors they reflect back yellow, orange, or reddish brown, according to the metal in question. This effect is also influenced by the finish. Glossy, or mirror-polished, finishes have a very high reflectance. Textured metallic finishes (also called satin or brushed) combine the reflectivity of polished metals with a microtexture (of tiny roughnesses) that breaks up sharp or smooth reflectivity. Metallics, like patterns, can be considered special cases, best evaluated in actual or simulated* samples.

Colors in Relation to Each Other

The actual space will also influence how colors appear. When seen against a larger background, small areas of color may alter in both value and hue. Light colors will appear lighter than they are when seen against a darker background, darks become darker against a light background (fig. 353). A medium tone can be made to seem either light or dark through contrast with its surroundings (fig. 354). Similarly, hues will seem to shift in

Metal foils, metallic papers, and plastic sheeting are often convenient substitutes for actual pieces of metal that may be unavailable or too difficult to use in color planning.

relation to surroundings. A neutral gray will appear warm when placed on a blue background and cool when placed on red (fig. 355). Stronger colors will seem to shift in hue in relation to background, with a small sample seeming to move toward the complementary of the background color. For example, a small area of strong green will seem more intensely green when placed on a reddish (pink) background; placed on a violet background, its hue will seem to shift toward yellow-green.

Effects of Color on Space

Conversely, color itself creates some surprising effects. Warm colors are said to *advance,* that is, appear closer than they actually are, while cool colors *recede,* appearing farther away. Light colors make objects look larger and lighter than they are, while darker colors make them look smaller and heavier. Placing sharply contrasting hues (that is, one advancing, one receding) together can cause a sense of *vibration* as the colors seem to move in opposite directions (fig. 356).

These effects can be used to advantage in interior design. A small space can be made to seem larger, an oddly shaped space to seem better proportioned by a judicious use of colors in ways that exploit these effects. A long, narrow room, for example, will seem more normally shaped if the end walls are of a strong, warm color while the sides are lighter and cooler in tone, so that visually the ends seem to come closer and the sides move away. A dark ceiling will tend to seem lower than the same ceiling in a light tone. A dark floor *and* ceiling can greatly reduce apparent height and may even seem oppressive. A door painted to match the color of the wall around it or a window curtained in a tone matching its surround will blend into their environment. The same elements treated in contrasting colors will be emphasized.

Similarly, furniture can be made recessive or prominent according to whether it matches or contrasts with its background. An ebony black grand piano will be striking on a light floor with a light wall behind it. It will appear smaller and less assertive against a floor and wall in dark tones. Trim moldings (baseboards, cornices, window and door frames) stand out and define form when painted to contrast with walls in hue, value, or both. Trim painted to match walls tends to be less noticeable, deemphasizing the shape and contributing to an effect of spaciousness.

Effects of Light on Color

For every use of color, it should be remembered that color and color effects are influenced by the presence of light, which is what makes it possible to see color at all. When working with

353

354

355

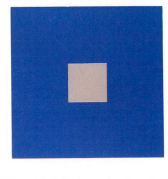

Daylight and incandescent light have enough in common to be almost interchangeable, keeping in mind that incandescent light is warmer, making cool colors appear more neutral and warm colors stronger than they appear in daylight. The human eye and brain accept this shift quite readily, since the relationship of colors remains otherwise unaltered. Fluorescent lights, HID, and other light sources are much less predictable in their impact on color. Inspection of a scheme under the actual light source is essential when such illuminants are to be used.

PRACTICAL APPROACHES

Having absorbed as much of the theoretical views of color as possible, actual work with color comes down to some methodical steps that can be applied to virtually any interior problem. A preliminary step involves collecting an adequate assortment of color samples, including samples of materials, in ranges of colors, that may become part of actual schemes. (Putting together such a sample collection is discussed in more detail later in this chapter, on page 265.) Assuming that samples are at hand, the steps to be taken are:

1. Note down in an orderly list the factors that will influence the scheme. *These might include such items as:*
The orientation and extent of windows or other daylight supply to the space.
The type and location of artificial lighting to be used.
The hours that the space will be used and the purposes it will serve.
The character or atmosphere desired, expressed in such general terms as calm, restful, stimulating, exciting, dignified, playful, and so on.

356

color in developing interior schemes, it is important that the light used match the light that will be normal in the actual built space. Working at the drafting table with daylight illumination when the built space will normally be artificially lit can lead to some distressing surprises. Conversely, a desk lamp can falsify a scheme that will most often be seen in daylight. Many interiors must serve with both daylight and artificial light. In such cases, proposed color schemes should be evaluated under both types of lighting and under combinations that simulate the light that will be present in the real space.

353. A small sample of a light tone on a dark background appears lighter than a larger sample of the same color. Similarly, a small, dark sample on a light background appears darker than a larger sample.

354. A dark background with a medium, light sample appears darker because of the contrasting tone than the same background with a dark sample.

355. Identical neutrals look different when placed on different backgrounds. The red makes the gray seem cooler and darker, while the blue background shifts the gray to a lighter, warmer tone.

356. Because the eye cannot focus simultaneously on an intense green superimposed on an intense red, the edge where the colors meet appears to vibrate. Since strong complementaries juxtaposed tend to produce this phenomenon, they are usually used only when an effect of intensity and tension is desired.

The personal preferences of users, if they can be ascertained. In residential design, the occupants can easily be queried about the colors they like and dislike. In public spaces, such individual preferences are not a factor, but generally accepted preferences of a whole population can often be identified through observation of common regional color usage.

Geographical location, both in terms of climate and in relation to regional preferences in color use.

2. Establish the general character of the scheme in relation to the factors outlined above. *This may include choosing among warm, cool, or neutral color, selecting the type of color scheme in theoretical terms (analogous, complementary, and so on), and deciding the dominant hue or hues. This step can be developed in words alone or together with color images. These may be actual color samples; imagery from color photographs of existing interiors; or other color materials, such as paintings or color combinations in natural objects or settings.*

3. Make selections of color for one or two of the major large areas, *such as floor, walls, and ceiling. Any major areas of predetermined color should be noted at this first step—existing furniture to be retained, for example, or large areas of material of a known color (brick, stone, or natural wood to be left unpainted), or any other color elements not subject to change.*

4. Add color selections for secondary items: *furniture, drapery, and other elements with significant color impact.*

5. Add selections of small areas of color that will act as accents. *These may be strong values of color already selected, in a contrasting color, or materials of a special nature, such as metallic elements, tinted glass, or mirror, that will have a significant impact on the total scheme.*

Once these basic selections are made, the scheme can then be adjusted, changing one or more items to improve or fine-tune the scheme. It is often wise to make several alternative schemes for comparison; sometimes elements from one scheme can be exchanged with those of an alternative as an aid in arriving at the optimum solution.

In going through this process, it often seems that choices can be extremely arbitrary—that one color can be as good (or as bad) as another and that the difficulty of arriving at good color can arise as much from this freedom as from any other problem. If that is so, several approaches that effectively limit or guide choices in what may otherwise seem a totally unstructured realm of possibilities may be considered. The following three approaches have a record of proven usefulness.

Natural Color

A decision to keep all materials in their own natural, unaltered color will generally produce a pleasing and harmonious result. Each material, whether brick, stone, wood, plaster, tile, or other, has a natural color that results from its growth or manufacture, a color that will be visible as long as no colorants, paints, or dyes are used to alter the basic color of the material itself. Such a scheme finds support from a certain school of thought that connects it to the issues of honesty and expressivity in design. The idea that all materials are best left in their natural color relates to the belief that the nature of materials should be central to the visual character of any constructed space.

In practice, most materials have natural colors in a warm neutral range, from the grays of stone and slate to the browns and reds of brick and tile, from the light grays and whites of plaster to the lighter browns and tans of woods. Textile fibers fall in a range of light neutrals (light grays and tans). Wool ranges from black and brown through grays and tans to near-white. A naturally colored interior will usually have a color character defined by these values. Stronger color can come from the greens and flower colors of plants or from the colors introduced by the clothing of occupants.

This kind of color can be seen in the work of Frank Lloyd Wright (fig. 357), his one-time student Harwell Hamilton Harris, and many modern architects and designers. It is also the color of many historic interiors, medieval castles and churches, European and American Colonial cottages and farmhouses. The introduction of strong accent color is a frequent modification of the strictly natural color scheme. Wright liked to use his favorite vermilion red in small spots, perhaps on some cushions or upholstery fabric, a small area of tile or paint. The stained glass of the medieval stone cathedral has a similar impact.

Modern synthetic materials that can hardly be said to have a natural color introduce quandaries into the natural color scheme. What is the natural color of the plastic of floor tiles, laminate furniture tops, or plastic chair shells? What of surfaces, such as steel, that require paint for protection? In the all-natural color scheme, the usual answers are to select plastic colors that use a minimum of artificial colorants—grays, tans, and neutrals like those of so many natural materials—and to select paints that are basic pigments, such as white lead and red lead, choosing them for their durability and protective qualities rather than for their varied color. White plaster may be painted white for protection without altering its color. Red lead primer or the rustlike finish of Cor-ten steel are relatively natural choices for steel that must be finished. Wax, oil, and some clear lacquers protect wood with minimal change in color.

357. In all his work, Frank Lloyd Wright respected the intrinsic qualities of his materials, including color. The pleasing, warm, and humane atmosphere of his interiors derives in large measure from this commitment to natural hues. Here, in the 1922 Storer House in Los Ange- *les, the tones of only the rug and couch do not derive from their materials; however, they remain largely within the color range set by the natural materials. (Photograph: Carlos von Frankenberg/ Julius Shulman Associates)*

358

Natural color is generally very safe since its colors are basically neutral, precluding harsh, unpleasant, or clashing combinations. Its record of success in both historic and modern interior design is impressive. In spite of its generally limited range, it rarely seems monotonous, perhaps because it stays close to the natural color range of the outdoor landscape, a range that has an almost universal appeal.

All-Neutral Color

This approach, which might also be called the neutral-plus color scheme, has much in common with the all-natural color approach but is arrived at without specific concern for the natural colors of materials. It is a type of monotone or monochrome scheme (see page 252) based on the idea that neutral colors, those close to the central gray axis of the Munsell color solid, are always safe and nonclashing, generally acceptable in any situation. A neutral scheme may be based on true neutral grays in the white-to-black range or may be warm, using beiges and tans as dominant colors, or cool, using grays of greenish, bluish, or violet tint. Of all the neutrals, white is probably the most useful and most widely used. Whites too can be cool or warm or, with colored pigment added, tinted toward cream, as in the many paint colors offered with names such as off-white, linen-white, or oyster-white. Schemes using white, grays, and black are of this type.

The notion of *neutral-plus* adds to the neutral scheme some limited areas of strongly chromatic color, often one or more true primaries. Such schemes were favorites of early modernism,

358. Neutral colors are usually thought to be safe in that they avoid any risk of harsh clashes—a fundamental consideration in exhibition spaces, where objects on display often present strong color. The Tilghman Gallery in Boca Raton, Florida, developed by Rex Nichols Architect & Associates, Inc., in 1986, furnishes an ideal setting for the artworks there. The chair in the foreground is a design of Robert Venturi (see also fig. 254). (Photograph: © Steven Brooke)

suggesting the paintings of Mondrian and the work of various designers connected with the De Stijl and Bauhaus movements. White and neutrals plus primary accents remains a useful formula for color schemes that can hardly go wrong while offering possibilities for varied color through the use of strong color tones in the accent areas. An all-neutral scheme with only plants as a source of accent color is also frequently adopted.

Neutral schemes are very satisfactory in places where strong color will come from sources other than basic interior color, as in museums and galleries (fig. 358), where a neutral surround best sets off paintings or objects. They are similarly useful in restaurants, where the table settings and costumes of diners will provide color, or in transport design (vehicles, such as airplanes or trains, and terminals), where an environment of quiet neutral color character provides the most restful setting for the changing light, view, and occupants.

Functional Color

This is probably the approach most widely used in developing color schemes. It is based on an analysis of what color is expected to *do* for the interior space in an active sense. Overall color tonality is chosen to enhance or offset environmental factors of climate or orientation. Warm color is welcome in cold climates or spaces with a northern orientation that will never receive direct sun. Cool colors are helpful in hot and sunny locations. Difficult spatial shapes can be modified, with small spaces made to look larger, oddly shaped spaces made more reasonable through color distribution, based on the known facts of color perception. Elements can be emphasized or visually diminished through the selection of color and messages subtly conveyed through selection of colors that attract, repel, or express specific attitudes. A white door in a white wall will seem to disappear. A bright red door invites attention and suggests importance.

In general, a functional approach to color permits, even encourages, a very free use of color elements, demanding only that every color decision be purposeful in one or another specific way. Functional use of color can interlace with the concepts of color theory and can overlap neutral and natural color use. It is particularly appropriate to modern concepts of overall design rooted in functional intentions.

WORKING METHOD

Putting together a color scheme at the drawing board involves making color charts and material charts. These convert color scheme ideas into visual forms that can be evaluated and, when accepted, realized.

Collecting Color Samples

The process requires a readily available stock of color samples that can be viewed, placed in trial relationships, and then pinned down to form visual records of schemes as they develop. Preparing a collection of such samples is a key preliminary step in color work.

It is generally most convenient to work first with abstract color schemes, that is, representing all colors with flat paper swatches devoid of texture, pattern, and other special characteristics of real materials. Colored papers, which come arranged in systems,* offer a suitable medium. Available index booklets of such color paper systems are an ideal means of bringing a full range of color to the worktable.

The color stock can be augmented with large sheets of color papers and color paper samples cut from packages, printed brochures, advertisements, and any other sources that may turn up. The habit of clipping and filing colored papers and cards leads quickly to a highly useful collection of samples ready for use in working on color schemes. Metallic papers, glossy flint papers, and textured papers can be added to a sample collection to increase its range. In addition, one can mix colors (using tempera, gouache, or designers' colors) in small quantities and brush the mix onto cards to create additional color samples. Preparing samples in this way was standard practice some years ago, when color materials were less widely available. With modern color systems in general use, this method has become a last resort.

Preparing Color Charts
USING COLORED PAPER SAMPLES.

With an adequate sample collection at hand, it is a simple matter to begin making up any desired color scheme by grouping together sample swatches to represent the chosen colors (fig. 359). In doing this, it is important to lay out the samples so that each color covers an area roughly proportionate to the actual space it will take up, so that large sample areas represent large areas, appropriately small swatches stand for small accents. Again, it is essential that the work of color charting be done under light having the same color characteristics as the light that will be normal in the real space, including all the types of light to be used, alone and in whatever combinations may occur in the actual space.

Insofar as possible, color samples should be arranged in the same order that they will occupy in the actual space, that is,

*Color-Aid, Normacolor, and Pantone are trade names of some of the available color system papers. Color-Aid is a particularly complete and useful system.

floor color should go at the bottom of the chart, walls above, colors for furniture and other objects in corresponding relationships, and ceiling color on top. It is important to include samples of *all* colors that will be present; a white ceiling, for example, should not be ignored but should be represented with an appropriate area of white sample. As it is developing, the scheme should be viewed against a neutral background—white, black, or, best of all, a neutral gray. Samples should be placed side by side, leaving no background visible between them. As a scheme is brought together into a final color plan, samples can be glued down to a mount to form an established record (fig. 360). Such an abstract color chart can be used for review with a client or as a basis for color sketching or rendering.

Another method of color charting uses a floor plan, usually at $\frac{1}{4}'' = 1'\text{-}0''$. An extra print of the furniture layout plan works best as the basis for a color chart. Actual colors of flooring, furniture, and built-in elements are shown by pasting down samples cut to fit the plan indication of the element in question. Wall colors and the colors of drapery and other materials on vertical surfaces are indicated by diagrammatic color lines (in pencil or marker), which are then keyed to sample swatches placed adjacent to the plan (fig. 362). In this way, color is seen more or less in position as it will occur in the real space.

A further extension of this technique places a plan with wall elevations adjacent to the plan indication of the wall surfaces. Plan and elevations then both become the basis for pasting in color samples (or pencil or marker indication of colors), displaying all colors in correct relative location and area. By cutting out such a plan and elevation drawing chart and folding the wall elevations up into a vertical position, a kind of abstract model of the space, called a *maquette,* is created. Traditional decorators often made such a color presentation by rendering (usually in watercolors) the floor plan and each wall surface. While lacking the full three-dimensionality of a model, this maquette is often helpful in visualizing how colors will actually relate in the completed space.

Still another technique of color charting uses a perspective drawing, usually only a geometric layout without detail, as a basis. Color samples cut to fit the areas in the layout are pasted down to form a collage color chart that approximates the appearance of the constructed space as seen from a certain viewpoint.

USING ACTUAL MATERIALS. The color chart can be taken a step further by translating the abstract colors into real materials and finishes (fig. 361). Once again, a collection of samples is extremely useful. Wood and laminate finishes available from furniture makers and samples of basic material colors (brick, concrete, terrazzo, metals, woods, and so

on) are needed along with samples of tiles, floor coverings, and other materials. For materials not easily kept on hand, such as brick, stone, and other bulky materials, color illustrations may be substituted. It is important to have samples of the actual carpet and textiles in order to take into account the impact of textures and patterns. Large samples of carpets, textiles, and other major material areas should be viewed in relationship to try to offset the misleading tendency of tiny samples viewed only at the drawing table.

Large *memo square* samples of textiles, usually a yard of whatever width the fabric is produced in, large samples of carpet, and panels of wood finish are available from manufacturers. It may be necessary to carry the more portable materials to a showroom where a more bulky item is on display in order to observe the relationship. Textiles, carpet, and paint color samples, for example, might be taken to a furniture showroom or to a supplier of brick or marble. Larger design firms often operate a sample room storing large samples of frequently used materials, which can be spread out on a large table and viewed under suitable lighting.

Sample Boards

Charts called *sample boards* can be made up using real materials along with color swatches representing paint and other solid color areas. Such charts, like the abstract charts, should show materials in areas proportional to their real use and in appropriate relationships. The accepted chart becomes a record of the color selections for items to be purchased and for paint and other colors to be applied on site. A written record of pattern and color numbers should be made and a set of samples should be put away in a folder or envelope representing the scheme settled on for each space of a total interior project.

Realizing the Color Scheme

Realization then becomes a matter of placing orders for products (furniture, draperies, and so on) with correct color specifications, relaying specification information for materials and items that are built-in (architectural materials, hardware, and light fixtures), and, for the painter, preparing a plan color chart showing where each color is to be applied, with a key to a set of sample swatches.

SPECIALLY MIXED COLORS. It is important to remember that color choices are not limited to the available standard colors offered by the makers of paints, fabrics, carpet, and other products. Carpets and textiles can be dyed to order, paints mixed to match any sample swatch. Ready-mixed paints are usually limited to a range of banal tints, although some

---

359. This color scheme was initially developed using a selection of colored papers.

360. Here, the same scheme shows the papers arranged with their areas proportionally equivalent to their final organization in the interior and ordered to correspond roughly to their ultimate placement. Thus, the rug color occupies the bottom of the chart, the ceiling color

the top, and the wall, upholstery, and drapery colors the area in between. The papers have been taped down in a neat band because the scheme will be presented to a client for discussion.

361. In this stage, the scheme takes the form of a chart of the actual materials, laid out as they will be used in the completed space.

362. The same scheme is shown here in a paste-up, or collage, floor plan. Fabrics are cut out and fixed in place to represent upholstered furniture. Papers are used to show the floor color; the colors of furniture materials (wood, marble) and other elements (such as walls) are usually indicated in colored pencil. This

type of plan does not portray the total, three-dimensional impact of wall, ceiling, drapery, and other colors, and it should be studied along with other color charts for a balanced impression of overall color. Nevertheless, it helps to analyze the effect of color on certain key features of a space.

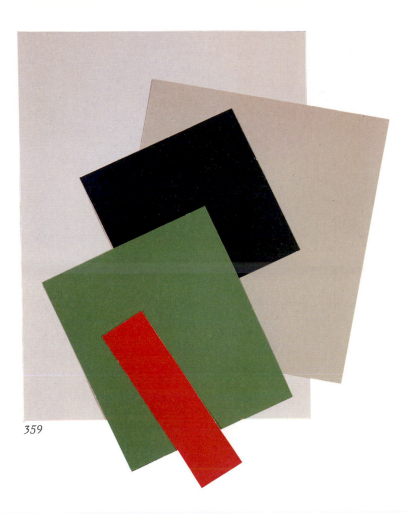

359

360

361

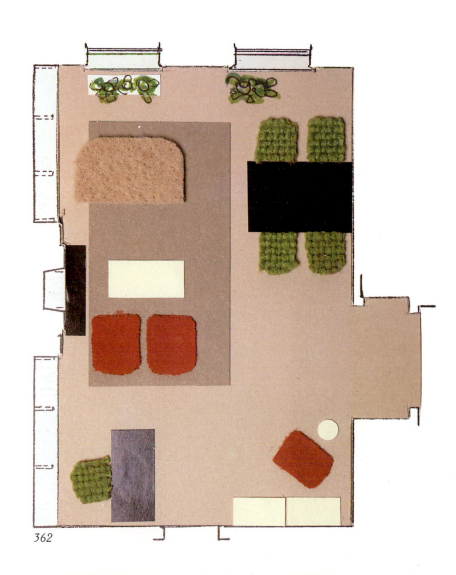

362

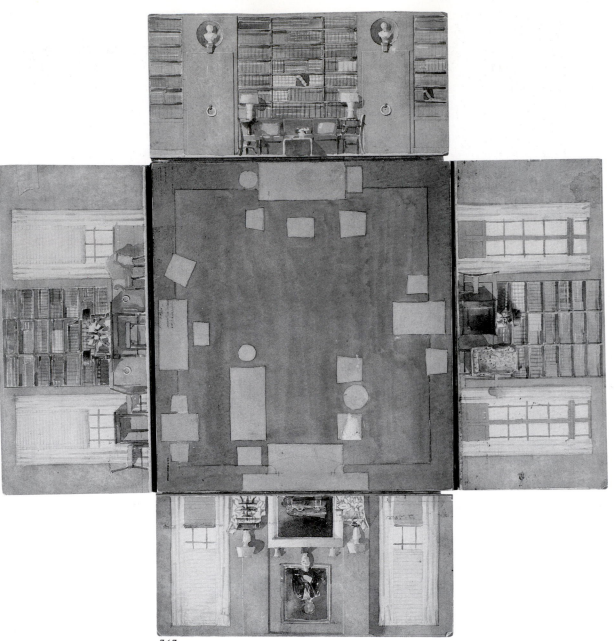

363

paint color systems offer a much wider range, including strong colors often identified as decorator colors. A competent painter can mix color to match any requirement, except, perhaps, color desired at an extreme level of intense saturation (very high or full chroma). Dyeing carpet and fabric to order offers only the limited risk that a large area matched to a small sample may be a visual surprise—for better or for worse.

EVALUATING COLOR ON SITE. In following a project on site, it is important not to be upset by the impression given by one or another color or finish before all the

related elements are in place and seen under the specified lighting. Colors influence one another so strongly that it is quite common for some one color, perhaps a painted area or a floor color, to look all wrong until the other elements that make up the total color scheme are in place. Some on-site adjustments of color can be made, although only to certain elements, the most flexible being paint color. A prime coat can be viewed and changes considered before a final coat is applied. Still, it is important to remember before making adjustments to paint color that the color areas to be delivered later (carpet,

363, 364. A room of a New York apartment of 1948 is here presented in the form of a maquette. The floor plan (in the center) is surrounded by elevations of the four walls, all realistically rendered in watercolors. If each wall is folded up to form a box, the result suggests the three-dimensional view given by a

model. Any one or two walls can be folded down so that the interior can be studied at eye level. This example is the work of Grace Fakes of McMillen, Inc. The actual room as constructed (fig. 364) closely matched the scheme proposed in fig. 363. (Photograph: Hans van Nes, courtesy McMillen, Inc.)

364

upholstery) will influence the way painted areas will appear. Hasty changes and adjustments made on site when the total scheme is not yet in place are often unwise. In general, if a well-proportioned color chart viewed under appropriate light has seemed satisfactory, the finished space will probably look as good. Sticking to a well-conceived plan until all elements are in place is usually the sensible course of action.

Common Color Problems

The following lists common problems in color use that cause disappointing color results:

- *RANDOM ACQUISITION OF ITEMS AND COLOR DECISIONS NOT RELATED TO A CAREFULLY CONCEIVED COLOR PLAN.*
- *TOO MUCH AND TOO VARIED COLOR. Restricted color schemes are usually safe; schemes using many hues run greater risks. A full rainbow scheme using many or all hues will almost certainly fail, appearing as chaotic as the random color arrived at without planning.*
- *TOO INTENSE COLOR USED IN LARGE AREAS. This may work in spaces used only briefly; otherwise, it is likely to become tiring over a period of time.*

- *TOO MUCH CONTRAST IN LARGE COLOR AREAS can also be problematic. In complementary schemes in particular, near-equal areas of contrasting color in near-equal intensity set up a tension that is usually unpleasant. It is best if one or the other color is dominant in intensity or in area. Most often it is best if small areas of high intensity are used in relation to larger areas of lesser intensity.*

  At the opposite extreme from the problems mentioned above is the potential problem of drabness and monotony. Institutional-green color schemes and use of beiges, tans, and browns carry safe color too far, producing depressing results. In restricted color schemes, strong accent color is particularly useful in avoiding this kind of problem.

Successful color depends, above all, on the planning of a total scheme with all elements, in swatches or samples of whatever sort, viewed in relationship to one another in proportional areas and under appropriate light. The amateur's failure to create a well-conceived color relationship is usually the result of piecemeal color decision-making. Whether the planned scheme is derived from some form of color theory or simply improvised intuitively, it will have a basis in systematic coordination. This is the only reliable way to approach color planning.

CHAPTER TEN
ART AND ACCESSORIES

A completed interior of outstanding design with all materials, furniture, and equipment in place will often seem in some way incomplete, in a sense, unoccupied. Spaces come to life with the addition of elements expressive of individual character—the character of the users or occupants of the space or character developed by the designer to express the less personal individuality of an organization, corporation, or institution. These elements can generally be identified as belonging to one of two classes: works of art or accessories. The dividing line is not absolute; some things fall into an overlapping area.

Works of art are most familiar in the form of mural paintings or two-dimensional pictures hung on walls, but three-dimensional sculpture, bas-relief or in the round, can be fully integrated into interior space. While painting is regarded as the primary art form of a two-dimensional nature, the other two-dimensional mediums, such as the various printmaking techniques, weaving, photography, and other types of graphic art, are probably more often used than original painting to bring visual variety and interest into interior spaces.

The term *accessories* covers a vast variety of objects, usually smaller in scale than furniture, that may be introduced into a space to serve a practical purpose, for ornament or display, or for some combination of these purposes. Stage designers fully realize the importance of appropriate accessories in making a theatrical set express time, place, and character. Photographers photographing interiors often provide their own accessories and make a point of moving—or removing—small objects in order to show the space at its best.

In residential interiors, owners or occupants introduce objects or possessions that may be familiar and beloved or simply necessary and useful. The results vary from charming and interesting to cluttered and messy. The interior designer can affect the outcome by acting as an advisor, helping with placement, perhaps selecting new and different objects, and, frequently, suggesting the elimination of objects that cannot be successfully placed or that detract from the visual effect of the space because of poor design quality. This last function calls for special tact and persuasive ability.

Although public spaces such as lobbies, restaurants, and shops do not involve such personal issues, providing art or decorative objects is an important way to add warmth. The interior designer may play a role in selecting or suggesting art, as well as useful accessories. Private offices fall in a middle ground between public and personal spaces, with occupants often anxious to differentiate their spaces from identical units by personalizing them. Motivated by a sense of responsibility and pride in a job well done, the designer will usually direct and control the choice and placement of art and accessory

elements rather than leave all this to the occupants. Many clients want and appreciate help with these matters.

Both artworks and accessories are often treated as incidentals added almost as an afterthought. This approach may work when only a few practical necessities are required, but it is usually wise to give more design attention to these elements. A major work of art can dominate a space and influence all other design decisions (about color, materials, and furniture placement). An art collection can have a similarly important role, or it can be displayed as a more incidental, background contribution to the totality of a space.

Accessories, especially items such as wastebaskets and ashtrays, are more likely to play a background role, although a large collection of objects or a single object of strong character can also become a major design focus. A handsome clock, a ship model, or a framed map or chart can, like an artwork, dominate an interior.

Of all the elements of an interior, artworks and accessories are among the easiest to relocate, remove, or replace. For example, a painting can be relocated or removed; a ship model can be replaced by a clock; new vases can replace old. Such flexibility makes decisions about these objects less binding—but no less important than decisions about more lasting elements.

Dealing with art and accessories involves several interrelated concerns:

It is helpful to anticipate various practical needs and provide for them in order to avoid makeshift and unattractive solutions later on. For example, it is possible to include such items as umbrella holders, coat racks, calendars, bulletin boards, signs, and displays in ways that enhance a design. If forgotten, ad hoc approaches to dealing with such needs can be unfortunate.

It is important to provide for specific objects of a personal or sentimental value that occupants of spaces want on view in a way that satisfies their owners without compromising the design. These may include inherited pieces, trophies, or souvenirs that may or may not have aesthetic merit. A collection of shells, boxes, or toys, a hunting or fishing trophy, a framed document can usually be fitted into an interior if planned for. If not, they may later be inappropriately placed, creating visual clutter.

The introduction of well-chosen artworks and accessories can add to the interest and aesthetic quality of a space while reducing a sense of bareness or incompleteness. Making good choices in these areas is part of the designer's job. A well-chosen artwork placed in an inviting space satisfies everyone who sees it. At the same time, it preempts a less appropriate display.

365. Commissioned for the bathroom of a Manhattan apartment, these paintings are clearly based on ancient Roman motifs as they appear on excavated interior walls in the ruins of Pompeii. David Fisch was the painter. (Photograph: © Jeff Blechman)

366

ACCESSORIES

This term refers to the incidental objects, useful, decorative, or both, that may be added to the interior over and above basic furniture and equipment. Such objects are usually portable and subject to frequent change. Many of the items in this class are small, even trivial, so that discovery of sources for well-designed examples may take some searching. Sources may include consumer retail outlets (department stores and mail-order houses, for example), craft shops, and galleries, as well as reputable, design-oriented showrooms. It is helpful to build up a file of sources with brochures, advertisements, and magazine tear sheets. The most serviceable file will include a wide range of stylistic types in every object category. Some interiors, especially true period rooms, demand accessories that match their styles and periods. On the other hand, in many modern interiors, smaller objects from earlier traditions may fit very well. Vases and candlesticks, clocks, or ship models from some past era can be made very much at home in an otherwise totally contemporary interior.

Practical Accessories

Practical accessories should be considered in relation to the particular functions of each space in which they will be placed. The designer has an obligation to aid in the selection of items

that will be fixed in place or built in, and will often have a role in choosing things that will be movable but in regular use. Other, more transient objects may or may not come under the designer's province. The selection of linens and tableware, for example, often an important part of a restaurant's design, may become the designer's responsibility, while residential clients may want to make their own choices of these items, may already own these objects, or may want design help in selecting them.

Reviewing a checklist of accessory items for various kinds of spaces may help to make such objects a planned part of the design rather than intrusions in a space (see Table 12 on page 274).

Decorative Accessories

Decorative accessories other than works of art exist in infinite variety, often combining some degree of usefulness with a primarily decorative role. Objects may be modern, antique, primitive, or of craft origins, and they need not always match the style of an interior. An antique or primitive object will often look very well in an otherwise contemporary interior. Choices may be based on the preferences or interests of the occupants (as with personal collections, trophies, or heirlooms) or may relate to the character and use of the space. A collector of old

366. In a Manhattan loft designed by Mary Emmerling, a neutral space has been transformed by a collection of accessories that share an American old-time country flavor. Linen bed curtains, homespun bed canopy, cushions and coverlet, earthenware jugs for flowers,

boxes and baskets—all pull together to display a collector's favorite things, and convert an impersonal, even cold and industrial, interior into something pleasant and unique. (Photograph: Chris Mead, courtesy House Beautiful)

367

367. In the architectural offices of Peter L. Gluck and Partners, AMEV Holdings, Inc. (1984), a corridor treated as a gallery for the display of art both relieves the monotony of the long, narrow space and expresses the firm's interest in values beyond its normal business concerns. Peter L. Gluck and Partners, designer. (Photograph courtesy Peter L. Gluck and Partners)

TABLE 12. CHECKLIST OF ACCESSORIES

ENTRANCE AREAS:

  Coat racks or hangers
  Umbrella and overshoe holders
  Protective mats or runners for the
    floor
  Bell pushes, intercom plates,
    closed-circuit TV
  Mailboxes or trays, message board
  Signs, bulletin boards
  Nameplates

LIVING SPACES:

  Small tables or stands
  Stools, hassocks
  Cushions
  Bookshelves or racks
  Music and video components;
    record, tape, and cassette
    storage
  Ashtrays
  Wastebaskets
  Flower containers
  Planters and plants
  Clock
  Frames or other display devices
  Telephone, intercom
  Answering machine

DINING SPACES:

  Serving cart, trays
  Place mats and/or tablecloths
  Flatware and holloware
  Dishes and serving pieces,
    glassware
  Candlesticks or holders
  Trivets or hot pads

KITCHEN AND PANTRY SPACES:

  Storage/display for cooking pots
    and utensils
  Storage/display for staples, bottled
    items
  Canisters
  Storage/display for dishes,
    glassware, and other tableware
  Racks or other holders for towels,
    potholders
  Cutting, rolling, mixing boards
  Scales

  Spice rack
  List and memo pads
  Cookbook storage
  Clock/radio
  Telephone
  Small and larger appliances
  Special plumbing hardware
    (faucets and so on)

BEDROOMS:

  Bedcovers, quilts, blankets, and so
    on
  Pillows, cushions
  Bedside stands or tables
  Clock
  Radio/TV
  Mirror(s)
  Dressing accessories (brushes,
    combs, and so on)
  Telephone

BATHROOMS

  PRIVATE:

  Towel rack(s)
  Soap dish(es), toilet-paper holder,
    toothbrush and glass holder
  Medicine cabinet
  Mirror(s)
  Scale
  Towels, mats

  PUBLIC:

  Paper-towel dispenser, discard
    container
  Liquid-soap dispenser
  Coat hooks

OFFICES:

  Desk accessories (pads, holders
    for pens, pencils, paper clips,
    scissors, and so on)
  Ashtray(s)
  Telephone(s)/intercom unit
  Clock
  Calendar
  Computer and associated
    equipment
  Typewriter/business machines
  Tack board/chalkboard
  Letter trays

  Address and phone number
    directories
  Radio/music and video
    components

GENERAL (ITEMS THAT MAY BE
  CONSIDERED FOR ANY SPACE):

  Portable lighting (lamps: task,
    ambient, accent)
  Telephone and directories
  Ashtrays and sand urns
  Wastebaskets
  Flowers and vases
  Plants and planters
  Terrarium
  Tack (pinup) surfaces
  Storage (books, magazines,
    papers, records, tapes,
    special purpose)
  Fireplace tools, fire screens,
    wood basket
  Display pedestals (plaster or
    glass cases, panels)
  Mirror
  Clock
  Computer
  Typewriter/printer

SPECIAL-PURPOSE SPACES

  PUBLIC SPACES:

  Directory, signs, location plan
  Graphic materials (brochures,
    menus, wine lists, printed
    forms)

  CHILDREN:

  Toys and toy storage
  Play equipment

  PETS:

  Bird cage
  Aquarium
  Bed
  Litter box
  Scratching post
  Dishes

  MUSIC:

  Instruments
  Music stand
  Music storage

369

368

370

368. Roger Zenn Kaufman's Becker desk organizer turns the familiar miscellany of calendar, calculator, pencil, pen, and clip holders, major components of typical desk-top clutter, into an ornamental and positive object—perhaps a bit of a status designator as well. (Photograph courtesy Sointu, New York)

369. Many modern designers have come to view minor, functional accessories as worthy territory for the introduction of creative ideas into general circulation. This magazine rack, by Dutch designer Ann Mae, has an active, sculptural quality that enhances its simple utility. (Photograph courtesy Sointu, New York)

370. In a bathroom of the Middleton Inn, South Carolina, Clark & Menefee Architects have converted a rather austerely architectural environment into an inviting space by realizing the potential aesthetic value of familiar bathroom accessories. As arranged here, towels, a basket of washcloths, and the soap and soap dish are understood as vehicles for bringing color and texture into the room. (Photograph: © Tom Crane)

371

372

373

371, 372. Wall systems contain and organize the various odds and ends that modern living calls for and that may otherwise turn into clutter. Here, audio equipment, TV, books, bottles, and glassware become decorative when they fit into a planned wall system, made by Cy Hymann Designs (fig. 372). A sliding, mirrored closure makes them invisible when not in use (fig. 371). (Photograph courtesy Cy Hymann Designs)

373. The offices of the innovative architectural design firm SITE Projects Inc. in an older New York City loft building are divided by semitransparent screen walls of slats. An eclectic collection of objects and artworks mounted on these dividers gives this space an individuality that ex- presses SITE's unusual design directions. The project model on the table in the foreground becomes an accessory that connects the creative work of the firm with its setting. SITE Projects Inc., designer. (Photograph: © 1985 Peter Aaron/ESTO)

374

toys or tools may want to display some or all of a collection; an enthusiastic gardener will want vases and other containers for cut flowers. A ship model might be appropriate in the office of a shipping or engineering company; restaurants often display objects that relate to a national or regional style of cookery or to other menu elements (nets and nautical objects have become clichés of seafood-restaurant design).

Live plants are a particularly attractive decorative accessory. Even one small plant in a room tends to make the space seem pleasant and civilized. Larger plants, groups of plants, even growing trees can find a place in larger spaces. When selecting plants, their light, temperature, and watering needs, continuing care required, and, possibly, ease of replacement must be considered. The provision of containers, planters, plant boxes,

374. In an authentically traditional interior, period accessories create a consistent character. This is easier to achieve in a museum display than in an environment in daily use. The Federal period room illustrated, from the Phelps-Hathaway House, built c. 1765 and redone in 1788–89, in Suffield, Connecticut, preserves its original details. It is now installed at the Henry Francis du Pont Winterthur Museum, Winterthur, Delaware. (Photograph: Lizzie Himmel)

375

even whole greenhouse or conservatory areas is a normal part of the designer's work. Plant selection may be done by the designer alone, the designer and client together, or by a specialized consultant (see Table 13 on page 285).

A list of possibilities could be endless, and choices are not generally specific to any particular functional use. The following short list offers only a small sampling of the kinds of objects that may be considered. Some of the items on this list duplicate items listed above as useful. They reappear here as decorative when they can be considered in either or both roles.

Baskets
Bird cages
Books and magazines
Bottles
Bowls
Boxes
Brassware
Candlesticks
Ceramics
Clocks
Collections (for example, of coins, mounted but-

terflies, eggs, obelisks)
Figurines
Frames (containing photographs, curios, and so on)
Games (for example, chess sets)
Glassware
Instruments (scientific, drafting, musical)
Kites
Lamps

Mirrors
Models (for example, ships, trains, architectural)
Paperweights
Pillows and cushions
Pitchers
Plants
Pottery
Quilts
Rugs
Sewing boxes, baskets

Shells
Silverware (bowls, pitchers, boxes)
Tapestries
Tools
Toys
Trophies
Vases
Weapons
Weavings

375. A lamp, pictures, and books are familiar decorative accessories. Here, high up on the wall, a more surprising collection is on display—handbags in the changing styles of bygone fashion. The ladder allows access for close inspection and rearrangement and itself acts as an accessory that draws attention upward to the display. Stephen Levine, designer. (Photograph: © Norman McGrath)

376

377

376. A collection of small carved-ivory objects and an ivory model of a ship become a decorative display set out on tables, with a ceramic tureen and candlesticks as background and a framed hunting scene above. Designed by the owner. (Photograph: Lizzie Himmel, courtesy House Beautiful)

377. As collections of objects grow, their display can become a chaos of clutter. The studio of the famous Italian writer Gabriele d'Annunzio is crowded with possessions that each had special meaning for their owner. Their quality and the obvious concern with which they have been collected and displayed turn them into a fascinating reflection of personality. We are attracted by what could, in other circumstances, seem excessive. A similar density of accessories of lesser quality, chosen at random, would make a space look crowded and busy. (Photograph: © Robert Emmett Bright, Photo Researchers, Inc.)

378

379

378. In the home of a professional musician, musical equipment plays an essential role. The piano—a strikingly handsome object—becomes an important piece of furniture, here surrounded by music stands and recording apparatus. The library of music scores in this New York apartment strikes a decorative note; the seating furniture is properly angled for listening. Melvin Dwork, designer. (Photograph: Jaime Ardiles-Arce)

379. Restaurant design often takes its cue from the region associated with the featured menu, as in this Mexican restaurant, Café Marimba, in New York. Pottery and woven hangings enliven the architectural details and materials, making the space a memorable and attractive setting with an atmosphere that supports and enhances the regional cuisine. Sam Lopata, designer, 1985. (Photograph: © Peter Paige)

380

381

382

380. The equipment of dining, particularly formal dining, belongs to a special class of decorative accessories that are also functional. An elaborate table setting is an object display that adds greatly to the ceremony of a meal. In this table setting for two, attractive groupings of plates and napkins, glassware and silver, candles and flowers make it clear that the meal to come will be an occasion. (Photograph courtesy Gourmet)

381. In a log house by woodworker Steve Cappellucci, hollowed-out logs are used as window boxes inside the large windows. Here, they are filled with flowering plants, appearing to be a natural outgrowth of the overall design concept. (Photograph: © 1985 Michael Skott)

382. The garden atmosphere of the Tavern on the Green restaurant in New York's Central Park is largely created by the presence of growing plants. In this glass-enclosed terrace, a 1976 renovation by Warner LeRoy, latticed boxes stretch along the length of the room and also function as a room divider. (Photograph: © Elliott Kaufman)

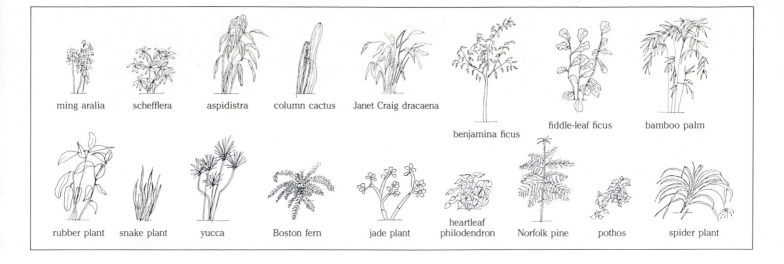

ming aralia   schefflera   aspidistra   column cactus   Janet Craig dracaena   benjamina ficus   fiddle-leaf ficus   bamboo palm

rubber plant   snake plant   yucca   Boston fern   jade plant   heartleaf philodendron   Norfolk pine   pothos   spider plant

TABLE 13. INDOOR PLANTS

	Plant Name	Height	Width	Pot Diameter	Light Required	Water Required
Floor plants and trees	Aralia (Ming)	12–48	8–24	6–14	H	M
	Schefflera	18–96	10–48	6–17	M	M
	Aspidistra	18–40	12–36	6–14	L	M
	Cactus (Candelabra)	4–30	8–18	6–14	M	D
	Cactus (Column)	4–20	6–18	6–17	M	D
	Dracaena (Janet Craig)	16–60	12–28	6–17	M	M
	Ficus (several varieties)	18–240	12–60	6–48	H	M
	Ficus (Fiddle-leaf)	36–84	12–30	10–17	H	W
	Palm (Bamboo)	14–28	8–24	8–21	M	M
	Palm (Dwarf Date)	24–54	18–42	8–21	H	W
	Palm (Kentia)	36–72	12–24	10–17	M	M
	Palm (Lady)	26–120	20–60	10–21	M	W
	Rubber plant	24–96	18–40	6–16	M	M
	Sansevieria (Snake plant)	12–36	8–16	6–14	M	D
	Yucca	15–96	8–24	6–17	M	D
Smaller table and hanging plants	Ferns (various)	12–28	12–36	6–12	H	W
	Ivy (Grape)	6–10+	R	6–10	M	M
	Jade plant	12–30	12–28	5–10	M	D
	Philodendron (Heartleaf)	6–10+	R	6–10	L	W
	Pine (Norfolk)	12–30*	10–24	5–10	M	M
	Pothos	6–10+	R	6–10	L	M
	Spider plant	variable size			M	W
	Flowering plants (various)	variable sizes, range, and requirements				

Heights and widths are given in inches

Light requirements: L = 50–75 fc (footcandles), M = 75–100 fc, H = 200+ fc

Water requirements: D = less than average, M = average, W = more than average

R = runner plant, variable width and form

*Can grow into full-size tree

383. In the home of a serious art collector, pieces are often displayed as they would be in a gallery or museum. In this entrance area of a private home in Sands Point, New York, art objects are exhibited and lighted with care. Raised on a transparent stand, the Calder mobile at the left shows its lines to best advantage, while the Picasso ceramic in the foreground occupies a museum-style case. Myron Henry Goldfinger was the architect of this 1981 project. (Photograph: © Norman McGrath)

384

385

384. Flowering plants in pots used as a decorative accent combine with bright painted colors to make an otherwise ordinary stairway in a house in New Orleans pleasant and cheerful. R. Clay Markham, architect; Tom R. Collum, interior designer. (Photograph: © Jacques Dirand, courtesy House & Garden)

385. Plants in pots establish space division between inside and outside in a California house designed by Mark Mack and Andrew Batey, architects. The flowers are appropriate accents in a design that is inspired by Italian villas and the influence of Mexican architect Luis Barragan. (Photograph: Joel Rosenberg, courtesy Metropolitan Home Magazine)

386

387

386. Plain walls and large windows define the space in this modern Italian building. The paintings, rugs, small sculptures, and other decorative objects create warmth, liveliness, and interest and show up particularly well in the otherwise reserved setting. (Photograph: Guy Bouchet)

387. In a Dallas interior, designer Dan Nelson has used photography as framed, wall-hung art. Four prints in matching frames are hung on the facing wall next to an early-nineteenth-century highboy. Above the stairwell, a band of six related photographs has been framed together in a long ribbon. (The daybed at the left is an old Thonet piece now used as a sofa.) (Photograph: Louis Reens, courtesy Metropolitan Home Magazine)

388

389

Arbitrarily introducing decorative accessories for no reason other than to fill space or add interest may well add nothing more than clutter. In doubtful situations, it is usually best to omit display. Errors of omission are far less common than errors of excessive inclusion. Inclusion should perhaps be reserved for times when occupants demand certain objects on display or when the projection of a particular atmosphere or spirit calls for visual support.

ART

The practice of including works of art as integral parts of interiors has a long history. Prehistoric cave paintings, the wall paintings and bas-reliefs of Egyptian tombs, the wall paintings at Pompeii, and the great frescoes of the Renaissance—all bear witness to the continuing human urge to make art an important element of our surroundings. During the Renaissance, the framed easel painting became the most popular form of artwork

388, 389. An interesting comparative study: four small drawings have been placed in matching frames and hung as a group. In fig. 388, the usual rule of hanging at eye level has been followed, with the result that the works seem to float off upward, unrelated to the other objects. In fig. 389, the same four works have been lowered to a position closer *to the chair and table, where they become easy to view from a seated position and enter into a relationship with the real objects placed on the table—the bottles, teapot and cup, and dish of fruits—which are more transitory accessories. (Photograph: Michael Luppino, courtesy Metropolitan Home Magazine)*

in interiors, and it has remained so, with murals, sculpture, and a wide variety of art forms other frequent choices.

It seems to be widely felt that an interior is not really complete until the process of "hanging some pictures" has filled up any blank wall areas. In practice, the habit of putting up indifferent or bad works that have no special value or meaning for the occupants of a space often does nothing but add pointless clutter to the visual scenes. Bare walls can be handsome and restful, and a truly fine work of art is usually seen to best advantage displayed in uncluttered surroundings (see fig. 393).

Selecting Artwork

The selection of artwork generally follows one or both of two patterns. When works are already on hand—owned, borrowed, or previously chosen for purchase—further selection may be necessary to decide which to display, which to store, which to dispose of. Works to be displayed must then be placed, although available display space may well influence the choice of certain works. Alternatively, works are selected and purchased for particular locations.

The first situation arises when the occupants of a space are art collectors, who may own far more than can possibly be put on view at one time. Other occupants insist on displaying certain works that they are attached to, such as family portraits, works by a friend or relative, or simply favorites, even aside from their artistic merits. In the corporate world, such works as portraits of a founder or former officials, a view of important buildings or events, and similar materials, valued for historic or sentimental reasons over aesthetic merit, may be selected by the client for display.

In private homes or private offices, it is usually possible to find locations where such materials can be put on view to the satisfaction of the occupants. If the spaces are used by visitors or the general public, the designer may try to discourage, exercising ingenuity and tact, display of inferior materials. Failing this, it may be possible to turn such material into something of a historical exhibit rather than an art display. Fortunately, many modern corporations have become major collectors of high-quality artworks. In this case, it is usually easy to place good works in prominent locations and to find more obscure placement for less attractive works that still are wanted on display.

When art is to be specifically acquired for a particular interior project, designer and client must work together to make choices and plan placement. Specialized consultants can help to steer a course through the often confusing world of art markets, both in terms of finding suitable works and giving advice related to costs and budgets. Such consultants may assist significantly in developing a major collection of valuable works. In any case, it is extremely important to verify the consultant's credentials, since the art world, like all businesses, has its share of unscrupulous business practices.

PAINTINGS. A great variety of artworks may be considered for acquisition and display. Paintings often come to mind as the most suitable works for wall hanging. Certainly, almost any subject matter, size, shape, color tonality, period, or style can be found amid the vast output of artists who have worked or are currently working in this form. Major works by important artists, whether old master or modern, have become very costly. They are sold through art auctions, well-known galleries, and eminent dealers. While no guarantees can be given, they may turn out to be excellent investments.

Works of lesser-known artists, secondary historic figures, and younger living artists who have not made major reputations are more likely to be available at affordable prices. As investments, they carry an even more uncertain future. Even so, modestly priced works selected for their visual merit rather than for name value and price will often be a more workable choice, especially if an unlimited budget is not available.

There is also a seemingly endless supply of inferior work, banal, glibly illustrative, and cliché-ridden. This all too often appeals to the unaware who simply want a spot of color to fill a given space. One can learn to distinguish good art from bad by studying high-quality work directly in museums, major galleries, and through reproductions in books. This does not mean that all the work of unknown artists is bad, but those who have no background in art might do well to avoid the unknown in favor of artists backed by a reputable gallery or by critical approval. This applies to works of art in all other mediums as well.

DRAWINGS AND PRINTS. Works on paper, usually classified as drawings even if they are in watercolors or pastels, are generally smaller in scale and more delicate in character than oil paintings. They are entirely suitable to smaller and more intimate interior spaces. They tend to cost less than larger works by the same artist; in fact, drawings by artists of major reputation are sometimes priced at levels accessible to medium-level budgets.

Prints, or, as they are now often called, *multiples,* are works in one or another medium that permits the making of many copies of a work through some printing technique. Original prints are made from a printing medium such as the copperplate of the engraving and etching, the crayoned stone of the lithograph, or the stencil screen of the silk-screen print worked directly by the hand of the artist or under the artist's direct supervision. The artist signs and numbers each perfect print with figures that indicate the total number of copies printed (the edition) and the order in which the particular print was made (for example, 30/100 indicates the thirtieth impression in an edition of one hundred). After printing, the plate, stone, or screen is destroyed so that additional, possibly inferior, prints cannot be made. Editions are usually small, in the range of 50 to 500 copies. Prints of lesser quality are sometimes produced in large numbers without the participation of the artist, without a signature, with a signature printed from the plate or stone, or even with a forged signature.

A print's monetary value usually depends on the number and signature, but the visual value can be evaluated by simple inspection. Prints produced in large volume, reasonably priced, are often an excellent choice for spaces such as hotels or large office projects that need many artworks. People of average means who wish to start an art collection do well to begin with prints, since works of good quality at affordable prices are available and because an extensive collection can be compactly stored in a small space. Such collectors may put a few works on display in rotation.

Photography is another medium that produces prints. The investor should again look for signed and numbered originals printed by the photographer or under direct supervision in limited editions. While photography is a relatively young medium, its practitioners already include a great many established artists whose work is of serious merit, as well as an increasing number of young photographers working in creative ways.

REPRODUCTIONS. All of the methods of producing original works, whether unique or in multiples, must be distinguished from *reproductions*, that is, versions of an original in which the artist had no role. These are usually different from the original in size, medium, and technique. In quality, they range from very inferior to quite good. One method of reproduction is the hand copying of known paintings, often by artists of some skill. The results are nevertheless generally of disappointing quality and should not be considered worthy of display except, possibly, as a kind of theatrical prop in some commercial spaces—restaurants or bars, perhaps, where a particular character is sought.

The more common form of reproduction is by modern photomechanical means on color printing presses, usually in large quantities. The original work is photographed, and plates or films are made with a screen, which creates the tiny dots of halftone printing. Full-color printing requires four color inks, each printed from its own plate or film. Such color reproduction, commonplace in books and magazines, is used to make the cards and reproduction prints sold in museum shops and other art outlets. The process can always be easily identified by looking through a magnifying glass for the halftone dot pattern.

Reproductions relate to original artworks much as records or tapes relate to live musical performance. They may be of excellent quality and make works accessible for study and enjoyment at any place or time, yet they are undeniably different from the original they reproduce and can never successfully pretend to be anything but reproductions. When and if reproductions should be used for display in an interior is a somewhat debatable question. There is a certain absurdity in framing and hanging a reproduction of a major work; if bad, it makes a poor substitute for the original, if excellent, it involves a level of pretense best avoided.

Reproduced art certainly can offer beauty and satisfaction, but it should always be used in a way that makes its status clear. This may be why posters that reproduce an artwork often seem the most attractive form of reproduction. Those produced by museums and galleries are usually graphically well designed. A poster with its printed legend included also may serve as a reminder of a trip, an exhibition visit, or some other event that connects the artwork with personal experience. Posters have become collectors' items, with prices ranging from modest sums for modern posters to substantial sums for old and rare examples.

OTHER ARTWORKS. Many other kinds of artwork can be considered for interior display. Some functional objects of superior visual quality become art-worthy when they are displayed in a way comparable to other art forms. The following list suggests several of the many possibilities:

Advertisements (for example, posters)	Quilts
	Rugs
Architectural drawings	Sculpture:
Architectural ornaments:	Ceramic
Iron or bronze	Glass
Stone	Metal
Terra cotta	Mixed materials
Arms and armor	Mobile
Autographs, letters, documents	Stone
	Wood
Blankets (for example, American Indian)	Tapestries
Implements (industrial, agricultural)	Technical (engineering) drawings
	Textiles
Manuscripts, music	Tools (antique)
Maps and charts	Weavings
Primitive artworks	

When art purchases of any magnitude are contemplated, it is wise to seek advice from disinterested experts. The art world is

390

not immune to dishonest practices. Traps for the unwary to guard against include unscrupulous dealers who try to pass off copies, prints, reproductions, and other works of little value as originals and the buying of forgeries or stolen works. Even expert collectors and major museums are sometimes taken in by frauds. Expert opinion is the buyer's best protection, including a second opinion when called for. Besides art consultants, museum curators and collectors with a good knowledge of a particular field and its prices are qualified experts.

Framing and Placing Artwork

In addition to a role in selecting and possibly purchasing art, the designer is likely to be involved in decisions about mounting and framing art. The way museums and galleries frame and hang works provides guidance in these areas. Historic art is often displayed with framing contemporary with the work, often of considerable, even excessive, elaboration. With modern art, the tendency is to use simple, even minimal, framing or to omit frames entirely in favor of the simple edge strip or a frameless mount. Art supply shops stock many

different types. A number of systems offer frames in standardized sizes that serve very well for framing smaller works, including prints, drawings, and photographs. If mats are used, they should be of a paper quality that will not damage the displayed item. Better frame shops are also helpful in suggesting suitable framing for a particular work and can aid in the selection of mats and similar details. The recommendation of a gallery or dealer is often the best way to find a good framing shop.

Choosing the location, background, and hanging position for artwork is very much part of the interior designer's work. Traditionally, art was often hung on elaborate backgrounds of cloth or wallpaper, crowded together to show a maximum number of works, and placed too high for comfortable viewing. Modern practice is to allow generous wall space around each work and to provide a neutral background that will not compete with the art. White or other light neutral colors and smooth or unobtrusive textures are preferred. Standard hanging height today brings works down, with their center near average eye level (figs. 388, 389). If the space has good general lighting, no

390. When a large number of smaller artworks—prints, drawings, or paintings—must be accommodated in a limited space, a time-honored technique is to arrange them into a mosaic-like pattern that almost covers the available wall surface. Mac II, designer. (Photograph: © François Halard, courtesy House & Garden)

392

special lighting is necessary, although special concealed lighting or track lighting like that used in many galleries might be considered to emphasize the work. Individual lights attached to the tops of frames are now obsolete and rarely used.

Hanging works from a picture molding or a modern concealed hanging strip is one way to avoid nail holes in a wall, especially if pictures will be rotated. Arrangements of

works in symmetrical groups of three or in stepped rows, a traditional placement, now appear forced and unattractive. It is acceptable to cluster a large number of small works together into a kind of mosaic, which serves to display many works in a limited space (fig. 390). Another way to display art in a limited space is to provide a location, perhaps with a ledge or shelf, where individual pieces can be interchanged from time to time

391. *In this bedroom of his own apartment (1982), architect Preston Phillips balances a wall-hung artwork on the right with art placed on a long, continuous shelf that also acts as a headboard. Since these pieces are not hung, they can be easily rearranged, replaced, or* *removed without worrying about wall damage from nail holes. Anyone with an extensive collection of smaller works and a desire to make frequent changes in the display will find this solution both convenient and attractive. (Photograph: Tom Bersten)*

392. *In this view of the living area designed by Cliff May, architect, for his own home, Mandalay, in Santa Monica, California (1953), a display of primitive sculpture appears in the foreground. (Photograph: © 1986 Tim Street-Porter)*

(fig. 391). This also avoids putting nail holes in the wall.

Sculpture and other three-dimensional works, if they are small, may be simply placed on a table, shelf, or other horizontal surface (figs. 392, 394). If the work is too large or it requires protection, a glass or plastic case, which usually tops a pedestal base of some kind, may be used (see fig. 383). Generally, the simplest of frameless cases look best, with similarly simple boxlike pedestal bases. The moving sculptures called mobiles must be suspended, usually from the ceiling, and need to be located to prevent a possibly dangerous collision that could damage either the mobile or the colliding person. This usually entails hanging the work beyond human reach or providing a barrier (furniture or a railing) that makes contact impossible. Here, too, the practices of major museums and better galleries are a good guide.

Positioning works of art involves relating the spaces available, the objects to be displayed, and the desired level of viewers' attention. A major work, especially if it is large, calls for a focal location—for example, centered on an uncluttered wall (fig. 393). Certain locations, including the chimney breast above a fireplace mantel or the blank wall above a low chest or bookshelf, seem to invite the display of art. Works placed in these locations will tend to draw attention and can even dominate a room. Less important works may be best fitted into locations that draw less attention, such as smaller wall areas, the walls of corridors, or other incidental spaces, or may be grouped so that no one work has a dominant position. A collection can be seen to advantage in a circulation space, where objects come to attention in a planned sequence as the viewer walks past (see fig. 367).

Another possibility in acquiring artwork that has not yet been discussed is the commissioning of work for a particular place (see fig. 365). The practice boasts a noble history. Some of the great masterpieces—including the Sistine Chapel frescoes by Michelangelo, the metopes of the Parthenon (now known as the Elgin marbles), or Matisse's stained-glass windows in the chapel at Vence—are works commissioned to occupy a particular location. Today, commissioned artwork is most often created for important public spaces; some public buildings built with public funds are even legally required to have it. Occasionally, competitions, more or less formal, are undertaken to select an artist or a work in such situations.

A specially commissioned work always involves some element of risk, since there is no sure way to predict how the end result will actually look in the space until it is complete. Commissions are usually granted on the basis of an artist's reputation and, often, after a preliminary small-scale sketch or model has been considered and evaluated. Murals painted to fit a particular space and monumental architectural sculpture are almost always commissioned. They may be executed on site or, when the scale and medium allow, in the artist's studio, to be delivered to the intended location and installed. A specially commissioned work calls for understanding and cooperation among artist, designer, architect, if involved, and client. It may happen that the results disappoint the commissioning individual or agency, possibly leading to conflicts.

While designers expect to have an important role in the selection and placement of art and accessories in typical projects, it should be recognized that in some situations the user may have preferences quite different from those of the designer. This pattern arises in large projects where there are many private rooms, including office projects, dormitories, and spaces, such as school classrooms, where users actually produce art and other decoration. In such cases, it is best to provide locations where art and objects can be placed according to the occupants' wishes without doing either physical or aesthetic damage to the space. A tackable surface and an empty horizontal shelf or other surface allows placing a picture without damaging a wall and can be used for a favorite family snapshot, a potted plant, or a souvenir.

Since the desire to have such things about in any space that can be regarded as personal territory seems to be nearly universal, the wise designer accepts this reality and supports it, whether the actual selection and placement is part of the project or must be left to the inclinations of occupants.

393. A truly fine, major work of art such as this Picasso is generally best given an important location in a simple and uncluttered setting. The painting clearly dominates and sets the character of this otherwise subdued, traditionally detailed space, with furniture placed to emphasize the importance of the work. Emily Landau, designer. (Photograph: © Henry Bowles, courtesy House & Garden)

394. This 1982 New York apartment highlights a collection of diminutive three-dimensional pieces in a well-designed and -lighted display case. Bromley/Jacobsen Designs, designer. (Photograph: Jaime Ardiles-Arce)

393

394

CHAPTER ELEVEN

KITCHENS, BATHROOMS, STORAGE

Although the basic issues involved in interior design are the same for every kind of space, the areas for food preparation, sanitation, and storage merit special attention from the points of view of both user and designer. In residential design, kitchens and bathrooms attract particular interest on the part of those who will occupy a house or apartment. Builders have long known that an attractive kitchen and bathroom plus adequate closets will do more than any other features to sell a home. Renovation of a kitchen or bath is often the first (and sometimes the only) project that new owners or occupants plan on when moving to a new home.

Bathrooms and kitchens are design problems of unusual complexity because they pose specific and demanding functional considerations, they make use of specialized fixtures and appliances, and they call for special material and finish selections. In most projects, they are the only areas in which the various trades of plumber, electrician, cabinetmaker, and tile installer must all be coordinated and in which so many special details must be worked out. While less technically complex, storage still requires careful thought and planning if it is to be truly convenient and efficient.

Professional kitchens for restaurants, hotels, and other larger dining facilities are so specialized in nature as to fall outside the concern of most interior design work. Therefore, this chapter deals only with residential kitchens. On the other hand, the design of public and semipublic toilet and restroom facilities often falls to the interior designer, so it is discussed here.

The interior designer usually confronts preplanned spaces, that is, already in existence or planned on paper in terms of size, shape, and general layout. The designer's first task is to evaluate the space and decide whether the existing (or planned) spaces can be accepted and worked with in terms of more detailed layout and design or whether more basic replanning should be done. In the latter case, the constraints of walls, doors, windows, adjacent space requirements, and plumbing locations must be taken into account and balanced against the time and budget available.

Common reasons for replanning are given in Table 14. In addition to all the practical reasons to redesign these spaces, there is the desire to make them visually attractive, well lighted, and cheerful. Specific suggestions for dealing with these issues follow.

TABLE 14. REASONS FOR REPLANNING

Kitchens	Bathrooms	Storage
Older kitchens are often too large, oddly subdivided, and inefficient, having been intended as work areas for a servant or staff. Modern kitchens are often too small, having been planned as "efficiency" units with little conception of family living patterns and modern ideas of gourmet cookery.	New bathroom spaces—an additional bath, a new lavatory (toilet and washbasin only), or a powder room (a popular euphemism for a lavatory with some luxury dressing features such as mirrors, counter with washbasin insert, or both)—may be required.	Insufficient and badly planned closet spaces are among the most common causes of complaint about house and apartment plans. Finding locations for additional storage space is a frequent interior design problem. Closet space is adequate, but the given shape, layout, and equipment do not work well. Deep, narrow closets are hard to use efficiently. In wide closets with a narrow door, the side spaces are hard to reach. The customary provision of hanging space in all closets except, perhaps, for one linen closet with shelves does not answer the varied and specific storage needs of modern living patterns.
The layout of counters and appliances is often thoughtless, impractical, and antiquated. Modern appliances are often different from their older equivalents: refrigerators are larger; stoves break up into cook tops and wall ovens; multiple sinks and dishwashers have new spatial requirements. New functions may call for new features, including informal dining areas, laundry facilities, or some kind of office-like work area within the kitchen space.	The typical three-fixture bath may need to be replanned into a different configuration to accommodate reorganized or new functions. For example, the compartmented bath, separating toilet from bathing, often works best for family use. Additional or different fixtures (multiple fixtures, counter lavatory, extra stall shower, larger bathtub) may be desired. Older bathrooms are often crammed into the minimum of space, while modern ideas about hygiene and relaxation suggest more spacious and versatile plans. New functions, such as exercise and rest or recreation, may call for a larger and more luxuriously planned bath.	General storage space, which used to be provided by the cellars and attics of older houses, is often entirely missing, leaving no place to store such bulky items as bicycles, unused furniture, trunks, and boxes. This need may call for a special planning effort.

395. Lavish bathing is a sensuous amenity at the Middleton Inn, a resort hotel in Charleston, South Carolina. Clark & Menefee Architects, designer. (Photograph: © Norman McGrath)

396

397

396. The Colonial American kitchen was a highly functional work center. In New England, it also served as the main living and dining space of the house. In the South, with its warmer climate and highly stratified social system, the kitchen did not function as a social area. Illustrated here is the kitchen of the Wythe House in the restored town of Williamsburg, Virginia. (Photograph: Langdon Clay, courtesy the Colonial Williamsburg Foundation)

397. In the kitchen of a large residence modernized in the early 1900s, the tiled floors, walls, and ceiling and the well-organized storage cabinets indicate a high level of concern for sanitation and efficiency, but the utilitarian character of the space is clearly determined by the expectation that only professional staff—servants—will work here. (Photograph courtesy Museum of the City of New York)

KITCHENS
Programming

It is unfortunate that a complete, somewhat standardized kitchen is normally built into every house or apartment. The needs of individuals and families differ so widely that such ready-made kitchen spaces are rarely ideal for any user. Therefore, the designer's work properly begins with a careful review of the real needs and desires of the actual users. This means developing answers to the following questions:

What meals are to be prepared?
Breakfast only
Breakfast plus an occasional dinner
Breakfast and dinner daily
Three meals a day

How many people will be served, normally and at maximum?
One alone
Two people
A family: how many?
Occasional, or frequent, guests: how many?
Maximum number:
  Seated
  Buffet style
  Party service

How many people will work in the kitchen, normally and at maximum?
One person
Two people working together
One or two with helpers (children, relatives, guests)
A servant: normally, or for special occasions only

Will meals be served in the kitchen?
Breakfast
Lunch
Snacks
All meals
Occasionally; always

Is the kitchen to be an isolated work center; a room accessible to family and guests; totally open to dining or living areas?

Is the kitchen to accommodate any special functions in addition to food preparation?
Laundry
Ironing
Plant and garden care
Sewing
Other

For each regular user, what is:
Optimum counter height (32"–38"; standard: 36")
Maximum high shelf reach (72"–76")
Need for handicapped use, if any

Desired appliances (general type and any specific preferences), storage requirements, special needs?

With all of this data in hand, the designer works out the amount of space needed, going on to the general plan layout and the selection of appliances and equipment, finally proceeding to the detailed design of counters and cabinets, choices of finishes, colors, and similar details, as discussed in the following pages.

Planning

Historically, the big Colonial kitchen, with its huge fireplace, had been the main room of the house and the center of family activities (fig. 396). The Victorian kitchen, at least in larger houses, provided a spacious work area for servants as well as (when they chose to use it) for the ladies of a family (fig. 397).

Until recently, ideas about kitchen design have been colored by the thinking of the Depression years of the 1930s, when the decreasing use of household help, the need to scale down construction costs and size, and the appearance of more varied and improved appliances and equipment led to the "streamlined" kitchen of minimum size, designed with a laboratory-like neatness for efficient work patterns (fig. 398). This small, efficient kitchen had been planned for use by one person—the "typical housewife"—whose burden of work, it was thought, would be reduced by the compact, assembly-line layout, with appliances and sink embedded in a continuous line of counters, favoring neatness and easy cleaning. Storage space was usually enclosed by doors.

This concept still influences modern kitchen design, although its assumptions have come into question. To begin with, a small kitchen is likely to be inconvenient with more than one person working; closed storage makes for the endless opening and closing of doors; a uniform counter line tends to place storage and appliances too high or too low for many users.

In addition, today's life styles have outgrown the "laboratory kitchen." The modern tendency is toward open kitchen plans that permit easy communication with family or guests. The standard kitchen layout cannot accommodate other activities, such as eating, children's play or study, sewing, or laundry. Eating habits have become varied, too, ranging from quick snacks and prepackaged TV dinners to gourmet cookery

398

requiring more space and equipment than the "average" meal uses.

Whatever the functional requirements for a particular kitchen may be, planning will follow some basic concepts. First of all, plumbing limitations must be considered. It is always most economical to stay close to existing piping or, in new construction, to group plumbing fixtures close together, back-to-back when possible. If piping can be run freely below the floor (as, for example, when the basement is below the kitchen space), plumbing can be located as desired, although a close grouping minimizes the cost of plumbing installation. If access to the space below is difficult or impossible (as, for example, in multistory apartment buildings), it is essential to stay close to existing plumbing riser locations. Pipes can extend a few feet in one direction or another, but long horizontal runs are impractical. (See also Chapter 18, pages 482–83.)

The placement of architectural elements usually imposes constraints as well. Planning must take account of window location, for example, to make the best use of it. Most users prefer a window over a sink. If the design places it behind a refrigerator or a tall cabinet, it will be blocked off. Door location is somewhat more flexible, although any change, particularly of an outside door, may be costly. Kitchens designed for the disabled call for special consideration (see Chapter 14, figs. 511, 519–21).

PRIMARY WORK CENTERS. With these constraints in mind, and with a program of needs established, the designer can consider the different plan layouts possible. All of these, from the smallest to the most elaborate, will feature three primary work centers, each related to one of the basic pieces of kitchen equipment.

RECEIVING AND STORAGE. *The refrigerator is the primary item of equipment, with space for unpacking and spreading out groceries and storage for packaged and canned goods close by (fig. 399). Some serving from this center (for ice, cold drinks, and cold foods) can also be anticipated.*

FOOD PREPARATION. *This center comprises work counter space and the sink (or sinks) for washing, mixing, chopping, and so on (fig. 400). After meals, it becomes the center for cleanup. Dishwasher and disposal unit, when they are provided, logically belong here, along with conventional trash and garbage containers. Adjacent storage holds utensils, cleaning supplies, and possibly some cooking and serving items.*

COOKING. *The range and/or cook top and oven plus, possibly, the popular microwave oven are the obvious equipment. Adjacent counter space is used for some preparation and for serving. Storage for pots and pans and serving dishes should be at hand.*

398. In the 1930s, as households employed fewer servants and the kitchen became increasingly the province of the homemaker, kitchens became much smaller and more finished in appearance. At the same time, however, industrial designers of the period focused on efficiency, introducing appliances and cabinetry of almost labora-tory-like aspect. The "streamlined" kitchen became a showplace in the modern house—although it did not prove to be the ideal workplace. This example is in the Butler House of 1936 in Des Moines, Iowa, designed by Kraetsch and Kraetsch, architects. (Photograph: Hedrich/Blessing)

399

400

399. *A wall refrigerator (at right) and well-planned cabinets make up the receiving and storage area of a modern kitchen. Note also the window placed over the sink (at left)—a popular location. This New Orleans house is the work of R. Clay Markham, architect, and Tom R. Collum, interior designer. (Photograph: © Jacques Dirand, courtesy* House & Garden)

400. *In this modern kitchen in a house in Bryn Mawr, Pennsylvania, the island holds the primary preparation surface with sink, with a secondary surface and another sink in the counter space on the left. The cooking area is straight ahead; a wall oven is on the right. The laboratory-like, continuous counters of the 1930s have now been humanized, and natural wood finishes have replaced white enameled metal. John Caulk, designer, 1984. (Photograph: © Tom Crane)*

Storage for dishes and glassware may relate to either food preparation or cooking. Secondary functions (such as laundry equipment and eating space) are logically given peripheral locations.

KITCHEN LAYOUTS. Ideally, kitchen planning places the three centers in sequence, starting with receiving and storage, proceeding to preparation, and ending with cooking and serving, with the idea that this corresponds to the actual sequence of meal preparation, minimizing wasted movement. This leads to a typical layout with refrigerator, sink, and range in that order, spaced out with work counters and storage between the major appliances.

The most favored arrangements are:

STRAIGHT LINE. The three centers are lined up in order, ideally with service entrance at one end and access to dining at the opposite end (fig. 403). This is the most common plan for a minimal or very small kitchen or kitchenette. An in-line plan in a larger facility may stretch the elements out across an overly long walking path.

L-SHAPE. The centers, in the same sequence as above, are bent around a corner to fit the space available and to reduce paths of work movement. This plan places two of

the centers in a line with the third at a right angle. Occasionally, the preparation center is placed at the bend, sometimes with an L-shaped or diagonal sink.

U PLAN. This plan, in which the three centers make up the three sides of the layout, is probably the most popular and most often recommended (fig. 404). This plan is particularly efficient for one person working alone who stands within easy reach of a work triangle formed by the three sides. Its problems include the two corner areas, often difficult to use well, and the somewhat constricted space within the U if more than one person will work in the kitchen.

OTHER PLAN TYPES. More or less variations on the basic layouts, these include the parallel, or corridor, plan *and* plans incorporating an island. *In the first, a straight line is cut into two parts, placed to face one another across the work aisle, or a basic straight line is paralleled by a storage line opposite (fig. 405). An island is usually added to an L or U plan to make either the range or the sink accessible from several directions (fig. 402). It is particularly suitable to larger kitchens and situations in which several people will work together at meal preparation.*

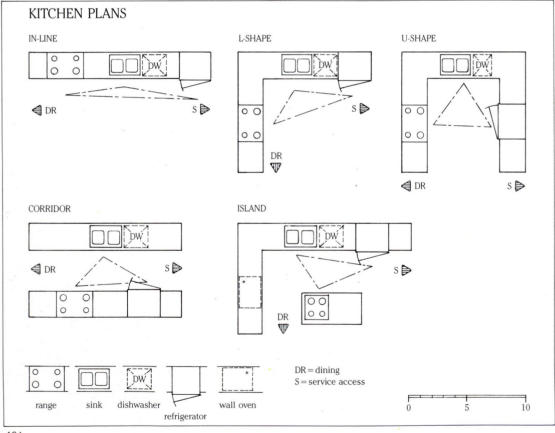

KITCHEN PLANS

IN-LINE

L-SHAPE

U-SHAPE

CORRIDOR

ISLAND

range   sink   dishwasher   refrigerator   wall oven

DR = dining
S = service access

0   5   10

401

401. Different kitchen layouts are illustrated here, from upper left: in-line, L-shape, U-shape, corridor, and island. The work triangle outlines the walking path created by the layout of the three centers. The arrows point to service access and dining room. The architectural plan symbols for the major fixtures and appliances are given below.

402. In this kitchen, an island holds the sink and some preparation space and also supports an L-shaped dining counter that seats five. Shelton, Mindel & Associates, designer, 1986. (Photograph: Jeff McNamara)

403

404

405

403. This three-center, in-line kitchen graces a California house. Here, the refrigerator is not in the line but facing it on the left. (Photograph: © Philip L. Molten)

404. In this compact version of a highly efficient U-shape kitchen plan, the refrigerator (running out of the picture at the extreme left) begins the receiving and storage area at the left. The sink and preparation area is on the right, with the cooking center at the middle of the U. The most common U-plans place the sink at the end and the range on the right, but here the narrowness of the sink area would be too constricting. This plan is very practical for one person—less convenient, perhaps, for more than one. Lee Harris Pomeroy Associates Architects, New York, designer. (Photograph: © Norman McGrath)

405. In a corridor kitchen, the work space is between two parallel lines of counters, appliances, and storage units. Service access is usually at one end of the corridor, access to the dining room at the other end. This kitchen was designed for maximum efficiency by its owners, Jim and Christopher Hirsheimer, the latter a caterer. (Photograph: John Waggaman, courtesy Metropolitan Home Magazine)

406

Kitchen Elements and Materials

After selecting a basic plan layout and incorporating additional elements, such as laundry or eat-in table or counter, the designer moves on to the detailed planning of work surfaces, storage, and equipment selection and placement. A number of kitchen systems offer excellent counter and storage products (fig. 406) and, often, an advisory service as well, making solutions almost certain of success. Some appliance manufacturers offer related storage elements. The many cabinet lines, in wood, metal, and combinations of materials, vary from excellent to indifferent in both design and construction quality.

It is also entirely possible to custom design all kitchen installations, incorporating only a sink and appliances of standard manufacture (fig. 408). While it takes considerable effort, this latter course makes it possible to provide for specific, possibly unusual needs. It is often more economical than high-quality standard product systems.

This phase of design involves the following choices:
COOKING APPLIANCE. The common choice is between a unit range, or stove, or separate cook top (fig. 411) and oven or ovens. Large restaurant, or professional, ranges

have come into use in kitchens designed for serious cooks (fig. 407). Cooking devices such as microwave ovens, electric frying pans and casseroles, toaster-ovens, and so on often serve as auxiliaries to the basic range.

FUEL. The choice between gas or electric fuel depends upon both economics and the cook's personal preference. Even the obsolescent wood stove can be considered, usually with a gas backup, in rural locations where wood is an economical fuel.

REFRIGERATOR TYPE. Models come with freezer space at the top or, more convenient but requiring more space, alongside. When space permits, a separate freezer of cabinet or chest type may be a good choice. Wall-recessed refrigerators of fine design are also available.

SINK TYPE AND MATERIAL. Types may be single, double, multipurpose; of stainless steel or enameled cast iron; with or without a drain board configuration (fig. 413). Faucet type and design must also be selected (fig. 412), as well as dishwasher and disposal unit, if included. Space, budget, and user preferences are determinants in selection.

406. The most compact possible kitchenette—a single unit incorporates sink and burners in the counter top, refrigerator below, and microwave oven above. (Photograph courtesy Dwyer Kitchen Products)

407

408

409

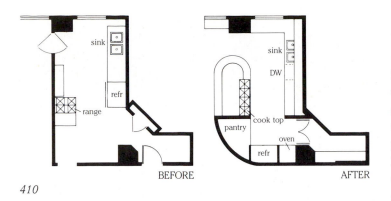

410

BEFORE AFTER

The choice of wood or metal as a primary material is not a simple one, as each material offers its own advantages. Wood doors and drawers, with their quiet operation and their warm feel, texture, and appearance, may create a more comfortable, or homelike, atmosphere. Metal is stronger, easier to clean, and suggests sanitation and durability. Finishes on metal are usually tough, but once damaged they are hard to repair, with the possibility of rust developing. Natural finishes on wood are less likely to show damage and are easier to repair. Paint finishes on wood are less durable than similar metal finishes, but repainting is comparatively easy. Plastic laminate is a durable alternative. Since neither material has an overall clear advantage, selection is primarily a matter of personal taste. A possible compromise is the use of metal cabinets with wood door and drawer fronts.

STORAGE PROVISION. Closed cabinets are a favorite, but open storage deserves consideration for items that are not messy and require no protection (figs. 416, 417). Open shelves and hanging pots and utensils avoid the inconvenience of constantly opening and closing doors. Open wire shelves and baskets (fig. 414) and systems for hanging pots and tools (fig. 415) are convenient and inexpensive storage alternatives. Dish and glassware storage may be part of a kitchen plan or may be placed in or adjacent to the dining space. Drawers, cabinets with rotating shelves, and ingenious special units for specific storage needs, including cleaning supplies and equipment, are available in most kitchen systems (figs. 419, 420).

COUNTERS. The standard height of 36 inches will not serve all tasks and all users, but it is widely adopted as a compromise norm. Many surface materials are possible, each with various advantages and disadvantages. Favorite choices include plastic laminate, wood (butcher block), linoleum, tile, stainless steel, and special synthetic composition materials such as Corian.

FLOOR MATERIALS. Linoleum, resilient tile, ceramic tile, quarry tile, and slate all lend themselves to the

411

407. *Designer Mary Emmerling designed this kitchen for her Manhattan loft. The efficient, gleaming look of the professional restaurant range and large wall refrigerator is offset by baskets on a high shelf and the country-style rug, furniture, place settings, and accessories, all working together to make a useful, comfortable, and original cooking and dining area. (Photograph: © Chris Mead)*

408, 410. *Custom-made under-counter and overhead cabinets of coordinated design organize all of the elements of this spacious, renovated kitchen (fig. 408). Fig. 410 shows its plan. Charles Morris Mount, designer. (Photograph: William P. Steele)*

409. *The architect Eva Jiricna designed this tiny kitchen for her own apartment. The materials and colors are highly unusual: wall and counter-top surfaces are a strong green; the dimpled rubber sheet is most often used as a flooring material. Details are carefully considered—accent colors are bright yellow and red; the faucets are by Danish designer Arne Jacobsen; all storage is open and accessible. (Photograph: © Richard Bryant)*

411. *In this "kitchen idea" from Abaco, designed by Giovanni Offredi, cupboards make up an unbroken wall at the far end of the counter. Sinks and burner top are set into the counter; its curved back-splash is surmounted by a continuous luminous band that provides working light directly above the work surface. (Photograph courtesy Abitare)*

412

413

kitchen environment. Wood and carpet specially made for wet-location use may also be considered.

WALL SURFACES. Paint, plastic sheet material, plastic laminate, and tile are popular choices (fig. 409).

CEILING MATERIALS. Sheetrock, plaster, and acoustical materials are choices.

MISCELLANEOUS ITEMS. Other details that call for consideration include lighting, ventilation, and a variety of accessories and gadgets. A central globe light, often provided for general illumination, tends to place the user in his or her own shadow and gives an overall effect of bleakness. The most effective lighting comes from strips concealed under wall cabinets or shelves. Downlights directed at counters also work well. A range hood, ideally outside-vented, is the best cure for kitchen smells and deposits of cooking fumes and grease. A window fan or ceiling fan is an inferior alternative. Accessories such as towel racks, pinup boards, clocks, spice racks, and many other popular gadgets will become items of clutter if not planned for (fig. 418).

Appearance

It is a curious fact that the appearance of residential kitchens is most often spoiled by efforts at beautification, usually realized in one or both of two ways: by importing an artificial charm, which may derive from inappropriate period décor, fussy elements such as patterned curtains, overdecorative tile, and other ornamental materials, and accessories such as clocks in the form of teapots or cats, or by using imitative materials. Modern cabinets faced in imitation—or even real—knotty pine or with French provincial details; linoleum that imitates Spanish tiles, flagstone, or brick; wallpapers that simulate Dutch (or any

414

412. *A single-control, or mixing, faucet displays an exceptionally neat and elegant design. (Photograph courtesy Kroin)*

413. *A double kitchen sink of acid-resistant enameled cast iron supports, in one basin, a removable wooden cutting board. The person working pushes scraps through the hole into a container in the sink below. A single-control, or mixing, faucet is an alternative to the two-control installation shown. (Photograph courtesy Kohler Co.)*

414. *An open wire-grid storage system, used here to hold a food processor's various attachments, can accommodate a variety of hooks, holders, racks, and shelves, making it possible to arrange a custom-storage assembly for almost any imaginable collection of small items. (Photograph courtesy Heller Designs, Inc.)*

415. *In this unusual, glass-roofed kitchen by James Rossant, racks of tin-lined copper pots and pans become accessories on display—and in handy reach. The stainless-steel cabinets are rubber-lined to deaden noise. (Photograph: © 1985 Wolfgang Hoyt/ESTO)*

416

417

418

416, 417. In this 1982 house in Belvedere, California, architect Hank Bruce used the most basic storage solution—open shelving (fig. 416), ideal when objects are attractive and do not need to be protected. Other storage—here shown open—is enclosed (fig. 417). The doors, themselves lined with shallow shelves, close over the fixed shelves to conceal cans and packaged items that can appear untidy. (Photograph: © Philip L. Molten)

418. An imaginative L-shape kitchen uses a standard cabinet system that includes many functional accessories. The narrow vertical shelf unit supports one end of a dining surface—an unusual variation within an L-shape plan. (Photograph courtesy Siematic)

419

420

419. The doors of this kitchen storage unit have glass inserts to provide a glimpse of the items stored within. The solid faces of the cabinet are of Color-core laminate, a plastic surface material in which the face color is carried through the thickness of the laminate so that the edges are the same color as the face. (Photograph courtesy Formica Corporation)

420. Roll-out shelves make items stored near the rear of an under-counter storage unit easily accessible, forestalling the need for stooping and groping. The small spice shelves above the counter top at the rear store the diminutive jars neatly. (Photograph: Diane Padys)

other) tiles—all these set a tone of falseness and visual clutter. Such elements are all too often featured in consumer publications that advise on kitchen design. In fact, a more practical and straightforward design will hold up better, both in use and in attractiveness, over a period of time. This approach eliminates neither comfort nor, at best, genuine beauty.

BATHROOMS

Like kitchens, bathrooms are usually given the minimum of space and designed according to formula, with a few "special features," such as a counter lavatory, possibly added to soften the effect. While bath functions are less complex than those of kitchens, they deserve more attention than the formula layouts devote to them.

Residential Bathrooms

The modern bathroom has its origins in the Victorian introduction of modern plumbing (fig. 422). The toilet owes its alternative name *water closet* to its frequent introduction, quite literally, into an existing closet. The bathroom most often began as an existing room, perhaps a small bedroom or storage room, and was converted by the installation of the three standard fixtures (toilet, washbasin, and bathtub).

Placing these fixtures together in one room has a certain logic, since the privacy of all three functions is ensured with one closable door to the room. The disadvantage, of course, is that one user ties up the entire room as long as the door remains closed. Moreover, modern bathroom use often calls for, in addition to the basic three fixtures, a shower (or substitutes this for or combines it with the bathtub), twin washbasins, perhaps a bidet (common in France but unusual elsewhere), provision for exercise, rest, or special bathing facilities (such as a sauna or Jacuzzi), and, occasionally, laundry facilities.

One bathroom can hardly accommodate all of these elements. Also, if there will be more than one user, two or more units have clear advantages. A number of possible combinations can be considered (fig. 428), including adding a *lavatory* or *powder room* (without tub or shower) accessible to guests as well as family; creating a *split bathroom,* for example, with toilet or toilet and wash basin in a unit separate from a bathing unit; and providing two or more complete bathrooms.

Whatever their layout, all bathroom spaces must connect to plumbing, most economically with pipes shared by another bath or kitchen, ideally back-to-back. The toilet requires a larger drainpipe called a *soil pipe,* which can pass through only a thick partition wall or pipe chase space. Efficient plans usually line up all fixtures with pipes along one wall. Minimal

421

dimensions are well-known standards, widely published. However, these make for rather cramped facilities; actual use patterns give a better guide to dimensions.

Available standard fixtures—toilet, washbasin or lavatory, bathtub and shower stall—are far from ideal, but few alternatives exist: basins can be installed in counter units set at the proper height for actual users; tubs can be installed in a designed surround; and showers can be built to order. In luxury baths, the tub may become a specially constructed pool-like unit.

All bathroom spaces require ventilation as well as heat. The former may be by means of either a window or skylight or a fan and duct, or by a combination of both. Details of a bath include provision for soap, towels, toilet-paper dispensers, medicine cabinet, mirror, and suitable lighting. Materials need to be selected for water-resistance. Tile, slate, and marble are more durable than plaster, wood, and wallpaper, which, although commonly used, must be regularly renewed.

Bathrooms have a bad record as locations for accidents. The presence of slippery surfaces, water (particularly hot water), soap, electric outlets, and, often, glass-enclosure elements, alone or in combination, create a variety of hazards, particularly for children, the elderly, and handicapped persons. Glass shower enclosures should be avoided, mirrors placed with care to avoid

421. An Eileen Gray mirror is an elegant feature of an uncluttered bathroom designed by Andrée Putman. Note the band of decorative tile and the glass-block wall of the shower alcove. (Photograph: © Grant Mudford, courtesy House & Garden)

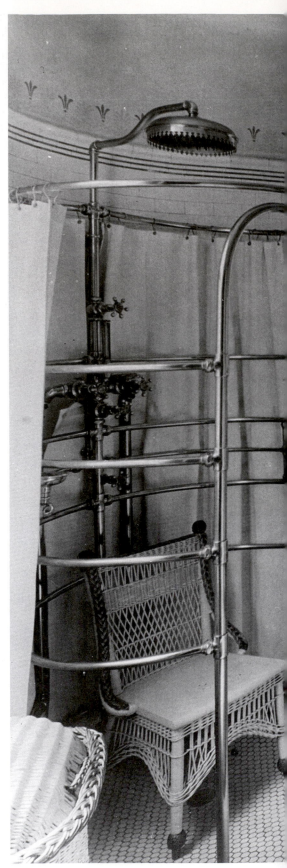

422

422. This luxurious, late-Victorian bathroom dates from the beginning of this century. Note the fireplace with stained-glass window above, the chandelier, and the marble washbasin counter and back-splash. The extraordinary arrangement at the left offers seated comfort while showering. Museum of the City of New York. Wurts Collection

423

423. Here, polished marble and rough-cut stone create a sumptuous contrast of textures. The natural colors of these materials, the green plants, and the accents of towels and small accessories make this elegant bathroom a visual delight. John F. Saladino, designer. (Photograph: © Norman McGrath)

424

accidental breakage, nonskid surfaces and grab rails provided, and electrical outlets of safety type specified.

Space and budget permitting, bathrooms can become outstandingly attractive with good daylight, night lighting, growing plants, space and equipment for rest and exercise, and handsome materials and colors. Small details such as faucets, soap dishes, and towel racks—even the towels themselves—can add to the design quality of a bathroom. Storage space for towels, soap, and similar items can be provided within or adjacent to a bath. Dressing and makeup facilities could be combined with or located adjacent to a bathroom.

Nonresidential Bathrooms

Bathrooms for hotels and motels, dormitories, hospitals, and the "executive washroom" now often provided in office facilities (fig. 425) follow home practice, with appropriate modifications for the special needs of these situations. Public toilets, or *restrooms*, for offices, stores, restaurants, and other public situations demand more complex planning, with stalls, basins,

425

424. At the Phoenix Level Restaurant (1985) of the Garden State Racetrack, Cherry Hill, New Jersey, a richly detailed public toilet displays strong colors and opulent materials, which transform a necessary utility into a dramatic space. Ewing, Cole, Cherry, Parsky, designer. (Photograph: © 1985 Tom Crane)

425. Executive washrooms have become favorite status symbols in business office complexes. Handsome materials and details add to the sense of opulence in this example, designed by Gwathmey Siegel & Associates, architects, for the offices of FDM Productions, New York. (Photograph: O. Baitz, Inc., courtesy Gwathmey Siegel & Associates)

426

427

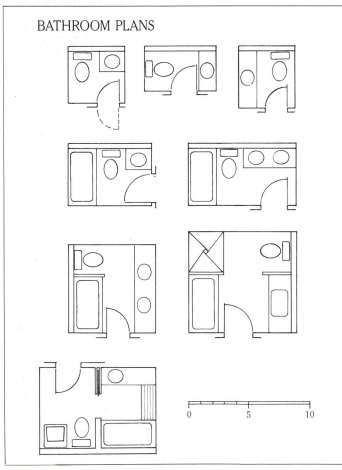

428

BATHROOM PLANS

counters, vestibule, and detail items (such as paper-towel dispenser or air-dryer and waste container) laid out in a logical pattern for sequential use and in ways that establish adequate privacy (fig. 424). Choice of materials and design details also follow home practice, with extra consideration for durability, easy maintenance, safety, and handicapped access (see Chapter 14, pages 385–86, and figs. 515–17).

STORAGE
Residential Storage

Closets make up the primary storage provision in modern residential practice, although shelving, cabinets, files, and even entire storerooms may also be called for. Intelligent design begins with a careful estimate of what is to be stored and a consideration of where suitable storage spaces should go. Commonly, a coat closet is needed near each primary entrance to a dwelling, a clothes closet for each bedroom (ideally double for double occupancy), and at least one linen closet to hold bedding, blankets, and bathroom linens. In addition, the great variety of things that modern families accumulate—sports gear, toys and games, photography equipment, records and tapes, luggage, even such bulky items as bicycles, snow tires, and skis—demands general storage space.

Conventional closets must be large enough to provide hanging space for clothing and require full front access through

426. A surface pattern makes "standard" bathroom fixtures of unusual, sculptural design even more original. Cactus Cutter is the name of the pattern. (Photograph courtesy Kohler Co.)

427. An oval lavatory sink of handcrafted, hammered metal with a polished nickel finish becomes a striking design element. (Photograph courtesy Eljer Plumbingware)

428. Here are layouts of typical bathrooms, ranging from the minimal lavatory or powder room to complete baths, in minimal, simple, and split-bath arrangements. Pipes are hidden in the walls indicated with a double line.

429

429. In a New York apartment designed by Noel Jeffrey, a large bathroom has a pool-like tub incorporating the popular Jacuzzi. (Photograph: © Norman McGrath)

430

430. Ward Bennett was the interior
designer of this dressing room in a 1982
New York apartment. Simple, elegant
forms are accentuated by the Josef
Hoffmann chair, of Vienna Secessionist
vintage. Note the stainless-steel washbasin with hospital-type faucet controls.
(Photograph: Jaime Ardiles-Arce)

sliding or accordion doors. Shelves, shoe racks, built-in drawer units, and other specialized provisions can make storage space more efficient and convenient. Such storage arrangements can be specially detailed and built or can be developed through the use of widely available ready-made systems of closet accessories (fig. 431). More extensive storage arrangements include the walk-in closet, actually a small room with hanging space and other storage fittings on both sides of an aisle, and the dressing room, in which closets and other storage are combined with space and equipment for dressing, grooming, and makeup, including good mirrors and lighting (fig. 430). A dressing room is often used as a transitional element between bedroom and bath.

There are several ways to introduce extra storage space into a plan that lacks adequate closets:

- *REPLACING A WALL BETWEEN TWO ROOMS WITH A LINE OF CLOSETS.* The storage wall usually goes between two bedrooms and is divided so that each room gains half (or some other fraction) of the total. Each space loses only one-half the total closet depth while otherwise retaining its shape.
- *STORAGE FURNITURE.* This can be placed (or built in) where needed (figs. 432, 433). Wardrobes and armoires, widely used in Europe in place of built-in closets, are available as imports, often as elements of storage systems that also provide drawers, shelving, and special-purpose elements such as desks, bars, and TV/audio equipment arrangement.
- *THE POPULAR ROOM DIVIDER AND WALL UNIT.* These are also furniture approaches to adding storage. (See Chapter 6, page 172.) They are best suited to the storage of smaller objects such as books, records, dishes, and glassware rather than clothing. A room divider is used, as the name implies, between two spaces—where there is a large opening, where an opening can be created by the

431

432

433

431. A closet system provides drawers, shelves, and multilevel hanging spaces. Such planned fittings can multiply the usable space of conventional closets. (Photograph: Rothschild, courtesy Closet Systems)

432. Eileen Gray's ingenious storage cabinet with pivoted swinging bins in place of conventional drawers is here realized in lacquered wood and nickel-plated metal. (Photograph courtesy Ecart International/Palluco)

433. When storage is made from transparent plastic, it becomes easy to locate any stored item. Sliding trays in a see-through box are a practical and attractive part of a complete wardrobe. Leonardo Fiori, designer; Zanotta Poltrone, Italy, manufacturer, 1968. (Photograph courtesy The Design Council)

434

435

removal of a wall, or where one large space can be divided to serve multiple functions (fig. 434). The most usual locations are between living and dining areas and between dining area and kitchen. Wall units stand against, and may be attached to, a blank wall. Both types of units are usually made up of modular elements, available in a range of sizes and with varied functions. This means that the complete unit can be custom-designed to fit particular needs, even though the elements are factory-made. Similar units can also be specially designed and custom-built, often at a lower cost than a similar installation of ready-made elements. Storage walls can often accommodate bulky items—sporting gear, hobby equipment, and so on (fig. 437).

- WHERE SPACE IS LIMITED, INGENIOUS WAYS TO USE SPACE CAN OFTEN PROVIDE EXTRA STORAGE. Drawers or rolling box units under beds are one example (see fig. 222). Closets often contain waste space above the normal hat shelf, which can be developed for dead storage of rarely used objects. Shelves or cabinets high up on walls, while inconvenient, can hold items needed only occasionally if a suitable stepladder or stool is accessible. Space above standard kitchen wall cabinets may be used in this way, thus avoiding the problem of dirt collecting on cabinet tops at the same time. In a garage, it is often possible to develop storage space at an upper level over the hood of a parked car or even over the car itself with some arrangement for a lowerable rack or container.

434. Executive work stations at American Capital, Houston, in a semi-open plan are separated by large, custom-built wall units, some with central openings. The units provide storage as well as defining individual offices. ISD Incorporated, designer. (Photograph: Charles McGrath, courtesy ISD Incorporated)

435. A storage system makes good use of the often wasted triangular space below the sloping jib of a staircase. Open boxes store childrens' toys in a bi-level play and bedroom space designed by Ari Bahat, architect. (Photograph courtesy Ari Bahat)

436

437

438

Nonresidential Storage

Storage provisions for hotels, motels, and dormitories follow residential practice, although, obviously, it is impossible to design for unique, individual needs. Office storage in executive and managerial offices also follows similar patterns in providing closets and space for books and equipment. For general and open offices, hanging space is necessary for outdoor clothing and for smaller items, jackets, handbags, and personal possessions. Wardrobe units are often placed close to general work spaces, with a lockable drawer or locker compartment nearby. Larger coat rooms located near entrances pose security problems that have discouraged their use.

Offices present special problems in the storage of records, documents, computer-related materials, and supplies. File cabinets, the traditional basis of office storage, are produced in a great variety of sizes and types by a number of manufacturers. Most file systems also offer utility cabinets, wardrobes, and other storage units in modular sizes that make it possible to assemble neat banks of storage elements, which may also be used as space dividers. For file rooms and archives, systems with banks of files on roller tracks are available; the units are solidly packed with no aisle space except at a single location where the banks are rolled apart to permit access.

Adequate provision of general storage—for supplies, equipment, and odds and ends such as sample products—is important if office spaces are to maintain a sense of neatness and order. Papers and objects that cannot be discarded but do not fit any available storage space contribute greatly to the chaos that all too often characterizes office interiors.

Kitchens, bathrooms, and storage facilities are special-purpose spaces—spaces used for specific purposes, with their own unique set of design problems—that appear in almost every interior project. Most residential interiors include other special-purpose spaces. The following chapter deals with a variety of such project types.

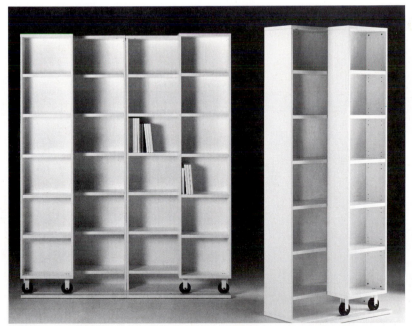

439

436. Another use for the space under a stairway: in this instance, fitted stacks of drawers are as pleasing visually as they are functional. (Photograph: Guy Bouchet)

437. The most traditional wall storage—bookcases—can be installed wall to wall, floor to ceiling, or both. Shown here is a 1981 New York apartment designed by Gwathmey Siegel & Associates, architects. (Photograph: Norman McGrath, courtesy Gwathmey Siegel & Associates)

438. Compactly stacked, this washer and dryer—and a tiny home office—occupy less space than is usually required for a laundry center alone. (Photograph courtesy the Maytag Company)

439. A mobile system of double-banked bookcases can greatly expand the storage capacity of a given lateral space. The front units roll in tracks to give access to the units behind. (Photograph courtesy Punt Mobles, S.L.)

CHAPTER TWELVE
SPECIAL-PURPOSE SPACES

The interior designer occasionally encounters special types of interior spaces. Some of these gain their special character from a particular kind of building or plan type, others from a special function. This chapter presents a survey of such spaces.

Historic Preservation and Adaptive Reuse

Interior design for buildings with historic detail presents a special set of interesting problems. Many excellent older buildings survive, displaying either the styles of design current at the time of their construction or imitations of older historic styles. In Europe, structures built as far back as the Middle Ages, as well as buildings ranging through all the historic styles since, can be found. In America, all of the historic styles are represented, sometimes in combination, in the eclectic, imitative architecture of the late nineteenth and early twentieth centuries, while genuine examples of Colonial, Federal, and Victorian periods are not uncommon.

For many years, it was common practice to gut older buildings and reconstruct them in an entirely new way. Old farmhouses, older city row houses, and many stores and office buildings have been given such "face-lifts." Some of the results were of excellent quality, but too often fine older work was replaced with inferior modern substitutes. Many older buildings were designed with detail of fine aesthetic quality and built with craftsmanship that is now difficult or impossible to equal. When such older buildings become neglected and shabby, it is often tempting to modernize them totally, but in many cases it is wiser and cheaper to restore existing work, making appropriate changes to adapt it to modern uses and needs.

Recent years have seen an upsurge in historic preservation and what is called *adaptive reuse,* that is, the preservation of structure and some details with modifications to permit ongoing modern use. Many places now designate historic buildings or districts as *landmarks,* legally protecting them against destruction or inappropriate modernization. Although the landmarking of interiors has increased, usually only exteriors are protected. Nevertheless, the preservation and intelligent adaptation of interior space in preserved buildings, even when not required by law, are usually advisable. The modern movement toward professional specialization in historic preservation includes interior design as an important aspect.

Dealing with preserved interiors presents several special problems. These include adaptation to modern uses, needs, and expectations, and the practical matters of obtaining appropriate materials and workmanship. These problems appear in various ways according to the functional purposes of the particular

space. The answers to the following questions will influence and guide the interior design approach to buildings with historic detail:

Is the historic detail of such good quality and in sufficiently good condition that it should be preserved?

Is the detail of basic merit, but in bad condition? If so, can it be and should it be restored?

Should the style of the interior design elements—furniture, color, lighting, and so on—follow the style of the building, as a type of restoration *interior similar to the period rooms in many museums? Is this technically and economically practical? Will it be possible to obtain actual antique elements of the appropriate period or will reproductions be used?*

Will it be best to retain and restore the existing historic elements while introducing modern elements (furniture, lighting, color) for reasons of economy, practicality, and comfort? How can this be done to avoid conflicts of style?

Is the existing older work of such mediocre or poor quality or in such bad condition that the best solution is to totally reconstruct it into a modern space?

These questions must be worked out with the owner or client after the condition of the given space has been evaluated. *RESIDENTIAL PROJECTS.* In residential projects, while basic living patterns remain largely unchanged, many of the details of day-to-day living are quite different from those of the past. For example, the Colonial interior tends to have small windows, big fireplaces, and very limited storage facilities. Bathrooms, modern kitchens, and modern lighting, not to mention any kind of electronic equipment, were all unknown until recent years. Most people today do not find ladder-back chairs and hard benches for dining seating adequately comfortable. As a result, a genuine Colonial house poses problems about what to preserve and what to modify. Total preservation, with a giant cooking fireplace and candle and oil-lamp illumination, is usually possible only in museum-like exhibition situations. To use such buildings for actual living, ways must be found to introduce more comfortable furniture, bathrooms, and modern heating and lighting. Kitchens must be totally renovated, tucked away in some hidden place, or, possibly, placed in a modern wing.

Victorian and later periods, with ideas of comfort and convenience closer to present-day standards, are less problematic. Victorian kitchens and baths may have outmoded equipment, but otherwise they are often quite practical, permitting modernization without much visual change. Gas

440. Original architectural details have been preserved and emphasized in a 1984 adaptive reuse of an older building for modern office purposes. Here, a bank building of the 1880s has been reconceived by architect Glave Newman Anderson to house the information and processing center of a state-run money-management facility for retirees, the Virginia Supplemental Retirement System, in Richmond. (Photograph: Whitney Cox)

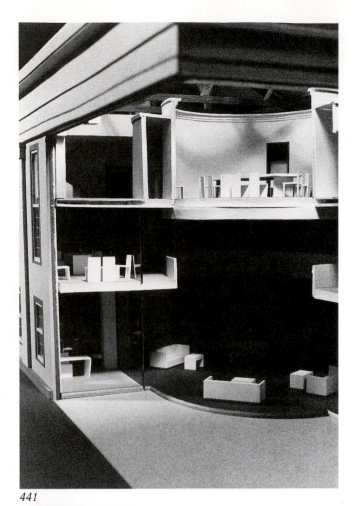

441

CASE STUDY 3

ADAPTIVE REUSE
Alumni Hall, Alfred University, Alfred, New York

PROJECT DESIGNER: PHILIP B. PRIGMORE, ARCHITECTURAL CONSULTANT

ARCHITECTS AND ENGINEERS: FRED H. THOMAS ASSOCIATES, P.C.

INTERIOR DESIGNER AND FURNITURE CONSULTANT: JOHN PILE

The center edifice of the Alfred University campus—an 1851 Greek Revival structure—was originally built as a church that served the university and town. Over the years, however, it underwent several changes in purpose, its final incarnation being a gymnasium. With the arrival of a new university president, it was decided to rehabilitate the building and endow it with a function appropriate to its focal location on campus. Today, Alumni Hall is a reception center for prospective students, and

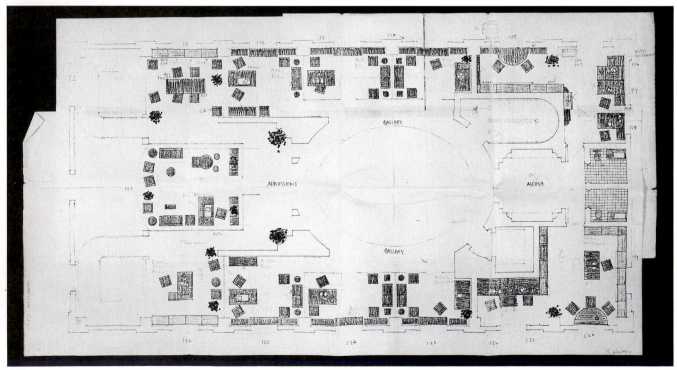

442

441. A very detailed model of this project was built as a visual aid in explaining the total concept. The exterior shell can be lifted off to reveal the complete planned interior.

442. Rough furniture plans were developed by the designer after he conducted extensive interviews with the staff members, deans, and faculty members who would be the future users of the space. Having obtained comprehen-

sive data on work and storage needs, he surveyed with a consultant the roughly two hundred office systems available and narrowed them down to ten product lines. Although no specific furniture choices were made at this stage, the plans served as the basis for selection when the manufacturer was chosen. The final selection was made on the basis of versatility: it offered both conventional furniture for partitioned offices and system furniture for open spaces.

443. Samples of actual materials—color swatches for paints, wood finishes, and drapery material—are spread out here on prints of the architectural construction plans. The colors and textiles generate a reserved yet lively scheme that conveys a delicately balanced sense of tradition and stability along with an energetic and forward-looking orientation that reflects the present character of the university. (Photograph: George Hein)

444. This view of a main area in the finished project looks from the first-floor rotunda toward the entrance, which is flanked by twin stairways. The contemporary furniture—Circolo sofa and Acorn chairs designed by Massimo Vignelli—strikes a modern note but also harmonizes with the tradition and stability implied in the restored and reconstructed details of the historic building. (Photograph: Bill Kontzias, courtesy Sunar Hauserman Systems and Furniture)

also houses the admissions and related offices, as well as exhibition and meeting spaces.

The exterior of the building was painstakingly restored; the interior, long in decay, was gutted and totally reconstructed. The result is a new structure nested into the old shell. While the new interior does not attempt to reproduce the historic original, it retains a relationship to the 1850s design in its quiet symmetry and its choices of materials and colors. The twin winding stairs to the four upper levels were the pride of the original building, while the double-height rotunda embodies the monumentality of the period.

The completed project forms a striking physical theme for the institution as a whole, a warm and welcoming starting point for incoming students and their parents and an active center for internal administrative functions.

445

lighting can be electrified (it usually already has been) without greatly changing its appearance.

Whatever its age, the historic interior has probably been subjected to some unfortunate changes. Over the years, different owners remove fireplaces, alter windows, paint over woodwork, damage plasterwork and wood moldings—and destroy other period details while making repairs. Decisions about what to restore, replace, or simply accept depend on an evaluation of the space's condition, budget limitations, and practical issues. Fortunately, many new techniques and products make it possible to restore old detail, remove inappropriate finishes, and generally refurbish historic interiors to the limit of the owner's desires and budget.

Many difficult decisions remain. Should furniture be genuine antiques, which tend to be rare, expensive, and not the most practical choice; antique reproductions, which are also expensive and cannot avoid a quality of artificiality; or modern, which carries the danger of clashing with the space's period? The last alternative often works out surprisingly well, with the modern movable objects forming a pleasant contrast with the

446

445. A studio–office space occupies a Roman building with rich historic detail. The interior design incorporates an eclectic collection of furniture and objects, all serving modern uses effectively. Designed by Adriano Magistretti, of Pediment Design, Inc., for his own home (see also fig. 1). (Photograph: Isidoro Genovese)

446. Modern furniture in a Victorian setting is an example of adaptive reuse in a living room. Stephen Levine, designer. (Photograph: © Norman McGrath)

period background (fig. 446). Should dark Victorian woodwork be preserved and complemented with dark and florid Victorian wallpaper, or should brighter modern colors and finishes be used? There are no absolute answers. The judgment and taste of the owner and designer will enter into the resolution of every such question that arises in a particular project.

NONRESIDENTIAL PROJECTS.

Nonresidential historic buildings present some other problems, depending upon the building type (figs. 440, 447). Religious buildings, for example, can usually be preserved or restored without much change, except to heating and lighting systems. Introducing modern levels of lighting without resorting to inappropriate fixtures or inappropriately dramatic effects requires discretion and judgment. Theaters and auditoriums often need improved and more comfortable seating, but care must be taken not to harm acoustics when making changes. Safety requirements dealing with exits, stairs, and certain materials may also be an issue.

Many public buildings include large and monumental spaces that may seem depressing (creating a gloomy atmosphere that can be corrected by improved lighting) or simply wasteful in terms of modern economics. How to deal with such spaces in courthouses, post offices, and banks, for example, is a special concern, but it is clear that making new ceilings, carving out commercial shop space, and similar courses of action are usually destructive and unwise. Some building types—for example, the railroad station—have become largely obsolete. An appropriate new use must first be found for them before design issues can be addressed. Many good examples of intelligent adaptive reuse are appearing (see fig. 476).

Lofts

A loft is simply an open space, usually unfinished in detail, intended for utilitarian uses such as manufacturing or storage. In larger cities, loft buildings provide space in multifloor configurations similar to the open areas typical of large office buildings. Artists in search of studio space were the first to recognize that, with the addition of kitchens and baths, loft space could serve as living space as well as for studio use. As

447

447. Among the more startling and amusing touches of the Virginia Supplemental Retirement System project by Glave Newman Anderson (see fig. 440) is a bank vault—complete with its massive door—that has been turned into a conference room. (Photograph: Whitney Cox)

manufacturing and warehousing activities have tended to move out of central city locations, first artists and then others looking for spacious city living space have gradually taken over loft buildings and whole loft neighborhoods, converting them to studios and/or living space.

A typical loft is large, high-ceilinged, often generously windowed, and has one or more details characteristic of older industrial or mill buildings (fig. 448). There may be large exposed wood or cast-iron columns, exposed beams or so-called tin (pressed-metal) ceilings, sprinkler pipes, rather crude heating and lighting arrangements, and, of course, no partitioning into rooms for normal residential use. The new occupants, with their designer and (often) architect, must introduce the kitchen, bath, storage, and partitioning to make the space useful and comfortable, all in ways that comply with building laws and the occupants' budget (fig. 449).

The results can range from open studio space with a minimal bath, kitchenette, and sleeping alcove or raised platform tucked away in a corner of the space to the luxury loft, which, aside from its unusually large space, can be quite similar to a conventional apartment. The big spaces characteristic of lofts, which lend themselves to social gatherings, performances, and exhibits, call for special attention to suitable furniture and finishes. Many typical residential elements (furniture, textiles, wallpapers) are on a small scale that looks out of place in open loft spaces. Simple materials, strong colors, and unpretentious kinds of furniture tend to work well in lofts. Large paintings and other works of art appear to advantage.

Studios

The term has come to designate a one-room apartment, generally small, but the studio in its original sense is discussed here—an actual work space for an artist, musician, dancer, or other creative person who needs a special and fairly large place to work. Lofts often are studios or incorporate studio space, but a studio may also be a special room in a house or apartment. Traditionally, the studio of an artist or photographer is placed to make north light available through large windows or, best of all, from a north-facing skylight.

The interior design of a typical artist's studio is totally simple (fig. 450). White walls and ceiling are the norm, with a floor of neutral color. Even the floor is often painted white, to reflect light and minimize any visual impact from a particular chromatic color. Furniture, usually minimal, may be improvised or "found" in character. Visual interest usually derives solely from work in progress and the artist's props and collection of necessary materials. It is surprising how often this direct and unplanned interior becomes a beautiful and exciting space. The

448

448. Older loft buildings frequently offer particularly fine opportunities for adaptive reuse. In this case, the high ceilings permit the addition of a new mezzanine floor, while the elaborate, Corinthian-style cast-iron column capitals supply welcome decorative detail. Michael S. Wu, architect, converted the space in a Manhattan loft building into a sculptor's home and studio. (Photograph: Gilles de Chabaneix)

449

studios of well-known artists are often photographed; those of some earlier famous artists can be visited as museums (for example, the studios of Cézanne, Monet, and Renoir). Such studios, with their lively and simple but expressive qualities, provide fine examples of studio space at its best.

Workshops

With do-it-yourself and other hobby activities becoming increasingly popular, the demand for home workshop space has increased (fig. 451). For many years, homeowners have commonly devised some sort of basement workshop. Now, more and more inhabitants of small houses or even apartments have begun to insist on having workshop space. Although the interior designer is rarely responsible for the design of such space, some thoughtful planning can have a significant effect on making a workshop useful.

For hobbies that require a large area—such as serious woodworking, boat-building, or work on cars—basements,

449. A cavernous one-time garage was transformed into office and studio space for Jeff Kerns, a graphic designer in Hollywood. The wooden trusses and roof structure of the old building remain exposed; low partitions define the office and studio. Part of the original red-brick wall (right) and new ochre-tinted partition walls provide a background for Kerns's private office. The large painting on the left is by Jean-Michel Basquiat, the small paintings are by Chuck Connolly. Frederick Fisher was the architect. (Photograph: Tim Street-Porter)

450

451

garages, or, when they exist, barns are often used as workshops. It is important to plan the space around shop equipment so that tools and materials have adequate clearances. A circular saw in a woodworking shop, for example, requires clearance for feeding and removing work, calling for a considerable clear area when such large pieces as 4-by-8-foot plywood or 16-foot lengths of wood are being cut. The size of projects must also be taken into account beforehand. Jokes about boats built in spaces too small to permit their removal are not so farfetched. Noise from power tools and fumes from painting and work with plastics and the fire risks associated with such materials also need attention.

Some hobbies do not need a large space but call for equipment that many home spaces cannot easily accommodate. The minimal requirement for firing pottery, for example, is an electric kiln that may need special heavy-duty wiring. Gas or wood-burning kilns need a chimney. Many craft hobbies, such as woodcarving, making model airplanes or boats, making guitars or violins, printing on a small scale, and weaving, make more modest demands on space and equipment, but still deserve some thought if suitable workshop space for any one or any combination of these activities is called for. Such hobbies may even use a closet, a storage wall grouping, or a foldaway piece of furniture as a workplace, arranged to make work convenient. Although the work space is clearly limited, it concentrates and confines equipment and the mess associated with the hobby.

Sewing

Ideally, this activity receives its own room, but it is most often combined with a laundry room, utility room, or, occasionally, a kitchen. Sewing requires good task light, good placement for a sewing machine with ample surrounding work space, a cutting table, an ironing board (a foldaway board may be used), and suitable storage.

Darkrooms

Many professional and serious amateur photographers require a home or studio darkroom (fig. 452). A bathroom or kitchen may serve as a makeshift space, but the most practical darkroom has its own space and facilities. An extra bathroom or a large closet can sometimes be successfully converted to a darkroom, but a space planned for the purpose works out best.

The need for darkening is obvious, with special arrangements at window and door to assure full light-tightness. Since excluding light usually means cutting off ventilation, some mechanical ventilation (or air conditioning) is essential. Running water and drainage are highly desirable, although

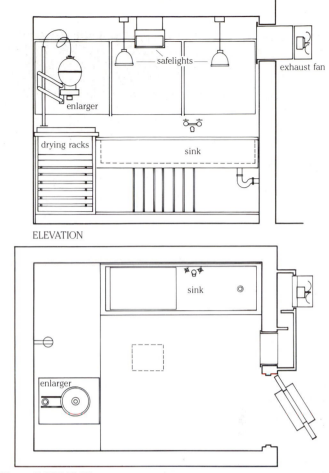

ELEVATION

452   FLOOR PLAN

improvised ways of doing without can be considered. Manuals addressed to photographers and photo technicians give comprehensive advice on the suitable arrangement of work counters, storage, electrical outlets, and similar matters, on which the user will usually have specific ideas.

Home Offices

Many careers are based at home or involve taking work home from the office with enough regularity to call for a special work space. Even the office-like chores of everyday life (writing letters, paying bills) can be facilitated by having a special place for doing and keeping paper work, files, a typewriter, and, lately, a personal computer as well.

A home office may be a single piece of furniture sharing space in a bedroom (fig. 453), library, living room, or kitchen. It may be a special built-in grouping in a study, an extra bedroom, or even a closet (fig. 455). If extended use is anticipated, it may become a room not unlike a typical private office in a larger office grouping (fig. 454). Suitable seating, good lighting, appropriate privacy, and ample storage space are the basic needs.

450. The vast proportions of Willem de Kooning's studio are appropriate to the large scale of the artist's work. The clutter, which resolves into signs of creative activity, becomes the source of the space's aesthetic quality. (Photograph: Jaime Ardiles-Arce)

451. A special-purpose home workshop is equipped to serve the needs of professional textile designer and weaver Jack Lenor Larsen. Both the worktable and loom are well lit and placed to allow a pleasing view of the garden outside. The workshop, designed by Larsen, is part of his home in Connecticut. (Photograph: Karen Radkai, courtesy House & Garden)

452. A photographic darkroom is a highly specialized workshop, much prized by enthusiasts, both amateur and professional. While makeshift spaces in bathrooms and kitchens are not uncommon, a complete, custom-designed facility—like the one shown in this drawing—is ideal for serious photographic work.

453

454

453. Juan Montoya designed this interior, a home office in a luxury bedroom in a New York apartment. (Photograph: Jaime Ardiles-Arce)

454. A more spacious home office occupies a terrace greenhouse, an extension of a Manhattan apartment. The wood table and ample shelves (at left) provide a comfortable, almost country-style work environment. Note the telescope on a tripod at left, indication of a personal interest. Shelton, Mindel & Associates, designer. (Photograph: © Bo Parker, New York)

Media Rooms

This new and developing functional room type is based on the special conference/meeting rooms utilized by many office facilities. The media room is really a small theater designed to provide a comfortable and convenient setting for viewing and listening to television and projected film and slides (fig. 456). A special space for these purposes is obviously a luxury only possible in a large house or apartment, although to someone who is professionally active in television, film, and related advertising fields, it may be a necessity.

Ideally, the media room is a specially dedicated space with arrangements for its own equipment, seating, and acoustics. If this is not possible, the required equipment may be built into or incorporated into the living room or entertaining space. Specialized consultants can be very helpful with technical requirements. Besides making the space attractive, the interior designer must deal with positioning complex equipment so that it can be easily concealed, if desired, as well as used.

Conservatories

A special room or alcove for plants has been a desired feature of many residential spaces at least since the Victorian era (fig. 457). Big windows, preferably south-facing, are the basic

455

456

455. A home office was carved out of a living room wet bar, and doors were added. A walk-in bedroom closet could provide a similar space. A roll-away file, a pull-out work shelf, and a wire-rack storage system on the right wall all expand the utility of the small room. (Photograph: Steve Smith, courtesy Metropolitan Home *Magazine)*

456. Architect Ari Bahat designed this media room, a functional space dedicated to video and audio monitoring, to accommodate all necessary equipment in ideal conditions. The space is a facility of the M.B.W. Advertising Network, New York. (Photograph: Phillip Ennis, courtesy Ari Bahat)

457

requirement for a conservatory. Shelves for plants and, for larger plants, a suitably water-resistant floor are needed. A conservatory that houses tropical plants must be isolated from other interior spaces and have its own separate controls to maintain the proper levels of heat and humidity. Glass partitions accomplish isolation without giving up visibility.

Greenhouses

A greenhouse is a special type of conservatory that has glass walls and roof to maximize the entrapment of solar energy for plant growth. Adaptations of the free-standing greenhouse used by professional nurseries, in forms that can be attached to a residence, have become popular. Adding a greenhouse to other living spaces, extending it into garden space or onto a deck or patio, is a pleasant way to open up interior space to light while providing space for growing plants. In fact, many people add greenhouse space simply to gain living space with a particular feeling of brightness and openness (fig. 460).

In order to put in a greenhouse, sufficient south-facing space with unobstructed light must be available. Issues that must be considered are how to handle the connection between greenhouse and existing walls; the type of opening for access and closure; and the type of flooring, taking into account the damp conditions. A greenhouse addition works well as an extension of living, dining, or kitchen spaces. The greenhouse used for serious plant cultivation, like the conservatory, needs isolation and separate atmospheric controls. At the other extreme, when no space is available for a larger, walk-in unit, tiny greenhouse units that fit into a window opening offer a limited greenhouse function.

Courtyards

A court is, in effect, an outdoor room, surrounded by adjoining enclosed spaces and differing from them only in being roofless. Courts have been a traditional element in home design in Mediterranean regions since ancient times, and they continue to be an attractive possibility in larger residential plans. A court is normally an element in a one- or possibly two-story building, but it is technically feasible at the top level of a taller building, too.

457. *This conservatory porch doubles as an informal living area. The hydraulically operated windows can be retracted into the basement, thus opening the space to the outdoors. The West Porch of Westbury House, Old Westbury Gardens, Old Westbury, New York, is a modern renovation of the 1906 mansion. (Photograph: Richard Cheek)*

458. *Architectural elements, such as the spiral staircase and the overhead beams, mediate between a pool in an open atrium and the residential structure itself. The result is an area that is both outdoor and indoor. The house in Del Mar, California, was designed by Batter Kay Associates, Inc., Architect, in 1983. (Photograph: © Mary E. Nichols, courtesy* House & Garden*)*

459. *A skylight surmounts an atrium with a central pool in a monumental space that acts as a formal focus for a multiple residence, the Colonnade Apartments in Philadelphia, renovated in 1985 by David Beck, Architects. (Photograph: © Elliott Kaufman)*

458

459

460

A court may have a primarily garden-like character, or one closer to that of an interior room, or any possible mixture of these characteristics. Pools and fountains are favorite elements for inclusion in a courtyard (fig. 458). With the modern availability of glass or window walls, an open court can be seen and enjoyed even in the cold months in more northern climates. The materials and furniture used in a courtyard, like those for terraces, decks, and patios, must be selected for the special qualities that outdoor service demands. In addition, unless the courtyard is at ground level, the construction must ensure that there is no water leakage into spaces below. Some kind of lighting may be desired for nighttime use.

Atriums

The word *atrium* (its preferred Latin plural is *atria*) is simply Latin for *courtyard*. It has recently come to refer to a large interior space roofed over with glass—an interior courtyard that is actually a special kind of interior room. The atrium has become a much-favored element in large new hotels and in some corporate office headquarters buildings. In a private house, an atrium plays almost the same role as the courtyard, with the difference that it is independent of the effects of weather and climate (fig. 459). Introducing an atrium into an older, conventional row house is one way to open up the interior into a more modern set of special relationships. Incidentally, it can also help to bring daylight into what might

460. Here, the addition of a greenhouse has brought light and openness into an otherwise conventional bedroom. The art in view includes a Botero sculpture and a Nevelson wall construction (right). Noel Jeffrey was the interior designer of this 1982 Manhattan project. (Photograph: Kari Haavisto, courtesy House & Garden)

461. In the pool house of a residential project in Llewellyn Park, New Jersey, whimsical Post-modern elements give the space a playful quality appropriate to its recreational function. Robert A. M. Stern Architects, designer, 1979. (Photograph: © 1981 Peter Aaron/ESTO)

461

otherwise be dark interior spaces. An atrium is often used as an indoor garden or conservatory, where growing plants up to the size of small trees can thrive.

Pools

A swimming pool has become a popular luxury feature of homes located on sufficient land to make space available (fig. 461). Most pools are out-of-doors, but enclosure is a possibility that makes a pool, at least occasionally, an interior element, perhaps in combination with a gym or other exercise facility. A fully indoor pool in a room of its own is possible, but usually an outdoor pool is enclosed with a glass housing similar to a greenhouse. This makes the pool available in all seasons and all weather conditions and minimizes the cleaning problems typical of outdoor pools.

A glass enclosure may pick up excessive solar heat in summer, making some means of shading (with blinds, awnings, or special heat-resistant glass) desirable. The pool space should have its own source or controls for heat, cooling, and humidity. Materials for floor surfaces and furniture must be water-resistant. Floors should also be nonskid.

Terraces, Patios, Roofs, Decks

Although these are not, strictly speaking, interior spaces, their function as outdoor living rooms and their close relationship to adjacent interior spaces often bring them into the concern of interior design (figs. 463, 464). The concept of indoor and outdoor space flowing together, primarily through the use of large glass window walls, has been a favorite idea of modern architecture. This concept can be strengthened by choosing floor and/or wall materials suitable to both indoor and outdoor use, so that the space appears to pass through the window wall and continue into the out-of-doors. In general, masonry materials, such as brick, stone, and tile, serve best. While wood can be used out-of-doors, it will weather and eventually decay unless it is kept painted or treated with a special preservative.

Furniture for decks and terraces also presents some special problems. Sun, rain, winter weather, and dirt are all hard on furniture. Even furniture made especially for outdoor use will eventually deteriorate if left out year-round. A special class of *indoor-outdoor furniture* has been developed that is intended to hold up with moderate outdoor exposure, to be suitable in appearance for indoor use, and to be sufficiently portable to be pulled or rolled in or out as needed (fig. 462). The most durable materials include metals (aluminum stands up best), some plastics, glass, marble, tile, and certain woods. Cedar, redwood, and teak have an oil content that makes them more weather-resistant than most other woods. Cushions and other upholstery elements are best made removable and brought indoors when not in use.

Outdoor spaces can also be designed to include permanent, built-in-place elements, such as benches, seats, tables, pools, and fireplaces (favorite elements for cookouts), of durable architectural materials. The familiar interior elements such as walls, ceilings, and doors are joined, out-of-doors, by additional elements such as fences, hedges, gates, awnings, and umbrellas. The profession that has special concern with this vocabulary of design is landscape architecture, a field usually associated with the use of plant materials in garden and landscape design. The landscape architect works with paving, steps, walls, and fences, as well as outdoor lighting, and will often be a helpful consultant or collaborator in dealing with outdoor spaces as they become of concern to the interior designer.

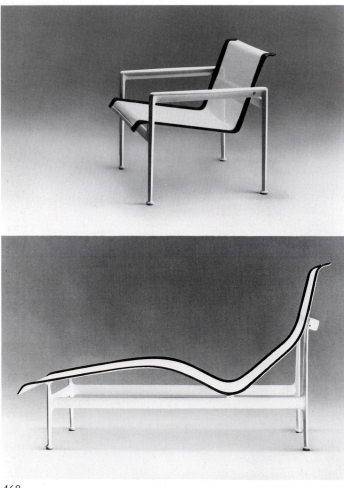

462

462. Outdoor furniture must be both weather-resistant and suited to the relaxed style associated with open-air living. In this armchair and lounge, part of a group designed in 1966 by Richard Schultz, plastic-coated frames of cast and extruded aluminum support seating surfaces of woven Dacron mesh with vinyl straps. Rainwater runs off through the mesh, and all of the materials are conceived to withstand exposure. Like all outdoor furniture, however, these pieces should be covered or brought indoors in inclement weather. (Photograph courtesy Knoll International, Inc.)

463. Tennessee twig chairs bring the rural outdoors to a Manhattan roof terrace. (Photograph: © 1985 Michael Skott)

464. This porch of a landmark Victorian house on Long Island, New York, was renovated in 1983 by Mark Hampton, designer. Like many traditional porches, this one functions as an outdoor room, for which the choice of furniture and fabrics is no less important than for an indoor living room. (Photograph: Peter Vitale, courtesy House & Garden)

463

464

CHAPTER THIRTEEN
PUBLIC INTERIORS

As mentioned earlier, interior design work separates into two main fields described as *residential* and *contract*. The first term is self-explanatory, but the second term merits a closer look. It comes from a semiobsolete business practice in which nonresidential projects were often taken on under an inclusive contract to provide all the needed elements, similar to the kind of contract usually entered into for building construction. The term has come to refer to all interior design work that is *not* specifically related to private residential space—that is, the kinds of spaces that are discussed here as *public interiors*.

Residential design is characterized by generally small-scale projects and a close working relationship with the client (in fact, the client may even be his or her own designer). The resulting space has been carefully tailored to the needs, desires, and tastes of the person or people who will be the occupants and users of the completed project.

Nonresidential interior design tends to have a different character. Projects are generally larger, sometimes huge. More often than not, users are not the clients of the designer but some segment of a public that may include staff, workers, employees, executives, and professionals, plus, in many projects, outsiders from a general public of customers, visitors, travelers, guests, and casual passers-by. Their relationship to the project may vary from quite close (for example, occupants of a dormitory, patients in a hospital, or workers in an office) to very tenuous (for example, customers in a shop, visitors to a museum or gallery, or passengers to a depot or terminal).

Public interiors are accessible to a large range of users and include highly visible, even spectacular spaces that attract interest and excitement. Professional interior design has, in recent years, come to focus on contract work, partly because it includes large and lucrative projects, partly because such projects almost always require the services of design professionals. A high proportion of residential spaces are still put together, for better or for worse, without help from any trained specialists. This used to be the case with public spaces as well. Some years ago, a typical office was simply furnished with whatever the office manager thought necessary to make work possible. A restaurant was often designed by the contractor who built the installation, while major public buildings (courthouses, churches, libraries, and museums) received furniture and lighting almost as incidental details.

Various factors have brought an increasing number of public spaces into the sphere of interior design. These include a new awareness of environmental influences on human behavior: the way in which an office interior influences work performance, for example, or the way in which the design of a restaurant impinges on the satisfaction of the restaurant's customers. This latter case illustrates how design has come to be seen as an important factor in the commercial success of many enterprises. The good design of a store, bank, hotel, or office makes an impression on the people who visit the spaces, raising their confidence and encouraging a return visit. Bad design can have an opposite and highly negative impact.

Designers aim to make public spaces serve their purpose well, that is, to be comfortable and convenient for both the public and the staff. A second, equally important goal is to create pleasant, exciting, and memorable spaces. This may serve strictly commercial ends in bringing in (or bringing back) customers, or it may serve wider purposes in building morale and confidence in an institution, an organization, a town, or a nation.

In working on such projects, the interior designer is guided by the same concerns that govern residential projects: the functional issue of having a space work in a practical way; choosing materials and constructional techniques to serve the practical requirements; and resolving the first two issues in a way that makes an aesthetic impact.

Contract design is often quite specialized. Some designers concentrate on certain fields, for example, offices, hotels, restaurants, or hospitals. While specialization tends to build efficiency and skill in a particular field, it can also lead to repetitious formula design. A designer who tackles a new kind of project for the first time is more likely to come up with a fresh approach than a designer who works on an endless stream of similar projects. Still, many modern assignments have such specialized technical requirements that some specialization seems necessary. Hospitals and health-care facilities, for example, demand technical expertise, but a specialized consultant or an association with a designer experienced in such a field can bring the necessary skills into a firm taking on such a project for the first time. The skills that lead to first-rate work in one kind of project are generally transferable to even highly specialized projects when all the necessary specialized knowledge is drawn into a project team.

The increasing variety of projects that come to the attention of interior designers has extended the range of practice in this field to make it a more varied and lively profession than it was only a few years ago. Such seemingly unlikely interiors as those of spacecraft, submarines, laboratories—even jails—are now appropriate areas for professional design concern. An extensive literature deals with the specialized problems of various interior types, including offices, hotels, restaurants, hospitals, museums, and retail stores. It is impossible to go into detail about every one of these fields here. Instead, this section offers a survey of typical projects in a wide range of types, with some brief comments about each area of practice.

465. In the atrium of One Magnificent Mile, a central city shopping center in Chicago (1983) by Himmel Bonner Architects, small shops fall into place in relation to the large, central space, which employs lively geometric elements to suggest both an Art Deco flavor and a contemporary, high-fashion orientation. (Photograph: Barbara Karant)

466

Shops, Shopping
Centers, Showrooms

In the modern, aggressively commercial world, shopping is an important activity, and shops form the setting for a wide range of practical and emotional experiences. People expect to be lured, charmed, and entertained in the process of selecting and buying goods.

SHOPS. The design of a shop is expected to convey a variety of messages about style, quality, and attitudes toward its products and services at the same time that it provides a practical setting for the display, storage, and actual sale of goods. The shop designer is expected to grasp the special character of a particular store—sometimes to help invent that character—and then project it visually in a concrete way that the customer and potential customer can feel, remember, and enjoy.

All of these features can be studied in some fine older shops in many of the world's great cities. The special qualities of these stores have been arrived at through tradition and the individual shopkeeper's particular sense of what appeals to a particular type of customer. Lacking a tradition, the shop designer must find ways to put across comparable impressions, and to do it with the more impersonal realities of most modern merchandising.

The nature of the goods to be sold, their price level, and the style of marketing will all influence the design. A shop may be conservative (fig. 466) or avant-garde (fig. 467), it may present a masculine or a feminine aspect, it may impart a sense of bargains waiting to be snatched up in a hurry or a feeling of leisurely and careful service. Small shops can convey a highly

466. The leisurely atmosphere of an old-fashioned exclusive shop, with overtones of residential elegance (in the tables, flowers, plants, small objects, the cozy armchairs, rugs, and so on), is recreated for the fashionable modern Polo/Ralph Lauren Store, New York, 1986. *The opulence of the setting implies good quality in the merchandise offered for sale. Naomi Leff and Associates, Inc., designers, with Ralph Lauren and staff. (Photograph: François Halard, courtesy Naomi Leff and Associates, Inc.)*

467

467. In contrast with the conservative atmosphere of the shop illustrated in fig. 466, the Esprit store in West Hollywood, California (1985), with High Tech accents in the fans and lighting and its use of Memphis furniture (foreground), suggests a lively and energetic avant-garde orientation. Joseph Paul D'Urso, designer. (Photograph: Tim Street-Porter)

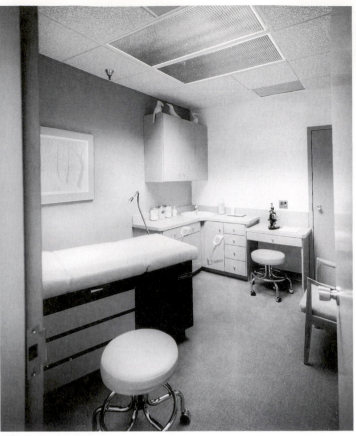

468

distinctive and personal feeling, while larger stores, such as major department stores, must provide varied settings for different departments and still suggest an overall character that can catch and hold customer loyalty. Along with all of this, display techniques, color, and lighting are deployed to make merchandise look its best and, for shops that sell apparel and related goods, to flatter the customer as well. Even fitting or dressing rooms call for consideration in this respect.

SHOPPING CENTERS. The shopping center, plaza, and mall are new types of commercial centers that have rapidly become extremely popular public gathering places. At their best, they offer exciting, even beautiful interior spaces that easily attract crowds, although many people come without intending to shop. This makes it highly advantageous for the individual shops within the shopping center or mall to develop design that will offer special attractions in such a highly competitive environment (fig. 465).

SHOWROOMS. The use of design as a tool for competitive selling has also become an important factor in the showrooms maintained by manufacturers of products and materials used by the design professions in their architectural and interior projects and in the showrooms serving the fashion trades. The showroom not only displays goods, it is also a source of design stimulation, an expression of company attitudes and philosophy, and almost a kind of theater for the projection of new ideas associated with products that often have a strongly fashion-related character. A well-designed showroom or display space may be as important to sales as the design of the actual products offered for sale.

Office Design

Modern business now generally regards the drab and often depressing quality displayed by business offices in the early part of the twentieth century as unacceptable. It has been realized that appearance makes a difference: visitors to an office form impressions and draw conclusions about the business's character and quality based on the design of the offices they see; the setting in which employees spend their regular working days heavily influences their attitudes toward their employers.

The offices of major corporations and other big modern organizations (such as governmental agencies) have become large, even vast complexes sometimes occupying many floors or

468. Pale colors, pinks and greens, soften the otherwise clinical atmosphere of an examining and consulting room in a gynecologists' office suite in Texas. Kenneth Jorns & Associates, Inc. (Kenneth Jorns), designer. (Photograph: R. Greg Hursley)

entire buildings. Planning such office projects is a demanding and specialized activity, and office design and planning has become an important field of interior design practice. Decisions about layout, the sizes of offices, the provision for privacy through partitioning (fig. 470) or (often in modern practice) without partitioning (fig. 471) must be balanced against the requirements of the work function, the projection of individual rank and status, and the overall style and objectives of the organization. Large office groupings also usually include special-purpose spaces, conference and meeting rooms, libraries and board rooms, lounges and dining facilities.

Some offices are primary contact points with the public. This is true of ticket offices, the consumer service offices of insurance or loan companies, brokerage offices, and the public offices of different organizations where people come to apply for credit, make complaints, or confer about other matters. In all of these situations, the ambience of the office itself conveys a strong impression about the nature and quality of the organization.

The waiting rooms, office or consulting rooms, and treatment rooms of the professional offices of doctors (figs. 468, 469), dentists, lawyers, and similar individual practitioners (whether in practice alone or as part of a group or firm) strongly influence the patient or client. An ugly, cramped, or depressing waiting room and office can add to a patient's nervousness and tension or lower the confidence of a client. In the end, professional competence is more important than appearances, but an appropriate and attractive setting reinforces confidence in professional skills and improves the client's experience.

The design of all offices includes the selection of suitable work equipment and seating. Modern office furniture and equipment are available in great variety and are, at best, of very high design quality. Modern computer and communications equipment has brought new efficiency to office work, creating what is often called the *electronic office,* but it has created new

469

469. In this conference room in a doctor's office suite in a renovated older building, pale grays and white work with traditional carved wood details to create a near-residential atmosphere, in contrast to the cold and forbidding character too often typical of professional offices. John F. Saladino, designer. (Photograph: Peter Vitale)

470

471

problems as well. The need to maintain a fixed seating position can result in physical problems (muscular or back pains), while long hours working with the computer terminal under unsatisfactory lighting can cause eyestrain. A work pace set by the electronic equipment rather than by the worker's own normal habits can generate nervous and emotional problems. Research has shown that these can be minimized with careful design. Spatial arrangement, color, lighting, and acoustics influence the ease and efficiency of work and establish an atmosphere that can reduce stress, make work easier and less tiring, and support morale. The office designer has an opportunity (and an obligation) to achieve some of the best interior design work currently being produced.

Banks

The tradition of formal, temple-like architectural structures for bank facilities has been upset by the new competitive struggle among banks to attract depositors. The "friendly banking" movement has drawn banks toward the liveliness and attraction of a retail shop or display pavilion for their public spaces (fig. 473). This is no easy goal, considering that banks have no merchandise or products to display and that the growth of automation is gradually replacing human tellers and counter attendants with machines.

At its best, the interior design of today's banks ranges from a modern but still dignified formality to visually spectacular displays of light and color. Some of the most interesting of bank designs involve older bank buildings of fine design quality, even of landmark status. These have been modified internally to improve convenience and project a sense of contemporary vitality while still retaining and respecting the older setting with its architectural dignity (fig. 472).

In addition to the public banking room spaces, banks usually include semipublic spaces, such as a safety-deposit area, and

472

470. In an open layout in a renovated warehouse in Minneapolis, stepped-height screen partitions provide degrees of privacy for a group of designers' work stations in the office of SteinDesign (Sanford Stein, principal). Sanford Stein, designer. (Photograph: © 1986 Philip Macmillan James. All rights reserved)

471. Semiprivate work stations surround two informal conference areas. Playful accents in unusual colors suggest cheerful creativity in this toy-manufacturer's office. ISD Incorporated designed the offices for Mattel Inc., in Hawthorne, California. (Photograph: Toshi Yoshimi, courtesy ISD Incorporated)

472. Many bank facilities are designed to project a sense of dignified conservatism. This space, designed by John F. Saladino for the Chase Manhattan Bank of New York, is in a building constructed circa 1933 and renovated in 1986. The atmosphere suggests a Georgian residence or club, while the modern electric lighting from recessed ceiling fixtures provides illumination for contemporary working conditions. (Photograph: © Langdon Clay)

473

474

475

an office area with formal executive quarters and more utilitarian "backstage" work areas. All of these spaces can be examples of design excellence.

Public Buildings

Courthouses, city halls, capitols of states, and legislative buildings of nations have usually been designed to include some monumental and ceremonial spaces of strong architectural character. Offices and public service spaces (information counters, cashiers' windows, registries of public documents, and so on) in the same buildings are often drab, inconvenient, and unattractive. In recent years, public buildings of more modern design have appeared, and many of these have more functional, comfortable, and attractive interior spaces (fig. 474). In many older public buildings, improvements have been made through superior interior renovation. In some situations, a

change in use has stimulated an interior renovation that greatly improves the building while preserving the best aspects of its traditional character. For instance, the Jefferson Market Courthouse in New York has been successfully turned into a public library.

Museums, Galleries, and Libraries

These public and semipublic facilities often suffered in the past from an emphasis on monumentality at the expense of utility. Newer buildings invite creative solutions to providing genuine service to the public, while the renovation of older buildings can often greatly improve both the function and attractiveness of their interior spaces.

MUSEUMS. In recent years, many museums have launched an aggressive effort to attract a large public to exhi-

473. A neighborhood branch of the Chase Manhattan Bank in New York's SoHo district, a favorite location for artists' lofts and studios, features artwork in a gallery atmosphere in order to express a kindred orientation. Plants add another "friendly" touch. Skidmore, Owings & Merrill, designer. (Photograph: © Wolfgang Hoyt/ESTO)

474. The new City Hall built in 1969 in Boston, Massachusetts, is one of the most striking public buildings built in any American city in recent years. The interiors make no reference to any historic style: they convey a sense of dignity and permanence in an entirely modern idiom. The architects—who won the

commission in a competition—were Kallmann, McKinnell & Knowles, in association with Campbell, Aldrich & Nulty. The engineers were LeMessurier Associates, Inc.; interior space designers were ISD Incorporated. (Photograph courtesy ISD Incorporated)

475. This exhibition (of Elie Nadelman's sculpture) was designed by Joe Shannon for the Hirshhorn Museum and Sculpture Garden, Smithsonian Institution, Washington, D.C. The setting's simplicity and the track lighting's flexibility make it possible to provide ideal display conditions for changing exhibitions. The architect for the building was Gordon Bunshaft of Skidmore, Owings & Merrill's New York office, 1974. (Photograph courtesy Skidmore, Owings & Merrill)

476

476. In a remarkable conversion, a disused turn-of-the-century Paris railroad station was transformed into an exciting museum. The Gare d'Orsay in Paris was redesigned as the Musée d'Orsay by architect Gae Aulenti in 1986. (Photograph: J. Purcell, © Établissement public du Musée d'Orsay)

477

bitions planned and designed with a sense of showmanship comparable to that of the commercial world. Dramatic settings and use of color and lighting can convert a museum from a dusty warehouse of antiquities to a lively and exciting space in which educational values merge into entertainment (figs. 475, 476).

GALLERIES. Private galleries for the exhibition and sale of works of art and related objects are generally smaller in scale than museum spaces, and do not attempt to serve as large an audience. They share the need to show off exhibited objects to best advantage through intelligent planning of space, color, and lighting.

LIBRARIES. Libraries may be public institutions varying from very small to large and complex (fig. 477); they may also be specialized parts of a larger project such as a school, an office, or an institution. All must provide book storage and protection (plus provision for modern book alternatives, such as microfilm materials) along with space for the users of the facility to read, study, and take notes. Specialized libraries (law, music, or for children, for example) modify library basics to suit a particular need.

477. The New York Public Library, a famous work of 1911 by John Merven Carrère and Thomas Hastings, formerly draftsmen in the office of McKim, Mead and White, remains an outstanding example of classicism in the American architecture of its day. The area illustrated was restored and modernized in 1985 by Davis, Brody & Associates. Now the D. Samuel and Jeane H. Gottesman Hall, it is a monumental circulation space also used to display changing exhibitions. The original wood ceiling was carved by Maurice Grieve. The arches and columns are of Cipollino marble, the walls of white Danby marble. The modern, unobtrusive track lighting is easily adapted to the changing exhibits. (Photograph: © 1985 Peter Aaron/ESTO)

478

Exhibition Design

Exhibits ranging from small to vast are a ubiquitous part of the modern commercial and institutional world. Shows of automobiles, boats, various kinds of manufactured goods, even military hardware take place in exhibition halls built for the purpose (fig. 478). These structures are simply empty shells that shelter the material on display and the crowds of visitors that come to view it. Exhibits range from a small booth setting in such a structure to entire buildings with all their contents, as in the major exhibit pavilions at a world's fair.

The exhibit designer is a highly specialized kind of interior designer who must create settings that can be constructed quickly, that will communicate effectively in a competitive and often confusing environment, and, often, that employ standard and reusable elements. The temporary nature of exhibits sometimes offers the designer an extraordinary freedom to try out experimental and adventurous approaches that might seem

too risky for more lasting projects. Exhibit design can be an experimental showcase for future-oriented design directions, as it has proved to be in the past.

Theaters, Concert Halls, Auditoriums, Arenas

Auditorium spaces present special and interesting interior design problems. An audience numbering in the hundreds or even in the thousands must be seated in reasonable comfort within a space that provides good sightlines and satisfactory acoustical conditions for all. In addition, safety considerations impose very stringent demands, usually expressed in legal codes, on lengths of seating rows, aisle widths, arrangements of steps, and exit doors.

Along with the solution of these technical problems, the designer is expected to create a visual ambience appropriate to the events that will take place in the facility. The traditional opera house or theater is expected to present an atmosphere of festivity and opulence without overwhelming the performance that takes place within it (fig. 479). A more modern approach gives the hall a totally neutral and simple setting that focuses all attention on the performance event taking place. Ancillary spaces such as lobbies, lounges, bars, and cafés present a wide range of related design problems. Specialized consultants have

479

James Stewart Polshek and Partners, Architects brought the building up to modern standards of safety and performance, while preserving and refurbishing the period opulence of the interior. (Photograph: Jan Staller)

478. At the Montreal World's Fair, Expo '67, the U.S. pavilion was a giant geodesic dome built according to Buckminster Fuller's patented system of construction. The design firm Cambridge Seven developed exhibits on platforms that seemed to float in the vast space within the largely transparent structure. Escalators moved visitors from level to level. (Photograph: John Pile)

479. New York's Carnegie Hall, built in 1891 to the designs of William B. Tuthill (with William Morris Hunt and Dankmar Adler as consultants), has an international reputation for its fine acoustics. In a 1986 renovation and restoration, the architectural firm of

480

an important part in dealing with the problems of sightlines, acoustics, and lighting, as well as the complexities of backstage mechanics.

Large performance spaces, convention halls, and sports arenas tend to be more strictly functional in character, the enclosure, seating, and performance space dominating interior design elements (fig. 480). In such projects, however, color, lighting, and the design of access spaces present interior design problems of considerable scope.

Temples and Churches

Religious buildings have a tradition of monumentality and pure architectural expression. In referring to the great cathedrals or other historic religious buildings, one can hardly speak of interior design independent of the basic structural form. It is interesting to note the ways in which modern interior design ideas have come to play a part in the design of contemporary religious buildings (fig. 481). The same thoughtful interior design that goes into other, secular spaces has greatly influenced the success of many new religious buildings. The renovation and restoration of older buildings often call for new thinking about color, lighting, and functional issues concerning both ritual and public accommodation.

Along with the actual sanctuary space, religious buildings often include related spaces for teaching, social functions, and similar secondary uses that present design problems closely related to similar secular building types. Interior design can have a significant and creative role in making religious buildings both serviceable and inspiring in visual character.

480. The Ingalls Hockey Rink was designed by architect Eero Saarinen in 1958 for Yale University in New Haven, Connecticut, with an innovative structural system that gives the interior an exciting spatial quality. (Photograph: © Ezra Stoller/ESTO)

481

481. The altar and chancel of St. Matthew's Episcopal Church, Pacific Palisades, California, a 1983 project by Moore Ruble Yudell Architects & Planners, is shown here. Modern lighting, art, and architectural forms convey a strongly contemporary character, while certain key traditional forms clearly identify the structure's function as a church. (Photograph: Timothy Hursley, © The Arkansas Office)

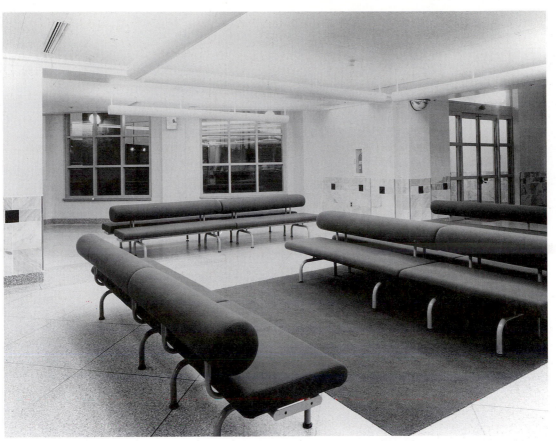

482

Institutional Buildings

To say that the design of a building is *institutional* is not
normally a compliment. The word suggests dreary corridors and
drab color schemes of green and brown. There is no reason
why institutional buildings should be any less attractive than
other buildings; in fact, it is increasingly acknowledged that
interior design of high quality can improve the function and
morale of every institutional type. Even so unpromising a type
as the modern jail, or correctional facility, can be shown to be
more effective when its interiors avoid depressing grimness.
Schools too often seem rather like jails, although the most
modest thought and effort could easily make them pleasant,
even exciting places.

Interior design has met with considerable resistance in many
institutional areas. Governmental agencies often feel that a
demonstration of respect for economy requires the most austere
and unattractive treatments that can be produced, while the
design of public health-care facilities (fig. 486), mental
institutions, and jails (figs. 482, 483) has often followed the even
more oppressive view that such places should contribute to the
suffering of occupants rather than to their needs. Modern
research has demonstrated that superior design for such places

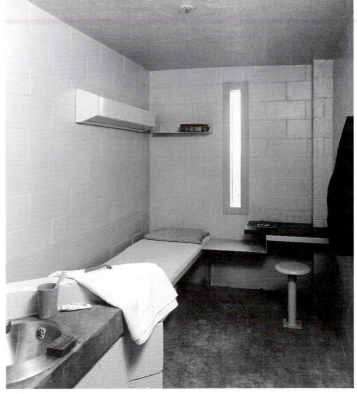

483

*482, 483. A jail cell may seem an
unlikely professional design project, but
the value of intelligent planning in such
facilities is receiving increasing recognition. The cell (fig. 483) and the public
seating area (fig. 482) were designed in
1986 by Ehrendrantz & Eckstut, architects, in collaboration with Jacob/Wy-
per Architects (Philadelphia) for the
Philadelphia Industrial Correctional
Center. (Photographs: © 1986 Paul
Warchol)*

484

can improve their effectiveness while making the life of staff and professionals easier, pleasanter, and more productive.

Historically, college and university buildings have often included beautiful and inspiring spaces. The interior design of these buildings, which include dormitories, lounges, small classrooms, lecture halls (fig. 487), auditoriums, offices, dining halls (figs. 484, 485), and libraries, should satisfy the minimum requirements of making the spaces function well, with good lighting, seating, acoustics, and color. It can go a lot further to create memorable, exciting, and inspiring spaces.

Residential facilities, dormitories, nursing homes, and facilities for the elderly also invite design treatment that will support the morale of their occupants, make for comfort and convenience, and allow users a degree of personal expression by providing a suitable balance between preestablished or fixed design elements and design details that can be modified, changed, and adjusted. The quality of life in such places is strongly influenced by the design of both private spaces (such as bedrooms) and the shared spaces of living or common rooms, dining halls, and circulation spaces.

484, 485. Exterior (fig. 484) and interior (fig. 485) of an unusual university dining hall designed by Venturi, Rauch and Scott Brown. The hanging lighting fixtures of curious shape are a strong visual element, while the tables and chairs recall more traditional academic interior spaces. Gordon Wu Hall, Butler College, Princeton University, 1983. (Photograph: Tom Bernard, courtesy Venturi, Rauch and Scott Brown)

486. A bright and active interior for the Columbus (Indiana) Occupational Health Center. The exposed structure, ducts, and piping become important design accents in a High Tech environment. Hardy Holzman Pfeiffer Associates were the architects. (Photograph: © Norman McGrath)

487. This university lecture hall derives its striking visual impact from the stepped, sweeping curves of the functional writing surface. It was designed by Peter L. Gluck and Partners for Uris Hall, the Business School, Columbia University, New York (1985). (Photograph: © Paul Warchol)

485

486

487

489

490

488. A modest restaurant can benefit from skillful interior design fully as much as a more elaborate eating place. Charles Boxenbaum, the architect and interior designer for the Pizzapiazza in New York (1983), made wide use of surfaces of Colorcore plastic laminate. Graphic design is by Milton Glaser. (Photograph: Norman McGrath, courtesy Formica Corporation)

489. Total restaurant design often includes tableware, linens, and glassware as well as graphic designs for menu covers, coasters, and matchbooks. A consistent theme helps to place a unique and memorable stamp on a dining environment. The tableware illustrated here was designed by Vignelli Associates for the Palio restaurant illustrated in fig. 490. (Photograph courtesy Vignelli Associates)

490. In the spectacular, high-ceilinged bar area for an elaborate—and expensive—New York restaurant called Palio, developed by Skidmore, Owings & Merrill, architects, in 1986, the large mural by Sandro Chia is the dominant design element. (Photograph: © 1986 Wolfgang Hoyt/ESTO)

491

Restaurants, Hotels, and Clubs

For these spaces, the importance of excellent interior design has long been understood.

RESTAURANTS. The aim of restaurant design is to create an atmosphere or ambience that supports the character of the food and service being offered and makes the experience of dining memorable, encouraging the customer to return and to recommend the restaurant to others (figs. 488–91, 494). Restaurants vary from simple to elaborate, from frenzied to leisurely, from cheap to staggeringly expensive. All of these possibilities have their usefulness and their own particular clientele.

Design, including that of private dining rooms, bars, lounges, and restrooms, must reinforce the best aspects of a restaurant's qualities while promoting functional efficiency, ensuring the comfort and pleasure of the diner, and serving the economic needs of the management to make the place a business success.

HOTELS, MOTELS, AND INNS. Hotels, motels, and inns range from the simplest of small guest houses to vast complexes, complete resorts, or urban meeting places on a major scale (figs. 492, 493, 495–98). At a minimum, hotel guests seek comfort. They have come to expect entertainment as well—the active entertainment of sports facilities, casino, or nightclub or the more passive entertainment of using interesting or exciting public spaces and occupying guest rooms that are more than mere places to sleep. Modern hotels and motels serve a variety of guests, ranging from the vacationer through the expense-account business traveler to celebrities who expect their lodging place to set off their personalities and styles.

CLUBS. Clubs combine, in various proportions, the qualities of meeting halls, restaurants, hotels, and residences. Their design needs to express the particular quality that has brought together a particular membership. The clubhouse is something of a secondary home at the same time that it serves

491. *Warm woods, subdued lighting, and accessories such as the large tapestry create an atmosphere of inviting elegance in a traditional dining room of the hotel Les Crayères in the Champagne region of France. French architect Pierre-Yves Rochon redesigned the interiors of the turn-of-the-century building in 1981. (Photograph: Langdon Clay, courtesy* Metropolitan Home *Magazine)*

492. *The famous Villard Houses, palazzo-like dwellings for wealthy New Yorkers, were built in 1882–86 to designs of McKim, Mead and White in what is now a central midtown site. When they were incorporated into a new hotel complex, the Helmsley Pal-ace, in 1980, the lavish traditional interiors were restored, converted, and preserved. Sarah Tomerlin Lee of Tom Lee Limited turned spaces such as this salon—now a lounge—into rooms answering contemporary requirements. (Photograph: Jaime Ardiles-Arce)*

493. *In the Mansion on Turtle Creek, Dallas, the tropical and elaborate decorative treatment creates an atmosphere of luxury in a guest room. The hotel, attached to the original 1925 structure, was built by Shepherd & Boyd in 1979–80 and renovated by Hirsch/ Bedner & Associates. (Photograph: Jaime Ardiles-Arce)*

492

493

495

496

494. A former Lane Bryant clothing store was converted into a dramatic setting for the Max au Triangle restaurant in Los Angeles, California, designed by Stanley Felderman, architect, in 1985. (Photograph: Tim Street-Porter)

495. For Morgans Hotel, a modern small hotel in New York City, designer Andrée Putman replaced individual pieces of storage furniture with a built-in storage wall cupboard system in her design of 1984. (Photograph: © Paul Warchol)

496. The wood-board ceiling, fireplace with antique agricultural tools mounted above, and wicker furniture communicate a simple, rustic atmosphere in the restaurant lounge area of the Auberge du Soleil in Rutherford, California. The Auberge du Soleil was completed in 1986, the restaurant in 1981. Sandy Walker, architect; Michael Taylor, designer. (Photograph: Russell MacMasters, courtesy Auberge du Soleil)

498

the needs of such groups as golfers, business people, gamblers, yachtsmen, or whatever group has chosen to band together. The interiors of some older clubs are showcases of fine traditional design that modern design cannot easily equal.

Gymnasiums, swimming pools, and other kinds of health and exercise facilities formerly were of a strictly functional character. Today, their design has more and more come to emphasize their value as places for recreation and social contact (fig. 499). The growth of these facilities, both in connection with hotels, clubs, and institutions or independent, and the increasing importance of giving them a strong visual character have made them another field for interior design expression.

Transportation

Transport calls for two kinds of interior space, those in stations, terminals, ticket offices, and other fixed-base locations that serve transport, and the interiors of the transport vehicles themselves: buses, trains, airplanes, ships, and private automobiles. Some of these, for example, cars and planes, may seem to fall more in the professional territory of the industrial designer; nevertheless, as interiors they receive careful professional design attention.

While the day of the great ocean liners is drawing to a close, cruise ships prosper and proliferate, and their interiors receive the same kind of design attention called for by resort hotels (fig. 500). The interior space of aircraft is extremely limited and

497. A vast, several-story-high atrium has become a favorite feature of city hotels built in recent years. Such spaces transform a hotel stay into something of an entertainment experience. John Portman & Associates, architects, is generally credited with having introduced this concept into modern practice. Illustrated here is that firm's design for the Plaza Hotel, Renaissance Center, Detroit, 1977. (Photograph: Alexandre Georges)

498. The active, stimulating atmosphere of an Arizona desert resort hotel complex, Loews Ventana Canyon Resort near Tucson, Arizona, was conceived to serve both vacationers and business conference groups. In the Cascades lobby lounge, illustrated here, the rough-cut stone of the columns and

stepped geometric column and ceiling forms suggest the influence of Frank Lloyd Wright's Arizona desert work. Frizzell Hill Moorhouse Architects, San Francisco; Hirsch/Bedner & Associates, interior designers. (Photograph: Mary E. Nichols, courtesy Hirsch/Bedner & Associates)

499

restricted by the shape and size of the craft, by the need to pack in the maximum number of passengers, and by complex weight and safety restrictions. Despite these design limitations, intense competition among airlines and the increased use of private jets has led to an extraordinary effort to make airplane interiors special, attractive, and, insofar as possible, luxurious.

Long-distance passenger trains present similar design problems in a slightly less intense form, while commuter and subway trains and buses present special problems resulting from constant, long-term use and the threats of vandalism and other mischief.

Great railway terminals with dramatic interior spaces have become relics of the past, but modern rail and urban transit stations present challenging problems in aesthetics, functional utility, and security (fig. 501). Airport terminals vary from the strictly utilitarian to those with a monumental expressivity rivaling that of the older railway terminals. Practical issues of functional efficiency, economics, and new problems of security make these exciting projects with possibilities for impressive and user-satisfying results.

Interior design can even contribute to such unlikely spaces as the interiors of naval vessels and spacecraft. Long time spans in the cramped and sealed spaces of ships (submarines in

particular), airplanes, and spacecraft generate psychological stresses that intelligent design, including its aesthetic considerations, can do much to limit, through what is sometimes called *habitability*. This promotes efficient performance by maximizing functional convenience and comfort and minimizing the discomfort and stress involved in such spaces, thereby conserving human energy for the tasks that must be performed.

The design of automobiles, often called *styling* in the industry, contributes greatly to the product's commercial success. It is widely recognized that, in addition to the basic engineering design and the external form, a car's interior is a major factor in purchase decisions and in user satisfaction. Even the employment of famous designers, who contribute some visual improvements (and, perhaps, some element of snob appeal), has become commonplace with some automotive manufacturers.

Design issues obviously include comfort, ease of operation for the driver, and appearance. Safety considerations, long neglected in the auto industry, are receiving increasing attention. Interestingly, at its best, the design of the family car's interior is often far superior to that of the same family's house or apartment!

499. *Many modern corporate office complexes now include exercise facilities in order to encourage health and fitness among their executives, managers, and office staff. Since use of these facilities is voluntary, it is important that they be as attractive as possible. In the Cardiovascular Center at Chemical* Bank's *World Headquarters in New York, good lighting, pleasant colors, and growing plants contribute to an agreeable atmosphere. Haines Lundberg Waehler, Architects Engineers and Planners, designer. (Photograph: George Cserna)*

500

501

500. Generally, ocean-liner interiors historically express national style and spirit. This double stateroom aboard the British liner Queen Elizabeth II—familiarly known as the QE2, and sometimes called the last of the great liners—displays no national style, but it is neat, compact, and tasteful in its restraint. The porthole is the only reminder that the room is on a ship. Dennis Lennon and Partners, designer. (Photograph courtesy Cunard Line)

501. All too often, subway stations in large cities are dark, depressing, and even dangerous, although the new subways in Montreal and Washington, D.C., demonstrate that design excellence can make these areas both comfortable and attractive. Here, an older New York City station, at Fifth Avenue and 53rd Street, was rehabilitated and modernized by Lee Harris Pomeroy As-sociates Architects with Pentagram, graphic designers, in 1986. The double-layered metal-strip ceiling serves as an acoustic insulator and also controls water leaks. A display of back-lit transparencies provides local information and shows works from nearby museums and libraries. (Photograph courtesy Lee Harris Pomeroy Associates Architects)

502

Work Spaces

The interiors of factories, workshops, laboratories (fig. 503), and power plants rarely receive professional interior design attention. Their strictly functional purposes have kept them within the province of engineers and technicians. The exceptions suggest that there can be benefits in considering the aesthetic possibilities of such spaces. In industrial plants, color and lighting can be used to aid vision and to promote efficient work and safety. Interested visitors are always impressed by a steel mill, an auto factory, or a powerhouse, and the impression is heightened when the space is treated visually to make it understandable, exciting, and even beautiful.

Utility companies have found that inviting public inspection of power plants and control rooms is good policy. The power plants of the Tennessee Valley Authority have been consistently admired as examples of the beauty possible in industrial settings (fig. 502). The power plant at Kennedy airport in New York occupies an all-glass building, displaying its colorfully painted equipment to those driving by. The engine room of a ship is often one of the most handsome parts of the vessel. In all of these instances, strict engineering needs are, of course, primary, but concern for visual design can help to make the technical realities attractive, interesting, and exciting in a way that helps public understanding while supporting staff pride and morale.

503

502. An aesthetic of industrial technology, developed in the Tennessee Valley Authority projects of the 1930s, is evident in this generator room at the Pickwick Dam Powerhouse. Roland Wank of the Tennessee Valley Authority headquarters in Knoxville, Tennessee, was in charge of design. (Photograph courtesy Tennessee Valley Authority)

503. A research laboratory work space displays an open, luminous quality in the W. C. Decker Engineering Building of the Corning Glass Works, Corning, New York, by Davis, Brody & Associates, 1981. (Photograph: Robert Gray)

CHAPTER FOURTEEN
HUMAN FACTORS

Since all buildings are designed to serve some human purpose, it may seem strange that the study of human factors in relation to design has become a specialized field. Designers generally assert their intention to serve the users of their designs to the best of their abilities, and historically, it is obvious that the most admired projects are ones that have delivered a high level of satisfaction.

There is no escaping the truth, however, that many buildings and many interiors, even including some by skilled designers, fall far short of serving human needs in an optimal way. This can hardly be considered a recent problem. Throughout history, there have been cold and cramped cottages, depressing and comfortless temples and churches, mansions and palaces that must have been miserable to live in. Such problems, long viewed as inevitable evidence that "nothing is perfect," have been accepted more or less without complaint.

Over the years, several forces have emerged in protest against antihuman design. One such force, the theoretical school on which modern architecture is based, is *functionalism*. First developed in the 1930s, functionalism insists that the serving of function is the primary goal of all design efforts. Oddly, it has been the failure of many projects designed in the name of functionalism to deliver the promised satisfactions that has stirred up a new interest in understanding the relationship between human beings and the buildings that they build and use.

Several related disciplines, each with a highly specific interest in designing for human needs in a more careful and methodical manner than has been common in the past, have pulled together in recent years. Their first task has been to study existing buildings, to see how they work or, more often, fail to work for their users. Many modern offices, shops, restaurants, apartments, and houses are inconvenient, uncomfortable, or unsatisfactory in one or more ways (for example, poorly lighted, badly ventilated, or noisy). More and more stories circulate about widely published projects that photograph well—that even win awards—but have turned out to be unsatisfactory in use, some even bitterly disliked.

The causes of such failures are varied and often difficult to pin down. In some cases design simply has not caught up with the complexities of modern building technology, or technology may have been relied on for performance beyond its current capability (as with windowless buildings totally dependent on less-than-perfect air conditioning and other environmental controls). In other cases, design may have been directed by people or agencies with little awareness of the actual needs of users. Modern apartment houses and office buildings are designed more for the profit of the developer than for the satisfaction of occupants. Economic forces that run counter to

users' needs (for taller buildings, perhaps, or smaller rooms) exert formidable pressures, and mistaken assumptions about "what the public wants" take the place of genuine information about actual requirements.

A particularly disturbing accusation suggests that designers are often more concerned with using projects as vehicles to further their own careers than in designing for users' needs. In a world in which media exposure has become vital to success, there are certainly temptations to try for startling, spectacular, or glamorous effects, whether or not they coincide with the goal of serving real human needs.

Increasing criticism of the design professions, from both without and within, has stimulated a new level of attention to the aspects of design, whether of spaces or products, that directly affect the user. In the past, concerned designers attempted to deal with this issue through the improved programming of projects, observation of how people used the buildings they and others had designed, and the exercise of whatever special talent and intuition they could bring to their work. While this approach was certainly helpful, it has proven inadequate, since designers tend to assume that everyone shares their ideas, which are based on their particular background, education, and experience rather than on direct research.

As a corrective, the design profession has become open to the studies of other professions that deal with human needs, particularly to research findings from psychology, sociology, anthropology, and other disciplines that tend to be more rigorously scientific in their approaches than the largely empirical world of design. Since, however, this is not as yet a defined field but an interdisciplinary approach drawing on a number of specialized fields, there is some confusion of terminology. Such terms as *environmental psychology, architectural psychology, ergonomics* (relating human physiology to design), *spatial behavior,* and *proxemics* have come into use, each defining one way of investigating the relation of design to human use.

The term *human factors,* used as the title for this chapter, is something of an umbrella term intended to include all such specialized studies, which share the realization that human beings are powerfully affected by their particular environment and the related conviction that human behavior is in turn influenced by the environment in which it occurs. While it is widely believed that people feel, work, rest, eat, and think better in some spaces than in others, there is surprisingly little *exact* knowledge of what makes one place so much more satisfactory than another. Exact scientific knowledge about any issue generally comes from research involving carefully controlled experiments in which only one factor is varied while all other

504. Stanley Tigerman, architect, designed this stairwell of a residence in a northern suburb of Chicago. Because winders—the wedge-shaped treads of curving stairs—are often regarded as unsafe, special lighting on both sides, a sturdy handrail on the right, and a non-slip carpet were installed to offset possible safety hazards. (Photograph: Howard N. Kaplan © HNK Architectural Photography)

factors are kept constant. Controlled research of this sort is rarely possible in the complex situations of built environments, where too many factors interact and prove difficult to control.

For these reasons, research in human factors is usually based on observation and such techniques as surveys rather than on controlled experimentation. While the results are therefore less precise, they yield general guidelines that can significantly aid the designer in avoiding serious mistakes and increasing user satisfaction. Many of the insights in the area of human factors research have come from sociology and psychology, fields that work in similar ways in much of their methodology. At the same time, the movement called *consumerism* has increased public awareness of the need to evaluate the performance of products of every sort, including buildings and their interiors, in terms of both service to and protection of consumer-users.

Every designer should be familiar with the studies of such pioneers as anthropologist Edward T. Hall and psychologist Robert Sommer, as well as with the constantly growing literature that examines the relation between designed artifacts and spaces and their human users. Hall, in *The Hidden Dimension*, studies the ways in which different cultures have developed differing attitudes toward space between human bodies in various social contacts. He extends this to the ways in which people use rooms and furniture (see Table 15). In various articles and several books, including *Personal Space* and *Tight Spaces,* Sommer has related similar observations more directly to the planning of buildings and rooms. His observations of territorial behavior in public and private spaces have provided new insights for designers. In addition, ergonomic data provide more specific details about human bodily dimensions, muscular and sensory functioning, safety and security matters, and the special needs of handicapped individuals.

The ways in which a designer may use the study of human factors will vary with the nature and scope of individual design problems, but some typical applications can be listed to give an idea of the range of possibilities.

Background

Traditionally, design education has focused on aesthetic issues, often relegating functional matters to a secondary role. Even the designs of avowed functionalists more often seem aimed at creating a strong visual effect than at serving specific user needs. The study of environmental psychology or any other discipline in the field of human factors directs design attention to the specific ways in which design impinges on human life and makes the union of aesthetics and practical service in a mutually supporting relation a design goal.

TABLE 15. PERSONAL DISTANCES

	Close	Far
Intimate	0″–6″	6″–1′6″
Personal	1′6″–2′6″	2′6″–4′
Social	4′–7′	7′–12′
Public	12′–25′	25′ and over

The four terms are fairly explanatory in defining kinds of relationships. *Intimate* indicates the closest of personal relations—parents and their children and lovers. *Personal* contacts are one-to-one conversational relationships. *Social* contacts are those at parties, conferences, business meetings, typically with more than two people involved. *Public* contacts are those between speaker and audience, teacher and class, and similar person-to-larger group relations.

Based on E. T. Hall, *The Hidden Dimension,* 1966.

Visually exciting design that runs counter to human needs can be seen as wasteful, harmful, and destined to failure when put to use. The notorious Pruitt-Igoe housing project in Indianapolis won design awards but finally was demolished in response to its disastrous inadequacy as a living environment for its residents. A handsome building may contain offices or laboratories that are inconvenient and inefficient. A fine winding staircase may be the scene of dangerous accidental falls.

On the other hand, users' efforts to make spaces comfortable by rearranging furniture, introducing personal clutter, and similar modifications can undermine the visual quality of a designed space. Occupants are often quite content with houses of banal exterior and interior design. The thoughtful designer will make every effort to create a space that works for its users without sacrificing visual quality.

Programming

In this phase of design work, the specific needs that a design project is meant to serve are spelled out in detail (see Chapter 4, pages 75–79). Too often, programs are developed by designers and clients without direct contact with end users. Managers of businesses and organizations often assume that they have sufficient knowledge to develop programs without any firsthand exploration of user needs. This leads to housing hated by its occupants; offices depressing and inconvenient to workers; hospitals that frustrate patients, visitors, and medical staff; schools and colleges that act as inhibitors to learning; and airports built for aircraft and airlines rather than for travelers.

Better programming demands the methodical observation of existing projects of a comparable nature to discover what aspects work well and where problems and failures occur. Surveys can often go directly to users to discover what real needs and desires exist (fig. 505). Office workers will often have specific complaints about noise, lack of storage space, poor lighting, and similar issues. Vandalism and crime in a housing project have many causes, but design that avoids dark, hidden spaces and provides access routes in full public view has a favorable impact on such problems. It is, of course, not possible to reach every future user of a hospital, airport, or office building, but some sampling of potential users can be undertaken.

Since surveys can only discover opinions and desires based on the experience of those surveyed, their results require interpretive study. Motivations should be questioned and unrealistic desires separated from genuine needs. A desire for "more closets," for example, may indicate a need for other kinds of storage that will be more serviceable. A wish for a windowed corner office may come less from any practical need than from a desire for heightened status—a value that may or may not deserve consideration. All needs and desires must be brought into some realistic relationship not only with the project's budget and priorities but also with the underlying economic forces.

User Participation

Clients of designers and architects who will be occupants and users of the projects they commission (as in the case of a private house or apartment) are almost inevitably participants in the design process, which means they discuss proposals and approve plans. In larger projects where the clients are managers, officials, developers, or others without direct user roles, it may take a specific effort to obtain any user participation in the design process. In fact, designers often resist such participation as troublesome, time-consuming, or a needless interference in their professional work.

Actually, user participation in design, accomplished through review groups, worker committees, and/or sessions with sample groups of potential users, will often aid design by discovering real needs in detail, sorting these out from assumed requirements. It may even lead to better design and direct economies. Just as worker participation in factory management has been found to improve production, user participation in design can contribute to developing projects that improve the user's quality of life.

Participatory design depends on establishing a relationship between designers and users in which each educates the other. The resulting design should satisfy many sets of values. While participatory design can take some extra time and trouble, it has proven worthwhile in many projects. Among its benefits is

505. This programming questionnaire was administered to collect data for the design of a large corporate office facility. (Courtesy J. F. N. Associates)

the higher level of users' acceptance of the end result. When compromises must be made (for example, between desires and economic realities), users involved in the process find it easier to accept the result than if they had simply been presented with a solution on which they had no influence.

Giving choices of equally satisfactory alternatives is another technique through which participation can improve user satisfaction. Choosing a color scheme, furniture, or furniture arrangement makes users feel that the resultant space is their own in a way that a fixed scheme mandated by remote authority does not. Designers' work is often defeated or sabotaged by users who resent having had no input into what is provided; involvement in some aspect of the design process can disarm such hostility.

Use of Research Data

Many design decisions can be aided or guided by information developed by researchers in the fields dealing with human factors. *Anthropometric* data deal with bodily dimensions to establish clearances, heights of tables, counters, and shelves, and similar useful guidelines. To this, *ergonomic* data add a concern with body mechanics and sensory performance, thereby guiding the designer on such issues as seating comfort, ease of seeing and hearing, and thus lighting and acoustics as well (figs. 506–11). *Experimental psychology* studies sensory perception and deals with the ways in which spaces are experienced and the impact of color and light on both senses and emotions. *Anthropology* and *sociology* study human behavior in various cultures and contexts.

Even studies in animal behavior have been useful in understanding human attitudes toward privacy and communication and have aided understanding of territoriality, the desire for space defined in terms of individual and group privacy. *Proxemics* deals with the impact of spatial realities on social grouping and behavior. For example, crowding is known to increase levels of irritation and frustration, leading to interpersonal friction, arguments, and even crime. Human beings require suitable levels of privacy for work, meditation, and rest, as well as adequate settings for personal contacts, in both work and social situations. Appropriate spaces, walls, doors, and furniture selection all contribute to making daily life comfortable, satisfying, and productive.

Research in all of these fields is quite specialized, often pursuing observation or research on specific, narrow questions.

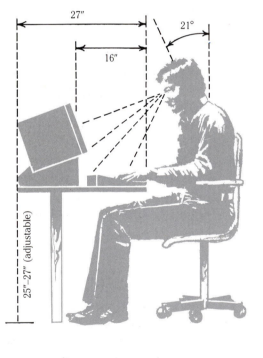

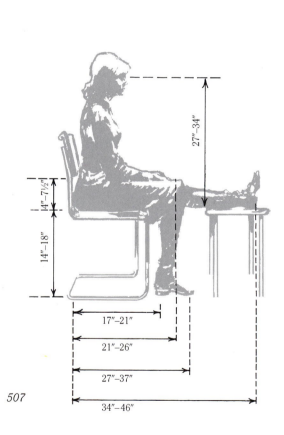

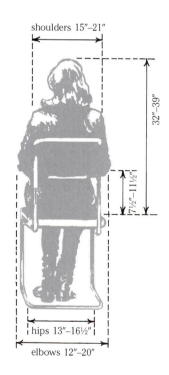

506

507

506. *Office tasks involving computer operation call for furniture thoughtfully sized—preferably adjustable—to make the workplace ergonomically suitable.*

507. *This diagram illustrates the dimensions required for ergonomically satisfactory seating.*

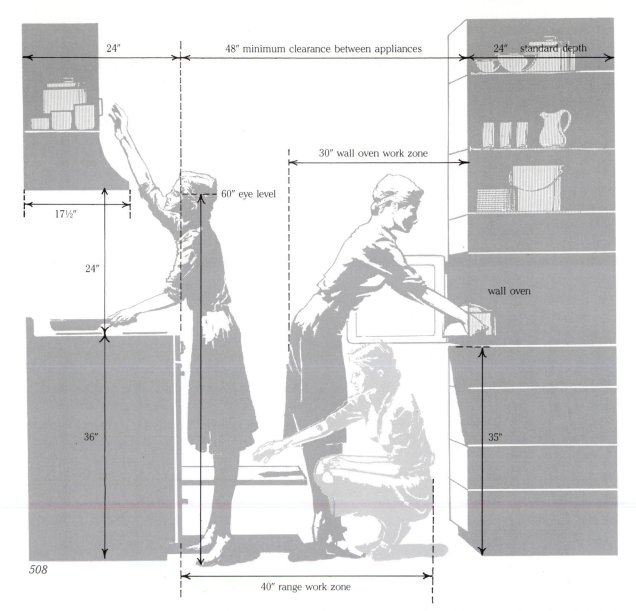

24"

48" minimum clearance between appliances

24" standard depth

30" wall oven work zone

60" eye level

17½"

24"

36"

wall oven

35"

508

40" range work zone

Many designers seem impatient with such studies, feeling that they do not deal with practical questions of designing specific projects. Actually, some studies have yielded very specific and useful "how-to" information relating, for example, to the design of good lighting and physiologically satisfactory seating. In other areas, such as the emotional impact of color or the role of space in influencing behavior, research data can have only a more general impact in promoting the better understanding of such matters.

It is not unusual to find that research data yield findings that may appear to be obvious; everyone knows something about the impact of warm versus cold colors, for example, or can guess that avoiding dark, hidden spaces in public areas will discourage crime and vandalism. Still, even such seemingly obvious issues are so often ignored that it seems important to focus attention on them. Designers also often find that in presenting design proposals to clients and committees, documented research findings offer support when the obvious becomes a matter for dispute.

Employment of Consultants

In many larger projects it is helpful to employ specialists in the fields of environmental psychology, sociology, or ergonomics. This transfers some responsibility from the designer to an expert with greater experience and more specialized knowledge in areas that lie somewhat outside the normal concerns of the designer. Just as specialists in engineering, lighting, or acoustics can be helpful to the overall success of a project, the specialist in human factors can function as a kind of spokesperson for a particular set of considerations.

508. These clearances, applied to kitchen design, are derived from studies of human proportions and movement, such as reach.

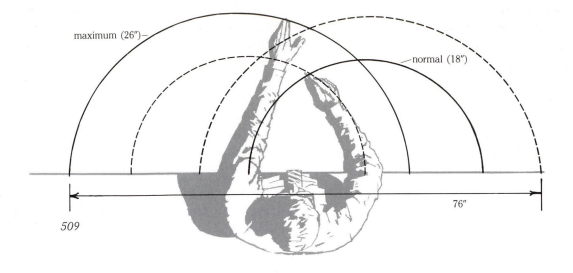

maximum (26″)

normal (18″)

76″

509

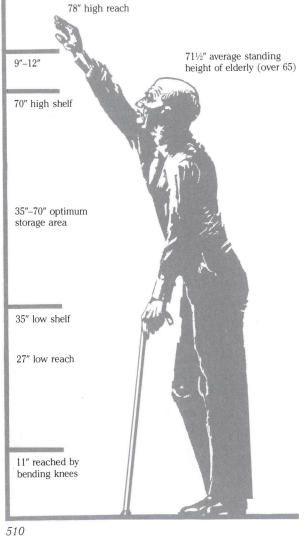

78″ high reach

71½″ average standing height of elderly (over 65)

9″–12″

70″ high shelf

35″–70″ optimum storage area

35″ low shelf

27″ low reach

11″ reached by bending knees

510

Scanning the available literature for studies and data germane to a particular project, setting up and conducting surveys or interviews, organizing user participation in design—these are all functions that a specialist can be expected to perform with a concentration that the designer can rarely achieve. Finding consultants who have expertise in their special fields as well as an adequate understanding of the goals and problems of design is not always easy, but current interest in this field is encouraging more and more qualified people to enter it.

The increasing use of interdisciplinary teams in the design of larger projects opens the way for including a specialist in environmental psychology as one of the team. Some localities legally require such a specialist, and this trend may well become general before too long. In the meanwhile, and in working on smaller projects, designers will have to continue to rely on their own knowledge and judgment about when to call on specialists.

Performance Evaluation

It is a curious reality that after design projects are put into use, they are seldom evaluated in any methodical way. Interesting projects may receive publication, commentary, and even criticism in the design press, but such comment is usually concerned primarily with aesthetic values. Furthermore, it is often based on information gleaned from drawings and photographs, sometimes supplemented by a brief visit to a space too new to have developed any clear user points of view. Designers themselves tend to move on to new projects, losing interest in jobs already completed. They may even avoid asking

509. An informed awareness of the mechanics of normal human reach is fundamental to the design of all work and storage areas.

510. This diagram gives average reaching dimensions for elderly males.

for evaluation for fear of stimulating complaints and criticisms that would otherwise be overlooked or suppressed.

This pattern has tended to inhibit the process of learning by experience, a process that has the potential to improve the levels of satisfaction delivered by the work of a particular designer and the work of the design professions collectively. The environmental fields have begun to make a practice of taking a formal evaluation after a project has been in use long enough to weed out problems related to the stresses of moving in and the resistances often set up by the strangeness of a new place. Making an evaluative study at intervals such as six months or one year can generate information about what has worked well and what has not that provides a basis for future improvement in design performance.

An evaluative study can be made on the basis of questionnaire or survey techniques; a more informal observation and report by a consultant with some experience in such

evaluations; or firsthand observation and interviews undertaken by the designer. The last approach has the obvious disadvantage of introducing the possibility of bias on the part of the designer, who is more likely to accept favorable comment than unfavorable criticism—although it is the latter that is most important in limiting future mistakes. Ideally, evaluation reports on a wide variety of projects should be made available to the entire design community, enabling all to learn from a common and growing pool of experience. At present, such general availability is unusual. However, from time to time journal articles provide some evaluative information of greater depth and seriousness than the rumors that frequently travel in design circles.

Human Factors in Relation to Smaller Projects

The outline offered above may seem to apply only to larger projects, such as airports, hospitals, and housing projects, and

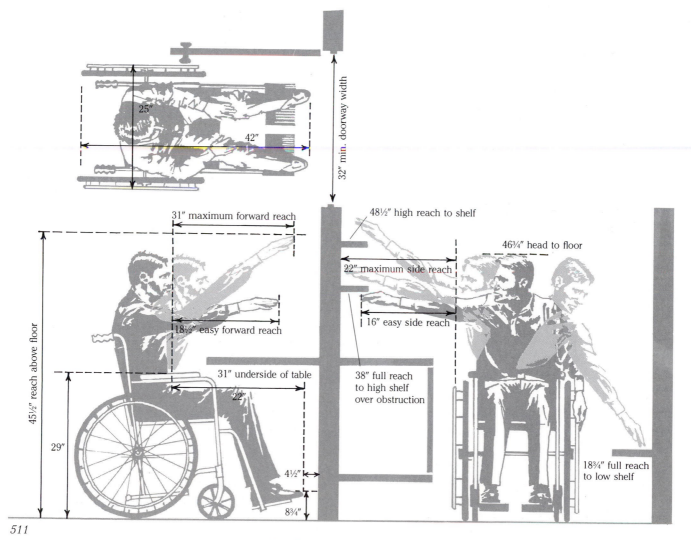

511

511. The reach of a person in a wheelchair and the clearance for the chair itself are important factors in adapting storage and work spaces to those so constrained. (See also wheelchair clearances in plan, fig. 518.)

large design organizations. It is certainly true that the need for formal and specialized study of human factors issues is greatest in such projects, in which direct user-designer contact is difficult and the often bureaucratic way in which projects are conceived, planned, and carried through seems to promote a rather inhuman organizational routine. Human factors issues are, however, every bit as important in small projects, even down to the design of a single room.

While room designations such as *living room* or *bedroom* or project descriptions such as *private office* or *cafeteria* may suggest a full and detailed program of "usual" functions, probing real user needs may lead to the discovery that the intended use is not at all standard. A living room may be used as a studio, a place for group meetings, or a conservatory for growing plants—or it may hardly be used at all, but kept as a

showplace or parlor. A bedroom may also serve as a study, a TV room, or an extra living room; it is vital to learn how many people will use it and what their relationships are. Many offices are conference rooms, TV-viewing rooms, or studios as well as offices. A cafeteria will often serve as a social club and lounge as well as for regular meal service.

While the design of spaces should respond to their intended use, it may also influence what the actual use will be. A dining room may impose formality or encourage relaxation. A cafeteria may impose a sense of rush, permit some ease and comfort, or turn into a "hangout" to what may be an undesirable degree. The planning of home kitchens has been found to be a factor influencing family relationships for better or worse. A cramped layout in which two people who share meal preparation constantly collide and get in one another's way puts nerves on edge and can even cause arguments, while a more accommodating layout might encourage cheerful cooperation.

Members of a family need to have suitable privacy and suitable gathering places to support pleasant relationships. Furniture arrangement can aid and encourage conversation or inhibit it. Color and lighting establish moods in a space and influence the events that take place there in subtle ways that often go unrecognized.

Many such issues may seem to be only what any competent designer would consider in the normal course of a design project. It is, however, the long history of their neglect that has made the subject of human factors a special field. In small projects where elaborate research and the employment of consultants is out of the question, the designer has a particular obligation to remember that the aesthetic aspects of a design must be related to the practical aspects that users will have to live with.

Human Factors in Relation to Specific Issues

In addition to the general planning and design considerations related to human factors, a group of more technical issues deserves attention. Both large and small projects can benefit from a concentrated review of the following matters:
S A F E T Y . The threat of accidents is generally associated with automobiles, travel, and public streets, but indoor accidents, particularly at home, are a major cause of injuries and death. Stairways and steps pose real dangers (fig. 504; see Chapter 5, page 144). Bathrooms, with their slippery surfaces, hard projections, mirrors, glass, and hot water, are notorious accident locations. Kitchens, with open flames, gas or electric elements, boiling water, heated fats, and sharp objects, present other risks. High locations, balconies, windows, and platform

512

512. Glass doors tend to prevent collisions between people entering and exiting, but can become dangerous when certain lighting conditions render the glass virtually invisible. Here, a decorative pattern of dots on a frameless glass door solves the problem. The entrance to the offices of A. G. Becker, Inc., in New York was designed by Jack L. Gordon Architects. (Photograph courtesy Jack L. Gordon Architects)

513. A hospice for terminally ill children contains an area for play and dance movement. The wood-floor stage is surrounded by benches; behind the benches, additional space can accommodate young spectators in wheelchairs. The facility at St. Mary's Hospital for Children, Bayside, New York, was designed by Breger Terjesen Associates, Architects, 1984. (Photograph: Andrea Brizzi, courtesy Breger Terjesen Associates)

514. Rooms and furniture for children must be designed with the users' size in mind, as were the tables, chairs, and storage shown here. Clear, bright, usually primary colors are generally considered the most appropriate to children's visual orientation. The United States Navy Child Center in Lemoore, California, was designed by Naomi Hatkin and Pamela Helmich of GHI Architects in 1985. (Photograph: Brenner Vandouris)

513

514

TABLE 16. SAFETY AND SECURITY PROBLEMS

Type of Hazard		Design Precautions
FALLS:	Slippery flooring	Avoid slippery materials, especially near outdoor access.
	Small rugs or mats	Avoid when possible. Use rubber antislip underlay.
	Bathrooms	Provide grab bars and use nonskid surfaces. Consider positioning the door to open outward in order to easily reach an injured person who may be blocking the door.
	Steps	Avoid level changes and single step if possible. If not, mark level change clearly through contrasting colors, material, or design. Provide rail and/or safety light.
	Stairways	Plan moderate (normal) angle of slope. Break long runs with landings. Provide handrails on both sides and, for wider stairways, in the center as well. Provide good lighting. Avoid slippery materials. Provide nonskid treads and/or nosings. Avoid winders. Mark beginning of stairway clearly through design.
	Windows	In high (upper-floor) locations, consider safety bars or rails. Use window type that restricts opening (but see fire safety problems below). Avoid low sills.
	Balconies, roofs	Provide adequate railings. Restrict roof access.
	Kitchens	Place all provisions and materials within easy reach if possible; if not, provide a secure step stool. Store knives and sharp objects well out of reach.
	Darkness	Provide adequate lighting, emergency light at key locations. Provide double switches at top and bottom of stairways. Install a light switch near the bed in bedrooms. Install a night light in bathrooms. Consider placing proximity or sonic switches in appropriate locations.
FIRE:	Prevention	Avoid highly inflammable materials. Store dangerous substances in fireproof enclosures. Use fire-safe materials near fireplaces, heating stoves, and kitchen ranges. Provide adequate and safe electric wiring.
	Control	Provide extinguishers, smoke alarms, alarm signals, bells where appropriate. Consider providing hose cabinets and sprinklers, particularly for high-floor locations, exit routes, high-risk locations.
	Exit and escape	Provide safe exits, two independent routes for upper floors and hazardous locations. Provide ample exits from public spaces with out-swinging doors, panic-bolt hardware. Provide exit signs and lights. Provide fire company access (avoid fixed windows, fixed window bars). Consider outdoor escapes, ladders, and so on. Provide emergency lighting.
ELECTRICAL:	Fire	Provide adequate and safe wiring. Also see "Fire" above.
	Shock	Avoid placing outlets near water. Provide ground-fault interrupt circuitry for bathroom and other wet locations.
WATER:	Bathrooms	Provide safe (thermostatically controlled) mixing faucets for tubs and showers. Avoid slippery floor surfaces (see "Falls" above), tubs, and shower bottoms.
	Pools	Control access. Consider installing railings, antiskid flooring.
AIR QUALITY:	Smoke	Provide adequate ventilation. Use smoke venting for enclosed meeting spaces. For spaces that carry special hazards (restaurant kitchens, theaters, and so on), consider smoke venting for use in case of fire.
	Cooking	Provide hoods and vents to remove cooking fumes.
	Chemical, bacterial	Check ventilating and air-conditioning systems to avoid retention and spread of pollutants. Provide adequate ventilation. Provide natural ventilation as backup in case of failure of mechanical HVAC systems.

Type of Hazard		Design Precautions
	Materials	Avoid materials that may give off air pollutants (plastics and other synthetics call for particular care). Avoid materials that produce toxic fumes when burning or smoldering.
MATERIALS:	Glass	Avoid glass and mirror in locations where collisions are possible. Mark or pattern glass walls and doors to aid visibility. Avoid sharp edges and corners in furniture applications. Avoid glass shower and tub enclosures. Consider use of tempered or shatterproof glass or nonshattering plastic alternatives where appropriate.
	Metals	Avoid sharp edges and corners in hazardous locations.
	Other	The location of all hard materials (tile, slate, stone) and rough materials (exposed concrete, rough wood boards) should be carefully considered as well as all their possible safeguards.
MISCELLANEOUS:	Furniture	Avoid small, low, and easily overturned furniture items, including chairs. Consider safety issues for movable furniture (on casters or rollers) such as low tables, plant stands, and so on. Furniture with rounded or padded edges and corners is safest.
	Children	Check bars and railings on stairways, furniture, and so on to avoid spacing that may catch a head, arm, or leg or allow the child to slip through. Steps, stairs, windows, and balconies all require safeguarding to prevent falls.
	Garage	Isolate to prevent possible exhaust pollution. Provide fireproof enclosure and good ventilation.
	Elevators and escalators	Check safety provisions, emergency stop, alarms, control of access.
SECURITY:	Intrusion	Provide suitable locks, gates, bars, and so on. Consider TV surveillance, intercom, computerized access control systems when appropriate. Plan to avoid hidden (blind) corridors, stairways, vestibule locations, and light these areas well.
	Burglary	Provide suitable locks, bars, automatic lights, and so on. Consider installing an alarm system.
	Pilferage and theft	Provide lockable storage, locking for individual rooms, and access and exit control points. Consider magnetic or other merchandise control systems for shops and stores.
	Vandalism	Consider use of resistant materials. Plan for maximum surveillance of risky locations.

515

516

517

515, 516. A "Lift" system renders a washbasin accessible to persons in wheelchairs and small children. The sink can be set at normal height (fig. 515) or lowered as required (fig. 516). It is available in eleven colors and can be used with basins of several different designs. (Photographs courtesy Villeroy & Boch USA)

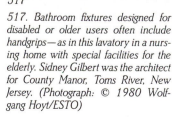

517. Bathroom fixtures designed for disabled or older users often include handgrips—as in this lavatory in a nursing home with special facilities for the elderly. Sidney Gilbert was the architect for County Manor, Toms River, New Jersey. (Photograph: © 1980 Wolfgang Hoyt/ESTO)

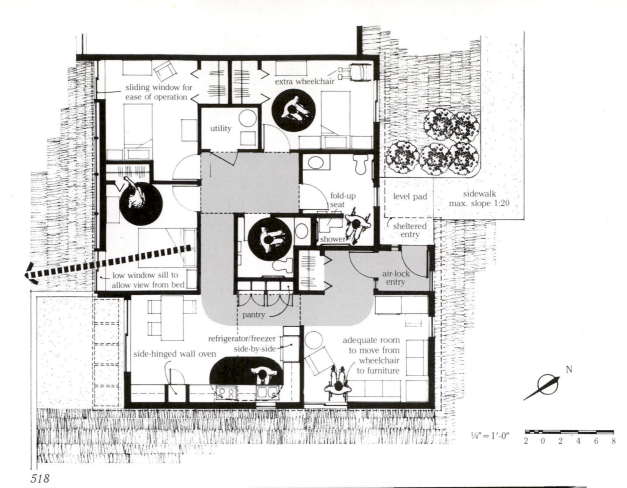

518–21. The floor plan (fig. 518) illustrates barrier-free strategies in a residential apartment designed to accommodate a disabled person. The shaded central zone indicates a circulation path for wheelchairs. The Nutting Apartments for Disabled Persons, Amherst, Massachusetts, was designed by Juster Pope Associates Architects & Planners, 1981. In an interior of the Nutting Apartments, the kitchen area (fig. 519) is designed to make appliances and work surfaces easily accessible to residents in wheelchairs. A low oven comes equipped with a pull-out shelf below, to facilitate use by a person in a wheelchair (fig. 520). The work surface pulls out from the counter to allow wheelchair clearance and provide a comfortable working height (fig. 521). (Photographs courtesy Juster Pope Associates)

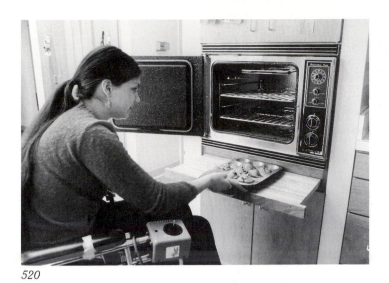

520

521

edges need the best possible guardrails or bars, marking, and lighting. Glass always poses a danger, particularly in the form of large windows and doors that can sometimes be virtually invisible (fig. 512). Polished floor surfaces are a hazard, especially outdoors or near entrances where water, snow, or ice can add to the risk. Nonskid surfaces will minimize these risks. Small rugs and mats and the edges of larger rugs can cause falls. Furniture edges, projecting legs, and objects that roll or overturn easily are also involved in a surprising number of accidents.

Fire safety is a special matter that calls for the observance of regulations concerning exit routes and equipment such as smoke detectors, fire alarms, extinguishers, and sprinkler systems and for the choice of materials for maximum fire-resistance. Many designers feel that fire-safety consideration stops at the minimal observance of legal requirements. Reports of actual fires make it clear that a far higher standard of fire safety is both easily obtainable and highly desirable. Many modern synthetic materials present particular risks because they give off toxic fumes when burning that can be more deadly than the fire itself. The dangers are multiplied by modern closed spaces with artificial ventilation, often on high floors where rescue access is difficult.

SECURITY. This is an issue closely related to safety and, unfortunately, an increasingly important consideration, particularly·in urban areas where social conditions have brought about an increase in robbery, vandalism, and even terrorism. Design cannot control every aspect of such problems, but both basic planning and suitable details and equipment can help to minimize risks. Dark halls and hidden areaways invite trouble, while open and visible access points are to some degree self-protecting. Oscar Newman's book *Defensible Space* explores the ways in which design and planning can discourage crime and vandalism in apartment buildings and public housing projects. Most of the recommended steps may seem to be obvious, common-sense precautions, but a systematic review of the risks that are inevitably present and the design steps that can be taken to control them is a commendable routine.

ENVIRONMENTAL PROBLEMS. Public awareness of environmental issues such as the effect of pollution on air quality has finally focused attention on the indoor environment. The surprising conclusion is that hazards may be greater inside buildings than outside. Sealed buildings with recirculated air-distribution systems tend to gradually concentrate bacterial contamination and air pollutants produced by many modern synthetic materials and by combustion (in cooking, heating, and smoking). Artificial lighting lacks some components of sunlight essential for the human body's best performance. Noise and radiation produced by many types of equipment present problems that are only now being explored for their possible harmful effects. While no designer can cope with all such problems in the modern world, designers can make it their responsibility to keep alert to such matters and respond to them as far as their skills and knowledge permit.

CHILDREN, THE AGED, AND THE HANDICAPPED. Designers tend to think of the typical user of any space as an "average person," but the real human population includes a high proportion of people who are "nonaverage" and who present special problems. Children from infancy to adolescence, for example, are smaller in bodily dimensions, active but, at least in early years, less coordinated than adults, and therefore subject to falls and other accidents. Designers should avoid selecting furniture with sharp corners, breakable parts, and details such as bars or rungs in which children's heads can be caught (figs. 515, 516).

Elderly people too are often poorly coordinated, suffer from reduced muscular control and strength, may be overweight, and may have problems with sight and hearing that make them vulnerable to falls and other injuries. The use of safety rails, handgrips (fig. 517), good lighting, and similar provisions for the protection of the aged will improve safety for everyone. With the constantly increasing proportion of the population in upper-age brackets, design with these special problems in mind is increasingly important.

There is also currently a new awareness of the needs of people with various physical disabilities, who find "normally" designed buildings and rooms difficult to use. While the proportion of the population with any particular disability (visually impaired, inability to walk, lack of muscular coordination, for example) may be small, a surprisingly large proportion of the population can expect to go through some period of disability as a result of injury, disease, or increasing age.

In addition to safety, access is a primary problem for these groups. The physically impaired, ranging from elderly people who have difficulty in walking to people in wheelchairs, obviously cannot negotiate steps or stairs. Adequate access can be provided by ramps, elevators, and wide doors that open automatically. (It is worth noting that the entry doors to many stores and office and public buildings are difficult for even a person of normal health, much less the physically impaired, to manage.) If changes in levels within a space cannot be avoided, ramps or elevators should be provided. Allowing clearances for wheelchairs throughout a space, particularly in congested spaces such as bathrooms, can often make the difference between self-sufficiency and dependency (figs. 518–22). Problems with seeing are common throughout the population and become more widespread among older age groups. Totally blind people depend on the tactile information given by flooring, railings, door hardware, and elevator and other control buttons (fig. 523).

While special-purpose interiors such as hospitals, nurseries, and institutions and residences for the elderly routinely acknowledge these needs in their planning, it should be remembered that almost all spaces are *sometimes* used by children, old people, or people with special handicaps. Organizations representing the disabled are increasingly vocal in pointing out that the disabled population would use all sorts of facilities more often and better if it had better access. Laws requiring provisions for access by the disabled in many public facilities are now being gradually introduced. Even where no such requirements exist, reasonable provisions seem a logical and humane step, particularly since they so often improve safety and convenience for everyone.

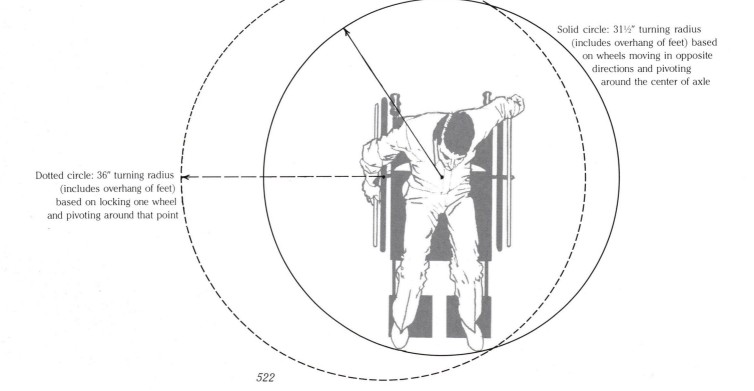

Solid circle: 31½" turning radius (includes overhang of feet) based on wheels moving in opposite directions and pivoting around the center of axle

Dotted circle: 36" turning radius (includes overhang of feet) based on locking one wheel and pivoting around that point

522

522. This diagram shows dimensional clearances for wheelchairs.

523. Planning for a sight-impaired client, the architects selected various flooring materials and strong wall textures that change from level to level or space to space, providing tactile information on location, while the flowing mahogany railing serves as a guideline. The sighted members of the family can enjoy the visual effect of these design details. The circulation and stair core of this house is also a conservatory, adding other sensory touches. The house near New York was designed by Charles Moore and Richard B. Oliver, architects. (Photograph: © Norman McGrath)

CHAPTER FIFTEEN
ARCHITECTURE

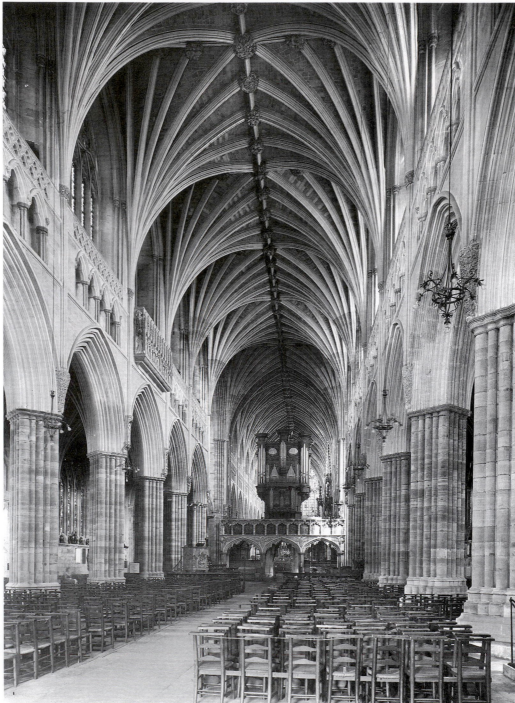

The ties between interior design and architecture are close and inevitable. It is impossible to think of the interiors of many great buildings apart from their architecture. Great buildings are designed in terms of internal space as well as exterior form. Experiencing them requires moving into and through the interior—movement that must take place in space and time. The finest architectural works (the Gothic cathedrals, for example) are those that most richly exploit this medium of space, time, and movement.

The relation of the interior designer to architecture is similarly close, but it takes various forms according to the situation presented by a particular design assignment. Architects often act as the interior designers for buildings that they design, or they work closely with interior designers to achieve a unity of design between exterior and interior. When a building is of a high level of architectural quality, the designer has an obligation to understand, support, and enhance that quality. Sometimes the architectural design of a building largely determines its interior character. In such cases, interior design becomes a matter of completing the given reality at a level of detail that architecture does not often address.

Historic buildings or older buildings of no significant historical value that are to be modernized or adapted for a new use present special problems. Interior design is closely related to the structure of the building shell and must take account of it even if its features are to be altered or hidden. Many older buildings have been seriously damaged by ill-considered modernization that has done more harm than good. Buildings of lesser architectural merit may call for design that makes the best of an indifferent or even bad situation. Minimizing faults of bad architecture is often part of the interior designer's work.

In other situations, interior design may be quite separate from architectural design. Many modern building types, whether of excellent, indifferent, or unfortunate design, are internally neutral—that is, having no particular character, requiring neither enhancement nor correction. This is true of office buildings, apartment buildings, and similar structures that rent or sell internal space to many occupants. Such interiors are deliberately designed to be as neutral as possible, leaving the specific design to each occupant to arrange as desired. In this situation, architecture influences interior design only to the extent that unchangeable features, such as ceiling height and columns and window locations, act as unavoidable constraints. Still, the kind of interior design that places Georgian rooms within a glass-sheathed skyscraper or an avant-garde apartment inside a Victorian mansion seems to be pointlessly insensitive to the relation between an interior and its context.

An understanding of architecture thus becomes basic to all work in interior design. Architecture is often regarded as the most basic of the visual arts, "the mother of the arts." Among the arts, architecture is unique in that it exists primarily to serve practical needs, with its role as art an almost incidental by-product of its production. In architecture, with only very rare exceptions, a building is designed to serve a specific need—as a house, a temple, a factory, or an office building. Certainly not every structure designed to fill such needs can qualify as a work of art, but the possibility is always present and in the mind of any skilled architect; at best, this goal is attained.

The ancient Roman architect, theorist, and writer Vitruvius, in his *Ten Books on Architecture* written in the first century B.C., seems to have been the first to articulate the goals of architecture clearly. He is most often quoted in the indirect form of an English-language paraphrase by the Elizabethan writer Sir Henry Wotton: "Well Building hath three Conditions; Commodity, Firmness, and Delight." The quaint terms can be converted, in modern language, to *function, structure,* and *aesthetics*—still as sound a summary of what architectural design must deal with as anyone has to offer. Understanding architecture in a general way and understanding any particular building involve considering these three aspects of design. While they interrelate very closely, each can be examined independently.

FUNCTION

The word *function* has come to serve architecture as the professional term meaning practical usefulness, the purposes that a particular building is expected to support. Architectural design begins with the study of a structure's intended function and the development of ways in which to satisfy the functions required of the building. The names of building types, such as house, school, church, hospital, or office building, describe in a general way a particular function, but the architect must move to a much more detailed analysis. A house has many functions—cooking, eating, bathing, sleeping, living, storage, and so on—each served by interior spaces, and each family or occupant will have a more specific set of needs for each of these. The internal function of modern building types, such as hospitals, airport terminals, or industrial plants, can be very complex, facing the architect with extremely difficult problems of planning.

As in interior design, the architectural process of providing for functional utility usually comes down to arranging spaces in order to make them as convenient and logical as possible. At its most basic, such planning may be thought of as creating a layout of rooms of appropriate sizes, suitably arranged. (In modern practice, not all spaces are rooms.) Creating a

524. The Gothic cathedrals of the Middle Ages used masonry construction—vaulting supported by exterior buttresses—to create interior spaces of great beauty and spiritual impact. To an observer facing east in the nave of the English cathedral of Exeter (circa 1280–1370), the many ribs of the vaults create patterns characteristic of fan vaulting, used in several English cathedrals. The screen with organ above interrupts the view into the choir, engendering a sense of mystery through spatial complexity. (Photograph: Copyright A. F. Kersting)

525

526

525, 526. In Le Corbusier's evocative church Notre-Dame-du-Haut in Ronchamp, France (1950–54), external and internal design make up an inseparable unity. The sculptural form of the exterior (fig. 525), with its upswept roof and pattern of window perforations, is carried into the equally sculptural interior hollow space. The tower-like form on the left encloses a chapel, one of three. (Photograph: Marvin Trachtenberg) Inside (fig. 526), Notre-Dame-du-Haut is as modern as its exterior, yet it suggests earlier architectural traditions. The lighted rectangles on the right are funnel-shaped apertures in the thick south wall, each filled with stained glass in brilliant color. The points of light in the wall behind the altar filter in through tiny windows. All of the interior details were designed by Le Corbusier. (Photograph: Lucien Hervé)

527

528

527, 528. Philip Johnson's own Glass House at New Canaan, Connecticut (fig. 527), was built in 1949. The glass perimeter wall of the house permits an unimpeded view of the interior, causing inside and outside to merge. (Photograph courtesy Philip Johnson) Despite the glass exterior walls, the interior of Johnson's New Canaan home (fig. 528) has a surprisingly sturdy character of its own, deriving from the discrete, simple elements: the brick drum, which encloses the bathroom (not visible here); the brick flooring, rug, and classic modern furniture; and the works of art displayed. (Photograph: Alexandre Georges)

convenient and logical layout can become a complex exercise when circulation patterns, needs for privacy, daylight, safety, and appropriate room sizes must be considered in relation to fitting an allotted space on a given piece of land, often in a building with many floors.

In functional planning, it is customary to speak of *needs* on one hand and *constraints* on the other. The latter are the limitations imposed by the available site, legal restrictions such as safety and zoning laws, and, probably the most influential, the financial considerations of available funds and predicted economic performance over the life of the building. The plans of a building, in the literal sense of its floor-plan layouts, are largely concerned with developing solutions to these functional requirements. At the same time, in order to be workable, they must also take into account the selection of appropriate structure.

STRUCTURE

In order to serve its purpose, a building must be made sturdy and lasting, practical to maintain, and economic in relation to its financial constraints. Modern technology has developed a great variety of structural approaches, from which the architect must select a suitable system for a particular building. In current practice, structural systems have become so complex that architects usually rely on help from the engineering professions to work out the structural details. The selection of the general structural system, since it is usually a vital part of the basic design of any building, remains the architect's responsibility.

Although buildings use a great variety of materials in special, secondary roles (for example, glass for windows; shingles, tiles, or asphalt for roofing; glass fiber for insulation), the materials available for basic structure—those that actually hold the building up—are surprisingly few. In fact, there are only four primary materials, two that have been known since ancient times and two that are modern, having come into use only since the Industrial Revolution of the nineteenth century. Each material and the structures suitable to it deserve some detailed discussion.

Wood

Timber is the most widely available, simplest, and most familiar of structural materials. Wherever there are trees, the use of wood for building becomes commonplace. For their huts and houses, primitive peoples used branches, poles, and logs in ways that minimized the need for precise joinery. As better tools became available, wood was worked with more precision into beams, planks, boards, and panels, creating characteristic historic building patterns.

Wood is limited by its source, trees, to a lengthwise strip material. This in turn limits timber building structure to a *frame,* that is, a cage or grid of long members put together with diagonal bracing members to form a sturdy structural support for whatever wall and roofing materials will be used. Walls and roofing may also be wood (in the form of vertical planks, clapboards, or shingles) or other materials, such as plaster and rubble for walls, tiles or tar paper for roofing.

Wood makes a reasonably durable, but not permanent, building material, being subject to decay, rot, insect damage, and fire. Wooden buildings over a few hundred years of age are rare, and none from ancient times survive, although we have knowledge of wood construction in ancient Egypt, Greece, and Rome from secondary sources such as paintings, written materials, and physical evidence in ruined structures.

Because of its lengthwise structure and comparatively light weight, wood was a favorite material for floors and roofs even when walls were made of stone or other more lasting materials. Many ancient ruined structures exhibit surviving masonry walls and columns, while wood roofing has been lost through one or another form of damage. Surviving wood roofing used for medieval barns, churches, and other large spaces often displays large wooden members assembled into triangular arrangements called *trusses* in order to span spaces wider than the longest available beams. The frames of heavy timber used for many smaller medieval structures are often exposed externally, creating the visual patterns of *half-timber* construction (fig. 529). In America, since exposed framing proved impractical because of climatic conditions, such framing in Colonial houses and other buildings was usually hidden by an external covering of shingles or boarding (fig. 531). However, if it was not covered by paneling or plaster, the framing was often visible inside.

The development of power saws and planers in more modern times has led to the practice of converting timber into neatly cut and sized units, referred to as *lumber.* Modern wood construction uses sawmill-cut lumber for the heavy framing, or, for smaller buildings, smaller members placed close together to form a light but strong frame. Small houses are commonly built with a structure of 2-by-4-inch studs placed 16 inches apart to form wall framing. Joists for floors and rafters for roofs are also 2 inches thick, but 8, 10, or 12 inches deep. They are also placed at the same 16-inch spacing. An outside sheathing and an interior finish together create a hollow "sandwich" assembly that provides reasonable strength with minimum material and labor costs. This system, called *balloon* or *western* framing, is

529

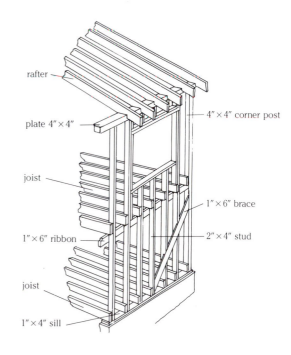

530

characteristically American and still in very common use for the construction of small houses (fig. 530). *Braced framing*, using heavy timber and bracing, also continues in use and has become popular with modern architects to form the structure for houses and other small buildings, particularly where large areas of walls are given over to glass.

The industrial processing of wood has added plywood and particleboard to the list of timber materials. These both convert wood into large sheets that minimize solid wood's tendency to warp, shrink, and split. Plywood is made up of layers of thin wood veneer, particleboard of wood chips and sawdust bonded together with an adhesive and pressed into flat sheets. Both materials make economical use of wood, and both are most useful for sheathing walls, roofs, and floors rather than as primary structural materials.

Although its use as a major building material is limited in modern practice by the combination of rising cost (resulting from diminishing supplies, as forests are cut more rapidly than

529. The Guild Hall at Thaxted, in Essex, England, was built in the second half of the fifteenth century. It is a fine example of half-timber construction, in which a structure's framework is exposed. The curving braces of the top floor are structural stiffening against side sway. The overhang is a characteristic medieval technique for gaining floor space in densely built towns. (Photograph: John Pile)

530. The structural system of wood framing known as balloon framing was developed in Victorian America. Small, lumberyard-sawed wood pieces are assembled in a frame that is easy and economical to construct. When they are vertical, these elements are called studs, when horizontal, joists, and when roof supports, rafters.

531

they are replaced with new growth) and restrictions introduced to reduce fire risks, wood seems assured a continuing role in the architectural construction of smaller buildings and as a secondary material in building using other materials for primary structure. Although wood structure is usually hidden, it influences the location and size of openings. When wood-frame members are exposed, they may become major visual design elements.

Masonry

Masonry is the general term for the other family of materials that played a major role in historic building and that continues in modern use. The term refers to construction with stone and manufactured materials such as brick, tile, concrete block—even the mud brick used in some ancient and primitive buildings. With the exception of mud brick, masonry materials offer excellent durability. The oldest surviving buildings are all of stone (the pyramids of Egypt, figs. 534, 535, and Stonehenge,

for example), and the ruins of ancient structures are usually the remaining stone portions of buildings that used timber roofing.

Use of stone requires available quarry resources and involves the tools and labor required to cut, transport, and erect this heavy material. Bricks and tiles are invented materials that have many of the qualities of stone, except that they can be made when and where needed and in sizes convenient to handle.

Masonry materials offer good strength under *compressive* loads (as in walls and columns), which tend to squeeze or crush the material in use. However, they have poor *tensile* strength for resisting stretching and are therefore not very satisfactory for use as beams or rafters in floor or roof construction. A *beam* is a structural member stressed in *bending* by the loads placed upon it. Bending stress combines compression at the top of a simple beam with tension at its bottom. Materials such as wood and steel make good beams because they are strong in both compressive and tensile stress. Masonry materials are strong only in compression.

531. The heavy, half-timber frame of the American Colonial house was faced with a skin of clapboards or shingles. In this 1759 example, the Vassall-Longfellow House in Cambridge, Massachusetts, the exterior also exhibits neoclassical details executed in wood and based on the Georgian architecture of England. (Photograph courtesy Essex Institute, Salem, Mass.)

532, 533. A wooden house of 1907, the R. R. Blacker House in Pasadena, California (fig. 532), was designed by Greene and Greene, leading American architects of the time on the West Coast. The structural and surface material largely determines the character of the interior. (Photograph: John Jacobus) The foyer of the R. R. Blacker House

(fig. 533) displays meticulously conceived (even the electric switch plates are of mahogany, with solid ebony push-buttons) and beautifully executed woodwork—a refined translation of the shingled exterior. (Photograph courtesy The Gamble House, Greene and Greene Library, University of Southern California)

534

535

A short stone beam called a *lintel* may be used to span a door or window opening in masonry construction, but the opening must be kept narrow in order to prevent the lintel from cracking under its own weight and the weight of the wall above. *Post and lintel construction* (fig. 537), in which columns are placed fairly close together to support lintels, creates an enclosure with the internal space filled only with columns, as, for example, in the hypostyle halls of Egyptian temples. Ways to roof over large open spaces with masonry did not come into wide use until the ancient Romans developed systems of arches and vaults that made possible the building of such structures as the Roman baths or the Pantheon (figs. 539, 540). Domes and vaults remained the only feasible and durable structural devices for enclosing large spaces until the development of the modern materials discussed below (fig. 538).

The building techniques of both domes and vaults require carefully cutting stones into complex shapes; using a temporary (usually wooden) structure called *centering* to support the structure while it is under construction; and massive walls or buttresses to resist the outward pressure, or *thrust*, exerted by arched forms as they convert the downward pull of gravity to an outward push. The Gothic cathedrals are spectacular exercises in masonry construction using vaulting and buttresses to produce lasting and dramatic buildings (fig. 524).

534, 535. The pyramids of Egypt are among the oldest surviving and most impressive of all stone constructions. About 2,300,000 stone blocks, weighing approximately two and a half tons each, make up the largest of the three pyramids at Giza, Egypt (fig. 534).

(Photograph: Hirmer Fotoarchiv) A detail of the Khufu, or Cheops, pyramid at Giza (fig. 535) shows how the component blocks fit together. A facing of finished stone once covered the monument. (Photograph: Roloff Beny)

536

536. In modern use, stone is a popular material for country houses. Architect Marlys Hann chose rough fieldstone for her 1985 house in the Catskill Mountains. (Photograph: © Paul Warchol)

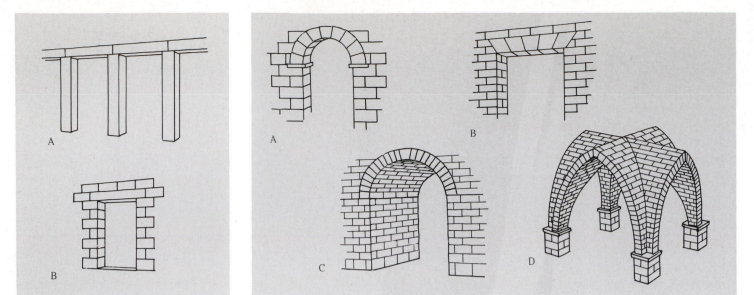

537

538

539

537. *A diagram of post-and-lintel construction (A) illustrates this most basic of building systems. Vertical posts, or columns, support horizontal members, the lintels, which span open spaces. (When the material used is wood, the system is described as post-and-beam construction.) The lintel shown in B is a stone insert spanning a window opening in a masonry wall.*

538. *In masonry, the development of the arch introduced an alternative to the lintel as a structural support over doors and windows. The semicircular, or Roman, arch (A) is the most familiar, but a flat arch (B) is also feasible. When an arch is extended horizontally in depth, the result is a vault. The simplest form of vault is a barrel vault (C). Geometrically, an arch form rotated around a central point generates a dome, which most often surmounts a circular space.*

In the Middle Ages, other types of vaults were developed that could be fitted over square or rectangular spaces and were supported only at four corner points (D).

539, 540. *The Pantheon in Rome (fig. 539) of A.D. 118–25 is one of the earliest domed, all-masonry structures with a vast interior space. (Photograph: Fototeca Unione) Beneath its coffered*

rotunda, the interior of the Pantheon (fig. 540), 142 feet high and 142 feet wide, is one of the most impressive of all domed masonry constructions, shown here in a painting by Giovanni Paolo Pannini of circa 1750. The bright disc on the wall is sunlight shining down through the oculus, the unglazed opening at the top of the dome. National Gallery of Art, Washington, D.C. Samuel H. Kress Collection

541

Vaulted construction has now generally become obsolete, replaced by newer materials that span large openings and spaces more economically. For bearing walls and columns, brick and concrete are in wider use than stone, which is often restricted to the exterior surfaces of walls in monumental buildings. Brick remains in wide use for walls of small buildings with wood floor and roof construction. Exposed brick (sometimes painted) has become a widely used interior surface. Exposed rough stonework is also still quite common for walls and chimneys, particularly in buildings in rural or suburban settings.

Steel

Steel is the modern material that has had the greatest impact on architectural design. In the nineteenth century, the Industrial Revolution brought metals into wide use to make machinery. Iron in both cast and wrought forms began to be employed for bridge building, for columns in mill structures, and then as a major structural material for the frames of train sheds (fig. 543), market halls, and other utilitarian buildings. Iron finally began to replace masonry in many types of large buildings, and was itself replaced by stronger steel (iron alloyed with carbon) as the latter became generally available. The high strength and moderate cost of steel made it an ideal material for railroad rails, engines and other machinery, and shipbuilding. Toward the end of the nineteenth century, it was recognized as the best available material for the structural frames of tall buildings.

The *skyscraper* came into being with the rising values of city real estate, but its technical realization depended on the development of the elevator and the use of steel framing. In steel

541. The restored Ishtar Gate of circa 575 B.C. of the city of Babylon now graces the State Museums in Berlin. Lacking stone suitable for building, ancient Middle Eastern civilizations turned to brick for masonry construction. The brick most commonly used, of unfired mud, lacked durability; fired bricks, painted and glazed for the facing, were reserved for important structures such as this gateway. (Photograph courtesy Berlin State Museums)

542. The 2-4-6-8 House in Venice, California, by Morphosis (Michael Ro-tondi and Thom Mayne), represents a modern use of masonry and concrete. Seen from different angles, the building appears to change in size, an illusion created by the progressively larger sizes of the four windows on the four sides of the house. (Photograph: © 1986 Tim Street-Porter)

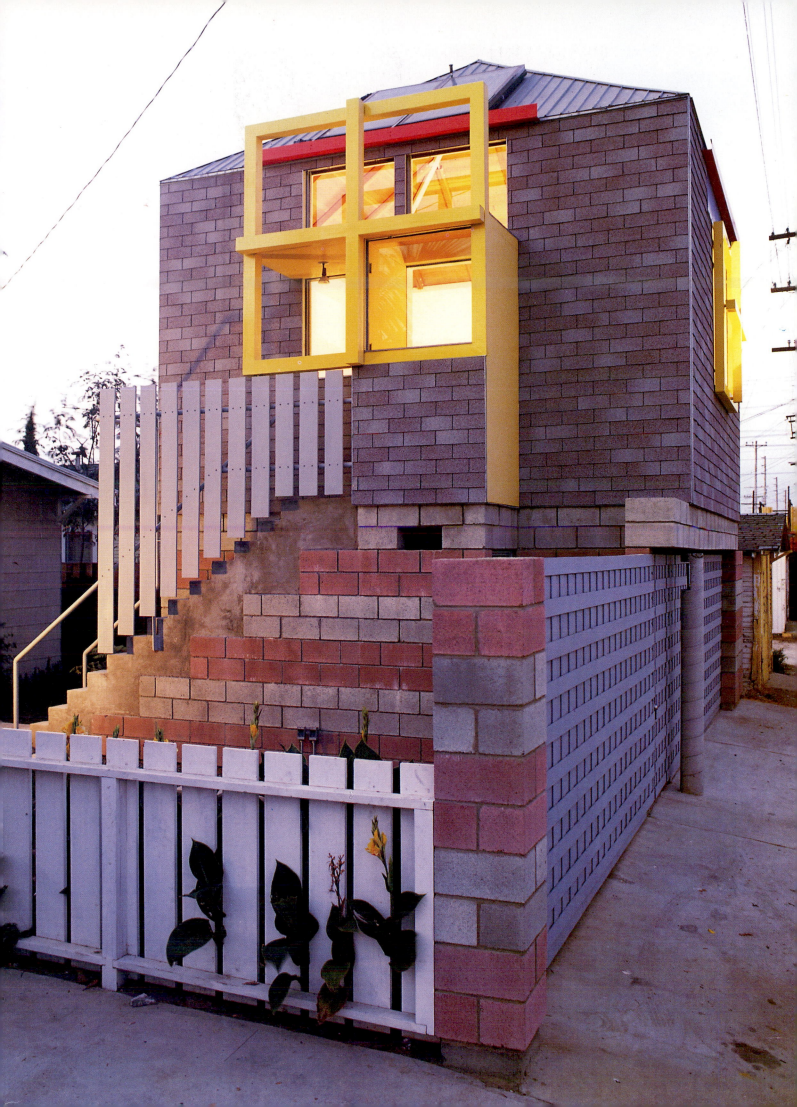

543

construction, walls do not ordinarily carry any weight (they exist strictly to provide enclosure), while columns at the wall line or standing freely support a grid of beams and girders that in turn support floor and roof-deck materials. The familiar I or H shapes of steel members provide a maximum of material where maximum compressive and tensile stresses at top and bottom of beams occur, while the thin connecting web uses a minimum of material. Steel structural members are cut and drilled at the mill and assembled on site with rivets or welding with surprising speed and seeming ease. While steel will not burn, the heat of a fire can soften it enough to lead to structural failure. Therefore, in multistory buildings it is always fire-proofed by covering it with masonry, concrete, or, in modern practice, sprayed-on insulating material.

In addition to forming a cagelike frame construction, steel can be used to make roof trusses to span wide openings. It is also the material for other types of constructions, including domes and *space frames*, roof structures in which many small

members create a grid using the rigidity of triangular forms to provide high strength with minimal material. Steel is a key material for some new and still experimental structural techniques, such as suspended structures using steel cable to support roofing in much the same way that cables of a suspension bridge carry a roadway over a wide open space.

Steel is currently the primary material for the structures of large buildings and is often used in small and light forms for parts of smaller buildings. *Open-web joists,* using steel rods to connect top and bottom steel elements, commonly form the roof structures for one-story garages, shops, warehouses, and factories. In small houses, steel may show up as a single floor beam or in the form of the tubular steel columns often used in a basement to support a main floor beam. Steel construction offers minimal obstruction to interior space and has been a primary force in the increased openness of modern planning. The only major rival of steel in modern building is reinforced concrete.

543. A vast train shed of iron and glass, Victoria Station in London of 1861 embodies the mid-nineteenth-century enthusiasm for the new industrial materials, which, along with modern engineering techniques, for the first time made possible wide-open spans and glass roofs. (Photograph: John Pile)

544

Concrete

The material concrete was known to the ancient Romans but then forgotten and not rediscovered until the eighteenth century. Made up of cement, sand, and small stones mixed with water, it hardens into a stonelike solid. This is *mass concrete,* the material of road surfacing and of the concrete block that is a favorite modern masonry material. Mass concrete, however, has little value as a major structural material, because of its weakness in dealing with tensile stresses. Only with the invention (in 1849) of *reinforced concrete* did concrete become a major modern structural material. Reinforced concrete is a hybrid material using steel rods embedded in concrete; the rods take tensile stresses while the concrete accepts compressive stress. This combination uses each material in the role for which it is best suited, resulting in economies and permitting structural design to exploit the variety of shapes that concrete can assume to suit each particular problem (fig. 545).

The first step in making reinforced concrete is building hollow, temporary, boxlike *forms,* usually made of wood, as molds into which concrete will be poured. Steel rods are placed in carefully engineered locations where tensile stresses are anticipated, and concrete is then poured into the forms surrounding the steel. When the concrete hardens, the forms are removed, leaving a structure of great strength, good economy, and inherent fire-resistance.

As compared with steel, concrete construction is more demanding of engineering design and, in the field, of labor, for form-building, reinforcement placement, and the processes of pouring, curing (hardening), and form-stripping. Its use of the cheap concrete material and reduced use of more expensive steel makes it economical in many situations. Deciding between steel or concrete as a primary structural material depends on careful calculations that take account of labor and material costs in a particular location at a particular time.

Reinforced concrete is likely to be the system of choice where large special shapes spanning wide spaces are required; where planning calls for the irregular placement of columns in high-

544. Most steel construction is masked with finishing materials, but in this example of High Tech architecture the structure is exposed as a vital part of the building's exterior design. Centre Georges Pompidou, Paris, was designed in 1976 by Richard Rogers and Renzo Piano, who were selected in an international architectural competition. (Photograph: Marvin Trachtenberg)

545

To the practical goals of architecture in solving functional problems and developing suitable construction techniques, a third element is added: aesthetic values. To be viewed as well designed or beautiful, a building must go beyond purely technical success. This opens up the complex issues of critical evaluation. What makes a building beautiful? Even architecture critics and art historians hold major differences of opinion, and architectural history records constantly changing views about the aesthetic goals of the architect from one era to the next.

Lasting aesthetic values emerge from the communication of ideas of some depth and significance. The architect's aim is to make the viewer aware of the thought, the purposes, and the meaning that went into the creation of the work. In architecture, these underlying issues are expressed through the ways in which a building fulfills its function; the ways in which it is put together as a physical reality; and more complex ideas about the society, in its time and location, that give the building a context, the forces that have called for the building, and the constraints that molded its design.

Those aspects of architectural design that can be called aesthetic transform the simple practical reality of a building into something that is memorable—an image that can be held in the mind and that can speak of the ideas that made the design what it is. The uses for which Greek temples were built and the technology of their construction are all obsolete, yet the design of these buildings remains vitally communicative of the ideas and character of their architects and the whole society that brought them into being. A sense of medieval life is more readily discoverable in surviving castles, churches, and walled towns than in the reading of historical accounts of kings, battles, and similar factual data. A Georgian house communicates something about the eighteenth century, its people, and its life style. The same designs imitated today communicate nothing about modern life, its technology, its business, and its quality.

Finding appropriate visual expression for the constantly changing realities of modern life while providing for practical needs is the primary goal of both architects and interior designers. For the interior designer, an understanding of the aims of architecture and a recognition of the need for close cooperation between interior and architectural design professionals are essential. Realization that success in architectural design is dependent on a relation between building form and interior space is equally important to interior designers, architects, and all of the other professionals who contribute to interior completion.

rise buildings; and wherever labor costs are low compared with the cost of steel (for example, in less industrialized parts of the world). Even in buildings using steel as the primary structural material, reinforced concrete is often employed for certain elements, such as floor or roof slabs or foundation walls.

When concrete is used to fireproof steel members, it can be difficult to tell by simple inspection whether the structure is steel or reinforced concrete. Columns, beams, and slabs appear much the same in both systems. The architectural and engineering drawings used in the construction of all major modern buildings will, of course, reveal what structural system is in use.

Such striking open and flowing building forms as Frank Lloyd Wright's Solomon R. Guggenheim Museum in New York (figs. 546, 547) or Eero Saarinen's TWA terminal at Kennedy airport, New York, could hardly have been conceived without the availability of reinforced concrete.

545. Architect Auguste Perret made one of the earliest uses of reinforced concrete in the Ponthieu garage of 1905–6 in Paris. Reinforced concrete not only makes up the building's structure, it also serves as a decorative part of the exterior. It is employed here somewhat conservatively: the columns and beams resemble earlier architectural materials—wood, masonry, and steel. Here, however, the construction elements are made by pouring the concrete mix into forms, that is, molds in which steel reinforcing rods have been placed. (Photograph: Dr. Franz Stoedtner)

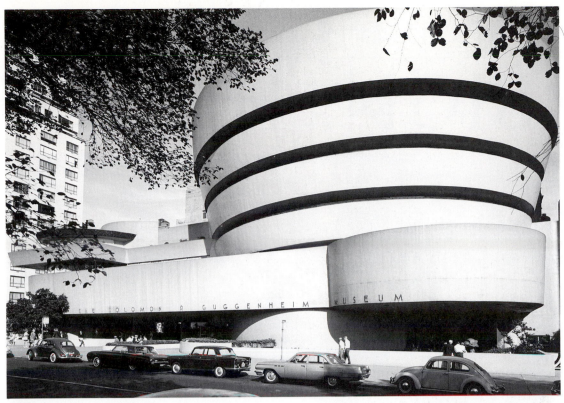

546

547

546, 547. A spectacular example of
reinforced-concrete construction, the
Solomon R. Guggenheim Museum in
New York (1956–59) was designed by
Frank Lloyd Wright, architect (fig.
546). The spiral ramp that dominates
the interior of the Guggenheim Museum
(fig. 547) is an outstanding example of
the expressive possibilities of reinforced-
concrete construction. (Photograph:
Roland Mates)

CHAPTER SIXTEEN
DESIGN HISTORY

The history of interior design draws upon several different fields of scholarly study. It is based in architectural history, but incorporates elements of the decorative arts, including furniture, metalwork, glass, ceramics, and textiles, which are often collected and displayed separately. Many books deal with one or another of these subjects, often emphasizing the interests of antiquarians and collectors over those of the practicing designer. For the interior designer, such fragmentation hampers an understanding of the unified way in which all of these things developed together in a particular historic period. Current interest in interior design history emphasizes understanding design as an expression of its own time and as a resource for stimulating new ideas.

A different approach treats historic interior design as a basis for modern imitation. This view of history, which has an extensive literature, was dominant from the end of the nineteenth century until well into the twentieth century. During that period, the study of interior design was largely a matter of learning the historic periods in order to adapt or imitate them in the interiors of the eclectic buildings of the time. While the leaders of modernism rejected this approach, they were usually devoted students of historical design. However, overenthusiastic followers, in their rebellion against imitative design, often seemed to encourage an indifference to historical study. The many educators among these followers passed this attitude down to their students.

Recent years have witnessed a renewed interest in historic design, not as a basis for imitation but as the foundation for a broad understanding of the lines of development that have led to current ways of thinking about design. Currently, designers are demonstrating a new willingness to make references to historic elements in a new, modern context. Even if references are sometimes picked up quite literally, the intention is never the direct imitation of whole rooms, or even whole buildings of the past. At the same time, there is a new interest in preserving and restoring historic buildings and interiors, work in which a detailed and precise knowledge of history is vital.

In the space available here, it is not possible to do more than give a general outline of the essential development of interior design, with names and terms important in describing historic work and the significant people who have influenced its direction. Reading in the specialized literature of architectural and design history—increasingly available in scholarly and well-illustrated books—is an important part of every designer's education. Visiting actual historic interiors, in museums and, especially, in surviving buildings, is the best as well as the most enjoyable way to become fully aware of historical design development.

PREHISTORIC AND PRIMITIVE DESIGN

It is not uncommon for the modern, sophisticated viewer to find greater interest in prehistoric and primitive design than in many of the familiar period works of the advanced cultures of the "civilized" world. Modern art has been strongly influenced by primitive art. While modern design may not have felt as deep an influence, there are often strong affinities between the directness of primitive design and the most respected of modern work. Weavings such as rugs and blankets, pottery and baskets and smaller household utensils from Africa, Oceania, and the Arctic and American Indian cultures are familiar examples of the kind of primitive design that seems vital and significant even in comparison with the best modern equivalents. There is little access, directly or through photographs, to the total interior in which such objects belong, but a sense of their complete environment can be generated from looking at both the individual objects and illustrations of the typical house structures.

THE ANCIENT WORLD *
Egyptian Design

The first major historic civilizations appeared in Egypt and in the Tigris-Euphrates valley in Asia Minor. Knowledge of interiors from the latter region is fragmentary because the primary building material was unfired mud brick of poor lasting quality. Egypt, however, has left lasting visual evidence of its design because many temples and tombs were built of stone, some even cut into solid rock, and have survived well. Temples are characterized by the vast *hypostyle hall,* a large space filled with rows of columns to support stone roofing, the forms of the stone columns based either on earlier columns of bundled reeds plastered with mud or other plant forms. The Egyptian custom of carving and painting walls with written and illustrated inscriptions gives further information on the ancient Egyptian environment.

Tombs have yielded up a wide range of objects, including furniture in good states of preservation, placed inside to accompany the body into an afterlife (fig. 549). The interiors of more everyday structures, such as houses, do not survive, but miniature models found in some tombs give an idea of the setting of Egyptian daily life (fig. 550). They suggest spaces with only minimal furniture, lively color in wall decoration and

Dates of the major cultural periods and design movements are given in the chronology on page 463.

548. *The eruption of Mount Vesuvius in* A.D. *79 buried the city of Pompeii in lava, which preserved a remarkable variety of ancient Roman remains. The atrium of the house of Menander, circa* A.D. *70, is an excellent example of Roman residential design, with its central* pool *and opening to the sky, its fine Roman Doric columns, and its partially surviving wall frescoes. Private living spaces open off the atrium on all sides. (Photograph: Deutsches Archäologisches Institut, Rome)*

woven materials, and, where they occur, the treatment of columns as strong decorative elements. Interiors were closely connected with the out-of-doors through open loggias and courtyards, even parts of rooms open to the sky with only cloth awning protection. The light and simple furniture, much of it folding and portable, could be extremely elegant, with fine proportions, restrained carved ornamentation, and, sometimes, colorful painted details.

Greek Design

Greek art and design is widely admired as a high point in aesthetic achievement. The Greeks built important buildings in stone but used wood for roofing, with the result that ancient Greek buildings survive only as ruins. Combined with such artifacts as pottery decorated with painted imagery, these ruins give a sense of early Greek interiors. The restored portions of the palace at Knossos on Crete (circa 1600 B.C.), including the great staircase with its columns and the throne room with wall painting decoration, present a vivid picture of early Greek design (fig. 551).

It is the later historic, high civilization of Greece that produced the famous temple architecture that has had such extensive influence throughout subsequent design history. The typical Greek temple is a simple, windowless, rectangular enclosure either surrounded by columns on all sides or with a front portico using columns designed according to a codified system called an *order*. The three major orders, Doric, Ionic, and Corinthian (each named for the supposed place of origin), are characterized by a particular column design and a well-standardized system of detailing the cornice (or *entablature*) above, which ornaments the stone lintels spanning from column to column (figs. 552–54). The details seem to be based on a translation into stone of an earlier system of wood building.

The simple Doric order has an austere column with no base and a plain block capital. It is usually considered strong, pure, dignified, perhaps the most beautiful of the orders. The Ionic order, with its spiral, voluted capital, is sometimes described as feminine, gracious and charming as compared to the sturdy and restrained Doric. The Corinthian order displays a more elaborate capital with acanthus-leaf decoration. In comparison with the others, it seems rich and elaborate.

Plans of ancient Greek houses can be reconstructed from excavated ruins (fig. 555), while knowledge of Greek interior design and furniture is surprisingly complete as a result of its frequent, detailed representation in vase paintings. The generally simple rooms used restrained moldings and details borrowed from the architectural systems. Strong color appeared in textile

549

550

549. The throne of Tutankhamen, from circa 1300 B.C., was discovered in the Pharaoh's tomb in 1922. Although it is elaborately carved and decorated to suit its ceremonial purpose, it exhibits the features of a classic Egyptian chair, most notably, the carefully joined wood-frame structure and seat. The open seat frame supports a woven-rush surface. The animal feet of the chair are raised slightly in order to remain visible above the rush floor covering used in most Egyptian interiors. Egyptian Museum, Cairo. (Photograph: Jean Vertut)

550. Our knowledge of the typical Egyptian house derives from beautifully detailed and painted models that were sometimes placed in tombs. This model of the house of Meket-Re, from circa 2000 B.C., shows a mud-brick house at the rear of a walled garden with a central pool. The columns, of bound papyrus reeds plastered over with mud, are painted in strong, bright colors. A hanging cloth and painted walls round out a characteristic color scheme. Metro-politan Museum of Art, New York. Museum Excavations, 1919–1920; Rogers Fund, supplemented by a contribution of Edward S. Harkness

551. The Queen's Chamber in the Palace of Minos at Knossos, Crete, dating from circa 1500 B.C., has been extensively restored. The columns, originally of wood (now replaced with stone), exhibit the downward tapering form typical of this time and place. They are

551

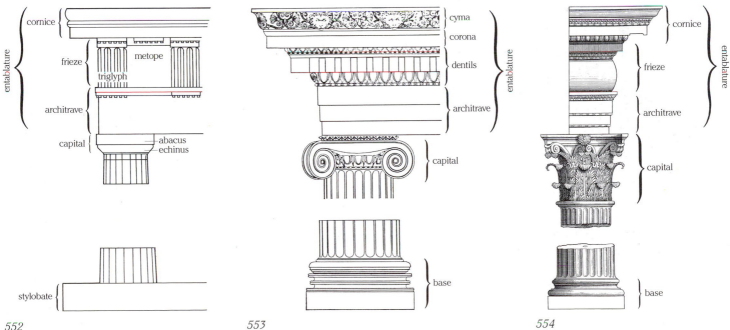

552

cornice

entablature

frieze · metope

triglyph

architrave

capital · abacus · echinus

stylobate

553

cyma

corona

dentils

entablature

architrave

capital

base

554

cornice

entablature

frieze

architrave

capital

base

painted black with red capitals. The Doric order, which emerged much later, may have evolved from this type. The restored wall paintings are based on traces of the original frescoes. (Photograph: Hirmer Fotoarchiv)

552–54. The three orders of architecture as developed by the Greeks are systems of columns and related details for use both outside and inside temples, as well as nonreligious structures. The

Greek Doric order (fig. 552), the simplest of the three, is often regarded as the most beautiful. The column has no base and simply rests on the three-stepped platform stylobate (continuous base). The entablature, which spans from column to column, is made up of three sections called, from top to bottom, architrave, frieze, and cornice. (Drawing after Grinnell) The Greek Doric frieze alternates panels called triglyphs and metopes. The famous Elgin

Marbles (British Museum, London) are the carved metopes from the Parthenon.

The Ionic order (fig. 553) is characterized by the spiral volutes of the column capital. Each column has a square base as well. In this example, from the Temple of Athena Polias at Priene, Turkey, circa 440 B.C., the entablature omits a frieze. The use of dentils and egg-and-dart moldings as decorative details is typical. (From Priene, by T. Wiegand and H. Schrader, 1904)

The third Greek order, called Corinthian, became a special favorite of Roman architects. This example (fig. 554) is a Roman version from the fourth-century San Giovanni Laterano in Rome, as illustrated in Palladio's The Four Books of Architecture of 1570. The elaborate column capital decorated with carved acanthus leaves is the identifying element of the Corinthian order.

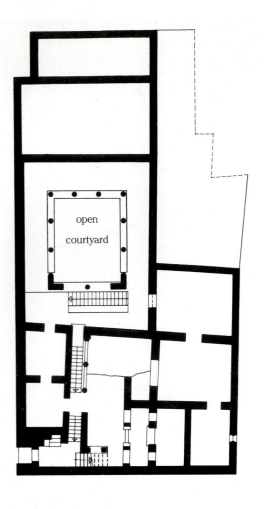

555

556

elements such as hangings, cushions, and coverings. Lesser utilitarian objects such as cups, dishes, and vases probably provided important decorative accents. The chair type called a *klismos* is characteristic of ancient Greece (fig. 556). Its outward-curving legs suggest that animal horns may have been a precedent, a form that is inappropriate structurally when translated into wood. Extended, the same basic design generated a couch or a bed. Tables and chests were of simple form, with unostentatious, often colored decoration.

Roman Design

After their military conquest of Greece, the Romans took over Greek concepts of art and design and, with their typically Roman energy, practicality, and engineering skill, made them their own. Roman architecture employed the Greek orders with certain changes, especially in the Doric order, modifying its proportions and adding a base. The Romans seem to have preferred the rich Corinthian order, and they adopted it as a favorite part of Roman design. Among their constructional innovations were an extensive use of good-quality brick and

concrete, arch construction, vaulting, and domes, which, for the first time, permitted buildings roofed over in masonry. Many Roman temples survive in good condition; the domed interior of the Pantheon (A.D. 120–124) remains a fine example of a monumental Roman interior (see figs. 539, 540).

The eruption of Mount Vesuvius in A.D. 79 served to preserve, by burying, entire neighborhoods in Pompeii and Herculaneum, providing an extensive knowledge of more modest Roman interiors. Houses were planned with rooms surrounding a central courtyard, or atrium, open to the sky (fig. 548). Larger houses may have had more than one such court, which supplied all or most of the building's light, since rooms had few or no windows. The more luxurious houses commonly displayed elaborate wall decoration using both marble inlays and painting, typically in black, gilt, and the shade of red often called *Pompeian* (fig. 557). Wall paintings were generally realistic, and their representation of everyday scenes gives information about furniture and other decorative details. The technique of mosaic became highly developed and provided decorative treatment of floors.

555. *A typical Greek house had rooms arranged around a central courtyard, a plan that became the norm of residential design in Mediterranean regions until modern times. This example is the House of Hermes at Delos, second-century B.C. From Roland Martin,* Living Architecture: Greek

556. *Accurate knowledge of ancient Greek furniture design comes from the detailed images that appear on painted vases and plates. The chair here, with its curved and splayed front and back legs, is a typical example of the* klismos. *The vase dates from circa 440 B.C. (Photograph: Alison Frantz)*

557

557. The walls in the Ixion Room of the House of the Vettii in Pompeii (A.D. 63–79) are decorated with frescoes, including some highly realistic perspective effects of architectural subjects. The colors are the typical dominating Pompeian red and black. (Photograph: Copyright by Leonard von Matt, Switzerland)

The books of Vitruvius—the first systematic handbook of architectural practice, written in the first century B.C.—were translated during the Renaissance and provided codified data about the orders of architecture. Roman architectural design, known from the surviving (and ruined) major buildings, from the excavation of lesser, domestic buildings of Pompeii and Herculaneum, and through Vitruvius's books, has had a recurring influence in the design work of Western societies, an influence that continues to be exerted, through both direct imitation (in buildings such as the old Pennsylvania Station in New York City; see fig. 601) and a more subtle and indirect incorporation of such concepts as symmetry and order in planning in the basic approaches to architectural thinking.

THE MIDDLE AGES

The decline and eventual breakup of the Roman Empire led to a comparable collapse in the Roman classical traditions of design. The lack of a strong central governmental force left Europe in a state of political anarchy and social misery. Religion took over as the central focus in almost every aspect of life, and design was almost exclusively at its service.

Medieval developments can be considered under four stylistic designations, the first two relating to the remaining aspects of Roman traditions, the latter two representing the formation of a new tradition destined to lead gradually toward the modern world.

Early Christian Design

As Christianity gained official acceptance, churches began to appear as a significant building type. The Roman court building called a *basilica* became the model for the Early Christian church, a central space with flanking aisles permitting a clerestory (a high, windowed wall) to light the central space. Arches and columns based on Roman practice were used, but their detail is less classical (in the sense of academically accurate) and systematic, with fragments of Roman orders used in an improvisational way; some of the fragments were bits of carving simply taken from older Roman buildings. The art of mosaic became a major decorative device for geometric floors and walls and in pictorial representations of religious subjects. The best examples of Early Christian work are in Rome.

Byzantine Design

Byzantine architecture developed from the Roman model after Constantinople became the capital of the Roman Empire in A.D. 330. It, too, is primarily a church-building development that employs Roman structural techniques and details along with an

559

elaborate mosaic decorative art. Byzantine building includes major domed structures, such as the famous Santa or Hagia Sophia in Constantinople (532–37), and reaches a level of elaboration and richness beyond the characteristic austerity of Early Christian work (figs. 558, 559). The Byzantine style returned to Italy to produce such buildings as the churches and tombs at Ravenna and San Marco in Venice (1063–94).

Romanesque Design

In spite of its name, Romanesque design has less connection with Roman architecture than do the styles described above. It is the style of the early Middle Ages, from about A.D. 800 to 1200 in Europe and, under the name Norman, in the British Isles. Surviving buildings, built in stone, are mostly churches, monasteries, and castles, the last the new building type so characteristic of the Middle Ages.

The typical feature of Romanesque stone structures is the semicircular arch and vault, a remnant of Roman structural technique. Monasticism produced a large number of building complexes, many surviving in reasonably good condition. In these, simplicity became a matter of religious conviction as well as a practical necessity, creating churches, chapter houses, cloisters, and dormitories with interiors of great beauty, emphasizing spatially impressive structure, minimally decorated (fig. 560).

Early medieval castles were often simple tower houses built in easily defended locations (fig. 561). Existing interiors with stone floors and roofs reveal such details as stone window seats at the small slitlike window openings, fireplaces for heat and cooking, and the generally unornamented functional character

558. The most spectacular of Byzantine interior spaces, the vast nave of Hagia Sophia in Istanbul, circa 532–37, is crowned by a 100-foot dome on pendentives. The pendentive is a curved, triangular element, introduced to fit a round dome over a square space be-

neath it. The original gilded and mosaic wall decoration, with its typical intricate and complex motifs, has been partially obliterated, but the overall richness and complexity remain impressive. (Photograph: Hirmer Fotoarchiv)

559. A detail of a column capital at Hagia Sophia displays the Byzantine interpretation of surviving memories of a Roman Ionic or stylized Corinthian order. (Photograph: Hirmer Fotoarchiv)

560

561

of Romanesque design. Furniture was minimal, partly because of undeveloped standards of comfort and partly because castle occupants moved from one location to another, maintaining their authority in the territory under their control through presence. Thus, the typical inventory of household fittings included plank-on-trestle tables, benches and stools of simple design, demountable, portable beds, trunklike chests for storage, and tapestries as wall coverings. Average people, the peasantry, had even less in the way of possessions and furniture of only the simplest sort.

Toward the end of the Romanesque era, larger churches began to show more elaborate decorative detail, and structural experiments in buttressed vaulting moved the style toward the development of Gothic architecture. Many buildings from the gradual transition period have earlier portions in the Romanesque style and later elements in the Gothic style.

Gothic Design

Gothic building is widely regarded as one of the great achievements of the Middle Ages. The characteristic feature of Gothic architecture is the pointed arch and vault, a technical development that made it possible to raise the height of the building and fill the walls with large window areas. At its peak, the Gothic cathedral became a skeletal stone cage with wall areas largely filled with stained-glass windows, which served as

560. *This austere interior of a Romanesque abbey church in Le Thoronet, in the southern French region of the Var, has changed little since its construction in circa 1175. The nave is roofed by a barrel vault, the aisles by half-barrel vaults. Only the very slight point of the almost semicircular arches foreshadows the later Gothic style. (Photograph: John Pile)*

561. *Although built near the end of the Middle Ages (circa 1519), the great hall at Cotehele, England, designed by Sir Piers Edgcumbe, retains the characteristics of the halls of earlier castles and manor houses, serving as the main living space for both domestic and ceremonial uses. Only minimal furniture and window detail soften the exposed structural stone walls and floor and wooden roof construction. (Photograph: © James Pipkin)*

both decorative art and illustrations of religious narratives (fig. 562). Sculptural carved detail was often used in the same way.

Castles and town fortifications survive in many locations, and some houses and other buildings of wood-frame construction (often with the exposed framing called *half-timber* work; see fig. 529), with interiors more or less as they were in the twelfth to fourteenth centuries, still stand. There is no typical medieval house plan. Layouts seem to have been improvised to suit site and function. Although complete rooms with furniture and lesser decorative details rarely survive intact, depictions of rooms in medieval art are often detailed and realistic in a way that makes it possible to visualize the Gothic interior quite accurately.

Decoration of Gothic stylistic character, with its ubiquitous pointed-arch forms, appeared in door and window moldings, around fireplaces, and in ceiling construction in a degree of elaboration that reflected the wealth and position of builders

and owners. Wood furniture of increasing quality, elaboration, and functional variety began to appear. Chairs and benches with designs that seem to derive from the simple box chest were made in considerable variety, usually with a frame of heavy members and thin inserted panels, generating the familiar appearance of *rail and panel* construction (fig. 563).

Considerable local variation in details gives Italian, French, German, and English medieval design their own unique qualities, while the Islamic influence makes Spanish work distinctive. The Crusades carried Gothic architecture and design into the Middle East and, in return, brought back into Europe an awareness of the art, design, materials, and techniques of that region. These varied influences combined to create the medieval design direction that can be thought of as the foundation on which all subsequent European design development has been based.

The influence is strong even in America, since the first

562

562. This view looking toward the west front in the nave of the Cathedral of Chartres (1194–1220) displays the Gothic arch, the ribbed stone vaults of the very high ceiling, and the color and light that shine through the stained glass—all elements of this most admired of medieval buildings. (Photograph: Hans Sibbelee, Amsterdam)

563

563. In the Middle Ages, the chair was an object with specific symbolic and ceremonial significance, denoting status or rank. This fifteenth-century French example is built up in a wood rail-and-panel construction derived from box construction. The tracery at the top relates the piece to Gothic architecture. Metropolitan Museum of Art, New York. Gift of J. Pierpont Morgan, 1916

settlers in the New World colonies brought with them traditions of European architecture and design that were formed in medieval times. The early Colonial house in America, with its heavy braced frame, similar to the typical North European half-timber building, and its minimal windows with leaded glass in small panes, is essentially a European late-medieval structure.

THE RENAISSANCE

Various changes and developments touching every aspect of Western culture and society led away from medieval ways of thinking toward the Renaissance. The Renaissance involved a new interest in the classical traditions of ancient Rome and Greece, a turning away from the domination of the Church and

its mysticism toward humanism, a more modern belief in the human ability to solve problems and deal with life in a rational way. A new, experimental attitude led to the beginning of modern science, the voyages of the early explorers, and modern ideas about trade and economic issues, all of which laid the foundations for the modern, industrialized, technological society of the twentieth century.

In design, these developments had several direct results. Interest in surviving classical Roman structures and study of Vitruvius's text on architecture led to the introduction of classical ideas (including the orders) into design. The more rational, scientific way of thinking, applied to construction, initiated a series of technological innovations that led to the modern understanding of engineering as a basis for structural

564

564. In the grand salon on the second floor (piano nobile) of the Massimi Palace in Rome (by Baldassare Peruzzi, 1535), the Roman Ionic pilasters, the elaborate frieze and ceiling, and the details of mantel and door frames combine to suggest a re-created interior of ancient Rome. The classical statuary adds to the effect, while the sparse use of furniture is typical of such ceremonial Renaissance interior spaces. From Letarouilly on Renaissance Rome *by John Barrington Bayley*

565

565. The architecture of the interior of the Villa Foscari—also called La Malcontenta—by Andrea Palladio at Mira, near Venice, circa 1556, is elegantly simple, while Giambattista Zelotti's elaborate frescoes wittily introduce rich architectural detail in illusionistic perspective. Balancing the real door on the left is a painted open door at the right, from which a figure seems about to step into the room. The furnishings are modern. (Photograph: Evelyn Hoffer)

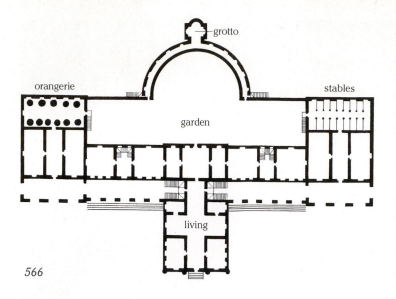

566

design. The invention and development of firearms made medieval defensive systems obsolete, eventually causing the castle to give way to the palace, château, and England's *great house,* although the houses and shops of the masses remained medieval in all but a few minor decorative details. The invention of printing, accompanied by an increase in literacy, accelerated the transfer of knowledge and made changes in the world of design increasingly rapid and extensive. At the same time, the changeover from the feudal system to more modern political and economic practices increased the variety of design requirements, with an emphasis on luxury and individuality of design.

Italy

The Renaissance began in Italy around the beginning of the fifteenth century and gradually spread north to France and England, then to other parts of Europe, including Germany, the Low Countries, and Spain, with a time lag roughly proportionate to the geographic distance. Art history customarily divides the Renaissance into three phases, early, middle (or High), and late (Baroque or Rococo). The term Mannerism, borrowed from the history of painting, is sometimes used to describe the transition from the High to Baroque phases in Italy.

EARLY RENAISSANCE. Early Renaissance work is characterized by a rather cautious application of classical Roman detail to buildings that are largely medieval in overall concept. Symmetrical planning appears in such buildings as the Florentine palaces (the Palazzo Medici-Riccardi of Michelozzo di Bartolomeo or the Palazzo Strozzi of Benedetto da Maiano, for example), which display a restrained use of classical moldings externally but a full use of Roman orders in the interior central

courtyards. The interior of the small Pazzi Chapel (begun circa 1442), usually attributed to Filippo Brunelleschi (1377–1446), gives a clear example of the way in which the detail of rediscovered Roman classical orders was used in Renaissance design. Such cautious introduction of Roman detail appears only in exceptional (and, in their own day, trend-setting) interiors as, for example, those of Brunelleschi.

While ordinary houses remained untouched by Renaissance ideas, the wealthy began to add decorative moldings, doors and door frames, and other details borrowed from Roman antiquity to the interiors of their houses and *palazzi.* Elaborate ceilings with structural beams made into patterns of squares (coffered ceilings), painted wall and ceiling decoration, and classical molding were often the main decorative elements in an otherwise simple room. Ceilings often included paintings, perhaps by major artists. Sculptural plaques or rondels (such as those of Della Robbia) appeared as wall decoration. Elaborate fireplace mantels began to include classical detail in their carving.

HIGH RENAISSANCE. The fully developed or High Renaissance moved toward a more sophisticated

567

566. *The plan of Palladio's Villa Barbaro at Maser appeared in a woodcut illustration in his influential* The Four Books of Architecture, *first published in Venice in 1570. The central living block houses a cross-shaped hall space with enclosed rooms (and stairs) at the four corners. The wings extend outward to farm buildings at left and right.*

567. *Renaissance furniture developed to suit the needs of an aristocracy with new and specialized functional demands —for the storage of varied objects of value and personal significance—and a taste for elaborate surface decoration. This walnut* stipo, *or cabinet, is made up of separable upper and lower sections for easy transport. The figures carved in relief are* bambocci, *or urchins. Florentine, sixteenth century. (Courtesy Sotheby's, New York)*

568. *The Italian Baroque at its most flamboyant is demonstrated in the huge baldachino under the dome of St. Peter's in Rome (begun 1624). Bernini's gigantic Corinthian columns are twisted and covered with decorative detail that almost conceals their Roman classical derivation. (Photograph: Copyright by Leonard von Matt, Switzerland)*

understanding of the concepts of Roman architecture with such consistently classical projects as the plan for St. Peter's in Rome by Donato Bramante (1444–1514), which would be altered and expanded over the following century. The modest-size Massimi Palace in Rome (1535) retains interiors in fairly complete states of preservation, while older engraved illustrations of these spaces give even more complete detail as to their design (fig. 564). Furniture was still used rather sparsely, in a manner reminiscent of medieval austerity, but there was a gradual increase in the variety and richness of furniture types (fig. 567). Classical detail, used with skill and confidence, provided wall decoration, moldings at doors and windows, fireplace mantels, and elaborately decorated ceilings.

The clarification and near-standardization of Renaissance design practice, as well as its geographical spread, were encouraged by architect-theorists such as Leon Battista Alberti (1404–1472) and Andrea Palladio (1508–1580). Both not only produced important work but also wrote illustrated books explaining their working methods. Alberti emphasized the mathematical and geometric basis of his designs while Palladio offered practical instruction along with illustrations of his own works, such as the Villa Rotonda (or Capra) at Vicenza (begun 1550) and the "Basilica" (begun 1549) in the same city, and accurate drawings of Roman architecture that formed the basis of his church designs, such as S. Giorgio Maggiore (begun 1566) and Il Redentore (begun 1576), both in Venice.

Palladian interiors are developed with the same sense of order and devotion to classical detail that governs the overall concepts of the buildings that house them. The churches use Roman architectural details for pilasters, cornice moldings, and door and window trim, usually in gray marble to contrast with the generally white wall and ceiling surfaces, thereby accenting form. The effect suggests that Palladio was trying to re-create, or at least make reference to, the great baths of ancient Rome.

Palladio's villas include many well-preserved interiors, which give an overview of his domestic work. The Villa Barbaro at Maser (circa 1555–59) has a main living area with a spacious cruciform central hall dividing the square plan, creating four large rooms in the four corners (fig. 566). The spaces are architecturally simple, but the walls are richly decorated with illusionistic paintings by Paolo Veronese in which architectural elements (arches, balustrades, doorways, trellises) frame scenes of distant landscapes. In the Villa Foscari at Mira (circa 1556), Giambattista Zelotti's frescoes include some doorways standing open with family members and servants, even a pet bird, looking in—all in trompe l'oeil painting (fig. 565). This kind of painted wall decoration suggests stage scenery.

Taken together, Palladio's work and books formed a demonstration of High Renaissance practice that became a basic model for classically oriented design for the next several centuries. Palladian influence can easily be traced to the American colonies, continuing to appear even today.

The urge toward systematic perfection so strong in the work of the High Renaissance gave way toward the end of the period to an interest in more experimental and personally expressive ways of designing. The term Mannerism is often applied to the style that marks a transition from the reserve and order of the High Renaissance to the elaboration of the Baroque, the third and final phase of Renaissance design. Mannerism is exemplified by such works as Michelangelo's Laurentian Library in Florence (begun 1524), with its extraordinary entrance hall and stairway. The architect used a classical order but pressed the columns back into recesses in the walls and filled the space with a great, exuberant stairway creating a dramatic sense of movement. Other interiors, such as the Palazzo del Te (circa 1526–34) of Giulio Romano (circa 1499–1546) at Mantua, similarly employed classical detail but introduced oddities, what seem to be mistakes (but are deliberate), and curious fresco paintings.

BAROQUE. Baroque, the term used for the third and last phase of the Renaissance, means, in everyday usage, elaborate or even overelaborate. The rich, sometimes excessive decoration of Baroque spaces led art historians of the last century to dismiss this work as decadent. Modern art historians have reinstated the Baroque as a significant phase, especially attracted to the Baroque interest in space, movement, effects of light, and sense of drama rather than its details of decoration. While classical detail was still used extensively, it was altered, even distorted, as in the spirally twisted columns of the Baldachin in St. Peter's in Rome (begun 1624; fig. 568) by Gianlorenzo Bernini (1598–1680). In smaller Roman churches, such as S. Carlo alle Quattro Fontane (1638–41) and S. Ivo della Sapienza (circa 1642–60), Francesco Borromini (1599–1667) carried Baroque ideas of spatial complexity to a further extreme.

The simple shapes—squares, circles, and rectangles—of the earlier, more restrained phases of Renaissance design gave way to more complex forms—ellipses, trapezoids, and spirals—in Baroque design. As these forms are developed in three dimensions and overlapped and interlaced, Baroque space takes on qualities of mystery and theatricality. It gives the effect of a richness that cannot be clearly comprehended but that vividly expresses drama, movement, and action. These design directions were encouraged and supported by the Counter-Reformation movement in the Catholic Church, where they joined with the other arts (including music) to make churchly events exciting and dramatic.

569

Central Europe

Over the next hundred years, Baroque ideas traveled north, reaching northern Italy in the work of Guarino Guarini (1624–1683) at Turin, in both churches and in secular buildings such as the Palazzo Carignano (1679–92), with its curving stairs and elliptical domed rotunda. Still later, Baroque concepts reached southern Germany and Austria and spread into Hungary and Czechoslovakia on the east and Switzerland on the west. Baroque churches by such architects as Johann Michael Fischer (1692–1766) and Johann Balthasar Neumann (1687–1753) are astonishingly complex and elaborate. German and Austrian palace architecture at the end of the seventeenth century and the beginning of the eighteenth combined Italian Baroque influences with the comparable French stylistic development, Rococo. Johann Lukas von Hildebrandt's Upper Belvedere Palace in Vienna (1700–23; fig. 569) and Neumann's Residenz at Würzburg (1719–44) are good examples.

France

In France, the Renaissance passed through the same three phases as in Italy, each occurring about fifty to a hundred years later than the Italian equivalent. The Early Renaissance in France appeared first in small details of ornament, door and window frames, and fireplace mantels in châteaux that are otherwise medieval in concept. Chambord (1519–47), the giant royal hunting lodge in the Loire valley, is full of classically derived detail and has a generally symmetrical plan, pointing toward growing acceptance of the Italian conceptual formality. The double spiral central staircase is a remarkable demonstration of geometric planning ingenuity. The much smaller château of Azay-le-Rideau is remarkable for its intact interiors, with furniture in place much as it must have been when the building was new (fig. 570).

With its square plan around a central court, symmetrical about both axes, the château Ancy-le-Franc, the work of the Italian architect Sebastiano Serlio (1475–1554), marks the arrival of a developed Renaissance style in mid-sixteenth-century France. By 1657 Louis Le Vau (1612–1670) was building the château of Vaux-le-Vicomte outside Paris (fig. 571). This building served as something of a model for the same architect's work for Louis XIV at Versailles, which was begun in 1661. Work continued there with Jules Hardouin-Mansart (1646–1708) succeeding Le Vau. The palace is a vast complex with many spectacular interiors, including a chapel, an opera house, and the famous Galerie des Glaces, or Hall of Mirrors.

570

570. A room in the château of Azay-le-Rideau (1518–27) in the Loire Valley retains a basically simple, medieval quality conveyed by the exposed wood ceiling beams. Italian Renaissance ideas are evident in the ornately carved fire-place with its classically inspired details. Fabric-draped walls and a curtained and canopied bed represent concessions to comfort. The demountable furniture could be adapted to specific circumstances.

571

572

571. This overwhelming, elaborately decorated bedroom was meant for the king, should he spend the night at the château of Vaux-le-Vicomte near Paris, built 1656–61 by Louis Le Vau. The painter Charles Le Brun and a team of plasterworkers and other artists produced an interior clearly based on Italian Baroque influences. (Photograph: Caisse Nationale des Monuments Historiques et des Sites. © ARCH. PHOT. PARIS/S.P.A.D.E.M.)

572. This room from the Hôtel de Varengeville, a town house on the boulevard St.-Germain, Paris, is a fine Rococo interior of about 1735. The soft color of the wood paneling and the rich gilded surface decoration are typical of the style. The central table, with its japanned lacquer finish and elaborate gilt decoration, was made in 1759 by the famous royal cabinetmaker Gilles Joubert (1689–1775) for Louis XV's private rooms at Versailles. Metropolitan Museum of Art, New York

573

574

Toward the end of the seventeenth century and in the eighteenth, French Renaissance design took on some of the character of Baroque design, particularly in the free and flowing use of curves. However, the last phase was more restrained in France than in Italy and Germany, meriting a different stylistic term, Rococo, to describe the elaborately decorative but classically ordered character of French Late Renaissance design. Such buildings as the Petit Trianon (1762–68) by Jacques-Ange Gabriel (1698–1782), among the finest examples of Louis XVI design, display a restraint and classical discipline characteristic of the Rococo style. The preserved salon from the Hôtel de Varengeville demonstrates how Rococo elaboration was adapted by aristocratic French society of the time (fig. 572).

Following the French Revolution of 1789, Rococo design shifted toward a more reserved and less florid direction, often called Neoclassic. The interior styles called Directoire and Empire (after the political developments of the time) introduced references to the styles of ancient Rome, partly as a result of interest in the findings of the excavations at Pompeii and, in the case of Empire work, partly to celebrate the exploits of Napoleon's era (fig. 573).

French Renaissance furniture and decorative elements are usually described with a terminology based on royal reigns, a reminder that these styles almost exclusively served royalty and the aristocracy, having relatively little impact on a wider public. French provincial furniture design, however, is a partial exception. In the seventeenth and eighteenth centuries, furniture makers of provincial France began to make everyday wooden furniture in simplified versions of French Renaissance "high

575

573. The French Empire style found its way to America with such craftsmen as the French-born and -trained Charles-Honoré Lannuier (1779–1819), who settled in New York and is believed to be the designer of this griffon-support console table (circa 1811). It is made of rosewood and ebony, with secondary parts of pine, poplar, and ash, and has gilded ornamentation and a marble top.

The Napoleonic decorative elements (eagles, wreaths, fasces) that give the Empire style its name were readily translated into symbols appropriate to the new federal government of the United States. 36½ × 42 × 18″. (Photograph: Helga Photo Studio, courtesy Bernard & S. Dean Levy, Inc., New York)

574. An oval library table of circa 1830 in the German Biedermeier style displays the style's characteristic combination of light, yellow-toned fruitwood and black edge trim. (Courtesy Didier Aaron Inc., New York)

575. The Long Gallery of Hardwick Hall, Derbyshire, England (1590–97), is a fine example of an Elizabethan great house interior, with its tapestried walls and strapwork plaster ceiling. The room runs the full length of the building, and the many large windows on the right flood it with light. The architect's identity is uncertain, but stylistic similarities to other buildings suggest Robert Smythson (circa 1535–1614) (Photograph: © 1985 James Pipkin)

576

style" prototypes. Such furniture, which struck a pleasant balance between simplicity and elaboration, has remained popular in France and is still widely collected elsewhere. (Unfortunately, the style has been abused by modern mass-produced imitations of poor quality, causing the term to become almost meaningless.)

The term Biedermeier designates German and Austrian furniture of the early nineteenth century based on French Empire design and interpreted by local craftsmen, who modified French design in the direction of traditional German peasant furniture. At its best, Biedermeier furniture can be simple, elegant, and handsome, with its use of various lighter woods and occasional painted (often black) detail (fig. 574).

England

English design of the Renaissance developed in a series of styles identified, as in France, with the reigning monarchs. Royalty did not influence design in any direct way, but designers, cabinetmakers, and other craftsmen seem to have felt that a change of rule offered a reason for introducing stylistic change that was already in the wind. Renaissance ideas first appeared in England in the sixteenth century during Tudor and Elizabethan times. Awareness of the new design developing in Italy came to England with travelers, with Italian craftsmen, and, indirectly, with craftsmen-designers from the Low Countries, where a somewhat modified version of Italian and Spanish design had appeared.

576. In St. Stephen's Walbrook (1672–79), one of Sir Christopher Wren's many London churches, a simple rectangular space becomes complex and visually rich, as the arrangements of columns, arches, and domes transform it into (in plan), in rising sequence, a *square, a Greek cross, an octagon, and a circle. This design may have served Wren as a preparatory study for St. Paul's Cathedral, Wren's largest and most famous work. (Photograph: Edwin Smith)*

The great house of Longleat (circa 1568–80), with its external symmetry and Italianate interiors, provides a complete example of Elizabethan Early Renaissance design. Robert Smythson (circa 1535–1614), one of several builder-craftsmen who seem to have acted as architects in this period, was probably responsible for Hardwick Hall of 1590–97, one of the finest of Elizabethan buildings to have survived (fig. 575).

A more sophisticated and consistent High Renaissance direction appeared in the work of Inigo Jones (1573–1652), who had visited Italy and was familiar with Palladio's work. He used a Roman temple concept for the English church of St. Paul at Covent Garden (1631), which presents an interior of classic simplicity characteristic of his other work as well.

Sir Christopher Wren (1632–1723) moved the Renaissance in England a step closer to the Baroque spirit. After the great fire of 1666 in London, he built a new cathedral of St. Paul, with its famous dome, and many small city churches. For these, Wren employed the classical vocabulary in a surprisingly varied way, each one a unique study in interior space and detail. St. Stephen's Walbrook (1672–79) is a particularly fine example (fig. 576). The building is crowded in among neighbors so that its exterior is scarcely visible, but its beautifully domed interior is one of Wren's greatest successes. Wren's work also included secular buildings; the Chelsea Hospital in London (1682–85), with its quiet brick exterior and handsome chapel and dining hall interiors, clearly influenced design in the American colonies.

Overall, the eighteenth century in England moved toward a more restrained and academic classicism, represented in buildings such as Lord Burlington's house at Chiswick (circa 1725–30), clearly based on Palladian precedents. The eighteenth-century style called Georgian developed a restrained and elegant way of using classical detail in large houses and in rows and squares of smaller city houses as well. Interior detail and furniture design exhibited some of the most admired of all historic work.

The famous English cabinetmakers Thomas Chippendale (1718–1779), George Hepplewhite (d. 1786), and Thomas Sheraton (1751–1806) became known for their fine products (figs. 577–80). The books they published illustrating examples of their work led to the development of styles in both England and America that take the names of their originators. The Adam brothers (James and Robert), working as architects, interior designers, and furniture designers, developed a personal style within the Georgian tradition based, in part, on Roman work as it was discovered in the excavations at Pompeii (fig. 582). (The excavation of Pompeii in the eighteenth century attracted wide attention in Europe and led to considerable imitation, more or less literal, in the decorative design fashions of that time.) Adam interiors such as the library at Kenwood (London, 1767–69), the drawing room at Home House (1772–73; fig. 581), or the sequence of great rooms at Syon House (1760–69), in their richness of color and delicate decorative detail, are among the most spectacular of eighteenth-century works.

577

578

579

577. This fine example of Thomas Chippendale's "ribband-back" side chair, of mahogany, dates from about 1755. The simple structure accommodates strong joints: for example, the section where the front legs meet the seat frame is larger than in other designs, allowing amply for joining. The carving, based on Rococo influences, converts the pristine form into something rich and elaborate. (Photograph courtesy Stair & Company, New York)

578. George Hepplewhite made these dining chairs in London about 1785, in both arm and armless versions, for a matching set of ten. The shield back is characteristic of Hepplewhite's work and that of his followers. These chairs are finished in black with polychrome decorative details. (Photograph courtesy Stair & Company, New York)

579. The style of Thomas Sheraton was more reserved than that of Chippendale, suggesting the Neoclassic influence of the Louis XVI style. His book The Cabinet-Maker and Upholsterer's Drawing Book of 1791–94 helped to make his style widely known. This mahogany chair was made about 1790. (Photograph courtesy Stair & Company, New York)

580

581

580. For his great house Stourhead, in Wiltshire, England (built 1718, reconstructed 1791–92), Sir Richard Colt Hoare commissioned Thomas Chippendale the Younger to refurbish the library in the high fashion of 1804–5. The result manifests the growing interest in Greek and Egyptian precedents that Chippendale discovered on a trip to Paris shortly before he undertook this project. His father's characteristic Georgian style here shifts toward the Empire of France. (Photograph: © 1985 James Pipkin)

581. The front drawing room (1772–73)—originally the music room—of Home House, 20 Portman Square, London, is a fine example of Robert Adam's unique style. To the period's Pompeian and French Rococo influences Adam added a particularly personal quality, especially evident in the unusual and elaborate decorative ceiling design.

582

583

584

THE UNITED STATES
Colonial Style

On the American continent, early settlers brought with them the design ideas from their former homes in Holland, France, Spain, and, of greatest importance, England. Colonial houses were generally modest and simple, almost medieval in character in that they were direct and functional with a minimum of decorative detail (fig. 583). Gradually, as the settlers became established and more affluent and were joined by newcomers of more aristocratic background, this early Colonial design vocabulary gave way to a version of more elaborate English style.

An American equivalent of eighteenth-century English Georgian design developed in which the influence of Wren and the great English cabinetmakers can be traced quite readily (fig. 585). Large houses such as Westover, Virginia (circa 1730), and the Governor's Palace in Williamsburg, Virginia (fig. 584), and churches such as Philadelphia's Christ Church (1731–44) adhered closely to the models provided by Wren and his contemporaries. Palladian details and academic classical design, learned from books imported from England, began to appear in buildings such as Thomas Jefferson's house at Monticello (1796–1809), clearly based on Palladio.

585

582. The work of the Adam brothers has always been admired for its bold and attractive use of strong color. This room by Robert Adam, removed from Lansdowne House in London (1762–68) to the Philadelphia Museum of Art, has recently been restored to the original colors, discovered under the many layers of paint applied over the years. Philadelphia Museum of Art. Given in memory of George Horace Lorimer by Graeme and Sarah Moss Lorimer

583. A bedroom of the Peter Wentz farmstead, built in 1758 in Montgomery County, Pennsylvania, and restored in 1971, exhibits the simple plaster walls, exposed wood structural ceiling, and uncurtained, double-hung window of its time and place. Below the chair rail, a surprising spotted pattern has been created with a paint-dipped sponge. (Photograph: Oberto Gili, courtesy House & Garden)

584. The Governor's Palace in Colonial Williamsburg, Virginia, dates from 1705–20 and was restored after 1930 (completed 1934). The classical Corinthian pilasters, paneling, and cornice trim of the dining room follow the Georgian English tradition, as do the furniture and details of ornament and table setting. (Photograph: Langdon Clay, courtesy the Colonial Williamsburg Foundation)

585. This highboy cabinet, made in Boston circa 1725 in the English Queen Anne style, is veneered in walnut and maple, the body made of pine. The ornamental detail is restrained, but the carefully matched veneers on the drawer fronts generate flowing, symmetrical patterns. $62\frac{3}{4} \times 40\frac{1}{2} \times 22\frac{3}{8}$". (Photograph courtesy Bernard & S. Dean Levy, Inc., New York)

586

Federal Style

The term Federal Style describes the furniture and interior design paralleling the architectural Greek Revival style in the newly independent United States around the beginning of the nineteenth century (fig. 588). The people of the young nation realized their government was the first democracy since the Athens of Pericles, inspiring an interest in the design of ancient Greece. While photographs were not available and travel to Greece was rarely attempted, such books as James Stuart and Nicholas Revett's *The Antiquities of Athens* (1762–95) made fairly accurate information about Greek architecture available. An effort to revive Greek architecture and adapt it to nineteenth-century needs produced many temple-like churches, public buildings, and even private houses (fig. 586). The interior design followed suit with related interior detail and furniture design suggested by images of Greek vase paintings. The American cabinetmaker Duncan Phyfe (1768–1854), well known for his designs based on the English Sheraton style, modified his pieces to reflect the Greek influence.

Gothic Revival Style

The Greek Revival was not confined to the United States. A parallel direction appeared in Germany and in England, and before long it led to a desire to revive other ancient styles. A Gothic Revival in both England and the United States followed on the heels of the Greek Revival, with many of the same architects simply shifting the sources that they imitated.

While Gothic architectural styles did not look out of place for churches, their application to hotels, public buildings, and houses produced many odd results (fig. 587). Gothic Revival furniture and interior design tended toward the curious and quaint. Its extension into simple country building led to the naive style called Carpenter Gothic. The term refers to country building with supposedly Gothic decorative detail added in the interest of fashion, with results sometimes charming, often simply amusing. The forms of pointed arches, tracery, and crockets ornamented ordinary household furniture. Houses and barns were decorated with forms vaguely resembling Gothic tracery cut out of wood by the increasingly popular scroll saw.

586. A watercolor rendering circa 1845 by the prominent New York architect Alexander Jackson Davis shows the double parlor of a New York City row house as it was to be furnished and decorated in the then-fashionable Greek Revival idiom. The Ionic columns and entablature have Greek echoes in the furniture; the side chairs are of the klismos *form seen in ancient Greek vase painting (see fig. 556). New-York Historical Society*

587

THE VICTORIAN ERA

The drastic changes wrought by the Industrial Revolution affected every aspect of life. In design, the modern world of mechanized production began to push aside the traditions of handcraft production in which design was an integral part of the making of things. Factory-made products were designed not by the people who made them but by managerial or professional sources only indirectly aware of the actual processes of manufacture.

At the same time, the efficiencies of industrial production began to create a new class of consumers, a middle class able to afford a certain level of luxury, especially at the modest cost that industrial production made possible. This pattern of cheap industrial production feeding markets that sought out elaborately ornamented objects, now easily produced by mass-production techniques, fueled the typically Victorian middle-class love for decorative excess generated without any clear aesthetic intention.

Victorian design is characterized by a kind of flamboyant elaboration borrowing from any and all historical origins in order to create interiors that were rich, crowded, and, more often than not, stuffy and incoherent (fig. 589). There can be a certain naive charm in Victorian elaboration, especially as it merges, now, into nostalgia, and its frequent originality somewhat offsets its excesses. Gothic, Renaissance, even Moorish and Oriental influences jumbled together coincided with the development of clever inventions (folding, reclining, and convertible furniture) and new uses of materials such as cast iron and metal tubing. The swivel chair, the brass bed, iron lawn furniture, and bentwood products are all Victorian developments.

The Great Exhibition of 1851 in London, a showcase for Victorian overdecoration, was, surprisingly, housed in a structure that pointed the way to modern architecture. This was the Crystal Palace, designed by Sir Joseph Paxton (1803–1865), built with a structural framework of iron and a glass skin in prefabricated parts, factory-made and assembled rapidly on site (fig. 592). This famous structure bore no resemblance to any

587. Lyndhurst (built 1838, renovated from 1864), a Gothic Revival mansion overlooking the Hudson River near Tarrytown, New York, is a markedly different example of the work of Alexander Jackson Davis, who designed the Greek Revival interior in fig. 586. The occu-pants of this dining room could imagine themselves to be characters in one of Sir Walter Scott's Romantic novels set in the Middle Ages—even though the atmosphere, with its dark, rich clutter, is more Victorian than Gothic. (Photograph: Bob Bishop)

588

earlier building, and it was a great popular success. After the exhibition ended, the building was dismantled and reassembled at Sydenham on the (then) edge of London, where it remained until destroyed by fire in 1936.

The Arts and Crafts Movement

While visiting the Great Exhibition, William Morris (1834–1896) found himself distressed by the quality of the objects exhibited there, and he felt impelled to become something of a design reformer. He believed the degradation of Victorian design lay in the separation of the design process from handwork in the industrial production of goods, eliminating the craftsman. He urged a return to handwork using materials honestly and with restrained and artistic decorative detail. Morris's critical writings and lecturing interested a group of followers who made up what

came to be known as the Arts and Crafts Movement.

Morris established a firm that sold Arts and Crafts products and took on interior design assignments (fig. 590). He himself designed textiles, wallpapers, some furniture, and many small objects. For textiles and wallpapers, Morris tended to concentrate on decorative surface designs. He used dense, allover patterns based on leaf, flower, and, occasionally, bird forms that were unusually respectful of their natural origins and accurate in their representation of detail (see fig. 155).

Morris's followers included architects and artists as well as what would now be called interior designers. Some of his followers concentrated on simple, well-crafted furniture and accessories while others were fine artists whose work was often incorporated into furniture designs. A chest or cabinet might carry a large and richly detailed pre-Raphaelite painting as frontal decoration. As these elements were combined in

588. The Greek Revival Roper Mansion of circa 1830 in Charleston, South Carolina, has been carefully restored with historically appropriate furniture and decorative details. In this bedroom, the warm gray walls have been painted with joints and veining to resemble stone. The Empire chair with gilded swan arms once belonged to the empress Josephine. The temple-shaped clock is Second Empire. (Photograph: Karen Radkai, courtesy House & Garden)

589

589. In 1894, this Victorian gallery in the New York home of Mrs. William Astor housed her collection of paintings. Far from being a neutral setting in which the art collection stands out, it is filled with lamps, a large chandelier, rugs, draperies, and furniture—all intended to create a sense of opulence. The actual paintings, displayed in tiers that rise far above eye level, seem to be no more than additional accessories. Photograph: Museum of the City of New York. Byron Collection

590

591

interiors, the effect often suggested the medieval style, but the work was never strictly imitative in the manner of the Gothic Revival.

In post–Civil War America, Morris's Arts and Crafts Movement, its name shortened to Craftsman Movement, formed the basis for what is often called the Mission or Golden Oak style (fig. 591), typified by the furniture of Gustav Stickley (1858–1942),

592

590. William Morris's firm, Morris & Co., produced the Green Dining Room in 1867 for the newly built Victoria and Albert Museum in London. The inclusion of stained-glass windows by the Pre-Raphaelite English painter Edward Burne-Jones demonstrates the Arts and Crafts Movement's aim to unify art, design, and craft. (Photograph courtesy Victoria and Albert Museum, London)

591. Gustav Stickley's Craftsman workshop, United Crafts, at Eastwood, New York, built this sideboard (circa 1906–10) from quarter-sawn white oak. Morris's Arts and Crafts ideals are evident in the clean lines of this honestly made furniture, with only hand-hammered copper hinges and pulls for decoration. $50\frac{1}{4} \times 70 \times 25\frac{1}{2}$". (Photograph courtesy Jordan-Volpe Gallery, New York)

592. Sir Joseph Paxton (with contractors Fox and Henderson and glaziers Chance and Company) produced, in 1851, what is often considered the first truly modern building, with its elegantly functional, prefabricated iron-and-glass structure. It housed the extravagant Victorian display that made up the Great Exhibition, an early type of world's fair, held that year in London. The illustration, a contemporary lithograph of Joseph Nash, shows the exhibition in progress. Victoria and Albert Museum, London. Crown copyright reserved

593

which found wide popularity around the turn of the century (see fig. 201).

Charles Eastlake (1836–1906) promoted some of Morris's ideas in his book *Hints on Household Taste*, published in England in 1868 and soon circulated in the United States as well. It is a manual urging the householder to accept quality and simplicity in preference to Victorian elaboration. Curiously, Eastlake's illustrations showing his own designs now seem as ornate as any other Victorian work. Many American interiors of the era display Eastlake-style woodwork in such elements as door and window frames and fireplace overmantels.

Morris's views, which continue to be influential, were eventually adapted by later designers involved in the development of modern design. The work that he and his followers produced remains some of the best of the Victorian age.

Shaker Design and Adirondack Furniture

A source of simple and restrained design that ran counter to the general Victorian love of elaboration came from the religious communities of the American Shaker sect. From the latter part of the eighteenth century through the nineteenth, this group formed colonies that built villages of great simplicity and beauty. Interiors were furnished with products designed and made by members in a functional, direct, and dignified style that hints at the direction that modern design was to take in the twentieth century (fig. 593). Shaker furniture and other products were sold to outsiders and gained considerable popularity, suggesting that Victorian taste was not restricted to the overelaborate style of the more commercial products of the

593. *The inspired simplicity of American Shaker design, exemplified by the Elders' Room of the Brick Dwelling House, Hancock Shaker Village, Pittsfield, Massachusetts (circa 1825–50), derived from religious belief rather than design theory. The bare floors, white walls, and hand-crafted, solid-wood fur-* *niture evince an aesthetic that is surprisingly modern in spirit. The peg strips allow the broom, clothing, and even chairs to be neatly stored. The small iron stove is remarkably fuel-efficient. (Photograph courtesy Hancock Shaker Village, Pittsfield, Mass.)*

time. Shaker products are now admired and valued antiques.

Another furniture design direction that stands outside the main line of development has come to be known as Adirondack furniture. The term describes rustic designs, usually of hickory left as natural sticks or logs—even, perhaps, with the bark left on—manufactured primarily by the Old Hickory Chair Company of Indiana, founded in 1898 (fig. 594). The stylistic term emerged from the popularity of the furniture for the rustic summer homes and lodges built in the Adirondack region by wealthy city dwellers.

ART NOUVEAU

In continental Europe, an aesthetic movement known as Art Nouveau surfaced at the end of the nineteenth century. Its primary bases were in Belgium, with such designers as Henri Van de Velde (1863–1957) and Victor Horta (1861–1947; fig. 597), and in France, with Hector Guimard (1867–1942). While the movement included art and architecture, it was particularly in interior design and in the design of furniture and smaller objects that it came into its fullest development. Art Nouveau is characterized by the abandonment of all historical references (which made it the first truly original style in a very long time), by adventurous exploration of new forms, and by the use of a rich and original vocabulary of decoration based on the curves and flowing lines of natural forms. Art Nouveau, like the Arts and Crafts Movement in England, revealed an awareness of Japanese design in its simple, flowing lines and freedom of form.

The movement spread rapidly, becoming known as Jugendstil in Germany and the Scandinavian countries, and it influenced

594

594. The term Adirondack Style is now applied to the rustic design of American camps and lodges built as far from the Adirondacks as the Pacific Northwest. Massive stone fireplaces, logs with their bark still intact used as structural members, and furniture made of tree branches are typical of the style. Color stays within a range of browns and grays. This living room, in the main lodge of Kamp Kill Kare on Lake Kora, New York, was built circa 1916–20. (Photograph: Adirondack Museum, Bluemountain Lake, N.Y.)

595

596

the work of Charles Rennie Mackintosh (1868–1928) in Scotland (see fig. 198) and Antonio Gaudí (1852–1926) in Spain (fig. 596). Each of these men developed a highly personal style quite unlike anything else that was being produced in their respective home cities of Glasgow and Barcelona, but with visual qualities that can now be seen to parallel closely the Art Nouveau of Belgium and France.

Art Nouveau design was strongly fashion-oriented, and its sudden rise in popularity was matched by its sudden decline and virtual disappearance by the dawn of World War I. Subsequently, Art Nouveau was generally dismissed as an eccentric fad; only in recent years has it been rediscovered and become an object of study and admiration.

Vienna Secession
In Vienna, a parallel new style directed toward the modern world arose. The Vienna Secession movement was begun by artists and designers who found the policies of the traditional academy too restrictive. In response, they set out to establish their own gallery. Josef Olbrich (1867–1908) designed their building, built in Vienna in 1898–99, in a style that mixed a certain symmetrical classicism with an original decorative vocabulary similar to Art Nouveau, although generally less curvilinear and more geometric in feeling. The work of Otto Wagner (1841–1918), Olbrich's teacher, included the Postal Savings Bank in Vienna (1904–6), with its steel and glass banking room. Josef Hoffmann (1870–1956) became best known for his Palais Stoclet of 1905 in Brussels, a large house with elaborate interiors in the innovative Secession vocabulary (fig. 597). Hoffmann's furniture and various decorative objects are highly original and give what is often called Vienna Moderne its special quality. Adolf Loos (1870–1933) pushed even closer to modernism in his work, which, at least in some examples, demonstrates his much quoted dictum, "Ornament is a crime."

597

595. The Art Nouveau designer Victor Horta developed every element and detail of the dining room of the Hôtel Solvay in Brussels (1895–1900) in the original Art Mouveau style, with forms based on nature's flowing curves. Furniture, fireplace mantel, window frames, light fixtures are all Horta's work, designed specifically for this project. (Photograph: Dotreville, Brussels)

596. The striking imagination of the Spaniard Antonio Gaudi is manifest in the dining room of a Barcelona apartment in a building Gaudí reconstructed in 1904–6 as Casa Batlló. The unusual forms of window and door woodwork, the curious twin columns, the ceiling rosette and hanging light fixture, and the custom-made furniture are all characteristic of Gaudí's work. (Photograph: MAS Barcelona)

597. The dining room of Vienna Secessionist Josef Hoffmann's Palais Stoclet in Brussels (1905) incorporates Hoffmann's own designs for rug, furniture, lighting, and ornamental silver pieces, with twin mural paintings by Gustav Klimt. The Wiener Werkstätte shops produced the decorative elements used throughout this elaborate mansion. (Photograph: Studio Minders, Ghent)

598

598. The work of the American Louis Comfort Tiffany is often associated with Art Nouveau. References to nature forms are obvious in this dragonfly table lamp from the early 1900s. The base, which encloses the fuel canister that feeds the original wick, is decorated with five dragonflies among arrowhead leaves and flowers on a mosaic ground. The colorful glass of the shade is a fine example of the Tiffany idiom. Height 18". (Photograph courtesy Christie's, New York)

599

Art Nouveau in the United States

In the United States, Art Nouveau and related influences can be traced in the decorative designs (lamps and glassware) of Louis Comfort Tiffany (1848–1933; fig. 598) and in the architecture and interior design of Louis Sullivan (1856–1924). Sullivan holds a complex role in design history. He was viewed as the first modern architect because of his use of steel-frame construction and glass, expressed as a design element in tall buildings. (He took the quotation "form follows function" as his guiding principle.) At the same time, his nature-based decorative vocabulary placed him closer than any other American to Art Nouveau (figs. 599, 600). Sullivan employed Frank Lloyd Wright and became his mentor before Wright established an independent practice. This connection forged a close link between Sullivan and the beginnings of the twentieth-century movement toward modernism.

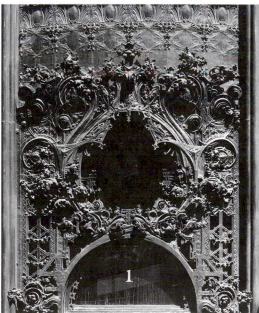

600

599. The Auditorium Building (so called because of the opera house at its center) of Chicago was designed by the firm of Dankmar Adler and Louis H. Sullivan (1886–89). The dining room shown here, in the adjacent hotel wing, has interior design by Sullivan himself. The floral decoration suggests an Art Nouveau influence. (Photograph courtesy Chicago Historical Society)

600. The elaborate decoration around the lower-floor windows of the Carson Pirie Scott Store in Chicago, a Louis H. Sullivan design of 1901–4, was actually detailed by George Elmslie, his young apprentice. The decorative vocabulary, however, is Sullivan's, and shows the influence of Art Nouveau on his work, which, at the same time, was developing in modern, functionalist directions. (Photograph: Sandak, Inc.)

601

THE TWENTIETH CENTURY

Four men—the American Frank Lloyd Wright and the three Europeans Walter Gropius, Ludwig Mies van der Rohe, and Le Corbusier—are now generally recognized as the key pioneers of modernism in architecture and design. Many others contributed significantly to the development of modernism, but any one of these four leaders alone might have taken design in that direction.

At the same time that they were developing their new style, most of the design in Europe and the United States followed the traditional historical styles.

Eclecticism

The ideas of Sullivan and Wright did not find wide acceptance in the United States of the early twentieth century. At the Chicago World's Fair of 1893, Sullivan's Transportation Building was considered more strange than beautiful, while the other buildings, of pseudo-Roman classical design, were greatly admired. American architects often went to France to study at the Ecole des Beaux-Arts and came home trained to produce buildings designed in the style now called Beaux Arts in recognition of its origin; the Paris Opera House by Charles Garnier, built 1861–75, is a fine example, with its rich overlay of

601. The majestic main concourse of the original Pennsylvania Railroad Station, New York, was inspired by the ancient Baths of Caracalla in Rome. Built in 1904–10 from designs by McKim, Mead and White, the terminal incorporated functional iron-and-glass train sheds (out of sight through the arch on the left) and eclectic borrowings from historic precedents. (Photograph: Geo. P. Hall & Sons, 1911, courtesy Museum of the City of New York)

602

603

602, 603. The pioneer professional decorator Elsie de Wolfe, in an 1898 renovation, brought about a dramatic change in the New York row house she occupied with Elisabeth Marbury. In 1896 (fig. 602), the dining room was the picture of late-Victorian and Edwardian stuffiness and clutter. With only fresh paint, some new furniture, and the elimination of extraneous bibelots, the 1898 interior (fig. 603) achieved the relatively clean, simple look that De Wolfe favored throughout a long career. Photographs: Museum of the City of New York. Byron Collection

florid, classically inspired decorative detail inside and out.

Most important buildings designed in America before World War II were influenced by the Beaux-Arts imitative way of working, often called Eclecticism. The word means "borrowing from many sources," and this was the leading characteristic of eclectic design. A museum or courthouse might be Roman in origin, a church Gothic or Romanesque. New York's Pennsylvania Railroad Station (1904–10; fig. 601) was designed by the firm of McKim, Mead and White in imitation of the Roman Baths of Caracalla! A style was chosen to suit each particular project; banks were often Greek or Roman, schools Tudor Gothic, clubs Renaissance palaces, private homes small châteaux or Georgian mansions. Modern steel structure was often concealed by the period-style exterior.

Interior design was expected to follow along, providing historically believable decoration in whatever style suited the building or the taste of the owner. The profession of interior decoration became focused on the ability to create rooms furnished with antiques (genuine or imitation) and related details in one of many styles. A somewhat degraded version of American Colonial interior design became a particular favorite in residential works.

The most positive development of the eclectic era in interior design was the emergence of a specialized profession called, at the time, interior decorating. Elsie de Wolfe (1865–1950) is often considered to be the first truly professional decorator (figs. 602, 603). Her clients were mostly wealthy New Yorkers, her work generally confined to tasteful borrowing from the historic periods. Her 1913 book *The House in Good Taste* served to popularize her thinking, which went far beyond stylistic imitation to probe more basic questions about aesthetic goals, even suggesting simplicity as a design objective. Her work opened the way for other decorators, such as Nancy McClelland (1876–1959), Ruby Ross Wood (1880–1950), Rose Cumming (1887–1968), and Dorothy Draper (1889–1969), who similarly adapted traditional styles to their clients' modern needs. The work of such designer-decorators as T. H. Robsjohn-Gibbings (1905–1976), Edward Wormley (b. 1907), and William Pahlmann (b. 1900) in the 1930s and 1940s had its roots in the style-oriented professional practice developed by the first wave of eclectic decorators.

Frank Lloyd Wright

Wright (1867–1959), building on the guidance of Sullivan, began early in the century to produce houses such as the Roberts house of 1908 and the Robie house of 1906–9 (figs. 605, 606) that, with their total rejection of historical references and their introduction of open and flowing interior space, define some of the primary directions of modern design. Concerned with every detail of the interiors of his buildings, Wright designed built-in furniture and lighting and, where the client would permit, movable furniture (fig. 604), even rugs as well. His interest in and respect for the character of materials recall the Arts and Crafts Movement. He always used wood in a natural finish and had plaster painted in its own cream-white color tones. These natural color tones, along with the natural colors of brick and stone (where they occur), created a soft, warm, natural color tonality, often enlivened by a strong, bright red, Wright's favorite accent color. He introduced more bright colors through inserts of stained glass in windows, in geometric patterns. Wright did not hesitate to use ornamentation in an abstract, geometric vocabulary.

Wright might be said to have had two careers, one up to 1915, when he left the United States for Japan to work on his Imperial Hotel in Tokyo (completed 1922), the second after his return to the United States. Much of his later work exhibits his awareness of traditional Japanese design (fig. 607). He produced a large body of work, including many houses (Fallingwater, a country house in western Pennsylvania of 1937, is probably the best known; fig. 608) and a variety of larger buildings with extraordinary interior spaces. The S. C. Johnson office building in Racine (1936–39; fig. 609), the Price office

604

604. Frank Lloyd Wright's swivel chair designed for the Larkin Company Administration Building (Buffalo, 1904), of painted metal and oak, represents an early effort to develop a chair suited to the modern office in both functional and aesthetic terms. Height 37½". The Museum of Modern Art, New York. Gift of Edgar Kaufmann, Jr.

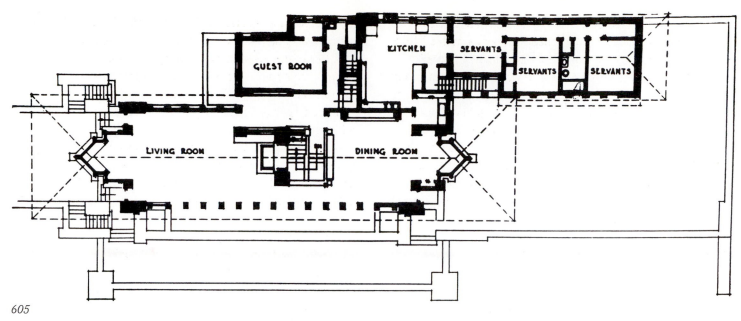

605

606

605, 606. Whenever his clients permitted it, Frank Lloyd Wright acted as his own interior designer. In the dining room of the Robie house (Chicago, 1906–9), his extraordinary table and chair group, built-in cabinets and shelves, lighting, ceiling treatment, carpet, and stained-glass windows together create a harmonious unity (fig. 606). While this early photograph suggests a gloomy massiveness, light and bright color actually prevail. In the plan of Robie house (fig. 605), the dining room appears at the left end of the main living space. A continuous ribbon of windows stretches across the front of the building; living and dining areas flow into one another, divided only by the freestanding fireplace and stairway. Decks and roofs on either side extend the long horizontals of the building. (Photograph: Chicago Architectural Photo Co.)

607

608

607. In his use of modular dimensional elements, simple geometric forms, and natural materials, Frank Lloyd Wright was strongly influenced by traditional architectural and interior design of Japan, exemplified by this interior, a work of the late sixteenth century by Nishi Hougan-ji.

608. The interior of Fallingwater, the famous house built for Edgar J. Kaufmann at Bear Run, Pennsylvania, by Frank Lloyd Wright (1936), combines warm colors and richly textured natural materials, which produce a remarkable sense of richness and comfort. Low ceilings and a strong horizontal emphasis are typical of Wright's residential work. (Photograph: Wayne Andrews)

tower in Bartlesville, Oklahoma (1953–55), and the Solomon R. Guggenheim Museum in New York (1956–59; see figs. 546, 547) suggest the scope and variety of Wright's later work.

As in his earlier work, Wright controlled, insofar as possible, every detail of interior design. His interest in ornament, while it grew more restrained, set his work apart from the International Style developing in Europe, giving it a much more personal, occasionally even eccentric feeling. The selection of materials, each used in its particular natural color, still controlled the interior's overall character, with the tones of brick, stone, plain concrete, and natural woods dominating (see fig. 357). A strong, bright red continued to be used as an accent color. Some of Wright's furniture designs move away from the craft-related use of wood. For example, the office furniture for the Johnson project employed painted steel as a primary material. However, the circle-related forms (even the desk drawers are round!) made his design distinct from standard factory-made products.

Walter Gropius

In Europe, meanwhile, modernism emerged in the work of three pioneers, all of whom had worked around 1911 in the office of the German premodernist Peter Behrens (1868–1940) and had probably become familiar with Wright's early work through its publication in Holland and Germany. Gropius (1883–1969), one of this famous threesome, is probably best known through the

609

609. The Great Room, or general office space, of the S. C. Johnson and Son, Inc., administrative office buildings in Racine, Wisconsin, was designed by Frank Lloyd Wright, 1936–39. The mushroom-shaped concrete columns make up most of the roof, with glass set between them to form a skylight ceiling. The furniture, which Wright designed especially for the project, remains in current use. (Photograph: Wayne Andrews)

610

influence of the German design school called the Bauhaus, established under Gropius's direction at Weimar in 1919 (fig. 611). The Bauhaus taught design in conjunction with modern art. In its design, spaces took on a quality related to the abstract character of the current painting and sculpture (Cubism and related movements). Ornament came solely from the visual effects created by combinations of materials and colors. The goal was to unify art and technology, creating an aesthetic suited to the modern mechanistic world by relating materials, form, and function in an abstract visual vocabulary.

The Bauhaus was a key influence on architecture, interior design, and industrial design in the 1920s and 1930s and, through the continued influence of its teachers and students, onward into recent times (fig. 610). The austere and unornamented "functional" modern interior with its tubular metal furniture and color palette of black, white, neutrals, and primary colors can be traced to Bauhaus origins.

After the closing of the Bauhaus in 1932, Gropius's influence continued through his work in England and, subsequently, in the United States, as well as through his leadership of the architectural department at Harvard University from 1937. Under Gropius's direction, Harvard became the first American design school to accept the ideas of the modern movement.

De Stijl

The Dutch movement called De Stijl (after the name of the magazine that was its mouthpiece) defined directions similar to those of the Bauhaus and had close connections to the work of the painter Piet Mondrian and the sculptor Theo van Doesburg. Gerrit Rietveld (1888–1964) is the best-known De Stijl designer, with his constructivist sculptural Schroeder house of 1924 in Utrecht (fig. 612) and his geometrically abstract furniture (see

fig. 203). The furniture of Marcel Breuer (1902–1981), developed at the Bauhaus, seems to parallel De Stijl thinking, although there was no direct link between the two centers (see fig. 251).

Ludwig Mies van der Rohe

The second major pioneer of modernism, who knew Gropius through their shared tenure in Behrens's office, Mies van der Rohe (1886–1969) followed Gropius as director of the Bauhaus in its final years. Mies tended to relieve the austerity of his work with rich materials, including onyx marble, travertine, chrome-plated steel, and natural or black leather (see fig. 240). The term Bauhaus style refers to either the austerity of Gropius or the richness of Mies's vocabulary of interior color, finish, and detail, or it can include both.

Mies van der Rohe's influence stemmed less from his academic positions than from his architectural design. The German pavilion at the Barcelona Exposition of 1929 (fig. 613) and the Tugendhat house of 1930 in Brno, Czechoslovakia, gave striking demonstrations of the modern view of interior space as

611

610. This teapot designed and made by Marianne Brandt in 1924 at the Bauhaus combines the clean geometry of machine-production with a craft aesthetic (in the flowing form of the handle). Nickel silver and ebony, height 3⅝". Manufactured at the Bauhaus metal workshop, Germany. The Museum of Modern Art, New York. Phyllis B. Lambert Fund

611. The director's office of the Weimar Bauhaus, designed by Walter Gropius in 1925–26, was furnished with a rug, wall hanging, and lighting created in the Bauhaus workshops and furniture of Gropius's own design. Here, the abstract qualities of modern art met the machine-inspired, unadorned simplicity of the Bauhaus aesthetic, to create a space characteristic of the developing International Style. (Photograph: Bauhaus Archiv)

612

613

612. The upper level of the Schroeder house, its main living floor, in Utrecht (1924), is one of the few complete examples of a De Stijl interior. It is the work of Gerrit Rietveld, an architect best known for his constructivist approach to furniture design. As in a Mondrian painting, the colors are restricted to white, black, and the three primaries. (Photograph: Die Neue Sammlung, Munich)

613. Perhaps the most famous of all modern interiors, the German pavilion at the 1929 Barcelona Exposition was demolished after the fair, but was reconstructed from the original plans in 1986. Shown here as originally built to Ludwig Mies van der Rohe's design, the pavilion combines travertine marble floors, polished-steel columns, and screen walls of glass and polished marble, rich materials characteristic of Mies's style. The Barcelona chair and ottoman are regarded as classic pieces of the modern era. (Photograph: Berliner Bild-Bericht, Berlin, courtesy The Museum of Modern Art, New York. Mies van der Rohe Archives)

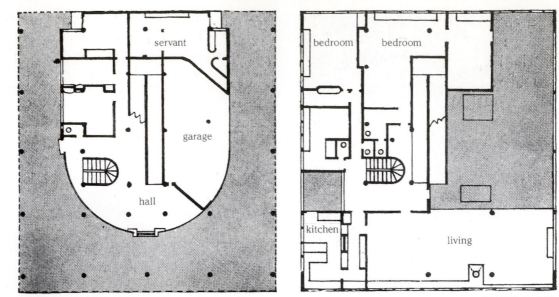

614   FIRST FLOOR   SECOND FLOOR

615

614–16. In the Villa Savoye, Poissy, France, of 1929–30, Le Corbusier (Charles-Édouard Jeanneret), with Pierre Jeanneret, created a vastly influential example of International Style modernism. The main living space (fig. 615) unifies outdoor and indoor areas by means of a rolling glass wall that allows the resident to define the flow of space. The nondescript original furnishings in this rigorously modern building reflect the unavailability of anything more appropriate at the time the house was built. (Photograph: Lucien Hervé, Paris) The new flow of space is apparent in the plans of the ground and main living floors (fig. 614). The main block of the house is lifted on columns, while

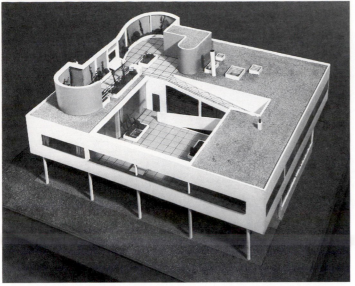

616

open and flowing, without division into boxlike rooms, without historical reference or applied ornamentation. Mies moved to the United States in 1938 to head the architectural school of the Illinois Institute of Technology, at Chicago. His phrase "less is more" is often quoted to summarize his design philosophy. He continued to influence modern design, producing a number of the major buildings of the 1950s and 1960s.

Le Corbusier

Although actually Swiss, Le Corbusier (Charles-Edouard Jeanneret, 1887–1965) is usually thought of as a French modernist, since most of his career was based in Paris. His influential book *Towards a New Architecture* of 1923 made him the primary theorist and publicist of the ideas of the modern movement, even before he had produced any major body of work. In his work of the late 1920s and 1930s, he demonstrated his conviction that the aesthetic of engineering (of ships, airplanes, and industrial buildings) formed a sound basis for all design in the modern era. His work was always regulated by an orderly, mathematical modular system that gave a special power and dignity to his design.

The Villa Savoye at Poissy-sur-Seine (1929–30), with the main block of the house elevated to the second-floor level on columns, is a good example of his work, shocking when it was built but now a respected key monument of the modern movement (figs. 614–16). Le Corbusier's early interiors generally shared the simplicity, austerity, and Cubist geometrics of Bauhaus design, although his use of color was somewhat more adventurous, perhaps drawing on his distinguished work as an abstract painter. He used not only strong primary colors but

the garage, entrance, and service space make up the small enclosed portion of the lower floor. A finely detailed exhibition model (fig. 616) was made of the house, in wood, aluminum, and plastic, 25½ × 22½ × 11⅛". The Museum of Modern Art, New York. Exhibition Fund

also tints (pink and blue) and secondaries—greens and oranges—and applied them in large, simple areas.

Because no modern furniture was available when the first Le Corbusier projects were designed, older, simple products, such as bentwood café chairs and plain restaurant tables, were often selected. Later, in cooperation with Charlotte Perriand (b. 1903), Le Corbusier developed furniture designs using steel tubing, leather cushions, and table tops and cabinet fronts of solid color (see fig. 250). Some of these designs continue in production and have come to be called *classic modern*.

After World War II, Le Corbusier's work changed in character, becoming less geometric and more sculptural or organic. The pilgrimage church at Ronchamp (1950–55) demonstrates this shift and also offers one of the finest religious interiors of the twentieth century (see figs. 525, 526).

The term International Style came to be used for the geometrically based, unornamented, and rather mechanistic work of the European pioneer modernists.

Art Deco

At about the same time that the International Style was developing, a more commercial and fashion-oriented kind of modernism was appearing, now usually called Art Deco. It had its origins in post–World War I France (fig. 618), where influences from primitive art and Cubist painting and sculpture combined with modern motifs such as electric power, radio, and skyscraper building (fig. 617). Ornament was accepted, but it was a modern ornament of stepped and zigzag forms often

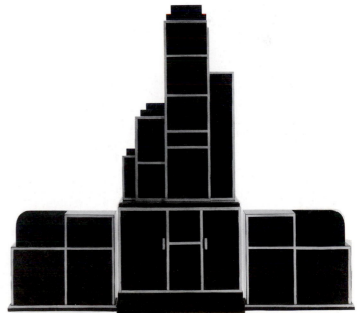

617

617. The Skyscraper bookcase, designed c. 1928 by Paul Frankl in black-lacquered wood with silver-lacquered front edging, refers explicitly to the skyscraper architecture of the period in its nonsymmetrical center element with its active setback forms. Setback and zigzag motifs are favorite elements of Art Deco design. (Photograph courtesy Phillips, New York)

618

619

618. This Art Deco bedroom by Paul Ruand (Paris, 1933) is furnished with semicircular Bibendum armchairs, a cube bed, and a decorative screen, all designed by Eileen Gray. With its African stool and zebra skins resting on a glass floor, the room exhibits an imaginative mix of Art Deco and more puristic, abstract geometric modern trends.

619. Tourist-class accommodations on the French ocean liner Normandie were modest only by comparison with those of first class. This smoking room is paneled in polished walnut with decorative inlays; the upholstery is red leather. Maison Marc Simon, designer, circa 1935. Photograph: Museum of the City of New York. Byron Collection

620. The meticulously preserved Art Deco lobby of the Pantages Theater, Hollywood (1929–30), displays the flamboyant forms and color of architect E. Marcus Priteca's decorative fantasy. Such modernistic design stands in striking contrast to the streamlined reserve of the International Style then developing. (Photograph: Carl Iri)

621

associated with the rhythms of jazz music, introduced more for commercial, fashion-oriented reasons than from any theoretical intent. This style became a favorite for theaters and exhibition buildings and was often used for public spaces, office building exteriors, and apartment buildings (fig. 620). New York's Chrysler Building (1930) and the structures of Rockefeller Center, including Radio City Music Hall (1931 and after), are rich in Art Deco detail. This style also had some popularity in England and, to a lesser extent, in other European countries. It was the decorative style of the interiors of some of the last great ocean liners, such as the *Normandie,* the *Queen Mary,* and the *Queen Elizabeth* (fig. 619).

Another influence in the 1930s came from the introduction of streamlining in dirigible and airplane design. The rounded shapes of streamlined aircraft were taken up by the practitioners of the new profession of industrial design and adapted to trains, automobiles, furniture, and even such unlikely objects as refrigerators and pencil sharpeners (see figs. 33, 34). Industrial designers produced interior design work—most often for trains, ships, retail stores, and showrooms—using some mixture of Art Deco and streamline styles.

Postwar Modernism

After World War II, professional design work by both architects and interior designers settled into a vocabulary of modernism largely based on the work of the prewar pioneers. The influence of Gropius and Mies as teachers combined with a widening acceptance and admiration of modern work led to the adoption of *functionalism,* or the International Style, as the basis for most public and commercial work (fig. 621). The availability of furniture design classics by the European leaders and a full range of more recent furniture and related products by postwar designers made the modern interior readily available everywhere. Modernism was far less widely accepted in residential interior design, which, for the most part, clung to imitations of traditional styles, with some limited inclusion of the craft-oriented Scandinavian furniture design often called Danish Modern.

FUTURE DIRECTIONS

In the 1970s and 1980s, several challenges to modernism have surfaced. Since this is a field for ongoing development, even struggle, it is not surprising that the several differing directions

621. In the 1950s, modernism's diverse influences came together in America in a widely accepted idiom easily adaptable to the facilities of large corporations. Florence Knoll Bassett, head of the Knoll Planning Unit, designed this executive reception area (1954–57) *for the offices of the Connecticut General Life Insurance Company in Bloomfield, Connecticut. Skidmore, Owings & Merrill were the architects. (Photograph: © 1957 Ezra Stoller/ESTO, courtesy Skidmore, Owings & Merrill, New York)*

622

High Tech

A somewhat different direction with a basis in modernism has come to be called High Tech. It places more emphasis on the exploitation and visible display of elements of science and technology, particularly the advanced technologies of the computer-oriented, aerospace, and automated industrial fields. Early modernism was closely allied with technology in its interest in the machine and its intention to create a design vocabulary suited to the modern, technological world. Devotion to the machine has gradually come to seem somewhat dated, a rather naive and romantic view of mechanization as the solution to every problem. High Tech design moves forward into the post-machine-age technology of electronics and space exploration to learn from the advanced technology of those fields and to search out an aesthetic in their products.

Prior steps in this direction can be found in the work of Buckminster Fuller (1895–1983), best known for the development of the geodesic dome structure, which has been used in many ways, including as the American exhibition pavilion at the Montreal World's Fair of 1967 (see fig. 478). Charles Eames (1907–1978) also hinted at this direction in his own house of

in competition for domination of future design work have engendered considerable conflict and confusion. The rather illogical term Post-modernism has been coined to describe whatever develops beyond the modernism of the recent past, but the term has come to be attached to a particular direction, only one of several quite different approaches. Whatever term is ultimately chosen, three distinct directions, each developing in a lively way, can be recognized and defined.

Late Modernism

Late modernism is a new term to define the most conservative of these directions. This work is firmly based on the modernism of the four famous pioneers, but it attempts to move forward into new forms, more adventurous and aesthetically more varied than the formula-like designs of the later generations of modernists. The work of I. M. Pei (b. 1917), such as the East Building of the National Gallery of Art in Washington, D.C. (1978), belongs to this category (fig. 622). The houses and other interior work of Richard Meier (b. 1934; fig. 628) and Charles Gwathmey (b. 1938; see figs. 153, 154, 200) also fall in a direct line of development from early modern roots.

622. The new (1971–78) East Building—popularly called the East Wing—of the National Gallery of Art in Washington, D.C., is a distinguished work by I. M. Pei & Partners. Stairs, landings, and decks lead to the various exhibition galleries, which overlook the main entrance area and central atrium. The simple geometric forms combined in complex angular relationships are typical of this architect's work. An Alexander Calder mobile forms a colorful focal point. (Photograph: © 1978 Ezra Stoller/ ESTO)

623

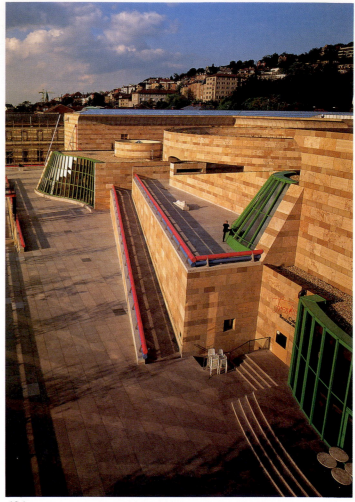

624

623, 624. The work of the British architect James Stirling is often described as High Tech. However, the Neue Staatsgalerie in Stuttgart, West Germany, by James Stirling, Michael Wilford and Associates, architects (1984), eludes easy classification: it is unique in its combination of High Tech, Post-modernism, and independent, creative directions. (Photographs: Timothy Hursley, © The Arkansas Office, courtesy House & Garden)

626. In this bedroom and related dressing area of a Palm Beach, Florida, home designed by Joseph Paul D'Urso in 1981, the rounded form of the divider between the spaces, the bare-bulb lighting, and the large mirrored area behind the twin beds point to High Tech, while the traditional furniture elements and an Oriental rug in the dressing area suggest a more eclectic approach. (Photograph: Tom Knibbs)

625. This kitchen is an example of the High Tech style in residential design. The sharp light of the helium-and-argon tubular fixture, the granite-covered counter tops, and the black-glass-covered appliances give this space, created by R. Scott Bromley and Robin Jacobsen for their own Manhattan loft in 1986, an individual, futuristic quality. (Photograph: Gilles de Chabaneix)

627. Early and late modern objects intermix with Memphis design in this living space in a West German home. The chair just visible on the left is a 1930s design by Alvar Aalto; the coffee table is a 1940s design by the sculptor Isamu Noguchi; on the coffee table stands a Columbina Descendens teapot and a Sherry Netherlands vase by Matteo Thun for Anthologie Quartett. The bookcase is by Ettore Sottsass. (Photograph: Peter Frank, courtesy Rainer Krause)

625

626

627

628

628. Richard Meier was the architect and interior designer for the Smith house in Darien, Connecticut, built in 1965–67 in the style now called Late Modernism. The simple, geometric forms and absence of ornament exemplify modernism's continuing dynamism. (Photograph: © Ezra Stoller/ESTO)

629

1949 (fig. 629), assembled from industrial building components, and in his well-known and widely popular furniture designs of 1946 onward (see fig. 212).

The mature style uses industrial materials, furniture, and equipment of technological character, simple forms, and little decorative or ornamental details (fig. 625). Its identification with advanced technologies tends to make High Tech work look futuristic. Architects and designers of this style include Renzo Piano (b. 1931) and Richard Rogers (b. 1933), whose Centre Pompidou in Paris (1971–77) has become an emblem of High

629. Charles and Ray Eames were the architects and interior designers for their home, built in 1949 on the Pacific Palisades near Venice, California. The double-height living room rises up to the open-web steel-joist structure and corrugated-steel roofing decking. Charles Eames was already famous at this time for his innovative furniture designs: the shelving and sofa—almost hidden under tigerskin and cushions—are his, but the rich mix of other materials and objects expresses the Eames' wide-ranging interests and tempers the industrial High Tech look. (Photograph: © 1984 Henry Bowles, courtesy House & Garden)

631

Tech (see fig. 544), and James Stirling (b. 1926; figs. 623, 624) and Norman Foster (b. 1935) in England. The work of the American interior designer Joseph Paul D'Urso (b. 1943), with its use of industrial and other mass-produced elements, is usually called High Tech, although D'Urso disavows any such narrow stylistic labels (fig. 626; see also fig. 467).

Post-modernism

The general term Post-modern has now come to identify one other new direction that grew from the theoretical position taken by Robert Venturi (b. 1925) in his influential book of 1966 *Complexity and Contradiction in Architecture*. In it, Venturi challenges the emphasis on logic, simplicity, and order characteristic of modernism, suggesting that complexity and ambiguity have a place in design. Following this dictum in his own work, Venturi has produced designs that sometimes seem

eccentric, disturbing, or banal (fig. 631; see also figs. 139, 254, 484, 485).

Post-modern design also departs from modernism in its willingness to include ornamentation and elements referring to historical styles. Such traditional elements are not intended to imitate past building styles but rather to act as references used out of context, often with humorous impact. Such *metaphors,* as these designers' figures of speech are often called, seem to question the seriousness of mainstream modernism. If the realities of the modern world sometimes seem to approach absurdity, Post-modernism offers us absurdities as serious creativity or, to look at this work in another way, presents serious work that can be viewed as absurd.

The American designer best known for Post-modern work (although he dislikes the term) is Michael Graves (b. 1934), whose witty and odd furniture and interior designs are now

630. Creeks Boutique in Paris, designed in 1986 by Philippe Starck, is a narrow and difficult space made usable and visually dramatic by its development in three levels, connected by a dramatic staircase. The wall on the left is mirrored *to enlarge the space visually and make the stair visible in its totality even to those walking up or down. The concept, clearly of the present, does not fit any one design direction. (Photograph: Tom Vack)*

631. In the dining room of Robert Venturi's Philadelphia home, which dates from the turn of the century, the owners have chosen to keep the original woodwork and leaded-glass cabinet doors. The stenciled walls and whimsical display of famous names above, the chairs of uncertain period, and the eclectic *collection of pictures and objects confer an inclusive, multifaceted personality on the space—a theme in the Venturi design theory that has informed the development of Post-modernism. Venturi, Rauch and Scott Brown, architect, 1983. (Photograph: © Paul Warchol)*

being joined by major architectural projects (fig. 632; see also figs. 79, 256). His Portland (Oregon) Public Service Building of 1980 has become one of the most controversial of recent building projects, attracting both extravagant praise and bitter condemnation. It is interesting to note that Philip Johnson (b. 1906), long a proponent of modernism in America, has moved toward Post-modernism in recent projects such as the A.T.&T. headquarters office building in New York (1984), with its references to Roman, Romanesque, and Georgian design elements.

In Italy, the group that uses the title Memphis has been energetic in developing furniture and interior design that share the Post-modern inclination toward arbitrary and whimsical uses of color and form (fig. 627; see also figs. 175, 227). Many designers in the United States have enthusiastically adopted this style.

The variety of different and often conflicting currents now running in the design world is characteristic of a period of change in which established norms seem to have outlived their usefulness while new norms have not yet taken clear form, similar to the Mannerist developments in Italy in the sixteenth century, when the established ascendancy of classical design systems came into question while the Baroque of the seventeenth century had not fully emerged. Mannerism was a style in transition, permitting experimentation, the testing of new and sometimes outrageous or extreme ideas, confusion, and rich development. If the present is also such a time, it is not surprising that untried and disturbing forms are emerging.

Living and working in design at such a time may not be as easy as it is in the middle of a well-established period, but the level of excitement and interest is higher. Public awareness of design issues and involvement in controversy increases at such a time and makes design a lively and vital field rather than a settled craft. The last decades of the twentieth century promise to become one of the most interesting of all historical design periods.

632

632. The Houston furniture showroom designed by Michael Graves, architect, in 1980 for Sunar Hauserman offers a stimulating setting for the display of modern furniture. An atrium-like space makes a Post-modern reference to classicism: paired columns support a simplified entablature that houses the indirect lighting. (Photograph: Charles McGrath)

TABLE 17. DESIGN CHRONOLOGY

Egypt *3100–311 B.C.*

Greece *650–30 B.C.*

Rome *753 B.C.–A.D. 365*

The Middle Ages
  Early Christian (c. A.D. 300–c. 500)
  Byzantine 323–1453
  Romanesque 800–1150
  Gothic 1150–1500

Italian Renaissance
  Early 1400–1500
  High 1500–1600
  Baroque 1600–1700

Spanish Renaissance *1400–1600*

French Renaissance and Later Periods *1485–1643*
  Louis XIV (Baroque) 1643–1700
  Régence 1700–1730
  Louis XV (Rococo) 1730–1760
  Louis XVI (Rococo/Neoclassic) 1760–1789
  Directoire 1795–1804
  Empire 1804–1815

German Biedermeier *1815–1848*

English Renaissance and Later Periods
  Tudor 1485–1558
  Elizabethan 1558–1603
  Jacobean 1603–1649
  Commonwealth 1649–1660
  Restoration 1660–1702
  Caroline (or Carolean) 1660–1689
  William and Mary 1689–1702

Queen Anne 1702–1714

Early Georgian 1714–1750

Middle Georgian (Chippendale) 1750–1770

Late Georgian 1770–1811
  (Adam 1728–1792)
  (Hepplewhite d. 1786)
  (Sheraton 1751–1806)
  Regency 1811–1830
  Victorian 1830–1901

American Early Colonial *1608–1720*
  Georgian 1720–1789
  Federal 1789–1830
  Greek Revival 1815–1840
  Victorian 1830–1901

Arts and Crafts *1851–1914*

Art Nouveau *1892–1905*

De Stijl *1917–1929*

Bauhaus *1919–1933*

Art Deco *1918–1939*

Modernism *1925–*

Post-modernism *1966–*

Note: Stylistic periods often have overlapping dates. Dates of royal reigns and dates of birth and death of individuals do not always correspond exactly to the related design periods.

CHAPTER SEVENTEEN
WORKING METHODS

"CLOVERLEAF"
TYPICAL LIVING-ROOM
LOOKING IN THROUGH WINDOWS

SHEET II
USONIAN HOUSES FOR THE USA PITTSFIELD MASS
QUADRUPLE SUN-DECK TYPE
FRANK LLOYD WRIGHT ARCHITECT

Every interior design project, no matter how small or simple, benefits from following a series of working steps that organize the designer's tasks. One of the striking differences between the amateur interior designer and the skilled expert is that the amateur tends to approach the project without any work plan. Making decisions without reference to a clear sequential order leads to revisions and mistakes. The end result often looks makeshift and poorly planned.

SETTING UP A WORKPLACE

Setting up a workplace where drawings can be made, samples and catalogs stored, and work in progress kept together is a wise preparatory step to the design process. A studio or office for design work alone is the best situation, but a corner of another room will serve. The essential piece of furniture is a sturdy desk or table for drawing. A drafting table made for the purpose is ideal, but a separate drawing board placed on a table or desk also works well and has the advantage of being portable so that it can be put away or moved easily. A large board on the sawhorses used for carpentry is an inexpensive way to make a drafting table. Drawing board or drafting table top must be large enough to accommodate the largest drawing to be made, preferably 30 by 50 inches, with 24 by 36 inches as a practical minimum.

A suitable chair or stool and good lighting are also needed. Windows give the best light, but a lamp will be needed for dark days and for evenings. The widely available adjustable Luxo lamp is a great favorite. The best version has a large reflector and a long arm and takes a 75- or 100-watt lamp (bulb). A large board may call for two Luxos. There must also be a straightedge whose length matches the width of the board. A T square is traditionally used for the purpose. Parallel rules attached more or less permanently to the board also answer this need. They may seem easier to use since, unlike the T square, they have no head (the crosspiece of the T square) to be held in place while drawing. The yet more elaborate drafting machine, highly favored for engineering drafting, is expensive and unnecessary for interior work but will serve well if available.

The other necessary tools and equipment are all fairly simple and inexpensive to acquire. Several will probably be found at hand already.

- TRIANGLES.   Two are needed, a 45° and a 30–60° of 8- or 10-inch size. A single adjustable triangle may be substituted.
- SCALE.   An architect's scale is needed. The triangular

variety with various scales along its three edges is the usual choice.

- TEMPLATES.   A circle-guide template is the most useful. A template with squares and hexagons in small sizes may be helpful, as will an ellipse guide with various ellipse shapes in a range of sizes. A furniture template with typical furniture units in plan at scale can be a convenience, as long as it does not tempt the user to avoid drawing furniture in more varied ways. Furniture manufacturers often give away templates for their own product lines.
- MEASURING TOOLS.   A yardstick, a carpenter's folding foot-rule, and a six-foot tape are essential. A hundred-foot tape may be wanted eventually.
- PENCIL SHARPENER.   A good crank-type is best, plus a small pocket-type for portability. An electric sharpener is a popular luxury.
- ERASER AND SHIELD.   Staedtler Mars No. 526 50 is the ideal plastic eraser. Bad erasers can damage or ruin a drawing and should be avoided. An eraser shield makes it easy to erase small details.
- MISCELLANEOUS ITEMS.   The board should be covered with sturdy paper or illustration board. An accessory metal edge for the board's left edge is helpful if a T square is used. A roll of drafting tape and a few thumbtacks and pushpins should be at hand. An adjustable curve or several French curves may be helpful, and a drafting compass may be needed occasionally. Drafting instrument sets in neat boxes, while attractive, will rarely be used and hardly justify their cost. Good scissors and a matte knife are vital.

Consumable materials can be acquired as needed. A basic stock for starting out would be the following:

- PAPER.   Tracing paper in rolls is most useful. Thin yellow (or canary) tracing paper is the norm for rough sketching. Twelve- or 18-inch rolls are convenient; stock plenty since it will be used in quantity. For more finished drawings, a good-quality white tracing paper in 36- or 42-inch rolls is standard. Avoid vellum papers. A pad of tracing paper and a white drawing pad may also be useful. Illustration board, in white on one side, gray on the other, is often used for presentation drawings and for color charts. Twenty by 30 inches is a convenient size.
- PENCILS.   Good-quality pencils are necessary. A few ordinary No. 2 pencils are useful, but drafting is usually done with special pencils that come in grades of hardness. Stock a few in grades H, F, HB, B, and 2B. Berol Turquoise is a good brand, Dexel Cumberland a fine

633. Perspective drawing helps planners—and users—to visualize spaces as they will appear in reality. Frank Lloyd Wright developed a unique and beautiful style for his architectural perspectives. This drawing illustrates the living space of one of the Usonian Houses he designed to be built in Pittsfield, Massachusetts, in 1942. (Photograph courtesy The Frank Lloyd Wright Memorial Foundation)

634

English alternative. Berol Draughting Pencil No. 314 is a
favorite for sketching (not, in spite of its name, for
drafting). A few colored pencils can be useful; a set in a
range of colors is a luxury. The Berol brand Prismacolor is
a good choice.

- *PENS.* Since ink drafting is rarely used for interior design
work in the United States, special pens and the technical
pen sets widely available are not needed. Felt-tip marker
pens, however, are widely used. A few thin-line markers
in black will be useful, and color markers are a favorite
sketching medium. Staedtler Mars 3000 series color
markers have a convenient flexible foam point and a fine
color range. A good fountain pen with nonclogging black
ink is a good sketching medium, but a disposable felt-
point pen can serve as well and is more convenient than
keeping a fountain pen in working order.
- *MISCELLANEOUS SUPPLIES.* Colored papers are often useful.

Color-Aid paper is a good brand; a book of samples is
available and full sheets can be bought as needed. Transfer lettering in a few styles may be helpful in making
neat titles. Duco cement is a good adhesive. Avoid rubber
cement. A box of single-edge razor blades is often useful.

Normal office supplies will also be needed from time to time.
Standard typing paper, lined yellow pads, index cards, file
folders, labels, tape, and similar supplies will be used
constantly. A good typewriter is basic to a working setup.
Papers, catalogs, and samples, which can expand to alarming
proportions all too easily, call for filing space. Drawings can be
rolled and stored in tubes until the quantity of work builds up
and calls for a flat file made for the purpose—an expensive
item. In another category, a camera, an exposure meter (built-in
or separate), a tripod, and photo lights will be useful. Almost
any kind of camera can serve, but the most versatile choice is a
35-millimeter single lens reflex.

*634. In this designer's office and studio,
drafting equipment, lighting, and storage
are all well placed to create effective—
as well as pleasant—working conditions. Note the generous work surface,
angled for efficiency. Charles Damga designed his own workplace in New York.
(Photograph: © Peter Paige)*

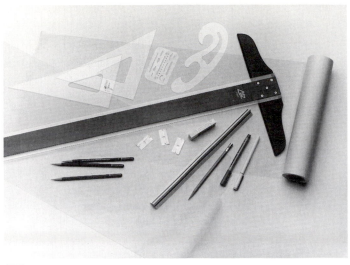

635

INTERIOR DESIGN DRAWINGS

With a workplace set up, tools and materials assembled, it is possible to turn to the most specialized aspect of interior design work, the making of drawings.

Everyone has made decisions about color choices or selected a piece of furniture and ordered it, and it is easy to understand how expanding such choosing, selection, and ordering to include everything that will make up an interior can turn into a complete project. Many such interior design steps actually rely on the everyday exercise of judgment combined with what might be called good business practices. Few people, however, have the training or skill to make drawings, especially the rather special sorts of drawings that the interior designer uses in planning and carrying out a project.

Drawings fall into two major categories. *Design drawings* develop the conceptual approach and visual form of a space. *Construction drawings* are made for use in taking bids and directing and controlling the work of contractor and workmen. Books and courses devoted to drafting, or (as it is often called in schools) mechanical drawing, are widely available. With a suitable book or two and the necessary tools at hand, it is possible to teach oneself to draw. However the skills are acquired, every interior designer will find some drawing ability helpful and useful.

THE DESIGN PROCESS

Every interior design project must be taken through a number of working steps in a logical order. The size of the project and the designer-client relationship will determine what steps are necessary. The simplest of projects—a single room, perhaps with the designer his or her own client—may hardly require any formal organization of work and may omit some steps that might seem overelaborate. Larger projects and projects that require client approval of design decisions call for more organization and systematization. In extensive projects involving many spaces and serving many people, orderly working methods are essential. They not only ensure efficient work processing, they also reassure corporate and institutional clients, who will certainly expect such methods.

For small projects, the designer may condense or even omit some steps, but even the smallest of projects will benefit if the designer goes through the basic working steps in a normal sequence.

Program

The first step of a working project involves determining the kind of work to be done and the needs and desires of the user or users. (See Chapter 4, pages 75–79, for a full discussion of the program.) The designer usually develops a general project statement and then conducts a survey (usually accomplished through interviews) to collect complete information on the client's requirements.

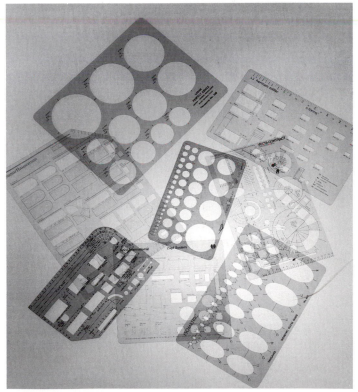

636

635. *The tools of the designer's trade include a T square, triangles, scale, French curve, eraser and eraser shield, an assortment of pencils, markers, and razor blades, and a roll of yellow tracing paper for sketching or preliminary drafting. (Photograph: George Hein)*

636. *Templates are employed in design and drafting to draw much-used forms to scale without measuring. Among the dozens available are circle and ellipse templates, shown here along with others provided by various furniture companies with cutouts geared to specific products. (Photograph: George Hein)*

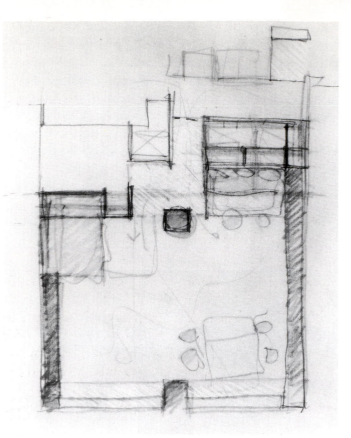

637

Space Allocation

Interview data can usually be translated into a listing of space requirements specifying rooms or other units in terms of approximate square footage. These area allocations, along with a list or chart of spatial relationships, form the basis of planning decisions. Before proceeding to any further design steps, obtaining an affirmative approval of a written program statement is recommended. Misunderstandings and contradictions dealt with at this point can eliminate possible future difficulties. This is also a good time to begin discussing budget considerations. While detailed budgets cannot be developed until later, the designer should discuss the client's budget limitations and deal with unrealistic expectations before they lead to future conflicts. Another issue to deal with is the assignment of project responsibilities.

> *How do interior designer, architect, consultants, contractor, and client share areas of responsibility?*
> *Who will select and deal with consultants, and how will payment be arranged?*
> *Will bids be taken for work? Who will select contractors and suppliers and approve their bids or prices?*
> *Who will provide on-site supervision of work, and how will responsibility for supervision be shared?*

638

637. This rough sketch, done in soft pencil on thin tracing paper, represents a living and dining area under development by interior designer Norman Diekman. Many such sketches are generated in the course of elaborating design ideas. (Courtesy Norman Diekman)

638. A perspective sketch by Mies van der Rohe shows a dining area on the left and living area on the right, as seen from an open court. The drawings of important designers and architects are often valued as works of art, collected and exhibited for their inherent beauty, as well as for their value as records of the design process. This drawing was part of a 1930 project for the Gericke house (unbuilt) at Wansee, Berlin. Pencil on illustration board, 19½ × 25½". The Museum of Modern Art, New York. Mies van der Rohe Archive. Gift of the architect

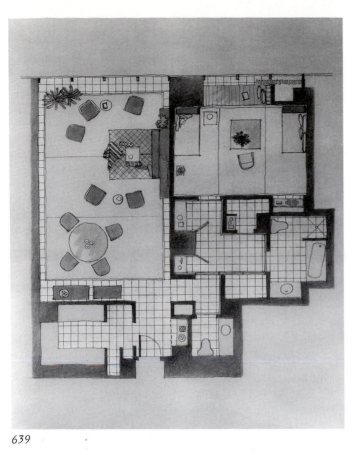

639

At what stages are there to be formal reviews of design proposals, budgets, and contracts? Who has authority to grant binding approvals?

Clarification of these issues with written notation of the decisions made will help to make a project run smoothly and avoid many troubles that can arise all too easily as a job progresses.

Preliminary Design

In this phase of work, the designer takes the accurate, scaled plan of the space in question and overlays it with yellow tracing paper, on which sketches of the interior in plan form can be drawn. (See Chapter 4, pages 82–95.)

Plan sketches provide an ideal way to study space allocations, placement of walls and openings, and location of major furniture elements with generally fixed locations (figs. 637, 638). Movable furniture can be shown in typical locations. Plans make it easy to see patterns of movement or circulation, using overlay diagrams to analyze these patterns and find ways to make them orderly, simple, and nonconflicting. At least one elevation or section at the same scale as the plan creates a sense of the three-dimensional proportion of the space being worked on.

640

639. In this neatly drafted plan of a city apartment by Norman Diekman, designer, the furniture and all other interior elements are drawn to scale. Color has been added, in pencil, pastel, and marker pen, to suggest the way the interior will actually look. (Courtesy Norman Diekman)

640. Here, the three-dimensional effect of N. M. McKinnell's accurate, measured perspective drawing is enhanced by shading in pencil. It shows the main entrance area of the Boston City Hall, a 1968 project of Kallmann & McKinnell. (Courtesy Kallmann & McKinnell)

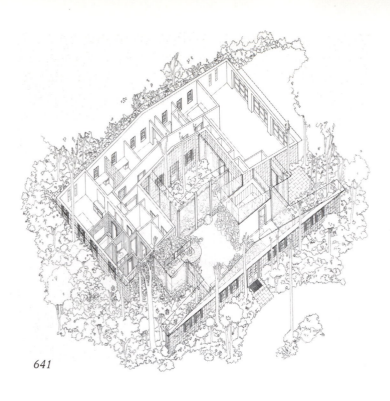

641

Preliminary design most often serves the designer, alone or with colleagues, while considering alternative ideas and moving toward specific proposals. The point at which sketches should be shown to a client is a matter of judgment. Some people may find design sketches hard to understand and become confused at seeing alternatives. Others may enjoy being included in the design process and indicate preferred directions to follow. In either case, the designer should assemble sketch plans that will give the client a clear idea of the design approach being taken. At the same time, the designer might present preliminary selections of color and materials to be looked at together with sketches. The goal is to gain the client's general approval before moving ahead to the next step.

Design Development

Once the design approach has been determined, the designer develops and refines it in more detailed design drawings, plans, elevations, sections, and, possibly, perspectives (figs. 633, 639, 640). These will be carefully drawn in black and white (pencil or ink), with straightedge and instruments where appropriate,

642

641. This axonometric drawing of a house with the roof removed resembles a model. It illustrates a highly unusual project by the imaginative, often experimental firm of SITE Projects Inc. The 1983 design was for a private dwelling to be built at Bedford, New York. The clients owned a wooded site and requested a house that would disturb the forest and other vegetation as little as possible—a house that blended into the site to become nearly invisible. The solu-

tion was a glass-block, false front wall with conventional, shuttered windows. The wall was set forward from the actual house, allowing the forest to penetrate into the dwelling's perimeter on either side. The house proper is thus half-hidden behind this natural screening; the woods dominate a central court as well. The drawing is in ink on a 36"-square sheet of mylar drafting film. © 1983 SITE Projects Inc., courtesy Max Protetch Gallery, New York

642. The Bedford house project by SITE Projects Inc. shown in fig. 641 is presented here in an interior perspective in ink and wash on paper. The rather loose, painterly approach to presentation communicates the concept of the house in the forest by making the forest itself the major visual presence. Note the rocks left in place on the right. Drawings of this kind are often works of art that also serve a practical function in the designer-client dialogue. © 1983 SITE Projects Inc., courtesy Max Protetch Gallery, New York

perhaps on sturdy white tracing paper. Such drawings can be reproduced as prints—which convey a quality of authority—suitable for mounting, pinup display, or mailing for client review. Color may be added to originals or prints with colored pencil or marker. Another way to combine color scheme and design is to make a kind of color collage on the plan, pasting down swatches of actual materials or colored paper slips to furniture or other items pictured in the plan.

Color samples and catalog sheets referring to furniture, light fixtures, and other purchased items can be assembled in folders, one folder relating to each space being worked on. This material can also be reviewed with a client while changes can still be made easily. This is also the time for a budget estimate as close as possible to anticipated realities.

Presentation

In design circles, this term describes a formal showing of design proposals to a client for approval. If designer and client have a close working relationship, this step may be managed informally or omitted entirely. Corporate clients, accustomed to

643

644

643. A model in cardboard and paper shows a grouping of custom-designed office furniture at a scale of 1" = 1'-0". Model and design by John Pile for Cosco Office Furniture, Inc. (Photograph: John Pile)

644. A model is most often built without a ceiling, in order to view it from above easily. It is one of the most convincing ways of illustrating a planned interior space. The example here, of cardboard, is a ¼" = 1'-0" miniature of the office area of a bank. Because it is to scale, even the very diagrammatic indication of furniture is accurate; colors and finishes are rendered very much as they will appear in the completed project. The model (and the design), for the Essex County Bank headquarters in Peabody, Massachusetts, is by John Pile, consultant designer to J. F. N. Associates. (Photograph: John Pile)

645

646

645, 646. *Two watercolors illustrate alternative color schemes for a living room in Robert A. M. Stern Architects' Villa in New Jersey, 1983–87. The base sheet is a carefully constructed perspective drawing in pencil by Thomas A. Kligerman, the associate in charge of the project. The watercolor was then added by William T. Georgis, also of the Stern office. (Courtesy Robert A. M. Stern Architects)*

the presentations made by advertising agencies, generally expect a similar performance, including an element of salesmanship, from the designer. Drawings of the design development stage are usually suitable for presentation (figs. 641, 642). Some rendered color perspectives, possibly the work of a specialist, may be added (figs. 645, 646). Color and material charts are usually carefully organized and assembled for showing. Large samples of actual materials, even examples of actual pieces of furniture, may also be shown.

Architects frequently use models as presentation elements; similarly, interior models can be effective presentation tools (figs. 643, 644). Although elaborate models can be very costly, they often prove the best means of putting across a design proposal. Some designers make their own models, others commission special craftsmen.

In recent years, designers have come to make increasing use of audio-visual techniques for presentation, particularly to groups that must approve larger projects. Slides, films, and videotapes all aid the viewer in understanding complex drawings and models. Photographs of models create an illusion of reality (and convey a certain charm, as well) that often helps to convince clients of a design proposal's success. The goal of a design presentation is securing approval to go ahead with the execution of the project. Given that approval, possibly with some minor adjustments, the remaining steps can proceed.

Construction Drawings

Working drawings, as they are often called (*blueprints* to laymen), will be used to obtain final cost figures and then by contractors and workmen constructing the project (figs. 647–50). Working drawings include scale plans, elevations, and sections, using notes and symbols together with large-scale details to spell out every particular of the work to be done. Written specifications give details of materials and methods of workmanship that drawings cannot fully show.

Interior design working drawings follow the general practice of architectural draftsmanship; indeed, architectural and interior drawings are often combined. At this point, coordination between designer, architect, and engineer is vital to avoid duplication and conflict. At the same time, this cooperative effort extends to all the specialists involved—lighting, acoustical, and other consultants. Electrical and plumbing details and, occasionally, heating and air-conditioning details must also be coordinated. The interior designer must now decide on finishes and prepare special charts of color chips and plans marked to show color locations for the painting contractor.

The way in which the project is to be contracted somewhat influences how complete the working drawings must be. If

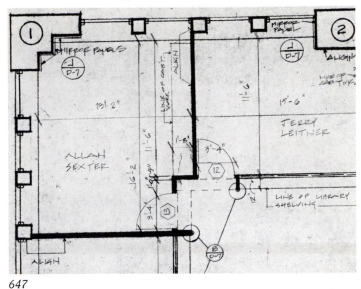

647

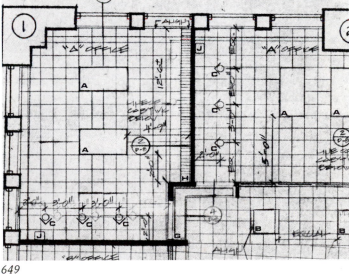

648

649

647–49. *A complete set of working drawings may include many sheets, each providing particular information. These details come from a set by Forbes-Ergas Design Assoc., Inc., interior designer, for a suite of law offices. Fig. 647 is from a portion of a basic construction plan giving dimensions, door sizes and types, and similar structural information. Fig. 648 shows the same area as it appears in a furniture layout sheet, with the locations and identity of each type of furniture item. Fig. 649 is from the reflected ceiling plan sheet, which details the layout of acoustic tile and the locations of ceiling lighting fixtures. (Courtesy Forbes-Ergas Design Assoc.)*

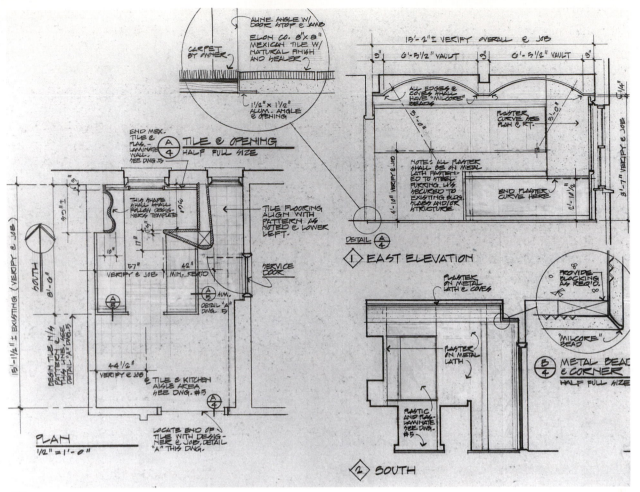

650

competitive bids are to be taken, drawings and specifications must be very complete and as precise as possible to assure that all bidders will be figuring on an identical set of requirements, leaving nothing to the imagination. For example, the indication "wood" can refer to softwood, hardwood, plywood, or even particleboard. Only totally specific drawings and/or specifications that clarify every such issue will serve to ensure that competitive bids are based on an identical set of requirements. If a contractor (or several contractors) is employed on a time and materials (or *cost-plus*) basis, drawings can be somewhat less inclusive, leaving details to be resolved later with the designer giving instructions on the job, verbally or in sketches. Good drawings always protect against later misunderstandings.

Estimates and Bids

Construction drawings may be sent for bids to several (often, three) equally qualified general contractors. One general contractor may bid on all aspects of the work, or separate bids may be taken from different trades (masonry, plumbing, electrical, and so on). The bidder who offers the best price wins the contract. For smaller projects and projects with tight deadlines, it is increasingly common to select one contractor without bidding, and to enter into a cost-plus contract in which payment is made on the cost of materials and workmanship plus a fixed percentage for overhead and profit. Besides being simple and convenient, this basis facilitates making additions and changes in a project as work progresses. While many people fear that an open-ended arrangement leads to higher costs than a fixed-price arrangement, experienced designers know this does not invariably happen.

Scheduling

In the design stages, the project probably progressed with informal schedules or instructions to advance "as rapidly as possible." Before actual work begins, the designer must make firm schedules to ensure that construction work proceeds without delays or conflicts. Scheduling also involves the architect (if there is one) and the contractor. Since interior design is the last phase of work, following schedules is crucial to the designer's success in delivering a job on time. Clients consider this the most important aspect of a project; they will sooner forgive cost overruns than a late completion date.

Trades must work in a logical sequence and purchased items must arrive when needed for the job to go smoothly. For example, when new stud or block walls are to be built, door frames (called *bucks* in the trade) must arrive and be set in place before the partition walls can go up. Plumbing and electrical work come before any surface finishes, but plumber and electrician must return to install fixtures *after* walls and ceilings are finished. Carpet is best installed last, although a painter may have to return after carpet installation to touch up any damage to walls that may have occurred. The interior designer has the additional task of providing a follow-up service to see that work schedules are maintained. Sophisticated management techniques such as PERT (Project Evaluation and Review Technique) and CPM (Critical Path Method), often using computer data management and display, can aid in handling the schedules of large and complex projects with their overlapping and intricate complexities. A simple CPM chart can help in working out schedules for more modestly scaled interior projects (see fig. 670).

Purchasing

Many of the elements that go into a typical interior are not made to order or made on site but purchased from manufacturers or dealers as standard items. These include rugs and carpets, wallpapers, furniture, light fixtures and lamps, and various accessories. Even antiques and unique works of art fall into this category. Making catalog selections, checking prices and delivery schedules, and issuing written orders for these purchases form a significant part of the interior designer's work. Complexities arise when, for example, upholstery fabric ordered from a supplier must go to a furniture manufacturer to cover particular items, and the finished pieces have to be delivered on a precise schedule. When clients prefer to do their own purchasing, the designer must still prepare the information on which the orders will be based. Coordinating delivery schedules will probably remain a design responsibility.

Supervision

Projects require on-site supervision to ensure the proper following of drawings and specifications and the quality of workmanship as well as to resolve any unanticipated problems that may arise. When a project site is close to the designer's base of action, frequent visits can provide adequate supervision without much difficulty. When a project is beyond the designer's travel range, it may be wise to make arrangements with a local designer to provide regular supervision. Supervision becomes crucial in the final phase of a job, when paint colors need to be checked (and sometimes revised), when furniture is being delivered and needs to be put in place, and when small details require constant attention.

Details

A project's success depends upon the handling of small details that complete a job: hanging pictures, acquiring and placing accessories, and possibly revising graphics and signs, to give a few examples. The designer has a special obligation to see such matters through, making sure that these details support the more major design concepts basic to the project. Mishandled details can hurt an otherwise strong design. At the same time, users of a space may be more likely to notice and be concerned with details close at hand than with the basic design. Issues involving details often continue to arise long after a project is completed in all major respects. Following through with minor changes, purchases of afterthought items, and dealing with complaints are important aspects of project completion.

Evaluation

Responsible designers carry out follow-up evaluation of completed jobs at reasonable intervals—for example, six months, one year, and two years—to determine how well the project is serving its users and meeting its goals. Many designers omit or ignore this step. This may be one reason why some well-known projects that photograph well and win praise from critics leave users with major dissatisfactions. Honest evaluation, together with a plan to provide revisions and corrections as needed, contributes to a project's success and to the designer's improved performance on future projects.

It often seems that *design* as the term is usually understood turns out to be a minor part of the total performance of the interior designer. It is important to be sure that the demands of project management never overwhelm design creativity and push it into the background. Nevertheless, a design success combined with poor management can leave behind an unhappy client and dissatisfied users who judge an aesthetic success poor compensation for assorted everyday complaints. The combination of poor design and good management is far more likely to satisfy clients. However, this is a choice that need not be made; excellent design and good project management together express a designer's concern for delivering quality design work.

CHAPTER EIGHTEEN

TECHNICAL ISSUES

Generally, the interior designer will not have to deal with excessively demanding technical issues in the course of most projects. Many residential and other smaller projects hardly make any technical demands at all. Larger and more complex projects may introduce issues of some importance. While the architect, engineer, and contractors will probably be responsible for resolving these, the interior designer should have a good general knowledge of technical fields, as an aid in talking with these and other professionals and consultants and as a basis for handling the impact these matters have on interiors.

The term *mechanical systems* describes the aspects of building technology of most importance. These are the electrical, plumbing, and *HVAC* (heating, ventilation, and air conditioning) systems. Lighting, a primary technical problem closely associated with interior design, has been covered in its own chapter (see pages 208–41). A few other technical matters relating to acoustics, safety and security, and communications are discussed here.

Typically, the interior designer faces such technical questions as: "Can a new sink be provided here?"; "Can this bathroom be relocated?"; "Can a new bath be added here?"; "Is the electrical service adequate for the new lighting and the appliances?"; "Can the ducts be concealed?" These questions may require consultation with specialized experts for firm answers, but a good sense of what such problems involve and of what questions to ask of whom is an important part of the designer's special skills. The interior designer often acts as a liaison between the architect, mechanical engineer, or contractor and the client.

HVAC

These concerns can be broken down into the three areas that the letters abbreviate.

Heating Systems

Heating systems are essential in all buildings in any but tropical climates. The interior designer is generally concerned only with the visible elements that deliver heat—radiators, convectors, registers, outlet grilles, and ducts or pipes. These must either be concealed or treated to minimize their effect on the interior design. The common heating systems are:
HOT WATER OR STEAM. These require radiators or convectors (similar to radiators), usually located under windows or in baseboards (fig. 652). The concerns are to conceal them with covers of inoffensive appearance as well as concealing the pipes connected to them.
WARM (OR ''HOT'') AIR. Such systems

circulate air from outlet grilles or registers (openings to admit air) in floors, baseboards, or ceilings. Concealment with covers of satisfactory appearance of these outlets is the primary concern. Ducts serving the outlets must also be placed in concealed or unobjectionable locations. When air conditioning is also provided, heated and cooled air are usually circulated through the same duct and outlet systems.
RADIANT HEATING. These systems use pipes or wires embedded in floors, walls, or ceilings, using few visible elements. However, they make more specific demands in terms of material choices. The heat-supply elements must be fixed in materials that conduct well (embedded in plaster or concrete; placed under stone, brick, or tile) and must not be blocked by elements that act as insulators. For example, rugs absorb heat from a radiant-heated floor, reducing effectiveness.

Radiant heating is often used as the back-up system for solar heating (which is another form of radiant heat). The same surfaces that conduct radiant heat can be used to absorb solar heat by day and radiate it back at night. Floors are particularly suited to working in this way, since sunlight normally falls on them.
SOLAR HEATING. This requires some basic architectural involvement in terms of orientation, the size and placement of windows and overhangs, and the choices of interior materials for floors and, in some systems, for ceilings.

Passive solar heating does not use mechanical equipment. Sun heat enters through windows and heats interior surfaces, primarily floors. In some systems, special blinds reflect the heat up to ceilings, where heat-absorbing panels are placed. The heated surfaces radiate heat back into the space, keeping occupants comfortable, and store heat so that the surfaces continue to radiate at night and on dark days (fig. 653). A back-up heating system, either radiant or conventional, is needed to provide additional heat when solar radiation is insufficient (in very cold weather or during protracted cloudy or stormy periods).

Active solar heating uses sun heat to heat air or water in collector elements. The heated air or water is then circulated by mechanical fans or pumps to deliver heat when and where it is needed. The circulating medium also heats a storage medium (a tank of liquid or, in some systems, a mass of stones), which radiates heat back into the system when solar output is insufficient. The same mechanical system that circulates the radiant heat is also used to distribute back-up heat provided by a conventional fuel.

The fuel used for any of the nonsolar heat systems is usually chosen on an economic basis and has no significant influence on interior design considerations.

651. Air-conditioning ducts—the large tubes visible in the upper portion of this photograph—are normally concealed above dropped ceilings, but in High Tech designs they are often exposed, even painted in strong colors, to become interior design details, as in the Columbus Occupational Health Center in Columbus, Indiana, designed by Hardy Holzman Pfeiffer Associates. (Photograph: © Norman McGrath)

Ventilation

Ventilation is essential to provide fresh air to replace air made stale by smoking, cooking, and the bodily functions (primarily breathing) of human occupants as well as to remove pollen, dust, and odors. In the past, the opening of windows and, perhaps, doors and the air leaks of ordinary construction generally provided adequate ventilation of all but totally internal (windowless) spaces. Modern warm-air heating and air-conditioning systems can provide fresh air and filter recirculated air. With other systems, separate mechanical ventilation may be required. Windowless interior spaces always need some provision for ventilation. This is usually a legal requirement for interior bathrooms, but other spaces may need smoke vents or other such arrangements involving ducts and fans (fig. 654). Meeting and conference rooms and places where many people gather are particularly in need of ventilation. The interior designer must remember to address ventilation needs in the design (fig. 655).

Air Conditioning

This has become a widely demanded comfort, particularly in areas where summer heat tends to be a problem. The term describes systems that provide cooling, controlled humidification (or dehumidification, as required), and air filtration and purification. Many modern buildings are windowless or have sealed windows, making mechanical air conditioning essential.

Built-in systems, which usually provide central locations for machinery, require only that the designer place the outlet ducts in inconspicuous locations and consider how to handle the return of exhaust air to the system. The latter often calls for doors with either vents or *undercuts* (a larger than normal clearance at floor level) to permit air to pass along corridors toward return air grilles. Supply outlets can often be provided as part of ceiling light fixtures described as *air-handling* or can be incorporated into many ceiling systems. Ducts, often large and intrusive, need to be concealed (usually above hung ceilings),

652

652. The lighting and acoustic qualities of this media room conceived for video and audio monitoring must meet the standards set by the complex technical equipment. Note the neat design of the radiator enclosure at lower right. Bromley/Jacobsen Designs for Kips Bay Showplace, New York, 1984. (Photograph: Jaime Ardiles-Arce)

653

653. Architect Marlys Hann installed large glass panels in the bathroom of her 1985 home in New York's Catskill Mountains to create a passive solar heat trap. The bathroom receives the sun's heat by day, retaining it in the tiled areas to reduce nighttime energy consumption. (Photograph: © Paul Warchol)

654

655

unless the designer chooses to expose and treat them as part of the interior design (fig. 651). Such exposed ducts are often prominent in High Tech interiors.

Providing air conditioning on a room-by-room basis is often the only practical means in older buildings or for projects with a limited budget. Window or under-window units are common, but larger *cabinet units* are sometimes better for such medium-sized spaces as shops, restaurants, or small offices. Finding suitable, unobtrusive locations is a planning responsibility.

While the details of air-conditioning systems are best left to experienced engineers, the interior designer must often act as coordinator in determining how the requirements for space, electrical service, water supply, and duct layout will be accommodated. This involves superimposing proposed layouts for the various systems on one plan drawing (and often in sections as well) to make sure that there is space for each system without any conflict. Lowered (*furred down*) ceilings (fig. 656), enlarged columns, thickened walls, and vertical pipe chases are the usual means for providing hidden space for these necessities. Suppliers of equipment often offer technical design services; however, except in the most minimal of projects, the designer must be careful to evaluate such self-serving advice. A better system for less money can often be developed by an independent expert who has no interest in promoting a particular product or brand.

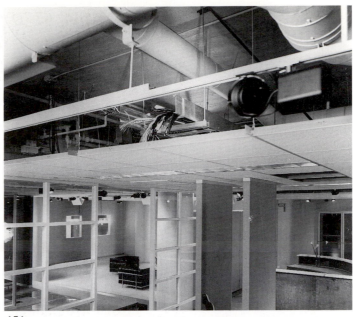

656

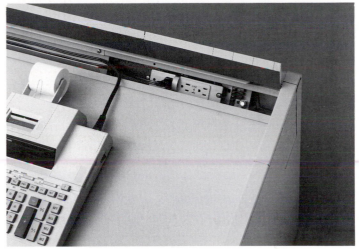

657

ELECTRICAL SYSTEMS

These usually offer few problems to the interior designer. After designing good lighting, the designer need only assure that adequate service and wiring are provided for lighting, incidental uses, air conditioning, and any special appliances. Some older buildings call for total rewiring to serve the electrical load demanded by modern lighting and other electrical devices. This is the responsibility of the engineer and contractor. For smaller projects, a licensed electrician, generally employed by the contractor, can usually deal with all electrical problems, including obtaining required inspections and approvals.

Some electrical details that may fall to the interior designer include the placement of switches, outlets, and circuit-breaker panels; the selection of dimmers, proximity switches, and other special controls; and the appearance of outlets, switch controls, and plates. The complexity of modern offices has made electrical provisions (for task lighting, office equipment, and computer hardware) a special concern. Many furniture and partition systems even offer special provisions for wiring (fig. 657). The designer may be responsible for evaluating the merits of such wiring systems and determining how power will be

carried to furniture locations through ducts or under-carpet wiring.

Designers must be familiar with the electrical symbols used on plans and understand how to read wiring diagrams that show the locations of fixtures, outlets, and switches as well as the functions of switches. (The standard symbols used are shown in Appendix 3, "Electrical Symbols.") In plan diagrams, dotted lines show the relation of switches to the fixtures they control. Studying a few such diagrams will make their meaning fairly clear. Complex wiring diagrams may seem confusing at first glance, but they are different only in the larger number of devices and circuits that they show. By simply following each symbol and line methodically, they can be understood quite readily (fig. 658).

654. *A large window fan provides ventilation, removes cooking odors generated in this open loft kitchen, and acts as a decorative element as well in a Manhattan loft by architect Michael S. Wu. (Photograph: Antoine Bootz)*

655. *Air-supply inlet grilles—the square, louvered units in the ceiling—are standard products widely used in HVAC installations. In this example, a cafeteria in Ferris Booth Hall, Columbia University, New York, the normally unobtrusive design of the grilles pleasingly echoes the four-sided lighting clusters atop the columns. Robert A. M. Stern Architects, designer, 1980. (Photograph: Ed Stoecklein)*

656. *A ceiling provides acoustical absorption and houses architectural lighting and air-conditioning outlets, while the hollow space, or plenum, above conceals wiring, ductwork, piping, and other mechanical and structural elements. The suspended ceiling is designed to facilitate access. (Photograph courtesy USG Interiors, Inc.)*

657. *Placing such standard office equipment as telephones, computer terminals, desk-top electronic devices, and task lighting together can result in an unsightly tangle of dangling wires. Many modern office systems provide neat, unobtrusive, and accessible locations for wiring—such as this trough at the rear of an office desk. (Photograph courtesy Steelcase, Inc.)*

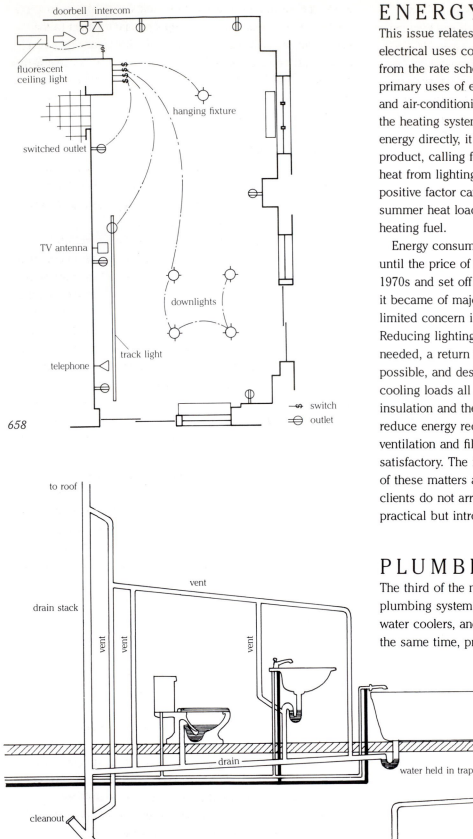

ENERGY CONSUMPTION

This issue relates to both HVAC and electrical matters. All electrical uses consume energy at a cost that can be determined from the rate schedules of the local electric company. The primary uses of electrical energy in buildings are the lighting and air-conditioning systems and, when electric heat is used, the heating system as well. Electric lighting not only consumes energy directly, it also generates heat as an unwanted by-product, calling for additional air conditioning in summer. The heat from lighting can reduce winter heating costs, but this positive factor cannot begin to offset the greater burden of the summer heat load. The other primary energy cost is for winter heating fuel.

Energy consumption was not considered an important issue until the price of energy in all forms climbed in the 1960s and 1970s and set off a movement toward energy conservation. Then it became of major significance in larger projects and of more limited concern in smaller, residential, and similar projects. Reducing lighting to reasonable levels and placing it only where needed, a return to the use of available daylight wherever possible, and design that minimizes winter heating and summer cooling loads all help to keep energy costs down. Good insulation and the sealing of windows and other openings can reduce energy requirements, but they call for extra concern for ventilation and filtration to ensure that the air quality remains satisfactory. The interior designer has an obligation to review all of these matters and to make sure that experts and uninformed clients do not arrive at systems that appear to be efficient and practical but introduce troublesome problems.

PLUMBING SYSTEMS

The third of the major mechanical systems of buildings, plumbing systems supply water to baths, kitchens, other sinks, water coolers, and any other situations that require water and, at the same time, provide drains from the same locations for waste

658. A floor plan with electrical outlet and switch locations uses the standard electrical symbols (see Appendix 3). The curving lines connect switch indications with the outlets they are to control.

659. Plumbing concerns water supply and drainage. Every drain requires a trap, that is, a curved section of drain-pipe that always holds water; this prevents the backflow of sewer gases and their offensive odors. Every trap also requires a vent—a pipe leading to the open air, usually at roof level, so that a rush of water down the drainpipe does not create suction and pull the water out of the trap. A typical bathroom requires drainpipes and traps for each fixture, as well as vent pipes connected to the drain stack that extends upward to the roof. Unlike drains and vents, which work by gravity and normal air circulation, water supply pipes are under pressure and can be placed virtually wherever desired.

water and sewage. Architects and engineers design building plumbing systems. The role of interior design in selecting and locating fixtures is covered in Chapter 11 (see pages 300–15). In addition, an interior designer should have some basic knowledge of how plumbing systems are arranged, since this influences decisions about relocating fixtures and moving or providing new baths, kitchens, or other facilities using water, including washer-dryer installations, wet bars, and darkrooms (fig. 659).

In most buildings, hot and cold water is supplied by a pressure system geared to the planned number of occupants and use of the building. This usually covers all demands except for the type of air-conditioning equipment that consumes water for cooling. In most localities, because of their concern with conserving water, the consumption of water for air conditioning is not permitted. However, systems that recirculate the water, since they do not add a major demand for water, present no problem. In older buildings, clogged pipes often reduce the available water supply, a problem that can be solved only by replacing the affected pipes.

Since water is supplied under pressure and supply pipes are quite small, it is usually fairly easy to supply water to new locations. *Risers,* the vertical lines of pipes running upward through a building from the basement, must be located (they are usually found adjacent to existing baths or kitchens) and then connected to the new pipes, which run horizontally to the new fixtures. The new pipes may be concealed by running them in walls, under floors, above ceilings, or in specially built enclosures.

Since drainpipes pose more difficulties, they will usually determine when and where new *wet facilities* can be provided. Drains use not pressure but gravity to steer waste downward to the pipes leading to a sewer or other disposal arrangement. Therefore, drainpipes must always slope downhill. Drains from basins and sinks need only slope down at a gentle angle, but the large soil pipes serving toilets must slope sharply to discourage clogging. New facilities must be placed close enough to vertical existing drains to make the required down slope possible without damage to spaces below the intended location.

Many people fail to realize that drains are also connected to upward *stacks* that must be carried up through the roof of a building. The stack is part of a safeguarding system that begins with a *trap* at each fixture. The trap holds water in such a way as to form a seal, preventing gases present in drainage pipes from entering living spaces and bringing objectionable odors. Beyond each trap, there must be a *vent* that prevents suction from pulling water out of the trap and that carries gases up and out to the air at roof level. Just as drains angle downward to a vertical stack, vents must angle upward and connect to the same stack as it travels up to the roof. This means that every drain location must allow for the provision (and concealment) of these upward vents without disturbing the spaces *above* it. In a single-story building, it is usually practical to provide water and drainage in almost any location, but in a multistory building, the impact of plumbing changes on spaces above and below can be significant. In tall buildings, it may be out of the question to install pipes, drains, and vents in a new location because of the need to pass pipes through spaces that may be occupied by other tenants or owners. In any case, even when possible, it may be prohibitively expensive.

The interior designer may have to turn to an architect, engineer, or plumbing contractor to arrive at a firm conclusion about whether a certain plumbing change will be easy, possible but difficult (and therefore costly), or virtually impossible, but the designer will find it useful to be able to make a reliable preliminary judgment. In general, it is easiest to locate new fixtures adjacent to walls where pipes already exist, that is, next to existing fixtures; close to the vertical shafts called *pipe chases;* or, in large buildings of steel- or concrete-frame construction, close to *wet columns,* structural columns that have an added space for pipes. Piping locations are sometimes difficult to identify on site, but building plans will show them very clearly.

Sprinkler systems form another plumbing installation in buildings where they are required by fire-safety regulations. They require supply pipes, or *mains,* shut-off valves, the actual sprinkler pipes, and sprinkler heads. Pipes can usually be concealed, but the heads must be exposed in order to serve their purpose. Modern sprinkler heads of reasonably neat and unobtrusive design are available.

Plumbing systems are subject to strict legal regulation. Plans and diagrams must be filed for approval for any significant plumbing work, which must be carried out by licensed contractors and inspected and approved when completed. Such work can entail high costs, surprising to many clients who have never had extensive plumbing work done before. Finally, it should be mentioned that since, unfortunately, all plumbing is subject to the possibility of leaks, access for repairs must be provided. This can be done by building access panels or locating pipes in closets or other semihidden spaces. This possibility also calls for judgment to avoid locating pipes above places where a leak could cause unusually costly or troublesome damage. Plumbers and engineers may not think of such issues, but a designer will be wise to point out any such problematic situations to a client.

660

ACOUSTICS

Although not a building system, acoustics can present several technical problems that have direct bearing on interior design. Major acoustical problems may call for the services of specialized consultants, but most can be dealt with by the interior designer quite simply through planning and material selection.

The common acoustical problems are of several types. They concern excessive noise levels; the transmission of noise from one space to another; guarding the privacy of individual spaces; maintaining the intelligibility of speech in relation to background noise; providing suitable background noise in certain situations; and, in the case of auditoriums and larger meeting rooms, the qualities that give the characteristics described as *good acoustics.*

Excessive Noise

Excessive noise can be disturbing in spaces where many people are present and involved in sound-producing activities. Offices, restaurants and cafeterias, and factory production spaces commonly present noise problems. The best way to limit general, ambient noise is through interior design decisions. Sound-absorbing materials for floors, walls, ceilings, and even furniture contribute greatly to reducing noise levels. Taken together, they will usually deal with noise problems at anything less than factory-machinery levels. Hard surfaces such as tile

floors, plaster walls or ceilings, and glass and metal surfaces not only reflect noise, they may even generate excess noise as feet and chairs scrape on floors or dishes and silver rattle on table tops.

Soft and absorbent materials include carpet or rugs for floors, fabric upholstery and drapery, mats or linens on table tops, and various special acoustical materials for walls and ceilings. Since floors and ceilings are usually the largest surface areas of a space, they become target areas for noise control. Carpeted floors have become widely accepted in offices and even in schools and hospitals largely because of their effectiveness in reducing noise levels. Various ceiling tiles and ceiling systems (fig. 660) offer noise reduction to a level of efficiency indicated by a numerical rating called a noise reduction coefficient, or NRC (see Table 18). Some of these acoustical materials, as, for example, the least expensive tiles, are unattractive, but many products of good appearance are now available. Another way to reduce noise levels is to identify major sources of noise (for example, typewriters or printers in an office) and place them in an isolated location or furnish some local sound control, such as an acoustic housing.

Residential spaces rarely need any noise level controls beyond the carpeting and upholstery that will normally be present. A space with hardwood or tile floors and large glass areas, especially in combination, may warrant the introduction of rugs, wall hangings, or some other absorbent surface to improve its acoustical quality.

TABLE 18. NOISE REDUCTION COEFFICIENTS (NRC)

An NRC rating is a single number indicating the effectiveness of a material in absorbing sound. With a range from 1.00 to .00, an NRC of .99 would indicate almost total absorption, .01 virtually none. The higher the NRC of a particular material, the more effectively it will absorb sound.

Material	NRC
Bare concrete floor	.05
Tile or linoleum on concrete	.05
Carpet (⅛″ pile)	.15
Carpet (¼″ pile)	.25
Carpet (⁷⁄₁₆″ pile)	.40
Plaster ceiling	.45
Metal pan acoustic ceiling	.60
Partition system surfaces	.55–.80 (.60 typical)
Carpet over padding	up to .65
Acoustical ceiling systems	up to .90

660. Sound-absorbent ceiling material is usually in the form of tiles, from 1 foot square to 2 by 4 feet. These, and the metal ribs that support them, make up a ceiling system that may also include light fixtures and air-conditioning outlets in a dimensionally coordinated assembly. The installation shown is typical of systems selected for offices, health-care facilities, and similar plants. (Photograph: Bob Shimer, Hedrich-Blessing, courtesy USG Acoustical Products Company)

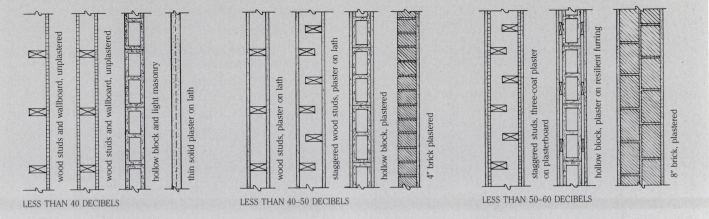

661

Transmitted Noise

Noise transmission from one space to another can be a source of annoyance and distraction. Traffic noise from outside, conversation from an adjacent bedroom, office, or hotel room, piano practice from upstairs, and the sounds from a nearby elevator or bathroom are frequent causes for complaint. Unfortunately, the problems of transmitted noise are more difficult to cope with than noise generated within a space. Despite their common use, acoustical materials on walls or ceilings give little improvement.

The easiest solutions to transmitted sound lie in prevention—through basic building structure and layout and planning decisions (fig. 661). Massive, heavy building materials, such as thick masonry or concrete walls, and heavy floor and ceiling construction are the best defenses against sound transmission (see Tables 18, 19), but interior design usually has little input into such matters. Failing this, double-wall construction, with separate studs for each side and insulation material packed in between, or building a false wall adjacent to but isolated from an existing wall can be useful in dealing with noise from plumbing, elevators, or a noisy neighbor. Radio studios are sometimes built as complete rooms within an outer shell with walls, floors, and ceiling all isolated on rubber cushions, but such a drastic step can rarely be justified or afforded in normal usage.

Double or triple glazing for windows, gaskets at the edges of doors or *sound-lock* double-doors, and acoustical treatment inside ductwork can also help to prevent sound transmission. Unfortunately, sound transmission through floors is particularly difficult to eliminate. Carpet and under-carpet padding in the space that is the source of the sound may be of some help, but when the source space is occupied by another tenant or owner

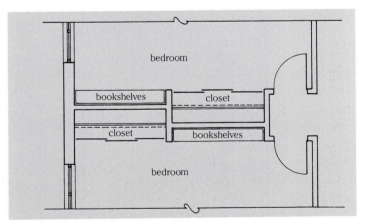

662

661. How partition walls are constructed determines how effectively they acoustically isolate the spaces on either side. It is hard to achieve perfect acoustical separation, but materials and methods can be rated in terms of an STC (Sound Transmission Class) factor (see Table 19). The types of construction illustrated are ranked by their STC number.

662. One of the best strategies for ensuring acoustical privacy is to avoid shared partitions between adjacent areas. Intelligent design situates bathrooms, corridors, or closets in place of common walls whenever possible. In the plan shown here, two adjacent bedrooms or offices are separated by a line of closets and storage shelves.

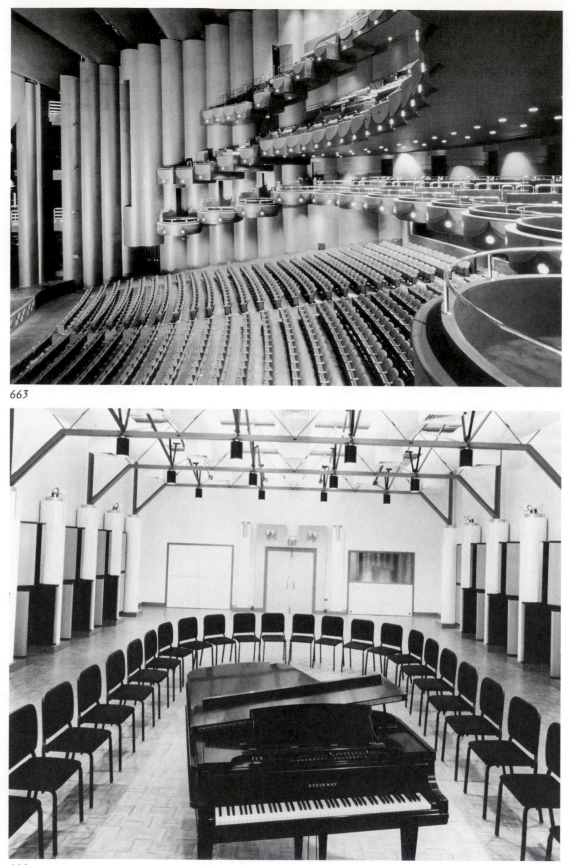

663

664

663. Theaters, auditoriums, and concert halls have special acoustical requirements. Walls and ceilings must be shaped so as to blend and distribute sound evenly throughout the audience space. A hall's size and form are also crucial factors in generating both an acoustic intimacy between audience and performers and a warm, well-balanced orchestral sound. Jaffe Acoustics was the consultant to Morris Architects in the design of the Brown Theater of the Gus S. Wortham Theater Center of 1987 in Houston. (Photograph: Paul Hester, courtesy Wortham Center)

664. Once used by a Masonic lodge, this renovated small meeting room in New York's Carnegie Hall building is now the J. M. Kaplan Space, used for rehearsals and sound recording. The cylinders along the side walls are filled with sand; they alternate with acoustical cabinets, which, together, control reverberation. They also contribute a strikingly rhythmic design element. The oversized ducts at ceiling height permit air conditioning to flow at low velocity, thus eliminating any audible hiss. Abraham Meltzer acted as the acoustical consultant to James Stewart Polshek and Partners, Architects, 1984. (Photograph: © Brian McNally)

it may not be possible to arrange. Ceiling treatment, such as replacing a ceiling with a hung ceiling with insulation above, may reduce sound levels but cannot totally eliminate the offensive sound.

Sound transmission between spaces can be controlled by planning. Potential sources of loud sounds should be located well away from spaces where quiet is desired. Bedrooms should not be placed next to TV or recreation rooms. Plumbing should be isolated or adjacent to the space it serves. Corridors and closets can act as sound buffers between spaces (adjacent bedrooms or offices, for example; fig. 662). Music practice rooms need to be remote from classrooms or offices. This applies to vertical as well as to horizontal adjacency. A piano in a room above a bedroom can be as much of a problem as in an adjacent space on the same level. Fortunately, noise does not transmit upward as readily as downward, but amplified music, television, or stereo may still be audible from a space below. Control through ceiling or floor treatment is usually inadequate.

Overheard Speech

In spaces that are generally quiet, such as private offices or bedrooms, another problem may develop: overhearing of intelligible speech in an adjacent space. This can be controlled by separating the spaces with partitions or a wall of solid (or double and insulated) construction and carefully plugging "sound leaks" around doors or through ducts, but, again, avoiding adjacency or using buffers such as closets works better. Fear of being overheard, a particular concern in doctors' consulting rooms, lawyers' private offices, and some business offices and meeting rooms where confidential conversations may take place, is the reverse of this problem, to which the same techniques for control apply.

In modern open-plan offices where no partitions are used, full acoustic privacy is difficult to achieve. Satisfactory conditions depend on the use of carpeting, an acoustical ceiling, screen panels with acoustical value placed between work stations, and a layout that adequately spaces out work stations. If necessary, an artificial, electronically generated background sound may be added to blend into the general sounds of activity to prevent conversation from being overheard. Similarly, in a busy restaurant, the general ambient noise makes it possible to talk without fear of being overheard at a nearby table.

Good Acoustics

In concert halls, theaters, auditoriums, and large meeting rooms, an opposite acoustical problem arises—making sound satisfactorily audible throughout the space. Achieving good acoustics in large halls presents complex problems in which the size and shape of the space and the placement of reflecting, absorbing, and diffusing elements play a part (fig. 663). An expert consultant is a virtual necessity, and architects and designers need to work closely with the consultant in order to arrive at the best possible results (fig. 664). Disappointments are not unusual, and remedial steps can be troublesome and costly.

Amplification systems are usually resorted to in large meeting rooms, ballrooms, and similar kinds of halls. They are, of course, routinely used in film projection and some kinds of music performance. "Sound reinforcement" is objectionable, however, for the performance of classical music, and should be avoided in churches, lecture rooms, and conference halls if at all possible. If amplification must be used in such circumstances, expert consultation is called for to make it as unnoticeable as possible.

WIRED SYSTEMS

Aside from electrical systems, discussed earlier, these include telephone, intercom, public-address, wired-music, and other sound systems, such as background sound and amplification (discussed above). Telephone wiring is often installed by

665

665. In this executive office, carpet squares and floor panels are raised to reveal the area beneath the visible, or access, floor. Access flooring is a surface of removable panels supported some distance—usually 6 to 18 inches—above the structural floor. The space generated can accommodate wiring, plumbing, and ductwork. Easy access from above makes this system particularly suitable to offices and workspaces where computers and computer-related equipment require complex wiring that needs frequent repair service or upgrading. (Photograph courtesy USG Interiors, Inc.)

telephone company staff as an after-the-fact improvisation. This serves well enough for simple installations, but more complex installations benefit from planning conduit and outlets, which makes for neatness in all situations. In larger buildings, *risers* are installed in special vertical chases leading to closets where wiring can be connected to horizontal runs, often in special under-floor ducts or, in the case of situations with extensive phone and other wiring needs, in hollow space provided beneath raised flooring. This latter system is particularly helpful in situations with extensive wiring for telephones, computer systems, and other communications needs. The raised floor is often installed in brokerage offices, reservations centers, trading rooms of banks and financial corporations, and computer centers (fig. 665). Wiring and speaker locations for sound systems are best planned as part of a project rather than added as an afterthought.

Special, and sometimes elaborate, audio-visual equipment has become a common requirement in business conference rooms and in presentation rooms of the kind required by advertising firms. This dictates special projection facilities for slides, film, and live or taped TV, often with rear projection as well as conventional projection arrangements. Sound and control systems (for switching equipment, dimming lights, and so on) can be quite complex, calling for special consultants to play a role in laying out and selecting equipment and planning wiring.

SAFETY SYSTEMS
The designer should be aware of items required by building codes or that may be otherwise needed for both safety and security concerns. Wiring and plumbing systems as well as separate elements may be involved. A checklist will include:

> Alarms:
>> Fire
>> Burglar
>> Exit door
> Extinguishers
> Locking hardware
>> (including magnetic
>> and computer-
>> controlled systems)
> Signs (exits)
> Sprinkler systems
>> (see Plumbing Systems, *above*)
> TV-surveillance systems

For larger buildings, a centralized control system that integrates safety, security, and other matters at a central console is now widely used.

VERTICAL TRANSPORTATION
Usually of concern only in larger buildings and large public spaces, this refers to elevators and escalators. Manufacturers of this equipment provide excellent planning advice to architects. Interior designers are usually concerned with the location and appearance of escalators and the design of elevator entrances, cab interiors, lighting, and signal systems (fig. 666). Coordinating these elements with centralized building control systems now in general use is desirable.

TABLE 20. ELECTRICAL BASICS

AMPERE (abbreviated to *amp*). The unit of measurement of the magnitude of an electrical current. The higher the amperage requirement of any device, the more current it will use.

VOLT. The unit of pressure (intensity) of electric current. In the United States, 115–120 volts is the standard. Heavy-duty appliances, including stoves, air conditioners, and other machinery, require a 220-volt current, separately wired.

WATT. The unit of power that results when a device uses a certain amperage at a particular voltage. Electrical devices carry a wattage rating that is based on their ampere requirement at the standard voltage. Electricity is sold on the basis of wattage consumed in relation to time. A device that requires 1,000 watts (1 kilowatt) when used for one hour will consume one kilowatt-hour (KWH). An electric meter measures KWH consumed so that the utility company can bill on this basis.

ELECTRICAL WIRING is normally planned to carry 1,200 to 1,320 watts in one *circuit*, or wiring loop. The total combined wattages of the devices connected in one circuit cannot exceed this maximum. A *fuse* or *circuit breaker* is provided for each circuit to protect it against an overload, which could cause overheating or fire. Groups of circuits are supplied by heavier wires or copper bars (called *busbars*), which are, in turn, protected by larger fuses or circuit breakers.

LOW-VOLTAGE (most often 12-volt) SERVICE is used for smaller electrical devices such as bells and buzzers and for some types of lamps (bulbs). A *transformer* is needed to convert normal voltage to the required low voltage. Since batteries deliver low voltages, a transformer is used when a battery device (such as a radio or tape recorder) is to be connected to regular power outlets.

666. Elevators can be more than the standardized units provided by a manufacturer. The cabs and entrances can be conceived instead as significant, interesting elements in a multistory building. A glimpse of elevator cab interiors, visible here, shows how they extend the lobby design. The Saddlery Building in Des Moines, Iowa, is the work of Douglas A. Wells, architect. (Photograph: © 1986 Frederick Charles)

CHAPTER NINETEEN

BUSINESS MATTERS

While interior design is primarily a field for artistic creativity, every project involves some business matters. Large interior projects may demand substantial business management. Problems, misunderstandings, even lawsuits are far more likely to arise from business than creative issues. Interior design benefits from employing sound business practices applicable to all types of businesses. At the same time, it introduces several unique considerations. Of the issues discussed here, some will be important only for large and complex projects and larger design firms, some will apply to smaller projects and to individual designers, while a few are important even to the individual who is his or her own client for a do-it-yourself project.

BUDGETS

Any project that goes beyond shifting furniture already at hand will involve costs. Planning for those costs—estimating and controlling them—is a primary need for almost every interior project. Since costs vary from place to place and change rapidly with the passage of time, it is not practical to provide specific figures here. The general basis for budgeting is, however, easy to review.

Estimating Budgets

A preliminary budget is usually calculated on the basis of the area, expressed in square feet, involved in a project. Once the extent of work to be done and the general level of quality desired are known, it is possible to arrive at an approximate cost for a project. The dollar cost per square foot may come from the designer's recent experience with similar projects; from costs for completed projects published in professional magazines; or from contractors or other professionals active in the field. Generating a cost range of low, average, and high figures can aid in setting the price goals for a project and in beginning to plan ways in which the project will be financed.

Clients often initiate a project with unrealistic ideas of prices and may need a period of adjustment to accommodate to the realities of current costs, either by modifying the project concept or rethinking the way they will handle the financing. With an approved preliminary budget in mind, design can be undertaken with a clear idea of the work to be done and the range of materials and products to be selected. An economy budget restricts the design in terms of both work and selection; a luxury budget places few limitations on design.

As design decisions are made, a detailed budget can be developed on an item-by-item basis. Construction work can be estimated (possibly with the help of a contractor) on the basis

667. The calculator joins the other tools of the designer in the business aspects of project realization.

TABLE 21. BUDGETING

A sample budget, proposed for the renovation of a living room in an apartment in 1986, is given below. Since prices vary in different regions and are subject to change, the costs given here cannot be considered a reliable guide, but the items and proportionate costs will probably remain stable.

General contract:	Demolition (remove existing closets)	$ 200
	Repair walls and floor	845
	Supply and install built-in bookshelves	420
	Electrical: new outlets and wiring	320
	Painting: walls and ceiling	530
	Refinish floor	275
Furniture and furnishings:	Sofa (existing, reupholstered)	625
	3 lounge chairs	1,125
	Dining table	460
	4 dining chairs	720
	Desk	625
	Desk chair	175
	Stereo/TV cabinet (custom-made)	825
	Rug (existing, cleaned)	210
	Blinds (2 windows)	200
Lighting:	Fixtures	416
	3 lamps	550
		8,521
Design fees (estimated):		1,200
Contingencies:		852
	TOTAL:	$10,573

of the square or linear footage of each item (ceiling, partitioning, plumbing and electrical work, and so on). Items to be purchased are selected and priced, the cost multiplied by the number of units desired and added up to give a reasonably firm final total. A cushion, or contingency allowance, should be included to allow for unexpected on-site developments, price changes, and similar surprises, almost certain to be in the upward direction. A skeleton outline for a typical budget follows:

> BASIC CONSTRUCTION (CONTRACTS):
> *Demolition*
> *General construction*
> *Electrical*
> *Plumbing*
> *HVAC*
> *Painting*

DECORATIVE ITEMS (PURCHASES):
  Floor covering (plus installation)
  Wall treatment (paper, vinyl, and so on)
  Furniture (plus cover fabrics and installation)
  Drapery (fabric plus makeup and installation)
  Lighting fixtures and lamps
  Accessories
  Art
FEES:
  Architectural and engineering
  Consultants
  Interior design
OTHER:
  Permits, insurance, and other items not included above
  Contingencies

Estimates, Bids, and Contracts

Following such budget estimating, actual prices are usually obtained from contractors. One general contractor or each trade separately can provide a figure based on time (the working time of employees on the job) and materials, plus allowances for profit and overhead, usually added as a percentage of time and materials. This is called a *firm estimate* if it is based on specific plans and specifications and put in writing. Similarly, suppliers of furniture and other purchased items will quote firm prices in writing.

In theory, the total of all such firm estimates will be the total cost of the project. In practice, this figure often turns out to be low, time and material costs rising to well beyond estimated levels. To obtain tighter controls, estimates must be converted to firm prices, or *bids*. This involves asking for prices from several potential contracting firms (usually three), each of which is provided with identical plans and specifications. All the bidders, chosen on the basis of reputation and recommendations, must be acceptable, ensuring that the low bidder's price and quality of work will be satisfactory. Taking bids for very small projects is rarely practical; even larger projects are often contracted on the basis of a firm, or *guaranteed*, estimate rather than through bidding.

Once bids or firm estimates have been accepted, it might seem that the cost of construction work would be fixed. In practice, design changes—additional or altered items; new choices of materials or finishes; even major replanning—may be necessary for one or another reason, each change entailing a cost adjustment, usually in an upward direction. Once the job has been contracted for, the contractor is under no pressure to minimize the pricing of such *extras*. Making many changes in design after work is under way will almost certainly lead to cost overruns. While some changes will almost inevitably be necessary, minimizing them is an important factor in keeping project costs under control.

The purchase of such items as furniture, floor covering, fabrics, and lighting fixtures usually does not involve bidding, since such items are unique. Those offered to the interior design and decoration field are generally assigned a *list price*, which is subject to a large discount when purchased by trade or professional buyers, usually ranging from 25 to 50 percent, with 40 percent common. The availability of such discounts is significant in encouraging clients to turn to professional design service rather than making direct purchases. Materials and objects available at retail are not subject to such discounts, a factor leading to the sharp separation between retail and "to the trade" suppliers. The same products are rarely offered in both markets.

Traditionally, interior decorators acted as specialized retailers, purchasing items at *trade,* or discount, prices and reselling them to their clients at marked-up prices. The difference between the purchase and selling prices provided the decorator's fee or profit. This way of working has been largely supplanted by the more professional practice of offering all trade or discount prices directly to the client and billing a designer fee clearly separated from the cost of products or construction services. The designer offers access to showrooms and trade sources, but the client, or end-user, makes purchases, either directly from the manufacturer or through authorized dealers who provide installation and other services figured into a firm price.

Suppliers are generally prepared to sell directly to client end-users on the basis of purchase orders written or authorized by designers. It is important to clarify credit responsibility, since suppliers are sometimes concerned about large orders when placed by designers or firms with limited financial responsibility. Payment in advance (with an order) by the client directly or through the designer's firm will usually allay any fears and make orders fully acceptable to trade sources.

Design Fees

Designers' professional fees can be arrived at in several different ways. A percentage of the cost of work—usually in the range of 10 to 15 percent—has some traditional standing but is now generally regarded as illogical. Simply choosing the color of a carpet may lead to a large purchase and, therefore, a large fee, while demanding work over small details may entail no purchases, therefore generating no fees. There is also always the concern that a percentage fee may motivate the designer to urge more rather than less costly solutions to every problem.

668. *Showroom displays of products used in interiors help designers and clients make the most suitable choices. Small samples of tile, for instance, do not give an accurate image of a total installation, and the nature of the material makes it awkward to move, file, or store.*

Here, the United Ceramic Tile Showroom in New York, designed in 1986 by Paul Haigh, architect, exhibits large areas of tile in many different colors and patterns. (Photograph: © Elliott Kaufman)

For these reasons, a fee based on working time expended, or *hourly rate,* has become more widely accepted as most truly professional. Such charges combine the actual salary costs for each person involved in a project with overhead and profit margins. Charges are billed on the basis of time-sheet hours and agreed-upon standard rates. A billing rate of between two and a half and three times the actual salary cost is usual. The solitary designer must establish an hourly rate related to this basis. Expenses (travel, telephone, making prints, and so on) are billed in addition.

For the many clients who are unwilling to enter into open-ended fee arrangements, designers will calculate an estimated fixed maximum based on anticipated working time. Such estimates often turn out to be the effective total fee, making

them similar to fixed fees, an alternative basis for design service compensation in which an agreed-upon figure is established on the basis of the work involved. It is a good idea to bill design fees on a monthly basis, so that any dissatisfactions with performance or billings will surface before the sums in dispute become major.

CONTRACTS

Two kinds of contracts are involved in interior design projects: between designer and client and between client and contractor or supplier. The latter is made for work or a product after a bid or purchase price proposal is accepted. The designer has a role in supervising such contracts to ensure that the terms are fair

669

669. *Top furniture manufacturers take pride in employing distinguished designers to develop spaces that are eye-catching in themselves as well as persuasive backgrounds for their products, often simulating possible typical uses. This Knoll International showroom in Atlanta was designed by Lee Stout with Hendrick and Associates in 1987. (Photograph courtesy Knoll International, Inc.)*

and carry no ambiguities that could later lead to disputes.

The contract between designer and client may take the form of a standardized agreement as developed by the various professional organizations or a simple letter of agreement in which the designer sets forth the terms on which work will be billed and the client makes an acceptance in writing. Strictly verbal agreements can be valid contracts, but since the terms are not recorded, they can readily become subject to dispute. Experience suggests that some agreement in writing is always best. For larger projects, a review of contractual documents by a lawyer familiar with the field is generally advisable.

It is important that the limits of the designer's responsibility be made clear to the client, since disputes often arise over such issues as perfection of work done or conformance to time schedules, which the designer cannot guarantee. Designers are also wise to carry insurance against being held liable for product failures or any risks that can possibly arise out of the complex events that a major design project can involve, from peeling wallpaper to major injury to a workman. The specifics of written designer-client agreements should establish the obligations that the designer assumes and the limits of these obligations.

If designers retain the services of consultants and other professionals, such as architects and engineers, and bill the consultants' fees to clients as expenses, they can become involved in any problems arising from such services. Therefore, while the designer will often aid the client in selecting consultants, financial arrangements are best made directly between client and consultant.

In general, the professional designer will find it best to limit all financial dealings with a client to direct professional fees while arranging for the client to pay for all purchases, professional fees, and any other costs directly, without going through the designer. This eliminates possible tax liabilities and many bookkeeping problems while keeping the possibilities for financial disputes to a minimum.

PROJECT MANAGEMENT

In addition to taking bids and awarding contracts, complete project management involves negotiating lease terms, scheduling, and expediting—coordinating the work of different trades, scheduling the delivery and installation of purchased items, and reviewing and approving all bills and invoices as they are received. The aim is overall control of performance in terms of both time schedule and costs. For large projects, project management may be assigned to a special person or a firm with experience in this field. Employing sophisticated

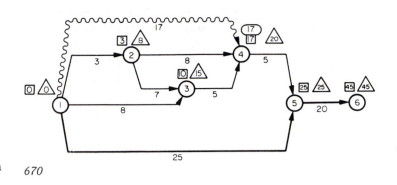

670

control systems such as CPM (Critical Path Method) or PERT (Program Evaluation and Review Technique), which make use of charts and, sometimes, computer techniques, can be helpful for complex projects (fig. 670). Interior designers and space planners may take on all or part of project management responsibilities in connection with smaller projects.

When space is to be leased in an office or loft building, project management usually begins with the negotiation of lease terms. Most such leases require the building owner to provide elements of interior finish (finished floors, ceiling, partitions, and lighting) to create usable space of a quality defined as *building standard*. Such standards usually allow for a minimal, utilitarian office installation, including a specified amount of partitioning, number of doors, and level of lighting. If the client

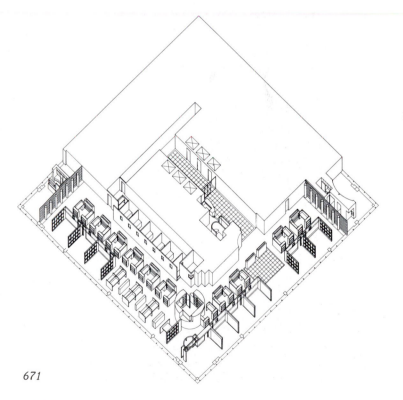

671

670. CPM (Critical Path Method) and PERT (Program Evaluation and Review Technique) are project management systems that organize scheduling by means of lists and charts that define the relationships between the steps of a project. In this CPM chart, lines represent activities or processes; circles, or nodes, represent the beginnings and ends of processes. Numbers indicate the duration of each step (in days or weeks). The critical path that gives the system its name is the route through the chart, from left to right, that adds up to the longest total time. This represents, therefore, the shortest possible time in which the project can be completed, if each stage remains on schedule, and so is the sequence most attentively monitored. Other paths allow some leeway in time —the float, indicated by numbers in boxes—and are thus not critical. From Critical Path Method by A. T. Armstrong-Wright.

671. An axonometric drawing illustrates an office design project. Building-standard interiors furnish a floor covering, utility-quality lighting, and a minimum linear footage of partition walls with doors. The glass-block walls, special partitions, and work-station units shown here raise this interior far above the building-standard level; the tenant must either pay for the enhancements or, if they are provided by the building owner, negotiate a higher rent than the base rent charged for building-standard space. This largely open office space was designed by Tod Williams and Associates, Architects, for B.E.A., an investment banking firm in New York, in 1979. (Courtesy Tod Williams and Billie Tsien Associates, Architects)

accepts building-standard work, the designer usually has no role beyond making a plan layout and selecting paint colors. In practice, most offices are designed for a quality level far above this standard (fig. 671).

A negotiated lease defines the work to be done by the owner, with costs covered by the negotiated rent, and the items to be paid for by the tenant. Tenants unfamiliar with interior projects often accept highly disadvantageous terms, exposing them to unexpectedly large costs for work that could have been covered under terms of the lease. A document called a *work letter* usually defines exactly the details of the work to be provided under a lease. Drawings and specifications are often made part of the lease terms. Once a lease is signed, any additional work becomes an *extra,* which is billed for on the basis of time and materials plus overhead and profit (a *cost-plus* basis). This poses another hazard for the unwary tenant, since the contractors are employed by the building owner and no restraints exist to keep the costs of extras down. As a result, such costs can easily mushroom, to disastrous effect on the project budget.

Good project management strives to minimize extras by establishing lease terms that define building-standard work as accurately as possible and by setting firm prices for all work beyond the standard covered in the lease. Changes in requirements that develop while a job is in progress and unforeseen conditions that surface after the lease is signed usually make some extras inevitable, but good planning keeps these situations to a minimum, thus avoiding cost overruns and many disputes as well.

Another major source of disputes is scheduling, an issue that involves move-in dates, when rent payments begin, and, if delays occur, the payment of double rents. When a project is in the planning stage, designers tend to be optimistic about rapid completion. Contractors anxious to be assigned work often give unrealistic completion dates. Whether acting as or working with project managers, designers have a responsibility to develop realistic schedules, leaving provision for the delays that always seem to occur, through late delivery of materials, the need to correct errors, changes made while work is in progress, and such unpredictable events as strikes, accidents, and storms.

While small projects involve lesser sums of money and fewer complexities of scheduling, the same problems may arise. Careful and realistic project management is just as important to the residential client undertaking a minor renovation as it is to a large corporation engaged in a vast project. The reputation of a designer often rests as much upon efficient handling of time schedule and money matters as upon the aesthetic success of the completed project.

HUMAN PROBLEMS

In addition to the many technical and practical problems already discussed, there is another group of problems rarely discussed in design schools. These are the problems created by people—by clients, by the designers themselves, and by the relationships between them that arise in the course of a design project. Any design professional will admit, at least unofficially, that people problems are more common and more difficult than technical problems. Among themselves, designers often grumble, "Design would be easy if it weren't for clients." While the human problems of design work have no clear solutions, they are worth reviewing in order to avoid or minimize them.

Every client-designer relationship—except when the designer takes both roles—begins with two strangers who have different backgrounds, training, and objectives. The client wants a design problem dealt with quickly, economically, and, often, in accordance with some preconceived ideas. The designer wants a project that will be, above all, a credit aesthetically, a source of professional satisfaction, and, perhaps, a link to additional projects. No designer wants to lose money or have a disgruntled client to deal with, but many designers consider publication in a respected professional magazine a more significant measure of success than monetary profits or even client satisfaction.

For many clients, the design project is their first such experience; in fact, it may be their only one. Clients face difficult decisions, perhaps involving troubling compromises and large sums of money. At the same time, they harbor desires and expectations that are likely to be a mix of realism, hopes, more or less realistic, and ideas, dreams, and notions that may be anything from useful to absurd. Projects are usually more complex, slower, and more expensive than they expect. In the modern world, it seems to be an unfortunate reality that the quality of workmanship constantly declines while costs and delays constantly increase. Clients' past experience of the lower prices and better-quality performance that were the norms of a few years ago tends to generate expectations that often cannot be justified under present conditions. Designers often find the temptation to tell the clients what they want to hear at the start of a project all too strong, inevitably resulting in disappoint-ments and recriminations.

It cannot be denied that some clients and designers are difficult—demanding, unrealistic, quarrelsome, arbitrary, and inconsistent. Every experienced designer can tell stories of clients who change their minds endlessly, who have wildly unrealistic ideas about money, who blame every trouble on their designer, and who fly into unreasonable rages, often leading to lawsuits. Stories of designers with comparable tendencies to make promises that cannot be kept, who overrun budgets by appreciable amounts, and who hide behind the screen of "artistic temperament" also have some unfortunate bases in fact. For a project to run smoothly, both client and designer must act reasonably, making an effort to understand the other's point of view and cooperate together, and, above all, to be honest in terms of communication, expectations, and actual dealings of every sort.

First meetings between client-to-be and designer are very important. Issues of taste and aesthetic preferences can be explored by looking at published illustrations of completed projects by the designer and others in magazines and books and making on-site visits to a designer's previous projects. If marked differences of opinion emerge in such sessions, they should be regarded as danger signals. At the same time, qualities of personality and compatibility can be smoked out to see if designer and client can set up a cooperative relationship. For the designer, any hint that a prospective client is contentious, suspicious, devious, mean, or cranky suggests that it is best to leave the project to someone else. It is not easy to pass up an interesting assignment voluntarily, but the strain of following through on a project under those circumstances promises to worsen rather than improve the relationship.

The term *client* implies an individual person, but many interior design clients are families, firms, organizations, or other groups of people. Dealing with groups multiplies the probabilities of human problems and calls for considerable tact. A business may be represented by an owner, by several partners, by one or more top executives, or by a committee representing various aspects of the client organization. These people are subject to change (through retirement, resignation, firing, illness, and death), and replacements may not be as sympathetic and cooperative as their predecessors. Committees and groups often have members with differing points of view or even direct conflicts. Steering a course between such members without succumbing to the politics involved can be very complex. The success of many well-known designers of large projects comes as much from their skill in this territory as from their design talent.

Residential clients present a less complex pattern but similar hazards. Many appear as couples, married or otherwise. A couple may approach a long-awaited new house or apartment with the expectation that they have totally matching desires, only to discover unexpected differences. Every designer with residential experience can tell stories of difficult and painful sessions, even quarrels and breakups generated by planning a home. Early discovery of such possible frictions is another danger signal to be heeded. The designer's tact and skill may be stretched to the limit in dealing with such problems.

672

Given reasonable and cooperative people on both sides of a client-designer relationship, avoiding problems is largely a matter of exercising good professional skills with particular emphasis on all matters relating to time schedule and to budget. Not surprisingly, money is one of the most common causes of difficulties and disputes. Following good business procedures meticulously and making sure that the client understands them is probably the most important key to satisfactory client relationships. Even when inevitable differences occur, good business practices will help to minimize the strains and avoid the unhappy problems of litigation.

DESIGN BUSINESSES
Every designer or design firm is a business that follows one of several organizational structures.

Sole Proprietorship
The individual designer usually starts out, and may continue throughout a career, as a *sole proprietor*. The designer simply owns his or her business and receives fees and pays bills out of a personal bank account or, often, from a separate business account maintained as an aid in keeping personal and business funds identifiable as clear entities. Sole proprietorship has the advantage of simplicity and directness; it requires no formal

672. This workplace answers all the professional and business requirements of a sole proprietor—a designer who works alone. Antine Polo designed his own office, in Englewood, New Jersey. (Photograph: © Peter Paige)

steps to start up and may serve well for many design businesses. A sole proprietor can, of course, hire employees and even build up a large organization.

An owner can even retire while retaining ownership of the ongoing business. In practice, however, the continuation of a business usually works out better through one of the other forms of ownership. A sole proprietorship is, at least in the design fields, usually a difficult business to sell if the owner wants to retire or give up the business for any other reason. Reputation and "good will" are usually so firmly attached to the person of the owner as to leave the business with little else of value beyond any outstanding contracts and some furniture and equipment.

Partnership

When a sole proprietor decides to share ownership with another person (perhaps an employee, another designer, or a business aide), or several people decide to establish a joint business, a *partnership* is the obvious form of organization. Several partners may bring various projects into a firm or may contribute a variety of complementary skills. Few individuals demonstrate equal abilities as designer, salesperson, office manager, and financial manager, while partners often represent such varied skills. A *silent partner* is someone who simply invests money in a partnership for profit, taking no part in the operation of the firm. Since design businesses rarely need large sums of money to start up, such investing partners are rare in design firms.

Usually, each partner invests some funds or contributes something else of value (such as a contract with a client) to the setting up of a partnership. This establishes each partner's share of ownership and forms the basis for the division of profits of the business. Partners may be equal, each with a half share, or may own different percentages of the business. The concept of junior and senior partnerships (with smaller and larger shares of ownership) is often used to give some share of ownership to employees who make a significant contribution to a firm. Partners normally take funds from the business through a *drawing account,* which provides regular payments similar to a salary for normal living expenses. At a longer interval, usually once a year, an accounting is made and any profits divided according to the terms of the partners' agreement. In small partnerships, the partners often adjust their rate of draw so as to take out profits on a continuing basis, leaving little to be divided annually.

Even when partnerships are started on a very informal basis, it is best to draw up a written agreement (usually with the help of a lawyer) that spells out the terms of the partnership in detail and covers such matters as the division of profits, the basis on which new partners may be taken in, and the terms for withdrawal of a partner or dissolution of the firm. Many design and architectural firms are partnerships, sometimes with the name of the founder (as in I. M. Pei & Partners) or with the names of all (or several senior) partners. A partner may retire while retaining an interest in the business or may sell an interest according to whatever terms may be agreed upon. Many partnerships have remained in business for many years, retaining the original name (for example, Skidmore, Owings & Merrill) after new partners join the firm and the founders retire.

The advantages of partnerships result from the adaptability of this form to group efforts and the ease with which ownership interest can be offered to new partners, allowing a firm to carry on almost indefinitely, even long after its founders have withdrawn. A matching disadvantage arises from the need for partners to get along well and agree about business decisions. Small partnerships (two or three partners) are particularly subject to trouble when a major disagreement occurs among the partners, often leading to the breakup of the firm. Differences in interests and styles, often the basis for making a partnership work, also commonly lead to problems that develop with the passage of time.

Incorporation

The third important format for a design business is *incorporation*. It is possible for one person to form a corporation, but it is a more generally used format for a firm with several principals or large firms with many owners. A corporation is an organization recognized by law as having an identity apart from its owners. Owners hold stock that represents their individual shares of ownership in the corporation. Profits are distributed as dividends, paid out at regular intervals. Most large businesses are *public corporations* whose stock is held by many investors and traded in a public stock market. Small corporations are usually *closely held,* that is, the stock is sold only to a restricted group—the original incorporators perhaps, or employees of the firm, or certain investors who have provided financial backing.

A corporation is controlled by a board of directors elected by the stockholders. The board elects officers who are usually the corporation's top executives. In a small corporation, the officers, the board, the stockholders, and the managers are often all the same people, perhaps those who would have been the partners if that form of organization had been chosen. Compensation to managers (as to employees) is generally through a salary and, possibly, bonuses instead of dividends. A corporation can accumulate undistributed income in ways that may have tax advantages and can provide funds for expansion, ownership of assets (such as cars or a building), investment in new ventures, and retirement income for managers. The corporate form of structure also shields the private assets of stockholders against any liability suits that may be brought against the firm.

Incorporation of small professional businesses has become increasingly popular in recent years because of the tax and other financial advantages that they can provide. It is important to consult legal and accounting advisers before deciding whether to incorporate a design business and in working out the details of incorporation. As in the case of partnerships, corporations can offer ownership shares to staff or to others and enable a business to continue beyond the involvement of any particular people. As prospective clients, big businesses and other large organizations are often reassured by this form of organization, which parallels their own organizational structures and avoids the more personal involvement of smaller firms. All of these factors tend to encourage the formation of design corporations.

Many designers are inclined to regard business matters as annoying and intrusive interruptions to creative work. They may therefore be tempted to deal with them grudgingly and carelessly. This attitude can all too readily lead to truly annoying and intrusive problems on a major scale. Time and effort devoted to the relatively small demands of good business practices pay off, in the long run, by making projects go smoothly, *freeing* time for creative work, and helping to build a reputation for skillful professional performance.

673

673. In the drafting room of the office of Robert A. M. Stern Architects, the typical layout of work stations with adjustable cantilever lamps over each drawing table is transformed by the addition of whimsical large, shaded lamps and an Ionic column, visible in the distance. (Photograph: © 1987 Peter Aaron/ESTO)

CHAPTER TWENTY

FUTURE DIRECTIONS

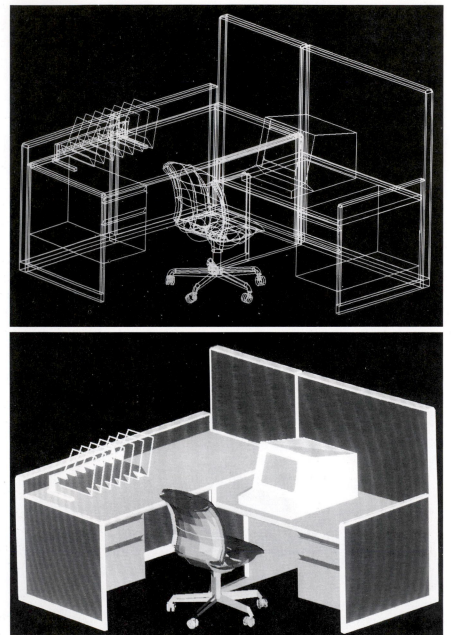

All attempts to predict the future are risky. It is a virtual certainty that even if predictions are basically sound, they will be wide of the mark in many details. The familiar case of Jules Verne's *Twenty Thousand Leagues Under the Sea* is a cautionary reminder; his prediction of the development of submarines was quite correct, but his yachtlike Victorian *Nautilus* is, in detail, totally unlike the modern reality. The future is not *something* already out there waiting to be foretold; it is, rather, a reality that will develop according to choices that people will make, singly and collectively, in interaction with uncontrollable events.

The future of interior design will be whatever its practitioners, their clients, and the public choose to make it. Each person involved in interior design or having any contact with the field can, by making decisions and choices, influence the direction that the field will take and so influence its future. Accepting or refusing a job or assignment, working in a particular way, selecting a certain material or product—all such steps make their own minute contribution to the aggregate of actions that becomes a trend, and thus a future direction.

Increasing Professionalism in Interior Design

It is not difficult, first of all, to identify a long-developing trend toward greater professionalism in interior design. This may make the field more serious and demanding, but it seems to be an inevitable drift in response to the complex demands of the modern world. The identification of the field with the amateurism of the eighteenth century and the craft traditions that stretch back into the distant past have largely broken down. Lord Burlington at Chiswick and Thomas Jefferson at Monticello were their own interior designers. Chippendale, Sheraton, and the Adam brothers were cabinetmakers, upholsterers, and, in the case of the Adam brothers, what would now be called contractors as well as designers. In the late nineteenth and early twentieth centuries, many well-known interior designers were simply self-taught amateurs who decided to become professional or fashion, display, or stage designers who drifted into the interior field. While this still happens occasionally, some professional training is now the norm, and a full four-year college course is available.

The pressure for full professional training comes from several sources: from the greater complexity and technical demands of many projects; the rising competitive standards within the profession; and the increasing formal requirements for accreditation and even licensing. A number of states now have licensing laws that attempt to ensure some level of competence among those who practice interior design. Most of these laws apply quite loose restrictions, but it seems certain that such restrictions will grow tighter as licensing laws become universal, gradually making interior design as closely controlled as architecture and engineering now are. In the meanwhile, there has been an increase in accreditation through self-imposed standards of training, experience, and competence, tested through examinations administered by the professional societies. A certificate from the National Council for Interior Design Qualification (NCIDQ) demonstrates a certain level of professional qualification, and more and more designers are volunteering to earn this badge of proficiency.

Setting higher professional standards is raising the level of design training and, in turn, the level of expectation on the part of prospective employers and clients. At the same time, clients such as major corporations and hotel and restaurant chains, having learned how much skilled interior designers can contribute, are employing them as *facilities planners*. Larger architectural offices now often include an interior design department staffed by designers whose professional status parallels that of the architects employed by the firm. All of these patterns of professionalism are quite new, and they can be expected to grow and spread.

It is also possible to observe a "trickle-down" effect in which the increasing professionalism of the design fields improves the quality of the interior design services offered by some furniture and department stores and by individual designers who work in the traditions of interior decoration, usually specializing in residential work. This has been accompanied by the wider availability of well-designed products, furniture, textiles, carpets, accessories, and other major components of interior design. Not too long ago, such good design was available only through very limited channels, often accessible only to accredited professionals.

Growing Public Interest in Design

Public awareness and acceptance of good design are on the rise, with more books, popular magazines, and newspaper home design pages joining with museum exhibitions to spread information on design excellence. While badly designed home furnishings remain commonplace, good alternatives are now readily available. Well-designed automobiles, stereo equipment, appliances, and similar products now have wide acceptance, while the success of well-designed home furnishings can be expected to encourage manufacturers to produce and distributors to stock better-designed products.

Computers and Design

A more specifically technical future direction relates to the constantly increasing involvement of computers and computer-

674. *A computer-plotted isometric drawing (above) illustrates an office work station. The hidden lines have not been removed, making this an X-ray, or skeleton, view. Color tones added to the module (below) block out the hidden lines. Not only is the result more realistic, but a nearly infinite range of color schemes can be reviewed on an appropriate monitor. (Courtesy Steelcase, Inc.)*

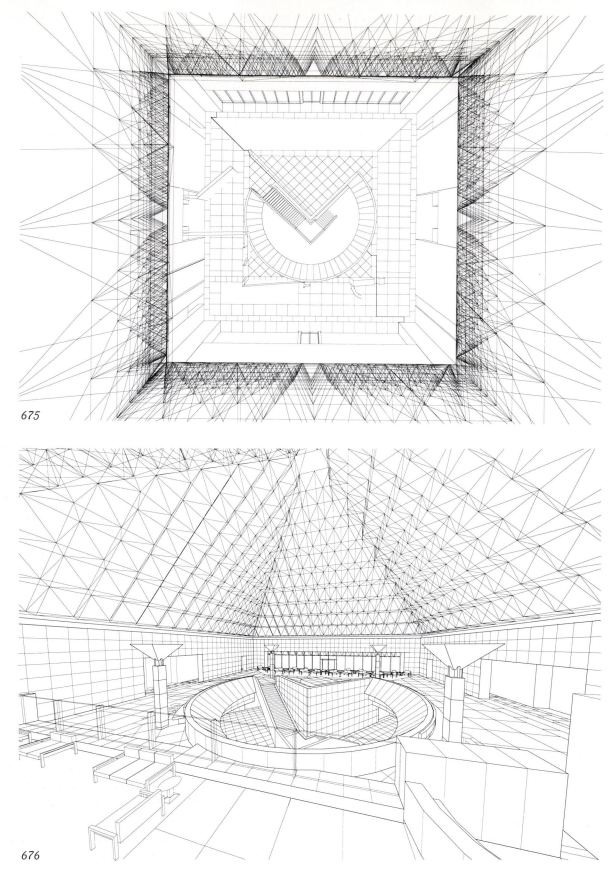

675

676

675–77. These three drawings were computer-generated. Once the basic data about an interior have been entered into the computer, any number of perspectives can be generated instantaneously, either on a screen or plotted on paper, as required. In fig. 675, a one-point perspective looks straight downward into a space—the floor plan of the atrium of an IBM building at Somers, New York, designed by I. M. Pei & Partners, 1986. Fig. 676 shows the plan at eye level. Fig. 677 shows the atrium in axonometric projection. (Courtesy CAD/East, Inc.)

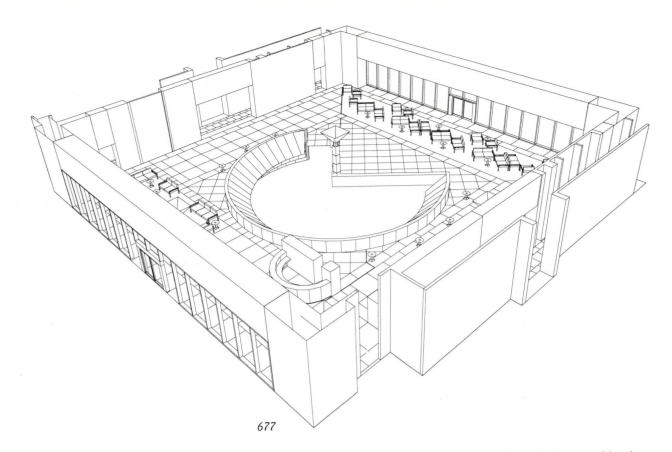

677

related techniques in all aspects of design work. Interior design is particularly well suited to computer applications because it so often makes use of repeated elements that are fairly well standardized (furniture, appliances, plumbing fixtures, doors, closets, and so on). By storing such elements in computer memory in plans, three-dimensional views, and such data as catalog numbers, manufacturer's identification, and price, this information can be called up as needed instantaneously for incorporation in drawings, specifications, estimates, and purchase orders. Until recently, such techniques have called for elaborate computer equipment and expensive programming hardly practical for the typical interior project, but increasingly small and inexpensive computer equipment is becoming available, bringing with it wider experience with computer techniques and greater acceptance in small- and medium-sized design firms.

It seems quite certain that the future will bring a rapid and widespread growth in the use of these computer-related techniques. The often expressed fear that computers will push aside human designers and make design work a mechanistic process seems to be subsiding as familiarity convinces more and more designers that computers are merely a tool to make routine work easier and more rapid and to aid human memory with reliable backup. Computers also have the potential to extend the capabilities of the designer, making larger projects more practical for the individual designer and small firms, thus giving them a wider range of outlets.

The design office tasks that computers can aid range from mundane business and clerical chores through drafting, specification writing, and perspective drawing to assistance in the actual planning process. The more complex tasks still demand large and powerful computer equipment, but the ever-expanding capacities of even the smaller computers, plus the ability of small-computer terminals to tap into larger computers over telephone wires, are making it possible to use highly sophisticated computer techniques with comparatively small and simple equipment.

A list of the things that computers can do now or will soon be able to do for interior designers is given in Table 22 on page 504. Taken together, these possibilities suggest that the typical design office will gradually become less a room filled with drafting tables and more a group of computer terminal work stations, with the drafting table an adjunct for occasional use. Many designers with a heavy investment in their knowledge of conventional planning and drafting skills fear that computer techniques will be unfamiliar and difficult, and therefore resist this idea.

In practice, these fears seem to have little basis. Many routine computer skills tend to become the province of specialists who

TABLE 22. COMPUTER TASKS

PERFORM OFFICE TASKS. Computers can expedite bookkeeping, payrolls, billings and purchase orders, tax returns and filing, and, through word-processing techniques, a considerable proportion of ordinary correspondence.

MAKE DATA BANKS OF INFORMATION INSTANTLY AVAILABLE. The information in manufacturers' catalogs and literature and the data in handbooks and journals together with legal codes and restrictions, often difficult to locate, use, and store, can be kept in compact memory and called up as needed. Central data banks can store vast amounts of such information and make it available to any subscriber over telephone lines. The centralized data will usually be kept constantly up-to-date to prevent the unintentional use of outmoded information.

DRAFTING. Placing and moving points and lines on the computer terminal screen, or monitor, builds up a constructed drawing similar to one done with pencil and instruments but accomplished with great rapidity and ease in making changes (figs. 675–77). Standard elements, plans of architectural elements, furniture items, and fixtures can be drawn from computer memory, moved about, and fixed in place. Lettering and dimensioning can be added with the same ease. Once completed at the computer, the drawing can be printed out by a printer or actually drawn by pen by a plotter, entirely mechanically, with a high level of precision and at great speed. Changes can readily be introduced in the computer memory and new prints produced as needed.

PERSPECTIVE DRAWING. Programs are now available that generate perspectives from basic plan and elevation data. The position of station point and angle of view can be changed, with the resulting varied perspective views instantly available on the monitor. As with other types of drafting, prints can be produced. Images of objects (such as furniture items) can be held in computer memory, to be called up and inserted into a perspective view, moved about, and shifted into the desired position. An interior thus developed in perspective can be redrawn as a plan or elevation and printed out in that form. Color tones can be added into such drawings for diagrammatic or realistic effect (fig. 674). Lighting can be inserted into a perspective and the visual effect of various positions and intensities of light sources studied visually in quite realistic images.

Fully realistic perspective imagery is still more of a future possibility than a current reality, but the technical means are already available to achieve this goal.

PLANNING. While this function remains at present largely a human monopoly, current programs will convert information about required areas and relationships into plan proposals. Although somewhat diagrammatic, these can form the basis for conventional planning. The ability of computers to hold and manipulate vast amounts of information makes these techniques particularly useful for very large and difficult projects such as airport terminals, hospital complexes, and large corporate and governmental offices.

ESTIMATING. With cost data in computer memory, it is possible to convert plan proposals into cost estimates almost effortlessly and instantaneously. As design progresses and various alternatives are considered, an ongoing estimated total, reflecting every new idea under consideration, can be constantly calculated.

SPECIFYING AND ORDERING. Catalog data, numbers, and prices held in computer memory, much as in estimating, can be used to prepare specifications and orders for products and goods such as furniture, light fixtures, carpeting, and fabrics. Orders can then be transmitted electronically directly to suppliers. This kind of electronic data transfer, in wide use in such fields as banking, financial markets, and even in the stock and inventory control of retail chains and mail-order houses, is still in the future for the design world. Its application to the design field is only a question of time.

---

work from the verbal or sketched instructions of designers, much as draftsmen now translate the ideas of architects to finished construction drawings. The aspects of computer use that serve creative design are generally quite easy to learn and, once the learning begins, turn out to be a source of pleasure and satisfaction to those willing to take the step. Computers and their associated programs constantly become less abstruse and more accessible to the nonspecialized user. The tasks desired are selected from a *menu* of choices displayed on a screen in easily understandable form, and processes that are slow and demanding when done by hand become quite easy and almost amusing with the aid of a computer.

Design schools are making computer techniques increasingly available to students, offering them basic familiarization, with a corresponding reduction in fear. The computer field is subject to such rapid development and change that techniques learned in school are virtually certain to be obsolescent by the time the graduated student is in office practice. Fortunately, learning current techniques takes only a few weeks of specialized study and practice at present, and as equipment and programming grow ever more accessible, it will become even easier.

For the designer who is not a full-time professional directing or working for a design office—the individual consultant designer, or the nonprofessional who wants to deal only with

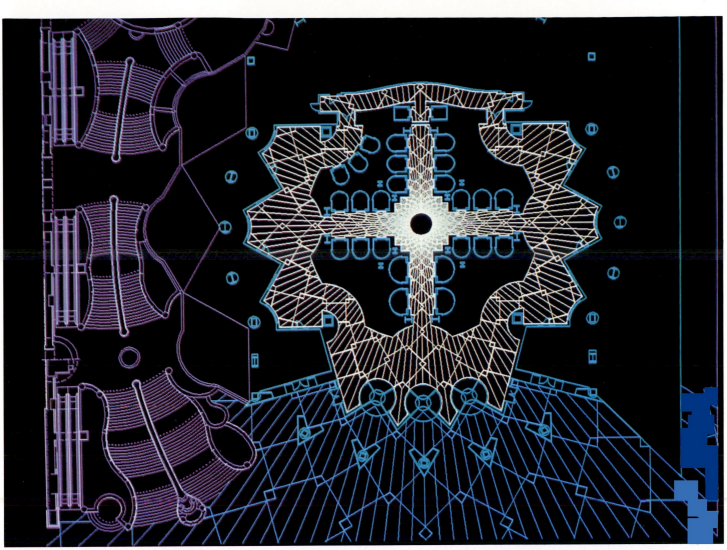

678

679

680

678–80. *These interiors, in different perspectives, were developed in color with computer graphic techniques. (Courtesy Skidmore, Owings & Merrill)*

681–83. Designer Michael Kalil—whose title in this project was Space Engineer—developed this futuristic office. The proposed space is capable of being transformed into almost any configuration to serve whatever function the occupant might wish. The prototype illustrated was built at the Armstrong World Industries Interior Design Center in Lancaster, Pennsylvania. When not in use, the room is a neutral box, its furniture and features stored beneath the flooring. Display screens can be activated (fig. 681); a horizontal, heat-sensor control bar emerges from the floor (fig. 682) to accept commands from the occupant's hand touch. A central seat is located between two posts that incorporate controls for lighting and furniture. The intention is to achieve universal flexibility and adaptability, with almost any imaginable configuration (fig. 683) temporarily available. Everything reverts to a neutral state when it is no longer required, just as a radio, TV, or computer becomes inactive when turned off. (Photographs courtesy Armstrong World Industries, Inc.)

smaller private projects—computer techniques may seem to have little significance. There is a strong possibility that some of these techniques will become available even at this level through connection into centralized equipment provided by manufacturing firms or by independent services. The typical home computer, for example, is not capable of producing complex interior perspective drawings, but access over phone lines to more sophisticated equipment enables the individual designer working at home to make occasional use of computer perspective drawing.

The showrooms of the larger manufacturers of interior-related products may offer computer services to customers, either directly or with the aid of specialists that the showroom might have on staff. When working with a client, designer and salesperson will often find it helpful to sit at a computer terminal and make instant visual comparisons between various possibilities, instantaneously calling up appearance data and relative costs.

TYPES OF FUTURE PROJECTS

The future of interior design involves more than computers. Once the computer is accepted and assimilated, its role will be clarified as an expediter of work processes. End results will remain a matter of the desires and intentions of clients and their designers. A more significant developing change in design practice is in some ways related to the increase in professionalism. This is the movement of interior design work toward two opposite poles that seem to grow increasingly far apart. These poles can be characterized, somewhat simplistically, as large and small projects.

The "large" end of the scale is dominated by projects with corporate, institutional, commercial, and governmental sponsors. Such work is almost always placed in the hands of larger firms with a staff headed by trained professionals, possibly licensed or accredited in some formal way as architects, engineers, interior designers, or planners. The actual designing is assigned to staff members at various levels of experience and training, often working in areas of specialization such as space planning, design, drafting, materials and color, or specification and purchasing. With architects increasingly active in interior design work, many architectural firms are developing interior design departments, which may work on buildings designed by the firm or take on separate interior design projects. Office planning, often called space planning, encourages the development of comparably large and specialized design organizations.

684

685

684. Much of the best in contemporary furniture is not available to the public in furniture or department stores, but only "to the trade" in the showrooms of manufacturers and importers. These showrooms, although open to the public, are generally known only to professional designers and architects and, through them, to their clients. The showroom illustrated here, Atelier International Ltd. in New York, is typical. Exposure to such displays is an important factor in acquainting a wider population with high-quality design. Stephen Kiviat, architect, with Skyline Architects, P.C.; Richard Penney, designer. (Photograph: © Norman McGrath)

685. More and more museums are recognizing well-designed furniture and other interior-related products as works of art, giving the museum-going public an opportunity to study objects to which they might otherwise not have access. The display illustrated is part of an installation, designed by R. Craig Miller, of twentieth-century furnishings in the Lila Acheson Wallace Wing's design and architecture gallery of the Metropolitan Museum of Art in New York. (Photograph: © Peter Paige)

The "small" project end of the scale includes residential design and the design of other small projects, such as smaller retail shops, individual professional offices, and single spaces within larger buildings. Such design work rarely interests larger design organizations, which find dealing with a client, offering supervision, and all of the other complications that go with even the smallest projects too troublesome in proportion to the fees. The individual private client usually expects a highly personal level of design service, which larger organizations are not equipped to offer even to their large clients.

This increases the opportunities for individual practitioners and very small firms, partnerships or individuals with one or two assistants. While this kind of design practice can also be highly professional, it is geared to a different scale and pace of work. The individual designer can give individual clients the personal attention they demand, and can do so at fee levels in line with the scale of the work in question. All of this suggests a future in which the medium-sized, all-purpose design firm will become rare, while both large, highly organized firms and individual designers and small firms will flourish.

USER PARTICIPATION IN DESIGN

In residential design, there is a new tendency for the user of the space, whether apartment, co-op, condominium, or house, not only to show more awareness of design excellence but also to claim a major role in the actual design process. Up to now, good interior design has generally been produced only by the professional decorator, designer, or architect, who could assert total control over a project. The costs of both professional design service and executing the professional's design are usually so high as to make this route available only to the well-to-do, the usual clients of architects and designers.

While this pattern still largely holds true, other forces are at work. Upward economic mobility in the general population, better and more widely available education, and an increasing recognition of the benefits of quality design are making design concerns more widely known. Subscriptions to design-oriented magazines, crowds attending design shows at museums, the sale of design books, and the success of retail shops devoted to home products of a high level of design excellence all point to a parallel trend toward the intelligent public's acceptance of a role in improving their home situations.

Self-help materials have been available in the field of interior design for many years, but most have consisted of watered-down versions of the more pretentious approaches of professional decoration. As their audience increasingly sees design as a tool for making life more comfortable and more attractive rather than as a way to display or attain status, the self-help books have responded. At the same time, design products have improved. Even an intelligent and well-informed householder is dependent on retail sources for well-designed products. Many of the unfortunate results of self-help owe as much to the badly designed merchandise in furniture and department stores as to any failure of public taste. As well-designed products become more widely available, known, and respected, the quality of the undesigned residential interior is certain to rise.

Even real-estate developers planning apartments, condominiums, and suburban houses (long known for their indifference to design standards) seem to be showing an increasing interest in design quality standards. Public awareness of design standards leads to demand for excellence. Realization that improved design quality can be a marketing asset may motivate a rising quality standard in the living spaces available to average occupants.

CONSULTANT SERVICES

In a related trend, consultant design services are being offered to the general public as an aid in smaller, generally residential projects. A consultant of this kind does not attempt to prepare complete plans for a space but offers instead an advisory service on an hourly or per diem basis to deal with aspects of an interior problem that need expert attention. This may include a visit to the space, discussions of how particular problems might be solved, advice about color and materials, suggestions for furniture selection, and any other issues the householder may find problematic. The consultant may provide plans or sketches, access to catalogs and showrooms, and references to tradesmen and contractors known to have a good record for quality performance.

This kind of service can be very helpful when the full services of an interior design firm are unnecessary or beyond the individual's means. It can deal with simple questions (the choice of a color, rug, fabric, or single piece of furniture) or with special problems such as built-ins (shelves or cabinets) or bathroom or kitchen renovations, or it can simply offer advice about practical issues that may be difficult for laymen to deal with. On another level, many people hesitate to turn over a project fully to professionals not only because of concern over costs but also because they wish to retain control of decisions about their own homes. A limited consultant service can be a highly satisfactory middle ground between totally unaided "do-it-yourself" design and full professional service.

686. Contemporary concepts of interior design, once the esoteric preserve of design professionals and their clients, are now broadcast, often only incidentally, to the wide film- and TV-viewing public. This set for the television program "Miami Vice" was designed by Robert Lacey, Jr., set decorator, and Jeffrey Howard, production designer; the influence of Memphis, Art Deco, and minimalism is evident. Public awareness develops through what is sometimes called a "trickle-down" effect. (Photograph: © 1985 Melyana)

687. Anne D. McCulley was the set decorator for this set for Ruthless People, a film that popularized the avant-garde imagery of Memphis furniture as only a mass medium can. (Photograph: © 1986 Touchstone Pictures)

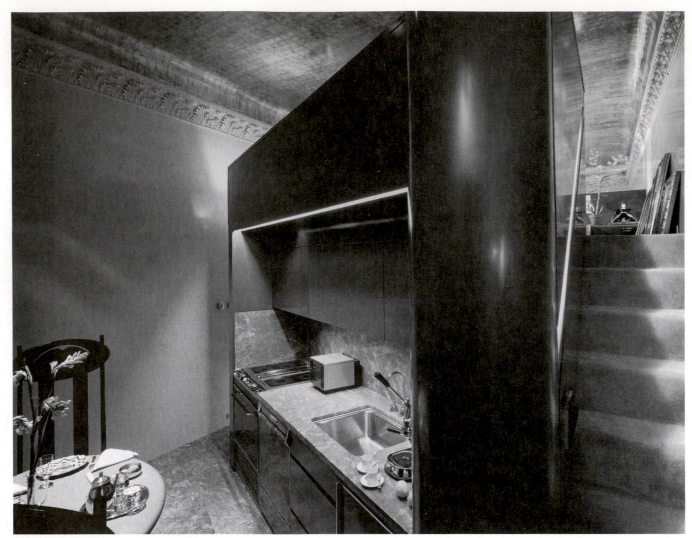

688

FUTURE TRENDS

Aside from these issues of how interior design services are offered, provided, and executed, there is also the interesting issue of what future directions will bring to the actual character, style, and look of spaces. Increasing populations will give rise to a greater concentration of people in cities and urban regions, leading to crowding and a reduction in the per capita space available. As resources are consumed faster than they can be replaced, the cost of materials and products will increase. At the same time, computerization and automation promise to make production more efficient and less dependent on manual labor. Office work and work in service fields have already outpaced agricultural and factory production work in developed countries.

Extracting predictions about design from these general trends, it seems that spaces for living and working are likely to get smaller, focusing attention on ways of gaining reasonable

comfort in smaller spaces. The costs of materials will probably reverse the long-term trend toward lowered costs for furniture and other products. This may well be offset by dropping costs in technological products whose construction relies more on complex elements suitable to automated production than on materials. Such trends are already apparent in the manufacture of automobiles, which have grown smaller in size while increasing in price. At the same time, new versions of electronic goods, such as stereo equipment, television sets, and computers, that are both smaller and functionally improved are constantly being offered at lower prices. Taken together, these directions should reverse the longstanding trend toward rapid obsolescence and society's "throwaway" orientation and lead to an increased concern for high quality and long life in the selection of materials and products.

688, 689. In an increasingly densely populated world, spatial compression inspires new design solutions. In a New York studio apartment, a cooking area (fig. 688) is tucked beneath a sleeping loft (fig. 689) reached by a short flight of steps. Although the space of this interior is used with maximum economy, individual design details are quite luxurious. Rosen Hochberg, designer. (Photographs: © 1983 Paul Warchol)

689

APPENDIX 1. *ARCHITECTURAL SYMBOLS*

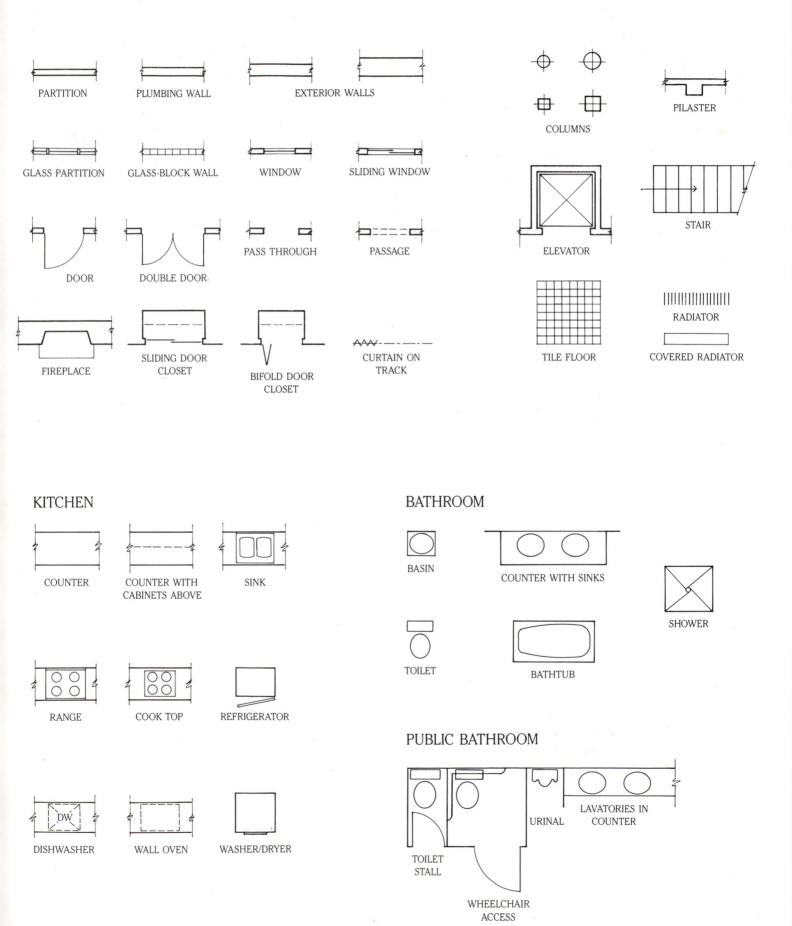

PARTITION

PLUMBING WALL

EXTERIOR WALLS

COLUMNS

PILASTER

GLASS PARTITION

GLASS-BLOCK WALL

WINDOW

SLIDING WINDOW

ELEVATOR

STAIR

DOOR

DOUBLE DOOR

PASS THROUGH

PASSAGE

TILE FLOOR

RADIATOR

COVERED RADIATOR

FIREPLACE

SLIDING DOOR CLOSET

BIFOLD DOOR CLOSET

CURTAIN ON TRACK

KITCHEN

COUNTER

COUNTER WITH CABINETS ABOVE

SINK

RANGE

COOK TOP

REFRIGERATOR

DW

DISHWASHER

WALL OVEN

WASHER/DRYER

BATHROOM

BASIN

COUNTER WITH SINKS

SHOWER

TOILET

BATHTUB

PUBLIC BATHROOM

URINAL

LAVATORIES IN COUNTER

TOILET STALL

WHEELCHAIR ACCESS

APPENDIX 2. *FURNITURE SYMBOLS*

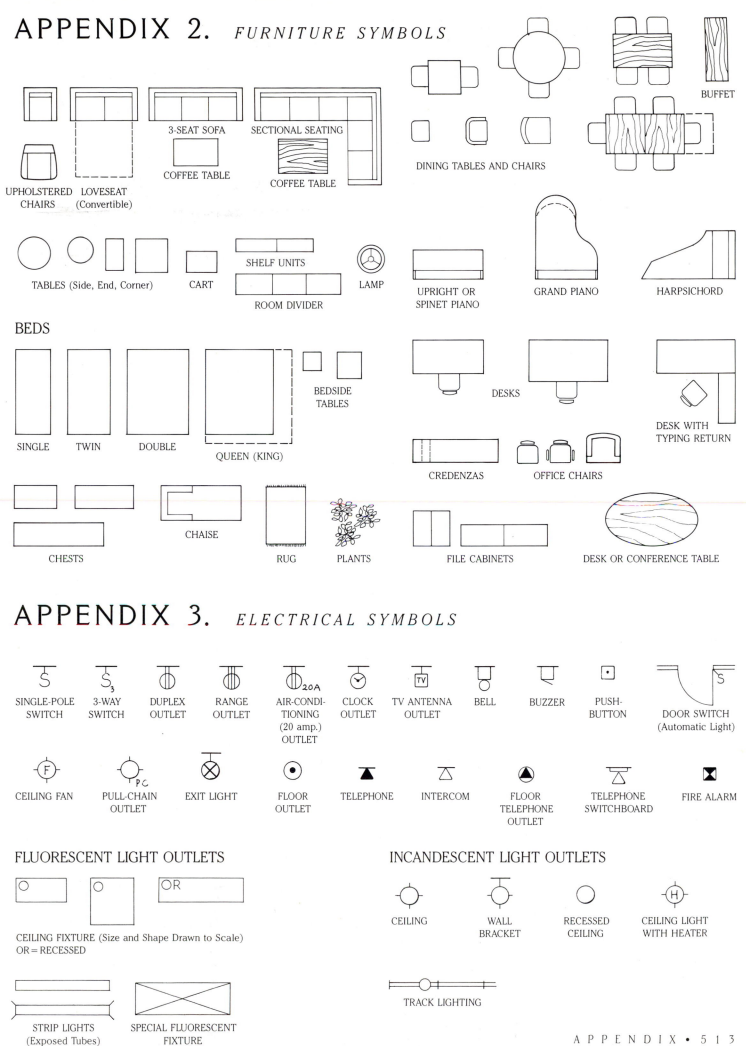

BUFFET

3-SEAT SOFA

SECTIONAL SEATING

COFFEE TABLE

COFFEE TABLE

DINING TABLES AND CHAIRS

UPHOLSTERED CHAIRS

LOVESEAT (Convertible)

TABLES (Side, End, Corner)

CART

SHELF UNITS

ROOM DIVIDER

LAMP

UPRIGHT OR SPINET PIANO

GRAND PIANO

HARPSICHORD

BEDS

SINGLE

TWIN

DOUBLE

QUEEN (KING)

BEDSIDE TABLES

DESKS

DESK WITH TYPING RETURN

CREDENZAS

OFFICE CHAIRS

CHESTS

CHAISE

RUG

PLANTS

FILE CABINETS

DESK OR CONFERENCE TABLE

APPENDIX 3. *ELECTRICAL SYMBOLS*

SINGLE-POLE SWITCH

3-WAY SWITCH

DUPLEX OUTLET

RANGE OUTLET

AIR-CONDI-TIONING (20 amp.) OUTLET

CLOCK OUTLET

TV ANTENNA OUTLET

BELL

BUZZER

PUSH-BUTTON

DOOR SWITCH (Automatic Light)

CEILING FAN

PULL-CHAIN OUTLET

EXIT LIGHT

FLOOR OUTLET

TELEPHONE

INTERCOM

FLOOR TELEPHONE OUTLET

TELEPHONE SWITCHBOARD

FIRE ALARM

FLUORESCENT LIGHT OUTLETS

CEILING FIXTURE (Size and Shape Drawn to Scale)
OR = RECESSED

STRIP LIGHTS (Exposed Tubes)

SPECIAL FLUORESCENT FIXTURE

INCANDESCENT LIGHT OUTLETS

CEILING

WALL BRACKET

RECESSED CEILING

CEILING LIGHT WITH HEATER

TRACK LIGHTING

APPENDIX 4. *MATERIAL INDICATIONS IN SECTION*

WOOD

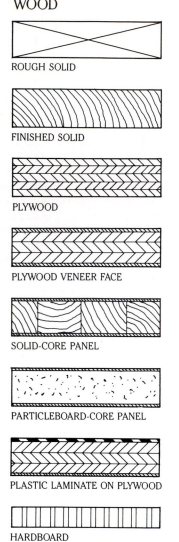

ROUGH SOLID

FINISHED SOLID

PLYWOOD

PLYWOOD VENEER FACE

SOLID-CORE PANEL

PARTICLEBOARD-CORE PANEL

PLASTIC LAMINATE ON PLYWOOD

HARDBOARD

MASONRY

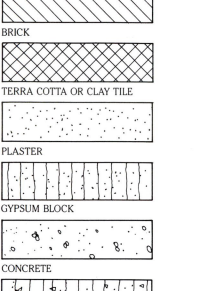

STONE

TERRAZZO

SLATE/BLUESTONE/SOAPSTONE

BRICK

TERRA COTTA OR CLAY TILE

PLASTER

GYPSUM BLOCK

CONCRETE

CONCRETE BLOCK

METAL

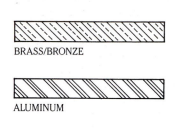

STEEL

BRASS/BRONZE

ALUMINUM

GLASS

CARPET

INSULATION

APPENDIX 5. *FURNITURE STYLES*

  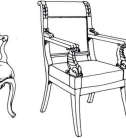    

GOTHIC   RENAISSANCE   LOUIS XV   EMPIRE   BIEDERMEIER   QUEEN ANNE

CHIPPENDALE   SHERATON   HEPPLEWHITE   AMERICAN COLONIAL (Windsor)   FEDERAL (Duncan Phyfe)   SHAKER   VICTORIAN

It is quite possible to work in interior design without making perspective drawings, and, indeed, to the uninitiated, what is merely a matter of technique may appear obscure and difficult. There are many excellent how-to books on the subject, but most emphasize drawings of objects or building exteriors rather than interiors. Since drawing in perspective is the most realistic and, hence, persuasive way to illustrate design proposals, it is a skill well worth acquiring.

In nature, objects far away appear smaller than nearer objects of the same size—an effect produced by the manner in which the lens of the eye projects an image on the retina. A camera lens similarly projects an image on film, resulting in the highly realistic quality of photographs, which are, themselves, accurate perspectives. Close observation of any scene can also, as artists know, be translated into accurate perspective. The familiar example of a road moving away across a barren landscape until its lines meet at a point on the horizon, while the telephone poles on either side become smaller and closer as they move into the distance (fig. 690), illustrates one of the basics of geometrically constructed perspectives: parallel lines converge toward a point on the horizon.

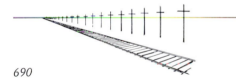

690

When the aim, however, is to illustrate an interior, possibly not yet built and certainly not yet furnished, direct observation will not serve. Instead, a specific, methodical process produces the desired drawing. Although the process may be followed entirely freehand, better results are obtained at a drawing board using the appropriate drafting instruments (see Chapter 17, pages 465–66). Going through the following routine with a few different examples will soon make the technique familiar.

1. Obtain a floor plan of the space to be illustrated. This may be an architect's construction drawing, a printed plan of the kind often provided by real-estate firms, or a plan

drawn for the purpose—even in freehand. Whatever its source, the plan must be to scale. Although ¼″ = 1′-0″ is often convenient, a ½″ scale may be preferable for a very small space and ⅛″ for a large area. If the available plan has been drawn accurately to a scale other than these common scales, it can still be used. Note down the ceiling height of the space and any other significant heights (such as windowsill and head [top], door height, or heights of shelves or mantels).

2. Decide where the imagined viewer will stand and mark this spot with a circled point or cross (fig. 691). This is the *station point,* usually marked SP. For most rooms, it is best to locate the station point near the corner farthest back from the part of the room to be shown so as to produce the most inclusive view possible. It can even be placed outside the walls of the room, although this will produce a view that cannot be seen in reality.

3. Decide on the direction in which the imaginary viewer will look and mark this direction with an arrow. An angle of 30° on either side of this arrow gives the widest view that can be drawn without distortion; this 60° cone of vision approximates normal vision. An angle of up to 90° (45° on either side of the line-of-vision arrow) may be used, if a bit of distortion at the edges of the finished drawing is not a problem. Several possible locations for the station point and several directions of viewing should be tried; it is often helpful to draw station points, viewing direction arrows, and indications of the 60° to 90° cones of vision on separate pieces of tracing paper so that they can be moved about the plan experimentally to ascertain the advantages of each.

4. Once the station point and direction of view have been marked, rotate the plan until the viewing direction arrow is vertical—that is, until it points straight up on the drawing board (fig. 692). Tape the plan down, making sure to leave ample space above it for the final drawing.

5. Draw a horizontal line across the sheet that touches the topmost corner of the rotated plan. This line represents the *picture plane,* or surface upon which the final drawing will be projected in the following steps.

6. Draw a line vertically upward from the topmost corner of the plan into the area

where the final drawing will be made. This will serve as the line along which all heights will be measured.

7. Along this *height line,* at a short distance above the plan, measure off the floor-to-ceiling height of the space to the same scale as the plan. This height will represent the most distant corner of the space that will be visible in the final drawing.

8. Measure upward from the bottom of this height line, to the same scale as the plan, a height that represents the eye level of the imagined viewer. This is usually about 5′0″ to 5′6″ for a standing person, less for a seated person, more for a raised point of view.

9. Draw a horizontal line through the eye-level point right across the drawing. (It will be parallel to the picture plane.) This is the *horizon line.* In an outdoor view it is the line

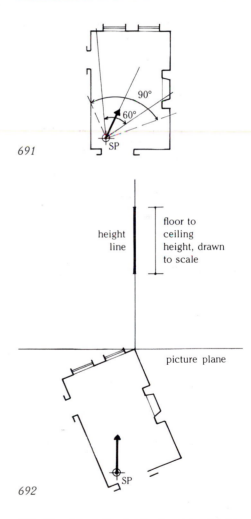

691

692

691. *A plan drawn to scale shows the space to be drawn in perspective, and the point marked SP indicates where an imagined viewer stands. An arrow indicates the direction in which the viewer is looking. Light lines indicate a 60° cone of vision, dotted lines the maximum 90° cone of vision.*

692. *The plan on the drawing board is rotated to render the direction of viewing vertical; a picture plane line is added. The heavy vertical line above the plan is a height line drawn to scale.*

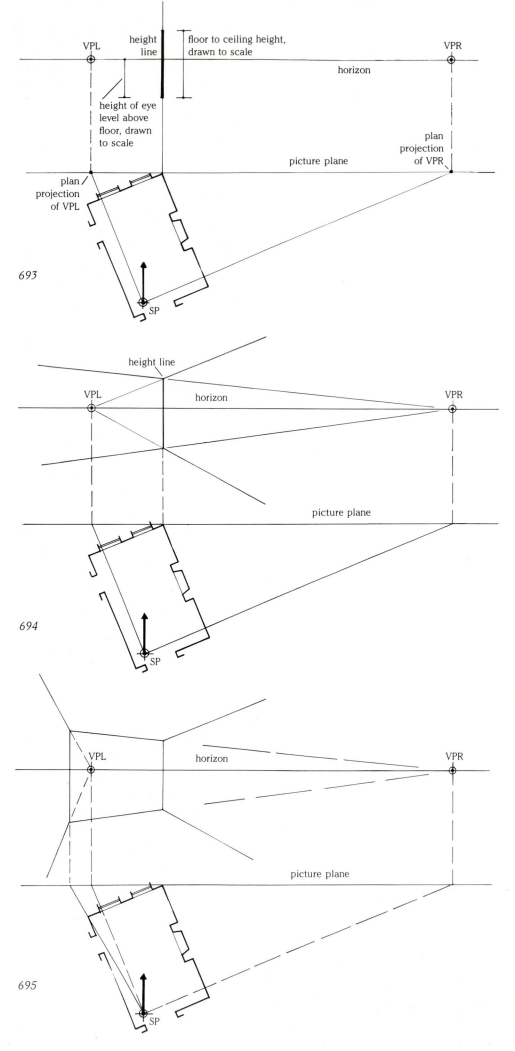

693

694

695

where earth and sky seem to meet—hence the name—but in an interior it is simply an important construction line, that is, a line used in the process of drawing a perspective that will be removed from the final drawing. (It will, however, give the level of the horizon should it be visible through a window or other opening.)

10. It is now possible to locate two *vanishing points,* one each to the right and left. This is done in two stages. First, in the plan, draw a line through the station point parallel to the side walls pictured in the plan, extending it to the picture plane line. Next, draw another line from the station point parallel to the front wall of the room in plan until it, too, reaches the picture plane. Mark these points.

11. From these two intersection points on the picture plane, carry a vertical construction line up to the horizon (fig. 693). These intersections are the two vanishing points that will be used to define the perspective. Mark them VPL and VPR. It often happens that one or the other of these points is so far to one side as to be off the drawing board. The point can still be marked on the desk top or even on an adjacent desk or table. If this is too inconvenient, however, go back to Step 4 and turn the plan to an angle that will keep both vanishing points on the drawing board.

12. Using the vanishing point developed by the line parallel to the front wall of the space, draw lines from the vanishing point extending toward the top and bottom of the height line (fig. 694). These lines will represent the intersections of the back wall with the floor and ceiling.

13. The height line forms one corner of the back wall; to find the other corner, draw a light construction line from the station point through the second back wall corner in plan to the picture plane (fig. 695). Extend a construction line vertically upward from this point across the perspective. The portion of this line that runs from the floor-to-ceiling lines of the back wall may be drawn heavily; it represents the second corner of the back wall and completes the trapezoid that depicts this wall in the final perspective.

14. From the second vanishing point (VPL), four lines can now be drawn outward to show the intersections of the side walls of the space with the floor and ceiling. The box image of the room is now complete.

15. Elements in or against the walls of the space, such as windows, doors, or fireplace, can now be added. The right and left sides are found by using construction lines in plan, the

693. The viewer's eye level is measured, to scale, from the height line. This point fixes the horizon line, parallel to the picture plane.

Lines pass through the station point parallel to each set of walls in the plan and extend to the picture plane. Dotted verticals from these points up to the horizon locate the right and left vanishing points, VPR and VPL.

694. Lines radiating from each of the vanishing points and extending to the top and bottom of the height line and beyond it are drawn to represent floor and ceiling intersections with the back and right-hand walls.

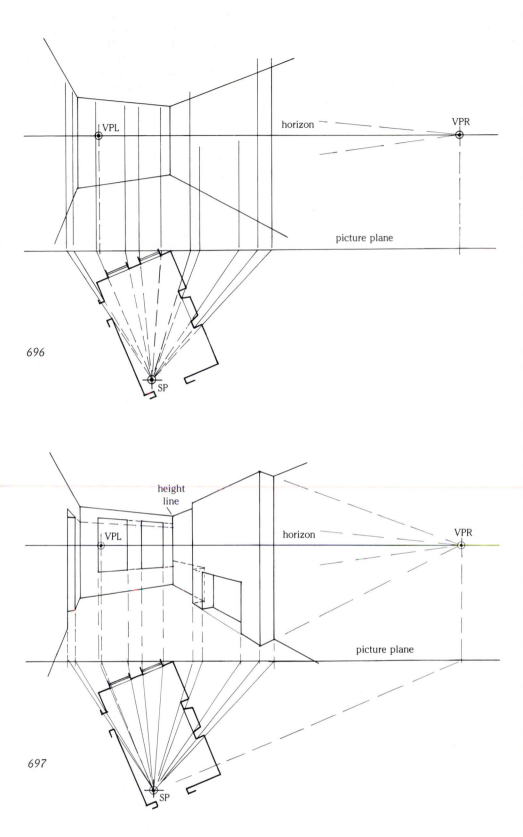

696

697

sight lines, that begin at the station point and run from each of the edges of the element to the picture plane, just as the corner was found in Step 13 (fig. 696). The top and bottom lines are found by measuring the required heights on the height line—the back, right-hand corner of the space—and carrying a line from the appropriate vanishing point through the intersection of the element's height on the height line to the element (fig. 697). The outline of these elements may now be drawn in heavily.

16. Objects adjacent to a wall and extending into the space are drawn by developing their intersection with the wall, as in Step 15 above, and extending lines outward until they meet the construction lines that locate the other corners (fig. 698). These are found with sight lines in plan that radiate from the station point, pass through those corners in plan, and continue to the picture plane. Verticals are then brought up into the perspective to locate the required corners. The corners are connected by lines radiating from the appropriate vanishing point.

The object's corners on the floor (for example, the table legs in fig. 698) are found by taking the sight lines through each corner in plan and finding their intersection with the wall. This gives two of the lower corners. These points are extended in lines running toward the farther vanishing point, and their points of intersection with the vertical sight lines from the opposite corners in plan locate the remaining lower corners on the floor.

Objects that do not touch any walls can, similarly, be drawn by tracing out imaginary lines along the floor to an adjacent wall, establishing a height at the wall, and extending horizontal lines outward at this height.

17. Objects at angles to the main walls of the space can be drawn by running sight lines through the corners of the object to the picture plane and thence upward vertically into the perspective (fig. 699). Imaginary lines from corners of the object intersect at right angles with the nearest wall. These intersections are given sight lines to the corresponding wall in the perspective. These lines will intersect with the dotted line radiating from the height line and extending down the same wall, and then they will be extended toward the opposite vanishing point until they meet the sight lines drawn from the actual location of the object in plan and extended upward into the perspective. These intersections give the location of two of the object's corners. Once these corners are thus

695. The left rear corner of the space is obtained by drawing a line from the station point through the top left corner in plan to the picture plane. A vertical carried upward from that intersection locates the left corner. Lines can now be added radiating from VPL extending to the top and bottom of the new corner line to represent the top and bottom lines of the left wall, completing the basic box of the space.

696. Elements in or adjacent to the walls are located by drawing lines from the station point through the edges of the elements in plan and extending these lines to the picture plane. Verticals carried up into the perspective locate the left and right edges of these elements.

697. Top and bottom lines for these elements are located by measuring the element to scale along the height line and carrying lines outward from the vanishing points through the heights established on the height line.

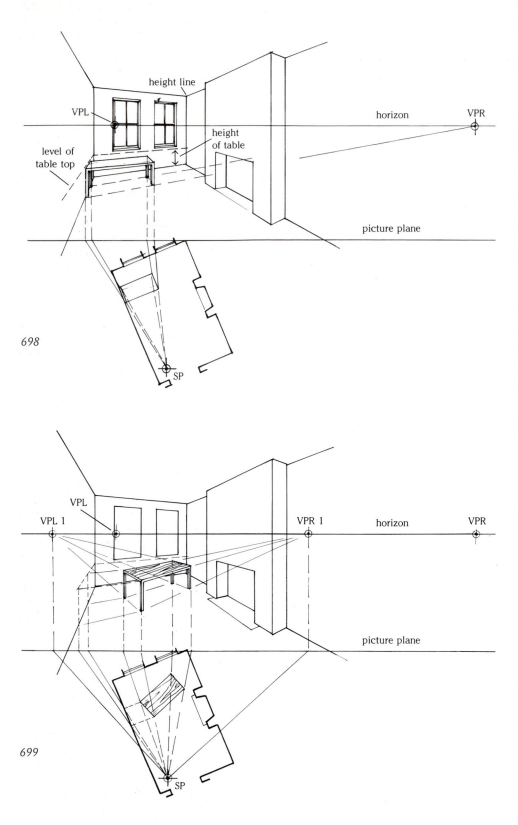

698

699

located, the other corners can be similarly located. When the corners are connected, a rectangle results that appears to stand in the space at an angle.

If the drawing has been made accurately, the edges of the rectangle will converge toward additional new vanishing points. This feature can be used as a shortcut in drawing or to check the accuracy of the drafting. Irregularly shaped objects, such as chairs or a piano, are best drawn by developing an enclosing box of lines within which the curved forms can be drawn freehand.

18. Circles require particular attention because the eye discerns even minute errors in perspective. A circle drawn in perspective appears as an ellipse, a geometric figure having longer and shorter dimensions—the major and minor axes—which divide it into four matching quarters. Ellipses vary from almost circular to almost linear, but they are always smooth, continuous curves. Even a very thin, or flat, ellipse does not come to a sharp point at the ends. The form of the ellipse can be studied with ellipse-guide templates, which provide a range of sizes and proportions, but it is unusual to find a template for the specific ellipse required for a particular perspective. The most practical way to put a circular form in perspective is to enclose it in a square, put the square in perspective, and then fit the appropriate ellipse into the resulting quadrangle (fig. 700). In doing this, however, it is important to observe the following two axioms:

> The major axis of any circle that lies in a horizontal plane will be horizontal; the minor axis will be vertical. This applies to tops of round tables, lamps, ceiling lights, round rugs, and all such elements.
>
> Any circle that lies in a vertical plane will have a minor axis that, extended, will pass through the vanishing point that serves the system of lines at right angles to that which represents the surface on which the circle lies. The major axis will be at a 90° angle to the minor axis. This rule applies to round windows, mirrors, clock faces, the portion of a circle that forms an arch, and similar elements.

If these rules are neglected, table tops will run downhill and arches will be oddly distorted. It may seem impossible to fit an el-

698. Objects adjacent to a wall and extending into the space, such as the table shown here, are placed by establishing their points of intersection with the wall and by bringing a level from the height line along the walls, here shown dotted. Outer corner locations are found with lines from the station point through the corners of the object in plan to the picture plane and vertical lines carried upward into the perspective. Horizontal lines can now be added that radiate from the vanishing points to complete the top and bottom lines of the object. The bottom lines are used here to locate the points at which the legs touch the floor.

699. Objects at angles to the walls are placed by locating each corner as above and establishing height by bringing imaginary lines outward from one wall. Lines representing the horizontals of the object will be found to converge toward new vanishing points, VPL 1 and VPR 1.

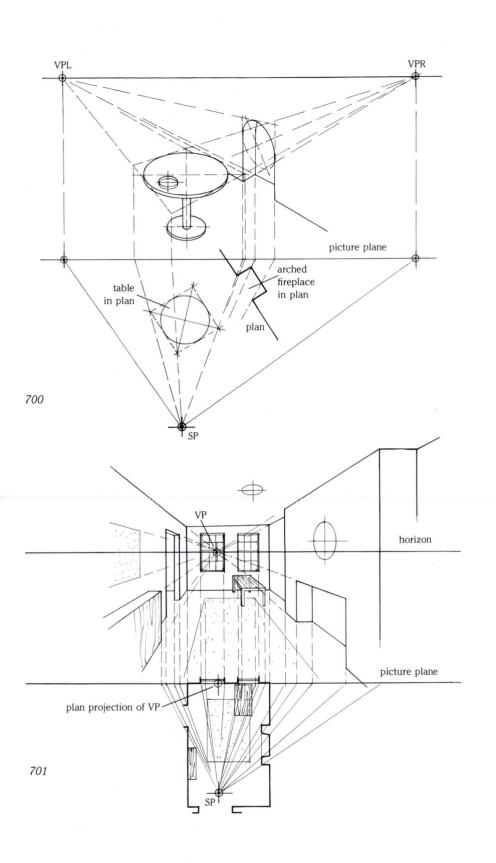

700

701

lipse into a constructed square, but it is preferable to have the ellipse correct than to have a fit that uses a skewed or mispositioned ellipse.

All problems of perspective—including a sloping ceiling, walls at angles, reflections in water, or mirrors—can be solved by variations on the basic method described here and above. Angled walls or ceilings, for example, are drawn by locating their beginning and ending edges and completing the figure by connecting the ends of the edges. Reflections are simply images that duplicate the actual space depicted in reverse, right to left or top to bottom.

19. The basic method described above is called *two-point perspective* because it uses two vanishing points, at right and left. *One-point perspective*, often recommended to beginners as being easier to learn, is merely a special case of the two-point method in which the second vanishing point has moved so far away as to be at the theoretical location of infinity, and is therefore unavailable. All lines that move toward this infinitely remote vanishing point are parallel.

In practice, a one-point perspective is drawn by placing the plan in use on the board with its main lines horizontal and vertical (fig. 701). Heights can be measured anywhere on the back wall; in fact, the back wall appears in true elevation. The single vanishing point, as in two-point perspective, is identified by running a line through the station point to the picture plane and bringing that line up to the horizon. (Like the two side walls of the plan, this line, which parallels these walls, will intersect the picture plane at a right angle.) All the other steps are the same as for two-point drawing, except that one set of horizontal parallel lines can be simply drawn as horizontals without concern for their vanishing point. One-point perspectives work well for formal, symmetrical spaces, but they can be monotonous and limiting if used indiscriminately.

Familiarity with geometrically constructed perspective techniques makes it easier to draw freehand perspectives that are reasonably accurate and look right. Once the essential procedure has been grasped, elements may easily be drawn by eye within a constructed drawing. The ability to design in perspective, beginning with sketches that show spaces as they will actually appear, is a fundamental technical skill for an interior designer.

700. Circles are represented by ellipses or sections of ellipses. In horizontal planes—the table top and base here—they will have horizontal major axes and vertical minor axes. In a vertical plane—such as the fireplace arch—a minor axis radiates from one vanishing point, with a major axis at right angles to the minor axis. Circular forms are most often located by enclosing the circle in perspective into a square and then fitting a suitable ellipse into the square as it appears in perspective.

701. In a one-point perspective, the plan is placed so that the wall lines are horizontal and vertical. Given a station point, the single vanishing point is located by a vertical line that runs upward from the station point to the horizon, intersecting at a right angle. Heights can be measured anywhere on the back wall, which is actually an elevation. Lines moving forward and backward in the space are drawn radiating from the vanishing point; lines that move sideways are drawn as horizontals. Elements are located with construction lines as described above for two-point perspectives.

Fabric

Before ordering drapery or upholstery fabrics or carpet, it is best to obtain an estimate of the quantity required from the firm that will install the material. A *drapery workroom* and installation contractor will take measurements and calculate the required yardage when quoting a price for the installation. Furniture manufacturers note in their price lists the correct yardage needed for "COM" (customers' own material) cover fabrics for each individual product. The contractor who will install the carpet computes the yardage needed and takes responsibility for making a correct estimate.

Interior designers must often make preliminary estimates for budget purposes before precise figures can be obtained. The budget may have to include the cost of upholstery fabrics before final selections of furniture have been made; or the approximate carpet yardage may be a factor in selecting carpet—or in comparing it with another floor covering. A pocket calculator can help in making such budget estimates.

DRAPERY YARDAGE

Drapery fabrics come in a number of widths, the most common being 36, 42, 45, 50, 52, 54, 56, and 118 inches. Since prices are quoted in linear (lengthwise) yards, it is necessary to determine, or at least assume, the width of the fabric to be used. Curtains are made up with *fullness*, that is, extra width to allow them to hang in folds; this means that the fabric must always be wider than the window or other space to be covered by the closed curtains. This fullness is expressed as a percentage; for example, 100 percent fullness means that the actual flat fabric will be twice the width it will cover when hung. Fullness usually ranges from 100 to 200 percent. Thin and sheer materials require more fullness than heavier materials. Estimating will follow these steps:

1. Measure (on site or from drawings) the width of the space the closed drapery will cover.
2. Multiply that width by the factor that gives the desired percentage of fullness: e.g., by 2, or twice the width, for 100 percent fullness, and by 3 for 200 percent.
3. Divide the resulting total width by the width of the fabric to be used. This gives the number of widths, or panels, required.
4. Measure (on site or from drawings) the total height of the drapery—from floor to ceiling, floor to window head, or sill to window head, according to the design planned. Add to this dimension an allowance for hems at the foot and head of each panel of made-up drapery. This will range from 6 to 16 inches, according to the details selected and the nature of the fabric. The result gives the total length, or height, of each panel *(width)* in inches.
5. Multiply this height dimension by the number of widths. Add a factor to allow for waste (usually 10 percent). Divide the total figure in inches by 36 to obtain yardage. If the pattern requires matching, allow an extra percentage factor for waste.

In addition to estimating the required fabric, the installation firm will quote a price for making up the curtains, including the cost of lining material, if any, and any decorative elements such as fringe, cords, and tassels. It will also price the hardware (track, traverse rods, and so on) and any related elements, such as valances or lambrequins, plus the cost of labor for on-site installation. Having drapery made up and installed usually costs at least twice the cost of the fabric (of average price) alone.

UPHOLSTERY COVER FABRIC

Even before making final furniture selections, it is possible to estimate the fabric yardage needed to cover a piece, given its general type and size, by looking in a manufacturer's catalog or price list. This will enable the designer to estimate cost before making final furniture selections. Typical requirements will be in the following ranges:

Small side chair (armless)	1–2 yards
Small armchair (unupholstered arms)	2–3½ yards
Executive office armchair	4–5 yards
Fully upholstered chair	3–4 yards*
Fully upholstered two-seat sofa	6–8 yards*
Fully upholstered three-seat sofa	8–12 yards*
Ottoman	2–3 yards

*Add 1½ yards for each fully upholstered arm.

Most upholstery fabrics are made in 52-inch widths. An allowance must be made for narrower widths. The matching of stripes or patterns calls for an extra allowance. Natural leather is priced in hides, not by the yard. The leather supplier can indicate the approximate yield in yards per hide, equivalent to yards of 36- or 52-inch-wide fabric, for any particular leather.

CARPET YARDAGE

Carpet, priced by the square yard, used to be made in widths of 27 or 36 inches. Now it is usually manufactured in various *broadloom* widths, commonly 6, 9, 12, and 15 feet. Since many room dimensions do not easily accommodate broadloom widths, it may take some ingenuity to work out an economical way to lay out widths so as to minimize waste. The easiest way to estimate the yardage required is to make a tracing paper overlay with lines spaced to indicate the bands of width and to move this about over the actual space plan to arrive at the best layout of widths and seams.

Once a rough layout is made, measure the length of each band in feet and add all the band lengths together. Multiply the total of the band lengths by the broadloom width in feet. Divide by 9 to convert the area in feet to yards. Add 5 to 10 percent for waste (the larger the area, the smaller the allowance) plus an allowance for matching if there is a pattern. Carpet squares or tile can be estimated simply by figuring the area to be covered and adding a small allowance for waste.

To the cost of the carpet alone, it is necessary to add the cost of any underlay or other installation materials and the cost of installation, which will vary with the location and size of the project. When quoting price per yard, a carpet manufacturer can usually give a fairly accurate estimate of the total cost, including installation in a particular location.

Wallpaper

Wallpaper is priced in units called *single rolls,* although it is produced and distributed in larger (double or triple) rolls as well. Allowing for waste, one single roll will cover 30 square feet of surface, found by measuring the actual ceiling or wall area and subtracting the dimensions of any openings. Very large patterns may call for 10 to 20 percent extra waste allowance to match the pattern properly.

Licensing for Interior Designers

Unlike other design professions—architecture and engineering, for example—interior decoration and interior design, until very recently, were unregulated fields. The realization that interior design can affect the safety and health of building occupants and users has led to licensing requirements that include giving evidence of training, experience, and competency.

Although only a few states—at the time of writing, Alabama, Connecticut, Louisiana, and the District of Columbia—have enacted licensing laws, a number of other states have legislation pending, and there is a clear trend toward gradual, near-universal adoption of such laws. Although they may vary from state to state, such laws generally restrict the use of the title *interior designer* to those who have met specific criteria. While others remain free to do interior work, licensed professionals can assure potential clients that their backgrounds and skills meet appropriate standards.

The typical licensing law requires that an applicant demonstrate a suitable combination of professional education and experience and that he or she pass a standard examination similar to those administered for entrance into other professions. Passing the examination, which is offered by the National Council for Interior Design Qualification (NCIDQ), is at present a condition for membership in several of the professional organizations listed below. In areas where licensing is not yet mandatory, an applicant may elect to take the examination and obtain a certificate of qualification. The examination includes sections that address:

Programming and planning
Theory
Contract documents and
  communication skills
Building construction and
  support skills
Materials
Business and professional
  practice
History
Design (through a ten-hour, jury-
  evaluated design problem)

Professional Organizations

Several organizations set standards for the profession by offering membership to individuals qualified in interior design and providing various services. The following organizations are national in scope:

American Society of Interior
Designers (ASID)
  1430 Broadway
  New York, NY 10018
Membership in this primary professional organization attests to the qualification of its members, who may use the initials ASID. It also conducts programs, monitors legislation, and coordinates interior design concerns with those of related professions.

Foundation for Interior Design
Education Research (FIDER)
  322 Eighth Avenue
  New York, NY 10001
This organization is concerned with design education and the accreditation of design schools and their programs.

Institute of Business
Designers (IBD)
  1155 Merchandise Mart
  Chicago, IL 60695
An organization for designers primarily involved in the office and contract fields.

Interior Design Educators
Council (IDEC)
  P.O. Box 8744
  Richmond, VA 23226
An organization of teachers and others involved in design education.

Interior Designers of
Canada (IDC)
  P.O. Box 752, Station B
  Ottawa, Ontario
  Canada K1P 5P8
The Canadian equivalent of the ASID.

National Council for Interior
Design Qualification (NCIDQ)
  118 East 25th Street
  New York, NY 10010
The organization that administers and scores the interior design qualification examination.

The following organizations serve the professions most closely related to interior design:

American Institute of Architects
  1735 New York Avenue N.W.
  Washington, D.C. 20006
The primary American architectural organization.

Industrial Designers Society of
America
  1142-E Walker Road
  Great Falls, VA 22066
The professional organization of the American industrial design field.

There are, in addition, state and local organizations concerned with various aspects of design, national organizations in other countries, and several international organizations that coordinate the activities of the national organizations.

GLOSSARY

Words or terms in *italics* within the definitions are also defined in the glossary.

ACCESS FLOOR/CEILING Systems of manufactured elements that provide accessible hollow spaces below floors or above ceilings, where any combination of wiring, piping, and *ducts* may be placed.

ACRYLIC A transparent *thermoplastic,* usually made up into sheets, rods, or tubes. It can also be thermoformed into complex curved shapes, made translucent, or colored. Plexiglas and Lucite are trade names.

ADDITIVE COLOR In lighting, color mixing that involves the addition of colors. The mixing of dyes or pigments, on the other hand, *subtracts* color through absorption. The additive *primary* colors are red, green, and blue.

AMBIENT LIGHT Also called general lighting, this is the overall level of light in a space, which should be adequate for comfortable movement and for seeing people and objects.

ANTHROPOMETRICS The study of the dimensions and articulation of the human body by means of systematic, statistical observation of large numbers of people.

ARCHITRAVE In the classical *orders* of architecture, the horizontal *molding* just above the capital of a column. Also, the molding around a doorway or other opening.

ART DECO A popular term for the stylistic development of the 1920s and 1930s that stemmed from Paris exhibitions called "Les Arts Décoratifs." These included interiors, furniture, and other objects designed in a modern style that came to influence architecture as well. At the time, this style was called Moderne or, in English, Modernistic.

ART NOUVEAU A stylistic development of the late nineteenth century centered in Belgium and France. Abandoning all historical references, this genuinely modern style used instead elaborately curved decorative detail, generally based on natural forms.

ARTS AND CRAFTS MOVEMENT An aesthetic inspired by the desire to reform design by closing the gaps between fine arts, crafts, and design in architecture, interiors, and decorative objects. It developed in England in the latter half of the nineteenth century, with William Morris as its primary spokesman. Subsequent design directions have close ties to Arts and Crafts theory and attitudes.

ASBESTOS A mineral fiber with excellent insulating and fire-resistant properties. Loose asbestos fibers present health hazards, which have led to a marked decrease in the use of this material.

ASHLAR Building stone cut into square or rectangular blocks; masonry construction made up of such stone blocks.

ATRIUM In classical Roman architecture, the central courtyard of a house; by extension, any central courtyard or open space around which a house is built. In current usage, the term describes an interior space roofed over with glass, as in more recently built hotels, office buildings, or other large projects.

AWNING WINDOW A window with a sash that pivots at the top and swings outward.

AXMINSTER A traditional carpet construction using a jute back and wool cut pile. Made by a now-obsolete mechanical weaving process, these carpets display a wide variety of colors and patterns.

BALLAST In electrical parlance, a *transformer* that converts the current in a circuit to that required by *fluorescent lamps.*

BALLOON-FRAME CONSTRUCTION A method employed primarily in building small houses of wood. Structural members are placed close together as framing; exterior sheathing and interior finishes create hollow spaces within walls and beneath floors that provide locations for pipes, wiring, and insulation. This simple, economical system was developed in mid-nineteenth-century America.

BALUSTER A vertical post or support for a railing, most often a stair rail.

BAROQUE The design of the latter part of the Renaissance, characterized by complex forms and elaborate decorative detail. Baroque design originated in Italy and was widely accepted in Germany, Austria, and related European regions, but less so in northern Europe. Most significant Baroque work dates from the seventeenth century.

BASEBOARD A band of protective or decorative trim or *molding* along the bottom of a wall where it meets the floor.

BAUHAUS A German school of art and design that operated from 1919 to 1932. Under the direction of Walter Gropius, the school exerted a profound influence on the development and practice of *Modernism* in art, architecture, and design. The name of the school has come to describe work in the severe, functional, and often mechanistic style favored at the school.

BENTWOOD The product of a technique in which thin strips of solid wood are softened by steam and bent around molds. Furniture made by this method was developed in the latter half of the nineteenth century by Michael Thonet.

BROADLOOM Carpet woven on a loom at least 54 inches wide so as to avoid the need to seam narrow strips.

BUILDING STANDARD The basic interior elements, such as partitions, floors, ceilings, doors, and light fixtures, provided without additional charge to tenants of large modern office buildings by the building owners.

BURL A marked irregularity in a wood grain resulting from abnormal tree growth. Burled wood is most often used to make a *veneer* with striking color and pattern.

CABRIOLE A furniture leg with a double, or S-shaped, curvature, often decoratively carved and ending in a more or less elaborate foot. The shape is used in many traditional furniture styles.

CALENDERING A process for finishing textiles or forming thin sheets, for example, of plastic, by passing the material between rollers under pressure.

CANDLEPOWER A unit of light intensity equal to the output of a standard candle.

CANTILEVER A horizontal projecting beam or structure anchored at one end only.

CASEMENT WINDOW A window hinged at the side and swinging open like a door, most often used in pairs.

CHAIR RAIL A molding, usually of wood, that runs along a wall at the height of chair backs, thus protecting the wall from being scraped or otherwise marred.

CHAISE LONGUE A reclining chair with a seating surface long enough to provide support for the sitter's legs. (Often corrupted to "chaise lounge.")

CHASE A vertical shaft that holds *ducts,* piping, or wiring.

CHROMA A color's purity, or saturation. In the *Munsell* color system, it is measured by a range of numbers from 1 to 14. The highest numbers indicate maximum intensity, although different hues reach maximum chroma at different numbers.

CIRCULATION The movement patterns of a space's occupants. The study of circulation patterns is particularly important in planning complex interiors made up of many rooms, corridors, or other areas.

CLERESTORY An outside wall, pierced with windows, carried above an adjoining roof, as in the upper walls of the nave of a *Gothic* church; also, a wall with a window or band of windows placed high.

COFFER Originally a chest or other box. By extension, coffers are the recesses that form three-dimensional decorative patterns in ceilings, vaults, or domes.

COLD-CATHODE LIGHT A light source that uses thin, luminous, gas-filled tubes similar to those of neon signs but that produces normal white light. The tubes are often custom-designed and permanently installed, usually in ceiling *coves.*

COLONIAL A term applied to early-American architecture, including a version of English *Georgian.* The same term is used, rather loosely, to describe more modern imitations of that design.

COLOR TEMPERATURE A single number expressed in degrees Kelvin (°K)— or, more currently, in kelvins (k)—that indicates the relative warmth or coolness of lighting.

COLOR WHEEL A circular arrangement of *hues* in their spectrum, or "rainbow," order of red, orange, yellow, green, blue, and violet. When colors are thus organized, each *secondary* color falls between the *primaries* that make it up, and all colors are directly opposite their complementaries.

CONSTRAINT   In design, any restriction that influences planning.

CONSTRUCTION DRAWING   A drawing made to aid in taking bids and for contractors or artisans to use in executing work; also called a working drawing or blueprint.

CONTEMPORARY DESIGN   Current or recent design work. The term commonly describes work that neither refers to historical precedent nor displays the strong stylistic austerity and simplicity associated with *modernism*. The term "transitional" is sometimes used, mistakenly, as a synonym for "contemporary" in a design context.

CONTINUOUS-SPECTRUM LIGHT   Light that contains all of the energy wavelengths—colors—that make up white light. When viewed through a prism or spectroscope, such light reveals a continuous rainbow band of colors. Sources of continuous-spectrum light include the sun, candles, *incandescent* electric light, and oil lamps.

CONTRACT DESIGN   All non*residential* interior design. Contract design includes the production and distribution of elements such as furniture, textiles, and light fixtures used primarily in larger commercial and institutional projects. These elements are purchased under contracts rather than through retail channels.

CONVECTOR   A heat-supply device similar to a *radiator* but designed to maximize the effective flow of heated air by convection, that is, the circular motion of air at nonuniform temperatures.

CORNICE   A horizontal band of projecting decorative *moldings* at the top of a wall or building. In the classical orders of architecture, the uppermost of the three bands that make up the *entablature*. Also, a projecting horizontal band placed above a window to conceal curtain rods.

COST-PLUS   A system of charging for construction work in which the final charge represents the actual costs of materials and labor, plus an established percentage for overhead and profit.

COVE   1) A trough or other recess, often part of a ceiling design, occasionally built into a wall. The cove conceals an *indirect light* source (cove lighting), usually *fluorescent* or *cold-cathode;* 2) a concave molding, particularly one placed where the wall meets the ceiling or floor.

CREDENZA   A horizontal chest or cabinet common in interiors of the Italian Renaissance. In modern usage, the term describes an office storage cabinet of dimensions similar to those of a desk, with doors and sometimes drawers.

CROSS-BANDING   In the construction of veneered *panels* for furniture, doors, paneling, and other interior elements of

wood, the layer beneath the exposed, or face, *veneer.* The grain of the cross-banding runs at right angles to the grains of both the solid-wood core and the face veneer, preventing splits and warping.

DADO   1) The lower part of an interior wall treated with paneling or other special surface materials; 2) in classical architecture, the middle band of a pedestal.

DESIGN DRAWING   A drawing made to illustrate or aid in the development of design. Normally, design drawings emphasize visual concepts and do not include the dimensions and details needed for construction.

DE STIJL   A movement (1917–29) in the development of *modernism.* Centered in Holland, it took its name from the magazine that was its primary organ. Gerrit Rietveld, Theo van Doesburg, and Piet Mondrian were the most active in defining this style.

DISCONTINUOUS-SPECTRUM LIGHT   Light in which only some wavelengths—colors—are present. Although such light appears to be white, a spectroscope shows bright lines of certain colors and blanks elsewhere along the spectrum. Gaseous-discharge lamps, such as *mercury* or *sodium* lights, produce discontinuous-spectrum light. *Fluorescent* light is a mixture of discontinuous- and *continuous-spectrum* light.

DISTRESSED FINISH   A trade term for a finish of reproduction antique furniture that has been deliberately damaged to imitate wormholes and other signs of age.

DOUBLE GLAZING   The insertion, in a window, door, or skylight, of two panes of glass with a dead-air space in between to provide insulation; the principle is that of the storm window.

DOUBLE-HUNG WINDOW   A window sash made up of two separate panes that slide vertically.

DOVETAIL JOINT   An element of wood joinery, made up of two interlocking pieces. Dovetails may be handcut, as in fine traditional cabinetry, or machine cut. A through, or slip, dovetail uses a lengthwise, wedge-shaped tab that slides into a matching groove.

DOWEL   A round pin, usually of wood. A dowel (or doweled) joint uses one or more dowels fitted into bored holes to form a wood joint widely used in cabinet-making.

DOWNLIGHT   A can-shaped housing that directs light from an *incandescent lamp* downward for general lighting. Downlights may be surface-mounted, recessed into a ceiling surface, or hung from a stem. *HID* versions are increasingly available for larger spaces.

DRYWALL   A technique in general use for building interior partitions. Large panels or sheets of *wallboard, gypsum* board, plasterboard, or Sheetrock are used in place of plaster to cover *studs* or other structural wall-support materials.

DUCT   An air passage, usually made of

sheet metal and usually rectangular, but sometimes round. In *HVAC* systems, ducts carry heated or cooled air to inlet grilles.

ECLECTICISM   Generally, the borrowing of ideas from many sources. In design, the term describes an architectural and interior design direction of about 1900–1940, which referred to historic precedents from the distant past, imitating them with considerable accuracy.

ELEVATION   An orthographic drawing showing a front, side, or oblique projected view in true or consistently scaled dimensions.

ENTABLATURE   The part of a classical architectural *order* that extends horizontally above the columns. It is made up of three bands, from bottom to top: the *architrave,* the *frieze* (sometimes omitted), and the *cornice.*

ERGONOMICS   The study of human body mechanics and sensory performance in relation to the designed environment, especially in work situations.

EYEBALL   An *incandescent* lighting fixture, usually recessed into a ceiling. The *lamp* is installed in a pivoting, spherical element that permits direct light to be focused as desired.

FEDERAL   An American decorative and furniture style associated with the *Greek Revival* movement in the first half of the nineteenth century.

FIBERGLASS   A hybrid material that uses glass fibers to reinforce a polyester *thermosetting plastic.* In translucent form, fiberglass is often employed for skylights or roofs. Other applications are automobile bodies, small boat hulls, chair bodies, and other furniture parts.

FILL LIGHT   Background, ambient, or diffused light that reduces the contrast between dark areas or shadows and primary or *task light.*

FLOCKING   A velvet-like surface made by applying fibers to an adhesive backing, often creating a pattern in relief. Flocking is sometimes used in the manufacture of economy-grade carpeting.

FLUORESCENT LIGHT   A combination light source that gives off light both from glowing gas inside a sealed *lamp* and from fluorescent phosphors that coat the inner surface of the lamp. The lamp is usually tubular, and, occasionally, circular, although fluorescent bulb shapes are also produced.

FOOTCANDLE   A unit of light intensity. The illumination of a surface at a distance of one foot from a standard candle equals one footcandle.

FRIEZE   In the classical *orders* of architecture, the section, often decoratively sculpted, of the *entablature* between the *architrave* and the *cornice;* hence, any horizontal ornamental band such as that often placed at the top of a wall.

FULL-SPECTRUM LIGHT   Light that contains the complete range of wavelengths present in daylight, including the invisible radiation at each end of the visible spectrum.

FURRING   The lining of a wall with wood, brick, or metal strips to support interior finish material, such as plaster or *wallboard.* The term also describes the strips of metal that support a lowered ceiling, which is then referred to as "furred" or "furred down."

GATELEG TABLE   A drop-leaf table in which a hinged leaf is supported by a leg unit that swings out in the manner of a gate.

GEORGIAN   The mid-to-late English Renaissance style developed approximately concurrently with the reigns of George I to George IV, about 1714–1800. The term is also used for the parallel American design of the same period.

GOTHIC   The architectural and decorative style of the latter half of the Middle Ages (about 1150–1500). Its most striking characteristic is the pointed arch and *vault,* used in stone construction and, in similar forms, other design work.

GREEK REVIVAL   An architectural and decorative style developed in imitation of ancient Greek design and paralleling the interior *Federal* style. It was popular in America, England, and Germany, and, to a lesser extent, other European countries from about 1800–1840.

GROUND FAULT INTERRUPTER A safety device for electrical circuits that shuts off power in case of a short circuit in order to prevent shocks. Its use is suggested where electrical outlets or devices are close to water or metal pipes, as in bathrooms or near pools.

GROUT   A cement mortar, or other material with similar properties, used to fill holes or as an adhesive for setting tiles.

GYPSUM   A mineral substance used to make plaster, block for building interior partitions, and gypsum board, a sheet wall-surface material also known as plasterboard, *wallboard,* or Sheetrock (a trade name), used in *drywall* partition construction.

HALF-TIMBER CONSTRUCTION Large-scale timber framing with an infilling of panels of brick rubble and plaster, resulting in a characteristic exterior of exposed dark wood beams against a lighter material. This was the primary system of wood construction in northern Europe from the Middle Ages until well into the eighteenth century. The same structure, but with an exterior facing, was continued in the American colonies.

HALOGEN LIGHT   See TUNGSTEN-HALOGEN LIGHT

HAND   The textural feel of a fabric.

HARDBOARD   A generic term for any of various types of fiberboard, made from pressed wood fibers and hardened in manufacture by heat and pressure. Masonite is the trade name for one kind of hardboard.

HID LIGHT   The abbreviation, in current use, for high-intensity discharge. HID *lamps* employ *mercury, metal halide,* or high-pressure *sodium* in a sealed globe to produce an efficient type of electric lighting.

HIGH TECH   A recent design direction that incorporates elements from industrial, aerospace, and other advanced technologies, giving it a characteristically sleek and gleaming mechanistic look.

HUE   The distinctive characteristics of a color described by a basic color name and assigned a particular position in the spectrum. There are three *primary* hues (red, yellow, and blue) and three *secondary* hues (violet, orange, and green).

HVAC   The abbreviation in current use for heating, ventilating, and air-conditioning systems.

INCANDESCENT LIGHT   The most common light source, from a *lamp* that produces light by means of an electrically heated wire filament within a sealed globe.

INDIRECT LIGHTING   Lighting directed against a reflecting surface, most often a ceiling. Such an arrangement generates diffuse, *ambient* lighting.

INLAY   A decoration set into the surface of an object and finished flush. Inlays of variously colored wood veneers and, occasionally, other materials such as mother-of-pearl or metals are elements in many traditional furniture styles.

INTERNATIONAL STYLE   A direction of post–World War I architecture and related interior design characterized by an absence of ornament, large glass areas and flat roofs, and an emphasis on functionalism. It originated in 1920s Europe, was developed by the *Bauhaus* school, and became the dominant modern style worldwide from about 1930 until recent years.

JALOUSIE   A window or door with an arrangement of overlapping, adjustable, horizontal slats, which controls ventilation, light, or both. Jalousie doors for interior use—such as closet doors—often have fixed slats.

KNIT   A fabric construction in which yarn is interlaced by means of needles. Hand-knitting is a traditional craft technique, but knitting machines have been developed for the industrial production of knitted fabrics.

LAMBREQUIN   A boxlike, usually fabric-covered trimming that holds and decorates drapery at the top or top and sides of a window or door. Also, a short decorative drapery along a shelf edge or window.

LAMINATE   Any product of the process of *lamination,* but the term most often describes a plastic sheet made of layers of paper soaked with *melamine* resin. The result is a tough surface material used for table and counter tops and other furniture that calls for resistance to wear and impact damage. Common trade names include Formica, Micarta, Colorcore, and Nevamar.

LAMINATION   The process of adhering layers of thin material to make up a thicker sheet. *Plywood,* flat or molded, is made by lamination. Plastic *laminate* is widely used as a table top, counter top, and general furniture surface material.

LAMP   In nontechnical usage, any portable lighting device, such as a floor or table lamp. In the lighting trades and professions, the term refers to the light source itself, the bulb or tube that converts electrical energy to light.

LATH   Thin strips of wood nailed to the *studs* of a wall to support a plaster or other surface. The term is now also used for metal mesh and perforated sheet serving the same purpose.

LINTEL   A short, horizontal member spanning an open space between columns or over a door, window, or other opening.

LOAD-BEARING WALL   A wall that provides structural support for a floor or roof.

LUMEN   A unit of light flow generated by the light of one standard candle.

LUMINAIRE   In the lighting trades or professions, a complete light fixture, including the *lamp* or lamps, power connections, and any enclosures, reflectors, lenses, baffles, or other elements.

MAQUETTE   An interior plan with related elevations—representing walls—placed around and adjacent to it; when the group is cut out and the elevations folded up, a boxlike model of the interior is formed.

MARQUETRY   Inlaid decorative detail on furniture and flooring using variously colored woods or other materials.

MELAMINE   A highly resistant *thermosetting plastic* used to make *laminates* for table or counter tops or other furniture applications.

MERCURY LIGHT   A type of gaseous-discharge *lamp* that uses mercury gas in a sealed tube. It is highly efficient, but its *discontinuous-spectrum light* is an unpleasant bluish color unsuitable for all but utilitarian purposes such as highway lighting.

METAL-HALIDE LIGHT   An economical *HID lamp* that provides high output.

MITER   A joint made by fitting together two pieces of material cut to meet at matching angles, usually 45°, to form a corner, usually 90°.

MODERNISM   A general term for design styles developed in the twentieth century that make little or no reference to earlier historic periods, characterized instead by functional simplicity.

MODULE   1) A standardized unit of measurement used in planning and construction, such as 8-inch bricks or 2-by-4-inch studs, to facilitate convenient and economical usage; 2) one of a set of standardized units in an integrated system that allows numerous combinations, as in a furniture set (a modular couch or storage system).

MOLDED PLYWOOD   *Plywood* that is shaped under pressure while the adhesive between its component layers is still malleable. Molded plywood is used in many modern furniture products.

MOLDING   An architectural band that covers and trims a line where parts or materials join or that creates purely decorative linear patterns. Moldings are often of wood, sometimes of metal, plaster, or plastic.

MORTISE AND TENON In wood-working, a joint in which a projecting element, the tenon, is fitted into a corresponding cavity, the mortise.

MULLION A vertical member dividing *panels* or panes of a door or window.

MUNSELL COLOR SOLID In the Munsell color system, the mass that results when the steps of *value* are arranged in a vertical axis, the *hues* form a sphere in the horizontal planes around the axis, and the steps of *chroma,* or saturation, radiate from the axis (least saturated) to the circumference (most saturated).

MUNTIN A vertical member dividing *panels* or panes of a door or window.

NEOCLASSIC A stylistic development based on a return to the principles of classic—ancient Greek and Roman—architecture and design. For example, neoclassicism characterizes French design of the period following the French Revolution and extending into the nineteenth century, including the Directoire and Empire interior styles.

NOSING The projecting front edge of the *tread* of a stair.

NRC (NOISE REDUCTION CO-EFFICIENT) A decimal number that indicates the ability of an interior surface material to absorb sound by giving the percentage of sound that will be absorbed. Hard materials have a low NRC, while materials with good sound-absorbent qualities have high NRC ratings, up to a maximum of about .90.

OPEN PLAN A layout with few or no walls or partitions. The term has become associated with a system of office planning that, instead of separate, enclosed offices, uses screens or other furniture elements to provide some degree of privacy within a single, open space.

ORDERS The classical systems of architectural detail and ornament based on columns supporting an *entablature.* Developed in ancient Greece and Rome, the most commonly found orders are Doric, Ionic, and Corinthian, named after their supposed places of origin.

ORIENTATION The placement of a building, room, window, skylight, or other relevant element in relation to the points of the compass.

OSTWALD COLOR SOLID In the Ostwald color system, steps of *value* are arranged in a vertical axis; the steps of *chroma,* or saturation, radiate outward from the neutral center (least saturated) toward the *hues* (most saturated), which form the outer layer on a horizontal plane. Unlike in the *Munsell* system, steps of variation in chroma are equalized to form a smooth, double-conical solid.

PANEL A rectangular unit of material, usually framed by some sort of border. Wood paneling is a popular wall treatment. Rail-and-panel construction is a system of making doors or parts of furniture by setting thin wooden panels into a frame of *rails.*

PARQUET *Inlaid* woodwork made up of small blocks of hardwood arranged to form a geometric design or pattern, often in contrasting colors, primarily used in flooring.

PARTICLEBOARD A sheet material made up of wood chips, sawdust, or both, bonded with a resin adhesive. Painted or *veneered,* particleboard provides a finished surface equal to *plywood* or solid wood.

PEDIMENT A triangular gable over a door, window, or portico; also, the *molding* edging on a gable roof.

PERSPECTIVE The system of realistic pictorial drawing representing objects and spaces in relative distance or depth. Distant objects appear smaller than nearer objects, and horizontal lines move into the distance, converging toward "vanishing points" on the horizon.

PILE A cloth or carpet surface of raised yarns, looped or cut flush. Velvet and terry cloth are two pile fabrics.

PLAN A depiction, drawn to scale, of a horizontal section of a building or other unit taken at or near ground or floor level. Such "ground plans" or "floor plans" are the most important drawings used in architectural and interior design. The term "planning" refers to the development of such plans and, by extension, any subsequent systematic design actions.

PLASTERBOARD See WALLBOARD

PLENUM A hollow space above a ceiling or below a floor, often used for return air circulation in an *HVAC* system or for placing architectural lighting fixtures.

PLYWOOD A sheet material made by *laminating* layers of *veneer* (veneer plywood) with their grains running at right angles. Some types of plywood contain a solid-material core and are finished with a good veneer. The first is most commonly used for carpentry or, *molded,* for furniture; the second, for furniture.

POINT-SOURCE LIGHT Lighting that comes from a concentrated source virtually identical to a point in space. The sun, the flames of candles and oil lamps, and the filaments of *incandescent lamps* give point-source light, as distinguished from the diffuse light of cloudy skies, *fluorescent* tubes, and luminous or *indirectly lit* ceilings.

POST AND LINTEL A system of construction in which upright members—posts—support horizontals—*lintels*—to form a structural frame or grid, usually in timber or stone masonry.

POST-MODERNISM A term recently coined to describe stylistic developments in architecture and design that diverge from the precepts of *modernism.* Eccentric ornament, historicism as metaphor, and a certain whimsical quality are characteristic of this direction.

PRIMARY COLOR One of a group of colors from which all other colors may be generated, but which itself cannot be made by mixing. The *subtractive* (pigment or dye) primaries are red, yellow, and blue; the *additive* (colored light) primaries are red, green, and blue.

PROGRAM An initial, verbal statement of objectives and requirements for a design project.

PROXEMICS A recently coined term for the systematic study of the psychological impact of space and interpersonal physical distances.

QUARTERED Wood from a log that has first been cut into lengthwise quarters in order to maximize the yield of boards at or close to a radial position in the log.

RABBET A cut or groove in the edge of a material, usually wood, that fits a corresponding cut in another piece so as to form a joint.

RADIANT HEAT A system in which surfaces are heated by water passed through warming coils or by electric heat elements. Unlike *convection,* which circulates heat throughout a space, this system radiates heat directly into a space. Radiant heating is often used in combination with solar heating.

RADIATOR A heating device made up of a coil, pipes, or a hollow metal unit through which hot water or steam is passed, radiating heat into the surrounding air and space. The term is somewhat misleading, since the common radiator distributes heat more by convection (spreading heat through the movement of air) than by radiation (the direction emission of heat energy).

RAIL A horizontal element such as a stair rail or a wooden frame member combined with *panels* in rail-and-panel construction.

REINFORCED CONCRETE A hybrid structural material combining concrete, which resists compressive stresses, with embedded steel rods and mesh, which resist tensile stresses.

RESIDENTIAL DESIGN The design of houses and other residential projects and their interiors as distinguished from *contract design,* which addresses commercial and institutional spaces.

RETURN AIR Air that returns to air-conditioning equipment after circulating through a space. Grilles, for example, permit air to return to *ducts,* a *plenum,* or through corridors.

RISER 1) In stair construction, the vertical element of a step; 2) in plumbing or wiring, a vertical stretch of equipment, usually serving the upper floors of a building.

ROCOCO The stylistic developments in eighteenth-century French and, to a lesser extent, German and Austrian interior design, and decorative detail typical of the latter part of the French Renaissance. Rococo, although characterized by very elaborate surface decoration, retains relatively simple basic forms.

ROMANESQUE The architectural style of the early Middle Ages in Europe (circa 800–1150). Despite its name, it is not a Roman style, but is so called because of its prominent use of semicircular—or "Roman"—arches. In England, such design is commonly designated "Norman."

SATURATION See CHROMA

SCALE 1) A measuring rule, such as an architect's scale, graduated in units applicable to scale drawing; 2) the system of representing objects or spaces in a compact drawing by reducing them by a certain proportion (e.g., ¼" = 1'-0"); and 3) the concept that all objects and elements of a design should convey proper and true size relationships.

SCONCE A wall-mounted lighting fixture, which generally directs light upward.

SECONDARY COLOR A color that results from mixing two *primaries*. The *subtractive* secondaries are orange, green, and violet.

SHEETROCK See WALLBOARD

SILL 1) In construction, a horizontal structural member; 2) the horizontal shelflike surface below a window, door, or other opening.

SODIUM LIGHT A gaseous-discharge light source that uses sodium gas in a sealed tube. Sodium light has a *discontinuous spectrum*, giving it a strong orange tone that makes it unpleasant for general use. Because of its high efficiency, however, it is sometimes used for street and highway lighting.

SOFFIT A lowered portion of a ceiling, or, generally, the underside of a structural element.

SPECTRUM The band of colors, ordered from longest wavelength (red) to shortest (violet), visible when light passes through a prism, as in a spectroscope. Daylight and other white, *continuous-spectrum* light produce a complete rainbow spectrum.

STACK In plumbing, a vertical waste pipe that extends downward to a sewer connection and upward to the open air to permit the venting of gases.

STC (SOUND TRANSMISSION CLASS) A number rating that indicates the effectiveness of a material or structure in preventing sound transmission. Low STC values (15–20) denote a poor sound barrier, higher values (40–60), a superior ability to block sound transmission.

STILE A vertical member in a door or window, usually combined with *rails* and *panels* in rail-and-panel construction.

STRETCHER A horizontal brace, or crosspiece, such as the member set between two legs of a chair or table.

STUDS Vertical frame elements in the construction of walls and partitions. Wood studs are usually 2-by-4-inch members placed 16 inches apart. In modern practice, metal studs are also used.

SUBTRACTIVE COLOR The colors of pigments and dyes absorb—that is, subtract—some of the light that strikes them, reflecting the color that results from this subtraction. Mixing pigments to produce tints and shades is a subtractive process.

SYSTEMS FURNITURE Furniture that is designed to combine with other elements. Furniture systems are most often developed in terms of storage walls and office *work stations* that may double as partitioning.

TAMBOUR A furniture front or top made with strips of wood adhered to a fabric backing that allows it to roll in curves. A tambour door slides in a track or groove, often into a hidden trough, to open.

TASK LIGHT Light necessary for specific kinds of work, or tasks, and installed close to a work surface so as to illuminate the area with minimal spill and thus with maximum energy efficiency.

TEMPLATE A guide used in drafting to trace given outlines. The templates most common in the design trade are cut-out plastic sheets with drafting forms such as circles, ellipses, or furniture shapes in scale.

THERMOPLASTIC Any plastic material that softens with the application of heat and hardens on cooling. *Acrylics*, vinyls, and polyethylene are thermoplastics.

THERMOSETTING PLASTIC A soft plastic that permanently sets, that is, hardens, with the application of heat. Phenolics, *melamines*, and polyesters are thermosetting plastics.

TONGUE AND GROOVE A joining technique used with wood and other materials in which a projecting lip, or tongue, is slipped into a corresponding channel, or groove. In wood boarding, the line of the joint is often emphasized with a cut *molding* to give a pattern or parallel lines.

TRACK LIGHTING A system of lighting in which a continuous fixed band, or track, supplies current and supports movable fixtures.

TRANSFORMER An electrical device that converts an electrical current to a lower voltage, in the case of such elements as doorbells or intercom units, and to a higher voltage for *fluorescent* and *HID* lighting units.

TRAP In plumbing, a curved section of pipe that connects a fixture to a drain. The trap permanently holds water, thus forming a seal that prevents sewer gases from escaping back into a bathroom.

TREAD The horizontal step surface of a stair.

TRUSS A structural framework made up of triangles that span wide spaces, supporting a floor or roof. Trusses may be of wood, steel, or a combination of these.

TUNGSTEN-HALOGEN LIGHT A recently developed *incandescent* light source that uses *metal halides* in compact, highly efficient *HID* bulbs, tubes, or reflectors. Because they generate a great deal of heat, halogen *lamps* require specially designed fixtures.

TURNING A round element, usually of wood, produced on a lathe.

UNDERCUT A clearance at floor level that is larger than normal, created by shortening a door to permit air in an *HVAC* system to return along corridors.

UPLIGHT Light directed upward toward ceilings or the upper sections of walls. The term is also used to describe floor lamps, or *torchères*, that cast all light upward.

VALANCE A short drapery concealing the tops of curtains. The term also describes any trim, of drapery or other material, hanging from an edge.

VALUE The lightness or darkness of a color in relation to a scale of grays ranging from black to white. Light values are tints, dark values, shades.

VAULT An arched roof or ceiling masonry construction. A barrel vault derives from the horizontal extension of an arch, a groin vault from the intersection of two arches.

VEILING REFLECTION Glare produced by the reflection of a light source off a glossy surface.

VENEER Wood (or other material) cut in very thin sheets for use as a surface material (face veneer), usually of fine quality, or as a component layer of *plywood*.

VENT An air inlet. In plumbing, a vent connects to a drainpipe just beyond each *trap*, to prevent suction from removing water from the trap and to provide an outlet for gases into the open air.

WALLBOARD A thin, manufactured sheet material used in the construction of interior walls and ceilings. The term is often used interchangeably with plasterboard or Sheetrock (a trade name).

WALL-WASHER A ceiling-mounted, adjustable lighting fixture that directs light sideways toward an adjacent wall, which is thus washed with more or less uniform light.

WELT A thin tube or cord of fabric used as a decorative trim and reinforcement along the edge of a cushion or other upholstery element.

WORK STATION Any of several systems of office furniture and equipment, often incorporating screens or other partitions to provide some degree of enclosure and privacy.

BIBLIOGRAPHY

Most of the books listed under the heading "General" may be consulted for information on specific topics.

GENERAL

Bayley, Stephen, ed. *Conran Directory of Design.* New York: Random House, Villard Books, 1985.

Brown, Erica. *Sixty Years of Interior Design.* New York: Viking Press, 1982.

Conran, Terence. *The House Book.* New York: Crown Publishers, 1974.

———. *New House Book.* New York: Random House, Villard Books, 1985.

Diamonstein, Barbaralee. *Interior Design.* New York: Rizzoli International, 1982.

Dreyfuss, Henry. *Designing for People.* New York: Simon & Schuster, 1955.

Faulkner, Ray, et al. *Inside Today's Home.* 5th ed. New York: Holt, Rinehart & Winston, 1986.

Friedmann, Arnold; Pile, John F.; and Wilson, Forrest. *Interior Design: An Introduction to Architectural Interiors.* 3d ed. New York: Elsevier, 1982.

Garner, Philippe. *Contemporary Decorative Arts.* New York: Facts on File, 1980.

Heskett, John. *Industrial Design.* New York: Oxford University Press, 1980.

Kleeman, Walter B., Jr. *The Challenge of Interior Design.* New York: Van Nostrand Reinhold, 1981.

Mumford, Lewis. *Technics and Civilization.* New York: Harcourt, Brace, and Co., 1943.

Museum of Modern Art. *The Design Collection: Selected Objects, 1970.* Introduction by Arthur Drexler. New York: Museum of Modern Art, 1970.

Naar, Jon, and Siple, Molly. *Living in One Room.* New York: Random House, 1976.

Ozenfant, Amédée. *Foundations of Modern Art.* Translated by John Rodker. Reprint. New York: Dover Publications, 1952.

Tate, Allen, and Smith, C. Ray. *Interior Design in the 20th Century.* New York: Harper & Row, 1986.

Weale, Mary Jo, et al. *Environmental Interiors.* New York: Macmillan, 1982.

Whiton, Sherrill. *Interior Design and Decoration.* 4th ed. Philadelphia: J. P. Lippincott, 1974.

DESIGN QUALITY

Kaufmann, Edgar, Jr. *What Is Modern Design?* New York: Museum of Modern Art, Simon & Schuster, 1950.

———. *Introductions to Modern Design: What Is Modern Design & What Is Modern Interior Design.* Salem, N.H.: Ayer Company Pubs., 1953. Reprint. New York: Museum of Modern Art Publication in Reprint Series, 1970.

Kepes, Gyorgy, ed. *The Man-made Object.* New York: George Braziller, 1966.

Lynes, Russell. *The Tastemakers.* New York: Harper & Bros., 1954. Reprint. New York: Dover, 1980.

Museum of Modern Art. *Machine Art.* New York: Museum of Modern Art, 1934. Reprint. New York: Arno, 1969.

Papanek, Victor. *Design for Human Scale.* New York: Van Nostrand Reinhold, 1983.

———. *Design for the Real World.* New York: Pantheon Books, 1971.

Pile, John F. *Design: Purpose, Form, and Meaning.* Amherst, Mass.: University of Massachusetts Press, 1979. Pap. New York: W. W. Norton, 1982.

Pye, David. *The Nature and Art of Workmanship.* New York: Van Nostrand Reinhold, 1971.

———. *The Nature of Design.* New York: Van Nostrand Reinhold, 1964.

Read, Herbert. *Art and Industry.* London: Faber & Faber, 1934.

DESIGN BASICS

Arnheim, Rudolph. *Art and Visual Perception.* Berkeley, Calif.: University of California Press, 1960.

De Sausmarez, Maurice. *Basic Design: The Dynamics of Visual Form.* New York: Van Nostrand Reinhold, 1983.

Doczi, György. *The Power of Limits.* Boulder, Colo.: Shambhala Publs., 1981.

Huntley, H. E. *The Divine Proportion.* New York: Dover Publications, 1970.

Itten, Johannes. *Design and Form.* New York: Van Nostrand Reinhold, 1964.

Kepes, Gyorgy. *Language of Vision.* Chicago: Paul Theobold, 1944.

MATERIALS AND ELEMENTS

Eiland, Murray L. *Oriental Rugs: A Comprehensive Study.* Greenwich, Conn.: New York Graphic Society, 1973.

Hornbostel, Caleb, and Hornung, William J. *Materials and Methods for Contemporary Construction.* 2d ed. Englewood Cliffs, N.J.: Prentice-Hall, 1982.

McLendon, Charles, and Blackstone, Mick. *Signage.* New York: McGraw-Hill, 1982.

Radford, Penny. *Designer's Guide to Surfaces and Finishes.* New York: Watson-Guptill, 1984.

Riggs, J. Rosemary. *Materials and Components of Interior Design.* Reston, Va.: Reston Pub. Co., 1985.

Schlosser, Ignace. *The Book of Rugs.* New York: Bonanza Books, 1958.

FURNITURE

Ambasz, Emilio, ed. *Italy: The New Domestic Landscape.* New York: Museum of Modern Art, 1972.

Boger, Louise Ade. *Furniture, Past and Present.* Garden City, N.Y.: Doubleday, 1966.

Boyce, Charles. *Dictionary of Furniture.* New York: Roundtable Press, 1985.

Bradford, Peter, and Prete, Barbara, eds. *Chair.* New York: Peter Bradford & Thos. Y. Crowell, 1978.

Emery, Marc. *Furniture by Architects.* New York: Harry N. Abrams, 1983.

Gandy, Charles D., and Zimermann-Stidham, Susan. *Contemporary Classics: Furniture of the Masters.* New York: McGraw-Hill, 1981.

Garner, Philippe. *Twentieth-Century Furniture.* New York: Van Nostrand Reinhold, 1980.

Hanks, David A. *Innovative Furniture in America from 1800 to the Present.* New York: Horizon Press, 1981.

Kaufmann, Edgar, Jr. *Prize Designs for Modern Furniture from the International Competition for Low-Cost Furniture Design.* New York: Museum of Modern Art, 1950.

Larrabee, Eric, and Vignelli, Massimo. *Knoll Design.* New York: Harry N. Abrams, 1981.

Logie, Gordon. *Furniture from Machines.* London: Allen & Unwin, 1947.

Lucie-Smith, Edward. *Furniture: A Concise History.* London: Thames and Hudson, 1985.

Mang, Karl. *History of Modern Furniture.* New York: Harry N. Abrams, 1979.

Meadmore, Clement. *The Modern Chair.* New York: Van Nostrand Reinhold, 1975.

Noyes, Eliot F. *Organic Design in Home Furnishings.* New York: Museum of Modern Art, 1941. Reprint. New York: Arno Press, 1969.

Page, Marian. *Furniture Designed by Architects.* New York: Whitney Library of Design, 1980.

Pile, John F. *Modern Furniture.* New York: John Wiley & Sons, 1979.

Russell, Frank; Garner, Philippe; and Read, John. *A Century of Chair Design.* New York: Rizzoli International, 1980.

Russell, Gordon. *Furniture.* West Drayton, Eng.: Penguin Books, 1947.

Sembach, Klaus-Jürgen. *Contemporary Furniture.* New York: Architectural Book Publishing Co., 1982.

Walker Art Center. *Nelson, Eames, Girard, Propst: The Design Process at Herman Miller.* Minneapolis: Walker Art Center, *Design Quarterly* (no. 98/99), 1975.

Wanscher, Ole. *The Art of Furniture.* New York: Reinhold Pub. Corp., 1967.

TEXTILES

Albers, Ann. *On Weaving.* Middletown, Conn.: Wesleyan University Press, 1965.

Hardingham, Martin. *The Fabric Catalog.* New York: Simon & Schuster, Pocket Books, 1978.

Hollen, Norman, and Saddler, Jane. *Textiles.* New York: Macmillan Co., 1964.

Larsen, Jack Lenor, and Weeks, Jeanne. *Fabrics for Interiors*. New York: Van Nostrand Reinhold, 1975.

Thorpe, Azalea Stuart, and Larsen, Jack Lenor. *Elements of Weaving*. New York: Doubleday, 1967.

LIGHTING

Kaufmann, John E., and Christensen, Jack F., eds. *IES Lighting Handbook*. 5th ed. New York: Illuminating Engineering Society, 1972.

Nuckolls, James L. *Interior Lighting for Environmental Designers*. New York: John Wiley & Sons, 1976.

Phillips, Derek. *Lighting in Architectural Design*. New York: Holt, Rinehart & Winston, 1968.

Rooney, William F. *Practical Guide to Home Lighting*. New York: Van Nostrand Reinhold, 1980.

COLOR

Albers, Josef. *Interaction of Color*. New Haven, Conn.: Yale University Press, 1971.

Birren, Faber. *Creative Color*. New York: Reinhold Book Co., 1965.

Evans, Ralph M. *An Introduction to Color*. New York: John Wiley & Sons, 1959.

Itten, Johannes. *The Art of Color*. New York: Van Nostrand Reinhold, 1961.

Munsell Color Company. *Munsell Book of Color*. Baltimore: Munsell Color Company, 1929.

ART AND ACCESSORIES

Emmerling, Mary Ellisor. *American Country*. New York: Clarkson N. Potter, 1980.

Furuta, Tok. *Interior Landscaping*. Reston, Va.: Reston Pub. Co., 1983.

Gaines, Richard L. *Interior Plantscaping*. New York: Architectural Record Books, 1977.

KITCHENS, BATHROOMS, STORAGE

Brett, James. *The Kitchen: 100 Solutions to Design Problems*. New York: Whitney Library of Design, 1977.

Conran, Terence. *The Bed and Bath Book*. New York: Crown, 1978.

———. *The Kitchen Book*. New York: Crown, 1977.

Kira, Alexander. *The Bathroom*. 2d ed. New York: Viking Press, 1976.

Nelson, George, ed. *Storage*. New York: Whitney Library of Design, 1954.

Wise, Herbert. *Kitchen Detail*. New York: Quick Fox, 1980.

SPECIAL-PURPOSE SPACES

Insall, Donald W. *The Care of Old Buildings Today*. London: The Architectural Press, 1972.

Kramer, Jack. *Garden Rooms and Greenhouses*. New York: Harper & Row, 1972.

Slesin, Suzanne, et al. *The International Book of Lofts*. New York: Clarkson N. Potter, 1986.

Tresidder, Jane, and Cliff, Stafford. *Living Under Glass*. New York: Clarkson N. Potter, 1986.

PUBLIC INTERIORS

Atkin, William, and Adler, Joan. *Interiors Book of Restaurants*. New York: Whitney Library of Design, 1960.

Backus, Harry. *Designing Restaurant Interiors*. New York: Lebhar-Friedman, 1977.

Edwards, Sandra, et al. *Office Systems*. New York: PBC International, 1986.

End, Henry. *Interiors Book of Hotels and Motor Hotels*. New York: Whitney Library of Design, 1963.

Harris, David A., et al. *Planning and Designing the Office Environment*. New York: Van Nostrand Reinhold, 1981.

Ketchum, Morris. *Shops and Stores*. New York: Reinhold, 1957.

Klein, Judy Graf. *The Office Book*. New York: Facts on File, 1982.

Mazzurco, Philip. *Media Design*. New York: Quarto, 1984.

Pile, John. *Open Office Planning*. New York: Whitney Library of Design, 1978.

Pulgram, William L., and Stonis, Richard E. *Designing the Automated Office*. New York: Whitney Library of Design, 1984.

Rutes, Walter A., and Penner, Richard H. *Hotel Planning and Design*. New York: Whitney Library of Design, 1985.

HUMAN FACTORS

Bennett, Corwin. *Spaces for People*. Englewood Cliffs, N.J.: Prentice-Hall, 1977.

Diffrient, Niels, et al. *Humanscale One-Two-Three*. Cambridge, Mass.: MIT Press, 1974.

———. *Humanscale Four-Five-Six*. Cambridge, Mass.: MIT Press, 1981.

———. *Humanscale Seven-Eight-Nine*. Cambridge, Mass.: MIT Press, 1981.

Goldsmith, Selwyn. *Designing for the Disabled*. 2d ed. New York: McGraw-Hill, 1967.

Gutman, Robert, ed. *People and Buildings*. New York: Basic Books, 1971.

Hall, Edward T. *The Hidden Dimension*. Garden City, N.Y.: Doubleday, 1966.

———. *The Silent Language*. Garden City, N.Y.: Doubleday, 1959.

Harkness, S., and Groom, J. *Building Without Barriers for the Disabled*. New York: Whitney Library of Design, 1976.

Lang, Jon, et al. *Designing for Human Behavior*. New York: McGraw-Hill, 1974.

Lee, Terence. *Psychology and the Environment*. London: Methuen, 1976.

Minimum Guidelines and Requirements for Accessible Design. Washington, D.C.: U.S. Architectural and Transportation Barriers Compliance Board, 1982.

Panero, Julius, and Zelnick, Martin. *Human Dimensions and Interior Space*. New York: Whitney Library of Design, 1979.

Perin, Constance. *With Man in Mind*. Cambridge, Mass.: MIT Press, 1970.

Proshansky, Harold M., et al., eds. *Environmental Psychology: Man and His Physical Setting*. New York: Holt, Rinehart & Winston, 1970.

Sommer, Robert. *Design Awareness*. San Francisco: Rinehart Press, 1972.

———. *Personal Space*. Englewood Cliffs, N.J.: Prentice-Hall, 1969.

———. *Social Design*. Englewood Cliffs, N.J.: Prentice-Hall, 1983.

———. *Tight Spaces*. Englewood Cliffs, N.J.: Prentice-Hall, 1974.

Sykes, Jane. *Designing Against Vandalism*. New York: Van Nostrand Reinhold, 1980.

ARCHITECTURE

Abercrombie, Stanley. *Architecture as Art*. New York: Harper & Row, 1985.

Blake, Peter. *The Master Builders: Le Corbusier, Mies van der Rohe, Frank Lloyd Wright*. New ed. New York: W. W. Norton, 1976.

Ching, Frances. *Building Construction Illustrated*. New York: Van Nostrand Reinhold, 1975.

Copplestone, Trewin, ed. *World Architecture*. London: Hamlyn, 1963.

Fitch, James Marston. *American Building*. 2d ed., rev. and enl. Boston: Houghton Mifflin, 1966.

Fletcher, Banister. *A History of Architecture on the Comparative Method*. 8th ed., rev. and enl. London: Batsford, 1928.

Giedion, Sigfried. *Space, Time and Architecture*. Cambridge, Mass.: Harvard University Press, 1941.

Heyer, Paul. *Architects on Architecture*. New York: Walker & Co., 1966.

Jencks, Charles, and Chaitkin, William. *Architecture Today*. New York: Harry N. Abrams, 1982.

Jordan, R. Furneaux. *A Concise History of Western Architecture*. London: Thames and Hudson, 1969.

Kostof, Spiro. *History of Architecture*. New York: Oxford University Press, 1985.

Pevsner, Nikolaus. *Outline of European Architecture*. New York: Penguin Books, 1943.

Rasmussen, Steen Eiler. *Experiencing Architecture*. Translated by E. Wendt. Cambridge, Mass.: MIT Press, 1962.

Trachtenberg, Marvin, and Hyman, Isabelle. *Architecture from Prehistory to Post-Modernism*. New York: Harry N. Abrams, 1986.

Wiffen, Marcus, and Koeper, Frederick. *American Architecture, 1607–1976*. 2 vols. Cambridge, Mass.: MIT Press, 1981.

HISTORY

General

Ball, Victoria Kloss. *Architecture and Interior Design: Europe and America from the Colonial Era to Today.* 2 vols. New York: John Wiley & Sons, 1980.

———. *The Art of Interior Design.* 2d ed. New York: John Wiley & Sons, 1982.

Banham, Reyner. *Theory and Design in the First Machine Age.* New York: Praeger, 1960.

Clark, Robert Judson. *Design in America: The Cranbrook Vision 1925–1950.* New York: Harry N. Abrams, 1983.

Fehrman, Cherie, and Fehrman, Kenneth. *Postwar Interior Design 1945–1960.* New York: Van Nostrand Reinhold, 1986.

Ferebee, Ann. *A History of Design from the Victorian Era to the Present.* New York: Van Nostrand Reinhold, 1970.

Hiesinger, Kathryn B., and Marens, George H., eds. *Design Since 1945.* Philadelphia: Philadelphia Museum of Art, 1983.

Hine, Thomas. *Populuxe.* New York: Alfred A. Knopf, 1986.

Kouwenhoven, John A. *Made in America: The Arts in Modern American Civilization.* Rev. ed. Garden City, N.Y.: Doubleday, 1962.

McCorquodale, Charles. *A History of Interior Decoration.* New York: Vendome Press, 1983.

McFadden, David. *Scandinavian Modern Design.* New York: Harry N. Abrams, 1982.

Pevsner, Nikolaus. *High Victorian Design.* London: Architectural Press, 1951.

———. *Pioneers of Modern Design from William Morris to Walter Gropius.* 2d ed. New York: Museum of Modern Art, 1949. Rev. ed. Harmondsworth, Eng.: Penguin Books, 1960.

———. *The Sources of Modern Architecture and Design.* New York: Praeger, 1968.

Phillips, Lisa, et al. *High Styles: Twentieth-Century American Design.* New York: Whitney Museum of American Art and Summit Books, 1985.

Praz, Mario. *An Illustrated History of Furnishing.* New York: George Braziller, 1964.

Rapoport, Amos. *House: Form and Culture.* Englewood Cliffs, N.J.: Prentice-Hall, 1969.

Schaefer, Herwin. *Nineteenth Century Modern.* New York: Praeger, 1970.

Smith, C. Ray. *A History of Interior Design in 20th Century America.* New York: Harper & Row, 1987.

Spence, Robin. *The Aesthetic Movement.* New York: Dutton, 1972.

Art Deco

Bush, Donald J. *The Streamlined Decade.* New York: George Braziller, 1975.

Sembach, Klaus-Jürgen. *Style 1930.* New York: Universe Books, 1971.

Art Nouveau

Amaya, Mario. *Art Nouveau.* New York: Dutton, 1960.

Brunhammer, Yvonne, et al. *Art Nouveau Belgium/France.* Houston: Institute for the Arts, Rice University, 1976.

Rheims, Maurice. *The Flowering of Art Nouveau.* New York: Harry N. Abrams, 1966.

Selz, Peter, and Constantine, Mildred, eds. *Art Nouveau.* New York: Museum of Modern Art, 1960.

Arts and Crafts Movement

Cathers, David M. *Furniture of the American Arts and Crafts Movement.* New York: New American Library, 1981.

Bauhaus

Naylor, Gillian. *The Bauhaus.* New York: Dutton, 1968.

Wingler, Hans. *The Bauhaus.* Cambridge, Mass.: MIT Press, 1969.

Marcel Breuer

Wilk, Christopher. *Marcel Breuer, Furniture and Interiors.* New York: Museum of Modern Art, 1981.

De Stijl

Jaffé, Hans L. C. *De Stijl, 1917–1931.* New York: Harry N. Abrams, 1967.

Overy, Paul. *De Stijl.* New York: Dutton, 1968.

Charles Eames

Drexler, Arthur. *Charles Eames Furniture from the Design Collection.* New York: Museum of Modern Art, 1973.

Eileen Gray

Adam, Peter. *Eileen Gray.* New York: Harry N. Abrams, 1987.

Walter Gropius

Fitch, James Marston. *Walter Gropius.* New York: Braziller, 1960.

Giedion, Sigfried. *Walter Gropius.* New York: Reinhold, 1954.

Hector Guimard

Graham, F. Lanier. *Hector Guimard.* New York: Museum of Modern Art, 1970.

High Tech

Kron, Joan, and Slesin, Suzanne. *High Tech.* New York: Clarkson N. Potter, 1978.

Josef Hoffmann

Sekler, Eduard F. *Josef Hoffmann: The Architectural Work.* Princeton, N.J.: Princeton University Press, 1985.

Le Corbusier (Charles-Edouard Jeanneret)

Besset, Maurice. *Who Was Le Corbusier.* Translated by Robin Kemball. Cleveland, Ohio: World Publishing Co., 1968.

Blake, Peter. *Le Corbusier.* Baltimore: Penguin Books, 1964.

De Fusco, Renato. *Le Corbusier, Designer: Furniture 1929.* Woodbury, N.Y.: Barron's, 1977.

Le Corbusier. *1929 sitzmöbel.* Zürich: Galerie Heidi Weber, 1959.

———. *Towards a New Architecture.* Translated by Frederick Etchells. London: The Architectural Press, 1927. Reprint. New York: Praeger, 1970.

Adolf Loos

Rukschio, Burkhardt, and Schachel, Roland. *Adolf Loos.* Salzburg and Vienna: Residenz Verlag, 1982.

Charles Rennie Mackintosh

Barnes, H. Jefferson. *Some Examples of Furniture by Charles Rennie Mackintosh in the Glasgow School of Art Collection.* Glasgow: Glasgow School of Art, 1969.

Memphis

Radice, Barbara. *Memphis.* New York: Rizzoli International, 1984.

Ludwig Mies van der Rohe

Glaeser, Ludwig. *Ludwig Mies van der Rohe: Furniture and Furniture Drawings.* New York: Museum of Modern Art, 1977.

Tegethoff, Wolf. *Mies van der Rohe: The Villas and Country Houses.* New York: Museum of Modern Art, 1985.

William Morris

Clark, Fiona. *William Morris: Wallpapers and Chintzes.* New York: St. Martin's Press, 1973.

Day, Lewis F. *Decorative Art of William Morris and His Work.* London: H. Virtue and Co., 1899.

Morris, William. *Selected Writings and Designs.* Edited by Asa Briggs. Baltimore: Penguin Books, 1962.

Parry, Linda. *William Morris Textiles.* New York: Viking Press, 1983.

Post-modernism

Klotz, Heinrich. *Postmodern Visions.* New York: Abbeville Press, 1985.

Shaker Design

Andrews, Edward Deming. *Religion in Wood: A Book of Shaker Furniture.* 2d ed. New Haven, Conn.: Yale University Press, 1939.

Sprigg, June. *Shaker Design.* New York: Whitney Museum of American Art/W. W. Norton, 1986.

Thonet

Wilk, Christopher. *Thonet: 150 Years of Furniture.* Woodbury, N.Y.: Barron's, 1980.

Henri van de Velde

Osthaus, Karl Ernst. *Van de Velde.* Hagen: Folkwang-verlag, 1920.

Frank Lloyd Wright

Hitchcock, Henry-Russell. *In the Nature of Materials.* New York: Duell, Sloan and Pearce, 1942.

Wright, Frank Lloyd. *An Autobiography.* New York: Green and Co., 1932.

WORKING METHOD

American Institute of Architects. *Architectural Graphic Standards.* 7th ed. Edited by Charles G. Ramsey and Harold R. Sleeper. New York: John Wiley & Sons, 1981.

Callender, John Hancock, ed. *Time-Saver Standards for Architectural Design Data.* 6th ed. New York: McGraw-Hill, 1986.

Diekman, Norman, and Pile, John F. *Drawing Interior Architecture.* New York: Whitney Library of Design, 1983.

————. *Sketching Interior Architecture.* New York: Whitney Library of Design, 1985.

Hornung, William J. *Architectural Drafting.* 4th ed. Englewood Cliffs, N.J.: Prentice-Hall, 1966.

Pile, John F. *Drawings of Architectural Interiors.* New York: Whitney Library of Design, 1967.

————. *Perspective for Interior Designers.* New York: Whitney Library of Design, 1985.

Ratensky, Alexander. *Drawing and Model-making.* New York: Whitney Library of Design, 1983.

Reznikoff, S. C. *Interior Graphic and Design Standards.* New York: Whitney Library of Design, 1986.

————. *Specifications for Commercial Interiors.* New York: Whitney Library of Design, 1979.

Wakita, Osamu A., and Linde, Richard M. *Professional Handbook of Architectural Working Drawings.* New York: John Wiley & Sons, 1984.

Wallach, Paul I., and Hepler, Donald E. *Reading Construction Drawings.* New York: McGraw-Hill, 1981.

Wright, Lawrence. *Perspective on Perspective.* London: Routledge and Kegan Paul, 1983.

TECHNICAL ISSUES

Loftness, Robert L. *Energy Handbook.* New York: Van Nostrand Reinhold, 1978.

Watson, Donald. *Designing and Building a Solar House.* Charlotte, Vt.: Garden Way Publishing, 1977.

BUSINESS MATTERS

Siegel, Harry, and Siegel, Alan M. *A Guide to Business Principles and Practices for Interior Designers.* Rev. ed. New York: Watson-Guptill, 1982.

FUTURE DIRECTIONS

Ballast, David Kent. *Practical Guide to Computer Applications for Architecture and Design.* Englewood Cliffs, N.J.: Prentice-Hall, 1986.

Kennedy, E. Lee. *CAD Drawing, Design, Data Management.* New York: Whitney Library of Design, 1986.

National Council for Interior Design Qualification. *NCIDQ Examination Guide.* New York: National Council for Interior Design Qualification, 1986.

Teicholz, Eric. *CAD/CAM Handbook.* New York: McGraw-Hill, 1985.

PERIODICALS

Abitare (Milan)
American Craft (New York)
Architectural Record (New York)
Designers West (Los Angeles)
Domus (Milan)
House and Garden (New York)
Interior Design (New York)
Interiors (New York)
Progressive Architecture (Stamford, Conn.)
Restaurant and Hotel Design (New York)

INDEX

Pages on which illustrations appear are in *italics*.

ACKNOWLEDGMENTS

The author is indebted to innumerable people and organizations who have contributed ideas, advice, photographs, and other illustrative materials to make this book possible. Special appreciation should be expressed to Donald Rorke of Knoll International, Inc., who first introduced author and publisher.

Thanks are also offered to Norman Diekman; Susan Forbes and Joel Ergas of Forbes-Ergas Design Assoc.; and Philip B. Prigmore, architectural consultant to Alfred University, who provided the information and illustrative materials for the three case studies. Richard L. Wagner of Knoll International, Inc., provided helpful suggestions and a careful fact-check of Chapter 7, "Textiles."

The many designers, architects, manufacturers, and photographers who have provided information, illustrations, and permission to use material have also made an appreciated contribution to this book.

At Harry N. Abrams, Inc., the efforts of many dedicated editorial and design staff members have been of essential importance to this project. Among these, the author is particularly indebted to senior editor Sheila Franklin Lieber who, as project manager, steered the project through countless difficulties and orchestrated the various elements that are part of a complex book. Lory Frankel, as editor, was exceptionally diligent and tireless in editing text and in coordinating the relationships of words and images. Picture editor Susan Sherman, responsible for the selection and organization of the visual materials that are central to the content of this book, made an extraordinary contribution through her special understanding of the ways in which illustration can support the framework of words. Bob McKee, this book's designer, gave graphic form to the combination of words and images with a special skill that makes a totality superior to the sum of its component parts. Sam Antupit, who as art director carries overall responsibility for the design of an Abrams book, has been a valued and trusted support. Margaret Kaplan, in her early encouragement of the project and for her support during manuscript preparation, also provided valuable help in this demanding undertaking.

John Pile

PUBLISHER'S NOTE

In the course of the lengthy and complex process of putting together *Interior Design,* the publishers have incurred several debts of gratitude.

The formidable task of gathering photographs was immeasurably aided by the patience and generosity of the designers and photographers who opened their files to us, especially Tim Street-Porter, Jaime Ardile-Arce, Peter Paige, Elliott Kaufman, Frederick Charles, Paul Warchol, Grant Mudford, Timothy Hursley, Norman McGrath, ESTO, Langdon Clay, Tom Crane, Jeff McNamara, Jacques Dirand, François Halard, Lizzie Himmel, Mary E. Nichols, Mark Ross, Eveyln Hoffer, Chris Mead, Michael Skott, Mark Hampton, John F. Saladino, Stuart Bromley of Bromley/Jacobsen Designs, McMillen, Inc., CAD/East, Gwathmey Siegel & Associates, ISD Incorporated, Knoll International, Inc., and Herman Miller, Inc.

The following people and organizations went out of their way to be helpful: Lorna Caine and Diana Edkins of The Condé Nast Publications, Inc.; Valerie Atlas of Crown Publications; Susan Butler of Clarkson N. Potter; Lester Dundes of *Interior Design;* Donald Karas of *Restaurant and Hotel Design;* Margot Dockrell of Brunschwig & Fils; Malcolm Forbes; and the staffs of *Progressive Architecture; Southern Accents; Metropolitan Home;* Christie's; Sotheby's; Sointu, New York; Stair & Co., New York; and Paul Smith, Inc., New York. At Abrams, photo researchers Pamela Bass and Jennifer Bright contributed greatly.

The editors are grateful to Andre Mirabelli and Drew Browning for providing them with specialized information. The work of turning the manuscript into a finished book could not have proceeded without the help of editor Alexandra Bonfante-Warren and, at Abrams, editor Ann Whitman and associate editor Margaret Rennolds. Special thanks are also due editorial assistant Suzanne Wagner, who energetically handled the complicated job of manuscript trafficking.

PHOTOGRAPHIC CREDITS

Our grateful thanks to the many photographers, publications, companies, and individuals, including those listed below, who provided us with material and kindly permitted its reproduction.

Fig. 17 Copyright Meredith Corporation, 1987. All rights reserved; fig. 23 Copyright © 1984 by The Condé Nast Publications, Inc.; fig. 45 Copyright © 1984 by The Condé Nast Publications, Inc.; fig. 50 from *The International Book of Lofts,* © 1986 by Suzanne Slesin, Stafford Cliff, Daniel Rozensztroch. Used by permission of Clarkson N. Potter, Inc.; fig. 61 from *Mary Emmerling's American Country West,* Copyright © 1985 by Mary Ellisor Emmerling. Used by permission of Clarkson N. Potter, Inc.; fig. 80 Copyright © 1984 by The Condé Nast Publications, Inc.; figs. 97, 98 Copyright Meredith Corporation, 1987. All rights reserved; fig. 119 Copyright Meredith Corporation, 1987. All rights reserved; fig. 120 Copyright Meredith Corporation, 1986. All rights reserved; figs. 144, 145 Copyright © 1984 by The Condé Nast Publications, Inc.; figs. 146, 147 from *Mary Emmerling's American Country West,* Copyright © 1985 by Mary Ellisor Emmerling. Used by permission of Clarkson N. Potter, Inc.; fig. 167 from *Freestyle* by Tim Street-Porter, published by Stewart, Tabori & Chang; fig. 169 from *Mary Emmerling's American Country West,* Copyright © 1985 by Mary Ellisor Emmerling. Used by permission of Clarkson N. Potter, Inc.; fig. 171 from *Caribbean Style,* Copyright © 1985 by Suzanne Slesin, Stafford Cliff, Estate of Jack Berthelot, Martine Gaume, Daniel Rozensztrock, and Gilles de Chabaneix. Used by permission of Clarkson N. Potter, Inc.; figs. 222, 257 from *Freestyle* by Tim Street-Porter, published by Stewart, Tabori & Chang; fig. 269 from *Mary Emmerling's American Country West,* Copyright © 1985 by Mary Ellisor Emmerling. Used by permission of Clarkson N. Potter, Inc.; fig. 285 Copyright © 1986 by The Condé Nast Publications, Inc.; fig. 326 from *Theory and Use of Color* by Luigina De Grandis, Copyright © 1984 Arnoldo Mondadori Editore S.p.A., Milan; fig. 338 Copyright © 1985 by The Condé Nast Publications, Inc.; fig. 342 Copyright © 1986 by The Condé Nast Publications, Inc.; fig. 348 Copyright © 1984 by The Condé Nast Publications, Inc.; fig. 366 Reprinted by permission from *House Beautiful,* copyright © September 1981. The Hearst Corporation. All Rights Reserved; fig. 376 Reprinted by permission from *House Beautiful,* copyright © August 1986. The Hearst Corporation. All Rights Reserved; fig. 380 Copyright © 1986 by The Condé Nast Publications, Inc.; fig. 381 from *Mary Emmerling's American Country West,* Copyright © 1985 by Mary Ellisor Emmerling. Used by permission of Clarkson N. Potter, Inc.; fig. 385 Copyright Meredith Corporation, 1986. All rights reserved; fig. 386 from *Italian Style,* Copyright © 1985 by Catherine Sabino and Angelo Tondini. Used by permission of Clarkson N. Potter, Inc.; fig. 387 Copyright Meredith Corporation, 1983. All rights reserved; figs. 388, 389 Copyright Meredith Corporation, 1986. All rights reserved; fig. 392 from *Freestyle* by Tim Street-Porter, published by Stewart, Tabori & Chang; fig. 405 Copyright Meredith Corporation, 1986. All rights reserved; figs. 408, 420 from *Creative Kitchens,* Copyright © 1984 by Knapp Communications Corp. Courtesy of *Home* Magazine; fig. 436 from *Italian Style,* Copyright © 1985 by Catherine Sabino and Angelo Tondini. Used by permission of Clarkson N. Potter, Inc.; fig. 448 from *The International Book of Lofts,* © 1986 by Suzanne Slesin, Stafford Cliff, Daniel Rozensztroch. Used by permission of Clarkson N. Potter, Inc.; fig. 451 Copyright © 1985 by The Condé Nast Publications, Inc.; fig. 455 Copyright Meredith Corporation, 1986. All rights reserved; fig. 460 Copyright © 1986 by The Condé Nast Publications, Inc.; fig. 463 from *Mary Emmerling's American Country West,* Copyright © 1985 by Mary Ellisor Emmerling. Used by permission of Clarkson N. Potter, Inc.; fig. 464 Copyright © 1983 by The Condé Nast Publications, Inc.; fig. 491 Copyright Meredith Corporation, 1987. All rights reserved; fig. 542 from *Freestyle* by Tim Street-Porter, published by Stewart, Tabori & Chang; fig. 551 from *Andrea Palladio: The Four Books of Architecture,* published by Dover Publications, Inc., New York, 1965; fig. 555 © Office du Livre, Fribourg 1967, Grosset & Dunlap, New York; fig. 583 Copyright © 1983 by The Condé Nast Publications, Inc.; fig. 588 Copyright © 1986 by The Condé Nast Publications, Inc.; figs. 625, 654 from *The International Book of Lofts,* © 1986 by Suzanne Slesin, Stafford Cliff, Daniel Rozensztroch. Used by permission of Clarkson N. Potter, Inc.